D0119297

CHAUCER:
A BIBLIOGRAPHICAL MANUAL

CHAUCER

A BIBLIOGRAPHICAL MANUAL

BY

ELEANOR PRESCOTT HAMMOND, Ph. D.

"O degli altri poeti onore e lume,
Vagliami il lungo studio e il grande amore
Che m'ha fatto cercar lo tuo volume."

STATE TEACHERS COLLEGE
LIBRARY
MARYVILLE - MISSOURI

New York
PETER SMITH
1933

39401

COPYRIGHT, 1908
BY THE MACMILLAN COMPANY

Reprinted by Special
Arrangement with
The Macmillan Company

PRINTED IN THE UNITED STATES OF AMERICA
BY THE COLONIAL PRESS INC., CLINTON, MASS.

821
C49Vh
1933

"And that sweet city with her dreaming spires"

PREFATORY NOTE

Suggestions or sketches for a bibliography of Chaucer have been made by J. E. B. Mayor in Notes and Queries 1876 II: 530; by J. Maskell in the same journal 1883 II: 381, 1884 I: 138, 141, 361, 422, 462, II: 3, 64, 422; in the Boston Literary World 14: 288 (1883); by Henry B. Wheatley before the Bibliographical Society in March, 1884, see their Transactions vol. II, pp. 11-12. The reference lists in Sonnenschein's Best Books and in Koerting's Grundriss zur Geschichte der englischen Literatur, 2d ed. Münster 1893, are avowedly brief and partial; and Courtney's Register of National Bibliography, 1905, has under Chaucer but five entries. The Chaucer-bibliography appended to Vol. II of the Cambridge History of English Literature, which appears just as this volume goes to press, is of necessity condensed; but its choice of entries is irregular and uncritical, and it is defaced by numerous misstatements; e. g. it lists editions of "Chaucer's Works" by Sir Harris Nicolas and by Tyrwhitt.

In the present work no attempt has been made to include annotation of the Chaucerian text; this, it is supposed, is the province of Chaucer-editions and concordances, and the few such passages treated here are included because of their recognized historical position as Chaucer-cruces. Further, this manual does not comprise a list of the allusions to Chaucer; a work on that subject is in preparation by the Chaucer Society. Nor does it attempt to record all the lighter "literary" essays contained in the files of periodicals appealing to the younger or the very general reader; again, the section upon the life of Chaucer does not comprise such third-hand biographies as are usually printed in school manuals of literature, but deals with those accounts of Chaucer based upon direct investigation, or presumably so based, with notes upon early biographies which age has now rendered curiosities of criticism. The book as originally planned included a section upon the fourteenth century and Chaucer's contemporaries, obviously however a separate and equally large subject.

The repetitions which occur have been permitted for the sake of lessening the great amount of reference from page to page, and

also because of the probable use of the work for consultation
rather than for continuous reading. To the custodians and owners
of English manuscript collections and art galleries my thanks are
due for their readiness to further every investigation.

E. P. H.

CONTENTS

SECTION I

THE LIFE OF CHAUCER

The study of Chaucer's life may be divided into two periods, that of the Legend, and that of the Appeal to Fact. The first period extends from Leland to Nicolas, the second from Nicolas to the Life-Records gathered by the Chaucer Society, and subsequently. Many actual documents were examined and printed by Godwin, earlier than Nicolas, but the spirit in which Godwin's work is written forbids its inclusion among genuine biographies. The soberer investigations of Nicolas have been greatly augmented by the discovery, under the auspices of the Chaucer Society, of a number of official records throwing light upon Chaucer's life. All these records, forming the authentic foundation for a biography of the poet, are printed by the Society as the Life-Records below noted.

The work of killing the legend has, however, been difficult; for a most interesting and important summary see Lounsbury, Studies in Chaucer, vol. 1, chap. 2, and his earlier article in the Atlantic Monthly 40 : 269, 592, entitled Fictitious Lives of Chaucer. The principal fictions regarding Chaucer, e. g. that of his imprisonment for conspiracy, are now well eradicated; but even among scholars still persist the tendencies to repeat statements without examination, to welcome an attractive but ill-founded suggestion, and to accept poetic commonplace as autobiography. See the slips in Skeat's Life as noted by Flügel in Anglia 21 : 245 ff., the discussion over Chaucer's meeting with Petrarch, and the dispute as to the reality of Chaucer's hopeless love; see under Clerk's Tale, Section III G here, and in Appendix (b) to this Section.

A. The Legend

[Reprint of the Life of Chaucer by Leland in his *Commentarii de Scriptoribus Britannicis*, Oxford 1709, pp. 419-426.]

CAP. DV. *De Gallofrido Chaucero.*

GALLOFRIDUS *Chaucerus*, nobili loco natus, & summae spei juvenis, *Isiacas* scholas tam diligenter, quam qui maxime, celebravit: id quod ut faceret, academiae vicinitas quodammodo invitavit. Nam quibusdam argumentis adducor ut credam, *Isiacam* vel *Berochensem* provinciam illius natale solum fuisse. Hinc acutus dialecticus, hinc dulcis rhetor, hinc lepidus poeta, hinc

I

39401

gravis philosophus, hinc ingeniosus mathematicus, (qua parte & à *Joanne Somaeo,* & *Nicolao, Carmelita Linensi,* viris in mathesi eruditis, quos in libro de *Sphaera* nominat, instructus fuit) hinc denique sanctus theologus evasit. Maxima equidem sum locutus; at quisquis ejus libros curiosa manu evolverit, me bonae fidei praeconem facile judicabit. Ingenue tamen fatebor sic eum *Isiaci* studuisse, ut & alibi etiam longo studiorum usu multa ad scientiae cumulum adjecerit. Constat utique illum circa postremos *Richardi* secundi, cui non incognitus erat, annos in *Gallia* floruisse, magnamque ex assidua in literis exercitatione gloriam sibi comparasse; tum praeterea eadem opera omnes veneres, lepores, delicias, sales, ac postremo gratias linguae *Gallicae* tam alte coimbibisse, quam cuiquam vix credibile. Laus ista *Gallofridum* in *Angliam* reversum sequebatur, tanquam comes ejus virtutis individua. Ejusmodi igitur laetus successibus forum *Londinense* & collegia leguleiorum, qui ibidem patria jura interpretantur, frequentavit, ut & ante *Galliam* cognitam forsitan fecerat.

Illis temporibus inter forenses clarissimus erat *Joannes Goverus,* cujus vitam praescripsimus, homo venerandae aetatis, & qui mirum in modum *Anglicae* linguae politiei studebat. Hic, perspecta indole & examinata *Gallofridi* probitate, illum in familiarem sibi accivit, illum ulnis amplexus est, illum etiam in honestis deliciis habuit, illum denique tanquam *numen aliquod* modo non veneratus est. Ut ego taceam, ipsemet *Goverus* in libro, qui titulo *Amantis* inscribitur, abunde satis declarat, quanti suum *Chaucerum* fecerit; quem accuratissime prius laudatum, eximium vocat poetam, & sui operis quasi *Aristarchum* facit. Ecce tibi, lector, pulcherrimum virtutis certamen, nam ut *Goverus,* homo parum sibi tribuens, lucubrationes, quas consummaverat *Gallofridi* judicio modeste submisit; sic rursus *Chaucerus* Amores Troili *Goveri* & *Strodaei* calculis subjecit. Sed quis hic *Strodaeus* fuerit, apud autorem nullum hactenus legi. At memini interim legisse me illustria de *Strodaeo, Maridunensis* societatis ad *Isidis Vadum* alumno, in poesi eruditissimo, qui & in catalogo *Maridunensium* postremis *Eadveardi* tertii annis adscribitur. Tantum apparet ex *Gallofridi* versiculis philosophiae studiosum fuisse. Adde huc, quod quemadmodum *Chaucerus* admirator simul & sectator *Goveri,* ita . . . . *Schoganus,* cujus sepulchrum *Visimonasterii* extat, vir ad omnes facetias & sales compositus, *Chauceri* admirator ac imitator fuit. At rursus, quanto discipulus *Chaucerus* major *Govero* praeceptore suo, tanto minor erat *Schoganus Chaucero.*

Nunc vero orationis series postulat, ut aperte doceamus quem scopum *Gallofridum* studiis praefixerit. Profecto ejus scopus unicus fuit, ut linguam *Anglicam* numeris omnibus quam ornatissimam redderet, viderat enim *Goverum* in eodem negotio belle processisse. Quare nullum non movendum sibi lapidem putabat, quo ad supremam felicitatis metam perveniret. Et quoniam poesim praeter caetera semper dilexit, amavit, coluit; visum est ei vel commodissimum per illum ad ipsa eloquentiae culmina viam patefacere. Tale etenim est poesis, ut tropos, elegantias, ornamenta, copiam, & quicquid venerum & leporum est, non modo admittat, verum, quod multo majus, suo quodam jure poscat. Adde huc, quod *Italos* & *Gallos,* qui plurima suis linguis terse, nitide, ac eleganter scripserunt, in partem operis evocaverit. Tantum est inclytos habere duces, quos sequaris. *Petrarcha* circa haec tempora in *Italia* claruit, cujus opera lingua ibidem vernacula eo elegantiae perducta est, ut cum ipsa *Latina* de eloquentiae palma contenderit. Quidam etiam *Alanus* linguam *Gallicam* infinitis modis expoliebat. Uterque istorum (multos alios clarissimae notae homines, qui eadem fecerunt, omitto) calcar *Chaucero,* alioqui sua sponte satis currenti, addidit. Bonis igitur avibus incepto operi incubuit, nunc libellos *Gallica* lingua compte, ornate, diserte scriptos in patrium sermonem transferens; nunc *Latinos* versus *Anglicis,* sed docte, sed apte, sed canore exprimens; nunc multa è suo capite nata, & *Latinorum* felicitatem aequantia, victuris chartis commendans; nunc lectori ut prodesset nervis omnibus contendens, & vicissim ut eundem delectaret sedulo curans; nec antea finem fecit, quam linguam nostram ad eam puritatem, ad eam eloquentiam, ad eam denique brevitatem ac gratiam perduxerat, ut inter expolitas gentium linguas posset recte quidem connumerari. Itaque in libris meorum *Epigrammaton* his versibus ejus gloriae assurgo:

> Praedicat *Aligerum* merito *Florentia Dantem,*
> *Italia* & numeros tota, *Petrarche,* tuos:
> *Anglia Chaucerum* veneratur nostra poetam,
> Cui veneres debet patria lingua suas.

Et rursus:

> Dum juga montis aper, frondes dum laeta volucris
> Squamiger & liquidas piscis amabit aquas:
> *Maeonides, Graecae* linguae clarissimus autor,
> *Aonio* primus carmine semper erit.
> Sic quoque *Virgilius Romanae* gloria musae
> Maxima, vel *Phoebo* judice, semper erit.
> Nec minus & noster *Galfridus* summa *Britannae*
> *Chaucerus* citharae gratia semper erit.
> Illos quis nescit felicia saecla tulisse,
> Hunc talem & tantum protulit hora rudis.
> Tempora vidisset quod si florentia musis,
> Aequasset celebres, vel superasset avos.

Neque hic pigebit in medium adducere Hendecasyllabos, ex eodem fonte petitos, quos aliquot abhinc annis, orante *Thoma Bertholeto,* typographo cum diligenti tum erudito, scripsi:

Cum novum brevis *Atticus* leporem
Invenisset, & undecunque *Graecam*
Linguam perpoliisset, insolenter
Barbaros reliquos vocare coepit.
Cujus vestigia impiger *Quirinus*
Ter certo pede persequens, *Latinum*
Sermonem bene reddidit venustum;
Et cum *Graeco* alios rudes vocavit.
At quanto mihi rectius videtur
Fecisse officium suum disertus
Chaucerus, brevitate primus apta
Linguam qui patriam redegit illam
In formam, ut venere & lepore multo,
Ut multo sale, gratiaque multa
Luceret, velut *Hesperus* minora
Inter sidera; nec tamen superbe
Linguae barbariem exprobravit ulli.
Quare vos juvenes manu *Britanni*
Laeta spargite nunc rosas süave-
Spirantes, violasque molliores,
Et vestro date, candidi, poetae
Formosam ex hedera [citi] coronam.

Sed jam satis nostrarum nugarum adposuimus. Alius ille fortis homo erat, quam ut meae praeconio musae meritas laudes accipere queat. O quanto citius sub aequo judice à suis operibus justam consequetur laudem. Ideoque optarem quidem nostram linguam poetis *Latinis* familiarem esse: tunc facile inquam, facile in meam sententiam irent. At quoniam quod opto vix fieri potest, tantum exoratos volo, ut mihi *Latinarum* literarum amatori aliquid in hac parte fidei habeant. Quo auspicio non gravabor ejus lucubrationum inscriptiones *Latinitate* donare; ut sic saltem leonem, quemadmodum in proverbio est, ex ipsis aestiment unguibus.

Quanquam priusquam id, quod modo sum pollicitus, praestitero, non alienum meo erit instituto palam facere *Gulielmum Caxodunum,* hominem nec indiligentem, nec indoctum, & quem constat primum *Londini* artem exercuisse typographicam, *Chauceri* opera, quotquot vel pretio vel precibus comparare potuit, in unum volumen collegisse. Vicit tamen *Caxodunicam* editionem *Bertholetus* noster opera *Gulielmi Thynni;* qui, multo laßore, sedulitate, ac cura usus in perquirendis vetustis exemplaribus, multa primae adjecit editioni. Sed nec in hac parte caruit *Brianus Tucca,* mihi familiaritate conjunctissimus, & *Anglicae* linguae eloquentia mirificus, sua gloria, edita in postremam impressionem praefatione elimata, luculenta. eleganti. Sequar igitur codicem paucis ab hinc annis impressum. & promissum adponam syllabon.

Fabulae *Cantianae* XXIV.

quarum duae soluta oratione scriptae; sed *Petri Aratoris* fabula, quae communi doctorum consensu *Chaucero,* tanquam vero parenti, attribuitur, in utraque editione, quia malos sacerdotum mores vehementer increpavit, suppressa est.

De Arte amandi, alias *Romaunce of the Rose.*
Amores *Troili* & *Chrysidis* lib. 5.
Testamentum *Chrysidis,* & ejusdem Lamentatio.
Amores Heroidum.
De Consolatione Philosophiae, soluta oratione.
Somnium *Chauceri.*
Chorus Avium.
Flos Humanitatis,
qui libellulus a multis, tanquam nothus, rejicitur.
De Pietate mortua, & ejus Sepultura.
Chorus Heroidum.
De Astrolabio ad *Ludovicum* filium suum, prosa.
Querela Equitis cogn. *Nigri.*
Encomium Mulierum.
De Fama lib. 3.
Testamentum Amoris, lib. 3.
Threni *Magdalenae.*
De Remedio Amoris.
Querelae *Martis* & *Veneris.*
Epistola *Cupidinis.*
Cantiones.

Hactenus de nomenclatura ejus librorum, qui hodie passim leguntur. Praeter illos tamen, quos ego recensui, ipsemet in prologo, *Amoribus Heroidum* praefixo, fatetur se scripsisse libellum de *Morte Blanchae* ducis: tum etiam *Origenis de Magdalena* opusculum transtulisse: quod ego, (si modo *Origenes* tale quidquam scripsit) idem esse arbitror cum *Lamentatione Magdalenae,* de qua superius in syllabo mentionem feci.

Forsitan hic aliquis finem dicendi à me expectaret, sed ego pauca adhuc habeo, quae *Chaucerum* posteritati magnifice commendabunt. Nam, quemadmodum *Richardo Burdegalensi, Anglorum* regi, cognitus, & virtutum nomine charus fuit; ita etiam *Henrico* quarto, & ejus filio, qui de *Gallis* triumphavit, eisdem titulis commendatissimus erat. Quid quod & tota nobilitas *Anglica* illum, tanquam absolutum torrentis eloquentiae exemplum, suspexit. Accessit insuper ad ejus gloriam, quod sororem habuerit, quae *Gulielmo Polo,* (nisi me nomen fallit) *Sudovolgiae* duci, nupsit, ac magno in splendore *Aquelmi* vitam egit; ubi postea, fatis sic volentibus, diem quoque obiit, &, ut ego aliquando accepi, sepulta est.

Inter haec *Chaucerus* ad canos devenit, sensitque ipsam senectutem morbum esse; qua ingravescente, dum is *Londini* causas suas curaret, mortuus est, & *Visimonasterii* in australi insula basilicae, D. *Petro* sacrae, sepultus. *Ludovicum* autem reliquit fortunarum suarum, quas utcunque amplas habebat, haeredem, & praecipue villae suae *Vodestochae*, regiae admodum vicinae. Aliquanto post tempore *Gulielmus Caxodunus Chauceri* monimentum hoc disticho inscribi fecit:

> *Galfridus* CHAUCER vates, & fama poesis
> Maternae, hac sacra sum tumulatus humo.

Hi duo versus desumpti fuerunt ex quadam naenia, quam *Stephanus Surigonus, Mediolanensis,* poeta suo tempore clarus, rogante *Gulielmo Caxtono,* scripsit. Qu.re juvat totam ipsam naeniam, quoniam tersa, canora, & rotunda est, in praesentia recitare. Sic enim *Chaucerus,* qui re vera maximus fuit, nobili testimonio externi scriptoris major videbitur:

> *Peirides* musae, si possunt numina fletus
>   Fundere, divinas atque rigare genas,
> *Galfridi* CHAUCER vatis crudelia fata
>   Plangite; sit lacrymis abstinuisse nefas.
> Vos coluit vivens, at vos celebrate sepultum:
>   Reddatur merito gratia digna viro.
> Grande decus nobis est docti musa *Maronis,*
>   Qua didicit melius lingua *Latina* loqui:
> Grande novumque decus CHAUCER famamque paravit,
>   Heu quantum fuerat priscra *Britanna* rudis!
> Reddidit insignem maternis versibus, ut jam
>   Aurea splendescat, ferrea facta prius.
> Hunc latuisse virum nil, si tot opuscula vertes,
>   Dixeris, egregiis quae decorata modis
> *Socratis* ingenium, vel fontes philosophiae,
>   Quicquid & arcani dogmata sacra ferunt:
> Et quascunque velis tenuit doctissimus artes
>   Hic vates parvo conditus in tumulo.
> Ah! laudis quantum praeclara *Britannia* perdis,
>   Dum rapuit tantum mors odiosa virum,
> Crudeles Parcae, crudelia fila sorores,
>   Non tamen extincto corpore fama perit.
> Vivet in aeternum, vivent dum scripta poetae,
>   Vivant aeterno tot monimenta die,
> Si qua bonos tangit pietas, si carmine dignus,
>   Carmina qui cecinit tot cumulata modis.
> Haec sibi marmoreo scribantur verba sepulchro,
>   Haec meneat laudis sarcina summa suae:
> *Galfridus* CHAUCER *vates, & fama poesis*
>   *Maternae, hac sacra sum tumulatus humo.*
> Post obitum CAXTON voluit te vivere cura

Guilhelmi CHAUCER clare poeta, tui:
Nam tua non solum compressit opuscula formis,
Has quoque sed laudes jussit hic esse tuas.

Habes nunc, humanissime lector, elegos in nivea tabella depictos,
quos *Surigonus Visimonasterii* columnae, *Chauceri* sepulchro vicinae,
adfixit. Tu saepe eosdem in nostri vatis gratiam legas. Sic tibi,
quisquis eris, faveat suadela, leposque.

Leland's work, though not published until 1709, was written
much earlier; he died in 1552. The sources of his data are unknown; he may well have acquired much or all during the peregrina-
tion of England which he undertook at royal command to gather the
collections called his Itinerary. His list of Chaucer's works follows
closely the order as in Thynne's edition of 1542, see the notes in
Section II A below. The lives of Gower and of Chaucer are
reprinted in Brydges' Restituta, vol. II, pp. 1 ff. A translation of
the life of Chaucer is in Lounsbury's Studies, I : 133 ff.; see *ibid.*
for comment on Leland's work.

[Reprint of the life of Chaucer by John Bale in his *Illustrium Maioris Britanniae Scriptorum—Summarium*, 1548, fol. 198. No heading to the Life.]

GALFRIDUS Chaucer, Anglus, eques auratus, uir tam bonis disciplinis quam armata militia nobilis, exquisita quadam Anglici sermonis eloquentia, aetatem suam multo quam antea ornatiorem reddidit. Praeter Mathesim quam ingenue callebat, poeta lepidus erat. Ac talis apud suos Anglos, quales olim fuere apud Italos, Dantes & Petrarcha. Patrij sermonis restaurator, potius illustrator (& merito quidem) habetur adhuc primus. Boetium de consolatione philosophiae transtulit ad filium suum Ludouicum Chaucerum, & poemate uario, in lingua materna perappositae ac compte tractatus hos fecit, ut partim uidi, partim ab amico quodam fideliter accepi,

> Trophaeum Lombardicum,   li. 1.
> De principum ruina,   li. 1.
> Emblemata moralia,   li. 1.
> Amatoria carmina,   li. 1.
> De curia Veneris, li. 1.   In Maio cum uirescerent, &c.
> Chryseidae testamentum, trac. 1.   Diuturnis horis donec dolo.
> Chryseidae quærimoniam, trac. 1.   O tristem & cruentam lethi.
> Laudes bonarum mulierum, trac. 1.   Mille uicibus accepi muli.
> Cleopatrae uitam, trac. 1.   Post mortem Ptolemei regis,
> Vitam Thysbes Babylonicae, trac. 1.   Babyloniae quam Semi-
>   rannis,
> Vitam Didonis Carthaginensis, trac. 1.   Tuo sit nomine Vergili,
> De Hipsyphile & Medaea, trac. 1.   Sinistri amoris radix Iason,
> Vitam Lucretiae Romanae, trac. 1.   Fingendum mihi est Romano,
> De Ariadna Cretensi, trac. 1.   Cretensium rex Minos infer,
> De Phylomela Atheniensi, trac. 1.   formarum fabricator, qui,
> De Phyllide Thracensi, trac. 1.   Tam argumento quam autori,
> De Hypermestra Aegyptia, trac. 1.   In Graecia duo fratres erant.
> Somnium Chauceri, trac. 1.   Admirari hercle sat nequeo,
> Volucrum conglobationem, trac. 1.   Tam breuis est uita, ars,
> Vrbanitatis florem, trac. 1.   In februario cum luna,
> De misericordiae sepultura, trac. 1.   Quaesitam a multis annis,
> Carmen facetum, trac. 1.   In somno semisepultus au.
> De Augea & Telepho, trac. 1.   Immitis belligerantium deus,
> Choream dominarum, trac. 1.   Dum in Septembri uirgulta,
> De Astrolabij ratione, trac. 1.   Fili mi Ludouice, certis,
> Quaeremoniam, nigri militis, trac. 1.   In Maio dum Flora regina,
> Foeminarum Encomion, trac. 1.   Quibus animus est de muli,
> Narrationes diuersorum, trac. 1.   In comitatu Lyncolniensi,
> De Troilo & Chryseida,   trac. 1.
> De Caeyce & Halcyona,   trac. 1.
> In obitum Blanchiae ducissae trac. 1.

Tragoedias graues,	*li. 1.*
Comoedias leues,	*li. 1.*
Satyras & Iambos,	*li. 1.*
Facecias & Iocos,	*li. 1.*
Elegias & poemata,	*li. 1.*

De ceteris nihil accepi. A Guilhelmo Whyte atque alijs tunc uerbi ministris talia hausisse fertur, quod monachorum otia, missantium turbam ingentem, horas non intellectas, reliquias, ac ceremonias parum probauerit. Ad annum humane redemptionis, 1450, uixisse perhibetur sub Henrico sexto.

This, Bale's earlier biographical work, is much briefer than the *Catalogus* discussed below. The life of Chaucer, like many of the accounts contained in both works, was entirely recast for the later and more extensive catalogue. Bale derived much of his information from Leland; the antiquary Burton says indignantly that "Leland has delivered things impartially and in smooth language, Bale quite contrary and full of scurrilities." The list of Chaucer's works here given is discussed in Section II A below. On Bale see Lounsbury's Studies, I: 149, III: 35.

Bale's autograph notebook, MS. Selden supra 64, was annotated and printed as *Index Britanniae Scriptorum* Quos ex variis bibliothecis non parvo labore collegit Ioannes Baleus, cum aliis (etc.) Edited by Reginald Lane Poole with the help of Mary Bateson. Oxford, 1902.

This notebook differs from the two biographical works published by Bale; he arranged it alphabetically, not chronologically, and gave in most cases references to the sources of his information. It was begun about 1549, and its latest note of time is just after the appearance of the 1557 *Catalogus,* q. v.

Little is said in this Index of the life of Chaucer; but the list of his works there preserved, pp. 74-78, is discussed below in Section II A (3).

[Reprint of the Life of Chaucer by John Bale in his *Scriptorum Illus-trium Maioris Britanniae—Catalogus*, Basle, 1557-59, vol. I, pp. 525-527.]

GALFRIDVS CHAVCER. XXIIII.

Galfridvs Chavcer, nobili loco natus, & summae spei iuuenis, Oxonienses scholas tam diligenter quàm qui maximè cele-brauit: id quod ut faceret, academiae uicinitas quodammodo inuitauit. Nam quibusdam argumentis adducebatur Lelandus, ut crederet Oxoniensem uel Barochensem prouinciam, illius fuisse natale solum. Hinc acutus dialecticus, hinc dulcis rhetor, hinc lepidus poeta, hinc grauis philosophus, ac sanctus denique theologus euasit. Mathematicus insuper ingeniosus erat, à Ioanne Sombo & Nicolao Lynna, Carmelitis Lynnensibus, uirisque in Mathesi eruditis, instructus: quos ipse in libro suo de Sphaera celebrat, & clericos reuerendos uocat. Constat utique, illum circa postremos annos Ricardi secundi in Gallijs floruisse, magnamque illic ex assidua in literis exercitatione gloriam sibi comparasse. Tum praeterea eadem opera, omnes ueneres, lepôres, delicias, sales, ac postremò gratias linguae Gallicae tam altè imbibisse, quàm cuiquam uix credibile. Laus ista Galfridum in Angliam reuersum sequebatur, tanquam comes eius uirtutis indiuidua. Eiusmodi igitur laetis successibus, forum Londinense & collegia leguleiorum, qui ibidem patria iura interpretantur, frequentauit, familiaremque amicum inter eos Ioannem Gouerum mox habuit. Horum duorum unicus erat studiorum scopus, ut linguam Anglicam numeris omnibus quàm ornatissimam redderent. Nec antea finem fecerant, quàm linguam illam ad eam eloquentiam, ad eam denique breuitatem perduxerant, ut inter ex-politas gentium linguas posset rectè quidem connumerari. Huius Chauceri lucubrationum inscriptiones non grauabor hic latinitate donare: ut sic saltem leonem, ut in prouerbio est, homines ex ipsis aestiment unguibus. Adponam ergo syllabon, composuit enim,

Fabulas Cantianas 24.	*Lib. 1. Olim erat, ut ueteres historae innuunt.*
Praefationes earundem,	*Lib. 1. Dùm imbribus suauibus Aprilis.*
Aratoris narrationem,	*Lib. 1. Agricola tulit aratrum, dum essent.*
De arte amandi, Romane,	*Lib. 1. Plerique fatentur in somnijs meras.*
Amores Troili & Chrysidis,	*Lib. 5. Vt demonstrarem Troili dupli-cem.*
Testamentum Chrysidis,	*Lib. 1. Diuturnis horis donec dolo.*
Lamentationem Chrysidis,	*Lib. 1. O gemitus, offella moerore im.*
Amores Heroidum,	*Lib. 1.*
De consolatione philosophiae,	*Lib. 5. Carmina quae quondam studio.*
Somnium Chauceri,	*Lib. 1. Admiror hercle plurimum, quali.*

Chorum auium,	*Lib. 1. Vita tam breuis est, artis tam.*
Vrbanitatis florem,	*Lib. 1. In Februario, cum cornuta esset.*
De pietate mortua,	*Lib. 1. Oh, quod pietatem tandiu quaesi.*
Heroidum Chorum,	*Lib. 1. In Septembri, dum folia uirgulta.*
De astrolabio, ad filium,	*Lib. 1. Fili mi Ludouice, certis signis.*
Querelam equitis nigri,	*Lib. 1. In Maio, dum Flora regina terram.*
Encomium mulierum,	*Lib. 1. Quibus animus est, mulieres.*
De fama, et eius domicilio,	*Lib. 3. Vertat nobis Deus somnia in.*
Testamentum amoris,	*Lib. 3. Multi sunt qui patulis auribus.*
Threnos Magdalenae,	*Lib. 1. Moestitiae lethiferae uoraginibus.*
De remedio amoris,	*Lib. 1. Viso multiplici incommodo, quod.*
Querelam Martis & Veneris,	*Lib. 1. Congratulemini amatores, pullu.*
Epistolam Cupidinis,	*Lib. 1. Cupido, ad cuius nutum gener.*
Cantiones quoque,	*Lib. 1. Mille historias adhuc recensere.*
De Meliboeo & prudentia,	*Lib. 1. Iuuenis quidam Meliboeus, pontem.*
De peccatis ac remedijs,	*Lib. 1. Hieremiae 6 State super uias.*
Laudes bonarum mulierum,	*Lib. 1. Mille uicibus ab hominibus atque.*
Cleopatrae uitam,	*Lib. 1. Post mortem Ptolemaei regis magni.*
Vitam Thisbae Babylonicae	*Lib. 1. Babyloniae quandoque contigit.*
Vitam Didonis Carthaginensis,	*Lib. 1. Gloriosum sit Vergili Mantuane.*
De Hypsiphile & Medea,	*Lib. 1. Dissimulantium amatorum radix.*
Lucretiae Romanae uitam,	*Lib. 1. Narrare nunc oportet auxilium.*
De Ariadna Cretensi,	*Lib. 1. Discerne, infernalis Cretae rex.*
De Philomela Atheniensi,	*Lib. 1. Formarum fabricator, qui formasti.*
De Phyllide Thracensi,	*Lib. 1. Tam argumento quàm authoritate.*
De Hypermnestra Aegyptia,	*Lib. 1. In Graecia aliquando duo fratres.*
Carmen Chauceri,	*Lib. 1. Probae educationis amantissima.*
Super impia domina,	*Lib. 1. Me dormientem aureus sopor.*
De Annelida & Arcyto,	*Lib. 1. Immitis belligerantium deus.*
De cuculo & philomela,	*Lib. 1. Amorum Deus, quàm potens.*
Octo quaestiones & responsa,	*Lib. 1. In Graecia quandoque tam nobili.*
Chronicon conquestus Anglici,	*Lib. 1. Ea aetate, ut ueteres annales.*
De curia Veneris,	*Lib. 1. In Maio cum uirescerent, &.*
Epigrammata quoque,	*Lib. 1. Fugite multitudinem, ueri.*
Narrationes diuersorum,	*Lib. 1. In comitatu Lyncolniensi fuit.*
De Ceyce & Halcyona,	*Lib. 1.*
In obitum Blanchiae ducissae,	*Lib. 1.*
De Vulcani ueru,	*Lib. 1.*
De leone et eius dignitate,	*Lib. 1.*

Vitam D. Ceciliae,	*Lib. 1.*
Hymnos amatorios,	*Lib. 1.*
Amores Palaemonis & Arcyti,	*Lib. 1.*
De Thisbae amore,	*Lib. 1.*
De castello dominarum,	*Lib. 1.*
Comoedias & Tragoedias,	*Lib. 1.*
Facetias & iocos,	*Lib. 1.*
Dantem Italum transtulit,	*Lib. 1.*
Petrarchae quaedam,	*Lib. 1.*
Origenis tractatum,	*Lib. 1.*

Aliáque plura fecit, in quibus monachorum ocia, missantium tam magnam multitudinem, horas non intellectas, reliquias, peregrinationes, ac caerimonias parum probauit. Inter haec Chaucerus ad canos deuenit, sensitque ipsam senectutem morbum esse. Qua ingrauescente, dum Londini causas suas curaret, mortuus est, & Vuestmonasterij in australi Basilicae parte sepultus. Vixit anno Domini 1402, ut in charta Cupidinis refert. In quodam libro suorum Epigrammaton his uersibus Lelandus illum celebrat:

> *Praedicat Algerum meritó Florentiae Dantem,*
> *Italia & numeros tota Petrarche tuos.*
> *Anglia Chaucerum ueneratur nostra poetam,*
> *Cui ueneres debet patria lingua suas.*

APPENDIX.

Ex Lelandi Catalogo: Illis temporibus inter Forenses, clarissimus erat Ioannes Gouerus, historicus ac poeta moralis, cuius uitam praescripsimus, homo uenerandae aetatis, et qui mirum in modum Anglicae linguae politiei studebat. Hic perspecta indole & examinata Galfridi probitate, illum in familiarem sibi acciuit, illum ulnis amplexus est, illum etiam in honestis delicijs habuit, illum denique tanquam numen aliquod propemodum uenerabatur. Et ut ego (inquit) taceam, ipsemet Gouerus in libro qui titulo Amantis inscribitur, abundé satis declarat, quanti suum Chaucerum fecerit: quem accuratissimé prius laudatum, eximium poetam uocat, & sui operis quasi Aristarchum facit. Ecce tibi lector, pulcherrimum uirtutis certamen. Nam ut Gouerus, homo parum sibi tribuens, lucubrationes quas consummauerat, Galfridi iudicio modesté submisit: sic rursus Chaucerus, Amores Troili, Goueri & Strodi calculis subiecit, &c. Et quoniam poesim praeter caetera semper dilexit, amauit, coluit: uisum est ei uel commodissimum, per illam ad ipsa eloquentiae culmina uiam patefacere. Tale etenim quiddam est poesis, ut tropos, elegantias, ornamenta, copiam, & quicauid uenerum et leporum est, non modò admittat: uerùm quod multo maius est, suo quodam iure poscat. Adde huc, quòd Italos & Gallos, qui plurima suis linguis terse ac nitidè scripserunt, in partem operis euocauerit. Dantes & Petrarcha Italicam linguam, Alanus Gallicam,

Ioannes Mena Hispanicam, atque alij alias, infinitis modis tunc expolierant: hi Chaucero calcar addiderunt. Bonis igitur auibus incœpto operi incubuit: nunc libellos Gallica lingua scriptos in patrium sermonem transferens: nunc Latinos uersus Anglicis, sed docté, exprimens: nunc multa è suo capite nata, & Latinorum foelicitatem aequantia, uicturis chartis commendans, lectorique neruis omnibus prodesse contendens. Accessit etiam ad eius gloriam, quòd sororem habuerit, quae Guilhelmo Polo Sudouolgiorum duci nupsit, ac magno in splendore Aquelmi uitam egit, &c.*

[Reprint of the Life of Chaucer from John Pits' *De Rebus Anglicis*, Paris 1619, pp. 572-575.]

DE GALFREDO CHAUCERO.

GALFREDVS Chaucerus apud Vvodstoc non longè ab Oxonio in Anglia claris parentibus natus, patrem habuit Equestris ordinis virum, & ipse tandem auratus factus est Eques. Vir belli pacisque artibus mirè florens. Cùm ab ipsa pueritia praeclaram ostenderet indolem, ad scholas Oxonienses excolendi ingenij causa adolescens missus est. Vbi tanta cum industria, tanta cum foelicitate florentes annos in optimarum litterarum studijs collocauit, vt nihil eorum omiserit, quae ad ornatum ingenij sui longè cultissimi facerent. Nam iam antequam virilem aetatem attigisset, erat Poëta elegans, & qui Poësim Anglicam ita illustrauit, vt Anglicus Homerus meritò haberetur. Rhetor etiam disertus, Mathematicus peritus, Philosophus acutus, Theologus denique non contemnendus. Exquisitissimos in his omnibus scientijs habuit praeceptores, quos & ipse propter miram animi alacritatem ad studia, & singularem ingenij promptitudinem ac fœlicitatem, ita consecutus est, vt eorum cuique in cuiusque facultate par & aequalis, si non superior, euaserit. In scientijs Mathematicis legentes audiuit Ioannem Sombum & Nicolaum Linnam Carmelitas Linnenses, viros per illa tempora pereruditos, & Mathematicorum illius aetatis facilè principes, quos Chaucerus in sua sphaera reuerenter admodum compellat, & cum honore nominat. Absolutis autem in Anglia studijs, transfretauit in Galliam, tum vt linguam addisceret, & exterorum mores videret, tum etiam vt nihil reliqui faceret ad accuratissimam scientiarum perfectionem, si quid ei forsan suppeditaret Gallia, quod Anglia non haberet. Ibi omnes hominis ingenium, eruditionem, vrbanitatem, morum suauitatem, aliasque insignes dotes admiratione simul & amore prosecuti sunt. Ille interim quae è re eius erat, non neglexit, didicitque linguam, lepores, sales, omnesque Gallorum argutas facetias. Qua supellectile cumulatè instructus, & quasi quibusdam floribus nitidè ornatus, redijt in Angliam. Deindè Londini agens patrijs iuribus studuit, & Collegia iurisperitorum illic inuisit, historias etiam non omittens, ad excolendam patriam linguam se contulit. Inter haec incidit in Ioannem Gouerum (de quo mox dicendum) virum nobilem, doctum Galfredo ferè per omnia similem, quique eundem prorsus habuit omnium studiorum suorum propositum finem. Deprehenditur facilè morum similitudo, initur citò amicitia, concurritur in idem propositum, coniunguntur labores, frequens sit congressus, quotidiana familiaritas, omnis conatus eò refertur, vt materna excolatur lingua, & in Anglico sermone eloquentiae Romanae expressa appareant vestigia. Et attulerunt certè hi duo viri nostro idiomati tantum splendoris & ornamenti, quantum ante illos prorsus nemo. Nam sibi mutuò calcar addiderunt, & vter patriae plus afferret honoris, vterque vinci & vincere ambiens, amanter contenderunt. Non solum memores, sed etiam imitatores illius

> Quod lingua Catonis & Enni
> Sermonem patrium ditauerit, & noua rerum
> Nomina protulerit.

Et quia sua vel patrum memoria nouerant multos iam linguas vulgares industria cultura exornasse: Nam Dantes & Petrarcha Italicam, Alanus Gallicam, Ioannes Mena Hispanicam linguas iam cultiores reddiderant: operae precium igitur putabant isti, idem in Anglica lingua praestare, quod viderant alios in suis linguis magna cum laude, & posteritatis incomparabili vtilitate gnauiter praestitisse. Itaque alia ex alijs linguis transferendo, alia imitando, alia inueniendo, & proprio Marte componendo, comptè, tersè, politè scribere Anglico idiomate conati sunt. Et profectò in multis Latinorum elegantiam, si non sint plenè consecuti, at certè non infœliciter imitati. Vterque tamen minùs sibi tribuebat, quàm alteri. Vndè factum est, vt alter alterius iudicio scripta sua mutuò subijceret, & si quid in altero deesset, alter suppleret, atque ità communicatis consilijs, vtriusque lucubrationes, saepiùs sub incude vocatae, emendatiores in publicum prodierunt. Vnum hic, licet à nostro proposito forsan alienum videri quibusdam poterit, adnotare non piget. Licet Chaucerus tantum esset ordinis Equestris, tamen sororem habuit Guilhelmo Polo Illustrissimo Suffolcensium Duci in matrimonio longè supra suam sortem fœlicissimè splendidissimèque collocatam. Quod connubium illa magis virtutibus & doctrinae fratris, quàm splendori suorum natalium habuit acceptum. Nunc restat videre quibus litterarum monimentis, hanc nominis immortalitatem, quam habet, consecutus sit. De quo Lelandus noster inter epigrammata sua sic scribit

> Praedicat Algerum meritò Florentia Dantem,
> Italia & numeros tota Petrarcha tuos.
> Anglia Chaucerum veneratur nostra Poëtam,
> Cui veneres debet patria lingua suas.

Scripsit autem cultissimus noster Chaucerus pleraque Anglicè, sed quoniam omnia ferè Latina facta sunt, operum titulos & exordia Latinè ponam.

De consolatione Philosophiae, Libros quinque. Carmina quae quondam studio.

Somnium suum, Librum vnum. Admiror herclè plurimùm, quali.

Fabulas Cantianas viginti quatuor. Cùm retractat. Anglicè. *Librum vnum.* Olim erat, vt veteres historiae innuunt. MS. in Lumleiana.

Praefationes earundem, Librum vnum. Dum imbribus suauibus Aprilis.

Amores Troili & Chrysidis, Libros quinque. Vt demonstrarem Troili duplicem. MS. Cantabrigiae in Collegio S. Benedicti.

Testamentum Chrysidis, Librum vnum. Diuturnis horis donec dolo.

Lamentationem Chrysidis, Librum vnum. O gemitus offella maerore in.

Testamentum amoris, Libros tres. Multi sunt qui patulis auribus.

Threnos Magdalenae, Librum vnum. Maestitiae lethiferae voraginibus.

De curia Veneris, Librum vnum. In Maio cum virescerent.

De Thisbae amore, Librum vnum.

Amores Palemonis & Arcyti, Librum vnum.

De remedio amoris, Librum vnum. Viso multiplici incommodo, quòd.

Querelam Martis & Veneris, Librum j. Congratulamini amatores pullu.

Epistolam Cupidinis, Librum vnum. Cupido ad cuius nutum.

De arte amandi Romanè, Librum vnum. Plerique fatentur in somnijs meras.

Amores Heroidum, Librum vnum.

Chorum Heroidum, Librum vnum. In Septembri dum folia virgulta.

Chorum auium, Librum vnum. Vita tam breuis est, artis tam.

De pietate mortua, Librum vnum. Oh quòd pietatem tam diù quaesiu.

Historiam Oedipi & Jocastae, Librum vnum.

Obsidionem Thebes, Librum vnum. Quem in versus Anglicos vertit Ioannes Lidgatus.

Vrbanitatis florem, Librum vnum. In februario cùm cornuta esset.

Oratoris narrationem, Librum vnum. Agricola tulit aratrum dum esset. Puto esse librum illum cui titulus Anglicè Pierce Ploumam: & habetur MS. Cantabrigiae in Collegio S. Benedicti, & Oxonij in publica.

Encomium mulierum, Librum vnum. Quibus animus est mulieres.

Querelam Equitis nigri,   *Librum vnum.* In Maio dum Flora Regina terram.

De fama & eius domicilio,   *Libros tres.* Vertat nobis Deus somnia in.

Cantionum,   *Librum vnum.* Mille historias adhuc recensere.

De Melibaeo & Prudentia,   *Librum j.* Iuuenis quidam Melibaeus, pontem.

De peccatis & remedijs,   *Librum vnum.* Hieremiae sexto, state super vias.

De Astrolabij ratione Anglicè ad filium suum Ludouicum,   *Librum vnum.* Fili mi Ludouice, certis signis. MS Cantabrigiae in Colle. S. Benedicti.

Origenis quendam tractatum transtulit,   *Librum vnum.*

Laudes bonarum mulierum,   *Librum j.* Mille vicibus ab hominibus atque.

Cleopatrae vitam,   *Librum vnum.* Post mortem Ptolemaei Regis magni.

Vitam Thisbae Babylonicae,   *Librum vnum.* Babyloniae quandoque contigit.

Vitam Didonis Carthaginensis,   *Libr. j.* Gloriosum fuit Virgili Mantuane.

De Hypsiphile & Medæa, Librum vnum. Dissimulantium amatorum radix.

Lucretiae Romanae vitam,   *Librum vnum.* Narrare nunc oportet auxilium.

De Ariadna Cretensi,   *Librum vnum.* Discerne, infernalis Cretae Rex.

De Philomela Atheniensi,   *Librum vnum.* Formarum fabricator qui form.

De Phyllide Tharsensi,   *Librum vnum.* Tam argumento quàm auctoritate.

De Hypermnestra Aegyptia,   *Librum j.* In Graecia aliquando duo fratres.

Super impia domina,   *Librum vnum.* Me dormientem aureus sopor.

De Aunelida & Arcito,   *Librum vnum.* Immitis belligerantium Deus.

Carmen Chauceri,   *Librum vnum.* Probae educationis amantissima.

Epigrammatum,   *Librum vnum.* Fugite multitudinem veri.

De Cuculo & Philomela,   *Librum vnum.* Amorum Deus quàm potens.

Octo quaestiones & responsa,   *Librum vnum.* In Graecia quandoque tam nobili.

Chronicon conquestus Anglici,   *Librum vnum.* Ea aetate, vt veteres annales.

Narrationes diuersorum,   *Librum vnum.* In Comitatu Lincoln-
iensi fuit.
Hymnos amatorios,   *Librum vnum.*
De castello dominarum,   *Librum vnum.*
De Ceyce & Halciona,   *Librum vnum.*
De Vulcani veru,   *Librum vnum.*
De leone & eius dignitate,   *Librum vnum.*
In obitum Blanchae Ducissae,   *Librum vnum.*
Vitam S. Ceciliae,   *Librum vnum.*
Facetias & iocos,   *Librum vnum.*
Comedias & tragoedias,   *Librum vnum.*
Dantis Itali scripta transtulit,   *Librum vnum.*
Petrarchae quaedam transtulit,   *Librum vnum.*
Joannis Moni Angli librum de arte amandi quem Parisijs Gallicè
scripsit, in versus Anglicos transtulit, & operi titulum dedit The
Romaunt ob the rose. Alia etiam multa partim ipse scripsit, partim
ex alijs linguis vertit. Quae omnia Anglicè impressa fuerunt Lon-
dini anno Domini 1561. Londini senex obdormiuit in Domino, &
apud Vvestmonasterium honorificè sepultus est die vicesimo quinto
Octobris anno post salutem humani generis per Christum hominem
factum reparatam 1400, initiante regnum apud Anglos Henrico
quarto. Porrò post annos centum quinquaginta quinque, anno
videlicet gratiae 1555, gratiam hanc fecit nostro Chaucero Nicolaus
Brighamus vt eius ossa transferret, & in nouo marmoreo tumulo
in capella S. Blasiis plendidiùs collocaret, adiunctis versibus se-
quentibus :

> *Qui fuit Anglorum vates ter maximus olim,*
> *Galfredus Chaucer conditur hoc tumulo.*
> *Annum si quaeras Domini, si tempora mortis,*
> *Ecce notae subsunt, quae tibi cuncta notent.*
> *25. Octobris 1400.*

Pits begins his catalogue with Brutus, the mythical settler of
Albion, and closes it with himself, writing in 1614. His sketches
average in length one or two to the quarto page; the greatest amount
of space is given to the Venerable Bede,—11 pages. Richard Rolle
of Hampole, Gower, and Skelton, have two or three pages each;
but Chaucer receives more attention than any other English poet.
However, some sentences in the biography of Chaucer belong equally
to that of Gower, as Pits therein enlarges upon the friendly rivalry
of the two poets in their attempts to polish their own productions
and to refine the English tongue.

The tone of many of these biographies is very laudatory, but
the language used regarding Chaucer is somewhat more so than is

2

the description of any other poet, Lydgate coming nearest. In fact, one or two of the sentences descanting upon Chaucer's manifold abilities and on his work as a translator are closely reproduced in the biography of Lydgate.

———

[Reprint of the Life of Chaucer prefixed to Speght's 1598 edition of the Works.]
Titlepage of the Life:—
    The Life of Ovr Learned | English Poet, Geffrey Chaucer.

	Countrey. Parentage. Education. Mariage.	
So much as we can find by Herauldes, Chronicles, & Records, of his	Children, with their	Mariage. Lands. Seruice. Reward. Issue. Death.
	Reuenues. Seruice. Reward. Friends. Bookes. Death.	

Guilielmus Camdenus.

Gaufredus Chaucer sui saeculi ornamentum extra omnem ingenij aleam positus, & Poetastras nostros longo post se interuallo relinquens,

           . . . . iam monte potitus
    Ridet anhelantem dura ad fastigia turbam.

———

THE LIFE OF GEFFREY CHAUCER.

His Countrey.

THIS famous and learned Poet Geffrey Chaucer Esquire, was supposed by Leland[1] to haue beene an Oxfordshire or Barke-shireman borne: For so reporteth Iohn Bale in his Catalogue of English writers: *Quibusdam argumentis adducebatur Lelandus, vt crederet, &c.* Some reasons did moue Leland to thinke, that Oxfordshire or Barkshire was his natiue Countrey.

But as it is euident by his owne wordes in the Testament of Loue, hee was borne[2] in the Citie of London: For thus he writeth there: Also in the Citie of London that is to me so deare and sweete, in which I was foorth growen, and more kindely loue haue I to that place, then to any other in yerth (as euery kindly creature hath full appetite to that place of his kindly ingendure, and to wilne rest and peace in that stede to abide) thilke peace should thus there haue been broken, which of all wise men is commended and desired.

In the Records of the Guild Hall in London wee find, that there was one Richard Chaucer Vintener[3] of London in the 23. yeere of Edward the third, who might well be Geffrey Chaucers father.

Also there was a Nunne of Saint Hellens in London named Elizabeth Chaucer, in the first yeere of Richard the second, as it is in Record, which seemeth either to haue beene his sister, or of his kindred, and by likelihood a Londoner borne.

Moreouer in the eight yeere of the same King, Geffrey Chaucer was Controller of the Custome-house in London, as after out of Recordes shall appeare.

Other dealings hee had in the citie, as we may plainly see in the Testament of Loue, all the which may mooue us to thinke, that he was borne in London.

His Parentage.

For his Parentage and place of birth, although Bale termeth him *Galfridus Chaucer nobili loco natus, & summae spei iuuenis,* yet in the opinion of some Heralds (otherwise then his vertues and learning commended him) hee descended not of any great house, which they gather by his Armes, *De argento & rubeo colore partita per longitudinem scuti cum benda ex transuerso, eisdem coloribus sed transmutatis depicta sub hac forma.*

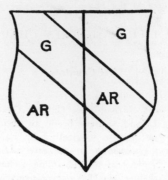

It may be that it were no absurditie to thinke (nay it seemeth likely, Chaucers skill in Geometry considered) that hee tooke the groundes and reasons of these Armes out of Euclyde, the 27. and 28. Proposition of the first booke: and some perchaunce are of that opinion, whose skill therein is comparable to the best.

And indeede both in respect of the name, which is French, as also by other coniectures it may be gathered, that his progenitors were Strangers.

But whereas some are of opinion that the first comming of the Chaucers into England was, when Queene Isabell[4] wife to Edward the second, and her sonne Prince Edward with Philip his new married wife, returned out of Henault[5] into England, at which time also almost three thousand Straungers came ouer with them (as by Chronicles appeareth) I can by no meanes consent with them; but rather must thinke, that their name and familie was of farre more auncient antiquitie, although by time decayed, as many moe haue been of much greater estate: and that the parents of Geffrey Chaucer were meere English, and he himselfe an Englishman borne. For els how could he haue come to that perfection in our language, as to be called, The first illuminer of the English tongue, had not both he, and his parents before him, been born & bred among vs. But what their names were or what issue they had, otherwise then by coniecture before giuen, wee can not declare.

Now whether they were Merchants, (for that in places where they haue dwelled, the Armes of the Merchants of the Staple haue been seene in the glasse windowes) or whether they were of other calling, it is not much necessary to search: but wealthy no doubt they were, and of good account in the common wealth, who brought vp their Sonne in such sort, that both he was thought fitte for the Court at home, and to be imployed for matters of state in forraine countreyes.

[Marginal Notes to the above are:] (1) *This Leland had commission from K. Hen. 8. to search all libraries in England for matters of Antiquitie: hee dyed in the daies of Edw. 6.*

(2) *About the second or third yeer of Edward 3. In the first booke & the fift Section.*

(3) *Vintner, quasi Winetunner, that is, a Merchaunt of the Vintrey, which sold by whole sale.*

(4) *This Queene Isabell beeing sent into Fraunce with her yong sonne Edward by the King of England her husband, to confer about matters with her brother the French King, would by no meanes returne, hauing conceiued a great hatred both against the Spensars, and also against the King for suffering himselfe to be misledde by their naughtie counsaile, but by all meanes stirred the people to rebellion, and in the ende came ouer her selfe with almost three thousand strangers besides Englishmen.*

(5) *Henault, a prouince lying betweene France and Flaunders.*

His Education.

His bringing vp, as *Leland* saieth, was in the Vniuersitie of Oxford, as also of Cambridge, as appeareth by his owne wordes in his booke entituled *The Court of Loue:* and in Oxford by all likelihood in Canterburie[1] or in Merton Colledge, with *Iohn Wickelife,* whose opinions in religion he much affected: where besides his priuate studie, hee did with great diligence frequent the publique schooles and disputations: *Hinc acutus Dialecticus, hinc dulcis Rhetor, hinc lepidus Poeta, hinc grauis Philosophus, ac sanctus Theologus euasit. Mathematicus insuper ingeniosus erat à Iohanne Sombo, &c.* Hereupon, saith Leland, he became a wittie Logician, a sweete Rhetorician, a pleasant Poet, a graue Philosopher, and a holy Diuine. Moreouer he was a skilfull Mathematician, instructed therin by Iohn Some & Nicholas Lynne[2] friers Carmelites of Linne, and men verie skilfull in the Mathematikes, whome he in his booke called *The Astrolabe,* doth greatly commend, and calleth them, Reuerend clerkes.

By his trauaile also in Fraunce and Flaunders, where hee spent much time in his young yeeres, but more in the latter end of the reigne of K. Richard the second, he attained to great perfection in all kind of learning. For so doe *Bale* and *Leland* also report. *Circa postremos Richardi secundi annos in Galliis floruit, magnamque illic ex assidua in literis exercitatione gloriam sibi comparauit. Domum reuersus forum Londinense, & Collegia Leguleiorum, qui ibidem patria iura interpretantur, frequentauit, &c.* About the latter end of King Richard the seconds daies he florished in Fraunce, and got himselfe great commendation there by his diligent exercise in learning. After his returne home, he frequented the Court at London, and the Colledges of the Lawyers, which there interprete the lawes of the lande, and among them he had a familiar frend called

Iohn Gower.² This Gower in his booke which is intituled *Confessio Amantis*, termeth Chaucer a worthie Poet, and maketh him as it were, the Iudge of his workes,

It seemeth that both these learned men were of the inner Temple: for not many yeeres since, Master *Buckley* did see a Record in the same house, where *Geoffrey Chaucer* was fined two shillings for beating a Franciscane fryer in Fleetstreete.

Thus spending much time in the Vniuersities, Fraunce, Flaunders, and Innes of Court, he prooued a singular man in all kind of knowledge.

[The marginal notes are:] (1)*Canterbury Colledge in Oxford founded by* Simon Islippe *Archbishop of Canterbury, was suppressed in the reigne of K. Henry the 8. & ioyned vnto Christs Church.*

(2) *Nicolaus de Lynna studiorum praecipuas partes in Mathesi collocauit, quae quatuor disciplinarum orbem complectitur: videlicet, Arithmeticam, Geometricam, Musicam, & Astrologiam. Bale.*

(3) Iohn Gower, *a Yorkshire man borne & a knight, as Bale writeth, studied not onely the common lawes of the land, but all other kind of good literature. Hee lyeth buried in Saint Mary Oueries in Southwarke, with his image lying ouer him in a habite of purple damaske downe to his feete: a collar of esses gold about his necke, and on his head a garland of yvie and roses, the one being the ornament of a knight, and the other of a Poet. Vnder his head he hath the likenesse of three bookes, which hee compiled: the first,* Speculum meditantis *in French: the second,* Vox clamantis *in Latine: the third,* Confessio amantis *in English.*

His Marriage.

He matched in marriage with a Knights daughter of Henault, called *Paon de Ruet*, king of Armes, as by this draught appeareth, taken out of the office of the Heraldes. This gentlewoman, whome hee married (whose name we can not finde) as it may be gathered by Chaucers owne wordes in his dreame, was attendant on Blanch the Duchesse in the Duke of Lancasters house, as also her sister Katherine was: or els waited on the Duchesse Maude sister of Blanch, who was married to William Duke of Bauare, Earle of Henault, Zeland, and Holland. But howsoeuer it was, by this marriage he became brother in law to Iohn of Gaunt⁴ Duke of Lancaster, as hereafter appeareth.

[Marginal Note:] (4) *Iohn Plantagenet, surnamed* Gaunt, *of Gaunt in Flaunders where hee was borne, was the fourth sonne of King Edward the third. Hee was Duke of Lancaster, Earle of Lincolne, Salisbury, Darby, and Leicester, King of Castile & Lyrne, and steward of England. He was also Earle of Richmond, Constable of Fraunce, and Duke of Aquitayne. He had three wiues,* Blanch, Constance, *and* Katherine. *He lyeth buried in the Quier of Poules.*

Stemma peculiare Gaufredi Chauceri | Poetae celeberrimi.

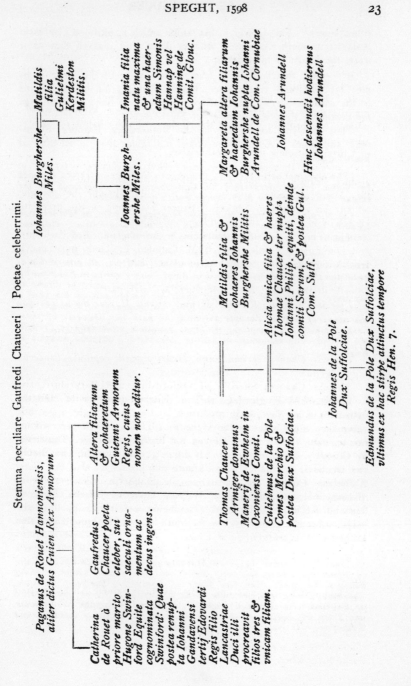

His Children, with their aduancement.

It should seeme, that Geffrey Chaucer had another sonne besides Thomas[1] : for in the Preface to the Astrolabe[2] he writeth to one, whome hee calleth his little sonne Lewys. Yet some hold opinion (but I know not vpon what grounds) that Thomas Chaucer was not the sonne of Geffrey Chaucer, but rather some kinsman of his, whome hee brought vp. But this pedigree by the hands of Master Glouer *alias* Somerset, that learned Antiquarie, as also the report of Chronicles shew it to be otherwise.

Some say that in recompence of Geffrey Chaucers seruice in France, being sent thither Embassadour, Edward the third gaue him this Maude daughter and heire of Sir Iohn Burghershe[3] Knight, whome he married to Thomas Chaucer his sonne to the great increase of his liuing, and amendment in blood.

This Thomas Chaucer besides his owne inheritance of Ewhelme[4] and Dunnington Castle[5] (which M. Camden Englands most excellent Antiquiographer termeth, *Quondam Chauceri, & postea Delapolorum Castellum exiguum*) was diuers waies preferred, as out of records in the Tower of London here we may partly see.

Vicesimo secundo Richardi secundi viginti Marcae datae Thomae Chaucer per annum durante vita.

Anno primo Henrici quarti idem donum viginti Marcarum confirmatum.

Thomas Chaucer primo anno Henrici sexti capitalis Pincerna regis Angliae.

Thomas Chaucer Sheriffe of Oxfordshire and Barkeshire, and Constable of Wallingford Castle[6] and Knaresborow Castle[7], and the forrest of Knaresborow during life.

Queene Iane[8] wife to Henry the fourth, the twelfth yeere of his raigne, gaue to Thomas Chaucer for his good seruice, *Manerium de Woodstocke, Hannebrough, Wotton, & Stuntesfield, cum omnibus membris & Hamlet. suis durante vita.*

Thomas Chaucer, the last heire male of the Chaucers, and owner of Ewhelme and Donnington Castle, the inheritance of the Chaucers, lieth buried in a blacke marble tombe in a faire Chappell in the parish Church of Ewhelme, in the south side of the Quier, with this Epitaph : *Hic iacet Thomas Chaucer Armiger, quondam dominus istius villae, & patronus istius Ecclesiae, qui obijt* 18. *die mensis Nouemb. anno Dom.* 1434 : *& Matildis vxor eius, quae obiit* 28. *die mensis Aprilis anno Dom.* 1436.

Thomas Chaucer had one only daughter named Alice, married thrice : first to Sir Iohn Phillip knight ; then to Thomas Mountacute Earle of Salisbury ; and the third time to William de la Pole[9] earle, and after Duke of Suffolke, who for loue of his wife and commodity of her landes, fell much to dwell in Oxfordshire and Barkeshire, where his wiues lands lay.

This William and his wife translated and encreased the Manor place of Ewehelme, and builded there a parish Church, and an hospitall called Godshouse, for two priestes and thirteene poore men to be sustained for euer. One of the priests to be master of the Almes house and Almespeople, them to instruct: the other Priest a Schoolemaster, freely to teach the children of the Tenants of the said Lordship their Grammar; and either of them to haue x pounds by the yeere. Also one of the poore men to be called Minister to present the faults of the other to the Master, and to ring their common Bell to seruice, and to haue sixteene pence the weeke, and the rest fourteene pence. To the which house they gaue the Manours of Ramridge in Hampshire, Conocke in Wiltshire, & Mersh in Buckinghamshire. They also founded an hospitall at Donnington Castle.

This Alice wife of Duke William suruiuing her husband, was after buried in the parish Church of Ewhelme, on the South side of the high altar, in a rich tombe of Alablaster, with an image in the habite of a Vowesse, & Duchesse crowned, lying on the same tombe: And another image vnder the tombe, so neare as may be, like vnto her at the time of her death, with this Epitaph: *Orate pro anima serenissimae principissae Aliciae Suffolchiae, huius Ecclesiae patronae, & primae fundatricis huius Eleemosynariae, quae obiit 20. die mensis Maii, anno Dom. 1475. Litera dominicali,* A.

This Alice had a daughter by her second husband Thomas Montacute Earle of Salisbury[10], named after her mother Alice, married to Richard Neuell sonne to Raph Earle of Westmerland, by whome she had Richard, Iohn, and George: Richard espoused Anne, sister and sole heire to the Lord Beaucampe and after Duke of Warwicke: in whose right he was created Earle of Warwicke.

Among many things that greatly renowned Geffrey Chaucer, this was one saith Bale, That he had a kinswoman, *Quae Gulielmo Sudovolgiorum Duci nupsit, ac magno in splendore Aquelmi vitam egit:* that is, which being maried to William Duke of Suffolke, liued in great honour at Ewhelme.

[Notes to the foregoing:] (1) *Written Anno domini 1391. Richar. secundi 14.*

(2) *Thomas Chaucer was borne about the 38. or 39. yeere of Edward 3.*

(3) *Bartholomaeus Burghershe, vnde hi fluxerunt, ab Edvardo 3. in ordinem Equestris Periscelidis cum alijs cooptatus erat in prima ipsius ordinis institutione.* G. C.

(4) *Ewelme olim Chauceri & Delapolorum, nunc Regiae aedes. Dum enim Iohannes Lincolniae Comes Gulielmo Delapolo è filio Iohanne nepos res nouas contra Henricum septimum moliretur proscriptus omnibus honoribus, & his possessionibus excidit: quae in patrimonium Regium transcriptae fuerunt.* G. C.

(5) *Donnington Castle standeth in a Parke in Barkshire not far from Newbery, where to this day standeth an olde oke called Chaucers Oke.*

(6) *Wallingforde in Barkeshire: Castrum admirandae amplitudinis*

& magnificentiae duplici murorum ambitu, duplici item vallo circun-
datum, in medio, moli in magnam altitudinem aeditae arx imponitur,
in cuius accliui per gradus ascensu fons est immensae profunditatis.
Incolae constructum à Danis credunt, alii à Romanis. G. Camden.

(7) *Knaresborow in Yorkeshire. Castrum rupi asperrimae impositum,*
quod Serlonem de Burgo fratrem Eustacij Vescij condidisse ferunt:
nunc patrimonii Lancastrensis censetur. G. Camden.

(8) *This Iane of Nauarr widow to Iohn of Mounford Duke of*
Britain, was maried to Henry the fourth, in the fourth yeere of his
raigne.

(9) *The Pooles were thus aduanced. William de la Pole merchaunt*
of Hull, for that he did frankely and freely lend to K. Edward the
third, a great summe of money at Mortaigne in Fraunce, when he was
greatly distressed, had not onely the same paid againe, but was also
honoured with the girdle Militarie and made Baneret, and endued with
1000. Markes by the yeere: and his successours after were aduanced
to be Dukes of Suffolke, as in Chronicles appeareth. William de la
Pole was first secretely maried to the Countesse of Henault, by whome
hee had a daughter, and after being divorced from her, publikely to T.
Chaucers daughter Countesse of Salisburie, who proued this daughter
being maried to one Barentine a bastard. The which Barentine after-
ward for a ryot made against the Countesse, was condemned, and lost
an hundred pounds by the yeere. In the 28. of King Hen. 6. 1450. this
William de la Pole was banished the Realme for 5. yeers, to pacifie the
harde opinion which the commons had conceiued against him. In his
iourney to his banishment hee was taken and beheaded, and his body
cast vp at Douer sands, and buried in the Charterhouse at Hull.

(10) *This Tho. Montacute, called the good Earle of Salisbury, was*
slaine at the siege of Orleance with shot as he loked out at a window.

His Reuenues.

Bvt now to returne to Geffrey Chaucer, although he had lands
and reuenues in diuers places, and that to the yearely value, as
some say, almost of a thousand pounds, yet the place of his most
abode was at Woodstocke in a faire house of stone next to the
Kings place, called to this day Chaucers house, and by that name
passed by the Queene to the tenant, which there now dwelleth.
Chaucer tooke great pleasure to lie there in regarde of the Parke,
in sundry of his writings much by him commended: as also to be
neare the Court, where his best friends were, and they who were
able to doe him most pleasure: By whose meanes hee had sundry
rewards bestowed vpon him, and that worthily for his good seruice,
which often he performed, and whereof in Chronicles we may partly
read thus:

His Seruice.

In the last yeare of King Edward the third, he with Sir Richard
Dangle², and Sir Richard Stan, was sent to Montreuill to mooue
a marriage to bee had betweene Richard Prince of Wales, and the
Lady Mary daughter to the French King. Some write that he with
Petrarke was present at the marriage of Lionell Duke of Clarence
with Violant daughter of Galeasius Duke of Millaine: Yet Paulus
Iouius nameth not Chaucer, but Petrarke he saith, was there.

And yet it may well be: for it is in record that twice or thrice he was emploied in foraine countries: which if it be true, wel might the man be at such charges and expences as he might stand in need of king Richard the seconds protection (as after shall appeare) till he had better recouered himselfe. But for his seruice he was not vnrewarded.

[Note on the above:] [1] *This Sir Richard Dangle, a knight of Poictu, came ouer with the Duke of Lancaster, who for his valiancie and tried truth to the King of England, was made knight of the Garter.*

His Rewards.

Edward the third hauing seised the lands of Edmond Staplegate, and also the said Edmond in his Minority at the death of his father for the manor of Bilsington in Kent, committed the said body to Geffrey Chaucer: to whom he paid 104 pounds for the same: as appeareth in the Book of Fees and Sergiancies in the Exchequer.

Anno. 8. Richardi 2. Galfridus Chaucer Contrarotulator Customariorum & Subsidiorum in portu ciuitatis nostrae London.

Anno. 17. Richardi 2. Viginti librae datae Galfrido Chaucero per annum durante vita.

Vigessimo secundo anno Richardi secundi concessum Galfrido Chaucero vnum dolium vini per annum durante vita, in portu ciuitatis London per manus capitalis Pincernae nostri.

Anno primo Henrici Quarti Galfrido Chaucero Armigero literae patentes confirmatae pro viginti libris nummorum per annum durante vita & vno dolio vini.

Eodem etiam anno concessae adhuc & datae eidem Galfrido Chaucero Quadraginta marcae per annum durante vita.

[Beside these Latin notes, in margin:] *Out of the Records in the Tour of London.*

His Friends.

Friends he had in the Court of the best sort: for besides that he alwaies held in with the Princes, in whose daies he liued, hee had of the best of the Nobility both lords & ladies, which fauoured him greatly. But chiefly Iohn of Gaunt Duke of Lancaster, at whose commandement he made the Treatise *Of the alliance*[1] *betwixt Mars and Venus:* and also the booke of the Duchesse. Likewise the lady Isabel daughter to king Edward the third, and wife to Ingeram De Guynes, Lord De Coucy: also the lady Margaret daughter to the same King, maried to Iohn Hastings Earle of Penbrooke, did greatly loue and fauour Geffrey Chaucer, and hee againe did as much honour them, but specially the Lady Margaret, as it may appeare in diuers Treatises by him written. Others there were of great account, wherof some for some causes tooke liking of him, and other for his rare giftes and learning did admire him. And thus hee liued in honour many yeares both at home and abroad.

Yet it seemeth that he was in some trouble in the daies of King Richard the second, as it may appeare in the Testament of Loue: where hee doth greatly complaine of his owne rashnesse in following the multitude, and of their hatred against him for bewraying their purpose. And in that complaint which he maketh to his empty purse, I do find a written copy, which I had of Iohn Stow (whose library hath helped many writers) wherein ten times more is adioined, then is in print. Where he maketh great lamentation for his wrongfull imprisonment, wishing death to end his daies: which in my iudgement doth greatly accord with that in the Testament of Loue. Moreouer we find it thus in record.

In the second yeare of Richard the second, The King tooke Geffrey Chaucer and his lands into his protection. The occasion wherof no doubt was some daunger and trouble whereinto he was fallen by fauouring some rash attempt of the common people. For liuing in such troublesome times, wherein few knew what parts to take, no maruell if he came into some danger, nay great maruell that hee fell not into greater danger. But as hee was learned, so was he wise, and kept himselfe much out of the way in Holland, Zeland, and France, where he wrote most of his bookes.

[Beside this last paragraph the marginal note is:] *Out of the Records in the Toure.* [(1) is annotated as follows:] *Some say hee did but translate it: and that it was made by sir* Otes de Grantsome *Knight, in French: of my lady of Yorke daughter to the King of Spain representing Venus: & my lord of Huntingdon sometime Duke of Excester. This lady was younger sister to Constance Iohn of Gaunts second wife. This lord of Huntingdon was called Iohn Holland, halfe brother to Richard the second: he married Elizabeth the daughter of Iohn of Gaunt Duke of Lancaster.* [Observe that Speght or Stow derives this note, as to Chaucer's having but translated the Mars, from Shirley's heading, preserved in MSS R 3, 20 and Ashmole 59; see reprint of headings in Chaucer Society Parallel Texts of the Minor Poems, p. 121, p. 412. Cp. Skeat, Oxford Chaucer, I : 65, 560.]

His Bookes.

Chaucer had alwaies an earnest desire to enrich & beautifie our English tongue, which in those daies was verie rude and barren: and this he did following the example of *Dantes* and *Petrarch,* who had done the same for the Italian tongue; *Alanus* for the French; and *Iohannes Mena* for the Spanish: neither was Chaucer inferior to any of them in the performance hereof. And England in this respect is much beholden to him, as *Leland* well noteth:

Anglia Chaucerum veneratur nostra poetam,
Cui veneres debet patria lingua suas.

Our England honoureth Chaucer poet, as principall
To whome her country tongue doth owe her beauties all.

Besides those bookes of his which we heretofore haue had in print, he wrote diuers others: as,

The Flower and the Leafe, neuer till now printed.

In obitum Blanchiae Ducissae, neuer before published: which seemeth rather to be his Dreame: and that other called his Dreame, The complaint for Blanch: as after the perusing of them both, any meane Reader will iudge:

De Vulcani veru.
De Leone & eius dignitate.
Comoedias & Tragoedias.
Facetias & Iocos.
Dantem Italum transtulit.
Petrarchae quaedam transtulit.

Others I haue seene without any Authours name, which for the inuention I would verily iudge to be Chaucers, were it not that wordes and phrases carry not euery where Chaucers antiquitie.

Now, concerning those bookes which we haue in print: the Canterburie Tales for the most part were of his owne inuention, yet some of them translated, and penned in King Richards daies the second, and after the insurrection of Iacke Strawe, which was in the 4. yeere of the same king: for in the Tale of the Nunnes priest, he maketh mention thereof.

The Romant of the Rose was translated out of French.

Troilus and Creseid called *Throphe* in the Lumbard tongue, translated: not *verbatim,* but the Argument thence taken and most cunningly amplified by Chaucer.

Mary Magdalen translated out of S. Origen.

The balad, *Fly from the prease:* made by Chaucer on his death bed.

The Letter of Cupid is none of Chaucers doing, but was compiled by Thomas Occleue[1] of the office of the priuie Seale, sometime Chaucers scholler. The which Occleue for the loue he bare to his Master, caused his picture to be truly drawen in his booke *De Regimine Principis,* dedicated to Henry the fift: the which I haue seene, and according to the which this in the beginning of this book was done by Iohn Spede, who hath annexed thereto all such cotes of Armes, as any way concern the Chaucers, as he found them (trauailing for that purpose) at Ewhelme and at Wickham.

[In the margin:] *Iacke Vpland is supposed to be his. But the A. B. C. called* Priere de nostre Dame, *is certainely Chaucers doing.*

[1] *Thomas Occleue,* vel *Ockelefe, vir tam bonis literis, quam generis prosapia clarus exquisita quadam Anglici sermonis eloquentia post Chaucerum, cuius fuerat discipulus, patriam ornauit linguam. Iohannis Wicleui, & ipsius Berengarij in religione doctrinam sequebatur. Tractatus hos fecit: Planctum proprium. Dialogum ad amicum. De quadam Imperatrice. De arte moriendi. De coelesti Hjerusalem. De quodam Ionatha. De regimine principis.*

Occleue in that booke where hee setteth downe Chaucers picture, addeth these verses:

> Although his life be queint, the resemblaunce
> Of him hath in me so fresh lifelines
> That to put other men in remembraunce
> Of his person, I haue here the likenes
> Doe make, to the end in sothfastnes
> That they, that of him haue lost thought & mind
> By this peinture may againe him find.

His Death.

Geffrey Chaucer departed out of this world the 25. day of October, in the yeere of our lord 1400, after he had liued about 72. yeeres. Thus writeth Bale out of Leland: *Chaucerus ad canos deuenit, sensitque senectutem morbum esse: & dum causas suas, Londoni curaret, &c.* Chaucer liued til he was an old man, and found old age to be grieuous: and whilst he followed his causes at London, he died, and was buried at Westminster.

The old verses which were written on his graue at the first, were these:

> *Galfridus Chaucer vates & fama poesis*
> *Maternae haec sacra sum tumulatus humo.*

But since M. *Nicholas Brigham* did at his owne cost and charges erect a monument for him, with these verses:

> *Qui fuit Anglorum vates ter maximus olim*
> *Gaufredus Chaucer conditur hoc tumulo:*
> *Annum si quaeras domini, si tempora vitae*
> *Ecce notae subsunt, quae tibi cuncta notant.*
> *Anno Domini 1400. die mensis Octob. 25.*

Now it shall not be amisse to these Epitaphes, to adde the iudgements and reports of some learned men, of this worthy and famous Poet. And first of all Thomas Occleue, who liued in his daies, writeth thus of him in his booke *De Regimine Principis.*

> But welaway so is mine hart woe
> That the honour of English tongue is deed,
> Of which I wont was counsaile haue and reed.
> O master dere and fadre reuerent,
> My maister Chaucer floure of Eloquence,
> Mirror of fructuous entendement,
> O vniuersall fadre of Science:
> Allas that thou thine excellent prudence
> In thy bed mortall mightest not bequeath.
> What eyld death: Alas why would she thee sle.

O death thou didest not harme singler in slaughter of
    him
But all the land it smerteth.
But nathelesse yet hast thou no power his name sle
His hie vertue asterteth:
Unslaine fro thee, which ay vs lifely herteth
With bookes of his ornat enditing
That is to all this land enlumining.

The same Author againe in the same booke:

My deare maister, God his soule quite,
And fader Chaucer faine would haue me taught,
But I was young, and leered lite or nought
Alas my worthy maister honorable.
This lands very treasure and richesse
Death by thy death hath harme irreparable,
Vnto vs done: her vengeable duresse
Dispoiled hath this lond of the sweetnesse
Of Rhetorige: for vnto Tullius
Was neuer man so like amongs vs
Also who was heire in philosophy
To Aristotle in our tongue but thou
The steppes of Uirgill in Poese
Thou suedest eken men know well inough.
That combre world that thee my maister slough
Would I slaine were: Death was too hastife
To renne on thee, and reue thee thy life
She might haue tarried her vengeance a while,
To that some man had egall to thee be
Nay lat be that: she knew wele that this Ile
May neuer man forth bring like vnto thee:
And her office needs do must she,
God bad her so, I trust all for the best,
O maister, maister, God thy soule rest.

Dan Iohn Lidgate[1] likewise in his prologue of Bocchas of the
fall Princes, by him translated, saith thus in his commendation:

My maister Chaucer with his fresh comedies
Is dead alas chiefe Poet of Britaine,
That whilome made full pitous Tragedies,
The faule also of Princes he did complaine,
As he that was of making Soueraine,
Whom all this land should of right preferre
Sith of our language he was the Loadsterre.

[Note:] [1]Iohn Lidgate Monke of Burie an excellent poet: he
traueiled Fraunce and Italy to learn the languages and sciences.

Afterward in the same place do follow fourescore and three verses in the commendation of Chaucer, and the bookes that he made particulerly named.

In a booke of *Iohn Stowes* called Little Iohn (but I knowe not who was the Authour) I find these verses:

> O fathers and founders of enornat eloquence
> That enlumined haue our great Britaine
> To soone we haue lost your lauriat science
> O lusty licoure of that fulsome fountaine,
> O cursed death, why hast thou those poets slain,
> I meane Gower, Chaucer, and Gaufride
> Alas the time that euer they fro vs dide.

Iohn Lidgate againe in a booke which hee writeth of the birth of the Virgine Mary hath these verses:

> And eke my maister Chaucer now is in graue,
> The noble Rethore, poet of Britaine,
> That worthy was the laurel to haue
> Of poetry, and the palme attaine
> That made first to distill and raine
> The gold dew drops of speech and eloquence
> Into our tongue through his excellence.

> And found the floures first of Rethoricke
> Our rude speech only to enlumine,
> That in our tongue was neuer none him like:
> For as the sunne doth in heauen shine,
> In midday spere downe to vs by line,
> In whose presence no sterre may appeare
> Right so his ditties withouten any peare,

> Euery making with his light distaine,
> In soothfastnesse, who so taketh heed:
> Wherefore no wonder though my hart plaine
> Upon his death, and for sorrow bleed
> For want of him now in my great need
> That should (alas) conuay and eke direct,
> And with his support amend and correct.

> The wrong traces of my rude penne,
> There as I erre, and goe not line right.
> But that for he, ne may me not kenne,
> I can no more but with all my might
> With all my heart, and mine inward sight
> Praieth for him that now lieth in chest
> To God aboue, to giue his soule good rest.

About William Caxtons time Stephanus Surigonus Poet Laureat
of Millaine, did write this Epitaph vpon Geffrey Chaucer, in Latin.

[Marginal note:] *This William Caxton of London Mercer, brought
printing out of Germany into England about the year 1471, in the 37
year of Henry the sixt, and practised the same in the Abbey of S.
Peter at westminster. It was first found in Germanie at Magunce by
one Iohn Cuthembergus a knight: and brought to Rome by Conradus
an Almaigne.*

Epitaphium Galfridi Chaucer, per poetam laureatum Stephanum
Surigonum Mediolanensem in decretis licenciatum.

> *Pyerides musae, si possint numina flaetus*
> *Fundere, diuinas atque rigare genas:*
> *Galfridi vatis Chaucer crudelia fata*
> *Plangite: sit lachrimis abstinuisse nephas.*
> *Vos coluit viuens: at vos celebrate sepultum,*
> *Reddatur merito gratia digna viro.*
> *Grandè decus vobis est docti musa Maronis,*
> *Qua didicit meliùs lingua latina loqui.*
> *Grande, nouumque decus Chaucer, famamque, parauit:*
> *Heu quantum fuerat prisca Britannae rudis.*
> *Reddidit insignem maternis versibus, vt iam*
> *Aurea splendescat, ferrea facta prius.*
> *Hunc latuisse virum nil, si tot opuscula vertes,*
> *Dixeris, egregiis quae decorata modis,*
> *Socratis ingenium, vel fontes Philosophiae,*
> *Quicquid & arcani dogmata sacra ferunt.*
> *Et quascumque velis, tenuit dignissimus artes*
> *Hic vates, paruo conditus hoc tumulo.*
> *Ah laudis quantum, praeclara Britannia, perdis,*
> *Dum rapuit tantum mors odiosa virum.*
> *Crudeles Parcae, crudelia fila sororum:*
> *Non tamen extincto corpore, fama perit.*
> *Viuet in aeternum, viuent dum scripta poëtae:*
> *Viuent aeterno tot monumenta die*
> *Si qua bonos tangit pietas, si carmine dignus,*
> *Carmina, qui cecinit, tot cumulata modis,*
> *Haec sibi Marmoreo scribantur verba sepulchro,*
> *Haec maneat laudis sarcina summa suae.*
> *Galfridus Chaucer vates, & fama poësis*
> *Maternae hac sacra sum timulatus humo.*
>
> *Post obitum Caxton voluit te viuere cura*
> *Guillelmi, Chaucer clare poëta, tui.*
> *Nam tua non solum compressit opuscula formis,*
> *Has quoque sed laudes iussit hic esse tuas.*

3

And as for men of later time, not onely that learned gentleman M. William Thynne, in his Epistle Dedicatorie to the Kings Maiestie, but also two of the purest and best writers of our daies: the one for Prose, the other for Verse, M. *Ascham* and M. *Spenser,* haue deliuered most worthy testimonies of their approouing of him. Master *Ascham* in one place calleth him *English Homer,* and makes no doubt to say, that hee valueth his authoritie of as high estimation, as euer he did either Sophocles or Euripides in Greeke. And in another place, where he declareth his opinion of English versifying, he vseth these wordes: *Chaucer and Petrarke, those two worthy wittes, deserue iust praise.* And last of all, in his discourse of Germanie, hee putteth him nothing behind either *Thucidides* or *Homer* for his liuely descriptions of site of places, and nature of persons both in outward shape of bodie, and inward disposition of minde; adding this withall, That not the proudest, that hath written in any tongue whatsoeuer, in these pointes can carrie away the praise from him.

Master *Spenser* in his first Eglogue of his Shepheardes Kalender, calleth him *Titirus,* the god of Shepheards, comparing him to the worthinesse of the Romane Titirus Virgil. In his Faerie Queene in his discourse of friendship, as thinking himselfe most worthy to be Chaucers friend, for his like naturall disposition that Chaucer had, hee sheweth that none that liued with him, nor none that came after him, durst presume to reuiue Chaucers lost labours in that vnperfite tale of the Squire, but only himselfe: which he had not done, had he not felt (as he saith) the infusion of Chaucers owne sweete spirite, suruiuing within him. And a little before he termeth him, Most renowmed and Heroicall Poet: and his Writings, The workes of heauenly wit: concluding his commendation in this manner:

> Dan Chaucer, Well of English vndefiled,
> On Fames eternal beadrole worthy to be filed.
> I follow here the footing of thy feet,
> That with thy meaning so I may the rather meet.

And once againe I must remember M. *Camdens* authority, who as it were reaching one hand to Maister *Ascham,* and the other to Maister *Spenser,* and so drawing them togither vttereth of him these words. *De Homero nostro Anglico illud verè asseram, quod de Homero eruditus ille Italus dixit:*

> . . . . *Hic ille est, cuius de gurgite sacro*
> *Combibit arcanos vatum omnis turba furores.*

And that wee may conclude his praises with the testimony of the most worthiest Gentleman that the Court hath afforded of many yeares: Sir Philip Sidney in his Apologie for Poetry saith thus of him. Chaucer vndoubtedly did excellently in his Troylus and Creseid; of whom truly I know not, whether to meruaile more,

either that he in that mistie time, could see so clearely, or that we
in this cleare age walke so stumblingly after him. Seeing therefore
that both old and new writers haue carried this reuerend conceit of
our Poet, and openly delared the same by writing, let vs conclude
with Horace in the eight Ode of his fourth booke:

Dignum laude virum musa vetat mori.

FINIS

In the 1602 revision of the Speght Chaucer, some minor changes
are made in the life of the poet, viz.: The italicized paragraph under
the diagrammatic shield of Chaucer's arms is altered, thus, "But
this is but a simple coniecture. For honorable houses & of great
antiquitie, haue borne as meane Armes as Chaucer: and yet his
armes are not so meane, ether for Colour, Charge, or Partition as
some would make them." Note that this change from the "geometrical" interpretation of the 1598 ed. was suggested by Thynne,
see the Animadversions, ed. Furnivall, p. 15. John and Elias
Chaucer are mentioned; it is said that the name Chaucer is "one
of Office or Occupation", and that "the Role of Battle Abbey
affirmeth Chaucer to haue come in with the Conqueror."

Various slight alterations are made in the section on Chaucer's
Children; that on Rewards is expanded; and under Friends, after
the mention of the Lady Margaret, it is said that Chaucer "did
specially honour her, as it may appeare in divers Treatises by him
written: As in the Prologue of the Legend of good women vnder
the name of the Daysie, and likewise in a Ballad, beginning, In
the season of Feuerier."

Under Bookes, after the six Latin titles, "Others I haue seene
without any Authours name, in the hands of M. Stow that painefull
Antiquarie, which for the inuention" etc. And "M William Thynn
in his first printed booke of Chaucers works with one Columbe on
a side, had a Tale called the Pilgrims tale, which was more odious
to the Clergie, than the speach of the Plowman. The tale began
thus: In Lincolneshire fast by a fenne: Standeth a religious house
who doth it kenne. The argument of which tale, as also the occasion
thereof, and the cause why it was left out of Chaucers works, shall
hereafter be shewed, if God permit, in M. Fran. Thyns coment
vpon Chaucer: & the Tale it selfe published if possibly it can be
found." In the section on Chaucer's death, after Brigham's epitaph
is quoted, there is added: "About the ledge of whiche tombe were
these verses, now cleane worne out.

Si rogites quis eram, forsan te fama docebit.
Quod si fama negat, mundi quia gloria transit,
Haec monumenta lege."
When the seven-line stanza is cited, between the two extracts from
Lydgate, the "called Little Iohn" is cut out. A citation from
Gawain Douglas is added to the commendatory extracts, before
Surigon's epitaph. In the mention of the men of later time who
have praised Chaucer, the allusion to Thynne is expanded, "whose
iudgement we are the rather to approue, for that he had further
insight into him than many others."

Winstanley. Englands Worthies. The Liues of the Most Eminent
    Persons from Constantine the Great to Oliuer Cromwell Late
    Protector, (etc.) London 1660. By William Winstanley, Gent.
    —47 Lives in all, almost entirely those of kings or of men of
    political import. Chaucer's is the 12th Life, pp. 91-98. Merely
    a condensed reproduction of Speght.

Phillips. Theatrum Poetarum, or a Compleat Collection of the
    Poets, especially the most Eminent, of all Ages, etc. By
    Edward Phillips. London 1674.
    With a preface on poetry. The Ancient Poets fill pp. 1-192;
    the Modern Poets 1-196. A supplement extends from 197 to
    234, Ancient Poetesses from 235 to 252, Modern Poetesses
    253-261. Chaucer is found pp. 50-51. Phillips says: "*Sir
    Geoffry Chaucer,* the Prince and *Coryphaeus,* generally so
    reputed, till this Age, of our *English* Poets, and as much as
    we triumph over his old fashion'd phrase, and obsolete words,
    one of the first refiners of the *English* Language, of how great
    Esteem he was in the Age wherein he flourish'd, namely the
    Reigns of *Henry* the 4th, *Henry* the 5th, and part of *Henry*
    the 6th, appears, besides his being Knight and Poet Laureat,
    by the Honour he had to be allyed by Marriage to the great
    Earl of *Lancaster John* of *Gaunt:* How great a part we have
    lost of his Works above what we have Extant of him is mani-
    fest from an Author of good Credit, who reckons up many con-
    siderable Poems, which are not in his publisht Works; besides
    the Squires Tale, which is said to be compleat in *Arundel-
    house* Library."

Winstanley. The Lives of the most Famous English Poets, or the
    Honour of Parnassus . . . . from the Time of K. William the
    Conqueror to the Reign of his Present Majesty King James II.
    (etc. etc.) By William Winstanley. London 1687.

Chaucer, pp. 23-32; slightly enlarged from the previous Life by the same author. A paragraph on editions is added, and Phillips' remark about the Squire's Tale is repeated. To the statement that Brigham erected the tomb of Chaucer is added the fact that he buried his four-year old daughter near the grave on June 21, 1557,—which fact Winstanley probably took from Camden's *Reges*. Under the discussion of Lydgate Winstanley says that Chaucer wrote the *Story of Thebes* in Latin, and that Lydgate translated it into English verse; this he gets from Pits.

Blount. De Re Poetica: or, Remarks upon Poetry, with Characters and Censures of the most considerable Poets, whether Ancient or Modern. Extracted out of the Best and Choicest Criticks. By Sir Thomas Pope Blount. London 1694.

The first few paragraphs of the life of Chaucer are a compound of Winstanley and Phillips, except that Blount drops out the "evidence" as to Chaucer's London birth, and says that the conclusion of the Squire's Tale is not to be found. He then gives the "opinions" of Pits, Winstanley, Ascham, Sidney, Denham, citing a few lines of verse by Denham beginning "Old Chaucer, like the Morning Star", Savil (Preface to Bradwardine against Eligius), Sir Robert Baker, Camden, Sprat and Verstegan; the epitaph is then printed, p. 44.

Urry, in the Edition of Chaucer's Works, 1721. The Life of Chaucer for this edition was originally written by John Dart, but was revised and altered by William Thomas, whose brother Timothy had undertaken the completion of the work begun by Urry. See Tyrwhitt, Appendix to the Preface, note n; although the British Museum Catalogue credits "J. Thomas" with the life. See Dart's Westmonasterium for expression of his indignation at the alterations in his work. The groundwork of the biography is taken from preceding lives of Chaucer, and develops the stories of his college education, his complicity in John of Northampton's plot, etc.; but in spite of this large admixture of fiction, the Life contains much that is noteworthy and sensible. The Scrope-Grosvenor controversy, and Chaucer's testimony there, are first mentioned in this biography; a few of the non-Chaucerian poems of the black-letter editions are repudiated, and the tone of the whole is both sober and appreciative. Its statement, that the works of Chaucer were excepted from the 1546 Act of Parliament *For the Advancement of True Religion,* is endorsed by Furnivall, Ch. Soc. ed. of Thynne's Animadversions p. xiv footnote. The books specifically excluded from censure by this Act were

"Cronycles, Canterbury Tales, Chaucer's bokes, Gower's bokes
and Stories of mennes lives." Although this Life is not so
clearly an advance, in method and in thoughtfulness, over
preceding work, as is the Preface by Timothy Thomas which
appears in the same volume, it should be carefully sifted by
students of the history of Chaucer-criticism.

Biographia Britannica: or, the Lives of the most eminent Persons
who have flourished in Great Britain and Ireland, from the
earliest Ages down to the present Times: Collected from the
best Authorities, both printed and manuscript, and digested in
the manner of Mr. Bayle's Historical and Critical Dictionary.
Six vols., folio, London 1747-1763. Licensed 1744.
    The life of Chaucer is in vol. ii, pp. 1293-1308, in English.
Very extensive notes. Marginal references to Leland, Bale,
Pits, Speght, Hearne, Urry, Ashmole's Theatrum Chemicum
Britannicum, Camden's Britannia, etc.

Bibliotheca Britannico-Hibernica, (etc.) by Tanner, with Wilkins'
preface, London, 1748, gives on pp. 166-170 the life of Chaucer
in Latin, with extensive footnotes, one of which prints the table
of contents of the 1602 Chaucer. Tanner says: "Quae de vita
Chauceri notavi excerpta sunt ex *Vita* ejus per Thomam Speght
operum edit. Lond. MDCII fol. praefixa."

Bibliographia Poetica. A Catalogue of Engleish Poets of the
Twelfth, Thirteenth, Fourteenth, Fifteenth, and Sixteenth Cen-
turys, with a Short Account of their Works. Joseph Ritson.
London 1802.
    The account of Chaucer, pp. 19-23, is mainly a list of works.

Godwin. Life of Geoffrey Chaucer, the Early English Poet: in-
cluding Memoirs of his Near Friend and Kinsman, John of
Gaunt, Duke of Lancaster: with Sketches of the Manners,
Opinions, Arts and Literature of England in the Fourteenth
Century. By William Godwin, London, 1803, 2 vols., 4to.
Second edition 4 vols., octavo, London, 1804. Translated into
German by Breyer, 1812.
    Reviewed at length, with liberal extracts, Gentleman's Maga-
zine, 1803, II : 1141, 1229; at the close it is said that Godwin
"has cleared up some points in Chaucer's history, but his
partiality has been well supported by his imagination." The
excessive introduction of contemporary history is commented
upon, and Godwin's description of the Chaucer-Gower quarrel
is termed "a copious flourish of matter, without an iota of

proof." The Edinburgh Review of 1804, 3:437-452, is more severe. "The incidents of Chaucer's life bear the same proportion to the book that the alphabet does to the encyclopedia." Godwin's flourishes and vague suppositions are condemned, and his attitude towards Tyrwhitt is described as "that dignified contempt of his predecessors which especially becomes an author at the moment when he is about to avail himself of the information they afford him." The style is termed "uncommonly depraved." (According to Poole's Index, this review was written by Sir Walter Scott.)

Blackwood's, 10 : 295 (1821), says of Godwin's work:—"A most unwieldy and unsatisfactory brace of quartos, contemptible in criticism, absurd and visionary in its inferences from facts, and altogether unworthy of the genius of the biographer."

Modern critics have treated Godwin with amused contempt: thus Morley, Eng. Writers V : 215; Lounsbury, Studies I : 191-98; Skeat, Canon 98; Mather, Eng. Misc. 301.

But Flügel, Anglia 21 : 245, Lowes, Publ. Mod. Lang. Ass'n. 19 : 593, note 4, point out that Godwin sometimes gives facts correctly. For Godwin's animus against Tyrwhitt see the list of references under Tyrwhitt in III C below.

Todd. Illustrations of the Lives and Writings of Gower and Chaucer. Collected from authentick documents by the Rev. Henry J. Todd, M. A., F. S. A. London 1810.

Contains: a print of Thynne's Animadversions; a print of Gower's will, and of a deed signed by John Gower; an "Account of some valuable Manuscripts of Gower and Chaucer, which I have examined"; extracts from Gower's Confessio Amantis, with notes; extracts from the poetry of Chaucer, the text of the Prologue from Tyrwhitt, the Flower and the Leaf from a collation of Speght and Urry; "Poems supposed to be written by Chaucer during his imprisonment", taken from the flyleaves of the Ellesmere MS; a glossary, founded partly upon the work of Tyrwhitt.

Much of this work has been done over, and of course done better, since Todd; both the EETS and the Ch. Soc. have edited the Animadversions; Macaulay's edition of Gower has superseded all others; and in some respects modern students differ from Todd, e. g., the Flower and the Leaf is no longer considered Chaucer's, and the poems by Todd attributed to Chaucer are repudiated by Furnivall and by Skeat, see under Section V below. Nevertheless, the book has value and interest for students to-day; it is entirely free from the blemishes of Godwin's work, and breathes a spirit of genuine devotion to the subject.

STATE TEACHERS COLLEGE
LIBRARY
MARYVILLE - MISSOURI

B. The Appeal to Fact

Nicolas. The Life of Chaucer, by Sir Nicholas Harris Nicolas, was prefixed to the Aldine Chaucer of 1845 and later, as noted below, Section II D.

Minto, in the Encycl. Brit., art. *Chaucer,* says that the Life was published in 1843; Lounsbury, Studies I : 199, says 1844. No separate publication is noted in the Brit. Mus. Catalogue or in Lowndes; but as the Life is reviewed Athenaeum Feb. 10, 1844, Monthly Review of March 1844, and Gentleman's Magazine, January 1844, it is probable that there was a limited or proof impression before the issue of the Aldine; indeed, the Athenaeum speaks of the Life as "to be prefixed to the Aldine edition of Chaucer about to be published by Pickering."

Reviewed as noted above, seven columns in the Athenaeum; commended by Hertzberg, p. 7.

This is the first life of Chaucer drawn up on sound methods, and the first deserving serious consideration by students. Nicolas used the documents discovered by Godwin, with recognition of his predecessor's work; but he printed many more, and his study is entirely free from the extravagances of Godwin. Some errors he made,—the "eleven months" of Chaucer's stay in Italy, the "only four days" before Henry IV's grant to Chaucer,— see Flügel, Anglia 21 : 245 ff.; he treats as genuine some works now declared spurious, the Testament of Love, the Flower and Leaf, the Cuckoo and Nightingale; and he disbelieves Chaucer's knowledge of Italian, since overwhelmingly proved.

Nicolas' work was condensed in Wright's ed. of the Cant. Tales, 1847-51, used by Bell for the 1854 ed. of the Works, reprinted in the subsequent Aldine eds. and in the Pickering ed. of Romaunt, Troilus, etc., see Section IV B here. Owing to its presence in this latter, that collection is sometimes termed, like the 1845 Aldine, the "Nicolas" edition.

Chaucer Society. The investigations of Furnivall and the Chaucer Society (founded 1867-68) are reported from time to time in the columns of the Academy, Athenaeum, etc., and subsequently collected in the Ch. Soc. Life-Records, see below.

Minto. Encyclopedia Britannica, art. *Geoffrey Chaucer,* by William Minto.

The results of Furnivall's investigations are briefly given; much more space is devoted to literary comment. Bradshaw's rime-test for determining the authenticity of poems is dismissed contemptuously, and the genuineness of the Flower and the Leaf and the Court of Love is maintained. (See the subsequent altercation between Furnivall, Minto, and Swinburne, Athenaeum for 1877 I : 417, 447, 481, 512.) Prof. ten Brink's classification of Chaucer's works into periods is scouted, and much emphasis laid upon "spontaneous expansion." The influence of Italian writers, in particular, is minimized; see citation under Troilus, Section IV here. Without bibliographical equipment, and of no profit to students.

Ward. Life of Chaucer, English Men of Letters Series, n. d. (1879, 1895). Adolphus William Ward.

The chapters are: Chaucer's Times, Chaucer's Life and Works, Characteristics of Chaucer and of his Poetry, Epilogue on the Influence of Chaucer. Reviewed by Koch, Anglia 3 : 554-559; by Vetter, Anglia Beibl. 1896, p. 77; in Acad. 1880 I : 208 (Furnivall) ; in Amer. Jour. Phil. 1 : 497.

Cautious and non-committal. Of no independent value, but a useful book for the beginner who desires some idea of the fourteenth century, or for the general reader.

Morley. English Writers, by Henry Morley. London 1887 ff., 11 vols. Vol. V contains the discussion of Chaucer.

A very full treatment of the works separately, with citations and summaries. Includes poems now regarded as spurious,— Court of Love, Flower and Leaf, Cuckoo and Nightingale, Chaucer's Dream. Biographical details from the work of the Chaucer Society. A useful outline for the general student, written without special knowledge, but without extravagance.

Hales. Dictionary of National Biography, art. *Geoffrey Chaucer*, by J. W. Hales.

A disappointing piece of work, especially when compared with the space and effort given by Pollard to Lydgate in the same Dictionary. Hales refers to Ward, Morley, etc., instead of using firsthand evidence; he introduces conjectures as fact, and bibliographical information is wanting. For criticism of some details see Flügel, Anglia 21 : 245, 257; Toynbee in Athen. 1905 I : 210, cited under Clerk's Tale, Section III G here.

Lounsbury. The first chapter of vol. I of Lounsbury's Studies in Chaucer, N. Y. 1892, contains a summary of the facts about Chaucer known up to that time (1892) ; the second chapter is on the legendary life of Chaucer. There are some small inaccuracies (cp. Flügel, Anglia 21 : 245), but the presentation is an admirable survey of the progress from romance to fact in the biography of Chaucer.

Skeat. Skeat's life of Chaucer, in vol. I of his Oxford Chaucer, is based upon the Life-Records (see below). Some inaccuracies are noted by Flügel, Anglia 21 : 245.

Life-Records. In the publications of the Chaucer Society, 2d series, Nos. 12, 14, 21, 32. The last part, 1900, contains 58 pages of Forewords by R. E. G. Kirk, summing up all now known of the poet's life. In this collection is printed every document relating to Chaucer, forming the only authentic basis for his biography. Upon these, so far as then available, were founded the sketches by ten Brink in his Hist. Eng. Lit., and by Pollard in his Primer. Additional facts which have come to light since 1900 are mentioned N. and Q. 1902 I : 134, 1904 I : 28, 1905 II : 5; Athen. 1906 I : 233; Mod. Lang. Notes 21 : 224.

Kern. The Ancestry of Chaucer. A. A. Kern. diss. Johns Hopkins Univ., 1906, pp. 163. Reviewed Nation 1907 I : 432-3; Jour. Gc. Phil.

Rearranging, and in some details correcting, the material of the Life-Records dealing with Chaucer's ancestry. Reproduces in part the results of V. B. Redstone as to the Suffolk ancestry of the Chaucers, a family known in that county by the name Malyn; see Redstone's paper on "The Chaucer-Malyn Family" in Proceedings of the Suffolk Institute of Archaeology, vol. XII, briefly noted Athen. 1906 I : 233. See also Kern in Mod. Lang. Notes 23 : 52.

Appendix

a) Dates of Chaucer's Birth and Death

The date of Chaucer's death is known to us only from his tomb in Westminster Abbey, where the inscription, when legible, read "25 Octobris 1400". This tomb is said by Stow and succeeding writers to have been erected by one Nicholas Brigham; see the Life in the Speght Chaucer, as cited above, for the epitaph, with date, which Brigham is said to have added. But in Notes and Queries 1904 I : 28 Furnivall writes that he has found in MS Egerton 2642 the statement that "Hickeman" wrote the epitaph of Chaucer and got the tumulus decorated. And in Athen. 1850 II : 768 (cited N. and Q. 1850 II : 142) it is said that examination shows the altar tomb to be the original tomb; only the canopy was added by Brigham.

From this it appears that we have the date of Chaucer's death only on the evidence of either Hickeman or Brigham, regarding whose sources of information we know nothing, and both of whom lived more than a century after Chaucer. Also, the now obliterated inscription is repeated for us by Stow and by Camden; we have no earlier testimony as to its text. Tyrwhitt, without expressing doubt, speaks cautiously of the date of the poet's death, as of his birth. No fact has as yet been discovered, however, to invalidate the belief that Chaucer died in 1400.

The Speght-Stow life, see ante, also says that at the time of Chaucer's death he had lived "about 72 years." The date 1328, for his birth, was accordingly inferred, and repeated until Fiedler, in the introd. to his transl. of the Cant. Tales, see Section III E here, attacked it, arguing from the evidence given by Chaucer himself in the Scrope-Grosvenor trial in 1386.

The report of the proceedings at this trial, which was a controversy over the right to bear certain arms, was published by Sir Harris Nicolas in 1832, entitled The Scrope and Grosvenor Controversy. Chaucer's deposition is preserved among those of the many other witnesses called; he describes himself as being of "xl ans et plus", and states that he had been armed for 27 years. A translation of Chaucer's evidence is given by Skeat I : xxxvi-vii, mainly from Sir Harris Nicolas. The latter, in his Life of Chaucer, treating the "xl ans et plus" as a little more than forty, says that there are strong reasons for believing 1345 too late a date; these reasons are the passages in Chaucer's works alluding to his age, and the misstatements as to age of several of the witnesses at this trial. Here, however, it should be noted that Chaucer's remarks about his age are not to be interpreted too literally; and that the mistakes of the other witnesses, although accepted as such by Morley, Eng. Writers V : 93 ff., require further proof. It is a singular fact in this connection that the materials for vol. III of Nicolas' work have disappeared, see N. and Q. 1906 II : 328.

A piece of definite evidence toward the date of Chaucer's birth was presented by Walter Rye in Athen. 1881 I : 165, and Life-Records p. 125; see reprint Skeat I : xi-xii. A plea of 1326, by the guardians of Chaucer's father, John Chaucer, states that John Chaucer was in 1325 not 14 years old. See Furnivall, Acad. 1896 I : 117.

b) Supposed Love Affair

In Trial Forewords pp. 35 ff. Furnivall interpreted lines 37 ff. of the Book of the Duchesse to refer to a long and hopeless love by Chaucer. He was followed by Fleay in his Guide to Chaucer and Spenser, pp. 36-7, by Ward in his Life, p. 53, by ten Brink, Hist.

Eng. Lit. II : 48-49, by Wülker, by Garnett and Gosse; the interpretation was mentioned without question by Skeat, Minor Poems p. 236, but dubiously in Oxford Chaucer I : liii. The theory was strenuously opposed by Lounsbury in Atlantic Monthly 40 : 592 ff., Studies I : 211-224; and see in especial W. O. Sypherd, "Chaucer's Eight Years' Sickness", in Mod. Lang. Notes 20 : 240-43, where the conventionality of Chaucer's expression is argued.

c) Monument

Caxton, in an epilogue added to his print of the Boethius, speaks of Chaucer, and says: "of whom the body and corps lieth buried in thabbay of westmestre beside london to fore the chapele of seynt benet by whos sepulture is wreton on a table honging a pylere his Epytaphye maad by a poete laureat whereof the copye followeth" (Surigon's epitaph, see above).

This pillar and epitaph were raised by Caxton himself, see Blades p. 214.

In the edition of Gower's Confessio Amantis of 1532 by Berthelette, the *To the Reder* mentions the friendship between Chaucer and Gower, describes Gower's tomb, and then closes, "The other lieth buried in the monastery of seynt Peters at westminster in an ile on the south side of the churche. On whos soules, and alle cristen . . . ." etc. Berthelette's preface is reprinted by Todd, Illustrations pp. 138 ff., with a picture of Chaucer's tomb as in 1809, to face p. 144.

John Stow, in his Survey of London, 1598 and again 1603 (ed. Thoms 1876 pp. 171-2) says, speaking of the graves in Westminster Abbey, "Geffrey Chaucer, the most famous poet of England, also in the cloister, 1400, but since Nicholas Brigham, gentleman, raised a monument for him in the south cross aisle of the church; his works were partly published in print by William Caxton, in the reign of Henry VI" etc. On Stow's probable error (derived from Foxe's Acts and Monuments) in placing Chaucer's grave in the cloister, see Athen. 1902 II : 189-90, 288, 552.

William Camden, in his Reges, Reginae, Nobiles, et Alij in Ecclesia Collegiata B. Petri Westmonasterij Sepulti, London 1606, pp. 66-67, has this: "In Australi plaga Ecclesiae. Galfridus Chaucer Poeta celeberrimus, qui primus Anglicam Poësin ita illustravit, vt Anglicus Homerus habeatur. Obijt 1400. Anno vero 1555 Nicholaus Brigham, Musarum nomine huius ossa transtulit & illi nouum tumulum ex marmore, his versibus inscriptis posuit.

Qui fuit Anglorum vates ter maximus olim,
Galfridus Chaucer conditur hoc tumulo.
Annum si quaeras Domini, si tempora mortis,
Ecce notae subsunt, quae tibi cuncta notant.
  25 Octobris 1400.
Aerumnarum requies, Mors.
N. Brigham hos fecit Musarum nomine sumptus.

Si rogitas quis fueram, forsan te fama docebit:
Quod si fama neget, mundi quia gloria transit,
  Haec monumenta lege."

At the foot of p. 67 Camden notes: "Rachael Brigham, filia Nicolai
Brigham quadrimula obijt, sita est iuxta Galfridum Chaucerum.
Obijt 1557 21 Iunij." [See Athen. 1894 I : 541, 1902 II : 552.]

Pits, 1619, gives the epitaph and the account of Brigham's erection of the new monument, see above.

Weever, in his Ancient Funerall Monvments within the Vnited
Monarchie of Great Britaine, Ireland, and the islands adiacent
(etc.), London 1631, treats of Chaucer on pp. 489 ff. He quotes
Speght and Leland, mentions the erection of the monument "at
the cost and charges of Nicholas Brigham, gentleman, Anno 1555",
and the burial of Brigham's infant daughter beside the tomb; he
cites Hoccleve's lines of elegy, and on p. 490 gives "the Inscriptions
vpon his Tombe at this day" The epitaph is as in Camden; Weever
adds: "About the ledge of the Tombe, these verses were written",
and cites Si rogitas, etc., see ante. Eulogies of Chaucer, apparently
from Speght, follow.

Ashmole, in his Theatrum Chemicum Britannicum, London, 1652,
has upon p. 226, just under the Finis of Hermes Bird (Lydgate's
Churl and Bird) and facing Chaucer's tale of the Canon's Yeoman,
a cut of Chaucer's tomb, crowded on to the page; it is marked
"Vaughan sculp". It represents a canopy of four arches, with a
tomb below which is about two-thirds the length of the canopy; at
the back of the recess, under the canopy, the epitaph appears in
the central compartment, with a full-length figure of Chaucer on
one side, marked "Imago Chauceri", and the other side blank. The
epitaph reads as in Camden, except that the last word of the third
line is vitae, not mortis, and that the two and one-half lines of
Latin below the mention of Brigham do not appear. The date 1556
is below the line naming Brigham.
  Ashmole gives a life of Chaucer on pp. 470-72 of this same
work; he quotes Speght, Bale, Pits, and Stow, and says that

Chaucer "dyed at London 25 Octob. Ann. 1400, as appeares by the inscription upon his Tombe at Saint Peters in Westminster Abby in an Isle on the South Side of the Church. Mr. Nicholas Brigham built this Marble Monument to his Memory, the true Pourtraicture whereof I have caused to be exactly graved in Brasse, and placed in page 226. There was formerly round the ledge of the Tombe these following Verses, but now no remainder of them left.

Si rogites (etc.)

The Picture of Chaucer is now somewhat decay'd, but the Graver has recovered it after a Principall left to Posterity by his worthy Schollar Tho. Occleve, who hath also these Verses upon it. (Hoccleve is cited.) Before Mr. Brigham built the aforesaid Monument it seemes Chaucer had a Stone layd over his Grave upon which was ingraved this following Epitaph:

Galfridus Chaucer Vates & fama Poesis,
Materna hac sacra sum tumulatus humo."

Antony à Wood, in his Fasti Oxonienses, 1691-2, does not give epitaph or arms; he says, in his account of Cowley, "in the south cross isle, or large isle joyning to the south side of the choir, was buried near to the place where the reliques of Jeff. Chaucer had been lodged."

John Dart, author of the life of Chaucer first planned for the Urry Chaucer of 1721, includes in his Westmonasterium (etc.), 1743, a full page engraving of the monument, by J. Cole, to face p. 83 of vol. I. His discussion of Chaucer in the text is mainly a complaint of the changes made by the editors in his Life of the poet above mentioned, but he gives a brief biographical notice, in which he says that Chaucer was born in London in 1328; that "his father, as I take it, was one Sir John Chaucer, employ'd in foreign affairs by Edward III"; that Chaucer died in the second year of Edward III, aged 72, and was buried before the Chapel of St. Bennet, "where his stone of broad Grey Marble, as I take it, was not long since remaining, but was taken up when Mr. Dryden's Monument was erected, and sawn to mend the Pavement." Dart also says that "upon the corner Pillar of St. Bennet's Chapel hung antiently a leaden Plate" with Chaucer's epitaph by Surigonus of Milan; he records that Nicholas Brigham erected the present tomb "about the year 1555", and says that he put the tomb "in a convenient Place, as near his Grave as he could, on which was formerly painted his Picture in a Blank on the North side the epitaph, but now quite defac'd. It was exactly like the Painting of Ocklefe, printed before the old Editions, and was remaining in Mr. Ashmole's Time, who in one of his Treatises, has given us the Monument. . . . There was formerly round the

Verge of the Tomb these Verses " 'Si rogitas' " (etc. see above). "On the Inside of the Tomb was his Arms, now gone, but the same are painted over it under the Arch of the Church Wall."

The full-page engraving which accompanies the text shows the epitaph as cited above, four lines of Latin, the date, a single line of Latin, and the line giving Brigham's name; below this appears the date 1556. A shield of the arms is on each side of the epitaph, and in each of the sculptured quatrefoils on the front of the tomb; the epitaph is above the tomb itself, under the canopy, upon the wall at the back of the recess.

In Neale and Brayley's History and Antiquities of the Abbey Church of St. Peter, Westminster, London 1818-1823, II : 265, occurs the passage cited by Sir Harris Nicolas in his Life of Chaucer, upon Chaucer's tomb and epitaph. Neale and Brayley say: "In front of the Tomb are three pannelled divisions of starred quatrefoils, containing sculptured shields, on which the arms of Chaucer are alone distinguishable, through the partial decomposition and crumbling state of the marble: the same arms may be traced in an oblong compartment at the back of the recess, where also, are some remains of the following *Inscription,* now almost obliterated from similar circumstances"; (the epitaph is then given as by Camden above cited, but with *v* everywhere written for *u,* and the date 1550 below the line containing Brigham's name). It is then added that the whole of the recess and the canopy have recently been colored black.

In the Nineteenth Century for August, 1897, p. 336, Henry Troutbeck, coroner for Westminster, states that he examined Chaucer's bones when they were exposed in the digging of Browning's grave, and that from the measurements which he made of some of the larger bones, he judges the poet to have been about five feet six inches tall.

d) *Connection with Thomas Chaucer, etc.*

The filiation of Thomas Chaucer, a wealthy landowner and conspicuous political figure of the fifteenth century, to Geoffrey Chaucer, was first asserted by Thomas Gascoigne, died 1458, in his Dictionarium Theologicum, which is in MS in the library of Lincoln College, Oxford, and is not yet printed as a whole, though extracts were published by Thorold Rogers as Loci e Libro Veritatum, Oxford, 1881. The passage on Thomas Chaucer, not printed by Rogers, was quoted by Hales, Athen. 1888 I : 404, reprinted Folia Litteraria 1893 pp. 110-111. Skeat, I : l, quotes a sentence; and see Chalmers' English Poets, I, page x. In the life of Chaucer prefixed to the Speght of 1598, see ante, Thomas appears as Geoffrey's son in the stemma drawn up by the antiquary Glover. The remark

follows, by Speght or Stow, that "some hold opinion (but I know
not upon what grounds) that Thomas Chaucer was . . . rather
some Kinsman" whom Geoffrey Chaucer brought up. The Life-
Records, part IV, pp. 51-57, discuss the question at length, and take
up the theory mentioned by Speght or Stow; suggestion is even
made as to the real name of him who was called Thomas Chaucer.
A work upon the subject is announced by the Chaucer Society.

Furnivall published in Notes and Queries, 1872 I : 381 ff., a poem
by Lydgate addressed to Thomas Chaucer on the occasion of his
departure to France upon ambassade, in which no mention is made
of any relation between Thomas and Geoffrey; the same text is
printed in Mod. Phil. 1 : 331-5. Furnivall regards this as strong
proof against the filiation, since Lydgate's admiration for the elder
Chaucer would certainly lead him to mention the connection if any
existed. Kittredge, Na+ ᵕn 1894 II : 309, considers this inference
unnecessary, as Lydgate was writing a mere occasional poem. In
Acad. 1901 II : 597 Furnivall repeats his argument, opposing a
letter printed *ibid.* p. 572.

Minor notes are in N. and Q. 1872 I : 436, 468, 493, II : 15; 1884
I : 364; 1891 II : 47, 109, 215, 338; 1900 I : 146 and refs. there given;
Acad. 1874 I : 65, 94; Athen. 1888 I : 404, 436, 468.

Koch, Chronology, pp. 18-20, opposes filiation.

In the Bell Chaucer of 1854, vol. VIII p. 130, is a note on Thomas
Chaucer, as follows: "In searching the Bodleian Library for MSS
for this edition, a curious fact was discovered, which, though possibly known to Tyrwhitt, has not been mentioned by him or any
subsequent editor. In the volume marked Fairfax 16 are contained,
in addition to *The Compleynte of Mars and Venus,* and other poems,
by Geoffrey Chaucer, some short pieces by one Thomas Chaucer.
This person was probably the poet's eldest son or a kinsman, who,
according to a tradition prevalent in Speght's time, was educated by
his more celebrated relative. To this Thomas Chaucer, therefore,
might very probably be traced many of those short pieces published
by Speght, but properly rejected from later editions of the works
of Geoffrey Chaucer."

Bell is here in error. The MS Fairfax 16 contains no pieces
marked as by Thomas Chaucer, but in another Bodleian MS, the
Shirley codex Ashmole 59, the envoy of the Venus is marked in the
margin as by Thomas Chaucer, see Anglia 30 : 326-7.

In the New England Historical and Genealogical Register, vol.
LI, there is printed, to face p. 389, a genealogical tree of the Manning family, from which it appears that one Simon Manning de
Codham, Kent, who was living in the 46th year of Edward III and
the fifth of Richard II, married "Catharina soror Galfridi Chawcer

militis celeberrimi Poetae Anglicani." From this union several well known New England families, among them the Higginsons and Prescotts, claim descent. Henry F. Waters, the compiler of the notes to this tree, see *ibid.* pp. 403, 405 in especial, assigns MS Harley 1548 as the source of his information, which reference is correct. The Harleian Catalogue says that this MS was written and tricked by Richard Mundy, and that the copy of the Visitation Book of the County of Kent which it contains, whence this genealogy is taken, is from that made and taken in 1619, 1620, 1621 by John Philpot Rouge Dragon, for William Camden Clarencieux. A note by the cataloguer says: "Herein I find many enlargements by Mr. Mundy and by Mr. Robert Dale; but mostly by the former."

C. Portraits of Chaucer

The Chaucer Society published in their second series, 1900, "The Portraits of Geoffrey Chaucer", by M. H. Spielmann; this work was reviewed by Koch, Engl. Stud. 30 : 445-50.

Spielmann attaches by far the greatest value to the halflength executed by order of Hoccleve on the margin of leaf 91 in MS. Harley 4866. This he reproduces; reproductions are also to be found *e. g.* in Life Records, part II frontispiece, Skeat I, frontispiece, Garnett and Gosse's Engl. Lit. vol. I, to face p. 140. There is a description in Trial Forew. pp. 93-4, and one by Lowell in his essay on Chaucer, in My Study Windows.

Chaucer is depicted, from fancy, by painters of the Canterbury Pilgrimage, see under Pictures of the Pilgrims at the close of Section III here. A bust by George Frampton, R. A., exhibited in the Royal Academy, 1903, has been placed in the Guildhall, London.

Previous partial lists of Chaucer's portraits are in the Dict. Nat. Biog., art. *Chaucer.* Many allusions to portraits, usually of no authenticity, may be found in the columns of Notes and Queries.

D. Chaucer as a Character in Fiction

Chaucer appears as a character in Robert Greene's Vision (about 1590?); in Ben Jonson's masque of The Golden Age Restored (1615), in the first recension of Gay's Wife of Bath (see p. 298 here), in E. L. Blanchard's Friar Bacon (1863), in à Beckett and Stanfield's operetta of The Canterbury Pilgrims (1884), and in Percy Mackaye's Canterbury Pilgrims (1903). See also James White's Adventures of John of Gaunt, Dublin (1790), 2 vols., described Anglia 25 : 251; and Florence Converse's novel entitled Long Will, Boston, 1903.

Landor's Imaginary Conversations include one between Chaucer, Boccaccio, and Petrarch.

SECTION II

THE WORKS OF CHAUCER

A. Introduction: On the Canon of Chaucer

IN studying the work of a nineteenth-century poet, we have at
our command a text which has been prepared for the press by
the author himself or by his literary executor, so that we are
secure of our data when discussing the poet's vocabulary or verse-
peculiarities. If in various successive editions the author introduces
changes, as was true of Rossetti and Wordsworth and Tennyson, we
have all those dated editions at our disposal, and an essay like
Dowden's on the text of Wordsworth's poems becomes possible.
But Early English verse offers us few or no such certainties. There
is a sense in which it is true that we do not know what Chaucer
wrote.

The works of Chaucer, written before the era of printing, have
come down to us in a mass of manuscripts, mainly of the century
following his death. No one of these texts appears to be in the
poet's own handwriting, and notwithstanding the great amount of
penwork which Chaucer's position in the Customs required of him,
no written line or even signature by him has yet been discovered.
(See Life Records pt. IV, pp. xxiv, 233 note, 278 note. See query
in Athen. 1868 II : 370.) Further, there appears in Chaucer's case
scarcely any evidence of personal effort towards an accurate reproduction of his own works, such as Macaulay has pointed out to be
true of Gower; see Works of John Gower, II : clxvii. The only bits
of such evidence for Chaucer are the stanza of reproof to Adam his
scrivener, and the lines at the close of the Troilus, fearing its too
probable "mysmetring". Our text of the poems has to be obtained
from the uncorrected copies of fifteenth-century scribes made at
second or third hand or even further from the original. Francis
Thynne, in his Animadversions, tells of a manuscript of Chaucer,
known to his father, which bore the endorsement "Examinatur
Chaucer"; but, as Furnivall says, this more than invaluable manuscript has never been seen by any student. We not only have no

51

text in Chaucer's hand or corrected by him; we have no text which is indubitably transcribed from his copy, or of which we can trace the original.

The study of Chaucer as a narrator and literary artist is not seriously affected by these considerations, because of the very close agreement of all manuscripts in the general trend of the narrative. In some of the shorter poems the majority of the copies are identical except for the omissions and slight errors of transcription which a scribe always commits; in others there are differences in wording between one set of texts and another which lead some critics to the supposition that two versions by Chaucer were in circulation, one of which had been revised by him. See for instance under the Anelida and the Troilus, here. Some few manuscripts, again, have been deliberately altered by the copyist, as the Selden MS of the Parlement of Foules; but these isolated cases can usually be quickly recognized. So marked is the general agreement among the copies that even the keenest linguistic specialist would probably say, with Pollard (Athenaeum 1901 II : 631) : "I doubt if in all the Canterbury Tales there are more than twenty lines in which it is possible for editors to adopt readings making any really important change in the sense." Compare also Temporary Preface, pp. 86-7.

But with the increasing modern interest in English philology has appeared the desire to know not merely Chaucer's general narrative trend, but also the details of his verse-command and of his language. Every day adds to the number of students who wish for a truthful text of Chaucer even more than for a readable one; and every new monograph upon Chaucer confirms such students in the belief that the truthful edition, when it arrives, will be unchanged in richness of literary texture and in melody of verse, while offering us a more exact reflection of the poet's language and of the details of his verse-technique. For such an edition we must look, not to any "editor with a good ear", but to the existing manuscript copies of the poems.

The term "manuscript" is applied roughly to various sorts of Chaucer volumes written by hand. First, there is the volume containing but one work, such as the Canterbury Tales, executed by a professional scribe for some wealthy patron, beautifully written and decorated with colored capitals, chapter-headings, etc., and sometimes with miniatures of the persons and scenes described. Secondly, the volume written by some firm of copyists either on commission or to be sold over their counter, and containing (say) from six to twenty works by various authors; this is often written in different hands, the workmen either relieving each other from time to time or each making a separate copy of some one work, all of which were later sewed together into a volume. Thirdly, the "commonplace-book" of a collector, written perhaps by himself, perhaps by his amanuensis, and containing a mixed mass of any-thing in which he was interested,—narrative verse, didactic Latin prose, proverbs, medical and culinary receipts, prayers, notes on astrology or contemporary events, etc. Fourthly, any one of these volumes partly executed and then passed from owner to owner until it is filled with the handwriting of several generations. Fifthly, a mass of verse and prose by many authors and many copyists, not intended by the scribes as an unit, but forced into one volume by a later binder. Many of the manuscripts of Gower's Confessio Amantis belong in the first class, as Macaulay has pointed out, loc. cit., but the copies of Chaucer's poems rarely show such care, though a few are of this sort, e. g. the Ellesmere MS of the Canterbury Tales described below, Section III B 7. The second class mentioned above may be illustrated by the MS Tanner 346 of the Bodleian Library, or by the volume described by Chaucer himself in the Wife of Bath's prologue lines 669 ff. An unusually fine example of the third class is the codex Fairfax 16 of the Bodleian Library, with which may be compared any book written by Shirley, as for instance Ashmole 59; the fourth class might be exemplified by Ff 1, 6 of the Cambridge University Library, and the fifth by Harley 78 of the British Museum. All these volumes are discussed below.

The better fifteenth-century manuscripts, as again in the case of Gower's poem, often have a colophon or a heading, sometimes both, giving the title of the work and the author; occasionally the date of completion may be added. Transcriptions of Chaucer, however, show no such system. We almost never find the date of the copy and only irregularly the name of the author; and it follows from such indefiniteness on the part of the manuscripts that we are not in certainty as to the poet's genuine works. We cannot take the testimony of every manuscript as credible, and make up the list of Chaucer's works on this evidence, because of the plain error of some manuscripts in assigning to him, for example, verse in broad Scotch and of doggerel quality. Nor can we take the testimony of any one MS as to Chaucer's exact words in any given poem; for all scribes must and do err. Two problems therefore confront the student; the determining which are the genuine writings of Chaucer, that is, the establishment of the Chaucer canon; and the determining of the genuine text of Chaucer. Only after the settle-ment of the former question, a settlement now virtually complete, can Chaucer's use of his sources and his artistic methods be dis-cussed; and upon the settlement of the latter problem depends our knowledge of his language and his verse.

The establishment of the canon of Chaucer, a work of many years and still not complete in minor details, has been arrived at by the utilization of several sorts of evidence. Having no text in the poet's hand, and knowing little or nothing of the scribes who copied his verse, we have had to form our conclusions in each case by a grouping of data. First, from such lists as are given in the Man of Law's headlink, in the prologue to the Legend of Good Women, or in the catalogue by Chaucer's contemporary and imitator, Lydgate, can we identify any existing poem or poems? Secondly, among such works, identified with reasonable probability, is there an agreement in literary spirit, in command of language, and in management of rime and verse? Thirdly, are such poems, so identified and so agreeing, marked as Chaucer's in early and credible manuscripts? See for example the note on Authenticity under the heading Book of the Duchesse, Section IV here.

It must be observed that one of these sorts of evidence is insufficient unless supported by at least one other test. Thus, the "Retractation" and Lydgate's list of Chaucer's works mention a "Book of the Lion", which has never been found; but if a poem marked with that title were discovered, we could not declare it Chaucer's unless its language, verse, and style agreed broadly with his known works; and even if the poem were marked with Chaucer's name in the text in which it was found, we should still investigate most strictly the credibility of the scribe, and probably refuse to believe him if his statement stood alone against linguistic and metrical evidence to the contrary. Compare, for example, the long continued inclusion of the Lamentation of Mary Magdalen or of the Testament of Love in the canon of Chaucer, and their final rejection. Again, a poem not in any of the lists of Chaucer's works, such as the Mars, may be accepted as genuine, because marked with Chaucer's name in authentic MSS, and because agreeing in style and language with the known works. The doubtful cases are: (a) poems marked by a scribe as Chaucer's, and contemporary in language, but not characterized by the rime and technique of the admittedly genuine works; (b) poems of grace and cleverness equal to Chaucer's, and contemporary in language, but not mentioned in any list nor marked in any manuscript. In the former case, as above said, the vital point is the credibility of the scribe; in the latter case the basis of argument is a personal judgment by the critic who maintains Chaucer's authorship—the most inconclusive of all forms of evidence. Compare Acad. 1889 I : 179, where Pollard says of Skeat's attribution to Chaucer of several anonymous poems because of their smooth metrical flow,—"He is here laying down a new and very dangerous canon." And an additional complication in case (a) just mentioned is the possibility that Chaucer, like other artists, may not only have allowed himself different usages at different times, but may have occasionally deviated from his apparently general rule. Thus, in the discussion of his rimes, note that there are exceptions to the y-ye test, see Lounsbury, Studies I : 388 (opposed by Skeat VI : lvii), and to the nonriming of close and open or long and short vowels, see Skeat

VI : xxxi ff. Also, note that Northern forms may appear in rime, see Lounsbury, Studies I : 387.

But despite these lesser uncertainties, the canon of Chaucer is at present reasonably settled. There follow here prints of the lists given by Chaucer and by Lydgate, a parallel survey of the lists in Thynne, Leland, and Bale, and a sketch of the subsequent enlargement and modern revision of those lists. The only separate work avowedly devoted to the subject is:

The Chaucer Canon. With a discussion of the Works associated with the Name of Geoffrey Chaucer. W. W. Skeat, Oxford 1900.

Reviewed Anglia Beibl. 12 : 291-2 (Schröer); DLZ 1901, pp. 863-6 (Kaluza); Engl. Stud. 30 : 450-56 (Koch); Sat. Review 90 : 17 ff. Much of the material here presented was previously included in the Oxford Chaucer.

In N. and Q. 1874 I : 185-6 Skeat suggested the non-use of linked stanzas as a minor test; see Lounsbury, Studies I : 398, Skeat VII : lxxv.

----

1) *Chaucer's Own Testimony*

1. In the prologue to the Legend of Good Women, lines 405 ff. (A), Alceste defends Chaucer against the reproofs of the god of Love:

(MS Gg iv, 27, University Library, Cambridge)

He made the bok that highte the hous of fame
And ek the deth of Blaunche the duchesse
And the parlement of foulis as I gesse
And al the loue of Palamon & Arcite
Of thebes thow the storye is knowe lite
And manye an ympne for thour halydayis
That hightyn baladis roundelys & vyrelayes
And for to speke of othyr besynesse
He hath in prose translatid Boece
And of the wrechede engendrynge of mankynde
As man may in pope innocent I-fynde
And made the lyf also of seynt Cecile
He made also gon is agret while
Orygenes vpon the maudeleyne
Hym ouu3te now to haue the lesse peyne
He hath mad manye a lay & manye a thyng   etc.

Earlier, lines 255-267 (A), the god of love accuses Chaucer:

> Thow hast translatid the romauns of the rose
> That is an eresye a-geyns myn lawe
> And makyst wise folk fro me withdrawe
> * * * * * * *
> Hast thow nat mad in englys ek the bok
> How that Crisseyde Troylis forsok,   etc.
> * * * * * * *

The works here mentioned as by the author of the prologue are thus: the translation of the Romaunt of the Rose, Troilus and Cressida, the House of Fame, the Death of Blanche the Duchesse, the Parlement of Foules, "Palamon and Arcite", ballads, roundels, virelays, the translation of Boece, and of the "Wretched Engendering of Mankind", the life of St. Cecily, and Origen upon the Magdalen. The two lines which contain the allusion to the "Wretched Engendering", from Pope Innocent, are not in other MSS of the Legend of Good Women; see under the Legend, Section IV here, and also under the heading of Lost Works. Neither this translation nor Origen upon the Magdalen is now known. The life of St. Cecily is the Second Nun's Tale; for Palamon and Arcite see under the Knight's Tale, Section III G.

2. From the headlink to the Man of Law's Tale. The Man of Law is speaking.

(MS Ellesmere)

> I kan right now no thrifty tale seyn
> That Chaucer thogh he kan but lewedly
> On metres and on rymyng craftily
> Hath seyd hem in swich englissh as he kan
> Of olde tyme as knoweth many a man
> And if he haue noght seyd hem leue brother
> In o book he hath seyd hem in another
> ffor he hath toold of loueris vp and doun
> Mo than Ouide made of mencioun
> In hise epistles that been ful olde
> What sholde I telle hem syn they ben tolde
> In youthe he made of Ceys and Alcione
> And sitthe hath he spoken of euerichone
> Thise noble wyues and thise loueris eke
> Who so that wole his large volume seke
> Cleped the seintes legende of Cupide
> Ther may he seen the large woundes wyde
> Of Lucresse and of Babilan Tesbee
> The swerd of Dido for the false Enee
> The tree of Phillis for hire Demophon

The pleinte of Diane and of Hermyon
Of Adriane and of Isiphilee
The bareyne yle stondynge in the see
The dreynte Leandre for his Erro
The teeris of Eleyne and the wo
Of Brixseyde and the Ladomya
The crueltee of the queene Medea
Thy litel children hangynge by the hals
ffor thy Iason that was in loue so fals
O Ypermystra Penolopee Alceste
Your wifhede he comendeth with the beste
But certeinly no word ne writeth he
Of thilke wikke ensample of Canacee
That loued hir owene brother synfully
Of swiche cursed stories I sey fy   etc.

The works here mentioned as by Chaucer are: "Ceys and Alcione", by which is usually understood the first part of the Book of the Duchess, or possibly some still earlier work which Chaucer rewrote for that position; and the Legend of Good Women, the separate stories of which the Man of Law proceeds to enumerate. It must be noted that he omits two, Cleopatra and Philomela, of which we have the text, and that he gives eight of whom there are no legends in the poem as it has come down to us. See Skeat V : 137-139, list on p. 138; see Lowes, Publ. Mod. Lang. Assn. 20 : 818-19 note.

3. In the so-called Retractation, at the close of the Parson's Tale, the author says:

(MS Ellesmere)

Wherfore I biseke yow mekely for the mercy of god that ye preye for me that crist haue mercy on me and foryeue me my giltes. and namely of my translacions and enditynges of worldly vanitees the whiche I reuoke in my retraccions As is the book of Troilus The book also of ffame The book of the xxv Ladies The book of the Duchesse The book of seint Valentynes day of the parlement of briddis The tales of Caunterbury thilke that sownen in to synne The book of the Leon And many another book if they were in my remembrance and many a song and many a leccherous lay that crist for his grete mercy foryeue me the synne But of the translacion of Boece de consolacione and othere bookes of Legendes of seintes and Omelies and moralitee and deuocion that thanke I oure lord Ihesu crist and his blisful mooder and alle the seintes of heuene bisekynge hem þat they from hennes forth vn-to my lyues ende sende me grace to biwayle my giltes and to studie to the saluacion of my soule and graunte me grace of verray penitence (etc.)

The works here mentioned are: Troilus, the House of Fame, the Legend of Good Women, the Book of the Duchess, the Parlement of Foules, part of the Canterbury Tales, the Book of the Lion, many a song, etc., the translation of Boece, and other books of legends of saints, homilies, moralities, etc.

The Book of the Lion is no longer known; see under Lost Works.

On the Retractation see after the Parson's Tale, end of Section III G here.

2) *Lydgate's Testimony*

(From the Prologue to the Falls of Princes, Tottel's print of 1554.)

And semblably, as I ha told toforne,
my maister Chaucer did his busines,
And in his dayes hath so well him borne
out of our tong tauoyden al rudenes,
And to reforme it with colors of swetenes.
Wherfore let vs yeue him laude and glory,
and put his name with Poetes in memory

Of whose labour to make mencion,
wherethrough of right he should comended be,
in youth he made a translacion
Of a booke which called is Trophe
in Lumbard tong, as men may reade & see,
And in our vulgare, long or that he deyed,
gaue it the name of Troylous & Cresseyde

Which for to rede, louers them delite,
they haue therin so great deuocion,
And this Poete him also to quite,
Of Boecius booke the consolacion
made in his tyme an whole translacion,
And to his sonne that called was Lowis
he made a treatise, ful noble & of great price

Upon that labour in full noble forme
set them in order with their diuisions
Mennes wittes tapplien and conforme
To vnderstand by full expert reasons
by domifieng of sondry mansions
the roote out sought at the ascendent
Toforne or he gaue any iudgement

He wrote also ful many day agone,
Daunt in English him self so doth expresse
The piteous storye of Ceio and Alcion
and the death also of Blaunche the duches
And notably dyd his businesse
by great aduise his wittes to dispose,
to translate the Romaynt of the Rose.

Thus in vertue, he set al his entent
ydlenes and vyces for to flee:
Of foules also he wrote the parliament,
Therin remembring of royall Egles three
howe in theyr choyse they felt aduersitee
tofore nature profered the batayle,
Eche for his partie if it would auayle.

He did also his diligence and payne,
in our vulgare to translate and endite
Origene vpon the Maudelayn,
and of the Lyon a booke he did wryte,
Of Anneleida & of false Arcite
he made a complaynt doleful and piteous,
And of the broche which that Uulcanus

At Thebes wrought full diuers of nature,
Ouide writeth, who therof had a sight
For high desyre he should not endure
but he it had neuer by glade nor light
And if he had it ones in his myght
like as my maister saith, & writeth in dede,
It to conserue, he should aye liue in drede.

This poete wrote at the request of þe quene
a legend of perfite holines,
Of good weomen to find out nenetene
that did excell in bountie and fayrenes:
But for his labour and busines
was importable his wittes to encombre,
In all this world to fynd so great a nombre.

He made the booke of Caunterbury tales,
whan the pylgryms rode on pylgrimage
throughout Kent, by hilles and by vales,
And all the storyes tolde in theyr passage,
endited them full well in our language,
Some of knighthod, some of gentlenesse,
And some of loue, and some of perfitnes.

And some also of great moralite
Some of disport including great sentence
In prose he wrote the tale of Mellebe
and of his wife that called was prudence:
And of Grisildes perfect pacience,
and how the monke of stories newe & olde,
Pitous tragedies by the way tolde.

This sayed Poete my maister, in his dayes
Made and compiled ful many a fresh ditee
Complaintes, ballades, roundles virelaies
Ful delectable to hearen and to see;
For which men should of right and equitee,
Sith he of english in making was the best,
Pray vnto God to yeue his soule good rest.

Lydgate's list includes: "Trophe", which seems to be synonymous with Troilus and Cressida; the translation of Boethius, the Astrolabe, "Daunt in English", Ceys and Alcione, the death of Blanche the duchess, the translation of the Romaunt of the Rose, the Parlement of Foules, Origen upon the Maudelayn, the Book of the Lion, Anelida and Arcite, the Brooch of Thebes, the Legend of Good Women, the Canterbury Tales, the tale of Melibeus, that of Griselda, and the Monk's Tale; also "many a fresh ditee," etc.

Of these, Origenes upon the Maudelayn and the Book of the Lion are supposedly lost. "Ceys and Alcione" is generally interpreted to mean the first part of the Book of the Duchesse; and the "Brooch of Thebes" is understood as a portion of the Anelida, see Section IV here. Two of the remaining titles of the catalogue are still Chaucer-cruces,—"Trophe", and "Daunt in English." See under House of Fame, Section IV here, for the latter; for the former see under Lollius, II C 4 below.

For the testimony of John Shirley, the only fifteenth-century Chaucerian scribe known to us, see Section VII B here.

3) *The Lists of Thynne, Leland, Bale*

THYNNE 1542	LELAND	BALE 1557-9	BALE 1548
Canterbury Tales	Fabulae Cantianae 1	Fabulas Cantianas 1 Praefationes earundem	
[Plowman's Tale]	Petri Aratoris Fabula 2	Aratoris narrationem 2	
Romaunt of the Rose	De Arte Amandi 3	De Arte Amandi 3	
Troilus and Cressida	Amores Troili et Chrysidis 4	Amores Troili et Chrysidis 4	[see No. 20 below]
Testament of Cressida	Testamentum Chrysidis 5	Testamentum Chrysidis 5	[see No. 7 below]
Legend of Good Women	Amores Heroidum 6	Amores Heroidum 6	[see No. 8 below]
[Mother of Nurture]		[see No. 26 below]	
			Trophaeum Lombardicum 2
			De principum ruina 3
			Emblemata moralia 4
			Amatoria carmina 5
De Consolatione Philos.	De Consolatione Philos. 7	De Consolatione Philos. 7	De Consolatione Philos. 1
		[see No. 32 below]	De Curia Veneris 6
		[see No. 5 above]	Chrysidis Testamentum 7
		[see No. 25 below]	Laudes bonarum mulierum 8 [each legend separately named]
The Dream of Chaucer	Somnium Chauceri 8	Somnium Chauceri 8	Somnium Chauceri 9
Parlement of Foules	Chorus Avium 9	Chorum Avium 9	Volucrum conglobationem 10
Flower of Courtesy	Flos Humanitatis 10	Urbanitatis Florem 10	Urbanitatis Florem 11
How Pity is Dead, etc.	De pietate mortua 11	De pietate mortua 11	De misericordia sepultura 12
La Belle Dame		[see No. 27 below]	Carmen Facetum 13
Anelida and Arcite		[see No. 28 below]	De Augea et Telepho 14
Assembly of Ladies	Chorus Heroidum 12	Heroidum Chorum 12	Choream dominarum 15
The Astrolabe	De Astrolabio 13	De Astrolabio 13	De Astrolabij ratione 16
Complaint of the Black Knight	Querela equitis nigri 14	Querelam equitis nigri 14	Queremoniam nigri militis 17
Praise of Women	Encomium mulierum 15	Encomium mulierum 15	Foeminarum encomion 18
House of Fame	De Fama 16	De Fama et eius domicilio 16	
Testament of Love	Testamentum Amoris 17	Testamentum Amoris 17	
Lament of Mary Magdalen	Threni Magdalenae 18	Threnos Magdalenae 18	
Remedy of Love	De Remedio Amoris 19	De Remedio Amoris 19	
Complaint of Mars and Venus	Querela Martis et Veneris 20	Querelam Martis et Veneris 20	
Letter of Cupid	Epistola Cupidinis 21	Epistolam Cupidinis 21	

3) *The Lists of Thynne, Leland, Bale*

THYNNE 1542	LELAND	BALE 1557-9	BALE 1548
Ballad in Commend. of our Lady	Cantiones 22	Cantiones quoque 22	
Gower to Henry IV			
		De Meliboeo et prudentia 23	
		De peccatis ac remediis 24	
		Laudes bonarum mulierum 25 [see No. 6 above, No. 8 of 1548]	[see No. 8 above]
[See at close of No. 6 above]		Carmen Chauceri= Mother of Nurture 26	
		Super impia domina=La Belle Dame 27	[see No. 13 above]
		De Annelida et Arcyto 28	[see No. 14 above]
Cuckoo and Nightingale		De cuculo et philomela 29	
Scogan to the Lords, etc.		Octo questiones 30	
		Chronicon conquestus 31	
[Stedfastnesse]			
		De Curia Veneris 32	[see No. 6 above]
Truth		Epigrammata quoque 33	
Diuers Other Goodly Balades [=Fortune, Scogan, Go forth King, Purse, Wicked Tongue]		Narrationes diuersorum 34	Narrationes diuersorum 19 [=Pilgrim's Tale]
		[See No. 4 above]	De Troilo et Chryseida 20
		De Ceyce et Halcyona 35	De Ceyce et Halcyona 21
		In obitum Blanchiae ducissae 36	In obitum Blanchiae ducissae 22
		De Vulcani veru 37	
		De leone et eius dignitate 38	
		Vitam D. Ceciliae 39	
		Hymnos amatorios 40	
		Amores Palam. et Arcyti 41	
		De Thisbae Amore 42	
		De Castello dominarum 43	
		Comoedias et Tragoedias 44	Tragoedias graues 23
			Comoedias leues 24
			Satyros et Iambos 25
		Facetias et iocos 45	Facecias et iocos 26
			Elegias et poemata 27
		Dantem Italum transtulit 46	
		Petrarchae quaedam 47	
		Origenis tractatum 48	

From Bale's *Index Britanniae Scriptorum,*
ed. R. L. Poole, Oxford, 1902.[1]

Galfridus Chaucer, eques eruditus, ac Ioannis Gaweri socius, obijt
A. D. 1400. 4. nonas Iunij. Post mortem quieuit ad sanctum
Petrum in Westmonasterio ad partem australem.

Ex confessione amantis Gaueri.

Galfridus Chaucer, quiescit sepultus ad diuum Petrum in Westmonasterio, ad australe latus eiusdem ecclesie. Ad eius sarcopha-
gum hec carmina sunt relicta.
Galfridus Chaucer, vates et fama poesis
Materne, hac sacra sum tumulatus humo.

Ex collectionibus Edwardi Braynewode.

Galfridus Chaucer, scripsit,
De Meliboeo ac Thopa, li. i. Iuuenis Meliboeus nomine, potens
ac diues.
Narrationem Agricole, li. i. Agricole subduxit aratrum in Iunio.

Ex officina Guilhelmi Hylle.

Galfridus Chaucer, eques auratus, et poeta, scripsit,
Prefationes xxiiij, trac. i. Dum Aprilis imbribus suauibus.
Equitis narrationem, trac. i. Olim erat, vt veteres historie.
Molendinarij narrationem, trac. i. Cum eques auratus suam
finisset.
Exactoris narrationem, trac. i. Cum omnes risissent ad hanc
fabulam.
Coci narrationem, trac. i. Cocus Londinensis loquente adhuc.
Legisperiti narrationem, trac. iij. Noster hospes satis uidit.
Armigeri narrationem, trac. iij. Protinus hospes noster inquit.
Mercatoris narrationem, trac. i. Plorationes lamenta, curas.
Mulieris Bathoniensis narrationem, trac. i. Experientia etsi nulla
in.
Mendicantis narrationem, trac. i. Iste solennis terminarius est.
Apparitoris narrationem, trac. i. Sitator iste in equo se.
Clerici Oxoniensis narrationem, trac. vj. Oxonij clerice, dicebat
hospes.
Plebei narrationem, trac. i. Generosi et antiqui Britones.
Vesthalis narrationem, trac. i. Ministra ac nutrix vitiorum.
Canonicorum serui narrationem, trac. i. Dum finita esset Cecilie
vita.
Medici narrationem, trac. i. Erat, vt refert Titus Liuius.
Indulgentiarij narrationem, trac. i. Venerabiles viri, dum in ec-
clesia.

---

[1] Reprinted here by kind permission of the editor. For note on this work, see
p. 9 above.

Naute narrationem, trac. i.   Amici, consequenter dicebat.

Priorisse narrationem, trac. i.   Domine dominus noster, quam admirabilis.

Rithmum de Thopaso, trac. i.   Viri fratres attendite bono.

Monachi narrationem, trac. i.   Vt finem daret narratio di.

Capellani narrationem, trac. i.   Tace domine, dicebat eques.

Bursarij narrationem, trac. i.   Monialium capellane dicebat.

De Melibeo ac prudentia, li. i.   Iuuenis quidam Melibeus, potens.

De peccatis et remedijs, li. i.   Hierem. 6.   State super vias.

De rose pulchritudine, li. i.   Plerique fatentur in somnijs meras.

De Troilo et Chryseida, li. v.   Vt traderem Troili duplicem.

Aratoris narrationem, li. i.   Agricola tulit aratrum dum.

Chryseide testamentum, trac. i.   Diuturnis horis donec dolo.

Chryseide querimoniam, trac. i.   O gemitus, offula merore.

Laudes bonarum mulierum, trac. i.   Mille vicibus ab hominibus accepi.

Cleopatre vitam, trac. i.   Post mortem Ptolemei regis.

Vitam Thisbe Babylonice, trac. i.   Babylonie quandoque contigit.

Vitam Didonis Carthaginensis, trac. i.   Gloriosum sit, Vergili Mantuane.

De Hisyphile et Medea, trac. i.   Dissimulantium amatorum.

Lucretie Romane vitam, trac. i.   Narrare nunc oportet.

De Ariadna Cretensi, trac. i.   Discerne infernalis Cretensis.

De Phylomela Atheniensi, trac. i.   Formarum fabricator, qui.

De Phyllide Thracensi, trac. i.   Tam argumento quam autori.

De Hypermestra Aegyptia, trac. i.   In Grecia aliquando duo fratres.

Carmen Chauceri, trac. i.   Probe educationis amanti.

Boetium de consolatione transtulit, li. v.   Carmina que quondam studio.

Conclusiones astrolabij, li. i.   Fili mi Ludouice, certe signis.

Fame domicilium, li. iij.   Vertat nobis deus somnia.

Testamentum amoris, li. iij.   Multi sunt qui patulis auribus.

Somnium Chauceri, trac. 1.   Admiror Hercle plurimum.

Auium cohortem, trac. i.   Vita tam breuis est, artis.

Vrbanitatis florem, trac. i.   In Februario cum cornuta.

De misericordie sepultura, trac. i.   Oh, quod pietatem tamdiu.

De domina immisericordi, trac. i.   Me dormitantem aureus sopor.

De Annelida et Arcyto, trac. ij.   Immitis belligerantium deus.

Comitium dominarum, trac. i.   In Septembri dum folia vir.

Querimoniam nigri militis, trac. i.   In Maio dum Flora regina.

Foeminarum encomion, trac. i.   Quibus animus est mulier.

Threnos Magdalene, trac. i.   Mesticie mortifere fluctibus.

Remedium amoris, trac. i.   Viso multiplici malo quod.

Querimoniam Martis et Veneris, trac. i.   Gaudete amatores pulluli.

Cupidinis chartam, trac. i.   Cupido, ad cuius nutum.

Carmen de nostra domina, trac. i.   Mille historias adhuc re.

De cuculo et philomela, trac. i. Amorum deus, quam potens.

Octo questiones et responsiones, trac. i. In Grecia quandoque tam nobili.

Epigrammata quoque, trac. i. Fugite multitudinem, veri.

De Ceice et Halciona, trac. i.

Obitum Blanchie ducisse, trac. i.

Chronicon conquestus Anglici, li. i. Ea etate, vt veteres annales.

Vitam Cecilie, li. i.

De Vulcani veru, li. i.

De leone, li. i.

Hymnos amatorios, li. i.

Amorem Palemonis et Arcyti, li. i.

De Thesbis amore, li. i.

Originem de Magdalena transtulit, li. i.

De ciuitate seu castello dominarum, li. iij.

Dantem Italum transtulit, li. i.

Et alia plura.

   Obijsse fertur A. D. 1400. iiij. nonas Iunij.

Ex magno volumine eiusdem.

The list of Leland is a close following of the Thynne table of contents, with the omission of La Belle Dame sans Mercy and Anelida. The entry *Cantiones* with which it closes may be a title for the Balade in Commendation of Our Lady, or merely a summary of the remaining contents.

The 1548 Bale is a mixture. Although the Canterbury Tales and the Romaunt are omitted from the list, several entries are added from Lydgate, *e. g.,* nos. 2-5, cp. the "Trophaeum Lombardicum" translated from Lydgate's allusion; the title of the Legend of Good Women is changed and each legend given separately in addition; the Court of Venus is added as No. 6, and as No. 19 we have the Pilgrim's Tale. From Lydgate are also added the Book of the Duchess and Ceyx and Alcyone, as Nos. 21, 22, while the Dream of Chaucer is previously mentioned as No. 9. No. 3 seems to represent Lydgate's own Falls of Princes. Nos. 2-5 of this list are not in Bale's Index, which was not begun until after the appearance of the 1548 Summarium, see Poole's ed. of the Index, p. xxi.

The 1557 Bale extends the catalogue of Chaucer's works, making several double entries. The Book of the Duchess is again noted twice, and if De Castello dominarum means the Legend, that work is thrice entered. The Romaunt and the Canterbury Tales are now included, and Melibeus and the Parson's Tale appended as if separate works, cp. their appearance thus, from Hill's press, in Bale's Index. The Knight's Tale also figures again, as "Chronicon conquestus", while Palamon and Arcite is taken, with several more titles, from Lydgate's list. The "Broche of Vulcan" (Anelida?) is thus added, and a *Thesbe* which is probably the hasty reading of the *Thebes* mentioned in Lydgate's next line following. La Belle Dame and Anelida are added from Thynne's list. The Court of Venus is moved down near the Pilgrim's Tale; and it may be conjectured that the "Dantem Italum transtulit" is Bale's understanding of Lydgate's "He made also—Daunt in English", in which case Bale is the first of the many who have struggled with Lydgate's cryptic utterance.

5

4) *The Lists of Pits, Stow, Speght, Urry*

Pits' list is clearly derived from Bale's of 1557. Like Bale he gives the Legend of Good Women twice, also the Romaunt of the Rose. He adds the History of Oedipus and Jocasta, and the Siege of Thebes (Lydgate's), which latter, he states, Lydgate translated from Chaucer into English verse. The story of Oedipus and Jocasta fills the first book of the Siege of Thebes.

Stow, in 1561, added to Thynne's list a mass of short poems, printed together in the latter portion of his volume. The only poem of length in this catalogue is the Court of Love; of these additions, Gentilesse, Proverbs, and the Words to Adam are still considered genuine, the Complaint to his Lady and Newfangleness are debated. Many of these additions were taken by Stow from the MS Trinity College Cambridge R 3, 19. Stow also added at the close of the 1561 volume Lydgate's Siege of Thebes, stating its authorship. Most of his additions were condemned by Tyrwhitt in 1775, and were not reprinted after that date as Chaucer's.

Speght added in the 1598 Chaucer the Isle of Ladies, styling it Chaucer's Dream; also The Flower and the Leaf. Skeat, Canon p. 163, speaks of a ballad, perhaps by Lydgate, as also added in this edition; the stanzas printed as envoy to the Isle of Ladies are meant, see under that heading, Section V here. In 1602 Speght further added the ABC (still considered genuine), and the spurious Jack Upland.

Urry, in 1721, printed Gamelyn and Beryn, in addition to all the works collected by previous editors. But in the Life prefixed to that edition it was not only pointed out that Henryson was the author of the Testament of Cressida, but it was also remarked that several ballads were "justly suspected" not to have been written by Chaucer; *e. g.*—O Mossie Quince, and—I have a Lady. Francis Thynne, in his Animadversions, had already said that Chaucer did not compose the Testament of Cressida, the Letter of Cupid, or—I have a Lady.

5) *The Work of Revision*

With Tyrwhitt the process of elimination began. He rejected: the Plowman's Tale, the tales of Gamelyn and Beryn, Jack Upland, the Lamentation of Mary Magdalen, the Assembly of Ladies, Praise of Women, Remedy of Love, and most of the "heap of rubbish" added by John Stow. He also pointed out that several of the poems printed with the works by previous editors were expressly ascribed in prints or MSS to writers other than Chaucer; thus he ruled out the Testament of Cressida, La Belle Dame sans Merci, the Letter of Cupid, Gower to Henry IV, Sayings of Dan John,

Scogan to the Lords, and four ballads by Lydgate, viz., Wicked Tongue, Doubleness, Beware, and In Commendation of our Lady.

Tyrwhitt accepted some works since rejected:—the Romaunt of the Rose, the Court of Love, the Complaint of the Black Knight, the Isle of Ladies, the Flower and the Leaf (with some hesitation), the Cuckoo and the Nightingale (though rejecting the envoy to Alison), and the Testament of Love. In acceptance and in rejection Tyrwhitt was apparently guided by his own taste and judgment as to the literary quality of the various works. His opinions are expressed in his "Account of the Works of Chaucer . . . . and of some other Pieces which have been improperly intermixed with his in the editions", prefixed to the Glossary which he drew up for the Works of Chaucer and appended to his edition of the Canterbury Tales.

Singer, in his ed. for the Chiswick Press, 1822, followed pretty closely the opinion of Tyrwhitt, deviating from it only in his retention of the Praise of Women and the Envoy to Alison; he also added the Prophecy, from MS.

In the editions by Bell (1854-56) and by Morris (1866) there were included as Chaucer's:—Merciless Beaute, Orison to the Virgin, and two additional stanzas to Proverbs (Bell); Prosperity, Former Age, and Leaulte vault Richesse (Morris).

Bradshaw (see Temp. Pref. 107-8) then rejected from the canon:—the Court of Love, Cuckoo and Nightingale, Flower and Leaf, Isle of Ladies, Romaunt of the Rose, Complaint of the Black Knight, Mother of Nurture, Praise of Women, Leaulte vault Richesse, Proverbs, Merciless Beaute, Virelay, Prophecy. These were ruled out by Bradshaw mainly because of their false rimes. He appealed to what is known as the "y-ye test", that is, to the fact that Chaucer in his admittedly genuine works did not rime together words which etymologically end in -y and words which end in -ye, e. g., trewely with folye. See Skeat I : 5, Canon 45; Trial Forew. p. 6, and note on p. 108; Lounsbury, Studies I : 372-4, 388-93. This test was also used by ten Brink, see Trial Forew. p. 108 and his Studien p. 22; ten Brink agreed with Bradshaw in several of these rejections. Both after the appearance of ten Brink's work and after the revision of the Bell Chaucer by Skeat in 1878, objections were made to the removal of some poems from the canon, see under Court of Love, Flower and Leaf, Section V here.

The "y-ye test" has been especially emphasized by the disputants over the authenticity of the Romaunt. Saintsbury, in his Hist. of Criticism I : 450, and again in his Hist. of Eng. Prosody I : 145 note 3, will none of the test. See Skeat in Canon p. 46, in Acad. 1892 I : 206, 230. On the occurrence of "false rime" see under Rime of Sir Thopas, Section III G here; and see Lounsbury, Studies I : 388-89, criticised by Skeat VI : lvii and Acad. as above.

Bradshaw, Hertzberg, and ten Brink, also doubted the authenticity of the Testament of Love, see under that heading.

The Romaunt of the Rose has been the subject of special discussion, see under that heading. The Proverbs are still retained in recent eds. of Chaucer, as is Merciless Beaute, although doubts have been expressed, see under those headings, Section V here.

Skeat has added, in his ed. of the Minor Poems and in his Oxford Chaucer:—Ballade of Complaint, Complaint to my Mortal Foe, Complaint d' Amours, Complaint to my Lode-Sterre, To Rosemounde, Womanly Noblesse; see under each of these headings in Section V here. In his Chaucer Canon, pp. 63, 147, Skeat retracts his opinion as to the Chaucerian authorship of the Ballad of Complaint, and speaks dubiously of the Complaint d'Amours. It does not apparently occur to Skeat that his procedure in including poems because they conform to Chaucerian language and are of some interest in themselves is precisely parallel to the conduct of earlier editors which he so earnestly censures.

The present canon of Chaucer may be thus drawn up: The Canterbury Tales, Troilus and Cressida, the translation of Boethius, the Astrolabe, the Legend of Good Women, the House of Fame, the Book of the Duchesse, the Complaint unto Pity (with some doubt as to the authenticity of the Ballad of Pity which follows it in Shirley's copy), the ABC, Mars, Venus, Anelida, the Parlement of Foules, the Words to Adam, Former Age, Fortune, Truth, Gentilesse, Lack of Stedfastnesse, Scogan, Bukton, Purse. The evidence for Womanly Noblesse and Rosemounde is stronger than for any other of the poems printed by Skeat with the works of Chaucer. For the four lines of Proverbs regularly included by editors in the Canon the evidence is dubious; the excellent Fairfax MS, from which alone we derive our copy of Bukton, marks the lines as Chaucer's; but the copy in Shirley's hand has no ascription to Chaucer. Bradshaw doubted the genuineness of the bit.

It might be remarked that if Shirley's marking e. g. of the Ballad of Pity or the ABC is to be accepted as proof positive of the genuineness of verse, the two bits, or one of the two bits so headed in his MS Adds. 16165 should be included in the canon. See Mod. Lang. Notes 19 : 35-38 and the refs. to Furnivall's prints there given. On Shirley see Section VII B here, and Anglia 30 : 320-348.

6) *Lost Works, etc.*

Book of the Lion. Mentioned by Chaucer in the Retractation, see end of Section III G here; also by Lydgate. Perhaps a translation of Machault's Dit du Lion, see Tyrwhitt's note on the Retractation.

Book of the Twenty-five Ladies. Alluded to in the Retractation;

probably the Legend of Good Women, q. v. in Section IV here. Skeat prints "nynetene"; see his note, V: 475.

Brooch of Thebes. Mentioned by Lydgate, see above. The Mars, lines 245-262, may be meant, as Tyrwhitt remarked in his Account of the Works of Chaucer. Note the heading to the Mars, Section IV here.

Ceyx and Alcyone. Mentioned by Chaucer in the Man of Law's headlink; usually taken to mean the introductory part of the Book of the Duchess.

Dant in English, see under House of Fame, Section IV here.

Life of Saint Cecyle, = the Second Nun's Tale. Mentioned by Chaucer in the prologue to the Legend of Good Women.

Origenes upon the Maudelayne. Mentioned by Chaucer in the prologue to the Legend of Good Women, and by Lydgate. The Lamentation of Mary Magdalen, see Section V here, was printed as Chaucer's for generations, under the impression that it was the work referred to.

Palamon and Arcite. Referred to by Chaucer in the prologue to the Legend of Good Women; understood to mean the Knight's Tale, perhaps in an earlier form, see Section III G here.

The Saintes Legend of Cupid, in the Man of Law's headlink, evidently means the Legend of Good Women.

Wrecched Engendring of Mankind, alluded to by Chaucer in one version of the prologue to the Legend,—see Lounsbury and Lowes as cited under ML Tale here, Section III G.

B. Chronology of the Accepted Works

The available evidence upon which a chronology of Chaucer's works may be based is of several kinds:

(1) Mention within the poem of the historical occasion upon which it was composed, or of some contemporary event; allusions to persons or places which afford clue to the date. Thus, the Book of the Duchesse is dated with almost complete certainty immediately after the death of the Duchess of Lancaster in 1369; see Skeat I : 63 and the interpretation of lines 1318-19 of the poem in Acad. 1894 I : 191. The Nun's Priest's Tale must postdate 1381, because of the allusion in line 575 to the uprising of that year. The envoy to Bukton is dated after 1396 because of its allusion to imprisonment in Friesland, see Skeat I : 558.

Add here allusion by contemporary writers, in works of known date, to works by Chaucer, and *vice versa*. See Kittredge in Mod. Phil. I : 1 ff., Lowes in Publ. Mod. Lang. Assn. 19 : 593 ff.

(2) Allusion in one work to others, affording evidence of the earlier composition of poems so mentioned. Cp. the lists in the prologue to the Legend and in the Man of Law's headlink. Positive evidence, but not negative, is afforded by this test; thus, the prologue to the Legend must postdate the works which it names, but the non-appearance in its list of the Mars or the Anelida does not prove that those poems were still unwritten. The order of mention in such lists is sometimes adduced as evidence of order of composition, though not a safe basis for inference.

(3) Allusion to youth or age by the poet. Thus, in the Man of Law's headlink Chaucer says of himself "In youth he made of Seys and Alcion"; and if this refers to the first part of the Book of the Duchesse, it is an additional proof of the early date of that poem. The complaint of age by Chaucer must be taken with caution; cp. House of Fame II : 995. For compare Caxton's complaint in the epilogue to his Recuyell (printed in Flügel's Neuengl. Lesebuch p. 3), written when he was about fifty years old, with a new career of active usefulness opening before him, in which he was to labor for twenty years. And see Nation 1892 I : 246, Skeat I : xvi, Lowes in Publ. Mod. Lang. Assn. 20 : 783.

(4) Tone appropriate to events in the poet's life. An uncertain and easily misjudged form of evidence. Cp. Flügel's censure of Skeat and others, Anglia 21 : 255, for connecting parts of the poet's work with the loss of his wife. And note the very large dependence of Koch's Chronology of Chaucer's Writings upon this sort of evidence.

(5) Evidence of maturity or immaturity in verse and style, in mode of translation, use of simple or complicated verse-forms, etc.

(6) Change in poetic models, *e. g.*, from French to Italian.

These two sorts of evidence are the most extensive available to

us, and have been the most discussed. They have however this
danger, the tacit assumption that a scale of Chaucer's work can
be constructed in a sort of geometrical progression, without regard
to the possibility that he, like other English poets, may have had his
moments of sudden expansion in youth or of dullness or compulsion
in maturity; or that, as in the prologue to the Legend, he may have
returned to French models long after those of Italy had become
familiar to him. Also, Skeat has argued (III : 382-84) that
stanzaic poems must be earlier than work in the heroic couplet, a
position not provable in detail. See Pollard's Primer, pp. 53-54.

The division of Chaucer's works into periods, according to the
models principally employed and in less degree according to the
verse-form used, was first worked out in detail by ten Brink, in
his Chaucer-Studien, 1870. Flügel remarks (Dial 18 : 117) that a
French period was first noted by Pauli, in his Bilder aus Altengland,
see *ibid.* chapter VII, but the allusion is very slight. Furnivall,
Trial Forew. p. 6, said that ten Brink's division "let in a flood of
light upon the subject", and all subsequent investigators have
worked from ten Brink's basis, though differing from him in some
details.

Ten Brink dated the influence of Dante and Boccaccio upon
Chaucer after Chaucer's first journey to Italy in 1372, and consequently put all works showing these influences after 1372. But
Lounsbury, in the introd. to his ed. of the Parlement of Foules,
and Morley, Eng. Writers V : 156, 187, suggested that Chaucer
was sent on the Italian missions because of his previous knowledge
of Italian, thus opening the way for an earlier dating of the
"Italian period"; while Mather, Nation 1896 II : 269, and Pollard,
Globe Chaucer p. xxii, consider that the Italian period of Chaucer's
work cannot be dated as beginning earlier than the poet's second
journey to Italy in 1378-79.

Ten Brink marks three "periods" in Chaucer's work. (1) The
work before his going to Italy, done mainly under the influence of
French models. (2) The work translated from or alluding to Italian
authors. (3) The works of his greatest period, from 1385 to 1400.

To this Furnivall would add a period of decline, "from, say,
1390 to 1400." See Trial Forew. p. 6 footnote. In this period
Furnivall puts, *e. g.,* Venus, Bukton, Scogan, Gentilesse, Stedfastnesse, Fortune, Purse, the finishing of the Parson's Tale; he also
remarks that "the dull Canterbury Tales" are either quite early,
or later than 1386. See his letters Athen. 1871 II : 16-17 and 494-5;
a summarized table is on p. 495, cp. Trial Forew. pp. 15 ff.

Koch, in his book on the Chronology of Chaucer's Writings,
Ch. Soc. 1890, has done little or no independent work; his remarks

are often unclear, but he seems to follow upon ten Brink and Furnivall.

Pollard, in his Chaucer-Primer, Lond. 1903, pp. 57-60 in especial, divides the Works into four periods: (1) to 1380, (2) the poems showing Italian influence, (3) the Canterbury Tales, (4) the few brief poems of Chaucer's "decline".

Skeat I : lxii-lxiii, prints a conjectural chronological list of Chaucer's works; *ibid.* p. xxx-xxxi he says: "It seems reasonable to date the poems which shew a strong Italian influence after Chaucer's visit to Italy in 1373."

Upon this long-accepted chronology two American scholars are now making modifications. See:
John L. Lowes' two papers on the Legend of Good Women, cited under that heading, Section IV here, especially the second; and see
J. S. P. Tatlock's Development and Chronology of Chaucer's Works. Chaucer Society, 1907.

The work of Robert K. Root on the Poetry of Chaucer, Boston, 1906, is commended by the Nation 1906 II : 370-71 for its "conservatism in rejecting the ingenious speculations aimed at revolutionizing the generally accepted chronology of Chaucer's poems."

C. Sources of Chaucer's Works

Chaucer's "learning" was by his biographers of the sixteenth century treated as immense, see the lives by Leland and by Bale reprinted ante; and the notion of his great erudition persisted down to modern times. Not until the appearance of Professor Lounsbury's Studies, in 1892, was a full investigation of the question carried out; and this essay, in volume II of the work, remains the only good survey of the subject, though much has been added in recent years, e.g. the use by Chaucer of Froissart and Deschamps, as demonstrated by Kittredge and by Lowes, see under Legend of Good Women and House of Fame, below.

The student to-day sees in Chaucer an eager reader of books, a man who read and translated easily both French and Latin (though with occasional errors, see Lounsbury, Studies II : 205, Stewart's Boethius pp. 222 ff.), a man possessed also of what was very unusual in his time, a knowledge of Italian. Some books, as we can perceive, he had chewed and digested,—the De Consolatione Philosophiae of Boethius, the Roman de la Rose, the Metamorphoses of Ovid, the Filostrato and Teseide of Boccaccio. But some of the authors whom he names he shows no clear sign of having read; and as Lounsbury has remarked, "Chaucer's quotations from writers exhibit a familiarity with prologues and first books and early chapters which contrasts ominously with the comparative infrequency with which he makes citations from the middle and latter parts of most of the works he mentions." (Studies II : 265.)

On this point I would add that in more than a few cases—Juvenal, Persius, etc.—the bits which Chaucer uses may have come to him through medieval Florilegia, or collections of Elegant Extracts, see below under C 4. Or mere school textbooks, the Ecloga of Theodulus or even the Priscian and Donat of Chaucer's boyhood, may have given him stray sentences cited by the grammars as illustrative quotation. This I might take yet further, and, in direct opposition to a theory like that of Rambeau regarding the House of Fame, I would question whether Chaucer's knowledge of Dante argues a reading of the whole Commedia.

The indebtedness of Chaucer to French poets was first fully discussed in :

Étude sur Chaucer considéré comme Imitateur des Trouvères.
E. C. Sandras. Paris, 1859.

Rev. by Ebert, Jahrbuch 4 : 85-106, and this review translated in Ch. Soc. Essays part I. Rev. by Macray, Gent. Mag. July 1865, pp. 24-30. Rev. by Hertzberg, Jahrbuch 8 : 145-153. Rev. (severely) by Furnivall, Athen. 1872 II : 147, and see Trial Forew. pp. 43 ff.; see Lounsbury, Studies III : 407 ff.

Chaucer's knowledge of Italian writers was for a time denied. Thynne, in his Animadversions (1598) remarked that the Knight's

Tale was an adaptation of Boccaccio's Italian; and both Warton and Tyrwhitt added further facts as to Chaucer's use of Boccaccio. Cary, in his translation of the Commedia, 1805 ff., referred in his notes to Chaucer's use of many passages. But Sir Harris Nicolas, in his life of the poet, doubted Chaucer's knowledge of Italian, in which he was followed by Craik, in his history of English literature. Fiedler, reviewing Craik in Blätter für literarische Unterhaltung, 1846, nos. 154-156, disproved this assertion, and remarked that Hippisley, in his Chapters on Early English Literature (Lond. 1837), had already noted Chaucer's debt to Italian writers; passages of Fiedler's review are cited Archiv 47 : 320. Protests were also made by Pauli, Bilder aus Altengland, by Hertzberg, Jahrbuch 4 : 86 ff., and Lemcke, Jahrbuch 8 : 100-105. The analyses of the Filostrato and the Teseide for the Chaucer Society by Rossetti and by Ward have amply proved Chaucer's use of Boccaccio; and Cary and ten Brink have pointed out passages taken by Chaucer from Dante. The only general study on Chaucer's indebtedness to Italy is:

Chaucer in seinen Beziehungen zur italienischen Litteratur.

Alfons Kissner. diss. Marburg, 1867, 81 pp.

Rev. by Hertzberg, Jahrbuch 8 : 153-64; by Lemcke *ibid.* pp. 102-105; praised by Eitner, Shakspere Jahrbuch 1868 p. 277.

Of less value is:

Introduzione allo studio dei fonti italiani di G. Chaucer.

P. Bellezza. Milan, 1895, pp. 59.

Reviewed Engl. Stud. 22 : 288 (Koch); Anglia Beibl. 7 : 103; Archiv 97 : 230 (Fraenkel), very severe.

For other studies on the indebtedness of Chaucer to individual Italian writers see under Dante, Boccaccio, etc., below.

(1) *Chaucer's Use of English Writers*

This question has not received special treatment. Chaucer's use of Anglo-Latin authors is discussed below, but his reading in his own language, with the exception of Gower and of the romances, is as yet uninvestigated in detail.

Gower, John: Died 1408. Chaucer's contemporary, and for part of their lives at least, his personal friend. For account of the conjectured break in their relations see under Man of Law's Tale, Section III G below; and for the legend of Chaucer's pupilage or rivalry to Gower see the Latin biographies reprinted ante. Gower was author of the Vox Clamantis (Latin), the Speculum Amantis or Mirour de l' Homme (French), and the Confessio Amantis (English); also of minor French poems. His works are ed. by Macaulay, 4 vols., Oxford 1899 ff. Macaulay had previously discovered the supposedly lost French work, see Acad. 1895 I : 315.

The possible relation of Gower's Mirour de l' Homme and Chaucer's Prologue to the Canterbury Tales is discussed by Flügel, Anglia 24 : 437-508; and the date of the Mirour in Appendix A to Tatlock's Development and Chronology of Chaucer's Works. See also Koeppel, Engl. Stud. 20: 154.

Between the Canterbury Tales and the Confessio there are four agreements in stories, viz., the story of Virginia, of Constance, of Phoebus and the Crow, and of Florent (cp. the Wife of Bath's Tale). The story of Ceix and Alcyone (see Book of the Duchesse) is also narrated by Gower, as is that of Jephthah's daughter, retold in the Doctor's Tale. Of these the treatment of the Constance story is by far the most striking, and when taken in conjunction with the censure in the Man of Law's headlink of two plots used by Gower, has furnished food for the theory of a quarrel between the poets.

Romances, Early English Metrical: Outside of the burlesque romance The Rime of Sir Thopas, Chaucer's allusions to romantic persons and subjects are as follows: Alexander is mentioned in general terms in the BoDuch lines 1059-60 and in the HoFame 1413, cp. MancTale line 122. The story of Alexander is briefly and generally told MoTale 641 ff., but in the HoFame 915 ff. there is a specific reference to a story concerning him recounted in the Wars of Alexander; see Skeat's note, III : 262 and his ed. for the EETS. Arthur is four times alluded to in the WBTale, the scene of which is supposedly laid at his court. Knights connected with the Arthurian cycle are Gawain (SqTale 95), Lancelot (SqTale 287, NPTale 392). Tristram is mentioned as a typical lover in PoF line 290 and in To Rosemounde line 20. Charlemagne is alluded to in MoTale 397, and Octovian, in a sense more historical than literary, in BoDuch line 368 and in LGW (Cleopatra) line 45. Were it not for the full knowledge of the English metrical romances displayed in the Rime of Sir Thopas, we might have assumed that Chaucer had done no reading in that field, and had picked up the allusions to Gawain as courteous, Tristram and Lancelot as typical lovers, and Arthur's court as the centre of chivalry, from the literary commonplace of his time. See under Rime of Sir Thopas, Section III G here.

The Middle English metrical romances have been partly listed, with summaries of plot and brief bibliographical notes, in Guide to the Middle English Metrical Romances, by Anna H. Billings, N. Y. 1901 (Yale Studies). See the mass of information in Ward's Catalogue of Romances in the Department of Manuscripts in the British Museum, 2 vols. Collections are:

Halliwell. The Thornton Romances. Camden Soc. 1844.
   (Perceval, Isumbras, Eglamour, Degrevant.)
Ritson. Ancient Eng. Metrical Romances, 3 vols. Lond. 1802, new ed. 1889-90.
Ellis. Specimens of Early Eng. Metr. Romances, ed. Halliwell, Lond. 1848.
Weber. Metrical Romances of the 13th, 14th, and 15th Centuries, 3 vols., Edinb. 1810.
See also Percy Folio MS, ed. Hales and Furnivall, 1867-68. For eds. of the single English romances, see under Rime of Sir Thopas, Section III G here.

"Romantic stories" among the CT are the MLTale, the CLTale, the WBTale, the FrankTale, the unfinished SqTale, and the burlesque Sir Thopas.

(2) *Chaucer's Use of French Writers*

Adenès le Roi: author of the Cléomades, a romance of the 14th century; for the connection of this with the Squire's Tale see Jones in Publ. Mod. Lang. Ass'n. 20 : 346.

De Guileville, Guillaume: Flourished 1330-60. Author of an elaborate tripartite Pilgrimage; part I, Pélèrinage de la Vie Humaine or de l'Homme; part II, Pélèrinage de l'Ame; III, Pélèrinage de Jésu Christ: all edited for the Roxburghe Club by J. J. Sturzinger, London 1893, 1895, 1897, with reproduction of illuminations, etc., from various MSS. Part I was twice written by De Guileville, first in 1330, revised in 1335-6; the former was Englished in prose about 1430, ed. for the Roxburghe Club in 1869 by W. A. Wright; this is the poem which may have been known to Bunyan. The revision of 1335-6 was

turned into English verse by Lydgate in 1426, ed. for the EETS
by Furnivall. The second part of the French work was Englished in 1413 in prose, and is to be ed. for the EETS; of part
III of the French no Englishing is yet known. See Furnivall's
introd. to the EETS publication, and the work of Miss K. I.
Cust, The Ancient Poem of Guillaume de Guilleville, entitled
Le Pélèrinage de l'Homme, compared with the Pilgrim's Progress of John Bunyan, London, 1858; and a prose translation of
the Pélèrinage de l'Homme, London 1859. See Ward, Catalogue of Romances I : 558 ff.

De Guileville's extensive work includes addresses and prayers,
one of which, an alphabetical hymn to the Virgin, was translated by Chaucer, and is known as his ABC; see Section IV
here. In Shirley's copy of the prose transl. of Part I, Chaucer's
ABC is inserted at the proper place; other copies of the ABC,
unmarked, are also found in MSS of the Pilgrimage.

Deschamps, Eustache: 1346?—1406? Works, in 11 vols., ed by de
Queux de St. Hilaire (vols. 1-6) and G. Raynaud (vols. 7-11),
Paris 1878-1903. A biography is prefixed to vol. 11. On
Deschamps see also E. Hoepffner, Eustace Deschamps, Leben
und Werke, Strassburg 1904, pp. viii, 233.

Deschamps addressed a ballad to Chaucer, hailing him as
"grand translateur"; this is printed by Paget Toynbee, Acad.
1891 II : 432, with notes, and in the Works as No. 285, reprinted
thence by Skeat I : lvi-lvii. Chaucer's knowledge of and probable literary relation with Deschamps are discussed by Kittredge, Mod. Phil. I : 1 ff., and especially by Lowes, in his first
paper cited under Legend of Good Women, Section IV here.
Earlier and less illuminating refs. are ten Brink, Hist. Eng.
Lit. II : 192; Lounsbury, Studies II : 217, III : 14; Skeat I :
lvi-lvii, 563.

Fabliaux:—French or Latin fabliaux or folk-stories, in circulation
either orally or written, are probably the source of several of
the Cant. Tales, viz.,—The Miller's Tale (Skeat III : 395 ff.),
the Reeve's Tale (Skeat III : 396-99), the Shipman's Tale
(Skeat III : 420), the Pardoner's Tale (Skeat III : 439 ff.), the
Wife of Bath's Tale (Skeat III : 447 ff.), the Summoner's Tale
(Skeat III : 452), part of the Merchant's Tale (Skeat III : 460),
the Manciple's Tale (Skeat III : 501). See further under each
tale, Section III G here.

Froissart, Jehan:—1333?-1419. Best known by his Chroniques, but
author also of a romance, the Méliador, and of a considerable
body of lyrical verse. See Oeuvres de Froissart, ed. Scheler,
Brussels, 1870; Froissart, Étude Littéraire, by Kervyn de Letten-

hove, Brussels 1857; Macaulay in Macm. Mag. Jan. 1895; Petit
de Julleville, Hist. de la langue et litt. française, II, Paris 1896;
Gröber, Grundriss II, part 1, pp. 1049-50; Froissart, by Mary
Darmester, Paris 1894; Besant in Essays and Historiettes, London 1903.

Chaucer's knowledge of Froissart is evident in the Book of
the Duchesse and in the prologue to the Legend; see Kittredge
in Engl. Stud. 26 : 321-336 and Lowes' papers as cited under
Legend of Good Women, Section IV here.

Granson, Otes de:—Died 1397. At the end of the Venus Chaucer
says that he is with difficulty following "Granson, flower of
them that make in France." Shirley's copies of the poem, MSS
Ashmole 59 and Trin. Coll. Cambr. R 3, 20, term Granson in
the headings "that worthy knight of Savoy", and "knight
Savoyen." See Piaget, Oton de Granson et ses Poésies, in
Romania 19 : 237, 403 (1890), where, among others, the ballades
translated by Chaucer are printed, and are reprinted by Skeat
I : 400 ff. See also Trial Forew. p. 123.

Lapidaire:—Referred to HoFame 1352; see Skeat III : 274, Lounsbury, Studies II : 343.

Lorens, Frère:—It was until recently believed that the source of the
Parson's Tale was the Somme des Vices et des Vertus of this
writer. See however the monograph of Miss Petersen under
the heading Parson's Tale, Section III G here.

Machault, Guillaume de: 1284?-ca. 1370. Works ed. by Tarbé,
Reims and Paris, 1849. On Chaucer's knowledge of Machault
see Sandras, Étude, pp. 75 ff., 288-94; ten Brink, Studien 7-12,
197-205; Lounsbury, Studies I: 423, II: 212-15, III: 409; Skeat
VI : 387; and especially Lowes' papers as cited under Legend
of Good Women, Section IV here.

Marie de France:—See under the Nun's Priest's Tale, Section III G
here. Cp. the remarks of Rajna, Romania 32 : 204-267, on the
Franklin's prologue and that of Marie's Equitan; see also
Foulet, Ztschr. f. roman. Phil. 30 : 698-711.

Meung, Jehan de: Of the 13th century, author of lines 4000 ff. of
the Roman de la Rose, of Le Testament de Jehan de Meung,
and of La Complainte de Nature à l'Alchymist Errant. All
these were known to Chaucer, and the effect of the first upon
him and his work was profound. The Roman is accessible in
two eds., that of Méon, 4 vols., Paris 1814, and that of Michel,
2 vols., Paris 1864; of these, that of Méon is the better. The

text of Michel, with readings from MSS, is reprinted by
Kaluza in his book on the Romaunt of the Rose, see Section
V here; the text of Méon, as far as line 1705 of the English,
is reprinted by Skeat, I. The other two poems are printed at
the end of Méon's edition; for their influence upon Chaucer
see Skeat, Acad. 1888 I : 239. To the notes in Skeat I upon
echoes of de Meung in Chaucer add Koeppel, Anglia 14 : 238-
267, Cipriani in Publ. Mod. Lang. Assn. 22 : 552-595. For de
Meung's transl. of the Liber Consolationis, used by Chaucer for
the Melibeus, see under Albertanus Brixiensis in (4) below.

Chaucer himself, in the prologue to the Legend, states that
he translated the *Roman,* but whether the existing incomplete
Middle English version be his or not is still warmly debated,
and will probably remain unsettled unless additional MS
evidence be found. See Section V here under Romaunt of the
Rose. The depth of de Meung's influence upon Chaucer is
unsurpassed by that of any other writer except Boethius; and
indeed the effect of de Meung upon medieval thought generally
is profound. Brunetière, in his Manual of the History of
French Literature, 1898, p. 26, says that de Meung is one of the
very few authors of the Middle Ages of whom it may be said
that their works are epoch-making. On de Meung see Brunetière as cited; Gaston Paris, La litt. franc. au moyen-âge,
chap. 5; Petit de Julleville, Hist. de la langue et de la litt.
franc., Paris 1878-1900, II : 105-160; Paulin Paris in Hist. litt.
vol. 23, pp. 1-61; Besant in French Humorists (1873) and
Brit. Quart., 1871 II : 359; Morley, Eng. Writers IV : 1 ff.;
Lounsbury, Studies II : 217 ff.; Skeat I : 16-20.

A transl. of the *Roman* into English by F. S. Ellis is pubd.
in the Temple Classics, 3 vols., London 1900. It is executed
in five-beat couplets, and is decidedly "classical" in treatment.
A review is in the Athen. 1900 II : 440, and Root, Poetry of
Chaucer p. 50, alludes to it favorably.

See Langlois, Origines et sources du Roman de la Rose, Paris
1890; Joret, La Rose dans l'antiquité et au moyen-âge, histoire, legendes, et symbolisme, Paris 1892. See Soltoft-Jensen
on Alanus and the Roman, Nord. Tidskr. 10 : 3 (this ref. from
Flügel, Dial 18 : 117).

Roman de Carité:—See under Knight's Tale, Section III G below.

Roman de Renart:—See Miss Petersen's monograph on the Nun's
Priest's Tale, cited Section III G here.

Roman de la Rose, see Meung, Jehan de.

Sainte-More, Benoît de:—Of the latter half of the twelfth century;
author of Le Roman de Troie, ed. by L. Constans for the Soc.

anc. textes franc., vol. I, 1904, vol. II, 1906, vol. III, 1907; previous ed. and study by Joly, Benoît de Sainte-More et le Roman de Troie, Paris 1871. As Tyrwhitt and Douce remarked (see Lounsbury, Studies II : 311), this was the original from which Guido delle Colonne (see under 4 below) worked. The question whether Chaucer used Benoît or Guido as the secondary source for his Troilus is still discussed, see under Troy-saga in (4) below, and under Troilus in Section IV here.

Trivet, Nicolas:—Flourished 1330-50. Author of an Anglo-Norman chronicle in prose, from which both Chaucer and Gower took the story of Constance, used by Chaucer as the Man of Law's Tale; extracts are printed Ch. Soc. Orig. and Anal. Trivet was a voluminous writer, especially of commentaries; the influence of his Boethius-commentary upon Chaucer is pointed out by Miss Petersen in Publ. Mod. Lang. Assn. 18 : 173 ff.; and he has left also commentaries on the tragedies of Seneca and upon Walter Map's Valerius ad Rufinum, see under (4) below.

(3) *Chaucer's Use of Italian Writers*

Boccaccio, Giovanni:—1315-1375. Boccaccio is the Italian writer most used by Chaucer, although Chaucer never mentions his name, see under Lollius in (4) below. He wrote in both Latin and Italian; his principal works were:

La Teseide, in verse, ottava rima, about 1340; see under the Knight's Tale, Section III G here.

Il Filostrato, in verse, ottava rima, about 1347; see under Troilus and Cressida, Section IV here.

Il Decamerone, prose, about 1349. Chaucer's knowledge of this work has been a moot point among students. No direct contact of the CT with the Decameron has been shown; the resemblances are the facts that both are sets of stories in a framework, and that five of the CT stories occur also in Boccaccio. But for one of these, the tale of Griselda, Chaucer used the Latin translation by Petrarch of Boccaccio's Italian: and the differences between the tales of Reeve, Merchant, Franklin, and Shipman and the narratives of the Decameron are such, in the opinion of most present-day critics, as to indicate rather a common folklore origin known to both authors. For divergent opinions on this point see Section III A here.

Boccaccio's principal Latin works, all in prose and all written after 1349, are:

De Claris Mulieribus, De Casibus Virorum Illustrium, De Genealogiis Deorum. Chaucer's Monk's Tale was apparently modeled on the De Casibus, as was first remarked

by Tyrwhitt; although the fables of Hyginus, from which
Boccaccio perhaps got his plan, may have been known to
Chaucer. This work and the Claris Mulieribus contain
many of the stories told by Chaucer's Monk and in the
LGW, but no close translation of Boccaccio by Chaucer has
yet been proved here. Chaucer's knowledge of mythology
seems often derived from the Genealogiae; but a detailed
examination of the subject is still lacking. See ten Brink,
Studien pp. 48 ff., Hist. Eng. Lit. II : 63 ff., 88 ff., 139-41;
Landau, Beiträge zur Gesch. der italienischen Novella,
1875; Lounsbury, Studies II : 225-36; Skeat III : 371, 427 ff.,
V : 227 ff.; Child in Mod. Lang. Notes 11 : 476 ff.; Koeppel
in Anglia 14 : 233; Lowes in Publ. Mod. Lang. Assn.
19 : 618; Young in Mod. Phil. 4 : 169; Tatlock, Devel. and
Chronol. of Chaucer's Works, chaps. I, III, and appendices
B, C.

Boccaccio's Italian works are obtainable in the ed. by Moutier,
17 vols., Florence 1827-34. The Decameron has been separately
pubd. in very many forms; and the two Italian poems first mentioned above may be had separately, e. g., the Filostrato ed. by
Baroni, Paris 1789, the Teseide as printed at Venice in 1858;
but the former is termed by Rossetti "portentously slipshod",
see p. 8 footnote of his Ch. Soc. study of the Troilus.

None of the Latin works has been reprinted since 1600; the
1511 ed. of the Genealogiae costs about $12.00; the De Casibus
may be obtained, in the undated ed., somewhat more cheaply.
For discussion of the Latin works, with bibliography, see Hortis,
Studj sulle Opere Latine del Boccaccio, Trieste, 1879. A paper
on Boccaccio's (Latin) Defence of Poetry, by Elisabeth Woodbridge, is in Publ. Mod. Lang. Assn. 13 : 333-349. The monograph of Koerting, Leipzig 1880, is the best available summary
of Boccaccio's literary activity. A thorough investigation of
Chaucer's debt to him is a great desideratum in Chaucer-study.
Of no value are:

Geoffrey Chaucer: seine Zeit und seine Abhängigkeit von
Boccaccio. F. Mamroth. Berlin, 1872, pp. 60.
Boccaccio and Chaucer. P. Borghesi. Bologna, 1903, pp. 70.

Dante:—1265-1321. The use of the Divina Commedia by Chaucer
was first pointed out by Cary in his transl. of the poem, 1805 ff.,
although the expression of Lydgate regarding "Dant in English" has been interpreted to mean use of Dante by Chaucer, see
under House of Fame, Section IV here. Dante is referred
to by name in Chaucer's works five times, HoFame 450, LGW
prol. 336, MoTale 471, WBTale 270-71, Friar's Tale 222.
Knowledge by Chaucer of any work of Dante's other than the
Commedia has not yet been demonstrated.

6

For the influence of Dante upon Chaucer see under HoFame,
Section IV here; under PoFoules, Section IV here; see also
ten Brink, Studien 78, 125, Hist. Eng. Lit. II : 103; Kissner
op. cit.; Lounsbury, Studies II : 236 ff.; Koeppei in Anglia
13 : 184-86; Tatlock in Mod. Phil. 3 : 367-72; Torraca, Jour.
Compar. Lit. 1 : 82-84; Toynbee *ibid.* 345-65, Mod. Lang. Review 1 : 9 ff. General works upon the influence of Dante in
English literature are:

> Dante and the English Poets from Chaucer to Tennyson.
> Oscar Kuhns. N. Y. 1904. Rev. Nation 1904 II : 279, not
> favorably.

> Dante in English Literature from Chaucer to Cary.
> Paget Toynbee. According to the Nation, 1907 I : 519, the
> publication of this work is delayed by the discovery of a
> mass of new material.

The article on Dante in Chaucer and his Followers, by Plumptre,
in Contemp. Rev. 40 : 859-864 (1881) is of little value.

Skeat omits remark upon several lines derived from Dante: some of
these are pointed out by Cary, viz., LGW 2638 from Inferno 7: 64;
MoTale 487 from Inferno 5: 56; HoF 201 ff. cp. Purgatorio 28: 9 ff.;
Troilus 5: 549 cp. Purgat. 23: 31; Troilus 3: 1693-4 cp. Parad. 19:
8; HoFame 505-6 cp. Parad. 1: 62-3; BoDuch. 880 cp. Inferno 4: 84.
The line Kn. Tale 903, often repeated by Chaucer, is by Toynbee paralleled with Inferno 5: 100. And note the transl. of Troilus 2: 64-66
from Purgat. 9: 13-15 (Koeppel, Anglia 13: 184). It is very probable
that a close investigation would show many more echoes of Dante in
Chaucer than have yet been pointed out; but it is remarkable that, with
the exception of the Ugolino story and the invocation to the Virgin
(of the Prioress' Tale), the usages of Dante by Chaucer appear in
scattered lines and phrases, often of small interest. They might be
classified, so far as our research has yet gone, into:—Invocations, cp.
HoFame 2: 10 and Inferno 2: 7; Prioress' Tale and prol. to Second
Nun's Tale with Parad. 33: 1-12, 16-21; HoFame 3: 1-19 and Parad.
1 : 13-27 (ten Brink); the address to Virgil, LGW Dido 1-3 and Purgat.
22: 66. Descriptions,—the approach of twilight, Inferno 2: 1 and
PoFoules 85; the approach of dawn, Purgat. 1-19 and KnTale 635;
flowers, Troilus 2 : 967 and Inferno 2 : 127 (but Cary says cp. Filostrato 2: 80); the song of Procne, Troilus 2: 967 and Purgat. 9: 13
(E. P. H.). Mere phrases, Troilus 5 : 549 and Purgat. 23: 31 ; Troilus
3 : 1693 and Parad. 19: 8; LGW 2638 and Inferno 7: 64; MoTale 487
and Inferno 5: 56 (but Toynbee says cp. Orosius). Note also longer
bits;—on envy, LGW prol. 358 and Inferno 13 : 64; on gentilesse,
WBTale 269 and Purgat. 7: 121; and see the extracts in the PoFoules
from Dante, 127 ff., 169 ff. With line 155 ten Brink, Studien p. 126
suggested a Dante likeness which he could not exactly parallel, see
Klaeber, Das Bild bei Chaucer p. 156, for ref. to Parad. 24 : 41. Outside this last possibility, the usage of Dante by the PoFoules is noticeably
of the Inferno, and of Cantos 1, 2, and 3, the early parts of them.
When we remark the apparent preference of the Troilus and the
HoFame for the Paradiso and the Purgatorio, an interesting question
might arise regarding Chaucer's different taste at different times, or his
varying access to books. I have previously suggested the query if the
whole Divina Commedia were known to Chaucer. The relation of Dante

and Chaucer is yet to be investigated; and a necessary prelude to such inquiry is the investigation how far Dante MSS were available in England in the fourteenth century, and what knowledge or opinion of Dante existed among Chaucer's contemporaries. See notes on "Dant in English" under House of Fame, Section IV here.

Verbal comparison between Chaucer and Dante may be facilitated by use of Fay's Concordance to the Divina Commedia, Boston 1888. The standard eds. of Dante are that of the Commedia by Scartazzini, Leipzig 4 vols., 1874-90 and in 1 vol. Milan 1896, or that by Moore of the complete works, Oxford 1894 and later. Cary's verse transl. is accessible in the Bohn Library with all the original notes; Norton's prose, in 3 vols., Boston 1891-92. Moore's Studies in Dante, 3 vols., London 1896 ff., includes in the first volume valuable information as to Dante's indebtedness to earlier writers, which might serve the Chaucer student tracing the connection of Dante and Chaucer with Virgil or Boethius.

There has been very little discussion of Dante's prosody; but see the paper by Tozer appended to Moore's Textual Criticism of the Divina Commedia, 1889, at pp. 713-723; see also Bartsch in the Jahrbuch of the Deutsche Dante Gesellschaft, 1871, pp. 303-367, and H. Zehle's diss. on Laut und Flexionslehre in Dante's Divina Commedia, Marburg 1885. Tozer's essay treats Dante's lines as accentual.

L' Intelligenza, an Italian allegorical poem of the early 14th century (?), of uncertain authorship. See Gaspary. Gesch. der ital. Litt., ed. 1885, I : 205 ff.; and G. Bellrich, Die Intelligenza, Breslau 1883, severely reviewed by Kölbing in Archiv 86: 86. Koeppel, Engl. Stud. 20 : 156-58 (1895) pointed out Chaucer's use of a bit of this poem in Troilus II : 19 ff.

Petrarch, Francesco, 1304-1374:—Author, in his earlier years, of sonnets and poems to "Laura", upon which his fame now rests, although he himself laid far more stress on the Latin verse of his maturity and on his Ciceronian correspondence with friends. Chaucer refers to Petrarch by name in the Monk's Tale 335, the Clerk's prol. 31 and Clerk's Tale 1191. Note also under Lollius in (4) below. Petrarch's Latin transl. of Boccaccio's story of Griselda, which Chaucer used for the Clerk's Tale, is accessible in Ch. Soc. Orig. and Anal. pp. 151-172, but is unfortunately reprinted from the Basel ed. of 1581 instead of from MSS. See G. L. Hendrickson in Mod. Phil. 4 : 179, and under Clerk's Tale here. Other borrowings from Petrarch are in the Troilus, I : 400 ff., see Skeat II: 464; Lounsbury, Studies II : 224.

The question of a possible meeting between Chaucer and Petrarch has been warmly discussed; see under Clerk's Tale, Section III G here.

On Petrarch see Koerting in vol. I of his Gesch. der ital. Lit., 1878; Zumbini, Studij sul Petrarca, 1895; Robinson and Rolfe, Petrarch, N. Y. 1898; de Nolhac, Pétrarque et l'Humanisme, Paris, 1892. The best ed. of the Canzoniere is that by Mastica,

1896. The Latin Epistolae Familiares are ed., with transl. into Ital., by Fracassetti, Florence 1859-63; the eds. of the *Opera,* Basel 1554 and 1581, are very faulty.

Villani:—In N. & Q. 1897 I : 205, 369, it is said that Villani's Chronicle was used for the Ugolino story, as well as Dante. See under Monk's Tale in Section III G below.

(4) *Chaucer's Use of Latin and Anglo-Latin Writers*

(With notes on some writers merely referred to by Chaucer, and on his knowledge of Greek and Science.)

Aesop:—Chaucer twice refers to stories which are narrated by Aesop; in Kn. Tale 319-22 and in Truth line 12. The third allusion cited by Skeat VI : 384, in Troilus I : 257, seems merely proverbial. There is apparently another allusion in WB prol. 692. Chaucer does not mention Aesop by name.

Agaton .—Referred to in LGW prol. 526; see Skeat III : xxxii; Lounsbury, Studies II : 400; Sandras, Étude p. 115, and for the same explanation Toynbee in Mod. Lang. Quart. 1 : 5.

Alanus de Insulis, or Alain de l'Isle:—Died 1205. Two of his works, the De Planctu Naturae and the Anticlaudianus, were known to Chaucer; the former is referred to and used in PoFoules, the latter is referred to in HoFame 986. Hales, Acad 1881 II : 384, pointed out the imitation by Chaucer in the PoFoules, and cited the passage. Skeat I : 74 prints the Latin of that portion from the text of Wright, see below.

The works of Alanus are printed in the Patrologia vol. 210, and the two above-mentioned are printed by Wright, Anglo-Latin Satirical Poets, Rolls Series, II : 268.

See Lounsbury, Studies II : 344-352; Koeppel, Archiv 90 : 149-151; Sandys, Hist. Class. Scholarship 531-2.

See O. Leist, Der Anticlaudianus, Seehausen, 1878.

Albertanus Brixiensis, or Albertano of Brescia:—Died ca. 1270. His Liber Consolationis et Consilii, in a French version by Jehan de Meung, was used by Chaucer for the tale of Melibeus; his De Arte Loquendi et Tacendi is referred to in the MancTale, see Skeat V : 442-3; his De Amore et Dilectione Dei is referred to in the MerchTale, see Skeat V : 355, 358. See in general Skeat III : 426-7, Koeppel in Archiv 86 : 29-47.

The Liber Consolationis was ed. for the Chaucer Society by Sundby, 2nd Series, No. 8; the De Arte Loquendi is printed as

Appendix 2 to Sundby's Brunetto Latini's Levnet og Skrifter, Copenhagen, 1869, accessible in an Italian transl. by Renier, Florence 1884; the De Amore is cited by Koeppel, Archiv 86: 29-47, *q. v.*, from MS.

See the ed. of the Melibeus in Maetzner's Altenglische Sprachproben; Skeat as above; Lounsbury, Studies II : 384.

Albricus:—Of the 13th century Author of a brief treatise entitled De Deorum Imaginibus, which is perhaps used in KnTale, see Skeat V : 78, 82, and in HoFame lines 130-133. According to Lounsbury, Studies II : 381-2, Albricus' work is printed in Van Staveren's Auctores Mythographi Latini, Leyden 1742.

Alexander-saga:—The legend of Alexander is alluded to in HoFame 915, MoTale 641 ff. In the WBprol. 498 a passage of the Alexandreid, a Latin poem by Philippe Gualtier, is mentioned. See Lounsbury, Studies II : 303-5.

Almansor:—A marginal note in the Ellesmere MS to WBprol. 613 refers to a work recognized as Almansoris Propositiones; no date given by Skeat V : 306, 310, but ref. to a print of 1641.

Ambrose:—Died ca. 397. Referred to in the ParsTale, see Skeat V : 448. Works ed. Patrologia vols 14-17.

Anselm:—1038-1109. Cited ParsTale, see Skeat V : 450. Works ed. Patrologia vols. 158-159.

"Arnold of the Newe Toun"—Arnoldus Villanova, died 1314:—His Rosarium Philosophorum, a treatise on alchemy, is quoted CYTale, lines 875-6. See Skeat V : 432; Lounsbury, Studies II · 393.

The Rosarium is printed in Ashmole's Theatrum Chemicum Britannicum of 1632.

Arthur-saga:—The legend of Arthur is alluded to at the opening of the WBTale and in the SqTale line 95. Lancelot is referred to in the SqTale 287, NPTale 392. Tristan and Isolde are mentioned HoFame 1796, PoFoules 290, LGW prol. 254; see also the poem To Rosemounde, Section V here.

Some of these refs. seem commonplaces in imitation of the lists of characters so frequent in the Middle Ages. For a misunderstanding of the word Isolde by annotators see Section VI G here. See Lounsbury, Studies II: 304-5.

Augustine of Hippo:—354-430. Chaucer alludes to brief passages of Augustine's writings in LGW 1690, in DoctTale 117,

ParsTale 100, 150, 183, 303, 484, 535, 562, 678, 694, 741, 1020; these refs. are according to Skeat VI : 384; see Miss Petersen as cited on the sources of the ParsTale, Section III G here. Augustine is also alluded to in Melibeus line 2833 and Prol. 187-88. See Lounsbury, Studies II : 297-99.

The works of Augustine are accessible Patrologia vols. 32-47, etc.

Aurora, *see* Petrus de Riga.

Bernardus Silvestris:—Of the 12th century. Author of the Megacosmos and Microcosmos, the former of which is used MLTale 197 ff.

Skeat V : 147 mentions an ed. of the work by Barach and Wrobel, Innsbruck 1876, and a MS Bodley 1265. See Lounsbury, Studies II : 385; Sandys, Hist. Class. Scholarship 514-16.

Bible:—See the list of Chaucer's uses of the Vulgate in Skeat VI : 381-84. A paper on the Bible in Chaucer, by Charles Noble, is in the Faculty Corner, Grinnell, Iowa, 1901, pp. 157-167, repr. from the Unit, an Iowa College paper, 1898-1901.

A note by Root, Nation 1904 II : 315, is commented on by Lowes, Publ. Mod. Lang. Assn. 19 : 668-669 footnote.

Boethius:—?470-525. Author of works on astronomy, music, etc., and, while imprisoned by the Emperor Theodoric previous to his execution, of a prose treatise De Consolatione Philosophiae, which was unboundedly popular in the late Middle Ages. It was translated into English by King Alfred and by Chaucer, beside other versions later, see Section IV here. Several of Chaucer's shorter poems are founded upon it, *e. g.*, Former Age, Fortune, Gentilesse; and there are constant allusions to and echoes of Boethius throughout the longer works, cp. the Monk's Tale, the discourse upon predestination in the Troilus, Book IV; see the list by Skeat, VI : 385 and the notes II : xxviii-xxxvii, also in especial Stewart's Boethius, an Essay, Lond. 1891, appendix B. Boethius exerted more influence upon the intellect of Chaucer than any other writer except perhaps Jehan de Meung.

The Opera are in the Patrologia, vols. 63, 64. The best ed. of the Consolatio, by Peiper, Leipzig 1871, is out of print and hard to get; see that in the Delphin Classics, Lond. 1823.

On Boethius see:—Gibbon, Decline and Fall, ed. Bury IV : 197-204; Ebert, I : 485 ff.; Hodgkin, Italy and her Invaders III : 4, chap. 12; Hauréau, Hist. de la philosophie scolastique, 1872, I : 112 ff.; Taylor, Classical Heritage of the Middle Ages, pp. 51-56; Ker, Dark Ages, pp. 103 ff.; Stewart

op. cit. above; Sandys, Hist. Class. Scholarship, pp. 237-243.
For Boethius' influence on Dante see Moore, Studies in Dante,
I : 282-288.

Bradwardine, Thomas:—Died 1349. Author of the De Causa Dei,
mentioned NPTale 422; the work was ed. London 1618. See
Lounsbury, Studies II : 382-3.

Caecilius Balbus: Sententiae
Cassiodorus: Variarum

{ Used in the original of the
Melibeus, see ed. by Sundby as
cited under Albertanus Brixiensis
above, and Skeat V passim under
Melibeus.

Cato:—The so-called Disticha of "Dionysius Cato" (4th century?),
one of the most popular handbooks of the Middle Ages, is
frequently alluded to by Chaucer, see list of refs. Skeat VI : 385.
See Lounsbury, Studies II : 358-61.

Text ed. by Hauthal, Berlin 1869. The old Provençal has
been discussed by Tobler, diss. Strassburg 1897 pp. 104. For
notes on the popularity of the work in the Middle Ages see
Manitius in Philologus 51 : 164-171. Burgh's 15th century English version of the work is ed. by Foerster, Archiv 115 : 298-
323, 116 : 25-40.

Charlemagne-saga:—Ganelon is referred to BoDuchess 1121,MoTale
399, NPTale 407.

Cicero:—B. C. 106-43. According to Lounsbury, Studies II : 271-3,
Chaucer refers to Cicero (Tullius) in the Frankl. prol. and in
Scogan; but all he seems to have known of Ciceronian texts
are the Somnium Scipionis (see under Macrobius below) and
the De Divinatione as used in the NPTale. Skeat VI : 385 adds
to this a number of citations in Melibeus, received of course
from the original. For the WBprol. see Skeat V : 312.

See Sandys, Hist. Class. Scholarship pp. 623-27.

Claudian:—Close of the 4th century. Lounsbury, Studies II : 254-8,
says that Claudian is twice mentioned by Chaucer in the HoFame
and once in the MerchTale, with reference to his De Raptu
Proserpinae; according to Skeat V : 70, a passage of the KnTale
is from Claudian; one bit of the PoFoules is transl. from him,
see Lounsbury, Studies II : 257, Skeat I : 509; and he is mentioned LGW prol. 280.

Claudian's works are ed. Hirt, Monumenta Germanica, Berlin
1892, and Koch, Leipzig (Teubner) 1893.

Constantinus:—About 1080. His work De Coitu and himself are

alluded to MerchTale 566-67; Tyrwhitt in his note on the passage says his works were printed at Basel in 1536. His name
appears Gen. Prol. line 433.

Corinne:—Mentioned in Anelida 21, see Skeat I : 531; Lounsbury,
Studies II : 403-5. I have queried if a MS could have given
Chaucer *Corinnus* instead of *Corippus;* see Sandys, Hist. of
Classical Scholarship 436; but there appears no evidence of
Corippus' influence.

Chrysippus, as alluded to in WBprol. 677, Tyrwhitt could not identify; Skeat V : 309 says Chaucer caught the name from Jerome's
treatise Adversus Jovinianum.

Dares Phrygius and Dictys Cretensis:—A supposed Greek and a
supposed Phoenician writer upon the Trojan war, the former
from the Trojan, the latter from the Greek point of view.
Latin works professing to be translations of these histories,
Dares in 44 short chapters, Dictys in six books and about twice
as long as Dares, have come down from perhaps the sixth
century, and are the ultimate sources of the Trojan legend as
known to the Middle Ages. They served as basis for the work
of Benoît de Sainte-More (q. v.), upon whose poem the Historia Trojana of Guido delle Colonne (q. v.) was founded.

See Ward's Catalogue of Romances I : 9-26; Lounsbury,
Studies II : 305 ff.; Skeat I : 489-90, III : 277; Morley, Eng.
Writers VI : 118; Warton-Hazlitt II : 127, III : 81. Editions
of both, according to Ward, in Valpy's Delphin Classics, London 1825; of Dictys by Dederich, Bonn 1833, and by Meister,
Leipzig (Teubner) 1872; of Dares by Dederich, Bonn 1835, and
by Meister, Leipzig (Teubner) 1873. See Koerting, Dictys
und Dares, Halle, 1874; Griffin, Dares and Dictys, diss. Johns
Hopkins, 1907; and other references under the Troilus, Section
IV here. Chaucer alludes to Dares and Dictys in the Book of
the Duchesse line 1070, the Troilus I : 146, V : 1771, the House
of Fame line 1467; but his allusions do not imply knowledge of
their text rather than of their later imitators, says Lounsbury,
Studies II : 314.

"Daun Burnel the Asse", *see under* Speculum Stultorum below.

"English Gaufride", mentioned HoFame 1470, is Geoffrey of Mon-
mouth, 12th century, author of the Historia Regum Britanniae.
See Schofield, English Literature from the Norman Conquest
to Chaucer, 1906, pp. 37-39.

Exempla:—Short stories used to "point a moral" were in the Middle Ages styled exempla, and collected for the use of clerics as adjuncts to sermons. See Miss Petersen's Sources of the Nonne Prestes Tale, pp. 97-100 note, and refs. given *ibid.*, viz., Exempla of Jacques de Vitry, ed. T. F. Crane, London 1890, Herolt's Promptuarium Exemplorum, 1492, Thomas of Cantimpre's Speculum Exemplorum, 1487, Flores Exemplorum, Cologne 1656, Magnum Speculum Exemplorum, Cologne 1747, also Holkot's Super Libros Sapientie and his Moralitates in Usum Predicantium, 1580; Bromyard's Summa Predicantium, 1518. The Friar's Tale and the Pardoner's Tale find partial analogues in such collections; and Miss Petersen remarks that Chaucer's use of example-books offers an interesting field for speculation. See Crane's art. *Exempla,* in Johnson's Cyclopedia.

Florilegia:—Anthologies, or collections of extracts from favored authors, must have been made with especial zeal in the Middle Ages, when books were scarce and the respect for antiquity immense. The subject has not been historically treated, so far as I know, but I note a few facts.

Keller and Holder, in their ed. of Horace, mention several Florilegia which contained abundant extracts from his writings; *e. g.* that which is in MS in the library of Notre Dame Cathedral, the Florilegium compiled by Nicholas Cusanus in the 12th century, the Florilegium Veronense, and Florilegium Basiliense. The Florilegia of Göttingen and of Saint Omer are alluded to in Bibl. de l'École des Chartes 60: 569 ff.

Earlier florilegia in MS are enumerated by Manitius in his Analekten zu Horaz, see pp. 35, 57, 75, 105. And a Greek one compiled by Stobaeus in the 5th century is ed. Meineke, Leipzig 1855-56, 4 vols.

Later and better known anthologies are the Fiore di Filosofi, formerly ascribed to Brunetto Latini; this collection, according to Gröber, Grdr. II:3, p. 43, is based upon Vincent of Beauvais. Vincent's extracts, in the Speculum Historiale, are sometimes extensive, including hundreds of lines from Seneca or Ovid, 40 from Horace's Ars Poetica alone; but sometimes very small, *e. g.* Persius.

These collections took a moral rather than literary turn: cp. the Fiore di Virtù discussed in Studi di filol. roman., vol. VI, or Les dits moraux des philosophes, transl. by Earl Rivers and printed by Caxton, see Blades pp. 189-91. Or note the Adagia of Erasmus, see Emerton's Erasmus, chap. IV.

It is very possible that some of Chaucer's Latin bits, especially those from Horace and Juvenal, perhaps from Claudian, may have reached him in such a way, or through works like John of

Salisbury's Polycraticus and Epistles, strewn with citations almost as liberally as is Burton's Anatomy of Melancholy, which Thackeray makes his hackwriter use (Pendennis ch. 33) as a repository of classical quotations. Further, the citation of lines by grammatical and prosodical writers like Isidor of Seville or the writers of Ars Dictandi, the commentators on the Eclogues of Theodulus, etc., must not be forgotten as the possible means of transmission of many a stray quotation which in the Middle Ages hardened into a proverb. See Skeat II : lii, III : 278. See Moore, Studies in Dante, I : 205.

Florus, L. Annaeus:—Of the 2d century, author of an Epitome de Gestis Romanorum, used by Chaucer for some details in the Cleopatra of the Legend of Good Women. See Skeat III : xxxvii, 313; Lounsbury, Studies II : 288.

    An ed. was published at Florence in 1524.

Gesta Romanorum:—A collection of anecdotes and stories, historical or pseudohistorical, largely of famous characters, which served as source for many medieval narratives and moral illustrations. There is no proof, according to Lounsbury, Studies II : 317-20, that Chaucer directly used this book, but he refers to "Roman gests" three times, in the Merchant's Tale line 1040, in the MLTale 1126, and the WBprol. 642. See Skeat V : 360-361 for a passage which he considers derived from the Gesta.

    On the Gesta see diss. IV in Warton-Hazlitt. See ed. by Oesterley, Berlin 1871.

Godfrey of Viterbo:—Bech, Anglia 5 : 340, says of LGW lines 1896-8 that the notion of Athens current in the Middle Ages may have come from such a passage as one which he cites from the Speculum Regum of this author.

Greek:—"Like his contemporaries, Chaucer was totally ignorant of Greek. There are some nine or ten quotations from Plato, three from Homer, two from Aristotle, and one from Euripides; but they are all taken at second hand, through the medium of Boethius. The sole quotation from Herodotus in the Canterbury Tales is copied from Jerome." Skeat VI : xcviii.

    Plato is mentioned by name in HoFame 759, 931, also in Prol. 741, MancTale 207, CYTale 895 ff. The last is an erroneous attribution to Plato of an anecdote usually connected with Solomon, see Skeat's note. The two other cases in the CT are repetitions of the saying from the Timaeus already transl. by Chaucer in the Boethius III prose 12, line 152. In the Boethius Plato is cited or mentioned seven times.

Aristotle is named HoFame 759, Gen. Prol. 295, SqTale 233.
There are three refs. to him in the Boethius, each more than
the mere mention which Chaucer gives.

Homer is mentioned in Troilus I : 146, V : 1792, HoFame
1466, FrankTale 715. In HoFame 1477 it is remarked that
some assert he made lies in his story. He is thrice mentioned
in the Boethius, and one passage, the allusion to Jupiter's two
tuns, was disseminated partly by Boethius and partly by the
Roman de la Rose deriving from Boethius.

A bit of Herodotus is cited, from Jerome, without the name
of either author, in WBprol. 782.

Euripides is twice quoted in the Boethius, once by name, and
once as a "tragedien", III, prose 6.

Gregory, Saint and Pope:—554-604. Referred to and cited several
times in the ParsTale, see Skeat VI : 386.

Guido delle Colonne:—Of the latter half of the thirteenth century.
It was first remarked by Tyrwhitt, note on CT 15147, that the
Historia Trojana of Guido (to which Chaucer refers as listed
by Skeat VI : 386), was probably a transl. of Benoît de Sainte-
More's Roman de Troie (see under Sainte-More above).
Douce, in his Illustrations of Shakespeare, 1807, restated the
fact; but the proofs were not presented until Joly's work of
1871, for which see under Troilus, Section IV here; see *ibid.*
for notes and refs. on the question whether Chaucer used Guido
or Benoit. See Lounsbury, Studies II : 309 ff.; Ward, Cat. of
Romances I : 35 ff. The Historia Trojana was first printed
1477.

Helowys, Héloise:—Referred to WBprol. 677; see Skeat V : 309,
and note that according to Woollcombe, Ch. Soc. Essays part
III, the letters of Héloise to Abelard avow the use of Jerome
Adversus Jovinianum, which may account for their appearance
in the same volume in the Wife of Bath's narrative.

Hermes:—A marginal note to WBprol. 613, in the Ellesmere MS,
refers to Hermes in libro fiducie; see Skeat V : 306.

Holkot:—See ante under Exempla, and especially Miss Petersen on
the Sources of the Nonne Prestes Tale, pp. 100 ff.

Horace:—Lounsbury, Studies II : 261-4, combats the tendency to
ascribe to Chaucer a knowledge of Horace. (The only earlier
editor whom I find tracing Chaucerian passages to Horace is
Bell, 1854, cp. his ed. III : 240.) Lounsbury gives "only three
instances" of such attribution to Horace; the story of Amphion,

at the beginning of the MancTale, and Troilus II : 1028-43. To these Skeat adds a passage in Melibeus, see his V : 219, another in the MancTale, see his V : 443, and another in Troilus II : 22, see Skeat II : 468. In citing these Skeat remarks II : 468 that this was probably borrowed at secondhand, remarks V : 443 that Chaucer got the line through Albertano or from the Roman de la Rose, says V : 439 that the passage reached Chaucer through the Roman de la Rose, and refers simply to Horace in II : 472. In VI : ci he says that we may be sure Chaucer's quotations from Horace and Juvenal were taken at secondhand. See II : lii-liii.

On the subject of secondhand quotations see under Florilegia above. On Horace in the Middle Ages see M. Manitius, Analekten zur Geschichte des Horaz im Mittelalter bis 1300, Göttingen, 1893. See Moore, Studies in Dante, vol. I, 1896, pp. 29, 197-206. See Sandys, History of Classical Scholarship, pp. 612-14.

The best ed. of Horace for students of literary history is that of Keller and Holder, Leipzig 1864, 2 vols., second ed. vol. I, 1899. At the foot of each page are given testimonia, or notes on the citation of Horatian passages by medieval writers and compilers of anthologies.

Hyginus:—Died 17 A. D. His Fabulae were perhaps known to Chaucer, see Skeat I: 464, III: 333-4; Lounsbury, Studies II : 287.

Pope Innocent III:—1161-1216. One of the greatest and most influential of the Popes, a writer as well as an administrator. His prose treatise De Contemptu Mundi sive de Miseria Conditionis Humanae, was known to Chaucer; and in the A-version of the prologue LGW, lines 414-5, it is said that the poet has translated "of the Wrecched Engendryng of mankinde As men may in pope Innocent yfynde." Of a complete independent translation of this work by Chaucer we have no copy; and Prof. Lounsbury, who first pointed out Chaucer's debt to Innocent, Nation 1889 II: 10-11, thinks that possibly no more was ever done than is to be found in the Man of Law's Tale and its prologue, and in the Pardoner's prologue. See also Lounsbury, Studies II : 329-336, I : 426, and Skeat's notes V : 141-2, 154, 160-1, 165. See in detail Koeppel in Archiv 84 : 405 ff. Cp. Lowes in Publ. Mod. Lang. Assn. 20 : 795-6.

The Latin passages used by Chaucer are printed by Skeat, by Lounsbury II : 332-3, and by Koeppel passim. Innocent's treatise is accessible in the works as ed. Migne, Patrologia vols. 214-217, and the De Contemptu has been translated into German by F. Rudolf, Arnsberg 1888.

Isidor of Seville:—Died 636. Referred to in the Parson's Tale, see Skeat V : 448. On him see Ebert I : 588-602, Sandys 442-4.

Jacobus a Voragine, *see* Legende Aurea.

Saint Jerome:—331-420. Called the most learned and eloquent of the Latin Fathers of the Church, and a voluminous polemical writer. Chaucer knew especially Jerome's treatise against Jovinian, a contemporary monk who doubted the excellence of celibacy; he used its Part I in the WBprol., the FrankTale, and the A-prol. LGW, where lists of loyal or disloyal women are found. Jerome, while denouncing marriage and women, cites noble examples from antiquity to show the degeneracy of his own time; hence the treatise yielded Chaucer material of both sorts. Part II of the treatise, which is on fasting, was but little used by Chaucer; see Skeat I : 541, 545, V : 278-9; see Lounsbury, Studies II : 292-97.

Jerome's works are contained in Migne's (Latin) Patrologia, vols. 22-30. The Adversus Jovinianum is in vol. 2 of the Works. The passages used in the WBprol. were translated by Woollcombe, Ch. Soc. Essays pp. 293 ff.; Koeppel adds a little in Archiv 84 : 414 note; and see his paper Anglia 13 : 174-181.

On Jerome see Ebert, Gesch. Lat. Litt. I : 184 ff., Sandys 219-222. The influence of Jerome's treatise has not yet been discussed. Note *e. g.* that Héloise's objections to marrying Abelard are avowedly taken from it, see above under Héloise; and cp. de Bury's Philobiblon, ed. Thomas, chap. IV.

John of Salisbury:—?1120-1180. The most remarkable intellectual figure of the early Middle Ages. Already Tyrwhitt, in a note on CT 12537, pointed out that Chaucer there apparently used John of Salisbury's Polycraticus sive De Nugis Curialium, although other similar passages (see his notes on lines 5817, 9172) were not from John but from John's original. This first-mentioned passage, in the Pardoner's prologue, is annotated Skeat V : 282-3; and Lounsbury, Studies II : 362-4, sees no further evidence that Chaucer used the Polycraticus. In N. and Q. 1899 I : 224 it is pointed out that the "maxime Lolli" passage of Horace may have reached Chaucer through the Polycraticus (vii, chap. ix). See under Lollius below; Woollcombe, Ch. Soc. Essays 295 ff., argues that Chaucer did not borrow from John of Salisbury.

John of Salisbury's works are accessible in the Patrologia vol. 199; on him see Schaarschmidt, Joannes Saresberiensis, Leipzig 1862; see chap. VII of R. L. Poole's Illustrations of the History of Medieval Thought, London 1884, and Sandys, History of Classical Scholarship pp. 517-522.

Juvenal:—Died 140. Mentioned and cited in Troilus IV : 197, WBTale 336. Skeat on these passages says "from Juvénal"; VI : 387 he says "probably taken at secondhand." Lounsbury, Studies II : 260, thinks Chaucer was familiar with at least a part of Juvenal's writings. See Sandys, Hist. of Class. Scholarship, pp. 619-20.

Legenda Aurea:—A compilation of the lives of the Saints by Jacobus a Voragine, who flourished in the latter half of the 13th century. This was used by Chaucer for part of the Second Nun's Tale, as Tyrwhitt pointed out. See Skeat III : 486-8; Lounsbury, Studies II : 320-1. Jehan de Vignay's French translation of the life of St. Cecilia is reprinted Ch. Soc. Orig. and Anal. pp. 190 ff. See Kölbing, Engl. Stud. 1 : 215. The Legenda Aurea is edited by Graesse, Leipzig 1850.

Lives of the Saints:—Saints' names frequently occur in Chaucer, but often as interjections or in slight allusions, cp. the use of Christopher, Frideswide, James, Julian, Leonard, Loy, Madrian, Maur, Peter, Ronyan etc.; and some mentions of saints' names apply to their literary work as known to Chaucer,—Augustine, Bernard, Gregory, or Isidor. Of anecdote or illustration from saints' lives the amount is not very great; and whether the poet cites from oral tradition or written work we do not know. See Lounsbury, Studies II : 321-9, and Skeat's list VI : 359 ff. under Ambrose, Antony, Dunstan, Edward, Hugh, Kenelm, Mary of Egypt, Thomas of India.

Livy:—B. C. 59—A. D. 17. Author of a history of Rome. Mentioned by Chaucer in connection with the stories of Lucretia and of Virginia; see LGW prol. 280 and lines 1683, 1873; Doctor's Tale line 1; Book of Duch. line 1084. See Lounsbury, Studies II : 279-84. Skeat VI : 387 says Livy is almost certainly quoted at secondhand; see III : 330, 435.

Lollius:—This name, apparently that of an earlier writer, is mentioned by Chaucer as follows:—In Troilus and Cressida I : 394 he professes to quote "myn auctour called Lollius", when he gives the song of Troilus, translated from a sonnet by Petrarch; he introduces it into a poem in which he is evidently following Boccaccio's Il Filostrato. In the same poem V : 1653 he speaks of Diomed's coat and its fate "as telleth Lollius"; the incident is in the Filostrato. Again in the House of Fame line 1468, he mentions Dares, Tytus (*read* Dictys), Lollius, and others as writers on the history of Troy. The question is additionally complicated by the fact that Chaucer nowhere alludes to Boccaccio, even when translating from him; he alludes to Petrarch only in the Clerk's headlink and Tale, when he assigns to him the Griselda story, translating it from his Latin, and in the Monk's Tale, where also he refers to Boccaccio's Latin as by Petrarch. He does not credit Petrarch with the sonnet which he renders in the Troilus; nor does he anywhere mention Boccaccio. An explanation of "Lollius" should cover a Trojan historiographer, Boccaccio, and Petrarch.

Dryden, in the preface to his "Troilus and Cressida", said that "the original story was written by one Lollius, in Lombard verse, and translated by Chaucer into English." This he derived, it is probable, from the note in Speght's glossary— "Lollius, an Italian Historiographer borne in the citie of Urbine"; and Speght's comment probably came ultimately from the only source of information which we have regarding Lollius, the single sentence in the Life of Antoninus Diadumenos, written by Aelius Lampridius about 400 A. D. This Life is one of those collected under the title Scriptores Historiae Augustae, and esteemed by the Middle Ages as of equal value with Suetonius' Lives of the Caesars, to which they formed a continuation. Lampridius mentioned Lollius as if he were a wellknown writer,—"Lollius Urbicus in historia temporis sui dicit"; and as the Augustan history was written during the reigns of Diocletian and Constantine, Lollius has been considered as of the third century. Warton (Warton-Hazlitt II : 327-8) remarked that he had never seen the history of Lollius, though noting that the Troilus is "said to be founded on an old history written by Lollius"; he cites also the statement of Lydgate (see Section II A here), that the Troilus was called "Trophe in Lumbard tongue." Theobald, in his notes on Shakspere's Troilus and Cressida, referred to Lollius without query. Tyrwhitt, in a note on the Recantation, said "How Boccace should have acquired the name of Lollius, and the Filostrato the title of Trophe, are points which I confess myself unable to explain." Godwin, in a note in his chap. 37, said "Considering that the stories of Troilus and Creseide, and of Palamon and Arcite, were both translated by Boccaccio and by Chaucer; that the original author of the latter is wholly unknown; that they were the work of the same age; and that Lollius is placed so familiarly by Chaucer upon a footing with the greatest writers; it is not very improbable that they were both the production of this author, and that Chaucer translated the one and the other from the Latin in which he had composed them." Douce, in his Illustrations of Shakespere, under Troilus and Cressida, begins thus:—"Of Lollius, the supposed inventor of this story, it will become every one to speak with diffidence. Until something decisive relating to him shall occur, it is better to conclude, with Mr. Tyrwhitt, that Chaucer

borrowed the greater part of his admirable story from Boccaccio's Philostrato; and that he either invented the rest
altogether, or obtained it from some completer copy of the
Philostrato than that which we now possess. What Dryden
has said of Lollius is entirely destitute of proof, and appears
to be nothing more than inference from Chaucer's own expressions." Isaac Disraeli, in his Amenities of Literature,
chap. On Gothic Romances, alludes to this passage of Douce.
Both Douce and Disraeli are cited N. and Q. 1849-50 I : 418,
where E. F. Rimbault says positively, "Lollius was the real or
fictitious name of the author or translator of many of our
Gothic prose romances." Sandras (1859), Étude pp. 45, 127,
and Henry Bradshaw, were the first to assert that in citing
"Lollius" Chaucer was merely indulging himself in a deliberate
mystification of his readers, "carrying out his habitual practice
of concealing his real authority and substituting the name of
some other author, often, as in this case, one whose works
were entirely lost." (Memoir of Bradshaw by Prothero, p.
216.) This view has since been advocated by Macaulay, Acad.
1895 I : 297; Courthope, Hist. Eng. Poetry I : 261; Schofield,
Hist. Eng. Lit., p. 293.

In the Athen. 1868 II : 433 Latham suggested that the appearance of Lollius as a historian of Troy was due to Chaucer's
misunderstanding the lines of Horace "Troiani belli scriptorem, maxime Lolli, Dum tu declamas Romae, Praeneste
relegi", from the epistle to Lollius; in N. and Q. 1899 I : 224 it
was pointed out that Chaucer (who probably knew nothing of
Horace) could have seen this passage in John of Salisbury's
Polycraticus, vii, chap. ix. Chaucer then, according to Latham,
believed Lollius to be a writer on the Trojan war. (Note that
this explains only the House of Fame allusion, not those in the
Troilus.) Latham was followed by Rossetti, Athen. 1868 II :
465, Rossetti retracting his suggestion already made *ibid.* p. 401
that by Lollius was meant Laelius, a name belonging to
Petrarch, whom Chaucer believed to be the author of the
Filostrato. Ten Brink, Studien pp. 87-88, adopted Latham's
view, with some additions; Skeat III : 278 considers the suggestion "quite reasonable"; Macaulay loc. cit. objects. Note
that already Bradshaw (see Prothero's Memoir p. 216) had
made the same suggestion as did Latham.

Hertzberg p. 44 note 71 said that "no one knows" Lollius.
Peiper, in Fleckeisen's Jahrbuch für Philologie und Paedagogik
97 : 65 (1868), would read Sollius. Kissner, *op. cit.* p. 9, maintains that Lollius is a pseudonym for Boccaccio, invented by
Chaucer to give the dignity of a Latin original to his work.
Kissner instances other cases of pretended authorities referred to
by Chaucer; but see Toynbee on "Agaton" in Mod. Lang. Quart,

1 : 5 (preceded by Sandras, Étude p. 115), Flügel on the Almagest in Anglia 18. Kissner is supported by Eitner in Shaksp. Jahrbuch 1868, pp. 277-78.

Koch, Engl. Stud. 1:291 ff. and Ch. Soc. Essays 411-414, declared that we have no right to impute capricious intention to Chaucer; he asserted that Chaucer did not know Boccaccio's name, a fact easily explainable from the frequent anonymity of medieval MSS. This explanation Morley, Eng. Writers V : 216 considers "incredible", Schofield, Hist. Eng. Lit. p. 293, "hardly credible." Morley thinks the word Lollius a coinage from *lolium* a tare, expressing Chaucer's sense of Boccaccio's wickedness. Borghesi, in his (valueless) Boccaccio and Chaucer, Bologna 1903, thinks that Chaucer left Boccaccio unmentioned because Boccaccio was known as a man of loose habits, and the English king might have disapproved of Chaucer's treating him as a master. Some Italian scholars have considered that Chaucer was afraid to acknowledge how much he owed to Boccaccio, and suppressed mention of him; thus Hortis *op. cit.* p. 581, Segrè as cited by Rajna in Romania 32 : 245.

Bright, Publ. Mod. Lang. Ass'n 19:xxii, suggests that Chaucer may have intended Loll-ius as a rendering of the somewhat difficult and unpleasing name Bocc-accio. (Here we might perhaps compare Dante's translation of Petrus Comestor into Pietro Mangiadore, Paradiso 12; or Leigh Hunt's version of Shelley as Conchiglioso.) In Mod. Lang. Notes 22:51-52 I have offered an explanation based, like Koch's, upon possible MS conditions: a marked work by Lollius may have been the first in a volume, and the Filostrato following unmarked, hence attributed by Chaucer to Lollius. To this paper Bright appends a note. Tatlock, Devel. and Chronol. p. 160 note 3, thinks Chaucer's silence as to Boccaccio's name must be attributed to ignorance.

Students who assert the deliberate use by Chaucer of authorities he knew to be incorrect will agree with Burton, who in his Bookhunter says: "I believe that if one of those laborious old writers hatched a good idea of his own, he could experience no peace of mind until he found it legitimated by having passed through an earlier brain, and that the author who failed thus to establish a paternity for his thought would sometimes audaciously set down some great name in his crowded margins, in the hope that the imposition might pass undiscovered."

The various theories upon this puzzling point may be classed as follows: (1) That Chaucer did know Boccaccio's authorship, and tried to conceal his debt; here Kissner and various Italian students would give one reason, Bright another, while Sandras and Bradshaw regard it as caprice, "a deliberate mystification."

On the lastnamed Lounsbury has said, Studies II : 413-14, that
the critics who dispose of Lollius in this way should offer more
conclusive evidence that such deception was practised by Chaucer.
(2) That Chaucer did not know Boccaccio's name. In this case
we must believe the attribution to Lollius due to mistake, arising
either from MS conditions or from Chaucer's belief that Petrarch
was the author of all Boccaccio's Latin writings; on this see
Tyrwhitt, note on CT 14253, and Rossetti in his Ch. Soc. study
of Troilus, p. vii. If the latter view be held, we should have to
say that Chaucer gave Petrarch now his own name, now that of
Lollius.

Trophe

To the above I may add an extreme flight of conjecture, that
if this supposititious volume of my theory entitled its work by
Lollius as " . . . *trophium"*, the name Trophe might then be
applied both to the unmarked Filostrato of the same volume and
to the preceding Latin (of Lollius) cited by Chaucer in the Monk's
Tale line 127. Cp. the words in . . . *trophium* in Du Cange's
Glossarium, *e. g.,* Orphanotrophium, Xenotrophium, etc. On this
suggestion, the reference in the Monk's Tale, . . . "as saith
Trophee", would refer to Lollius' book; and the reference by
Lydgate (see Section II A here) to the Troilus as from an
original called Trophe "in Lumbard tongue" would have reference
to the Filostrato under the title of the work by Lollius preceding
it in the MS, it also, as above conjectured, being ascribed to
Lollius' authorship. A reconcileable supposition is that Lollius'
work began "Ille vates Chaldaeorum Tropheus", a line cited by
the Ellesmere and Hengwrt MSS in the margin beside the Monk's
Tale passage. Note other refs. by the Ellesmere MS, probably
emanating from Chaucer himself, but uncomprehended as yet by
us; see Lounsbury, Studies II : 415.

On Trophe see Hertzberg, Jahrbuch 8 : 155; Morley, Eng.
Writers V : 188 note; Skeat II : lvi note; Tyrwhitt, in his note
on the Retractation, professed himself unable to explain the point.

Lucan:—39-68. Author of the epic poem Pharsalia. He or his
work is referred to by Chaucer MLTale 303, MoTale 729,
HoFame 1499, Troilus V : 1792. See Lounsbury, Studies II :
253-4. Note also the passage KnTale 767-8 with Pharsalia
I : 92 (Hammond) ; cp. also Rom. Rose 487 from Ovid, Metam.
II : 846 (Mather). Chaucer's knowledge of Lucan was first
discussed by Fiedler, Archiv 2 : 390-402 (1847).

Macrobius:—ca. 400. Author of a prose commentary on the
Somnium Scipionis, originally contained in Book VI of Cicero's
De Republica. This portion of Cicero's text has not come down
to us except in the annotated version of Macrobius, which
was widely read in the Middle Ages, and furnished the
model for much of the medieval dream-literature. It was used
by Chaucer in the PoF, and alluded to in the NPTale 303,
the HoFame 514, and the BoDuch 234. See Skeat I : 505;

Lounsbury, Studies II: 276-78; Sandys, Hist. Class. Scholarship 224-27.

Macrobius is ed. Eyssenhardt, Leipzig (Teubner) 1893; it was translated into French by Nisard, Paris 1883.

See E. P. Anderson, Some notes on Chaucer's treatment of the Sommium Scipionis. Trans. Amer. Philol. Ass'n 33 : xcviii ff. (1902).

Mapes or Map, Walter:—Flourished 1200. English. Archdeacon of Oxford. Famous as wit and satirist; his bestknown work, the De Nugis Curialium, is satirical, and includes a brief treatise written earlier, the Valerius ad Rufinum de non ducenda uxore. To this Chaucer refers WBprol. 671, LGW prol. (A) 280. See Lounsbury, Studies II: 367-370; Koeppel in Anglia 13: 181-3.

The Ad Rufinum was included among the supposititious works of St. Jerome, and printed in the Patrologia, vol. 30; it is ed. by Wright in the De Nugis, London 1851, for the Camden Society. To Map is also ascribed much of the "Goliardic" verse, printed by Wright for the Camden Society, London 1841, as Latin Poems Attributed to Walter Mapes; see Manly on Familia Goliae, in Mod. Phil. 5 : 201-210. He has also been credited with a share in the Arthurian romances. On Map see art. in Dict. Nat. Biog.; Ward's Cat. of Romances I : 218, 734-41; the eds. of the Carmina Burana by Schmeller, Breslau 1883 and by von Bärnstein, Würzburg 1879; Langlois, La Littérature Goliardique, in the Revue Bleue, Dec. 24, 1892 and Feb. 11, 1893; and the references on the romance-question given in the Dict. Nat. Biog. and in Ward. See also G. Phillips on Map in Sitz. ber. der Akad. der Wiss. (philos.-hist. Classe), Vienna, 1853, X: 319-99.

Marbodus:—See under Lapidaire above.

Martianus Capella:—Flourished 480. His De Nuptiis Philologiae et Mercurii was one of the most popular compendia of the Middle Ages. "Marcian" is mentioned HoFame 985, and his work Merch. Tale 488-94. See Lounsbury, Studies II : 356 ff.; Ebert, Gesch. Lat. Lit. I : 482-5; Sandys, Hist. Class. Scholarship 228-30.

Capella is ed. Eyssenhardt, Leipzig (Teubner) 1866.

Martinus Dumiensis is cited in Melibeus; see Skeat's notes, passim.

Maximian:—Of the 6th century. Lines 399-405 of the Pard. Tale are imitated from Maximian's first Elegy, as Kittredge noted, see Am. Jour. Phil. 9 : 184; Skeat V : 287.

Messahala:—An Arabian astronomer who flourished towards the end of the 8th century. His Operatio Astrolabii was one of the sources of Chaucer's Astrolabe, as was remarked already by Selden in his preface to Drayton's Polyolbion, see Skeat III : lxx note 1. The Astrolabe has been edited by A. E. Brae, London 1870, by Skeat for the EETS, London, 1872, and by Skeat in the Complete Works, Oxford 1894, vol. III. See Lounsbury, Studies II : 397 ff.; Skeat III : lxix ff.

Metaphrastes:—A partial source of the Second Nun's Tale is the life of St. Cecilia by Simeon Metaphrastes, for note on which see Skeat III : 486 ff., and especially Kölbing, Engl. Stud. 1 : 215 ff. Metaphrastes was printed in the Historiae de Vitis Sanctorum of Al. Lipomanus, Louvain 1571.

Mythographers, *see under* Monk's Tale, Section III G here.

Nigel Wireker, *see* Speculum Stultorum below.

Origen:—One of the early Church Fathers, of the third century. According to Chaucer's own statement, prol. to LGW lines 417-8, "He made also . . . . Origenes upon the Maudeleyne." This was supposed by early editors to be the poem printed by them as the Lamentation of Mary Magdalen; see Section V here and Skeat III : 308. The translation is now considered as lost.

Ovid:—B. C. 43—A. D. 17. Chaucer's knowledge of Ovid was very extensive. See Skeat's list of references, VI : 387-8; see Lounsbury, Studies II : 251-2. The poet's knowledge of Ovid was first discussed by Fiedler, Archiv 2 : 151-169 (1847). See in general Bartsch, Ovid im Mittelalter, prefixed to his ed. of Albrecht von Halberstadt, Bibl. der gesammten deutschen Nationalliteratur, 1861.

Ovid's works are ed. by Merkel, 3 vols., Leipzig (Teubner) 1897. Translation in Bohn's Library, 3 vols.

Pamphilus:—Referred to FrankTale 382. Author (?) of De Amore, or, De Arte Amandi. See Skeat V : 391; Lounsbury, Studies II : 370-72; print referred to by Skeat.

Pennaforte, Raymund of:—
Peraldus, Guilelmus:—

{ According to the investigations of Miss Petersen, see under Parson's Tale, Section III G here, the source of that tale is, ultimately, the Latin Summa of these two writers, rather than, as previously supposed, the French of Frère Lorens. See under Lorens above.

Persius:—Of the first century. One passage of Chaucer, in the Franklin's prologue, is from the prologue to Persius' Satires. See Lounsbury, Studies II: 264-5; Skeat V: 387.

Petrus Comestor:—Of the 12th century. Author of the Historia Scholastica, perhaps alluded to in the Pardoner's Tale line 160. See Skeat V: 278; Lounsbury, Studies II: 372-4. Skeat refers to the Hist. Schol. as ed. Paris 1518.

Petrus de Riga:—Of the 12th century. Author of the Aurora, a Latin metrical version of parts of the Bible, apparently referred to in the Book of the Duchesse line 1169. According to Tyrwhitt, note in glossary under Aurora, extracts from the work are printed by Leyser, Hist. Poet. Med. Aevi, Halle, 1721. See Skeat I: 492; Lounsbury, Studies II: 334-6.

Physiologus:—The work thus referred to in the Nun's Priest's Tale line 451 was probably that by Theobald or Thetbald, whose date is not known. It is of 296 verses, published in Hildeberti Turonensis Archiepiscopi Opera, ed. D. A. Beaugendre, Paris 1708, p. 1174. For other Latin Physiologi or Bestiaries see references in Mätzner's Altenglische Sprachproben, I : 55 ff., where is printed the Early English version of Theobald; the French Bestiaire of Philippe de Thaun is printed in Popular Treatises on Science during the Middle Ages, London 1841. See Ebert, Gesch. Lat. Lit. III : 76 ff.; Lauchert, Gesch. des Physiologus, Strassburg 1889; Lounsbury, Studies II : 336-7.

Ptolemy:—Of the 2d century. Chaucer several times refers to the Almagest of Ptolemy, viz.: in the Wife of Bath's prol. lines 180 ff.; in the Miller's Tale line 22; in the Summoner's Tale line 581. These passages were somewhat lightly dismissed by Tyrwhitt, in his note on CT line 5764; and Skeat V : 295, 300, citing Tyrwhitt, asserts that it is unnecessary to search Ptolemy for quotations ostensibly from his Almagest, evidently viewing the Wife of Bath's quotations as "mystifications" on the part of

Chaucer. Lounsbury, Studies II : 395-7, is more cautious. Flügel, in Anglia 18 : 133-140, Ueber einigen Stellen aus dem Almagestum des Cl. Ptolemei bei Chaucer und im Rosenroman, cites the original of the Chaucerian passages from a version of the Almagest printed at Venice in 1515, and censures Skeat, p. 135. See further Boll, Anglia 21 : 222 ff.

Ptolemy's Almagest is also quoted in Les Lamentations de Matheolus, see ed. Paris 1892, I : 107.

Science:—See Lounsbury, Studies II : 389-399.

"Secree of secrees", CYTale 894:—The Secreta Secretorum termed Aristotle's; see Skeat V : 433.

Seneca:—Of the first century. Chaucer gives an account of his death in the Monk's Tale lines 505 ff., and mentions him and his moral wisdom in various other passages, see Skeat's list VI : 388. See Lounsbury, Studies II: 267-271; Hauréau in Notices et Extraits 33 : 208, 227.

Seneca's works are ed. Haase, Leipzig 1887-92.

Senior:—Alluded to CYTale 897; see Skeat V: 433; Lounsbury, Studies II : 392.

Simeon:—See Metaphrastes ante.

Speculum Stultorum:—By Nigel Wireker, canon of Canterbury, who flourished about 1190. The work is cited by Chaucer, under the title of Daun Burnel the Asse, in the Nun's Priest's Tale lines 492 ff. The Latin is printed by Wright, Anglo-Latin Satirical Poets, Rolls Series, I : 3 ff. See Herford, Literary Relations of England and Germany in the Sixteenth Century, chap. VI; see Lounsbury, Studies II : 338-40; Skeat V : 256; Ward, Cat. of Romances II : 691, 695; Dict. of Nat. Biog. under *Nigel*.

Statius:—Of the first century. His Thebais is frequently referred to by Chaucer, especially in the Knight's Tale, see notes by Skeat V : 61, 62, 63, 79, 80-81, 82, 87, 92, 93; also mentioned in Anelida lines 530-1, in Mars 504, in Pity 62, in House of Fame 1460, in Troilus V : 1792; and evidently alluded to in Troilus II: 108 ff. The Thebais is ed. Leipzig (Teubner) 1876-98, 3 vols.

One phrase apparently derived from the Thebais, the *shippes hoppesteres* of Kn. Tale line 1159, has occasioned much annotation. See under Knight's Tale, Section III G here.

Suetonius:—Of the first century. Author of a history of the twelve Caesars. He is referred to twice in the Monk's Tale, for the lives of Nero and of Julius Caesar, lines 475, 730. See Skeat V: 242, 244-5; Lounsbury, Studies II: 284-6.

Suetonius is ed. Roth, Leipzig (Teubner) 1891.

Tertullian:—One of the Latin Fathers, died 230. Referred to WBprol. 676; see Lounsbury, Studies II: 289-291; Skeat V: 309. Tertullian's works are ed. Oehler, Leipzig 1863, 3 vols.; also in Patrologia and in Corp. Script. Lat. xx (1890).

Thebes Saga:—Lowes, Publ. Mod. Lang. Assn. 20 : 850-51, points out that the material of Boccaccio's Teseide was used by Chaucer in "both forms of the Knight's Tale", in the Ariadne of the Legend, in the PoFoules, in the Anelida, and in Troilus. Cressida, in Troilus II : 84, 100 ff., is evidently reading Statius' Thebaid; for question as to use of this work or of Boccaccio, see refs. under Statius ante; see Tatlock, Devel. and Chronol. of Chaucer's Works. Chaucer's refs., outside Anelida 53-63, KnTale passim, HoFame 1461, Troilus as cited and V : 601-2, are in Mars 245 ff., MLTale 102, 191, WBProl. 741, MerchTale 472, 476, MancTale 12-14. See Constans' ed. of the Roman de Thèbes, Paris 1890; Lydgate's Story of Thebes as noted Section V here.

Theodul* :—His Ecloga (ed. Beck, diss. Marburg 1836) was a schoolbook in Chaucer's time; for traces of influence on the House of Fame see Holthausen in Anglia 16 : 264-66.

"Theophrast":—Theophrastus, a disciple of Aristotle, died B. C. 287, was author of a treatise entitled the Liber de Nuptiis; this is lost, but a fragment is preserved in the work of Jerome against Jovinian referred to above. Chaucer used nearly all of the existing text, in the WBprol., see lines 235-378, in the Merchant's Tale, see lines 49-62, in the Manciple's Tale, see lines 43-59. See Skeat's notes V : 296, 298-9, 308, 354, 439; see Lounsbury, Studies II : 366.

The treatise is printed—a fragment—in Jerome as noted.

Thetbaldus:—See under Physiologus ante.

Trophe:—See under Lollius above.

Trotula:—Referred to in WBprol. 677. See Hamilton in Mod. Phil. 4 : 377.

Troy-saga:—Chaucer's usages of the legend of Troy are (1) the story of Dido as told in the Legend of Good Women; (2) the

summary of part of the Aeneid in HoFame 151-382, 427-465;
(3) the story of Troilus and Cressida, from Boccaccio's Filostrato. Otherwise Chaucer's refs. to personages of the Troy-
story are but mere mentions; see the description of the story of
Troy as wrought in windowglass, BoDuch lines 326 ff.

Troilus is but mentioned in Homer's version of the tale of
Troy. His celebration as a hero is made by Dares and Dictys,
see above, whose rendition of the Troy-legend seems to be the
ultimate source of the medieval versions, e. g., those of Benoît
de Sainte More and of Guido delle Colonne, q. v. The De
Bello Trojano of Joseph of Exeter, fl. 1190, is supposedly a
rendering of Guido's prose. The Gest Hystoriale of the Destruction of Troy, ed. Panton and Donaldson for the EETS, is
based on Guido, and the Troy Book of John Lydgate abounds
in refs. to Guido as its source. Boccaccio's Filostrato may owe
something to Guido, although the relation is not yet worked
out; and the possible debt of Chaucer to Guido is still disputed;
see under Troilus, Section IV here.

See Ward, Cat. of Romances, I : 1 ff.; Dunger, Die Sage
vom trojanischen Kriege in den Bearbeitungen des Mittelalters
und ihre antiken Quellen, Leipzig 1869; Greif, Die mittelälter-
lichen Bearbeitungen der Trojanersage, Marburg 1886; Gorra,
Testi Inediti di Storia Trojana, Turin 1887; Joly, Benoît de
Sainte More et le Roman de Troie, Paris 1871; ten Brink, Hist.
Eng. Lit. I : 168, II : 87 ff.; Lounsbury, Studies II : 305 ff.;
Skeat, introd. to Troilus, vol. II of Oxford Chaucer; Taylor,
Classical Heritage of the Middle Ages, chap. III. Work on the
sources of Chaucer's Troilus, by Dr. Young of Harvard Uni-
versity, is forthcoming.

Tullius, *see under* Cicero ante.

Valerius Flaccus :—Of the first century B. C. Traces of the
influence of his Argonautica are perhaps to be seen in
Troilus V : 8, see Skeat II : 495; and in LGW (Hypsipyle)
line 1453, see Skeat III : 326. Cp. Tatlock, Devel. and Chronol.,
p. 100.

The Argonautica is edited by Baehrens, Leipzig (Teubner)
1875. See W. C. Summers, A Study of the Argonautica of
Valerius Flaccus, Cambridge 1894; Schenkl, Studien zu den
Argonautica des V. F., in Wiener Sitz. ber. 68 : 271-382 (1871).

Valerius Maximus:—Of the first century. Author of the De Factis
et Dictis Memorabilium, referred to, though not by name, in
WBProl. 642, see Skeat V : 307, and used in WBTale 309, see
Skeat V : 320. "Valery" is mentioned LGW prol. 280, and
Monk's Tale 730; see Tatlock cited just above.

See Lounsbury, Studies II: 273-6; Miss Petersen on the

NPTale p. 110 note. The De Factis is ed. by Kempf, Leipzig (Teubner) 1888.

"Valery", *see under* Walter Mapes above, and Tatlock, Devel. and Chronol., p. 100.

Vincent of Beauvais:—Of the 13th century. Author of an enormous and widely read compendium of knowledge entitled the Speculum Majus; this is in three parts, the Speculum Naturale, Speculum Doctrinale, Speculum Historiale. The last of these, termed by Chaucer the "Storial Mirrour", is referred to LGW prol. (A-version) 307, and is perhaps used WBTale 339 ff., see Skeat V : 321; NPTale 344, see Skeat V : 255. See Lounsbury, Studies II : 375-381.

The Speculum was printed at Venice in 1494. The Historiale contains, besides masses of legends, miracles, and martyrdoms, curious accounts of Mahomet and of the Tartars, etc., lists of brief quotations from classical and patristic writings. Among others, Plato, Aristotle, Cato, Cicero, Virgil, Horace, Ovid, Seneca, Juvenal, Quintilian, and Claudian are thus excerpted, often very liberally, but usually with preference of "moralitees."

Vinsauf, Geoffrey de:—English? Flourished about 1200; author of a treatise on the art of poetry entitled the Nova Poetria, to which Chaucer refers NPTale 527-34. See Lounsbury, Studies II : 341-2; Skeat V : 257; Dict. Nat. Biog. under *Vinsauf.*

The poem is printed by Leyser, in his Hist. Poetarum et Poemarum Medii Aevi, Halle 1721, and separately Helmstedt 1724. There are many MSS in English libraries, *e. g.,* three among the Laud MSS, two among the Digby, one Bodley, and one Selden copy, all in the Bodleian; two in the library of Balliol College and three in Corpus Christi College, Oxford; two in the library of Trinity College, Cambridge, R 3, 29 and R 3, 51,—etc.

Virgil:—Died 19 B. C. Virgil is mentioned by Chaucer in HoFame 378, 449, 1244, 1483; in LGW (Dido) 924, 1002; in Troilus V : 1792, and in Friar's Tale 221. According to Lounsbury, Studies II : 250, Chaucer seems to have known only the Aeneid; this he partly summarizes in HoFame book I, and uses the story of Dido for the Legend.

It is a somewhat remarkable fact that more lines and phrases of Virgil do not appear in Chaucer. On Virgil and his influence see: Sandys, Hist. Class. Scholarship; Moore, Studies in Dante, vol. I; Comparetti, Virgil in the Middle Ages, Lond. 1895.

Vulgate:—See under Bible ante.

D. Editions of the Works or Poems

Introduction: On the Text of Chaucer

The gradual establishment of the canon has been, as described above, the work of many years. The so-called editions of Chaucer of the sixteenth and seventeenth centuries, as well as that of 1721, made no critical examination of the works which tradition or the editor's own verdict had connected with Chaucer's name; and each one of them added to the mass of spurious material printed in its predecessor. It has been the labor of Tyrwhitt, Bradshaw, Hertzberg, and Furnivall to separate the chaff from the wheat and present the evidence as to Chaucer's authorship or non-authorship of each poem.

Other tasks have been undertaken and wholly or partly accomplished in these years; the destruction of the legendary biography of Chaucer built up in the sixteenth century, and the substitution for it of the documentary evidence existing in English archives as to the poet's appointments, pay, and official missions. And, also, the foundations have been laid, by the establishment of the Chaucer Society in 1868, for the working-out of the text of Chaucer as it may have read in his own lost manuscript copies. This Society has reproduced, in parallel columns for purposes of comparison, and with diplomatic exactitude, the literal text of a large proportion of Chaucer's work as it stands in the existing manuscripts.

Since the founding of the Society the number of editions of the poet has greatly increased, keeping pace with the growing interest in Chaucer himself and with the widening study of the English language and of the Middle Ages. Editions both before and after this date have been of various types, and, barring out those which are popularized, modernized, or expurgated, we may distinguish three ways of presenting the Chaucerian text.

(1) The exact reproduction of some one manuscript. In such a treatment the "editing" is shown in the annotations, the suggested emendations, and in the appending of the noteworthy divergent readings of other MSS. Such an edition, nominally, was that of Thomas Wright, of the Canterbury Tales, in 1847-51.

(2) The building-up of a composite or "eclectic" text. Some or all MSS lie before the editor, and he selects now from one, now from another, according as he considers the text better. One MS may be followed for several lines, and then, when its reading seems confused or harsh to the editor, recourse may be had to another manuscript, and that manuscript's version of a line or a word may be incorporated in the edition. The resultant text is, of course, smooth and musical, for artificial selection has been exercised with that end in view; but every student should understand that it is obtained by an intrusion of the editor's personal judgment between

us and the author. The epoch-making edition of the Canterbury Tales by Tyrwhitt in 1775 was of this sort, as is that of Skeat.

(3) The third possible mode of editing is called the "critical." We know, to begin with, that no MS of Chaucer is without fault; No person, modern or medieval, could copy a long work without error. But unless two scribes are using the same original, it is highly unlikely that they will commit identical errors. Each man will become wearied, inattentive, stupid, in the course of his work; but no two men will show their weariness or misunderstandings in precisely the same way, if they are working from different originals. It is therefore the first problem of the "critical" editor to discover how far the texts before him are dependent upon or independent of one another in their errors; in other words, to construct the genealogical tree.

The definition of a critical text by M. H. Liddell, Athenaeum 1901 II : 597-8 is: "A text constructed in the light of all the critical evidence possible, regardless of the editor's personal opinion as to the inherent desirability, so to speak, of one reading over another. In such a use of the term no 'critical' text is possible until the mutual relations of the manuscripts have been ascertained."

To illustrate the above consider the text of Chaucer's Parlement of Foules. Of this poem we have fourteen MSS and a print by Caxton nearly equal in age to most of the MSS; all are printed by the Chaucer Society. Take a ruled notebook of large size and divide its pages into fifteen equal columns, beginning with an even page so that all fifteen readings can be spread out before the eye at once. At the head of each column put the name of a MS, and number the lines consecutively at the extreme left hand. If notes are then made, in each column, of the peculiarities of the MSS, it will appear, e. g., in line 5 that ten MSS have the word *wonderful* where the other five MSS have the word *dreadful;* in line 13 the same division of texts occurs, ten reading *I dare,* five *dare I;* in line 32 one group reads *seven it had,* the other *it had seven.* And when the entire poem has been worked through, the result is that in about fifty conspicuous cases the MSS divide in the same fashion, ten going one way and five the other. Such consistent agreement in deviation, in so many cases, cannot be by chance. We must consider that of the ultimate original, now lost, there were two main early copies, also now lost, differing in these points noted, and that these differences have been preserved in their existing descendants.

Notice here that numerical value is of no importance. The ten MSS are not twice as authoritative as the five; their agreement means one recension, and the agreement of the five means one.

A closer examination of the text will show, in the same way, differences within these two main groups; so that, on the basis of common divergences, we make subgroups within the principal groups A and Oxford. Each time that we find two or three MSS uniting in a set of minor differences from all the others, we must postulate a lost common original as the source of these special variations. Thus:

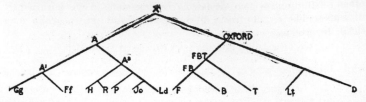

Here A, A¹, A², Oxford, FBT, FB, etc., are non-existent; we deduce the fact that they once existed from the idiosyncrasies of the known MSS, *i. e.*, Gg (Univ. Libr. Cambr.), Ff (Ff i, 6 of the same library), P (Pepys 2006), Jo (St. John's College Oxford), Ld (Laud 416), H (Harley 7333), R (R 3, 19 of Trin. Coll. Cambr.), D (Digby 181), Lt (Longleat 258), T (Tanner 346), F (Fairfax 16), B (Bodley 638). A¹ and A², FBT and FB, are obtained in precisely the same way as were A and Oxford. When, beyond these larger lines of distinction, we find two MSS such as D and Lt or Jo and Ld showing in common a number of petty mistakes and omissions not in even their nearest relatives, we have to suppose the existence of subdivisions in A or in Oxford to account for this.

This discussion is general and elementary; the possibilities of one existing manuscript's being derived from another also in existence, and the possibilities of contamination, are not entered upon here. Students desirous of pushing the question further may consult Westcott and Hort as cited below.

To the body of comparative evidence thus obtained, by the establishment of a genealogical tree, there must be added the intrinsic evidence. Which of these MSS are most prone to omit? to garble the text? It may sometimes happen that a very early copy, or a very well-written one, is derived from a careless text, or executed with less scrupulousness than is a copy a generation later; hence the date or the fine script of a codex does not determine its textual value, and is inferior in importance to evidence obtained by the comparative method.

In using this comparative evidence, it is plain that when A and Oxford (as represented by their existing descendants) agree, we have undoubtedly the text of X; but that when A and Oxford are in opposition, we do not know what X was, except in such cases as I have given in my paper[1] on the Parlement of Foules p. 9, where, by comparison with the Italian original, we can see what Chaucer

[1] Univ. of Chicago Decenn. Publ. VII : 1-22.

must have written, and see which group was right. Compare also
note on Troilus, Book I line 498, in the Nation 1894 II : 329.

It is not often, however, that such oppositions appear in a
Chaucerian text. Usually we find that one group and a part of the
opposed group show the same reading, and we can then see that the
other subgroup must have deviated. For example, in the Parlement
of Foules, line 65, the main group Oxford and the subgroup A^1
show the reading

> And was sumdel ful of harde grace

while the reading adopted by both Skeat and the Globe,—

> And ful of turment and of harde grace,

is found in the MSS of the subgroup A^2. But as it is not credible
that A^1 should independently of A^2 show one reading like Oxford
and not in A, and as it is credible that A^2 could have made an
alteration in the text, we must decide, critically, for the reading
given first above.

The possibilities of alteration in the text by the scribes are more
constant than is generally recognized. Deliberate attempt by the
scribe to make the sense clearer, or his desire to present his own
view on the subject of which he is writing, or even his wish to
improve upon the verse-flow of his original, may lead, and do lead,
to a number of minor changes in the text of medieval MSS. Thus,
the Chaucer-student John Shirley has introduced into his copies
not only a multitude of blunders, but also a definite proportion of
what may be attempted emendations, see Anglia 30 : 320-348. In
him, as in Caxton (see Modern Philology 3 : 174 ff.), is visible that
medieval conception of editorial duty which preserves the narrative
from change while paying no heed to variations in detail. Compare
the alterations in the text of a poem by Lydgate, and the probable
alterations in the Parlement of Foules text by MS Gg, discussed
in Univ. of Chicago Decenn. Publ. VII : 1-22. And note Foerster,
Anglia 20 : 140: "Dass es aber Schreiber gab, die durch Zusätze
oder sonstwie die Silbenzahl zu regeln trachteten, scheint mir trotz
Skeat's gegenteiliger Behauptung (Oxford Chaucer V : xxi) nicht
zu bestreiten."

The principles of textual transmission may be briefly digested
as follows:

(1) No copyist can escape error. As human character has been
the same in all ages, the tendency to error has manifested itself
in similar ways in all periods of history.

(2) Since, in spite of the general tendency to err, no two human
characters are alike in detail, no two scribes will show identical
errors if working independently. Persistent identity of error thus
implies identity of origin.

(3) If several or many copies of a lost original are preserved, a comparison of those texts may detect and eliminate the individual errors of each, and thus lead by exclusion to the construction of the archetype, or X. This construction we reach by determining the mutual dependence or independence of the MSS—by drafting the genealogical tree.

(4) In this comparison, no preconception as to the probable truth must interfere; the scribes are called as witnesses, and the comparison of their testimony must be made independent of all attempt to interpret. Interpretation or exegesis comes later.

Thus, if several varying versions of the same Chaucerian line, preserved in the MSS, are before the editor, he has no right to choose that one which seems to him likely in itself; if he does so, he is allowing a preconception to interfere, the preconception that his taste and Chaucer's must necessarily be in accord.

(5) The comparison must be of the whole, not of parts. See Moore as cited below.

(6) Of the various sorts of error, unconscious error is the most frequent. This results from weariness or carelessness; a word or verse may be omitted, a name misread, the eye may travel from the end of a line to a line ending similarly some distance below, and leave out all that intervenes, etc. The alterations of unconscious error are always for the worse, and can usually be recognized in even a cursory comparison.

(7) Semi-conscious error is more difficult to detect, and sometimes meets with the approval of uncritical editors. It arises in the case of a copyist who, reading the text before him and believing that he understands it, has fallen into a mental state in which he is no longer keenly examining his copy, but is letting his mind run free. In this condition he may hesitate for a moment at a word or phrase not quite familiar to him, and then write down what he thinks he sees, not what is actually there, "what is clearer and more satisfying to his mental state." Westcott and Hort, op. cit. below, point out that such changes usually "combine the appearance of improvement with the absence of its reality."

Thus, in Lydgate's prologue to the Story of Thebes, a "supplementary Canterbury Tale", the Host, calling upon Lydgate to narrate, bids him "Shet thy portos"; *portos* meaning a breviary carried by the monk, from which he had been murmuring prayers. The word was miswritten or misprinted *portes;* and Wülker, Altengl. Lesebuch II : 271, interprets it as doors or gates, used metaphorically for *lips.* If the change from *portos* to *portes* were semi-conscious, it was made by a scribe who substituted the known work for the unknown without realizing his deviation.

Compare the change of "fire and fleet and candlelight" into "fire and sleet", etc., see Athen. 1905 I : 400, etc.; though here a misreading of *f* to long *s* may have taken place. Semi-conscious error is allied psychologically to the phenomenon known as folk-etymology; see Greenough and Kittredge, Words and their Ways in English Speech, chap. 23, or Palmer, Folk-Etymology, Lond. 1882.

(8) Conscious error or deviation is still more likely to win the favor of uncritical editors. This is the deliberate alteration, by an intelligent or partly intelligent scribe, of the text before him, with the intention of bettering sense or metre. For the reason that human character has been alike in all ages, some of these changes are sure to seem to us, as well as to the scribe, improvements upon the reading offered by other MSS. Compare for instance line 353 of the Parlement of Foules, where all MSS but one concur in the reading:

> The swalow mordrer of the foules smale
> That maken hony on floures fresh of hewe,

and that one MS, R, reads *flyes smale*, a reading accepted and printed by Skeat and by the Globe Chaucer. If, however, we note the position of MS R in the genealogical tree, and note also the constant tendency of that MS to err or deviate, we shall recognize that it is impossible for it alone to have retained the archetypal reading at this point, and that the scribe, actuated by precisely the same impulse towards clearness and self-assertiveness which actuates the uncritical editor, has altered the text before him to remove what he believed an error Lounsbury, Studies I : 243, defended R's reading; but see Bright, Mod. Lang. Notes 17 : 220, Cook *ibid.* 21 : III-12.

(9) A full consideration of the tendency of some scribes to conscious error, and of the frequent possibility of semi-conscious error, in both of which there is usually present the appearance of improvement, leads us to the paradoxical rule that, unless a logical explanation be possible, we should, when editing, choose the more difficult reading. For example, returning to the diagram of MS-relations already given, if A^1 offers a "good" version of a line, and if the version in A^2 and Oxford can be explained as poor because of omission, *omission being a frequent failing of A^2 and Oxford*, we should have plausible ground for adopting the reading of A^1; but in such a case as line 65 above noted we have no right to take the reading of A^1 as against A^2 and Oxford.

This has been emphasized by Dr. Moore, in the prolegomena to his Textual Criticism of the Divina Commedia, a paper upon which too high a value cannot be put by intending Chaucer-editors. Dr. Moore says, *ibid.* pp viii-ix, "Copies of [the Divina Commedia] were multiplied with great rapidity, and unfortunately by copyists who were just able to take an unintelligent interest in what they were doing. . . The copyists were at the same time amateur, uncritical, and anonymous editors; and their experiments in 'restoration' have been as reckless and as fatal as any that we have had to deplore in other departments of art. It is indeed only in comparatively modern times that the true function of an editor or textual critic has been recognized to be the discovery of what the author actually *did write,* not the suggestion of what he *ought to have written.* . . . The textual critic has nothing to do with the superior correctness or clearness or elegance or taste of a reading. . . . . No writer is in every line perfect and infallible. There are times when even 'bonus dormitat Homerus'."

All of Dr. Moore's remarks in this paper, as well as his suggestions towards a Dante text, are of the utmost value. I select one or two of striking importance for Chaucer work. On p. xxxiii Dr. Moore speaks of Witte's complete collation of over 400 MSS for one canto of Dante, and says, "This method of selecting some one Canto as the basis of comparison has one most fatal defect . . . . that *the same MS exhibits very different characters of text not only in different Cantiche, but even in different Cantos of the same Cantica.*" This passage deserves especial stress in view of the recent attempt of Koch (following Zupitza), to construct a genealogical tree of the Canterbury Tales MSS on the basis of textual conditions in one Tale, that of the Pardoner. Although the number of Dante MSS is over ten times as great as that of Canterbury Tales MSS, so that it could less frequently have been possible for a Chaucer scribe to use several copies at one time, yet the greater separability of the English poem and the similar subdivided character of the work make Moore's dictum a priori probable for the Canterbury Tales. As ten Brink asserted for the Hengwrt MS, and as I point out below (Section III B) for a Royal, perhaps for a Selden codex, it is clear that a copy of the Tales could be written up to a certain point from an original of one type, and continued thereafter from a second archetype. It is also clear that touches of correction could be made in a copy, finished or unfinished, if another original came into the hands of the scribe. The result is so marked for Dante that Dr. Moore asserts, "If such a practice of copying . . . . were at all common, all hope of anything like a complete and systematic classification of MSS must be abandoned."

Dr. Moore is however speaking of an enormous mass of codices, nearer 600 than 500; and for the Canterbury Tales we have to do with less than 50 of approximate completeness. The unlikelihood, for Chaucer, of such alterations because of religious, political, or personal feeling as readily suggested themselves to Dante copyists, the freer and lighter movement of Chaucer's verse and thought, which thus presented less difficulty to the transcriber, have probably saved his text from some forms of distortion inevitable for Dante.

We may accordingly hope for a separation of the composite and the simpler texts of the Canterbury Tales after a comparatively small amount of effort, an amount far less than that to which Dante scholars have cheerfully addressed themselves. Perhaps the best method of arriving at this separation is by the selection of a body of test passages, which Dr. Moore recommends for Dante; and certainly the first step is a rough discrimination of the MSS according to the conditions of their Links, a procedure sketched by Bradshaw, and partly worked out in this volume, p. 243 and following.

This is true for the Canterbury Tales. In the Minor Poems we have a somewhat different problem, the approach to which lies, as I see it, only along the road of constructing for ourselves the personality of each copyist. A fairly large proportion of the Minor Poems have come down to us in commonplace books, collections of prose and verse written out by a dilettante or his copyist. From the ten to forty extracts which such a volume may contain, extracts often duplicated in other books where the Minor Poems are found,—it is possible to construct an idea of the individual workman, his intelligence, his scrupulousness, his ignorance, his self-assertiveness. We can and we should form conceptions of the principal copyists of the Minor Poems, of the Gg scribe, the Fairfax 16 scribe, the Tanner 346 scribes, and of John Shirley, before proceeding to the discussion of any single text existing in their script. Had the nineteenth century textual students of Chaucer applied to his poems half the energy and half the loyal resolve to find the true instead of the desirable, which has actuated Witte and Mussafia and Moore, we should to-day be able to claim more advance beyond Tyrwhitt.

References

Westcott and Hort's two-volume ed. of the New Testament in the original Greek, Lond. and N. Y. 1882; see the Introduction, in vol. II, part 2, on Methods of Textual Criticism, pp. 19-72 of the volume.

Moore's Contributions to the Textual Criticism of the Divina Commedia, Cambridge, Eng., 1889; see the Prolegomena, pp. v-xlvi

Editions of the Works, from Pynson to Skeat, etc.

Pynson, 1526. Blackletter. "Without a general titlepage, but containing three parts, seemingly intended to sell separately", Skeat I : 28. The copy in the Grenville Library of the British Museum has as titlepage for the first of the three parts, which are there bound together:—Here begynneth the boke of Troylus | and Creseyde | newly prin | ted by a trewe | copye |

(Woodcut of Troilus and Cressida)

Colophon:—Here endeth the boke of Troylus and | Creseyde / emprinted at London in | Fletestrete by Rycharde | Pynson / printer vnto | the kynges no- | ble grace

(On verso, woodcut of Pynson's device)

Titlepage to the second part:—Here beginneth the boke of Fame / made by Geffray Chaucer: | with dyuers other of | his workes |

(Woodcut of Fame below)

The House of Fame has the ending and epilogue written by Caxton. The Parlement of Foules follows, with no special titlepage, but a woodcut, above which is the heading, "The Assemble of Foules." Next, La Belle Dame sans Mercy, headed: This boke called la bele Dame Sauns | mercy / was translate out of Frenche | in to Englysshe by Geffray | Chaucer / flour of peo- | tes in our mo- | ther tong.—It has not the envoy or Verba Translatoris as in the form printed by Skeat VII : 325; but instead 6 stanzas of 7 lines, headed "Lenuoy de limprimeur", quite different, see under La Belle Dame in Section V below. There follow: Chaucer's Truth, headed "Ecce bonum consilium Galfredi Chaucer contra fortunam"; next, the Morall Prouerbes of Christyne, 202 lines in couplets, beginning "The great virtues of our elders notable"; the Lamentation of Mary Magdalen; the Letter of Dido to Aeneas; and Lydgate's Utter thy Language, headed "Thus endeth ye letter of Dydo to Eneas and here foloweth a lytell exortacion howe folke shulde behave them selfe in all companyes". Colophon:—Imprinted at London in Fletstrete | by Richarde Pynson / printer | to the kynges most no- | ble grace |

Titlepage to the third part:—Here begynneth the boke of Caunter | bury tales / dilygently and | truely corrected / and | newly printed |—(With a modified form of Caxton's proheme to his second edition.) Colophon:—Thus endeth the boke of Caunterbury / tales. Imprinted at London in flete- | strete / by me Rycharde Pynson |

printer vnto the kynges no- | ble grace: and fynis- | shed the
yere | of our | lorde god a M. CCCCC. | and xxvi. the fourth
| day of June. |

The printer's fullpage device occupies the recto of the last
leaf; the verso is blank. The book has running titles, but no
foliation; the first part has but one catchword (recto G4), the
second part has catchwords throughout, the third none. Leaves
11⅛ by 7¾ inches.

Upon Part II of this edition it may be noted:—The Moral
Proverbs of Christine, though correctly headed, are mentioned in
the colophon of La Belle Dame, which precedes them, as "And here
followeth certayne morall prouerbes of the foresayed Geffray Chaucers doyng." Ames, in his list of the contents of the volume,
accordingly gives "Certayne Morall Prouerbes of Chaucer", and
Skeat, citing Ames in Canon p. 160, footnote, notes the error without pointing out its source. Lounsbury, Studies I : 435, also refers
to the Moral Proverbs of Chaucer, quoting Urry's preface as his
authority for the list, and remarking that the next editor after
Pynson, Thynne, who did not reprint these or the Letter of Dido,
apparently exercised discrimination in the selection of what was to
be regarded as genuine. It should be noticed that the preface to
Urry gives the correct title, Morall proverbes of Christine; Lounsbury's error comes from some other source. These proverbs were
printed by Caxton, see Dibdin I : 72 ff. with a reprint of Caxton's
first page; Caxton added two seven-line stanzas stating that Earl
Rivers was the translator, for which also see Dibdin.

Upon Part III of this edition it may be noted:—Pynson apparently took his text of the Canterbury Tales from Caxton's second
or improved edition; Tyrwhitt remarks in the Appendix to his
Preface that such is the case, and that the material variations of
the 1532 and succeeding editions from this second text of Caxton's
are all for the worse. See the Urry-Thomas preface for Pynson's
proheme, where the contents of this edition are given.

See Dibdin, Typogr. Antiq. II : 515-520. A copy of this work
fetched £32 at the Ashburnham sale, see Athenaeum 1897 II : 67.

Of the works in this edition, La Belle Dame sans Mercy, the
Moral Proverbs of Christine, the Lamentation of Mary Magdalen,
the Letter of Dido, and Utter thy Language, are non-Chaucerian;
for notes on them see Section V here, and for notes on the genuine
works Sections III, IV.

Thynne, 1532. Blackletter. Titlepage:—The Workes of | Geffray
Chau | cer newly printed / with | dyuers workes whi | che were
neuer in | print before: | As in the table more playnly | dothe
appere. | Cum priuilegio |
(On the last recto, 383, at the top of the second column, before
Chaucer's epitaph, is the colophon:) Thus endeth the workes
of Geffray | Chaucer. Printed at London | by Thomas Godfray
| The yere of our lorde M. D. XXXII | Cum priuilegio a rege
indulto |—(The verso is blank.)

Contents:—Preface, in the form of a dedicatory letter by Thynne
(really by Sir Brian Tuke) to Henry VIII; the table of contents,
followed immediately by four short non-Chaucerian poems, viz.;
*Eight Goodly Questions with their Answers, *To the Kinges most
Noble Grace, etc., *When Faith Faileth, *It Falleth for a Gentleman. The Canterbury Tales (with a special titlepage); the *Romaunt of the Rose (with a special titlepage); Troilus and Cressida
(with a special titlepage); the *Testament of Cressida; the Legend
of Good Women; a *Goodly Balade of Chaucer (=Mother of Nurture); Boethius (with a special titlepage); the Dream of Chaucer,
with a special titlepage on the preceding verso (=the Book of the
Duchess, followed by Bukton, without heading and beginning "My
master &c"); the Assembly of Foules; the *Flower of Courtesy (its
envoy headed separately Balade symple); Pity (with a special
titlepage); *La Belle Dame sans Mercy; Anelida and Arcite; the
*Assembly of Ladies; the Astrolabe (with titlepage on the preced-
ing verso; the *Complaint of the Black Knight; *A Praise of
Women; the House of Fame; the *Testament of Love (with a
special titlepage); the *Lamentation of Mary Magdalen; the *Remedy of Love; the Complaint of Mars and Venus (with the Complaint
of Venus printed as the last part of the poem); the *Letter of
Cupid; *Ballad in Commendation of our Lady; *John Gower unto
the Worthy and Noble King Henry the Fourth; *the Cuckoo and
Nightingale (with the envoy to Alison appended, without heading);
*Scogan unto the Lords and Gentlemen of the King's House
(=Moral Balade); Stedfastness (without heading); Truth (headed
Good counsayle of Chaucer); Fortune (headed Balade of the Vyl-
lage without payntyng); Scogan (headed Lenuoye); *Go forth
King (without heading); Chaucer unto his empty Purse (the envoy
headed separately Chaucer vnto the King); Lydgate's *Wicked
Tongue (without heading). There follow the colophon, and
Surigon's Latin epitaph on Chaucer.

Spurious works, marked *, are discussed in section V here;
others in sections III, IV.

Lord Ashburnham's copy fetched £45, see Athenaeum 1897 II : 67.
Quaritch prices a copy at £57, see his Catalogue No. 193.

Reproduced in facsimile by the Oxford University Press, 1905,
as "The Works of Geoffrey Chaucer and Others. Being a Reproduction in Facsimile of the First Collected Edition 1532 from the
Copy in the British Museum, with an Introduction by Walter W.
Skeat, Litt. D., F. S. A." Skeat's introduction fills 44 pages.
Price of the work to subscribers, bound in Kelmscott boards, five
guineas; 1000 copies printed. See Nation 1905 I : 251-2.

The contents of this edition are given by Lounsbury, Studies I : 431-2. Furnivall, in his edition of Thynne's Animadversions, p. xlii, gives some bibliographical details in addition to those of the British Museum Catalogue. See Furnivall for particulars as to the life of Thynne, and the text of the Animadversions for Francis Thynne's account of his father's work.

It was noted already by Tyrwhitt, Appendix to the Preface note e, that the "preface by Brianus Tucca to Berthelet's edition" of Chaucer, praised by Leland in his life of Chaucer, was probably in reality the letter dedicatory prefixed to Thynne's edition. See Bradshaw's discovery of the truth of this surmise, in Furnivall's ed. of the Animadversions, Hindwords p. xxvi; and Lounsbury, Studies I : 266-7.

Tyrwhitt, in the Appendix to his Preface, commented on this edition, so far as its Canterbury Tales text is concerned, and re-marked that its material variations from Caxton's second edition are all for the worse.

The text of the Canterbury Tales presents some marked features, important because of the derivation of several successive editions from this by Thynne. The order of the Tales is Knight, Miller, Reeve, Cook (unfinished); Man of Law; Squire, Merchant, with Words of the Franklin assigned to the Merchant; Wife of Bath, Friar, Summoner; Clerk; Franklin; Second Nun, Canon's Yeo-man; Doctor, Pardoner; Shipman, Prioress, Rime of Sir Thopas, Melibeus, Monk, Nun's Priest (with epilogue); Manciple; Parson. The Man of Law's endlink (now called the Shipman's prologue), introduces the Squire in its line 17; there are spurious prologues to Doctor and to Shipman; the epilogue of the Nun's Priest does not introduce anyone; and there is no Retractation at the close of the Parson's Tale. Although the epilogue to the Nun's Priest's Tale is combined with the Manciple's prologue as in Caxton's second edition, differences exist in other ways between Thynne's arrange-ment and Caxton's. The assignment of the Franklin's Words to the Merchant, and the appearance of the spurious prologues, are departures from Caxton, in the direction of what is here termed, p. 247, the Corpus-Mm group of MSS; relations of MSS and prints are not yet worked out.

The House of Fame has a spurious conclusion of twelve lines, written by Caxton, and reprinted by Thynne with changes in the first few lines to adapt it to the longer fragment of the poem which he printed.

Previous to the issue of the above-mentioned facsimile, various texts of the 1532 Chaucer had been printed, viz.: By the Chaucer Society, the texts of the Book of the Duchesse, the House of Fame, the Legend of Good Women, Bukton, Stedfastnesse, the Pardoner's Tale; and the Romaunt of the Rose was announced as No. LXXXII.

The preface is printed in Flügel's Neuenglisches Lesebuch, pp. 304-6.

Skeat also based many of his texts in vol. VII upon the 1532 Thynne, viz.: the Testament of Love, John Gower unto the Worthy and Noble King Henry the Fourth, the Complaint of the Black Knight, the Flower of Courtesy, Ballad in Commendation of our Lady, To my Sovereign Lady (printed in Thynne as a part of the foregoing poem), Wicked Tongue (entitled Ballad of Good Counsel), La Belle Dame sans Mercy, Cuckoo and Nightingale, Assembly of Ladies, Mother of Nurture, Go forth King. Twelve of the twenty-nine selections in VII are thus from the Thynne of 1532.

On this edition see Lounsbury, Studies I : 265-70; Skeat, Canon, chaps. IX, X; Maskell in N. and Q. 1883 II : 381; 1884 I : 138.

The careless and inaccurate note of Courthope, Hist. Eng. Poetry I : 252, is censured by Kaluza, Engl. Stud. 22 : 271 ff.; Kaluza remarks that in Thynne's ed. 18½ poems are genuine and 22½ spurious.

William Thynne, editor of this work, who died 1546, was Clerk of the Kitchen to Henry VIII, favored by that sovereign, and apparently a man of means. He was an enthusiastic student of Chaucer and a collector of many MSS; his nephew, Sir John Thynne, built Longleat House and became the ancestor of the Marquesses of Bath; and as this Sir John was also a collector and one of the "overseers" of his uncle's will, there is a possible connection between the Longleat library and the 1532 Chaucer.

Thynne, 1542. Blackletter. Titlepage:—The workes of | Geffray Chau | cer newly printed, wyth | dyuers workes whych were | neuer in print | before: | As in the table more playnly | doth appere. | Cum Priuilegio | ad imprimendum Solum. | Printed by Wyllyam Bon- | ham dwellynge at the sygne | of the Kynges armes in | Pauls Church- | yarde | 1542.

(With woodcuts)

As noted by Quaritch, Catalogue No. 193 p. 20, the various copies of this edition bear the names of different booksellers, Toye, Kele, Petit, Bonham, Reynes, etc. At the Ashburnham sale a Petit copy fetched £18, a Bonham copy £20. This latter is priced by Quaritch loc. cit. at £36; the collations of it given ibid. are: A, 4 leaves, B-Z in sixes, Aa-Yy in sixes, AA-TT in sixes. See Nation 1907 I : 128 for sale of the Van Antwerp copy, "the finest known."

Quaritch, loc. cit., says: "The edition dated 1542 is frequently supposed to be identical with the undated edition, having the same booksellers' names, but it is a quite distinct edition and far rarer. The contents are the same as in Godfrey's text of 1532, *with the addition however of* the Plowman's Tale as the last eight leaves of the Canterbury Tales. It was printed here for the first time." [Not correct; Godfrey printed it, separately, previous to 1542; see Bradshaw as cited in Furnivall's ed. of Animadversions, p. 101.] On the contents see Skeat, Canon p. 93 ff. Skeat VII prints the Plowman's Tale and the Moral Balade from this edition.

Thynne, no date. Blackletter. Titlepage:—The workes of | Geffray Chau- | cer newly printed, with | dyuers workes whi- | che were neuer in | print before. | As in the table more playnly | dothe appere. | Cum priui | legio. [Colophon:] Thus endeth the workes of | Geffray Chaucer. | Imprynted at London by Thomas | Petit dwellyng in Paules churche | yarde at the sygne of the | Maydens heed. | Cum priuilegio ad imprimen- | dum solum. |
(With two woodcuts only, differing from those of 1542.)
Collations of a Petit copy, in Quaritch, Cat. No. 193, are: A, 8 leaves, B-V in sixes, X four leaves, Aa-Zz and Aaa-Ppp in sixes, Qqq five leaves. Priced by Quaritch *ibid.* at £32.
Dated in the Brit. Mus. Cat. "1545?"; by Quaritch *ibid.* "about 1547"; by Skeat, Canon p. 161, "about 1550." Lowndes speaks of the several eds. of the booksellers of "1542, 1546, 1555" etc. Hazlitt, Collections and Notes, 1867-76, s. v. *Chaucer,* insists that the undated ed. preceded that of 1542. Like the ed. of 1542, this bears the names of various booksellers.
Contents the same as in 1542 except that the Plowman's Tale is before the Parson's; see Thynne, Animadversions, ed. Furnivall, pp. 68, 69, for censure of this arrangement. On the ed. see preface to the Urry Chaucer; Maskell in N. and Q. 1883 II : 381-2; Skeat as cited.

Stow, 1561. Blackletter. Of this edition two issues exist. The earlier has as titlepage:—The workes | of Geffrey Chaucer, newlie printed | with diuers addicions, whiche | were neuer in print before: | with the siege and | destruccion of | the wor | thy | Citee of Thebes, compiled | by Ihon Lidgate | Monke of | Berie. | As in the table more | plainly doeth | appere | 1561. |

(This title in a woodcut border.)

The other impression has as titlepage:—The workes of Geffrey Chau- | cer, newly printed, with diuers ad- | dicions, whiche were neuer in printe before: With the siege and | destruccion of the worthy citee of Thebes, compiled | by Jhon Lidgate, Monke of Berie. | As in the table more plainly | dooeth appere. |

The lower two-thirds of the page is filled by a large woodcut of Chaucer's arms, with the couplet:

Vertue flourisheth in Chaucer still,
Though deathe of hym, hath wrought his will.

The colophons of the two impressions are identical, viz.:— Imprinted at Lon- | don by Jhon Kyngston for Jhon | Wight, dwellyng in Poules | Churchyarde | Anno. 1561. |

Both are printed in double columns; the former impression has in the prologue to the Canterbury Tales 26 woodcuts of the pilgrims, which, according to Quaritch, Catalogue No. 234, are printed from the same blocks as were employed by Pynson for his ed. of the Canterbury Tales. These cuts do not appear in the other impression of this ed. of "Stow." The earlier impression is the more valuable; Quaritch as cited prices them at £48 and £40; in his catalogue No. 243 he terms a copy of the second impression cheap at £21. [The library of Columbia University has a slightly imperfect copy of the earlier, that of Harvard University a copy of the later impression.]

In sixes. Text from A i-U vi, Aa-Zz, Aaa-Uuu vi, two more leaves. Upon the titlepage follows the letter of Thynne to Henry VIII; the table of contents: the four brief poems printed by Thynne at the close of his table of contents; an elaborate woodcut titlepage to the Canterbury Tales, showing in "tree" form the York-Lancaster ancestry of Henry VIII. The Tales are followed by the *Romaunt of the Rose; Troilus and Cressida; the *Testament of Cressida; the Legend of Good Women "with a balade",=*Mother of Nurture; Boethius; the Dream of Chaucer,=Book of the Duchesse; Bukton, (without a heading in the text); the Assembly of Foules; the *Flower of Courtesy; Pity; *La Belle Dame sans Mercy; Of Quene Anelida and false Arcite; the Complaint of Anelida to false Arcite; the *Assembly of Ladies; the Astrolabe; the *Complaint of the Black Knight; *Praise of Women; the House of Fame; the *Testament of Love; the *Lamentation of Mary Magdalen; the *Remedy of Love; the Complaint of Mars and Venus (with the Complaint of Mars and the Complaint of Venus as sub-headings); the *Letter of Cupid; *Ballad in Commendation of our Lady; *John Gower unto the Worthy and Noble King Henry the Fourth; *Saying of Dan John; *Yet of the Same; *Balade de bon Consail; *Cuckoo and Nightingale; *Scogan unto the Lords; Stedfastnesse (without heading); Good Counsaile of Chaucer (=Truth); Balade of the Village without painting (=Fortune); Scogan (headed Lenuoye); *Go forth, King (without heading); Chaucers Words vnto his emptie Purse (the envoy headed separately Chaucer vnto the Kinge); *Wicked Tongue (for heading see Section V here); *Balade in the praise and commendation of Geffrey Chaucer.

[After this:] "Here foloweth certaine woorkes of Geffray Chaucer, whiche hath not here tofore been printed, and are gathered and added to this booke by Iohn Stowe."

A balade made by Chaucer teching what is gentilnes, or whom is worthy to be called gentil.   [Gentilesse]

A Prouerbe against couetise and negligence.   [*Proverbs]

A balade which Chaucer made against Women Unconstaunt.

[*Newfanglenesse]

A Balade which Chaucer made in the praise or rather dispraise of
women for their doubleness.   [*Doublenesse]
The Craft of Lovers.   [*The Craft of Lovers]
A Balade.   [*Of their Nature]
The Ten Commandments of Love.   [*The Ten Commandments, etc.]
The Nine Ladies Worthy.   [*The Nine Ladies, etc.]
Alone Walking. (no heading)   [*Virelay]
A Ballade.   [*In the Season]
A Ballade.   [*O Mercifull]
How Mercurie with Pallas Venus and Minarva appered to Paris of
Troie, he slepyng by a fountain.   [*How Mercurie, etc.]
A Balade pleasaunt.   [*I have a Lady]
An other Balade.   [*O Mossie Quince]
A balade warnyng men to beware of deceitptfull women.   [*Beware]
These verses next following were compiled by Geffray Chauser and
in the writen copies foloweth at the ende of the complainte of
petee.   [*Ballad of Pity]
A Balade declaring that wemens chastite Doeth moche excel all
treasure worldly.   [*Chastity]
The Court of Love.   [*The Court of Love]
(Words to Adam.)   [Words to Adam]
(Surigon's Epitaph on Chaucer.)
(Lydgate's Story of Thebes.)   [*Story of Thebes]

In the above list of the contents the non-Chaucerian pieces are
marked with an asterisk, and may be found discussed in Section V
here, under the titles as given by Stow except for those pieces
added by him, which are here treated under the titles in brackets
at the right of Stow's. The other works are discussed in Sections
III, IV. Gentilesse and the Words to Adam, also (doubtfully)
the Proverbs, are the only additions made by Stow now admitted to
the canon.

Tyrwhitt, in his Account of the Works of Chaucer, says "It
would be a waste of time to sift accurately the heap of rubbish
which was added by John Stowe to the Edit. of 1561. Though we
might perhaps be able to pick out two or three genuine fragments
of Chaucer, we should probably find them so soiled and mangled, that
he would not thank us for asserting his claim to them." Skeat I :
31 ff., Canon 117 ff., gives elaborate analysis and discussion of this
edition; see also Dibdin IV : 469; Corser, Collectanea IV : 322;
Maskell in N. and Q. 1884 I : 141; Lounsbury, Studies I : 269, 437.

Whether Stow had any real share in this edition, further than
the appending of the body of poems above listed, is uncertain.
Many of these additions are found in manuscript in the codex
Trinity College Cambridge R 3, 19, from which it is highly probable
that Stow took them. His attribution of this "heap of rubbish" to
Chaucer casts suspicion upon his notes as to authorship made in
other cases, see Anglia 20 : 404-20.

John Stow, born 1525?, died 1605, was a London tailor. From
1560 on he devoted himself "to the search of our famous antiquities", and was an ardent book collector and copyist. His first
publication was the Chaucer just described, and he gave to Speght,

for the 1598 Chaucer, further notes and a list of the poems of John Lydgate, see below. The rest of his work was historical and antiquarian; like Cotton (see Section VII A here), he became an object of suspicion to Government because of the mass of documents he had collected, and his house was searched more than once. In his last years he was exceedingly poor, and James I granted him a license to beg, a printed copy of which is bound in the miscellaneous volume MS Harley 367. Most of his MSS are now in the British Museum; they passed at his death to Sir Symonds d'Ewes, and from him to Harley Earl of Oxford, thence to the nation as part of the Harleian collection. The codex Brit. Mus. Adds. 29729, partly in Stow's hand, partly in that of his scribe, is copied from various sources, one a Shirley volume, see under Shirley in Section VII B here. His possession of much of the work of Lydgate in MS is asserted in his heading to the list of Lydgate's works given to Speght. His notes are frequent in MSS owned or used by him; he wrote a tiny, scratchy hand, termed "uncommonly neat" in the Gent. Mag. 1837, I : 48-52. The codices Brit. Mus. Adds. 34360 and Trin. Coll. Cambridge R 3, 20, perhaps Fairfax 16, were at one time in his possession; but the statement in the Dict. Nat. Biog. that "Harley 2255, which contains transcripts by Shirley of poems by Lydgate and Chaucer, was once Stow's property", is wrong in every particular. The "Stowe MSS" of the British Museum have nothing to do with John Stow.

Speght, 1598. Blackletter. Titlepage: in a woodcut border designed as a portal with columns:
    The | Workes of our Antient and Learned | English Poet, Geffrey Chavcer, | newly Printed. | In this Impression you shall find these Additions. |
    1   His Portraiture and Progenie shewed.
    2   His Life collected.
    3   Arguments to euery Booke gathered.
    4   Old and obscure words explaned.
    5   Authors by him cited, declared.
    6   Difficulties opened.
    7   Two Bookes of his, neuer before Printed.
London, | Printed by Adam Islip, at the charges of | Bonham Norton. Anno 1598. |
[In a medallion at the top of the woodcut is in small italics :]

CHAVCER

Out of the old fields, as men sayth,
Commeth all this new corn, fro yere to yere;
And out of old books, in good fayth,
Commeth al this new science that men lere.

[At the foot of the design is:]

Ouid.

Seris venit vsus ab annis.

[In Notes and Queries 1862 I : 322 it is remarked that the edition has different titlepages. Others seen by me run as above except that the last portion is:]

London, | Printed by Adam Islip at the charges of | Thomas Wight, Anno 1598 |

or

Londini | Impensis Geor. Bishop | Anno 1598 |

The work was entered at Stationers' Hall in 1592 to Abel Jeffes, in 1594 to Adam Islip. See N. and Q. 1863 I : 2.

Contents :—Dedication to Sir Robert Cecil by Speght (one page) ; on the verso, "To the Readers" (two pages) ; a letter by Francis Beaumont the elder to Speght; on the verso of the fourth leaf a verse-dialogue of 20 lines between the Reader and Chaucer ; a leaf having on the recto, copperplate, Chaucer's full-length figure surrounded by the arms of various allied families, the verso blank; the life of the poet, filling b ii to c iii (eight leaves), and preceded by a special title page, b i; the "Arguments" mentioned on the title page of the work ; the Epistle of Thynne to Henry VIII, in blackletter ; the table of contents, A ii verso to mid of A iii verso. On the next leaf are the four short poems first printed by Thynne, viz.,—*Eight Goodly Questions with their Answers, *To the Kings Most Noble Grace, and (unmarked) the quatrains beginning respectively *When Faith Faileth and *It Falleth for a Gentleman.— There follow, from Ai-U in sixes, the Canterbury Tales, with a special woodcut titlepage of the English kings, York-Lancaster to Henry VIII; the *Romaunt of the Rose, with same titlepage ; Troilus and Cressida ; the *Testament of Cressida ; the Legend of Good Women ; *A Goodly Balade of Chaucer (=*Mother of Nurture) ; Boethius ; the Dream of Chaucer (marked in the table of contents as "otherwise called the booke of the Duchesse or Seis and Alcione, with a balad to his master Bucton") ; Bukton (without any heading) ; the Assembly of Foules ; the *Flower of Courtesy (its envoy separately marked Balade simple) ; Pity ; *La Belle Dame sans Mercy ; Anelida and Arcite (the Complaint of Anelida separately headed) ; the *Assembly of Ladies ; the Astrolabe ; the *Complaint of the Black Knight ; *A Praise of Women ; the House of Fame ; the *Testament of Love ; the *Lamentation of Mary Magdalen ; the *Remedy of Love ; the Complaint of Mars and Venus (with the Complaint of Mars and the Complaint of Venus as sub-headings) ; *Letter of Cupid ; *Ballad in Commendation of Our Lady ; *John Gower unto the Worthy and Noble King Henry the Fourth ; *A saying of Dan John ; *Yet of the Same ; *Balade de Bon Consail (=*If it befalle) ; the *Cuckoo and Nightingale (with the envoy to Alison following) ; *Scogan unto the Lords ; Stedfastnesse (without any heading) ; Truth ; Fortune (entitled Balade of the Village without painting) ; Scogan (headed Lenuoy) ; *Go Forth King (without heading) ; Purse ; Lydgate's *Wicked Tongue ; *Balade in the Praise and commendation of Maister Geffray Chaucer for his golden eloquence.

Then, on sig. Ppp ii recto, is the heading:—"Here followeth certaine workes of Geffray Chaucer, annexed to the impression printed in the yeare 1561: With an adition of some thinges of Chaucers writing, neuer before this time printed, 1597. All collected and adioined to his former workes by Iohn Stowe." Stow's additions, as in the 1561 Chaucer, with his headings, follow. After the *Court of Love is inserted,—

"Chaucers dreame, neuer before this time published in print. That which here tofore hath gone vnder the name of his dreame, is the book of the Duchesse: or the death of Blanch Duchesse of Lancaster."

This poem is now termed the *Isle of Ladies. It closes with stanzas apparently of another poem; see under *Fairest of Fair, Section V here.

The *Flower and the Leaf follows, then the Words to Adam, headed "Chaucers Words vnto his owne Scriuener." At the foot of the leaf, verso,—"Thus endeth the workes of Geffray Chaucer."

Lydgate's *Story of Thebes, with woodcut titlepage, Ttt v, follows; then, on the last leaf of Zzz, is a list of Lydgate's works, headed,— "A Catalogue of translations and Poeticall deuises, in English mitre or verse, done by Iohn Lidgate Monke of Bury, whereof some are extant in Print, the residue in the custody of him that first caused this Siege of Thebes to be added to these works of G. Chaucer."

From Aaaa (six leaves) through Bbbb (eight leaves) are found the explanation of old and obscure words, list of French phrases, list of authors cited by Chaucer, corrections and annotations, Faults Escaped.

The Canterbury Tales are in sixes, A-U; the signatures Aa-Tt are in sixes, Uu and Xx in eights, Yy and Zz in sixes. Aaa-Zzz are in sixes. Folio numbering begins with B i, at the opening of the Knight's Tale; at the head of that page is a woodcut of the Knight, and on the verso facing, after the close of the Prologue on the preceding recto, is a large cut of the arms of Chaucer, with the motto,—"Vertue flourisheth in Chaucer still   Though death of him, hath wrought his will."

The non-Chaucerian contents of this volume, marked with an asterisk as above, are discussed in Section V here, the genuine works in Sections III, IV.

This edition is often referred to as of 1597; it was probably published, as Todd says, in the January, February, or March of 1597-8.

Stow says of Chaucer, in his Survey of London, ed. Thoms, London, 1876, pp. 171-2: "His works were partly published in print by William Caxton, in the reign of Henry VI, increased by William Thinne, esquire, in the reign of Henry VIII; corrected and twice increased, through mine own painful labours, in the reign of Queen Elizabeth, to wit, in the year 1561; and again beautified with notes by me, collected out of divers records and monuments, which I delivered to my loving friend Th. Speght; and he having drawn the same into a good form and method, as also explained the old and obscure words, &c., hath published them in anno 1597."

Speght states in the Life prefixed to the edition that the pedigree there printed was drawn up by Glover, the Somerset Herald, and that the portrait and coats of arms are by John Speed.

The letter by Francis Beaumont is the work of Francis Beaumont the elder, see Athenaeum 1904 II : 766, where the error of Lounsbury in ascribing it to the dramatist is pointed out. This had been earlier remarked by Hazlitt, Collections and Notes, 1867-1876, s. v. *Chaucer,* and by Garnett in Am. Jour. Phil. 19 : 441-2 (1898).

The Life prefixed to this edition is reprinted ante Section I. A note on the Glossary will be found in Section VI G below.

Skeat VII prints the Flower and Leaf from this edition.

For comment on this edition see the Urry Chaucer of 1721; Edinburgh Review 132 : 9; Maskell in Notes and Queries 1884 I : 141; Corser's Collectanea IV : 322 ff.; Lounsbury, Studies in Chaucer I : 270, cp. 273, 275; Skeat, Canon 136 ff.

Immediately upon the appearance of this edition, Francis Thynne, son of the editor of the 1532 Chaucer, addressed to Speght, and dedicated to Sir Thomas Egerton, a long letter entitled "Animaduersions vppon the Annotacions and Corrections of some imperfections of impressiones of Chaucers workes (sett downe before tyme, and nowe) reprinted in the yere of oure lorde 1598 sett down by Francis Thynne." In this letter Thynne pointed out many misstatements and errors by Speght, especially in the explanation of words; the letter seems to have been communicated, in part at least, to Speght, and the edition of 1602 adopts some of the changes indicated. See below under discussion of the Glossary, Section VI here, and under discussion of the 1602 edition, next following here. The Animadversions were printed by Todd in his Illustrations, edited by Kingsley for the EETS in 1865, and re-edited with much addition by Furnivall for that Society and the Chaucer Society, 1876. See Ch. Soc. 2d Series No. 13.

Speght, second edition, 1602, blackletter. Titlepage:

The | Workes of Ovr | Ancient and learned English | Poet, Geffrey Chavcer, | newly Printed. | To that which was done in the former Impression, | thus much is now added. |

1 In the life of Chaucer many things inserted.

2 The whole worke by old Copies reformed.

3 Sentences and Prouerbes noted.

4 The Signification of the old and obscure Words prooued: also Caracters shewing from what Tongue or Dialect they be deriued.

5 The Latine and French, not Englished by Chaucer, translated.

6 The Treatise called Jacke Vpland, against Friers: and Chaucers A. B. C. called La Priere de nostre Dame, at this Impression added.

London. | Printed by Adam Islip | An. Dom. 1602. |

Contents:—Copperplate page with full-length figure of Chaucer surrounded by shields of alliance, this on verso, the recto blank; the titlepage as above, its verso blank; dedication by Speght to Cecil; To the Readers; the letter of Beaumont to Speght; The Reader to G. C.; two short poems, the first by Thynne; the life of Chaucer. The back of the leaf carrying the Stemma of Chaucer is blank. The life ends c iij verso; there follows another titlepage with the arms of Chaucer, its verso blank; the letter to Henry VIII; the table of contents; the four short poems as in 1598. These are on Ai; on Aii begin the Canterbury Tales. Double columns in sixes, A-Uuu; then two unmarked leaves, the second having on its recto a list of errata, its verso blank.

The differences between this edition and that of 1598 are:—The dedication to Cecil is rewritten, declaring, among other, that "both by old written Copies, and by Ma. William Thynns praise-worthy labours, I haue reformed the whole Worke, whereby Chaucer for the most part is restored to his owne Antiquitie." The "To the Readers" is rewritten, and contains the remarks on Chaucer's language censured by Hickes as below, also comment on Chaucer's versification cited p. 465 here. Thynne is thanked, and it is stated that much is due to his help and direction in restoring old words, correcting the text, and arranging the notes. The letter of Beaumont is altered; e. g. the 1598 says of Spenser that "his much frequenting of Chaucers antient speeches causeth many to allow farre better of him, then otherwise they would"; this passage runs in 1602, "his much frequenting of Chaucers auncient words, vvith his excellent imitation of diuerse places in him, is not the least helpe that hath made him reach so hie."

Changes in the Life of Chaucer are noted in Section I here, with the reprint of the 1598 Life.

The Arguments are removed from their 1598 position, and set at the beginnings of the corresponding works; there is no separate titlepage to the Canterbury Tales or to the Romaunt of the Rose. The works follow in sequence as in 1598; after the Flower and Leaf and before the Words to Adam are inserted:—

"Chaucers A. B. C. called La Priere de nostre Dame made, as some say, at the request of Blanch, Duchesse of Lancaster, as a praier for her priuat vse, being a woman in her religion very deuout." Jack Upland follows, then the Words to Adam, the colophon as in 1598, the Story of Thebes (without a separate title-page), the catalogue of Lydgate's works, the "Old and obscure words explaned", the Latin and French translated, and "Authours by name declared." The ABC is reprinted Ch. Soc. SPT.

It is noticeable, under the Works, that the heading of Purse and of its envoy are altered so as to attribute them to Hoccleve; —"Th. Occleue to his emptie Purse", and "Occleue vnto the King". The 1598 Chaucer has *Chaucer* in both cases; the 1687 follows 1602.

On this ed. see Corser, Collectanea IV : 325 ff.; Maskell in N. and Q. 1884 I : 142; Skeat, Canon pp. 141-2; Tupper in Mod. Lang. Notes 12 : 347-353 points out that Dryden used this Chaucer rather than that of 1598. Furnivall, ed. of Animadversions p. xvii, says that the changes in the 1602 glossary show that Speght had a copy of Thynne's letter. Lounsbury, Studies I : 275, compares the text of the Prologue in the two eds.; *ibid.* p. 343 he says that the 1602 ed. first attempted thorough punctuation, which "was fairly well performed." On the small share of Speght in the editing see Lounsbury, op. cit. I : 270.

Hickes, in his Thesaurus, sect. Grammatica Anglosaxonica, pp. 57 and 58, says of this ed., alluding to the prefatory "To the Readers",—"turpiter ignorans Editor Chauceri ita praefatur Lectorem—Chaucer many times understands his verb, as I *not* what men him call, for I know not." And again, "Editor Chauceri, nihil antiqui sapiens, dicit ipsum imitatum fuisse Graecos in vehementius negando per duo negativa."

To the non-Chaucerian contents of this ed. as listed under the Stow Chaucer and the 1598 Speght ante is here added Jack Upland. All these are discussed under Section V here; for genuine works see Sections III, IV.

Speght, 1687. Blackletter. Titlepage:

The | Works | of our | Ancient, Learned, & Excellent | English Poet, | Jeffrey Chaucer. | As they have lately been Compar'd with the best Manuscripts, | and several things added, never before in Print. | To which is adjoyn'd, | The Story of the Siege of Thebes, | By John Lidgate, Monk of Bury. | Together with | The Life of Chaucer, | Shewing | His Countrey, Parentage, Education, Marriage, Children, | Revenues, Service, Reward, Friends, Books, Death. | Also a Table, wherein the Old and Obscure Words in Chaucer are explained, and | such Words (which are many) that either are, by Nature or Derivation, Arabick, | Greek, Latine, Italian, French, Dutch, or Saxon, mark'd with particular Notes for | the better understanding their Original. | London | Printed in the Year, MDCLXXXVII. |

Contents:—Copperplate page with figure of Chaucer and shields of alliance, as in the earlier Speghts, its recto blank; the dedication to Cecil; To the Readers; the letter of Beaumont; the titlepage with the arms of Chaucer, its verso blank; the letter to Henry VIII; the table of contents; the four short poems first printed by Thynne; the Reader to G. C.; the two short poems to Speght, one being by Thynne; the life of Chaucer. On the recto following is an Advertisement to the Reader, signed J. H., the second paragraph of which says "whereas in the Life of Chaucer mention is made of a Tale, called the Pilgrim's Tale, which is there said to have been seen in the Library of Mr. Stow, and promis'd to be printed so soon as opportunity should offer; I have for the procuring of it, used all Diligence imaginable, not only in searching the publick Libraries of both Universities, but also all private Libraries that I could have access unto; but having no success therein, I beg you will please to accept my earnest endeavour to have serv'd you, and take what is here printed, it being all that at present can be found that was Chaucer's." The verso of this advertisement is blank; on the next recto the Canterbury Tales begin, with B. The contents fill B-Ssss in fours, the last two leaves blank; for list and arrangement see 1602 Speght, from which this is reprinted.

As in 1602, the Complaint to his Purse is said to be by Hoccleve, and the envoy is separately marked as by Hoccleve. The Isle of Ladies is marked Chaucer's Dream. At the end of the volume is printed an Advertisement, which calls attention to the recently discovered conclusions of the Cook's Tale and of the Squire's Tale; these are printed, twelve lines for the Cook and ten lines for the Squire. For notes on the spurious works, as marked under the 1598 and 1602 Speght, see Section V here; for the genuine, Sections III, IV.

Urry, 1721. Titlepage:

The | Works | of | Geoffrey Chaucer, | compared with the | Former Editions, and many valuable MSS. | Out of which, Three Tales are added which were never before Printed: | By John Urry, | Student of Christ-Church, Oxon. Deceased: | Together with a | Glossary, | By a Student of the same College. | To the Whole is prefixed | The Author's Life, newly written, and a Preface, giving an Account | of this Edition. |

[Below is a cut of Chaucer's tomb.]

London, | Printed for Bernard Lintot, between the Temple Gates. MDCCXXI. |

Contents:—Large engraving of Urry; titlepage as above; large engraving of Chaucer; the life of Chaucer, followed by Testimonies of Learned Men concerning Chaucer and his Works; the letter to Henry VIII as in Thynne and the Speghts; commendations of Chaucer; preface; table of contents; the four short poems printed by Thynne and in Speghts. On the last verso is the licence to print, facing the first page of the Canterbury Tales.

The Canterbury Tales; the *Romaunt of the Rose; Troilus and Cressida; the *Testament of Cressida, with Urry's statement that it is by "Henderson"; the Legend of Good Women; the *Mother of Nurture; Boethius; the Dream of Chaucer (=the Book of the Duchess); Bukton, headed "This seems an Envoy to the Duke of Lancaster after his Loss of Blanch", and beginning "My master, &c."; the Assembly of Foules; the *Flower of Courtesy; Pity, without the continuation; *La Belle Dame sans Mercy; Anelida; the *Assembly of Ladies; the Astrolabe; the *Complaint of the Black Knight; the *Praise of Women; the House of Fame; the *Flower and Leaf; *Testament of Love; *Lamentation of Mary Magdalen; *Remedy of Love; Complaint of Mars and Venus; Complaint of Mars; Complaint of Venus; *Letter of Cupid (with a heading saying that it is not Chaucer's but Hoccleve's); *Ballad in Commendation of Our Lady; *John Gower unto the Worthy and Noble King Henry the Fourth; *Saying of Dan John; *Yet of the Same; *Balade de bon Consail; *Cuckoo and Nightingale, with the *Envoy to Alison appended; *Scogan unto the Lords and Gentlemen of the King's House; Stedfastnesse (without heading); Gode Counsaile of Chaucer (=Truth); Balade of the village without painting (=Fortune); Scogan (headed L'envoye); *Go forth King (without heading); Purse (the envoy separately headed Chaucer unto the King) ; *Wicked Tongue ; *Ballad in the praise and commendation of Chaucer ; then Stow's additions, so headed ; these are, as before, with his headings :—Gentilesse ; *Proverb ; *Against Women Unconstant ; *Doublenesse ; *Craft of Lovers ; *Ballad (=Of their Nature) ; *Ten Commandments of Love ; *Nine Ladies Worthy ; *Alone Walking (=Virelay, no heading) ; *A Ballad (=In Feuerere) ; *A Ballad (= O Merciful) ; *How Mercury, etc. ; *Ballad Pleasant (=I have a Lady) ; *O Mossie Quince ; *Beware ; *Ballad of Pity ; *Chastity ; *Court of Love ; *Chaucer's Dream (=the Isle of Ladies, with the heading explaining its difference from the Book of the Duchess) ; the ABC ; *Jack Upland ; the *Mery Adventure and the *Tale of Beryn ; the Words to Adam. The Glossary, with special titlepage, follows ; then an explanation of some of the authors cited by Chaucer, additions to the Glossary, and errata. In folio, double columns, a-n, B-8R. Engravings of pilgrims at head of Tales, that for Rime of Sir Thopas following the table of contents.

For notes on the non-Chaucerian contents of the volume, marked with an asterisk in the above list, see Section V here; for the genuine works see Sections III and IV.

To the Canterbury Tales there were added in this edition not only the spurious tale of Beryn with its prologue, the Mery Adventure, but also two spurious Links, those preceding Doctor and Shipman; the Retractation, which had been omitted since the 1532 Thynne, here appears again. Lydgate's Story of Thebes is not reprinted. The Preface recognizes, though indistinctly, the existence of groups in the Canterbury Tales.

Hearne, Remarks and Collections VI : 95-96, says that Urry desired to use blackletter in this edition, and that the change to whiteletter was made after his death; this is the first edition of Chaucer not in blackletter. The original advertisement, in the Monthly Catalogue for Jan. 1714-15, reprinted N. and Q. 1875 I : 7, says, "A new Black Letter, Accented, has been cast on purpose for this Work, for the ease of the Reader."

Urry's agreement for publication is reprinted Gent. Mag. 1779, p. 438. Left unfinished by his death, the work was continued by Ainsworth, who also died before its completion; and the final revision and completion were entrusted to Timothy Thomas. According to Tyrwhitt, Appendix to Preface, the preface and glossary to this edition were by Timothy Thomas, though the Brit. Mus. Cat. speaks of the glossary as by "J. Thomas." See a letter by W. Brome published by Furnivall, N. and Q. 1874 II : 381. Tyrwhitt also says ibid. that the life of Chaucer for this edition was "very uncorrectly drawn up by Mr. (John) Dart, and corrected and enlarged by William Thomas." See Dart's complaint, in his Westmonasterium, I : 87, of the changes made in his biographical work without his consent. It is the retention of some of Dart's remarks in the Life, alongside of Thomas' remarks in the Preface, which cause the variety of opinion as to Chaucer's versification seen in this edition; cp. Lounsbury, Studies I : 290.

9

On the edition see Tyrwhitt, Appendix to Preface, Advertisement to the Glossary (last paragraph); Retrospective Review 14 : 314; Nichols, Literary Anecdotes I : 196-98; Todd, p. xl of introduction to Illustrations; Ellis, Specimens of Early Eng. Poetry I : 227; Horne, p. xl of introduction to the 1841 modernizations of Chaucer; Maskell in N. and Q. 1884 I : 142; Lounsbury, Studies I : 283 ff.; Skeat, Canon, chap. XIV. All critics have directed severe censure against Urry's treatment of the text. Thomas, in the preface, says that in "restoring Chaucer to his feet again" Urry had observed that "the discreet addition or omission of several initial or final syllables in use in Chaucer's time would often remedy the faults of unskilled transcribers"; that he accordingly exercised his judgment in that respect, and in the sounding or not sounding of the participial -ed, which he printed -id when it was to be taken as a separate syllable, and -ed when it was not. In the same way, "where the plural termination was quiescent", he printed it -es, writing it -is when it was distinct. "And in short I find it acknowledged by him that whenever he could by no other way help a Verse to a Foot, which he was perswaded it had when it came from the Maker's hands, but lost by the Ignorance of Transcribers, or Negligence of Printers, he made no scruple to supply it with some Word or Syllable that serv'd for an Expletive. But I find at the same time that he had once a design of enclosing such words in hooks . . . to distinguish them from what he found justified by the authority of MSS. But how it came to pass that so just, useful, and necessary a Design was not executed, I can not satisfy the curious Reader." See also extract printed under 1721 in Section VI A here.

On Thomas' work in the Preface, and on the Glossary, see Section VI G here. Corser, Collectanea IV : 328-330, says that the preparation of the glossary delayed the work more than two years.

The manuscripts used by Urry, with some additions and remarks by Thomas, are listed in Thomas' preface. Urry's I = Harley 1758; Urry's II = Harley 1239; Urry's III = Sloane 1685; Urry's IV = Sloane 1686; Urry's VII = Royal 18 C ii; Urry's VIII = Royal 17 D xv; Urry's XI = Univ. Libr. Cambr. Gg iv, 27; Urry's XIII = the Northumberland MS; Urry's XIV = the Lestrange MS, now the Devonshire MS; the Cholmondeley MS added by Thomas is now the Delamere; Thomas' Spelman MS is now a Phillipps MS, and Harley 34 B. 18 = Harley 78. Of the other Urry MSS, inquiry was made by Furnivall in N. and Q. 1871 II : 526 regarding the Chandos, Worseley, Canby, Norton, and Ely. The Norton is ncw Brit. Mus. Egerton 2863; the others are still unidentified.

***

Entick. In 1736 J. Entick issued proposals for an edition of

Chaucer; see print of extracts, with comment, by Furnivall in N. and Q. 1895 I : 126.

Johnson. In the list of publications projected by Dr. Johnson (see Hawkins' life of him, London 1787) is:
"Chaucer, a new edition of him, from manuscripts and old editions, with various readings, conjectures, remarks on his language, and the changes it had undergone from the earliest times to his age, and from his to the present. With notes explanatory of customs, etc., and references to Boccace and other authors from whom he has borrowed; with an account of the liberties he has taken in telling the stories; his life; and an exact etymological glossary."

Of which Lounsbury remarks (Studies I: 299): "An edition of Chaucer by Johnson could never have been an authority, but it would always have proved an entertainment."

Note on Collections of British Poetry

The first collected edition of British poets was by Blair of Edinburgh, from Milton down, filling 42 volumes duodecimo, published 1773. In 1776 John Bell undertook a more extended collection, from Chaucer down, to fill 109 volumes; some of these appeared more than ten years later. His collection was printed in Edinburgh and sold in London. In rivalry with his, the London booksellers put out the collection known as the Johnson, for which Dr. Johnson wrote the Lives of the Poets; this appeared in 60 volumes small octavo, 1779, comprising the poets from Cowley down, and being in reality little more than a re-edition of Bell. This edition was reprinted in 1790 with 15 additional volumes. Edinburgh booksellers then decided to extend the enterprise to include earlier writers, and produced the series edited by Anderson; in opposition to which the Chalmers edition was brought out by the London booksellers. This last was more extensive, and Chalmers was more frank as regards his debt to Johnson's Lives.
This note is from Sanford and Walsh: The Works of the British Poets with Lives of the Authors. Philadelphia, 1819, preface. The American series was projected for 50 volumes, 25 of which appeared; see comment below.
Cooke's edition of the British Poets, in 80 parts, n. d. (1798 ff.) was published at London, as was the 70-volume edition of 1805 by the Whittinghams; this latter did not include Chaucer. The two Whittinghams, uncle and nephew, founded the Chiswick Press in 1811, and in 1822 published the Chiswick edition of the British Poets, in 100 volumes; the Chaucer of

this collection is discussed below. After the death of the elder Whittingham, in 1840, his nephew became associated with William Pickering, who adopted, in 1830, the trademark and name of the famous Aldine printinghouse of Venice. The Aldine Series of the British Poets comprised 53 volumes, and was issued from 1835 to 1853; the Chaucer appeared, as noted below, in 1845. The business of this famous house later passed to Mr. George Bell. Robert Bell, 1800-1867, was not a publisher, but issued, from 1854 on, his edition of the British Poets, in 24 volumes, covering the poets from Chaucer to Cowper, but with gaps. This was the first annotated. edition of the poets; the Chaucer (noted below) appeared in 1854-56. The Edinburgh publisher, James Nichol, brought out, 1853 ff., a collection of the British Poets, largely edited by George Gilfillan; this included the Canterbury Tales.

Bell, 1782. In John Bell's The Poets of Great Britain Complete from Chaucer to Churchill, vols. 1 to 14, 24mo. Each volume has a general London titlepage, with designs various for each volume, and bearing dates from August 1, 1782 to May 29, 1783; this general titlepage is in each volume followed by a printed title dated Edinburgh 1782.

Reprinted London 1807, with a critique by Thomas Warton, condensed from the History of English Poetry. 14 vols. in 7.

Contents:—Vol. 1, Tyrwhitt's Essay and Introductory Discourse; an extract from Urry's preface; Thynne's dedication to Henry VIII, and four brief poems, *To the King's Most Noble Grace; *Eight Goodly Questions; *Prophecy; *It Falleth for a Gentleman;—then the lines The Reader to Geffrey Chaucer, prefixed to Speght's edition, and the lines to Chaucer by Thynne, from Speght. Vols. 2-5, the Canterbury Tales, text from Tyrwhitt; his notes are at the foot of the page. Vol. 6, *Gamelyn; the *Plowman's Tale; the *Mery Adventure; *Beryn. Vol. 7, the *Romaunt of the Rose. Vol. 8, the *Romaunt of the Rose; Troilus and Cressida. Vol. 9, Troilus and Cressida. Vol. 10, the *Testament of Cressida; the Legend of Good Women; the *Praise of Women; *La Belle Dame; the *Assembly of Ladies. Vol. 11, *Chaucer's Dream (=the Isle of Ladies); the Dream of Chaucer (=the Book of the Duchess); Bukton (headed "This seems an envoy to the Duke of Lancaster after his loss of Blanch"); the Assembly of Foules; How Pyte is Dede and buried in gentyle herte (with the continuation as noted here under Ballad of Pity); the *Cuckoo and Nightingale (with envoy to Alison); the Gode Counsaile of Chaucer (=Truth); Chaucer's ABC, called La Prière de Nostre Dame. Vol. 12, Anelida and Arcite; the *Complaint of the Black Knight; the Complaint of Mars and Venus (with the Complaint of Mars and the Complaint of Venus separately headed as parts of one and the same poem); *Lamentation of Mary Magdalen; *Flower and Leaf; *Court of Love;

*Remedy of Love; *A Saying of Dan John; *Yet of the Same; the
Motto to *Jack Upland. Vol. 13, the House of Fame; Certaine
Balades: =*Godely Balade of Chaucer (=*Mother of Nurture);
*Balade in Commendacion of our Ladie; *Balade de bon Consail
(="If it befalle"); Stedfastness (without heading); Balade of the
Village without Paintying (=Fortune); *Go forth King (without
heading); Scogan (headed Lenvoy); Purse (its envoy headed
separately Chaucer unto the King); Balade made by Chaucer teching what is Gentilnes; A *Proverbe against Covetise and Negligence; *Balade which Chaucer made against Woman Unconstaunt
(=Newfangleness); *Balade which Chaucer made in the Praise or
rather Dispraise of Women for their Doubleness (=*Doubleness);
the *Craft of Lovers; *A Balade (="Of their Nature"); the *X
Commandments of Love; the *IX Ladies Worthy; *Alone Walkyng
(without heading); *A Ballade (="In Feuerere"); *A ballade (="O
merciful"); *How Mercurie, etc.; *A Balade Plesaunte (="I have
a Lady"); *An Other Balade (="O Mossie Quince"); "A Balade
warnyng men to beware of deceitful women" (=*Beware); *A Balade
declaring that womens chastitie doth moche excel all treasure
worldly (=*Chastity); Chaucer's Words unto his own Scrivener;
*John Gower unto the Noble King Henry the Fourth; *A Balade
of Good Counseile (=*Wicked Tongue); *Scogan unto the Lords,
etc.,—Testimonies of Learned Men to Chaucer's Worth. Vol. 14,
Glossary.

The editing of these volumes appears in such traces as the
following: A note upon "How Mercurie, etc.", saying that
Juno has been substituted for Speght's and Urry's *Minerva;*
the placing of the supplementary Canterbury Tales to follow
the genuine tales; the rearranging of much of the material, the
poems to "ladies" being in vol. 10, the dreams, except the
House of Fame, in vol. 11, the complaints in 12, the ballads
in 13. The Ballad of Pity is moved up to follow Pity; the
"Dream of Chaucer" is made to follow "Chaucer's Dream";
the Remedy of Love is put next to the Court of Love. The
editor seems to have been guided more by agreement in sound
of titles than by the actual contents of poems. As compared
with Urry, the only omissions are the prose works (this being
specifically a poetical collection), the Flower of Courtesy, and
the Letter of Cupid. These two poems were shown in Urry's
edition to be the work of Lydgate and of Hoccleve; and the
Bell edition also relegates John Gower unto the King, Scogan
unto the Lords, and Lydgate's Ballad of Good Counsel to the
close of the collection, as if doubtful about including them.
However, the Testament of Cressida is reprinted, and no notice
taken of Tyrwhitt's rejections of many poems from the canon;
but his remark about the confusion of leaves in the Romaunt
of the Rose has been heeded by this editor. See Notes and
Queries 1894 I : 446.

The texts of poems other than the Canterbury Tales are
from Urry; the Tales are from Tyrwhitt. See Tyrwhitt's letter
in the Gentleman's Magazine for 1783, vol. I, p. 461, in which

he says that it is unwise to go to law for a property which is
attended with no profits, but that his name is used, and his text,
in this edition of Bell's, "without my consent, approbation, or
knowledge." The non-Chaucerian works of the above list,
marked with an asterisk, are discussed in Section V here, the
genuine in Sections III, IV.

The portrait of Chaucer prefixed to this edition is by Cook;
the 14 frontispieces were designed by Stothard.

See note on Cooke's edition of Chaucer, second entry below.

Anderson. The Works of the British Poets. With Frefaces,
Biographical and Critical, by Robert Anderson, M. D.
  Vol. I. Chaucer, Surrey, Wyatt, and Sackville. Edinburgh
1793 ff., London 1795.

Contents:—Life; Canterbury Tales, with *Gamelyn, *Plowman,
*Mery Adventure, and *Beryn at end after Parson; MISCEL-
LANIES, =*Rom. of Rose; Troilus and Cressida; *Testament of
Cressida; Legend of Good Women; *Praise of Women; *La Belle
Dame sans Mercy; *Assembly of Ladies; *Chaucer's Dream (=Isle
of Ladies); Dream of Chaucer (=Book of the Duchess); Bukton
(headed "This seems an envoy to the Duke of Lancaster after his
loss of Blanche", and beginning "My master &c."); Assembly of
Foules; *Cuckoo and Nightingale (with Envoy to Alison con-
tinuous with it); Pity (with the continuatory Ballad of Pity headed
as in Stow); Truth; ABC; Anelida; *Complaint of the Black
Knight; Complaint of Mars and Venus; Complaint of Mars, Com-
plaint of Venus; *Lamentation of Mary Magdalen; *Flower and
Leaf; *Court of Love; *Remedy of Love; *Saiyng of Dan John;
*Yet of the Same; *Motto to Jack Upland; House of Fame;
"CERTAINE BALADES &C". =*Mother of Nurture; *Ballad in
Commendation of Our Lady; *Ballad de bon consail (= If it be-
falle); Stedfastnesse (without heading); Fortune (headed Balade
of the Village without Painting); Scogan (headed Lenvoye); *Go
Forth King (no heading); Purse (its envoy headed separately
"Chaucer unto the King"); Gentilesse; *Proverbs; *Newfangle-
ness; *Doubleness; *Craft of Lovers; *Of their nature; *Ten
Commandments of Love; *Nine Ladies Worthy; *Alone Walking
(without heading); *In Feverere; *O Merciful; *How Mercury,
etc. (as in Stow); *Ballad Pleasant; *O Mossie Quince; *Beware;
*Chastity; Words to Adam.
  The Works of Surrey follow.

Anderson says in the Life of Chaucer prefixed: "The present
edition of the Canterbury Tales is from Tyrwhitt's incomparable
edition. The Plowman's Tale, Tale of Gamelyn, Adventure, and
Merchant's Second Tale, omitted by Tyrwhitt, have been
retained, though all evidence, internal and external, is against the
supposition of their being the production of Chaucer. The
genuine miscellaneous pieces of Chaucer are printed from
Urry's edition, exclusive of those pieces which are known to be
the production of other authors, and the anonymous composi-

tions which, from time to time, have been added to Chaucer's, in the several editions, without any evidence whatever."

Anderson's omissions are not however very extensive: the prose pieces, *i. e.*, Boethius, the Astrolabe, the Testament of Love, Jack Upland; the bits printed just after the table of contents by Urry and his predecessors; the Flower of Courtesy; the Letter of Cupid; Lydgate's Wicked Tongue; Gower to Henry IV; and Scogan to the Lords. All Stow's additions are reprinted except the Story of Thebes. Thus Anderson, as compared with Bell, cuts out only the bits after the table of contents, and the three poems relegated by Bell to the end of the collection. The non-Chaucerian works, marked with an asterisk in the above list, are discussed in Section V below.

Cook. Lowndes mentions, s. v. *Poetry* (British), an edition by Cooke, London n. d., (1798 ff.), 18mo. with plates, which contains Chaucer in 14 vols. This is apparently identical with Bell of 1782, above discussed.

Chalmers. The Works of the English Poets from Chaucer to Cowper, including the Series Edited, with Prefaces, Biographical and Critical, by Dr. Samuel Johnson; and the Most Approved Translations. The Additional Lives by Alexander Chalmers, F. S. A.   London 1810.

Vol. I, Chaucer. "In the present edition . . . Mr. Tyrwhitt's text has been followed for the Canterbury Tales; and for the remainder of his works, the black-letter editions, which, with all their faults, are more to be depended on than Urry's."

Contents:—Life by Chalmers; Canterbury Tales; *Romaunt of the Rose; Troilus and Cressida; *Testament of Cressida; Legend of Good Women; *Mother of Nurture; Dream of Chaucer (=Book of the Duchesse, followed by Bukton, the latter without heading and beginning "My master &c."); Assembly of Foules; Anelida; *Complaint of the Black Knight; *Praise of Women; House of Fame; Complaint of Mars and Venus, with sub-headings—Complaint of Mars, Complaint of Venus; *Cuckoo and Nightingale (with the Envoy to Alison in continuation, without heading); *Court of Love; *Chaucer's Dream (=Isle of Ladies); *Flower and Leaf; ABC; Certain Ballads (printed as if it were the heading to Stedfastnesse); Good Counsel of Chaucer (=Truth); Ballad of the Village without Painting (=Fortune); Lenuoy (=Scogan); *Go forth King (without heading); Purse; Gentilesse; *Proverb; *Newfangleness; Words to Adam. The "Prose Works of Chaucer" follow,—Boethius, the Astrolabe, the *Testament of Love.

"Poems Imputed to Chaucer or by Other Authors, and Usually Printed with his Works" follow. *Flower of Courtesy; Pity; *La Belle Dame sans Mercy; *Assembly of Ladies; *Lamentation of Mary Magdalen; *Remedy of Love; *Letter of Cupid; *Ballad in Commendation of our Lady; *John Gower unto the Noble King

Henry the Fourth; *Saying of Dan John; *Yet of the Same; *Ballad de bon consail (=If it befalle); *Scogan unto the Lords and Gentlemen of the King's House; Stedfastnesse (without heading); Fortune (headed Ballad of the Village without Painting); Scogan (headed Lenuoy); *Go forth King (without heading); Occleve to his empty Purse (=Chaucer's Purse); Occleve unto the King (=the envoy to Chaucer's Purse); *Wicked Tongue; *Ballad in the praise and commendation of Geffrey Chaucer.

"Here followeth Certain Works of Geffrey Chaucer annexed to the Impressions printed in the years 1561 and 1602. All collected and adjoyned to his Former Works by John Stowe."—Gentilesse; *Proverb; *Newfangleness; *Doubleness; *Craft of Lovers; *Of their Nature; *Ten Commandments of Love; *Nine Ladies Worthy; *Alone Walking (without heading); *In the season of Feuerere; *O Mercifull; *How Mercury, etc.; *I have a Lady; *O Mossie Quince; *Beware; *Ballad of Pity; *Chastity; *Jack Upland; *Story of Thebes; *Gamelyn; *Plowman's Tale; *Mery Adventure; *Beryn.   Glossary.

This list contains some repetitions and contradictions. Gentilesse, Proverb, and Newfangleness are twice printed, once in the first group of Chaucer's works, and again in the group of Stow's additions. Stedfastness, Fortune, Scogan, Go Forth King, and Purse, are twice printed, once as by Chaucer, and again among the Poems Imputed to Chaucer. The last-named poem is definitely assigned to Hoccleve when given for the second time, a fact which shows that Chalmers used the 1602 or 1687 ed. of Speght as well as the 1598, where this error is not made. Pity is included among the Poems Imputed to Chaucer. For notes on the non-Chaucerian works of this volume, marked with an asterisk in the above list, see Section V below; for others, Sections III, IV.

Cumberland. In Notes and Queries 1872 II : 86, L. B. Thomas asks "Who was the editor of a Chaucer in my possession, and when was it published?" The volume is described as Chaucer's Canterbury Tales and Other Poems, published by John Cumberland, 2 Cumberland Terrace, Camden New Town; 2 vols. small 12mo, no date, 926 pages of print; portrait and vignette titlepages, 21 cuts by J. Mills. Besides the poems, a sketch of English poetry, a life of Chaucer, extensive footnotes, and a glossary. The editor of N. & Q. adds that Cumberland published the British Theatre, etc., between 1823 and 1832; I assign the ed. conjecturally to a position just anterior to Singer's; cp. the note on Bukton as below.

This is probably the Chaucer alluded to in N. & Q. 1849 p. 30 as "Doble's", as it is printed by Thomas Dolby, Catherine St., Strand, London. A copy is in the Douce collection of the Bodleian Library. The preface,—without signature,—cites Tyrwhitt and Chalmers, and remarks that the ed. is limited to the well authenticated poems of Chaucer, omitting his translations, *e. g.,* Romaunt of the Rose and Troilus. Contents: Canterbury Tales, Legend of Good Women, Book of the Duchesse, House of Fame, *Complaint of the Black Knight, *Cuckoo and Nightingale, *Chaucer's Dream (= Isle of Ladies), ABC, Bukton, Ballad sent to King Richard (=Stedfastness), Good Counsel of Chaucer (=Truth), Scogan, Purse, Gentilesse, *Proverb, Words to Adam. Tyrwhitt's notes are liberally cited, but there seem many independent suggestions. On Bukton the editor notes that he puts it among the Minor Poems and gives it a title as in the Harleian MS; this, he says, has not been previously done. He also states that he has added extensively to Tyrwhitt's glossary. The editor's name does not appear.

For discussion of the non-Chaucerian poems of this ed., marked with an asterisk in the above list, see Section V below; for the genuine works, Sections III and IV.

Chiswick. The British Poets, including Translations. In One Hundred volumes. Vols. 1-5, The Poems of Geoffrey Chaucer. Chiswick, Whittingham, 1822.

The publisher's advertisement contains this statement: "In the course of time, and in consequence of printing from unrevised copies, innumerable typographical errors, fatal in many instances to the sense, had crept into the compositions of our poetical writers. To remove these blemishes, every poem has been minutely examined by a gentleman who is supposed to be competent to restore the purity of the text, and who, as he 'reverences the lyre', has naturally been zealous in the performance of his duty."

This "gentleman" was probably Samuel Weller Singer, who did much literary work for the firm of Whittingham, who wrote the life of Chaucer for this edition, and whose initials are appended to a note very near the close of vol. 5. The Life of Chaucer contains these paragraphs, by Singer: "It is with this edition (1532) and that of 1542, which are in general very correctly printed, that the minor poems of Chaucer have been collated for the present impression, with the exception of a few which appeared for the first time in Speght's edition of 1597. 'The Flower and the Leaf' is given from Mr. Todd's collation of Speght and Urry, and the 'Canterbury Tales' are given from Mr. Tyrwhitt's edition. . . . The unwarrantable liberties which have been taken in Urry's edition, in order to make the verse read smoothly to the modern unpractised ear, render that edition of little value. The time which a collation of manuscript copies with the printed text would occupy precluded the possibility of having recourse to their aid upon the present occasion; yet it is hoped, that the reader is here presented with a more correct copy of the minor poems than has been hitherto given to the public."

Contents :—Life of Chaucer by Singer ; the Canterbury Tales ; the *Romaunt of the Rose; Troilus and Cressida; Legend of Good Women ; *Mother of Nurture ; "The Book of the Duchess or the Death of Blanche, commonly entitled Chaucer's Dream"; Bukton (without heading, the first line reading 'My master, Bukton') ; Assembly of Foules ; Anelida ; *Complaint of the Black Knight ; *Praise of Women ; House of Fame ; Complaint of Mars and Venus (with subheadings—Complaint of Mars, Complaint of Venus) ; *Cuckoo and Nightingale (with *Envoy to Alison following without heading, after an Explicit) ; *Court of Love ; *Chaucer's Dream (=Isle of Ladies) ; *Flower and Leaf ; ABC ; Stedfastness (headed Ballad sent to King Richard) ; Truth ; Fortune (headed Ballad of the Village without Painting) ; Lenuoy de Chaucer a Scogan ; *Go Forth King (without heading) ; Purse ; Gentilesse ; *Proverb ; Pity ; *Virelai ; *Prophecy ; Words to Adam.   Glossary.

The Prophecy has a brief introductory note by Singer, stating where he found the text; at the close is appended "There follow some Monkish Latin Verses. S. W. S." As Furnivall has pointed out, Ch. Soc. PT p. 423, the 1845 Aldine Chaucer, using Singer's texts, copies this introductory note, altering its verb to the passive voice. At the end of the volume is reprinted Tyrwhitt's list of words and phrases not understood.

Singer has omitted from this ed. not only the prose works (Boethius, the Astrolabe, and the spurious Testament of Love accepted by Tyrwhitt), but also a number of poems rejected by Tyrwhitt, whose account of the works he evidently studied. Thus, he does not reprint the Testament of Cressida, the Flower of Courtesy, La Belle Dame, the Letter of Cupid, Gower to Henry IV, Scogan unto the Lords, the Sayings of Dan John, Wicked Tongue, Doubleness, Beware, the Ballad in Commendation of Our Lady, Lamentation of Mary Magdalen, Assembly of Ladies, Remedy of Love, the spurious Canterbury Tales, or the additions of Stow condemned by Tyrwhitt as a "heap of rubbish." Certain of these additions, following Tyrwhitt, he does retain, . . . the Court of Love, Gentilesse, Proverb, Words to Adam; and he reprints other poems now considered spurious, but still recognized by Tyrwhitt, the Complaint of the Black Knight, Chaucer's Dream (=Isle of Ladies), Flower and Leaf, Cuckoo and Nightingale, Virelai. In a few cases he goes against Tyrwhitt's verdict, . . . the Praise of Women, and Envoy to Alison; he also prints the Prophecy, from MS. On these works see under Section V below.

The Ballad of Pity, and Newfangleness, omitted by Singer, do not return to the canon until Skeat again includes them.

It should be noted that Singer, following Tyrwhitt, emends the first line of Bukton to its proper reading, wrongly given since 1532. Furnivall is incorrect in saying, Ch. Soc. PT p. 423, that the Moxon Chaucer first did this, and that the poem is not in the Chiswick or the 1845 Aldine; he emends this statement on a slip issued with the Ch. Soc. Odd Texts.

Dove. The Dove Chaucer, mentioned Athen. 1841 p. 107, I have not been able to trace.

Moxon. The Poetical Works of Geoffrey Chaucer, with an Essay on his Language and Versification, and an Introductory Discourse, together with Notes and a Glossary. By Thomas Tyrwhitt. London, Edward Moxon, 1843.

Reprinted 1851, 1855; 1860 and 1874 by Routledge & Sons, with another titlepage.

The misleading titlepage of this edition is corrected by Skeat, I : 30 note. Skeat there points out that the "works of Chaucer were not edited by Tyrwhitt, and that in this edition only the Canterbury Tales are from Tyrwhitt, the other texts from the blackletter editions." This note was first made by "F. N." in N. and Q. for August 3, 1889, p. 86, where the Saturday Review of June 8, 1889 is reprimanded for failing to notice the dishonest titlepage; the same omission was made in Athen. of 1843, p. 712. See also Skeat, N. and Q. 1889 II p. 133, and Hall *ibid*. p. 214. Skeat says "the book is all Tyrwhitt's down to p. 209, and again all Tyrwhitt's from p. 443 to end, which makes the deception so clever and so complete." Skeat's language otherwise is very strong: "cruel fraud," "indelible disgrace," etc. See his discussion V : xii ff. But the error is again made in the Cambridge Hist. of Eng. Lit. II : 515.

Compare for misleading titlepages the Blackwoods and the Crowell editions discussed under date 1880 below.

Contents :—Tyrwhitt's papers; the Cant. Tales; the *Rom. of the Rose; Troilus and Cressida; *Court of Love; Pity; Anelida; Assembly of Foules; *Complaint of the Black Knight; ABC; Book of the Duchess; House of Fame, with Thynne's conclusion; *Chaucer's Dream (=Isle of Ladies); *Flower and Leaf; Legend of Good Women; Mars; Venus; *Cuckoo and Nightingale; Minor Poems, =Bukton (headed L'Envoy de Chaucer a Bukton, and beginning "My master Bukton"); Ballad sent to King Richard (=Stedfastness); Good Counsel of Chaucer (=Truth); Ballad of the Village without Painting (=Fortune); Scogan; Purse; Gentilesse; *Proverbs; Words to Adam; *Virelai. Tyrwhitt's account of the works of Chaucer follows, then the Glossary.

The Moxon does not reprint some articles contained in the Chiswick, . . . Go forth King; Envoy to Alison; Mother of Nurture; Praise of Women; Prophecy; like the Chiswick,

it does not include Newfanglenesse, or the Ballad of Pity.
For its non-Chaucerian contents, marked above with an asterisk,
see Section V below.

Aldine. In Pickering's Aldine Poets, 6 vols., London, 1845. With
a memoir by Sir Harris Nicolas, see under Life of Chaucer,
Section I B here, and with Tyrwhitt's Essay. The text of the
Cant. Tales from Tyrwhitt; the other texts from the Chiswick
Chaucer, see Furnivall's note PT p. 423.

Reprinted 1852; revised by Morris in 1866; and the revised
edition reprinted with Appendices, 1870, n. d. (1872), 1880, 1891,
1893.

Contents:—Vol. 1, Nicolas' memoir, Tyrwhitt's Essay and Introd.
Discourse; Vols. 2 and 3, the Cant. Tales; Vol. 4, the *Romaunt of
the Rose, Troilus; Vol. 5, Troilus, Legend of Good Women, *Goodly
Balade of Chaucer (=Mother of Nurture), Book of the Duchesse,
Bukton (without heading), Assembly of Foules; vol. 6, Anelida, the
*Black Knight, *Praise of Women, House of Fame, Complaint of
Mars and Venus, Complaint of Mars, Complaint of Venus, *Cuckoo
and Nightingale (with Envoy to Alison appended), *Court of Love,
*Chaucer's Dream (=Isle of Ladies, with Tyrwhitt's assertion of
its genuineness), *Flower and Leaf, ABC, Certain Ballads, =
Balade sent to King Richard (=Stedfastness), Good Counsaile of
Chaucer (=Truth), Balade of the Vilage without Painting (=For-
tune), Scogan, *Go forth King (without heading), Purse, Gentil-
esse, *Proverbs, Pity (without the continuatory ballad), *Prophecy,
Words to Adam.

When this edition was revised by Morris, the texts were
taken from the MSS; the contents and arrangement of the eds.
1870 ff. are: Vol. I, Nicolas' memoir, Tyrwhitt's Essay and
Introd. Discourse, a paper on Chaucer's Pronunciation by A. J.
Ellis, a short paper on the genuineness of the Romaunt of the
Rose by F. J. Furnivall, one on the order of the Cant. Tales,
from Furnivall's Temporary Preface, and a Glossary. Vols. 2
and 3 contain the Canterbury Tales. Vol. 4, the *Court of Love,
the *Cuckoo and Nightingale, the *Flower and the Leaf, ABC,
*Chaucer's Dream (=Isle of Ladies), the Boke of the Duchesse,
Anelida, House of Fame, Legend of Good Women. Vol. 6
includes the *Romaunt of the Rose, the *Complaynt of a
Loveres Lyfe (=the Black Knight), Mars and Venus, a *Goodly
Balade of Chaucer (=Mother of Nurture), *Praise of Women,
and the Minor Poems, i. e., Pity, Fortune (headed Ballade de
Village sauns Peynture), Ballade sent to King Richard (=Sted-
fastnesse), Purse, Good Counseil of Chaucer (=Truth), *Pros-
perity, Ballade (=Gentilesse), Scogan, Bukton, Aetas Prima,
*Leaulte vault Richesse, *Proverbs, *Roundel, *Virelai,
*Prophecy, Words to Adam, *Oratio Galfridi Chaucer. In
an appendix are other texts of Fortune, Truth, and Aetas
Prima.

Morris' additions were: Prosperity, Aetas Prima, Leaulte vault Richesse. For the poems marked with an asterisk see Section V below.

Reprinted as noted above. For mention of the undated edition see Notes and Queries 1884 II : 4. Morris' allusion to "Sir Harris Nicolas' edition" is not correct; see description of the 1845 ed. above, in which the life of Chaucer alone is by Nicolas. The error is shared by Lowndes and by Skeat, Canon p. 116; but see Furnivall in PT p. 423, and under Nicolas' Life of Chaucer in Section I B here. Also Benjamin Disraeli, in a note to his father's essay on Chaucer, Amenities of Literature, says "Sir Harris Nicolas has produced an excellent edition of the poet." This edition was the standard until the appearance of Skeat's Oxford Chaucer; it has no notes. Many German critical monographs use it as basis, cp. Einenkel's Streifzüge. In vol. 12 of the Scott-Saintsbury Dryden are reprinted from this work the tales used by Dryden.

Reviewed Athenaeum 1867 I: 246; Jahrbuch 8: 94.

Bell, 1854. In Bell's Annotated Editions of the English Poets, 8 vols., London, 1854-56. The first volume of the Chaucer is dated 1854, the last 1856, the rest 1855. Edited by Robert Bell, assisted by John M. Jephson.

Contents:—Vol. 1, Memoir; introduction to the Canterbury Tales; text of the Tales, from Harley 7334 in the main; Vols. 2 and 3 also contain the Tales; Vol. 4 the Parson's Tale; the *Court of Love; the Assembly of Foules; the *Cuckoo and Nightingale; and *Flower and Leaf. Vol. 5 contains Troilus and Cressida, the text a collation of Harley 1239 and Harley 3943; the poem is completed in Vol. 6, which also contains *Chaucer's Dream (=the Isle of Ladies); the ABC; the Book of the Duchess; Anelida; and the House of Fame. Vol. 7 contains the *Romaunt, text from the Glasgow MS. Vol. 8 contains the *Complaint of a Lover's Life (Black Knight), with Tyrwhitt's assertion of its authenticity; Mars and Venus follow, printed as the Complaint of Mars and Venus, the Complaint of Mars, the Complaint of Venus. The Legend of Good Women follows, also the Minor Poems, Poems attributed to Chaucer, and a Glossary. The Minor Poems comprise Pity; Fortune (entitled Ballade de Village sauns Peynture); *Mother of Nurture (entitled A Goodly Balade of Chaucer); Stedfastness (entitled Balade sent to King Richard); Purse; Truth; Gentilesse (entitled A Ballad); Scogan; Bukton; *Proverbs.

The Proverbs have along with their text a print of the two stanzas beginning, the first "The world so wide," the second "The more I go," apparently by Lydgate, see Anglia 28:4. A note by Bell states that these stanzas, which appear in both Harley 7578 and Fairfax 16 as a continuation of Proverbs, are now printed for the first time. As will be seen from the Anglia reference, they had already been printed from Harley 7333 in Reliquiae Antiquae I: 234 (1841).

There follow a *Roundel (Youre eyen Two) from Bishop Percy's Reliques; the *Virelay (from the early prints) ; *Prophecy (from the early prints) ; Words to Adam (from the early prints) ; *Mother of God (from the text given in N and Q. 1855 II : 140). The poems attributed to Chaucer are: the *Lamentation of Mary Magdalen, *Praise of Women, *Go forth King, *Eight Goodly Questions, *To the King's Most Noble Grace, *It Falleth for a Gentleman.

A curious note as to poems by Thomas Chaucer, on page 130 of vol. 8, is reprinted under Section I Appendix (d) here. For poems marked with an asterisk see Section V here.

This edition has interest as the earliest attempt to annotate any poem other than the Canterbury Tales or the Troilus. Kynaston's notes upon which latter are still unknown. It is also the first edition to offer a text of the minor poems presumably drawn from the MSS. See Lounsbury, Studies I : 325, Skeat, Canon 26-29.

Bell's additions were Mother of God and the Roundel, already claimed for Chaucer, and the two stanzas printed with Proverbs, of which he asserted the Chaucerian authorship.

Bell is reviewed Fraser's Mag. 53 : 461.

This edition was revised, with an essay, by W. W. Skeat. London 1878, 4 vols. The spurious poems, i. e., Romaunt of the Rose, Court of Love, Cuckoo and Nightingale, Flower and Leaf, Complaint of a Lover's Life, and the group printed by Bell as Attributed to Chaucer, are here, for the first time, relegated to a volume by themselves; for this Skeat was praised by Furnivall, Academy 1878 I : 365. Skeat says in his preliminary essay, "In the main, with the exception of the rearrangement and some necessary corrections in the life of Chaucer in vol. 1, the edition remains the same as when completed by Mr. Jephson under the supervision of Mr. Robert Bell." For the poems excluded by Skeat, also the Isle of Ladies, Mother of Nurture, Proverbs, Roundel, Virelay, and Mother of God, see Section V here.

In N. and Q. 1884 I : 463 it is said that Griffin republished Robert Bell's edition in 8 vols. octavo n. d., as part of a complete edition of the English poets; that it seems less critical than the 1878 edition, and follows that of 1854 more closely. This ed. is probably of 1870-71.

Gilfillan-Clarke, see under Modernizations of the Canterbury Tales.

Routledge of 1860, see 1843 Moxon above.

Blackwood. In the Academy 1890 I : 373, Gunthorpe writes: "Blackwood has reproduced, as the Poetical Works of Chaucer, the one-volume edition by Wright of the Canterbury Tales,

apparently from old stereotype plates; added are the Cuckoo
and Nightingale, the Assembly of Foules, &c., from Moxon's
edition. Twelve genuine poems, including the Troilus and the
Legend of Good Women, are omitted." Nothing is said of the
date of the edition (1880?).

Crowell. The Poetical Works of Geoffrey Chaucer. A New Text,
with Illustrative Notes, by Th. Wright. T. Y. Crowell, N. Y.
n. d., (1880) 1 vol. 8vo. Contains Wright's introduction and
text of the Canterbury Tales, the Cuckoo and Nightingale, the
Assembly of Foules, Minor Poems, Glossary. Minor Poems
= Bukton, Stedfastness, Truth, Fortune, Scogan, Purse, Gentilesse, Proverbs, Words to Adam, Virelai.

It seems probable that this Crowell edition is from the
Blackwood mentioned just above. The titlepage of each is as
untruthful as that of the 1843 Moxon Chaucer, see ante.

Gilman. Poetical Works of Geoffrey Chaucer, to which are appended Poems Attributed to Chaucer. Edited by Arthur Gilman, M. A. 3 vols., Boston, 1880. Riverside Edition.

Contents:—Vol. I. Advertisement, The Times and the Poet,
On Reading Chaucer, Astrological Terms and Divisions of Time,
Biblical References. The Canterbury Tales.
Vol. II. The Canterbury Tales, the Minor Poems,—ABC, Pity,
Book of the Duchesse, Parlement of Foules, Mars, Anelida, Former
Age, Troilus and Cressida, Words to Adam.
Vol. III. Minor Poems (continued), = House of Fame, Legend
of Good Women, Truth, Orisoune to the Holy Virgin (= Mother of
God), Proverbs, Venus, Scogan, Bukton, Gentilesse, Ballad sent
to King Richard (=Stedfastnesse), Ballad de Vilage sauns Peinture
(=Fortune), Purse. Also, Poems attributed to Chaucer, as fol-
lows: The Romaunt of the Rose, the Court of Love, the Flower
and the Leaf, the Cuckoo and the Nightingale, Goodly Ballad of
Chaucer (=Mother of Nurture), Praise of Women, Chaucer's
Dream (=Isle of Ladies), Virelai, Prophecy, Go forth King. Index.

The advertisement states that use has been made of the
Chaucer Society's labors, and that the arrangement of works
devised by members of that Society is here adopted for the first
time. The Canterbury Tales are divided under three days.
Some of Tyrwhitt's emendations are adopted, and his work
commended; deference is shown to the work of Skeat. A few
notes, mainly interpretative of the text, are appended at the
foot of the page.

Not a sound work of reference; no longer of value to the
student. The Mother of God and the Poems Attributed to
Chaucer are now excluded from the canon, see Section V below.
Reviewed Atlantic Monthly 45 : 108 (Corson); DLZ 1880,
pp. 12-13 (Zupitza); N. and Q. 1884 I : 463.

Skeat. The Complete Works of Geoffrey Chaucer, edited by W. W. Skeat, Oxford, 1894. In six volumes.

A supplementary vol. VII, entitled Chaucerian and Other Pieces, Oxford 1897, contains many of the pieces formerly included in the works of Chaucer, and now known to be by other writers. This is referred to in this bibliography as Skeat VII, and the various volumes of the Oxford Chaucer as Skeat I, II, etc., without use of the title.

Contents:—Vol. I, General Introduction, Life of Chaucer, List of Chaucer's Works, introduction to the Romaunt of the Rose, introduction to the Minor Poems, text of the Romaunt, texts of the Minor Poems, appendix of three Minor Poems "probably genuine", notes to the Romaunt and to the Minor Poems. The Life of Chaucer contains two errors, see Flügel, Anglia 21: 247, 248; the text of the Romaunt is from the unique MS at Glasgow, collated with Thynne; the Minor Poems are: ABC, Pity, Book of the Duchess, Mars, Parlement of Foules, Complaint to his Lady (or Ballad of Pity), Anelida, Words to Adam, Former Age, Fortune, Merciles Beaute, To Rosemounde, Truth, Gentilesse, Stedfastness, Scogan, Bukton, Venus, Purse, Proverbs. The Appendix-poems are Against Women Unconstant, An Amorous Complaint, Ballad of Complaint. Vol. II contains the introduction to Boethius, the introduction to Troilus, the texts of Boethius and of Troilus, the notes to both. Vol. III contains the introduction to the House of Fame, to the Legend of Good Women, to the Astrolabe; the texts, and notes; also an Account of the Sources of the Canterbury Tales, pp. 369-504. Vol. IV contains the text of the Canterbury Tales, with an introduction of 23 pages discussing the MSS, and an appendix of the Tale of Gamelyn. Between the introduction and the beginning of the Prologue are inserted "Additions to the Minor Poems in vol. I", being—Womanly Noblesse, Complaint to my Mortal Foe, Complaint to my Lode-Sterre, and notes on the three texts. Vol. V contains the notes to the Canterbury Tales, with an introduction on the canon of Chaucer's works (26 pages), and an index to subjects and words explained in the notes. Vol. VI contains the general introduction, with discussion of phonology, metre, and grammar, a glossarial index to the works, separate indexes to the Romaunt and to Gamelyn, an index of proper names, of authors quoted by Chaucer, of books referred to in the notes, a list of manuscripts, a general list of errata in the edition, and an index of subjects discussed in the edition. A list of subscribers is appended.

Vol. I was reissued 1899. The Glossarial Index is separately issued Oxford 1899, 149 pages.

Contents of Vol. VII are:— Introduction, texts of the Testament of Love, the Plowman's Tale, Jack Upland, the Praise of Peace, the Letter of Cupid, To the King's most Noble Grace, To the Lords and Knights of the Garter, Scogan's Moral Balade, Complaint of the Black Knight, Flower of Courtesy, Ballad in Commendation of Our Lady, To my Sovereign Lady, Ballad of Good Counsel, Beware of Doubleness, Ballad warning Men to beware of deceitful Women, Three Sayings, La Belle Dame sans Mercy, Testament of Cressida, Cuckoo and Nightingale, Envoy to Alison, Flower and Leaf, Assembly of Ladies, Goodly Ballad, Go forth King, Court of Love, Virelai, Prosperity, Leaulte vault Richesse, Sayings printed by Caxton, Ballad in Praise of Chaucer. Notes, Glossarial Index of proper names and to some subjects explained in the notes, follow. List of subscribers is appended.

The Oxford Chaucer is reviewed: Amer. Jour. Phil. 19 : 439-445 (Garnett); Anglia Beibl. 6 : 321-3 (Hoops); Athen. 1894 I : 535, II : 313, 1895 I : 370; Dial 1895 I : 116-120 (Flügel); Engl. Stud. 22 : 271-288 (Kaluza); Nation 1894 II : 309, 329, 1895 I : 239 (Kittredge); Quarterly Review 1895 I : 521-548 (W. P. Ker), repr. Essays on Medieval Literature, 1905; Saturday Review 78 : 353; Speaker of March 17, 1894 (Quiller Couch), repr. Adventures in Criticism, 1896; New York Tribune, Feb. 24, 1895 (Lounsbury).

Chaucerian and Other Pieces is reviewed: Athen. 1897 II : 741; Nation 1897 II . 303.

Professor Skeat's great six-volume edition of Chaucer is acknowledged by his severest critics to be the best extant; but it has certain marked faults against which the student limited to its use should be warned. The issue of this elaborate work was preceded by Skeat's separate annotated editions of the Minor Poems, of the Legend of Good Women, of the Astrolabe, and of parts of the Canterbury Tales, the last frequently revised for school use. In this library edition of the Complete Works it was of course natural that Professor Skeat should avail himself of the results of his earlier labors; but it is often evident that those results are reprinted without the augmentation which every year makes necessary in a Chaucer-record, and even without revision.

In the method of text-construction, also, a weakness appears under which editions of Chaucer must labor until his editors recognize, as classical editors long ago recognized, that for a definitive edition the use of all the available evidence is indispensable. Great as have been the achievements of the Chaucer Society, and great as is the debt of students to Dr. Furnivall for his diplomatic reproductions of Chaucer-texts, an edition of the Canterbury Tales based upon the seven MSS (out of more than fifty) which the Society had issued when Skeat prepared his text, cannot be considered as final. (See Athen. 1899 I : 269, Dial 18 : 119.) In this matter of text-construction the limitation of the editor to a portion of the possible evidence is a more radical weakness than are the limitations above mentioned, since here the question is one of method. Moreover, although the text may upon this mode of procedure be satisfactory to the ear, we cannot follow the editor's reasoning in its establishment. For when after asserting that a certain group of MSS is "better" than another group—and here again we wish a reason—Skeat suddenly incorporates in his text readings from the "inferior" MSS, we look for an explanation,

10

which is not given. It is evident to any close student of the Canterbury Tales that Skeat has not devoted to the MSS such examination as Morell or Tyrwhitt made, and that his editorial procedure, a century and more after Tyrwhitt, is guided by the erroneous supposition that the true Chaucerian readings may be picked out intuitively, instead of by the laborious and impartial comparison of all the authorities. We find in him still the view of Bentley, "Nobis et ratio et res ipsa centum codd. potiores sunt." In the handling of the Minor Poems the same neglect of the evidence is visible. Flügel points out, Dial 18 : 119, that but seven of the seventeen texts of Truth are cited by Skeat; and his failure to search minutely his only authorities, the MSS, is frequently betrayed by such indiscretions as the sneer at MS Adds. 5140 for a reading which is due to the Chaucer Society prints, see Mod. Phil. 3 : 175 note, or the remark that the Ten Commandments of Love must be earlier than 1450 because of its inclusion in the MS Fairfax 16, into blank leaves of which this poem has however been inserted by a Jacobean hand. His meagre and hasty descriptions of the codices have long been a thorn in the flesh to students far from the English libraries, cp. Flügel in Anglia 22 : 510 ff.; and compare the dismissal of the undescribed de Worde Canterbury Tales of 1498 with the note "In the British Museum", while pages are wasted in elaborate and unnecessary "exposure" and denunciation of John Stow. The detailed censure of Stow for his accumulation of spurious pieces in editing Chaucer is the more out of place because Skeat himself has printed as Chaucer's several poems whose authenticity is questioned by other scholars and one of which, called by him "The Ballad of Complaint", he has since disavowed.

Lastly as to the Notes. It is here that Skeat appears at his best, and that his prolonged labors in medieval literature and in etymological pursuits enable him to speak as one having authority. The net result is a body of annotations by far the best accessible to students. Weaknesses do appear; as Kittredge has remarked, the "attempt to serve both the tyro and the adept" has resulted in unevenness and discursiveness. We could spare lengthy etymological comment upon verbal forms like *ought*, for example, and welcome more, *e. g.,* upon the history of annotation in the hands of Skeat's predecessors, upon the Brutus Cassius of the Monk's Tale, or the *goliardeys* of the Prologue.

But, as has been said by Kittredge, "after all that fault-finders can gather has been subtracted from the total merit of the performance, the edition will remain a monument of learning and sagacity which few similar works in English can rival."

Student's Chaucer. Edited by W. W. Skeat, Oxford 1895, again 1897, 1901. Text as in the Oxford Chaucer; a brief introduction, with life of Chaucer, remarks on phonology, etc., glossary, and at end of volume a few notes, mainly textual.

Reviewed Amer. Jour. Phil. 19 : 439-445 (Garnett); Anglia Beibl. 1895, pp. 196-199 (Pabst); Athen. 1895 I : 607; Engl. Stud. 22 : 287 (Kaluza).

Kelmscott. The Kelmscott Chaucer, edited by F. S. Ellis. Printed with "Chaucer" type in black and red, with 87 woodcut illustrations designed by Burne-Jones, and numerous woodcut borders and initial letters specially designed for this work by Morris and not used elsewhere. At the Kelmscott Press, 1896.

Colophon, p. 554, "Here ends the Book of the Works of Geoffrey Chaucer, edited by F. S. Ellis; ornamented with pictures designed by Sir Edward Burne-Jones, and engraved on wood by W. H. Hooper. Printed by me William Morris at the Kelmscott Press, Upper Mall, Hammersmith, in the County of Middlesex. Finished on the 8th day of May, 1896."

Contents:—The Canterbury Tales, ABC, Pity, Mars, Venus, Anelida, Words to Adam, Former Age, Truth (entitled Balade de Bon Conseyl), To Rosemounde, Proverb of Chaucer, Scogan, Bukton, Gentilesse, Lak of Stedfastnesse, Lenvoy to King Richard, Fortune (entitled Balades de Vilage sanz Peinture), Purse, Merciless Beaute, Complaint to his Lady, Womanly Noblesse, Romaunt of the Rose, Parlement of Foules, Boethius, Book of the Duchesse, Astrolabe, Legend of Good Women, House of Fame, Troilus and Cressida.

A page from the Troilus is reproduced by Garnett and Gosse, Eng. Lit., vol. I p. 145.

The Athen. of 1896 II : 444-45 says: "Mr. Ellis appears to have used the materials provided by the Chaucer Society for a one-text edition of the poet's works, based on what, at the time of issue, was considered the best manuscript of each poem, and to have seldom departed from this except with the sanction of Professor Skeat, whose courtesy, and that of the Clarendon Press, in allowing free use to be made of the text of the 'Oxford Chaucer', is duly acknowledged." Comment is then made upon the typography and upon the illustrations.

The Nation, 1903 I : 313-14, says: "It is by degrees becoming more widely known that the drawings for the Chaucer were really not by Burne-Jones. This artist made a series of rough pencil notes, suggesting the subjects and the composition, and they were then carried out by Mr. Catterson Smith and others. . . . . The book may be, or rather is, after its fashion, a truly magnificent example of printing, but, artistically, Burne-Jones had very little to do with it. . . . . And as it is partly for the illustrations that the book has been prized so highly, this fact must in the end make a difference."

Compare the facts as to prices. The work was published at £20, on paper; 13 copies were printed on vellum, of which 8 were for sale at £126. In October 1904 Quaritch priced a paper copy at £65; in March 1905, at Sotheby's, two paper copies brought £49 and £45, and George H. Boughton's vellum copy realized but £300, although the vellum copies sold in 1901 and 1902 fetched £510 and £520. For further notes and prices see Auction Prices I : 399; Nation 1896 II : 173 (Pennell); Mackail's life of William Morris, 1901, II : 278 ff.; Wheatley's Prices of Books, p. 258; Cockerell's description of the Kelmscott Press, 1898 (the last book printed at that Press); id. in Morris' Art and Craft of Printing, New Rochelle, N. Y., 1902, the Elston Press; Temple Scott's bibliography of William Morris, Lond. 1897.

Globe. The Works of Geoffrey Chaucer, edited by Alfred W. Pollard, H. Frank Heath, Mark H. Liddell, and W. S. McCormick. London 1898, reprinted 1899, 1901. 1 vol. octavo.

Contents:—The Canterbury Tales, ed. Pollard; the Earlier Minor Poems, ed. Heath, comprising Book of the Duchess, Pity, ABC, Mars, Complaint to his Lady, Anelida, Parlement of Foules; Boethius, ed. Liddell; Troilus and Cressida, ed. McCormick; Words to Adam, ed. Heath; House of Fame, ed. Heath; Legend of Good Women, ed. Pollard; Later Minor Poems, ed. Heath, comprising To Rosemounde, Former Age, Fortune, Truth, Gentilesse, Stedfastnesse, Scogan, Bukton, Purse, Proverbs. The Doubtful Minor Poems, ed. Heath, follow, viz., Merciless Beaute, Newfangleness, Compleynt Damours, Balade of Compleynte, Balade that Chaucier made (Womanly Noblesse). The Astrolabe is edited by Liddell; the Romaunt of the Rose by Liddell. A glossary follows, and there is a preface by Pollard, pp. vii-xi, with introductions by the various editors, pp. xv-lv.

This edition professes, in most cases, to offer "a critical text"; the preface states that the aim has been to produce "texts which shall offer an accurate reflection of that MS or group of MSS which critical investigation has shown to be the best, with only such emendation upon the evidence of other manuscripts as appeared absolutely necessary." The genealogical trees are constructed almost exclusively by Heath; see his paper before the Philological Society as reported Athen. 1896 I : 418.

Reviewed Acad. 1898 I : 303-4 (very readable notice); Amer. Jour. Phil. 19: 439-445 (Garnett); Anglia Beibl. 1899 pp. 304-307 (Wetz); Archiv 102:410-417 (Koch); DLZ 1899 pp. 464-66 (Graz); Athenaeum 1899 I: 268-9; Centrblatt 1899 pp. 629-30 (Wülker); Engl. Stud. 27 : 17-61 (Koch); see also Flügel in

Anglia 21 : 255-57, and Hammond in Decenn. Publ. Univ. of Chicago VII : 1-22. Brief notices in Nation 1898 I : 206, Romania 27 : 524.

———

Crowell. Chaucer's Complete Works, with an introduction by T. R. Lounsbury. New York, Crowell, 1900, 2 vols.

No notes; no mention of the source of the text.

The same work, with the introduction, is pub. by Crowell in one vol., 1900, in both the Astor Series and the Gladstone Series, the difference between which is merely one of price. The announcements of these series speak of the ed. as "Lounsbury and Skeat." The introd. is of 18 pages; there is a glossarial index.

World's Classics. The Poetical Works of Geoffrey Chaucer. London, Grant Richards, 1903 ff., 2 vols.

No notes. The text of Skeat, reprinted by permission. Very low-priced; even in limp leather costs but one and sixpence a volume.

Frowde. Works of Chaucer; in three vols., 12mo., Frowde, 1906.

One shilling a volume.

SECTION III

THE CANTERBURY TALES

A. Introduction

Stories in a Framework. This literary form is **Oriental** in its origin. The most conspicuous examples current in Europe in the latter Middle Ages are the Fables of Bidpai, the Seven Wise Masters or Seven Sages, and the Disciplina Clericalis. In the Fables of Bidpai or Pilpay, originally written in Sanskrit, the thread connecting the separate stories is didactic in character; the philosopher Bidpai narrates the tales to a king whose adviser he is. In many of the stories the personages are animals; some of the fables are Aesopic, and one or two have parallels in the Thousand and One Nights, or Arabian Nights, a work which did not reach Western Europe until after Chaucer's day. The work was translated into Latin about 1270.

See Max Müller, On the Migration of Fables, vol. IV of his Chips from a German Workshop. See Ward, Catalogue of Romances, II : 149 ff.

The Seven Wise Masters was a still more widely circulated medieval work. Its framework has somewhat more plot than that of the Fables. The son of the emperor Diocletian, falsely accused by his stepmother, is rescued from his father's anger by the narratives of the Seven Sages.

See Wright's edition for the Percy Society, 1845; Ellis, Metrical Romances, vol. III; Weber, Metrical Romances, vol. I; the dissertation prefixed to Warton-Hazlitt; Furnivall's summary in the Captain Cox volume of the Ballad Society; Ward, Catalogue of Romances II : 199 ff. and the references to Paris, Keller, Petras, etc., there given; Campbell's study of the Middle English versions, Publ. Mod. Lang. Ass'n 14 : 1-107 (1899), cp. Napier's note *ibid.* pp. 459-464; Fischer's dissertation, Greisswald, 1902.

The Disciplina Clericalis, a series of didactic narratives addressed by a father to his son, was written by Petrus Alfonsus, a converted Jew, in the 12th century.

See Ward, Cat. of Romances II : 235 ff., and the references there given.

These sets of framed stories are much earlier than the work of Chaucer; two compilations by his contemporaries invite closer comparison, the Decameron of Boccaccio and the Confessio Amantis of Gower; nor should we forget that Chaucer's own Legend of Good Women preceded his Canterbury Tales. In Boccaccio there is a very great advance in vivacity and picturesqueness of framework over any preceding set of framed stories. Ten young people, seven women and three men, all of rank, leave Florence to escape the horrors of the pestilence there raging, and pass ten days at a country villa, whiling away the time by telling stories. For each day there is chosen a sort of Master or Mistress of the Revels, who dictates the general subject of the stories for that day, and calls upon the group in turn. The superiority of this plan to any of those above mentioned will be recognized; first, the tales are not didactic, but narrated for amusement; next, there is some differentiation of character among the narrators, though this is not carried to any great extent; and in the choice of a "sovereign" for each day we may see a faint and far-off resemblance to Chaucer's Host. There is also in Boccaccio an atmosphere of out-of-doors not dreamed of in any of the Oriental compilations, which again reminds us of Chaucer. Nevertheless, the development of the framework-idea in Chaucer's hands is so great that no comparison can be made, even of the Decameron, with the Canterbury Tales. The choice of a pilgrimage as the scene, the only possible stage upon which all classes could then meet as equals; the variety and vividness of the figures introduced; the masterstroke which appointed as literary dictator the roughtongued, keenwitted Host, the faithful representative of the "hearty positive genius of the English people"; the skill with which the bits of framework between the Tales are differentiated from one another, here a quarrel, there the riding up of other pilgrims, here a comment or an interruption by the Host, and again the Knight, or the Merchant, or the Franklin, appearing as the critic; finally, the adaptation of most of the Tales to their tellers, from the coarse narratives of Miller and Reeve, the pious legends of the nuns, and the romance of the Squire, to the tale of disloyal love narrated by the Knight with a shrewd sideglance at his son,—such considerations as these have tempted many students into affirming the dramatic power of Chaucer.

Notwithstanding all this, some critics have opined that Chaucer was indebted to Boccaccio for his idea.—"It is probable that most of the Tales were written as so many distinct poems at different times . . . . and afterwards collected into one body in imitation of Boccace's Decameron, whence the Arguments of some of them were taken." (Life of Chaucer prefixed to the Urry Chaucer of

1721.)—"The Canterbury Tales was in all probability composed in imitation of the Decameron", said Tyrwhitt, Introd. Disc. § ii. —"Chaucer undoubtedly intended to imitate Boccaccio, whose Decameron was then the most popular of books." (Warton-Hazlitt, II : 336.)—"A performance with which Chaucer was familiarly acquainted." (Godwin, Life, chap. 35.) But Wright, ed. Cant. Tales p. xvi, says, "with which I think it doubtful if Chaucer were acquainted", and Sandras, Étude, p. 135, says "inconnu peut-être à Chaucer." Sandras thinks that collections such as the Disciplina Clericalis and the Seven Sages had more influence on Chaucer; Ebert, reviewing Sandras, rejects this opinion, see Ch. Soc. Essays pp. 26-28; Koch, Engl. Stud. 1 : 292, also disagrees with Sandras. Kissner p. 74 ff. thinks that Chaucer did know the tales of the Decameron; certainly the plan influenced him. Landau, in Beiträge zur Geschichte der italienischen Novella, Vienna 1875, treats Chaucer as an imitator of the Decameron, as do Hortis, op. cit., Rajna in Romania 32 : 244 ff. Ten Brink, Hist. Eng. Lit. II : 139, 141, does not decide. Lounsbury, Studies II : 229, asserts that "there is not the slightest proof that Chaucer had a knowledge of its existence"; Skeat III : 371, VI : xcix, considers it highly improbable that Chaucer knew the Decameron; and Pollard, Globe Chaucer p. xxvii, says there is "no shred of evidence to prove that Chaucer copied his plan from the very inferior plan of Boccaccio's Decameron."

The opinion expressed by Pollard as to Chaucer's superiority over Boccaccio is no more undisputed than is the theory of Chaucer's debt to Boccaccio. See for instance Dunlop's comparison of the Decameron and the Canterbury Tales, History of Prose Fiction II : 60; see Ginguené, Historie littéraire de l'Italie, III : 110. Landau, in his Beiträge above cited, says that Chaucer's wit is of a lower order than Boccaccio's, and that the English novelist is much more rarely lofty and touching, much oftener common and vulgar than is the Italian. See also the notes on the Troilus, the Knight's Tale, here, for comparisons of those poems with Boccaccio; but observe that Dryden felt that "Chaucer has refined on Boccaccio, and has mended the stories, which he has borrowed in his way of telling."

Another set of stories in a framework immediately contemporary with Chaucer was Gower's Confessio Amantis. This poem is in a prologue and eight books, with a total of nearly 33,500 lines in short couplets. The stories are related by a priest or confessor, admonishing a lover and narrating tales to point his monitions. The idea, as Macaulay says in his ed. of Gower vol. II p. xi, is no doubt taken from the Roman de la Rose, where "Genius" hears the confession of Nature. The prologue is not so closely related to the poem as in other framework treatments, and the plan is not worked out; as is frequently the case in medieval dialogues or disputes, no conclusion is reached; cp. the Owl and Nightingale, the Parlement of Foules, the Eye and Heart, the Assembly of Ladies, etc. The series of stories has much the character of the favorite medieval list, or accumulation of instances and authorities for any general statement, also seen in the example-books. Jerome's examples of unfaithful women, the lists of the fallen great in the poems on death or in Boccaccio's De Casibus and Chaucer's Monk's Tale, even the Processus Prophetarum of medieval miracleplay-cycles, are parallels to Gower's essentially medieval and didactic conception; his separate narratives, however, are often well told.

Chaucer's own Legend of Good Women, intended to consist of a prologue and 20 stories in praise of loyal women, was perhaps in hand when Gower's poem appeared, in 1390. From the fact that two forms of the prologue exist, it has been inferred that Chaucer worked upon the scheme at two different times; that he wearied of the less vivid and varied idea after that of the pilgrimage had occurred to him is very possible. This poem, like that of Gower, has much the effect of a list; the "surprise and contrast" so characteristic of the Cant. Tales plan are lacking. See Section IV here for discussion of the work.

The "framework" enclosing tales is found subsequent to Chaucer in many English works; a few are here mentioned.

Tarleton's Newes out of Purgatorie. About 1590, again 1630. To the writer in a dream appears Tarleton pale and wan, back from Purgatory; he is asked whom he saw there, and narrates the history of each. All the tales are in prose, except that of Ronsard; the only framework is Tarleton's remark, that he walked further and saw another personage, etc.

The Cobler of Canterburie. 1590, again 1608. The preface praises Chaucer and avows the imitation. A party sailing down the Thames tell the stories, which are in prose; descriptions of the narrators, in Skeltonic short couplets, precede the tales. The personages are: the Cobbler, the Smith, Gentleman, Scholar, Old Woman, Summoner. Frequent echoes or imitations of Chaucer appear in the descriptions.

Greene's Vision, by Robert Greene, shortly after 1590. To Greene asleep, after his penitent confessions of misdoing, appear Chaucer and Gower. Each is described in verse; 16 lines are given to Chaucer, beginning:

His stature was not very tall   etc.

The poets converse with Greene, each narrating a prose tale on jealousy; at the close of the dream Solomon appears and counsels wisdom.

Greene asserts to Chaucer that people have wrongly fathered the Cobler of Canterburie upon him, Greene.

The Tinker of Turvey. London 1630. Plan like the Cobler

of Canterburie, with similar verse descriptions of the personages inserted into the prose narrative, and songs interspersed. Running title "Canterburie Tales". The preface avows imitation of Chaucer; the narrators are: Trotter the Tinker, Yerker the Cobbler, Thumper the Smith, Sir Rowland a Scholar, Bluster a Seaman.

The Adventures of John of Gaunt. By James White. Dublin 1790. For an outline of this work see Cross in Anglia 25 : 251.

Canterbury Tales, by Harriet and Sophia Lee. Lond. 1797-1805, 5 vols. Seven stagecoach travellers are snowed in at Canterbury, and narrate tales to pass the time. Vol. I, by Harriet Lee, contains the tales of Traveller, Poet, Frenchman, Old Woman; vol. II, by Sophia Lee, the tale of the Young Lady; vol. III, by both sisters, the tales of Officer and Clergyman. Vols. IV and V were later added, and the preface requests the reader not to inquire too closely where the rest of the travellers came from. Vol. IV, by Harriet, contains tales by the German and the Scotsman; vol. V, also by Harriet, those of the Landlady, the Friend, the Wife. All in prose; no Links.

Crabbe's Tales of the Hall, 1819, are related to this literary type.

Wilkie Collins' Queen of Hearts, 1860. A collection of prose stories, supposedly by three old men, told to delay the departure of the "Queen" from their circle, into which her lover is expected unknown to her.

Collins' device for illuminating a mystery by giving the separate narratives of the various persons interested is best seen in his two masterpieces, The Moonstone and The Woman in White.

Arthur Hugh Clough was a careful student of Chaucer and of Early English. "In Mari Magno", of which six stories were written, was done in 1861.

Hawthorne's Wonder Book and his Grandfather's Chair are a simpler form of this literary type, with one narrator, like Gower and the Arabian Nights.

James Russell Lowell planned, largely at the suggestion of Clough, a series of framed stories, to be called The Nooning. This was but partly blocked out; the Voyage of Leif, Pictures from Appledore, and FitzAdam's Story, were episodes for it.

Henry Wadsworth Longfellow's Tales of a Wayside Inn. Part I, Boston 1863, Part II 1872, Part III 1873. See Andrae, Zu Longfellow's und Chaucer's Tales, Anglia Beiblatt 3 : 362, 4 : 244, 6 : 143, 9 : 141-152, cp. 276; 13 : 47-54, 298-309.

John Greenleaf Whittier's Tent on the Beach (1867) is modeled on Boccaccio rather than on Chaucer.

William Morris' Earthly Paradise. London 1868-70, 4 vols. Cheaper ed. in 1 vol. 1890, repr. 1895, 1896, 1898.

Charles Dickens partly made several frameworks for tales; cp. the Seven Poor Travellers, and Master Humphrey's Clock.

Maurice Hewlett's New Canterbury Tales and Robert Louis Stevenson's New Arabian Nights are the most recent collections of this type possessing literary merit. The "Sherlock Holmes" stories of Conan Doyle, the "Martin Hewitt" stories of Arthur Morrison, etc., are not in reality of this framework type, but belong more to the picaresque narrative, inasmuch as in these collections each story illuminates the personality or the intellectual acumen of one hero, the detective.

The student of framed narrative should also recognize by-forms like Browning's Pippa Passes and The Ring and the Book; with the latter cp. Wilkie Collins.

The sixteenth century Heptameron of Margaret of Navarre is said by her editor, Frank (1879), to be comparable in the dramatic character of its setting to Chaucer.

The title "Canterbury Tales" was abused by some scurrilous jest-books of the 17th and 18th centuries, viz.:

Canterbury Tales composed for the entertainment of all Ingenious Young Men and Maids at their Merry Meetings at Christmas, Easter, and Whitsuntide, or any other Time, especially the long Winter Evenings. Printed and sold in London.

Short prose anecdotes of the coarsest character, all placed at Canterbury. 24 pages, no date.

A work mentioned by Quaritch in his Catalogue No. 244 as Canterbury Tales by Chaucer junior. T. Norris on London Bridge, n. d.,—I have not seen.

For lists of personages in imitation of Chaucer see under Notes on the General Prologue, in G below.

Headlinks and Endlinks. The various stories constituting the Canterbury Tales are bound together by Chaucer's own narrative of the journey and by the Host's or other pilgrims' comments. These parts of the framework are most conveniently called, with Bradshaw, the Links. In many cases they serve two functions; they contain an epilogue, or a comment upon the story just narrated, and also the introduction of the next pilgrim; that is, they may be "Endlink" and also "Headlink". Cp. for instance the link between Knight and Miller, where Chaucer passes from the Host's enthusiastic comment to his call upon the Monk, and to the intrusion of the drunken Miller; this bit of the framework thus links both ways. Such double Links exist between Knight and Miller, Miller and Reeve, Reeve and Cook, Shipman and Prioress, Prioress and Chaucer's first Tale, this and Melibeus, Melibeus and the Monk, Monk and Nun's Priest, Doctor and Pardoner, Wife and Friar, Friar and Summoner, Clerk and Merchant, Squire and Franklin, Second Nun and Canon's Yeoman.

There are other cases in which Chaucer had not completed the connection of Tales, and where accordingly the Link serves but a single function. That before the Man of the Law's Tale is merely a headlink; we do not know what Tale was to precede; before the Squire, the Clerk, and the Manciple there is also a headlink only. The Doctor, the Wife of Bath, and the Second Nun, have no headlink, the Pardoner, Summoner, and Franklin no endlink. The Nun's Priest's Tale has in some MSS an endlink; but Chaucer had not decided who was to follow; the last line reads "another" instead of introducing a definite pilgrim. The Merchant and Pardoner have epilogues in which no one is brought forward as the next narrator. The conditions at the close of the Man of Law's Tale and of the Parson's Tale require special discussion, see under those headings below.

The variety of treatment in these Links deserves study. Although the Host is nominally in control of the course of the narration, he is by no means the only speaker or commentator. The quarrels of Miller and Reeve, of Friar and Summoner, form most of the connections between those Tales; and in the latter Link the Host does not speak at all. There is no comment by the Host after the Clerk's Tale; the Merchant catches up the Clerk's last words and begins his own story. The Franklin makes the comment at the end of the Squire's Tale, the Host then asserting his jurisdiction; and although the Host interrupts the Rime of Sir Thopas, it is the Knight, seconded by the Host, who stops the Monk. (For earlier variant form of this interruption, see under F below.) Three times the pilgrim called on by the Host does not narrate,—the Monk at the end of the Knight's Tale, the Parson at the end of the Man of Law's Tale, and the Cook before the Manciple's Tale. Add to these varieties the riding up of the Canon and his Yeoman, the altercation of the Friar and the Summoner at the end of the Wife of Bath's prologue, the description of the Cook's condition in the Manciple's headlink, the sermon of the Pardoner, and we may estimate the immense difference between Chaucer's framework to the Canterbury Tales and the unvarying, static scheme of Boccaccio.

Spurious links have been constructed in the Canterbury

Tales, viz.:—The Cook's Tale has in Rawl. poet. 141 four additional lines, no Tale of Gamelyn. It has in Bodley 686 twelve additional lines; see Urry and Tyrwhitt. A link Cook-Gamelyn of four lines is in Lansdowne; one of two lines is in Royal 18, Sloane 1685, Barlow, Hatton, Laud 739, Mm, Petworth, Egerton 2863, Hodson-Ashburnham. (The conditions in Ii, Christ Church, Trinity 49, are not known to me.) A link Merchant-Wife of 16 lines is in Barlow, Laud 739, Royal 18. A link Franklin-Doctor of six lines is in Harley 7335. A link Canon's Yeoman-Doctor of 14 lines is in Selden, Royal 17, Royal 18, Rawl. poet. 149, Petworth, Mm, Hatton, Sloane 1685, Barlow, Egerton 2863, Laud 739; one of 16 lines is in Lansdowne; there is a gap in Harley 1758 at this point. There is a spurious prologue to Thopas, four lines, in R 3, 3. A link of 12 lines Pardoner-Shipman is in Harley 1758, Rawl. poet. 149, Petworth, Mm, Hatton, Ii, Sloane 1685, Barlow, Laud 739, Royal 18, Egerton 2863; a link of six lines is in Lansdowne. There are eight spurious lines concluding the Squire's Tale in Selden and in Lansdowne; the latter has four more introducing the Wife of Bath, who follows.

The spurious link Cook-Gamelyn (Lansdowne) is printed in Wright's Cant. Tales I: 175; the 16-line link Merchant-Wife, *ibid.* I: 245-6 note; the spurious (Lansdowne) link Pardoner-Shipman, *ibid.* II: 283 note; the link Canon's Yeoman-Doctor is printed *ibid.* II: 245 note; the connection Squire-Wife (Lansdowne) *ibid.* II: 157 and I: 246 note.

The Host. Another point of superiority which the Tales possess over any similar set of stories is the figure of the Host. Already in the Biographia Britannica, 1747, art. *Chaucer,* note S, we find:—"Above all the character of the Host, who acts as a kind of Chorus in the ancient Drama, is most admirably kept up, and the same wit, spirit, and humour is preserved through the whole journey, that strikes and astonishes the reader so much at the very beginning, where the original character of this incomparable person is drawn at full length." Compare: "This type of a sturdy, well-to-do burgess, at a time when England still deserved the name of 'Merry England', was excellently fitted to play the part of the chorus in the varied drama of the procession to Canterbury. He represents most perfectly the magnanimous toleration, the serene benevolence, the easy and humane disposition which lend such a refreshing effect to Chaucer's magnificent poem." Ten Brink, Hist. Eng. Lit. II: 147. And, still better: "The hearty positive genius of the English people keeps watch, throughout this final masterpiece of Chaucer, upon the irresponsible literary and poetic instincts of rhetoric, sentiment, romance, which in later days have

habitually scorned its control." Herford, introd. to English
Tales in Verse, 1902, pp. xxix-xxx. On the Host see Todd
p. 265 ff.; Skeat V : 58 ff.

It has been noted, though not yet sufficiently discussed, that
in Chaucer's Links, and especially in the comments, are to be
found the beginnings of English literary criticism. Compare
Courthope's remark, Hist. of Eng. Poetry I : 259-60, and
Saintsbury, Hist. of Criticism I : 450; both of these observations are based upon the Rime of Sir Thopas, while a mass of
other material remains untouched.

The "Fragments" of the Canterbury Tales. Chaucer's plan for
the Canterbury pilgrimage included, as it is sketched in the
Prologue, two tales for each of the thirty pilgrims on the
outward journey and two on the return; this scheme he later
modified (Parson's headlink lines 15-16) by reducing it one-
half; but of even this diminished plan only some twenty-four
tales remain to us, several of which are incomplete. We cannot
doubt that he intended to arrange the tales in a certain definite
order, so as to obtain contrast and variety; note how the
Knight, the most dignified person in company, is followed by
the drunken and irresponsible Miller instead of by the person
next in rank, and how the Miller is angrily answered by the
Reeve. The whole body of tales, if the plan had been fully
worked out, would have been bound together by these Links,
and the Prologue at the beginning would have been balanced
by an account of the supper to the winner at the end of the
return journey. But in the incomplete sketch which remains to us
of this extensive plan, the twenty-four tales which we have are
not connected into a coherent whole; at a number of places a
gap occurs owing to the absence of any Link. Thus, the
Prologue passes directly into the Knight's Tale; the Knight is
followed at once by the Miller, and he by the Reeve; the Cook
then comments on the Reeve's tale and begins one of his own,
which however is left unfinished by Chaucer. We have therefore no certainty whose tale was to have come next, there
being no link; and this group of tales is generally spoken of as
Fragment A of the Canterbury Tales. The remaining stories
are similarly bound together into "fragments"; *e. g.*, there is a
link binding the tale of the Pardoner to that of the Doctor
which precedes it, but no link shows who preceded the Doctor
or who followed the Pardoner. And the whole mass of the
Canterbury Tales thus falls into ten fragments.

How Chaucer would finally have arranged these fragments
which remain we cannot with absolute certainty say. We can,
of course, recognize the first, or A-fragment, because of its
inseparable connection with the Prologue; and it is definitely

stated in the Parson's prologue that his Tale is the last of the
outward journey. But the sequence of the other eight fragments is matter for discussion. These fragments are, adopting
for convenience the lettering and order favored by the Chaucer
Society:

A. The General Prologue, the tales of Knight, Miller, Reeve,
and Cook, with the links connecting the several tales.
The spurious tale of Gamelyn is in many MSS found
just after the Cook's fragmentary tale.

B¹. The Man of Law's tale.

B². The tales of Shipman, Prioress, the Rime of Sir Thopas,
the tale of Melibeus, of the Monk, and of the Nun's
Priest.

C. The tales of Doctor and Pardoner.

D. The tales of Wife of Bath, Friar, and Summoner.

E. The tales of Clerk and Merchant.

F. The tales of Squire and Franklin.

G. The tales of Second Nun and Canon's Yeoman.

H. The Manciple's tale.

I. The Parson's tale.

In the groups E, F, and G, the first of the two tales which
each comprises is spoken of as E¹, F¹, or G¹, the second as E²,
F², or G².

Our uncertainty as to Chaucer's probable final arrangement
of the Tales is caused by the confusion which we find existing
in the manuscripts. One large body of texts has B¹ followed
by F¹; another, represented by the noble Ellesmere codex, has
D following B¹, and so on. We observe, however, that these
differences in arrangement are displayed by *groups* of MSS,
and that the codices do not vary irregularly from one another,
and in heterogeneous medley of Tales, but rather that they show
a systematic confusion by Fragments, or fascicules, as we may
also term them. In fact, if we try to imagine how Chaucer
worked over the Canterbury Tales, we are compelled to believe
that he must have had his papers in much such booklets or
fascicules as we now call "fragments." No poet could have
used as working copy a single large volume already bound;
his changes and additions could not have been carried out.
The differences among the existing MSS in arrangement of
Tales are, it seems to me, exactly such as would arise if the
Canterbury Tales were put into the hands of scribes in booklets, arranged and numbered tentatively by their author, but
recombined by copyists in accordance with their own judgment.
See discussion under Relative Dates of the Tales, Section III F
below.

In somewhat similar manner, the sequence adopted by modern
editors is based upon time and place allusions within the Tales

and the Links, without regard to the order seen in the MSS; this arrangement is not represented in any one manuscript, and depends for its validity upon the assumption that all these allusions were correct and final in Chaucer's intention. But in view of the occasional inconsistencies of the Tales, the feminine pronouns of the Shipman's Tale, the Second Nun's terming herself a "sone of Eve", the Man of Law's announcing that he is about to speak in prose, we can hardly assert that the time and place allusions are above doubt.

Evidence as to the Arrangement of the Tales. In a discussion of the probable order of these fragments, the following kinds of evidence are available:

(1) Allusions to place and time within Tales or Links.
(2) Allusions in Tales or Links to Tales in other fragments.
(3) The order as seen in the manuscripts.

1. *Allusions to Place.*

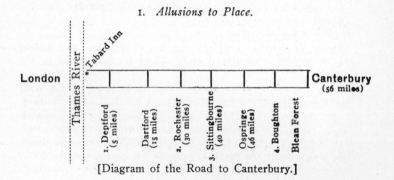

[Diagram of the Road to Canterbury.]

1. "Lo Depeford and it is halfway prime." (between 6 and 9 a. m.) Frag. A, Miller-Reeve link.
2. "Lo Rouchestre stant here fast by." Frag. B², Monk's prologue.
3. " . . . er I come to Sidingborne." Frag. D, Wife of Bath's prologue. The Summoner is speaking; cp. the last line of his tale, "we ben almost at toune."
4. "At Boughton-under-Blee us gan atake." Frag. G, introd. to Canon's Yeoman.
5. " . . . . a litel toun
   Which that ycleped is Bob-up-and-doun
   Under the Blee in Caunterbury weye".
                    Frag. H, Maniple's prologue.

Note that there is no place-evidence for the relative position of the C, E, or F fragment; but that such place-evidence as is given argues a sequence of fragments A, B², D, G, H.

2. *Allusions to Time or to Tales in Other Fragments.*

Note on the Duration of the Journey. Tyrwhitt, in a note on the opening of the Canon's Yeoman's prologue, line 16023 in his edition, remarked that some difficulties could be avoided by considering that the journey occupied more than one day; but he did no more than suggest. Furnivall, Temp. Pref. as cited below, decided for 3½ days, though at first favoring 2, see his note on p. 59 of Koch's Chronology. Koch there argues for 3; and see his ed. of the Pard. Tale p. xxi. Morley, Eng. Writers V : 310, still speaks of the journey as of one day; but see *ibid.* p. 312. And Skeat V : 132 seems to admit the one-day theory, though in III : 375-6 and V : 415 he follows Furnivall. Pollard, Chaucer Primer and Globe Chaucer, takes the opinion of Furnivall. Part of the evidence for the longer duration of the pilgrimage comes from the records of medieval journeys, part from the allusions in the Tales and Links themselves. For this latter sort of evidence, see below; for the former, see Temporary Preface 13-15, 41; Stanley's Historical Memorials of Canterbury, p. 237; Archaeologia 35 : 461; Notes and Queries 1892 I : 522, reprinted in Koch's Chronology p. 89; Oxford Chaucer V : 415; Academy 1896 II : 14; Flügel in Anglia 23 : 239; the Analogues of the Pilgrimage, Ch. Soc. 2d Series No. 36. See also under General Prologue, Section III G below.

It is generally considered that Chaucer intended all the tales for the outward journey; but Tyrwhitt, *ibid.*, said "I have sometimes suspected that it was the intention of Chaucer to begin the journey *from* Canterbury with the Nonnes tale." Ten Brink, Hist. Eng. Lit. II : 182, thought that the Manciple's tale was written for the beginning of the return journey.

First Day.

The Tales begin at once after a very early start, Prologue 822. "Lo Depeford and it is halfway prime", Frag. A, Miller-Reeve link.

Second Day according to Furnivall.

The hour 10 in the morning is given, introd. to the Man of Law's Tale, lines 1-14,—Frag. B¹.

"I can right now no thrifty tale seyn",—Man of Law's prol. line 46, compare "This was a thrifty tale for the nones", in the link between Man of Law and Shipman, line 3.

This agreement of the word *thrifty* furnishes Bradshaw, Furnivall, Skeat, and Shipley (as below), with strong argument for placing B² after B¹, an arrangement still more strongly supported by the fact that B² contains an allusion to Rochester which seems to place it before D with its reference to Sittingbourne, ten miles further from London. See however Modern Philology 3 : 164-65.

"I see wel that ye lerned men in lore   Can moche good"— Shipman's prol. lines 6, 7. Frag. B²

This was taken by Bradshaw and Furnivall to mean the Man of Law, whose tale has just ended; Shipley considers that it means Man of Law, Doctor, and Pardoner, and Furnivall, Acad. 1895 II : 296, agrees with him. Skeat III : 418-19 thinks that the Pardoner cannot be meant by this passage. Koch, Chronology p. 59, suggested putting C between B¹ and B², the phrase "lerned men in lore" then referring to Man of Law, Doctor, and Pardoner; but Shipley feels that the "thrifty" just noted makes B² inseparable from B¹, see Mod. Lang. Notes 10 : 260 ff.

Third Day according to Furnivall.

The Pardoner wishes to drink and eat a cake before beginning his tale; according to Furnivall, Temp. Pref. 25-6, this indicates an hour before breakfast; Shipley loc. cit. p. 272 thinks that Furnivall overestimates the point.

The Host says to the Clerk, introd. line 4, "This day ne herde I of your tonge a word". Shipley, loc. cit. p. 274, thinks this implies that much of the day has passed. Other critics have not noted the passage.

The Wife of Bath is alluded to in the Clerk's Tale, line 1170. Apparently E¹ must then follow D. In the Merchant's Tale, lines 441-2, reference is made to the Wife of Bath's discussion of marriage. E² must then follow D.

Fourth Day according to Furnivall.

"I wol not tarien yow for it is pryme". Squire's Tale, line 73.

In the Franklin's tale the subject-matter is so closely parallel to the tales of Wife of Bath and of Clerk, discussing marriage and "maistrye" and testing of wives, that we would infer the alliance of all these tales, and the position of D before E and F.

In the prologue of the Canon's Yeoman's Tale it is stated that the "lyf of seint Cecyle", or Second Nun's Tale, was just finished; the place Boughton-under-Blee is mentioned, and the Yeoman, who has ridden hard, to overtake the pilgrims, says:

" . . . . sires now in the morwe-tyde
Out of your hostelrye I saugh yow ryde".

This hostelry, according to Furnivall, was probably OsprInge.

In the prologue to the Parson's Tale it is stated that only this one narrative is now lacking, and that it is four p. m., "but hasteth yow the sonne wol adoun".

The above is Furnivall's time-scheme, according to which the

pilgrimage took four, or three and one-half, days. A journey
of three days is argued by Tatlock, Publ. Mod. Lang. Ass'n
21 : 478-486, following Koch, Chronology.

It may be remarked that the lapse of a night between the tales
of Fragment A and the Man of Law's headlink (Tatlock, loc.
cit. p. 482) is not certain. See p. 258 here, note.

On the absolute date of the pilgrimage see under Prologue in
Section III G below.

3. *The Order of the Tales in the MSS: Classification of the MSS.*

List of MSS of the Canterbury Tales, with the abbreviations by
which they are mentioned in this volume. For refs. to the
pages where descriptions may be found, see Index at close of
work. British Museum codices are described III B (1) below,
Bodleian codices in (3), Cambridge University Library in (5),
private property in (7).

Adds. 5140=Additionals 5140, British Museum.

Adds. 25718=Additionals 25718, British Museum.

Adds. 35286=Additionals 35286, British Museum. Formerly
Ashburnham 125.

Arch. Selden, see Selden.

Ashb. 124=Ashburnham 124, now (1907) in the hands of
Quaritch.

Ashb. 126=Ashburnham 126, private property.

Ashb. 127=Ashburnham 127, now (1907) in the hands of
Quaritch.

Barlow=Barlow 20, Bodleian Library, Oxford.

Bodl. 414=Bodley 414, Bodleian Library, Oxford.

Bodl. 686=Bodley 686, Bodleian Library, Oxford.

Cax. I=the original of Caxton's first edition.

Cax. II=the original of Caxton's second edition.

Ch. Ch.=Christ Church 152, in the Oxford college of that name.

Corpus=Corpus Christi College, in the Oxford college of that
name.

Dd=Dd iv, 24, in the University Library, Cambridge.

Del.=the property of Lord Delamere.

Dev.=the property of the Duke of Devonshire.

Egerton 2726, British Museum. Formerly the Haistwell.

Egerton 2863, British Museum. Formerly the Norton, then the
Hodson.

Egerton 2864, British Museum. Formerly the Ingilby, then the
Hodson.

Ellesmere=the property of the Earl of Ellesmere.

Gg=Gg iv, 27 of the University Library, Cambridge.
Glasgow=the copy in the Hunterian Library, Glasgow.
Harley 1239, British Museum.
Harley 1758, British Museum.
Harley 7333, British Museum.
Harley 7334, British Museum.
Harley 7335, British Museum.
Hatton=Hatton Donat. 1, in the Bodleian Library, Oxford.
Helmingham, private property.
Hengwrt, private property.
Hodson-Ashb.=Hodson-Ashburnham=Ashb. 124.
Hodson=Hodson 39, private property.
Holkham, private property.
Ii=Ii iii, 26 in the University Library, Cambridge.
Ingilby, now Egerton 2864, British Museum.
Lansd. 851=Lansdowne 851, British Museum.
Laud 600, in the Bodleian Library, Oxford.
Laud 739, in the Bodleian Library, Oxford.
Lichfield=Lichfield Cathedral.
Lincoln=Lincoln Cathedral.
Longleat=Longleat 257, the property of Lord Bath.
Mm=Mm ii, 5 of the University Library, Cambridge.
Naples, in the Royal Library, Naples.
New=New College, Oxford.
Northumberland=the Duke of Northumberland's MS.
Paris, in the Bibliothèque Nationale, Paris.
Petworth, the property of Lord Leconfield.
Phillipps 6570, private property.
Phillipps 8136, private property.
Phillipps 8137, private property.
Phillipps 8299, private property.
Phys.=in the College of Physicians, London.
R 3, 3,—R 3, 15=Trinity College Cambridge, R 3, 3—R 3, 15.
Rawl. poet. 141=Rawlinson 141, Bodleian Library, Oxford.
Rawl. poet. 149=Rawlinson 149, Bodleian Library, Oxford.
Rawl. poet. 223=Rawlinson 223, Bodleian Library, Oxford.
Royal 17=Royal 17 D xv, British Museum.
Royal 18=Royal 18 C ii, British Museum.
Selden=Selden B 14, Bodleian Library, Oxford.
Sion=the Sion College fragment, London.
Sloane 1685, British Museum.
Sloane 1686, British Museum.
Trinity 3=Trinity College Cambridge, R 3, 3.
Trinity 15=Trinity College Cambridge, R 3, 15.
Trinity 49=Trinity College Oxford, 49.

The above is the list as usually given, e. g., by Skeat or by Koch,
with the addition of three MSS recently acquired by the British

Museum, Adds. 35286, Egerton 2863, Egerton 2864. But if the Naples
or the Phillips 8299 MS, which contain only one of the Canterbury
Tales, is to be included in such a list, there are various other codices
containing a Tale or two which should be mentioned here. These are:—
Ee ii, 15 of the University Library, Cambridge; Harley 1704, Harley
2251, and Harley 2382 of the British Museum. Furthermore, Bernard
mentions a copy of Melibeus in a Gresham College, London, manuscript; and one of the Longleat MSS has fragments of the Parson's
Tale, according to the Hist. MSS. Comm. Report III, p. 181. Some
MSS named by Bernard which I have not been able to identify with
existing codices are:—Canby (or Prynne), Clarendon, Coventry School,
Gresham College above mentioned, Hodley, Worseley. Inquiry regarding the Canby and Worseley, as also regarding the Chandos, Ely, and
Norton MSS used by Urry, was made by Furnivall in N. and Q. 1871
II: 526. For the Norton MS see above under Egerton 2863; for the
Coventry School, not a MS of the Canterbury Tales, see Section IV
here under the ABC.

The Order of the Tales in the MSS. Tyrwhitt was the first editor
to give this point consideration, although according to Francis
Thynne (Animadversions pp. 68-9) his father, in the 1532
Chaucer, examined the Links carefully to see where the Plowman's Tale should be inserted. Tyrwhitt adopted the order of
what he called "the best manuscripts", *i. e.,* the Ellesmere and
its allies, making one difference in that he placed the ML endlink as the Shipman's headlink, see Introd. Disc. § xxxi. No
discussion of the matter appears in the Chiswick or the 1845
Aldine, both of which follow Tyrwhitt; Wright in 1847-51
printed the Harley 7334 text, the order of which is like the
Ellesmere except in the position of the G fragment. His text
was adopted by Bell, and by Morris in the revised Aldine, although neither of these editors discussed the question of
arrangement. In Notes and Queries 1865 II : 13 was printed
a letter from J. Dixon, asking for further light on the subject,
and in the same journal for 1868, II : 149, 245, appeared Furnivall's "Groups and Order of the Canterbury Tales"; these
results were afterwards printed in tabular form as Trial-Tables,
and prefixed to Part I of the Chaucer Society's Six-Text, with
a note of emendation by Furnivall. Taken in conjunction with
the Specimens of Moveable Prologues printed by the Chaucer
Society, these Tables afford clue to the arrangement and linking
of Tales in many, though by no means all, of the MSS.

Furnivall discussed the matter in detail in his Temporary
Preface, noted below, and added a condensed account to Warton-Hazlitt II : 379 ff. Bradshaw, who did not entirely agree
with Furnivall, made suggestions in a letter to him of Sept. 21,
1868, see Prothero's Memoir p. 350, and sketched a plan of
investigation in his Skeleton of Chaucer's Canterbury Tales.
Later editors have generally followed the conclusions of Furnivall; see references below.

A Temporary Preface to the Chaucer Society's Six-Text edition of Chaucer's Canterbury Tales, Part I, attempting to show the right Order of the Tales, and the Days and Stages of the Pilgrimage, etc., by F. J. Furnivall, M. A. Chaucer Society, 2d Series, No. 3. 1868.

Furnivall decides for the order of fragments as $AB^1 B^2$ CDEFGHI. His "Scheme" is reprinted as Appendix C to the revised Aldine Chaucer.

The Skeleton of Chaucer's Canterbury Tales. Henry Bradshaw. Published in Nov. 1871, and included in Bradshaw's Collected Papers, Cambridge, 1889, pp. 102 ff. Written in 1867. Bradshaw emphasized the necessity of regarding the various links or prologues to the separate fragments as the main line of action of the poem; he indicated lines of difference among the MSS, principally in the links, upon the strength of which he suggested MS-groups of three sorts, viz.:

I. "The least correct." Has the Tale of Gamelyn. At the end of B^1 the link is retained, and made to introduce the Squire. In E^1 there is no concluding stanza to the Tale, the stanzas of the envoy are transposed, and there is no link-stanza. The Merchant has no introductory link, and the link at the end of E^1 is perverted so as to introduce the Franklin. The endlink of the Squire is perverted so as to introduce the Merchant. Fragment G has the link at the end. The Monk's Tale has the modern instances wedged in; and the Nun's Priest's Tale has the endlink.

II. "The most authentic." Has Gamelyn. The link is retained at the end of B^1, though useless. The Clerk's Tale has the concluding stanza and the right order of stanzas, but not the link-stanza. The Merchant has an introductory link, and the Squire's endlink correctly introduces the Franklin. Fragment G occurs in its right place, and sometimes has, sometimes has not, the endlink. Fragment C has not the spurious link introducing the Shipman. The modern instances of the Monk's Tale are wedged in.

III. The order adopted by Tyrwhitt, and seen in the Ellesmere, etc. Agrees in the main with II, but the alterations seem to be the result of some editorial supervision exercised after Chaucer's death. Gamelyn is suppressed. The endlink of B^1 is suppressed. The Clerk's Tale has the concluding stanzas in the right order, and usually the endlink. In Merchant and in Squire the links are right. G is put between B^2 and H, and the endlink is suppressed. C has not the spurious endlink, and the Monk's modern instances are at the end of his tale.

Bradshaw though suggesting to Furnivall (in 1868) that B^2 should be lifted up to follow B^1, made no definite scheme of the

order of the tales; he contented himself with outlining the way
in which the evidence should be gathered and studied. For his
"lift" of B² see Furnivall, Temporary Preface p. 22, Academy
1874 I: 174, and Prothero's Memoir of Bradshaw p. 350.

The Chronology of Chaucer's Writings. John Koch. Ch. Soc. 2d
Series, No. 27. Dated London, 1890.

Pages 54 ff. discuss the order of the Canterbury Tales. The
subject is treated too hastily and with too much conjecture.
Shipley, in his paper mentioned below, says that it is often
"mere guesswork", and not always clear. Although suggesting
for the C fragment a position between B¹ and B², and for F a
position between B² and CD, etc., Koch seems finally to agree
with Furnivall.

In the Academy 1891 II: 96 and in the Oxford Chaucer III: 434,
Skeat takes up the question of the order of the tales. He says,
in his 1894 Chaucer, "I have been obliged to follow suit
(*i. e.,* to the Chaucer Society); but I wish to make a note that
the right order of the Groups is A, B, D, E, F, C, G, H, I."
See Furnivall, Academy 1894 II: 86.

Arrangement of the Canterbury Tales. G. Shipley. Mod. Lang.
Notes, 10 : 260 (1895). Shipley would place C before B.
Furnivall, Academy 1895 II : 296, adopts Shipley's theory;
Fleay writes, *ibid.* II : 343 that he had already proposed that
arrangement, Folklore Record 1879 II : 162, and adds that he
had then also advocated putting F before D. See Shipley,
Mod. Lang. Notes 11 : 290.

On the Order of the Canterbury Tales. Caxton's Two Editions.
Eleanor P. Hammond, Modern Philology 3 : 159 ff.

———

The Classification of the MSS. With the question of the arrangement of Tales in the MSS there is closely interwoven the question of the classification of the MSS, and the relation of their
groups. Bradshaw, as above, insisted upon the classification of
codices according to the state of their Links, that is, according
to their arrangement of the Tales; but his suggestion has not
been acted upon by any editor, and the order of Tales in
present-day editions is determined by the time and place
allusions contained in the Links, while the classification of MSS
made by Zupitza and Koch is in accordance with the state of
the text in one small portion of the work, that by Skeat
(nominally) in accordance with the order of Tales, although
Skeat does not permit this grouping to interfere with the
exercise of his judgment as to the Chaucerian text.

The classification of the MSS was very briefly treated by
Skeat in Academy 1891 II : 96 and Oxford Chaucer IV : xxiii.

He makes four main types, on the strength principally of the order of the Tales.[1] He does not use the other tests indicated by Bradshaw, nor even discuss them, though he departs materially from Bradshaw in his view of the Ellesmere group as "Chaucerian." He does not allow his election of this group as the most authentic to interfere with the moving up of B^2 or the adoption, at any time, of textual readings not sanctioned by that group; and he does not use all the MSS. His types are:

I: A, B^1, D, E, F, C, B^2, G, H, I.

This is the order of the Ellesmere and its allies; is the order adopted by Tyrwhitt; is the order due, according to Bradshaw, to a reviser.

II: A, B^1, D, E, F, G, C, B^2, H, I.

This is seen in Harley 7334; acording to Bradshaw this type is "the most authentic."

III: A, B^1, F^1, D, E, F^2, G, C, B^2, H, I.

As Skeat words it, this type "splits" F and separates its parts.

IV: A, B^1, F^1, E^2, D, E^1, F^2, G, C, B^2, H, I.

In Skeat's phrasing, a variety of III "with further splitting." For criticism of Skeat see Modern Philology 3 : 163.

A classification of the MSS was made by Zupitza, in his edition of the Pardoner's Prologue and Tale from all accessible MSS; his notes, interrupted by his death, are to be found in the introductions to Nos. LXXXI, LXXXV, LXXXVI, of the Chaucer Society's First Series. Mark H. Liddell, in the introduction to Part 4 of these Specimens (No. XC of the Society's Publications), presents in diagrammatic form on p. xlvii the genealogy of the Cant. Tales MSS, from Zupitza's results.

Liddell, in his edition of the Prologue and Knight's Tale, utilizes these results, and emphasizes that his edition is the first critical text of any part of the Canterbury Tales. See the correspondence Athenaeum 1901 II : 380, 597, 631, especially the editorial note on p. 598, mentioned below.

Professor John Koch, taking up Zupitza's unfinished work, edited the remaining parts of the Specimens for the Chaucer Society, Nos. XC, XCI, XCIII, XCIV. Koch then published: The Pardoner's Prologue and Tale. A Critical Edition. Berlin 1902, and adopted as a publication by the Chaucer Society.

[1] Skeat's paper on the Evolution of the Canterbury Tales (Ch. Soc. 1907) appeared after this book was in type.

In the introduction to this, Chapter VI, Koch discusses the relations of the MSS, pointing out on p. xxxv that in his grouping of them he only takes into account the text of the Pardoner, leaving aside the other Tales and their arrangement in the different MSS of the Canterbury Tales. On the same page he says that in his classification he deviates somewhat from Zupitza, and still more from Skeat. His grouping is:

(Type A) I: The Ellesmere-Dd group.
II: The Gg group.
These are classed together by Skeat, as I.
(Type B) III: The Harley 7334 group, including the Paris MS, Adds. 35286, and Harley 7335.
IV: The Selden group, Selden B 14 and Hatton Donat. 1.
V: The Tc group, Trin. Coll. Cambr. R 3, 15, Rawl. poet. 223, Glasgow, and Adds. 25718.
VI: The Co group, headed by Corpus, and composed of 8 MSS, the two Caxtons, and Thynne's print.
VII: The Pe group, the most numerous, headed by Petworth, and composed of 20 MSS.

The remark of the Athenaeum editor or reviewer, 1901 II : 598, when discussing Liddell's "critical" text of the Prologue, etc., is exceedingly applicable here also; that a "critical" text which assumes (1) the correctness of Zupitza's classification of the MSS of the Pardoner's Tale, and (2) the applicability of that classification to the Prologue, takes positions which are not beyond dispute. As said elsewhere, "In default of that detailed comparison of the entire mass of texts which lies in the future, we may base a tentative classification of the MSS of the Canterbury Tales upon these data:—The order of the Tales in every manuscript, accompanied necessarily by notes explaining whether that order be the original one, or whether the book shows signs of displacement; general notes upon the state of the text in every MS, with especial attention, as Bradshaw required, to the Links; minute notes upon the state of the text in some few portions of the text, portions taken preferably from different fascicules. A classification not based upon all these sorts of evidence must be regarded as unconvincing." See, for further discussion of the point and of Koch's method, Modern Philology 3 : 166 ff., and under F below.

I append a classification of the MSS made in accordance with Bradshaw's suggestions; for further discussion see under F

below. The curved line of connection between the names of
two fragments denotes the existence of a Link.

Group I. The order A B¹ D E F C B² G H I is found in:
Ellesmere, Gg, Dd, Egerton 2726, Devonshire, Egerton 2864,
Adds. 5140, Bodley 686, Hodson 39, Adds. 35286. To the same
group probably belong Paris, Harley 7335, Trinity 49, and the
archetype of Christ Church; and the Hengwrt MS, though a
hybrid, is allied to this type. The characteristics of these MSS
are: the absence of Gamelyn (present in Trinity 49), the absence of the ML endlink, the absence of spurious matter from
the links, the completion of the E and F links, and the place of
G between B² and H. The text is usually superior to that of
other groups; and although Bradshaw viewed this type as due
to some editorial supervision exercised after Chaucer's death,
I would venture to differ from that opinion, and to regard the
group as Chaucerian, because of the absence of spurious links
and the absence of the ML endlink, features, it seems to me,
which no copyist or imitator, only the author himself, could
have arranged. Furthermore, there is found in some of this
class of MSS one additional link, with which a few MSS have
tampered; at the end of B² is a connective of 16 lines, introducing only "another" and nameless pilgrim. This exists in six
MSS,—Dd, Christ Church, Egerton 2864, Hodson 39, Adds.
5140, and in Royal 17 (this last a hybrid MS); three of these
codices, Egerton, Hodson 39, and Adds. 5140, have six additional and spurious lines, introducing the Second Nun, whose
tale follows.

Laud 600, possibly a hybrid, has the order of Tales seen here,
and has no ML endlink; but it has Gamelyn, and its Clerk's
Tale does not end ready for the Merchant's headlink. This
group may be termed the Ellesmere Group.

Group II. The order A Gamelyn B¹ D E F G C B² H I is found
in:—Harley 7334. The special peculiarities of this enigmatic
MS are numerous; see Section III B (1) here. It agrees
with the Ellesmere group in the absence of spurious matter, in the completion of the links, and in the sequence of
fragments, except that G precedes C; but it retains the ML endlink, with the additional idiosyncrasy of showing in line 17 of
that link the name of the Summoner as the next speaker.
This latter trait is also found in Royal 17 and Rawl. poet. 223.

Group III. The order A D E¹ E² F¹ F² B¹ B² G C H I is represented in:—Selden B 14. This MS is the only known text
connecting Man of Law and Shipman, the former being
moved down to meet B². Clerk and Merchant, Merchant and
Squire, are united as in the Ellesmere group, but there are no
Words of the Franklin, and the Monk's endlink is in the short
form, see p. 242 below. No Tale of Gamelyn is present; there

is a spurious link GC. Selden's actual order is more confused than as above indicated, but the Links show the sequence $E^1 E^2 F^1$.

Group IV. The order A Gamelyn $B^1 F^1 E^2 D E^1 F^2 G C B^2 H$ I, with varying conditions of links, is found as follows: (a) Harley 7333 and R 3, 15, while linking Squire to Man of Law by the use of the Squire's name in line 17 of the ML endlink, and while dissociating the Merchant from the Clerk in position, have nevertheless the Clerk-Merchant link arranged, though broken. They have no Words of Franklin, *i. e.*, no link $F^1 F^2$, and no connective $E^2 F^1$. Further, they both show the short form of the Monk's endlink, see p. 242 below.

The same union Man of Law-Squire, the most important characteristic of this group, is in: (b) Corpus, Sloane 1686, Lansdowne. These have no bond $E^2 F^1$ nor $F^1 F^2$, a partial connection $E^1 E^2$, an imperfect form of Merchant's Tale, and in Corpus and Sloane the short form of the Monk's endlink. As the principal distinction between these and Harley 7333 is the latter's completed connection Clerk-Merchant, I would suggest that the two archetypes represent an almost identical stage in Chaucer's work.

The same union Man of Law-Squire is found in: (c) Harley 1758, Rawl. poet. 149, Sloane 1685, Lichfield, Hodson-Ashb., Egerton 2863, Royal 18, Laud 739, Barlow. But these MSS have added spurious connectives. The Words of the Franklin have been written in after the Squire, and altered (?) to fit the Merchant, whose Tale is next to Squire; a link has been constructed between Clerk and Franklin, composed either of the Verba Hospitis and the Squire's short prologue altered to fit the Franklin, or of the same plus a bit of the Merchant's epilogue. Spurious links GC and CB^2 have been written into most of these MSS, and in the last three above mentioned a link E^2D has been added. Of the class, Harley 1758 has the least spurious matter in its Links.

In Northumberland and in New College the order is A B^1 $F^1 E^2 D E^1 F^2 G C B^2 H I$, but the state of the Links is unknown to me. Bodley 414 is probably an imperfect copy of this class, as is R 3, 3.

The lift of Squire to Man of Law is also seen in: (d) Petworth, Mm, Hatton, Ii. This group places Merchant after Squire, like (a); but here the regular connective of Merchant-Squire, altered to introduce Franklin, appears after E^2 In Hatton and Ii the Franklin's Tale has been moved up between E^2 and D accordingly; in Petworth and Mm the order is as in Group IV, but the link $E^2 F^1$ stands, altered, in front of the Franklin; this arrangement was therefore probably the earlier, the Hatton-Ii archetype carrying the Franklin up to suit the

Link-conditions. The Mm archetype, as its occasional Tale-numbers indicate, closely resembled the archetype of Corpus. This group is here termed the Corpus-7333 Group.

Summarizing, we have:

    I. A B^1 D E F C B^2 G H I. Ellesmere Group.

          Ellesmere, Gg, Dd, Egerton 2726, Devonshire, Egerton 2864, Adds. 5140, Hodson 39, Adds. 35286.

    II. A Gamelyn B^1 D E F G C B^2 H I.

          Harley 7334.

    III. A D E^1 E^2 F^1 F^2 B^1 B^2 G C H I.

          Selden B 14.

    IV. (a) A B^1 F^1 E^2 D E^1 F^2 G C B^2 H I. The Corpus-7333 Group.

          Harley 7333, R 3, 15.

        (b) A Gamelyn B^1 F^1 D E^1 E^2 F^2 G C B^2 H I.

          Corpus, Sloane 1686, Lansdowne. [Delamere?]

        (c) A Gamelyn B^1 F^1 E^2 D E^1 F^2 G C B^2 H I.

          Harley 1758, Sloane 1685, Rawl. poet. 149, Lichfield, Hodson-Ashb., Egerton 2863, Royal 18, Laud 739, Barlow. (Northumberland, New??)
          There is no Gamelyn in Lichfield, New, Northumberland.

        (d) A Gamelyn B^1 F^1 E^2 D E^1 F^2 G C B^2 H I.

          Petworth, Mm.

        (e) A Gamelyn B^1 F^1 E^2 F^2 D E^1 G C B^2 H I.

          Hatton, Ii.

For fuller discussion see under III F below.

Manuscripts not included in the above classification are those containing but one or two Tales, as Harley 1704, Harley 2251, Harley 2382, Arundel 140, Ee ii, 15, Pepys 2006, Naples, Phillipps 8299, Longleat 257; those incomplete or confused, like Ashburnham 126, Adds. 25718, Harley 1239, Holkham, Rawlinson 141, Sion College; or MSS undescribed, such as Glasgow, College of Physicians, Helmingham, Lincoln, three Phillipps MSS, and Lady Cardigan's codex.

B. Manuscripts of the Canterbury Tales

(1) *In the British Museum*

Descriptions of British Museum MSS may be found in the catalogues listed by Madan, Books in Manuscript, p. 166 ff. Of these, the catalogues especially important to Chaucer-students are: that of the Cotton MSS, London 1802; of the Harleian, 4 vols., London 1812; of the Lansdowne, London 1819; and that of the Additional MSS, of which there has appeared at intervals since 1833 a "List of Additions to the MSS" etc.; some 38,000 codices are marked thus. This last catalogue and that of the Egerton MSS include most MSS acquired by purchase. For complete details and minor catalogues see Madan as cited. Some Chaucer MSS are described by Ward, Catalogue of Romances in the Department of MSS of the British Museum.

Additionals 5140: Paper quires in vellum covers; the first vellum leaf, a guard leaf, is lacking. The Canterbury Tales begin on 2a with a border. The hand changes with the Prioress' headlink, fol. 227a; this second hand has catchwords, which appear every 12 leaves. Of 423 folios, well executed, the first page with an elaborate capital and border, and the arms of Henry Dene, Archbishop of Canterbury temp. Henry VII, on lower margin. Contains the Canterbury Tales and Lydgate's Story of Thebes, the latter imperfect at close.

The Pardoner's Tale is printed Ch. Soc. Specimens part I; the Nun's Priest's endlink is printed Six-Text p. 301, the Merchant's headlink *ibid.* p. 442, the Squire's headlink *ibid.* p. 478, the Words of the Franklin *ibid.* p. 498, the Retractation *ibid.* for the Hengwrt MS. Folio 94b is reproduced Ch. Soc. Autotypes, dated 1475-1500. The MS was used by Tyrwhitt as Askew II.
Order of Tales:—A B^1 D E F C B^2 G H I.
There is no Man of Law's endlink (Shipman's prologue); the connections of E and F are as in modern editions; the Monk's endlink has been corrected from the shorter to the longer form, see p. 242 here; the Nun's Priest's epilogue is present, and has six additional spurious lines, not printed with it in the Six-Text as above. The MS belongs, roughly speaking, to the Ellesmere class.

Additionals 25718: Vellum, of 88 leaves 10½ by 7 inches. Fairly written in a XV century hand, with poor rubrication. An imperfect copy of the Canterbury Tales.

The Pardoner's Tale is printed Ch. Soc. Specimens part II.
Contains portions only of the tales of Knight, Miller, Man of Law, Summoner, Doctor, Pardoner, Clerk, Shipman, Prioress, Melibeus.

Additionals 35286: Vellum, of 238 leaves 12⅛ by 8¾ inches, of the beginning of the XV century. Carefully written; headings in red, and blue and red initials; names of owners. Lacks Prologue 1-153 and 234-396, also other portions. Was formerly Ashburnham 125; bought by the Museum in 1899.

The Pardoner's Tale is printed Ch. Soc. Specimens part V.
Order of Tales:—A B^1 D G^1 E F C B^2 H G^2 I. The Knight's

Tale is imperfect: there is no Man of Law's endlink (Shipman's prologue); a blank space is left after the Squire's Tale; there are gaps in B².

Skeat, IV: 5, 8, 12, remarks that the MS has points of agreement and points of difference as compared with the Ellesmere.

(The above is mainly from the Adds. Catalogue.)

Arundel 140: According to Ward, Catalogue II: 224 (*q. v.*), this MS contains an imperfect copy of the tale of Melibeus.

Egerton 2726: Vellum, 271 leaves 12 by 8¼ inches, containing the Canterbury Tales only. In a good early (?) hand, 40 lines to the page, with a 7-line capital at beginning. The latter part of the MS is apparently in a different hand, but I cannot say where it changes; there are catchwords in eights from 102b on, but not previously. A Jacobean copy of Gamelyn, for which there is no provision in the text, has been bound in after fol. 55, breaking into the text of the Cook's Tale; the leaves are numbered as if this Tale were part of the MS, 56 to 63. According to Furnivall, Athenaeum 1868 II: 248, this Gamelyn is copied from "Laud K 50", *i. e.*, from Laud 600.

The Pardoner's Tale is printed Ch. Soc. Specimens part II; the link Squire-Franklin is printed Ch. Soc. Specimens of Moveable Prologues p. 32. The MS is used by the Ch. Soc. to fill gaps in Cambridge Dd.

Formerly the Haistwell MS. Used by Tyrwhitt, and by him termed one of the best. Furnivall, Trial Tables, says the Haistwell=Askew I; Koch marks the Ingilby as Askew I.

Order of Tales:—A B¹ D E F C B² G H I. No Man of Law's endlink (Shipman's prologue); the Nun's Priest's endlink is present. The text seems good.

Egerton 2863: Formerly Norton, then Hodson-Norton. See under (7) below, Hodson

Egerton 2864: Formerly Askew I, then Ingilby, then Hodson-Ingilby See under (7) below, Hodson.

Harley 1239: Parchment; contains Troilus and Cressida, the Knight's Tale, lacking lines 1-34, the Man of Law's prologue and Tale, the Wife of Bath's Tale, the Clerk's Tale, an imperfect copy of the Franklin's Tale. (From the Harleian Catalogue.)

The Clerk's Tale is printed Ch Soc. Specimens part VI. A descriptive note is in the preface to Urry; this MS was his No. II. It was used by Tyrwhitt.

Harley 1704: Vellum and paper, a miscellaneous collection; no. 7, foll. 28a-31a, is the Prioress' Tale, somewhat modified.

Harley 1758: Vellum, given by Dean Atterbury, and containing "a very antient and fair Copie of Chaucers Canterbury Tales." (Harl. Cat.) Of 231 folios 13⅜ by 9⅛ inches, in eights, and beginning on fol. 1 of the first gathering. Fine illuminated initials, and border to page 1; this and a few subsequent leaves are somewhat battered. Some leaves are lacking, and there is a blank space of two leaves after the Squire's Tale, being the remainder of the tenth gathering. Words and passages are often added in the margin by the scribe.

The Tale of Gamelyn is printed Ch. Soc. Six-Text in the Appendix to Group A; also as appendix to the separate print of the Hengwrt MS. The Pardoner's Tale is printed Ch. Soc. Specimens, part IV. The link Man of Law-Squire is printed Ch. Soc. Specimens of Moveable Prologues, p. 10; the link Squire-Merchant is printed ibid. p. 40; the link Clerk-Franklin ibid. p. 53. The headlinks to Friar and Summoner are printed Six-Text p. 371, p. 383; the ending of the Merchant's Tale ibid. 473. The MS has the Retractation, printed Ch. Soc. Six-Text to fill out the Cambridge MS; and it and Sloane 1685 are used by the Society to supply other gaps in the Cambridge. Fol. 97b is reproduced Ch. Soc. Autotypes; there dated ca. 1450.

Descriptive note in the preface to Urry; this is Urry's MS I. Used by Tyrwhitt.

Order of Tales: A Gamelyn B¹ F¹ E² D E¹ F² G C B² H I. There is a spurious link Pardoner-Shipman of 12 lines.

Harley 2251: For list of contents and detailed discussion see Anglia 28 : 1 ff. The only Chaucerian articles of the codex are: the Prioress' Tale, with its prologue, and Fortune, Gentilesse, the ABC, the Complaint to his Purse. These latter are printed by the Chaucer Society as noted Section IV here under the Minor Poems. The textual value of the MS, as pointed out under the Anglia reference above and ibid. 30 : 320-348, is less than negative; the Harley, derived as it is in part from a lost Shirley (with its sister Adds. 34360), in part from an existing Shirley, Trinity R 3, 20, and in part from other MSS by Shirley anterior to the Shirley MS Ashmole 59, has further debased these untrustworthy sources by a number of freedoms of its own, which debar it from any consideration in the construction of a critical text.

Harley 2382: On paper, contains:
(1) Lydgate's Life of the Virgin, in 4 books, imperfect at the beginning.
(2) De Assumpcione Sancte Maria, in two books; the colophon says that they belong with the preceding article, but see Horstmann as below.
(3) Oracio ad Sanctam Mariam, beginning "Mary moder welle thou be".
(4) Testament of "Dan Johan Lydgarde", i. e., Lydgate.

(5) Fabula monialis de Sancte Maria, *i. e.*, the Prioress' Tale.
(6) Vita Sancte Cecilie, *i. e.*, the Second Nun's Tale.
(7) De Sancto Erasmo Martire. ed. Horstmann, Sammlung altengl. Legenden, 1878.
(8) Testamentum Cristi.
(9) The Childe of Bristow. Printed Retrosp. Review 1854, p. 198; in Hazlitt's Remains of Early Popular Poetry, I : 111-131; and in Horstmann, Altengl. Legenden, p. 315.

Harley 7333: Vellum, 211 leaves 17⅝ by 13⅛ inches. Contemporary pagination shows loss of 24 leaves at the beginning. Written in double columns in a large clear XV century script, not the hand of John Shirley, unless executed before Shirley's old age. Attributed to Shirley by Skeat, by Pollard in Dict. Nat. Biog., by Furnivall in Athenaeum 1871 I : 210 and in supplem. vol. of the Ballad Society p. 34; in the Ch. Soc. Autotypes, where fol. 37a is reproduced, Furnivall speaks of the MS as "probably copied by Impingham from Shirley." In this he follows Madden, see Orig. and Anal. p. 56. Dated in the Ch. Soc. Autotypes ca. 1450. See Foerster, Archiv 103 : 149 for disbelief of Shirley's hand in the MS. From the full "gossippy" headings and the occasional Shirleyan spelling, evidently copied from Shirley. List of contents in the Harleian catalogue; see Ward's Cat. of Romances I : 494; Meyer, John Gowers Beziehungen p. 64; Macaulay, Works of John Gower, II : cxlv. Used by Tyrwhitt.

    Contents:—Chronicle of Brut, impf. at beginning. Prose. (2) Burgh's Cato. Other MSS listed and grouped by Foerster, Archiv 101 : 45; text edited *id.* Archiv 115 : 298-323 and 116 : 25-40. (3) Lament of a Prisoner against Fortune, 21 stanzas of 7 lines. Also in Harley 2251 and Adds. 34360; there written as a continuation of Chaucer's Fortune. To be printed. (4) Lydgate's Pedigree of Henry VI. Printed by Wright, Polit. Poems, Rolls Series, II : 131; the "Roundel against the Coronation" which follows is printed in Ritson's Ancient Songs, 1877 I : 110, and in Skeat's ed. of Guest's English Rhythms, p. 646. (5) Lydgate's Guy of Warwick. Printed from Laud 683 by Zupitza, Vienna 1873; in 1874 he alluded to 3 other MSS, probably meaning the two in the Brit. Mus. and Trin. Coll. Cambr. R 3, 21. The last 78 lines of the poem are printed from Harley 7333 in Bishop Percy's Folio Manuscript II : 520. Ward, loc. cit., describes this MS and Lansdowne 699; the variants of the latter were printed by Kölbing, Germania 21 : 365. Robinson, in Harvard Studies V : 194, describes two more MSS, the Leyden, which is sister to the Lansdowne, and the Harvard Shirley. This last text and the text of Harley 7333 are of the same class, says Robinson. (6) Sellyng's "Evidens to be ware," see Warton-Hazlitt III : 169, Gaertner's John Shirley, p. 10, where a few lines are given. To be printed. (7) A French ballad by Charles of Orleans; see Foerster, Archiv 103 : 151 note. (8) The Canterbury Tales. With an elaborate Shirleyan heading printed by Furnivall Temp. Pref. pp. 115-116, and also, the spelling modernized, in Macmillan's

Magazine, 1872, p. 385, vol. 27; it is reproduced in Ch. Soc. Autotypes. Order of Tales, A B¹ F¹ E² D E¹ F² G C Prioress B²
H I. A fascicule is missing between E² and D, which breaks off
the text at line 874 of the Merchant's Tale, resuming at line 79
of the Friar's Tale. The tale of the Shipman is not in the MS, and
the Parson's Tale is unfinished. The link Man of Law-Squire is
printed Ch. Soc. Specimens of Moveable Prologues p. 11; the Verba
Hospitis, after Clerk's Tale, are printed *ibid.* p. 56; the Merchant's
headlink is printed Six-Text p. 442; the Clerk's in Specimens, part
VII p. 82. There is no link Squire-Merchant, *i. e.,* no Words of the
Franklin; the Merchant's Tale is defective at end by loss of leaves
105-112. The Monk's endlink is in the short form; for note on
this and on the probable genealogy of the MS see p. 242 below.
The Pardoner's Tale is printed Ch. Soc. Specimens part III.   (9)
Seven tales from Gower's Confessio Amantis; one of these, the
story of the Emperor Merelaus' wife, is printed Ch. Soc. Orig.
and Anal. pp. 57-70. After the first are inserted some proverbs
marked "Quod Impingham." (10) Chaucer's Parlement of Foules.
Printed Ch. Soc. PT pp. 49 ff. (11) Chaucer's Compleynt of Mars.
Printed Ch. Soc. PT pp. 101 ff. Unfinished; the second column not
filled out. The next two leaves are cut away. (12) Chaucer's
Anelida. Printed Ch. Soc. PT pp. 145 ff. and One-Text Print pp.
109 ff. (13) Complaint against Hope, 15 stanzas of 8 lines. Also
in Fairfax 16 and Bodley 638. (14) Complaint d'Amours. Also
in Fairfax 16 and Bodley 638; and in all three MSS the poems
occur together as here. This poem was printed by Skeat in Academy 1888 I : 307 as Chaucer's; also in his Minor Poems, and in
Oxford Chaucer I : 411, from this MS. (15) Lydgate's St. Edmund
and St. Fremund. Printed by Horstmann, Altenglische Legenden,
from Harley 2278, with variants from Ashmole 46. Horstmann
says, *ibid.* p. 376, that Fremund alone is in Harley 372; but that
MS contains both. The Ashmole version is, according to ten Brink,
Hist. Eng. Lit. III : 273, certainly not Lydgate's own. For other
copies see Cambridge Ee ii, 15, Harley 4826, Tanner 347, the Mostyn
MSS in Hist. MSS Comm. Report IV : 350, Warton-Hazlitt III :57;
bits in Ashmole 59, Harley 2255. (16) Lydgate's Complaint of
Christ, 15 stanzas of 8 lines. See Anglia 30: 330. (17) Chaucer's
Stedfastnesse. Printed Ch. Soc. PT pp. 433 ff. (18) Chaucer's
Gentilesse. Printed Ch. Soc. PT pp. 427 ff. (19) Chaucer's Truth.
Printed Ch. Soc. SPT pp. 153 ff. (20) Chaucer's Purse. Printed
Ch. Soc. PT pp. 447 ff. (21) Two balades by "Halsam Squiere",
see Anglia 28: 4. Printed from this MS in Reliq. Antiq. 1 : 234,
and by Flügel in Anglia 14: 463. Printed by Caxton; printed from
another MS in Bell's Chaucer, vol. 6. (22) Dialogue between Man
and Death, Latin rimes. (23) A bit from the English prose translation of De Guileville's Pilgrimage. (24) Lydgate's Verses on
English Kings, ending with Henry VI, and leaving space for another stanza. See Anglia 28: 6-7. (25) "Maister Benet's Christmas Game", see Warton-Hazlitt III : 134; four times printed, see
Foerster, Archiv 101 : 52-53. (26) Parts of the Gesta Romanorum,
in English prose. (27) Hoccleve's Dialogus inter Occliue et Mendi-
cum, see Furnivall's ed., EETS, of Hoccleve's Minor Poems, vol. I.

Harley 7334: Vellum, 286 leaves 14 by 9½ inches, in eights, beginning on the first leaf of the first booklet. Written in one clear,
handsome book-hand of the XV century. The first page has a
6-line illuminated capital and a border of foliage and flowers

conventionally treated, picked out in red and blue upon a gold ground. Similar illuminations mark the beginning of each tale, and the capitals throughout the volume are ornamented. Running titles in red. On the last folio are notes by former owners, with their names. Contains the Canterbury Tales only.

Printed entire by the Chaucer Society, 1885. The text was previously printed by Wright in 1847-51, this was reprinted in Cooke's Universal Library, n. d. (1853?), and in the undated eds. of Crowell, New York, and of Blackwood about 1880. Also reprinted in Bell's Chaucer of 1854, and by Morris in his revision of the Aldine Chaucer. No one of these, except the Chaucer Society print, really reproduces the MS, see Skeat, Chaucer Canon, pp. 25-28. The Man of Law's endlink is printed Ch. Soc. Specimens of Moveable Prologues, p. 3.

The Harleian Cat. makes but a two-line note on this MS; description in Ward I: 508 ff.; notes in Temp. Pref. pp. 70-85, where special readings of the Prologue are listed, and in the Forewords to the Ch. Soc. print; see also Wright's preface to his ed. Child's Observations were based upon Wright's text of this MS, to which he attributed greater accuracy than do later critics.

The order of Tales is:—A Gamelyn B^1 D E F G C B^2 H I. The Cook's Tale has but 48 lines; the Man of Law's endlink has not the last five lines, and introduces the Summoner; fragments E and F are fully connected, for although a fascicule is lost at end of Squire and beginning of Franklin, the line-count makes it probable that the Words of the Franklin were there. The Merchant's epilogue and Squire's headlink are on the last verso of a booklet, the Squire's Tale on the following recto. The Monk's headlink begins "When ended was my tale"; the endlink is of 54 lines; the Recantation is at close of Parson's Tale. The Knight's Tale does not contain the passage lines 1154-59.

This MS is, with Cambridge Gg, the most enigmatic of Chaucerian codices. In Prothero's Memoir of Bradshaw, p. 225, is a note stating that one of Bradshaw's reasons for abandoning an ed. of the Tales is believed to have been "his inability to account for the wide divergences which distinguish the Harleian manuscript." Pollard suggests (Introd. to Globe Chaucer p. xxix) that many of these readings may represent Chaucer's own corrections upon a finished copy, and that the Harley is a careless transcription of such a text. In the Athenaeum 1901 II : 631 Pollard speaks of "the eternal crux of Harley 7334." It might be conjectured from the completed connections of E and F and the full form of the Monk's endlink on the one hand, the lack of some lines and the presence of the Summoner's name on the other hand, that the Harley derived from A and B^1 fascicules of an earlier type, the rest of its text from revised work. A paper dealing with the MS was read before the Philological Society by Miss E. Morley, reported Athen. 1901 I : 216. A detailed study, by Tatlock is announced to appear in Modern Philology. See also Skeat's Chaucer Society paper, 1907, and Tatlock, Devel. and Chronol., p. 44 note 2.

Folios 1a and 103a are reproduced in the Chaucer Society's Autotypes, where the MS is dated 1400-25; dated in Ward "soon after 1400." 1a is also reprod. in Wülker's Gesch. der engl. Litt. between pp. 156, 157.

Harley 7335: Paper and vellum, 163 folios 11¼ by 8 inches; in eights, 34 lines to the page. Lacks about 1200 lines at beginning. In a small, narrow hand; frequent mutilations have been replaced in blank. No ornament.

The Pardoner's Tale is printed Ch. Soc. Specimens part II; the link Merch.-Squire, Six-Text pp. 476-478. Used by Tyrwhitt, and termed by him one of the MSS deserving most credit.
Order of Tales:—A B¹ D G¹ E F‿C impf. in Pardoner's Tale. Several other Tales are imperfect. There is a blank space after Part II of the Squire's Tale. A spurious link of 6 lines connects Franklin and Doctor; printed by Tyrwhitt, see his Introd. Disc. § xxviii, and his note on line 11929.

Lansdowne 851: Vellum, early XV century. The Canterbury Tales only.

The Tales are printed by the Chaucer Society in the Six-Text, and separately. The tale of Gamelyn is printed Ch. Soc. Appendix to the Six-Text, Group A, and also in their print of the MS; the link Man of Law-Squire is printed Ch. Soc. Specimens of Moveable Prologues p. 7.
Descriptive note in Ward I: 512; see Temp. Pref. p. 62. Folios 1a, 207a are reproduced Ch. Soc. Autotypes; there dated of the first quarter of the XV century; one page is reprod. in Garnett and Gosse's Engl. Lit. I: 166. Used by Tyrwhitt when the Webb MS.
Order of Tales:—A‿Gamelyn B¹ F¹‿D E¹ E² F² G‿C B² H I. There is a link of four lines Cook-Gamelyn; there are eight spurious lines at end of Squire, and four introducing the Wife; the Clerk ends ready for the Merchant, but there is no Merch. headlink; the Merch. Tale ends with line 1074, like Sloane 1686 and Corpus. No Merch. epil.; no Words of Franklin. Spurious links of 16 lines Canon's Yeoman-Doctor, and six lines Pardoner-Shipman, printed Ch. Soc. separate issue of this MS, p. 425, p. 456. It should be remarked of these spurious links that they are quite different from those in c) and d) MSS of the Corpus-7333 group (see p. 172 here), and that they are not present in Lansdowne's nearest relatives.

Royal 17 D xv: On paper, of 348 leaves 11¼ by 8¼ inches, imperfect at beginning, lacking 68 lines. The Canterbury Tales is bound with other works; its last leaves are mere strips, mounted. In two hands, changing at the beginning of a fascicule partway through the Clerk's Tale. The second scribe is the writer of much of Harley 2251 and Adds. 34360, see Anglia 28 : 1 ff.

The Pardoner's Tale is printed Ch. Soc. Specimens part IV; the Man of Law endlink is printed Ch. Soc. Specimens of Moveable Prologues p. 19. Two bits of its tale of Gamelyn are printed by the Ch. Soc. to supply gaps in Harley 1758 and Sloane 1685; see Ward, Catalogue I: 515, where may be found a brief note on the MS. The Nun's Priest's endlink is printed Six-Text p. 301; the Merch. headlink ibid. p. 442. Used by Tyrwhitt, and described in Urry's Chaucer, preface; Urry's MS VIII.

Order of Tales:—A Gamelyn B F¹ E² D E¹ F² G͜ C B² H I.
There are several noteworthy points about this MS. The Man of
Law's endlink has the Summoner's name, like Harley 7334; but
instead of the Squire's Tale following at once, as in so many MSS,
the Squire's Tale is preceded by the Merchant's epilogue and the
Squire's 8-line prologue; his Tale then follows. Although the
Merchant's Tale is out of position, the connections Clerk-Merchant
are present. There are no Words of the Franklin. There is a
spurious link of 14 lines Canon's Yeoman-Doctor; the Shipman
has no heading or assignment. The Nun's Priest has an epilogue
of 16 lines, printed as above.

The text is degenerate in the first hand, and frequently seems
arbitrary; if my conclusions as to the work of the Harley-Adds.
scribe in a scriptorium and from several archetypes are correct
(see Anglia 28 as above), this would explain the composite nature
of the Links in this MS. For note that although the ML endlink
mentions the Summoner, like the Harley 7334 type, the Squire is
next as in another large class of MSS; but the Squire's Tale has
been brought up accompanied by its own headlink and by the Merchant's epilogue. This would indicate, it seems, that in the Royal
a sequence Man of Law-Squire was followed (possibly dictated
by the numbering of an older codex), but that although the Squire's
Tale was moved in obedience to this numbering, its text was taken
from a properly arranged E and F group; and as the Squire booklet
there had (on its first recto?) the link Merchant-Squire, this was
unthinkingly copied by the Royal scribe. And, thirdly, the Nun's
Priest's epilogue is present as in the Ellesmere class of MSS.

Royal 18 C ii: Vellum, in eights, of 272 leaves 12¼ by 8½ inches.
Carefully written in two clear, inelegant hands of XV century,
the second beginning (?) at fol. 237. Contains only the Canterbury Tales. Some leaves in the ML Tale have been misplaced. The poem begins on the first recto of the first fascicule.

The Pardoner's Tale is printed Ch. Soc. Specimens part IV;
the tale of Gamelyn is printed Ch. Soc. Appendix to the Six-Text,
Group A, and as appendix to the print of the Ellesmere MS. The
link Man of Law-Squire is printed Ch. Soc. Specimens of Moveable Prologues, p. 8 and Six-Text p. 167; the spurious link Pardoner-Shipman is printed Specimens as cited p. 27; the link Merchant-Squire is printed *ibid.* p. 41; the link Clerk-Franklin is printed
ibid. p. 55; the Thopas endlink is printed Six-Text p. 199. Fol.
82b is reproduced Ch. Soc. Autotypes; the MS is there dated ca.
1450. Used by Tyrwhitt, and described in Urry's preface; Urry's
MS VII. Brief note in Ward, Catalogue I : 514.

Order of Tales:—A͜ Gamelyn B¹ F¹ E² D͜ E¹ F² G͜ C B² H I.
A spurious link of 16 lines connects Merchant and Wife; this
is also found in Laud 739 and Barlow 20. The Summoner's Tale
ends abruptly, and with two spurious lines, like Sloane 1685, Laud
739, Rawl. 149. The Clerk does not end ready for the Merchant,
nor is the Merch. headlink in the MS. The link Clerk-Franklin
is printed as above noted. There is a spurious link of 14 lines
Canon's Yeoman-Doctor, and one of 12 lines Pardoner-Shipman.
Retractation and colophon at close.

Sloane 1685: Vellum, 223 leaves 12 by 8⁵⁄₁₆ inches. Written in a
clear, coarse XV century hand, in eights, with occasional miss-

ing leaves; contains the Canterbury Tales only. Runs 36 lines to the page, and began originally on the first recto of a booklet, as the first 648 lines are missing, and the first catchword is on the 7th verso. (648÷36=18 pages, =9 leaves.) Capitals and running titles rubricated, and illuminated initial at the beginning of each tale. There is apparently a change in script on the first recto of the 7th fascicule. The last leaf is blank.

The tale of Gamelyn is printed Ch. Soc. Appendix to Six-Text, Group A, and also as appendix to their print of the Cambridge MS. The Pardoner's Tale is printed Ch. Soc. Specimens part IV. The link Man of Law-Squire is printed Ch. Soc. Specimens of Moveable Prologues p. 5 and Six-Text p. 167; the link Pardoner-Shipman is printed Specimens as cited p. 26; the link Squire-Merchant is printed *ibid.* p. 36 and Six-Text p. 498; the link Clerk-Franklin is printed Specimens as cited p. 51. The Reeve's headlink, Cook's Tale, link Shipman-Prioress, Monk endlink, Pardoner headlink, Clerk headlink, Franklin headlink, are printed in the Six-Text, where this MS is used to supply gaps, mainly in Cambridge Gg.

There is a descriptive note in Ward, Catalogue I : 514. The MS was used by Tyrwhitt, and was described in the preface to Urry; it is Urry's MS III. Folio 178a is reproduced Ch. Soc. Autotypes; there dated of the first third of the XV century.

Order of Tales:—A Gamelyn B¹ F¹ E² D E¹ F² G C B² imperfect. The Cook's Tale has two spurious lines connecting to Gamelyn; there is no epilogue to Merchant; the Summoner's Tale has the abrupt spurious ending; the connection Clerk-Franklin is of two seven-line stanzas; the Words of the Franklin are given to the Merchant, connecting him to the Squire; there is a spurious link of 14 lines from Canon's Yeoman to Doctor, and one from Pardoner to Shipman of 12 lines. There is no Thopas or Melibeus, though the Monk's headlink, following the Prioress' Tale, begins as usual. The beginning of the Man of Law's headlink is missing, also the latter part of the Nun's Priest's Tale.

Sloane 1686: Paper, in a fairly clear but loose hand. Runs 32 lines to page; begins imperfect, with line 63 of Gen. Prol., *i. e.,* lacks one leaf. Of 295 leaves 10⅛ by 7⁷⁄₁₆ inches, containing the Canterbury Tales only. Rubricated throughout, but the initials are very poorly executed. According to the Trial Tables, "a late MS."

The Pardoner's Tale is printed Ch. Soc. Specimens part III. The link Man of Law-Squire is printed Ch. Soc. Specimens of Moveable Prologues p. 12. The MS was used by Tyrwhitt, and by Urry; it is described in Urry's preface as his MS IV.

Order of Tales:—A Gamelyn B¹ F¹ D E¹ E² F² G C B² H imperfect. No connection Cook-Gamelyn; the Clerk ends ready for Merchant, but there is no headlink; the Merchant's Tale breaks off with line 1074, and the Franklin's prologue follows at once, no Words. The Monk's headlink begins "When ended was the tale—" etc.; and his ending is in the short form, see p. 242 here. The pages in the latter part of the MS are blurred and faded; copying ceases at the end of the Manciple's Tale, with "Deo gracias."

(2) *Other MSS in London*

College of Physicians: Paper, the Canterbury Tales, "Tales in the usual order", according to Hist. MSS Comm. Report VIII, Appendix p. 233. Tales of Prioress and Parson imperfect.

> The Pardoner's Tale is printed Ch. Soc. Specimens part VI suppl. 1. This is probably the volume described in Bernard 3579. 10 among the MSS of Fr. Bernard, "Collegii Medicorum Lond. Socius" as "Geoffry Chawcer's Works. Imperfect." Koch, ed. Pard. Tale p. xxxiv, speaks of this MS as "hitherto unknown to all Chaucerians."
> [I have not examined this MS.]

Sion College: In the library of Sion College, Victoria Embankment. On vellum, of 79 leaves about 8⅜ by 6⅜ inches; the last two blank except for an incomplete declaration written in "the first year of King Edward", and in a hand apparently later than the text. Script of the Canterbury Tales of the XV century, small and conventional; some traces of almost obliterated rubrics and capitals, other ink dark and clear. The great fire of London damaged these and other books of the library when at its former site. Contains only the Clerk's Tale, the Tales of Wife of Bath, Friar, and Summoner.

> The Clerk's Tale is printed Ch. Soc. Specimens part VI. Mentioned in Bernard 4091.27 as "Part of Geoffrey Chaucer's Poem of his Canterbury Tale, 4to." Described by Todd, Illustrations p. 125.
> This MS must be distinguished from the Sion College copy, written by John Shirley, of the prose English translation of De Guileville's Pilgrimage, which contains in its text a transcription of Chaucer's ABC. Skeat, I: 50, 59, mentions "the Sion College MS", meaning the Shirley; the "Sion College MS" to which he alludes IV: xiii is the copy of the Cant. Tales. The Dict. Nat. Biog., art. *Shirley* gives in the list of his MSS the "Sion MS of Chaucer"; this is incorrect.

(3) *In the Bodleian Library, Oxford*

> Catalogues of the Bodleian MSS are in Bernard, op. cit. The Ashmole MSS were catalogued by Black in 1845-67, the Tanner by Hackman in 1860, the Laud by Coxe, the Digby by Macray, who also catalogued part of the Rawlinson collection. See Madan, Books in Manuscript, pp. 172-75. The Bodleian collections not yet catalogued except by Bernard include the Fairfax, Bodley, Hatton, and Selden collections. Additions to the Library in the 18th and 19th centuries are described by Madan in his Summary Catalogue, vols. III-V; vols. I and II of this work are to be a revision of Bernard.

Barlow 20: Vellum, of 259 leaves 12½ by 8¼ inches, written in eights, 38 lines to the page. Begins imperfect with line 574, thus lacking probably one gathering, as the first catchword is on the 8th verso. In a clumsy XV century hand, with very wide margins and some ornament. Uses þ and ʒ. Ends with a booklet complete, the last verso blank; no Parson's Tale.

The Pardoner's Tale is printed Ch. Soc. Specimens part IV.
The link Man of Law-Squire is printed Ch. Soc. Specimens of
Moveable Prologues p. 6; the link Pardoner-Shipman is printed
ibid. p. *27*; the link Squire-Merchant is printed *ibid.* p. *35*; the link
Clerk-Franklin is printed *ibid* p. 54. Bernard notes the MS,
6420.8; it was used by Tyrwhitt.

Order of Tales:—A Gamelyn B¹ F¹ E² D E¹ F² G C B² H,
no more in MS. There is a spurious link of 16 lines Merchant-
Wife of Bath, as in Royal 18 and Laud 739; spurious links connect
Canon's Yeoman-Doctor and Pardoner-Shipman. Two lines connect Cook and Gamelyn.

The Man of Law's headlink and his endlink begin and end with
a fascicule.

Bodley 414: On paper, of 436 pages 11½ by 8½ inches, 434 pages
according to the old numbering, but 235 is trebled. In one
clear, compact hand ca. 1460-80. Spaces left throughout the
MS for initials; rubric headings to most of the Tales.

The Pardoner's Tale is printed Ch. Soc. Specimens part IV.
Order of Tales, not given by the Chaucer Society:—A, (no Cook's
Tale or Gamelyn), B¹ D E¹ F² G C B² H I. No Tale of Squire
or of Merchant. Spurious links Canon's Yeoman-Doctor and
Pardoner-Shipman.

(Description communicated.)

Bodley 686: Vellum, of 217 leaves 14⅞ by 9⅞ inches; first page
with large capital and illuminated border. In one hand of XV
century, stereotyped and clear; very wide margins, running
titles, rubrics, elaborate capitals, and some borders. The Canterbury Tales fill 1a to 184a. Order of Tales: A B¹ D E F
C B² in part, H G¹.

The text was used by Tyrwhitt. The Pardoner's Tale is
printed Ch. Soc. Specimens part II. The rest of MS, all by Lydgate,
contains: (2) Verses on English Kings, ending with Henry VI. See
Anglia 28: 6-7. (3) Stans Puer ad Mensam. See Anglia 28: 20.
(4) "For helth of body" etc., see Anglia 28: 7, to which list Foerster adds copies in Glasgow, Hunterian U iv 17, Sloane 989, Adds.
10099, Harley 5401, Rawl. A, 653, part in Harley 2252. See also
Rawl. poet. 35. The heading in this MS has a trace of Shirley
spelling. (5) "So as the Crab goes", see Anglia 28: 17. (6) Of
the Ram's horn, see Anglia 28: 15. (7) Wicked Tongue, see Anglia
28: 21. To that note it should be added that the last stanza of
Harley 2251 is not a part of the poem, but begins "Right as povert
causeth sobrenes," see under Prosperity, Section V here. This
poem has been printed by Skeat VII : 285, from Thynne. (8) Life
of St. Margaret, 74 stanzas of seven lines; also in Trin. Coll.
Cambr. R 3, 20 (a Shirley MS), and in Stow's copy from Shirley,
Adds. 29279. (9) Life of St. George, 35 stanzas of seven lines.
Also in R 3, 20, see above. (10) The Fifteen Joys of Our Lady,
followed by the Fifteen Heavinesses; in all 45 stanzas of seven lines.
In Harley 2255, Trin. Coll. Cambr. R 3, 21, Jesus Coll. Cambr. 56.
(11) The Dance Macabre, headed "The Daunce of Poules". The
text here copied is not Lydgate's direct translation from the French,
but has undergone some changes. The translated text is to be

printed in vol. 18, Sect. II of the Belles Lettres Series, Boston.
From the heading here given the poem, we may infer that the MS
is later than the painting of the fresco in Pardon Churchyard, St.
Paul's, which took place about 1430.

In the Canterbury Tales, the Cook's Tale has a spurious conclusion of 12 lines, printed in the 1687 Chaucer, and under Cook's
Tale here. The Man of Law's Tale has no endlink, and the E F connectives are complete, as in the Ellesmere type of MSS, except that
the loss of a leaf (S iii) at the end of the Squire's Tale renders it
doubtful if the Words of the Franklin were present. The Verba
Hospitis are at the end of the Clerk's Tale. At the end of Sir
Thopas follows the Manciple's Tale, marked not as his but as "a
lytel tretis of þe Crowe", and its pages headed "Lydgate." The
Second Nun's Tale is then copied, and no more of the Canterbury
Tales.

Hatton Donat, 1: Vellum, 257 leaves 10¼ by 7½ inches, in eights.
With headings and running titles in red, border around first
page and 8-line capital. In one small, neat XV century hand,
43 lines to page. Contains the Canterbury Tales only.

The Pardoner's Tale is printed Ch. Soc. Specimens part II.
The link Man of Law-Squire is printed Ch. Soc. Specimens of
Moveable Prologues p. 15; the spurious link Pardoner-Shipman is
printed *ibid.* p. 28, the link Merchant-Squire is printed *ibid.* p. 34.
Order of Tales:—A B¹ Cook Gamelyn F¹ E² F² D G C E¹ B²
H I. The Cook has his usual headlink, out of keeping with his
position here. His Tale is connected by two spurious lines to
Gamelyn. The Squire's Tale has a blank space of a leaf and a half
following it, and the Merchant begins a new fascicule. No Merch.
headlink; he has the Words of Franklin. There is a spurious link
of 14 lines Canon's Yeoman-Doctor, and the spurious headlink to
Shipman, connecting from Pardoner, is here out of keeping because
of the place of Clerk in front of Shipman. The connection
Merchant-Franklin here present is also found in Hengwrt, Petworth,
Cambridge Ii and Cambridge Mm. See Specimens of Moveable
Prologues, pp. 46 ff. The Retractation is present, and is printed
Six-Text to supply gap in Corpus.
From the Links it is plain that the order back of this MS was:—
A Gamelyn B¹ F¹ E² F² D G C B² H I, with E¹ probably follow-
ing D as in the Ii MS.

Laud 600: Vellum, of 304 leaves 11¼ by 8¼ inches, in eights,
beginning on 1a of first gathering. Illuminated initials, headings and running titles in red. Contains the Canterbury Tales
only; was originally in one clear, neat XV century hand, but
has suffered many mutilations, a number of which are supplied
on newer vellum by a hand of the early XVII century. Gaps
still existing are between Melibeus and Monk, Nun's Priest
and Manciple, Canon's Yeoman and Doctor, Doctor and
Pardoner.

The Pardoner's Tale is printed Ch. Soc. Specimens part IV.
The link Squire-Franklin is printed Ch. Soc. Specimens of Moveable Prologues p. 33 and Six-Text p. 498. This MS was used by

Tyrwhitt; it is described by Bernard 1476, Laud K 50 as "Geoffrey Chaucer his Canterbury Tales, except the Plowman's Tale."

Order of Tales:—A Gamelyn D E¹ B¹ E² F G C B² H I. The original order must have been as in the Ellesmere group, B¹ being misplaced.

The Wife's prologue opens a booklet; her first word is *Experiment*, as in Barlow 20, Lansdowne 851, Sloane 1686. There is no Man of Law's endlink (Shipman's prologue).

Laud 739: Vellum, 239 leaves 11⅛ by 7½ inches, in twelves, 33 lines to the page. Headings, running titles, glosses, additions, notes, and corrections by a Jacobean hand; the original scribe wrote in a large, coarse hand of XV century. No contents other than the Canterbury Tales. Breaks off imperfect in Sir Thopas; began on 1a of the first gathering.

The Pardoner's Tale is printed Ch. Soc. Specimens part IV. The link Man of Law-Squire is printed Ch. Soc. Specimens of Moveable Prologues p. 13; the spurious link Pardoner-Shipman is printed *ibid.* p. 28; the link Squire-Merchant is printed *ibid.* p. 39. This MS was used by Tyrwhitt; it is described in Bernard 1234, Laud G 69 as "Jeffrey Chaucer his Canterbury Tales."

Order of Tales:—A Gamelyn B¹ F¹ E² D E¹ F³ G C B² imperfect. There is a spurious link of 16 lines Merchant-Wife, as in Royal 18 and Barlow. The Summoner's Tale has the abrupt spurious conclusion, as in Petworth, Sloane 1685, Royal 18, Rawlinson 149. In this MS the Jacobean hand has crossed out the last four lines and written in margin "Hic desunt 2 folia." There is a garbled link Clerk-Franklin of two seven-line stanzas, as in Sloane 1685; spurious links also connect Canon's Yeoman and Doctor (14 lines) and Pardoner-Shipman (12 lines).

Rawlinson C 86: Paper, 189 leaves about 11 by 8½ inches, in various current hands, late and slovenly. Contents, 32 entries, partly Lydgatian; also Sir Gawain and Dame Ragnell, Guiscard and Sigismond, etc. The Chaucerian poems are the story of Dido, from the Legend of Good Women, marked as by Lydgate; the first 180 lines of the Prioress' prologue and Tale, without heading; and the Clerk's Tale, headed "Grysill" and ending (Envoy) with "I you counsell", followed by three spurious lines (see under Clerk's Tale in Section III G) and "ffinis Gryseld."

The Dido legend is printed Ch. Soc. OT pp. 133 ff.

Rawlinson Poetry 141 (fragmentary): Paper, ii plus 159 leaves 10½ by 7⅞ inches, in eights. Headings, running titles and initials in colors. In a clear, compact hand of the first half of the XV century, 32 lines to the page. Contains a part of the Canterbury Tales, beginning with line 1709 of the Knight's Tale, and breaking off imperfect in the Manciple's Tale.

The Clerk's Tale is printed Ch. Soc. Specimens part VI. The link Man of Law-Squire is printed Ch. Soc. Specimens of

Moveable Prologues p. 18. Described in Madan's Summary Catalogue III : 312.

Order of Tales:—A B¹ F¹ E¹ B² without the Nun's Priest, D Nun's Priest H imperfect. Parts only of the Summoner's Tale and Nun's Priest Tale are in the MS.

There is a spurious conclusion of four lines to Cook's Tale. The Clerk ends ready for the Merchant, but the Merch. Tale is not in the MS.

Rawlinson Poetry 149: Vellum, in one (or two) very small hand of the XV century. Of iv plus 138 leaves 11¼ by 8⅛ inches, in eights; written 49 lines to the page for part of the MS, then 74 lines to page. This change comes on the middle of a verso, in the ML headlink. Begins imperfect, with line 432 of the Prologue. Headings and some running titles in red, colored initials. According to note at end, written by William Stevens. At the foot of 136b is a short poem, ca. 1600, on the word *jest* scraped out of a lady's Chaucer; see the Glossary to Speght, s. v. *iape;* also see Urry, Glossary, and pp. 221, 507, here.

The Pardoner's Tale is printed Ch. Soc. Specimens part IV. The link Man of Law-Squire is printed Ch. Soc. Specimens of Moveable Prologues p. 20; the link Pardoner-Shipman is printed *ibid.* p. 30; the link Squire-Merchant *ibid.* p. 38. Described in Madan's Summary Catalogue III: 314.

Order of Tales:—A B¹ F¹ E² Gamelyn D E¹ G C B² H I. After the Squire's Tale is a blank of nearly one leaf; the Words of the Franklin, given to the Merchant, begin the next gathering, on K i. There is no Cook's Tale in A, and Gamelyn is imperfect at beginning, Merchant at end; a whole gathering seems to have been lost at that point. The Summoner's Tale ends abruptly, as in Royal 18, Sloane 1685, Laud 739. The Clerk does not end ready for the Merchant. There are spurious links Canon's Yeoman-Doctor (14 lines) and Pardoner-Shipman (12 lines.) The Monk's Tale breaks off in Hercules, and the Nun's Priest's begins imperfect. The Retractation is on the last verso.

Rawlinson Poetry 223, formerly Rawl. Misc. 1133: Vellum, xi plus 272 leaves 16⅜ by 11¼ inches, with rubrics and many beautifully illuminated large and small letters and borders, running titles in black, illuminated initials, figures of the Friar and of Melibeus. In one large, clear stereotyped hand of the XV century; writing and illuminating beautifully executed. Foll. i-x are a fragment, originally loose in the volume, of a XV century copy of Lydgate's Siege of Troy.

The Pardoner's Tale is printed Ch. Soc. Specimens part II. The link Man of Law-Summoner is printed Ch. Soc. Specimens of Moveable Prologues p. 14; the link Squire-Merchant is printed *ibid.* p. 37. The MS is described in Madan's Summary Catalogue III: 332.

Order of Tales:—A B¹ F¹ E² E¹ D Second Nun-Pardoner-Manciple-Sir Thopas-Melibeus-Nun's Priest-Doctor-Shipman-Prioress-Franklin's Tale given to Merchant-Parson.

The Man of Law's endlink introduces the Summoner, as in Royal 17 and Harley 7334; but the Squire follows, as in Royal 17. [I have not examined this MS.]

Rawlinson Misc. 1133, now Rawl. Poet. 223, see above.

Arch. Selden B 14: Vellum, of 309 leaves and two flyleaves 13 by 8¼ inches, in eights. Headings and running titles in red, occasional illuminated initials and borders. Written in one neat hand of XV century; said by Furnivall, Temp. Pref. p. 7, to be the "best of the disappointing Bodleian lot" of the Canterbury Tales MSS. The Tales are preceded by a "Kalendar" on foll. 1-3b, in the same hand. Unfinished lines occur often in this MS; thus, Mill. Tale 150, Summ. Tale 229, 230, 233, Pard. Tale 561, 562; proper names are often not written in the Monk's Tale of Zenobia or in Melibeus; blanks are left instead.

The Pardoner's Tale is printed Ch. Soc. Specimens part II. The link Man of Law-Shipman is printed Ch. Soc. Specimens of Moveable Prologues p. 2 and Six-Text p. 167; the Franklin's prologue *ibid.* p. 57; the Merchant's headlink is printed Six-Text p. 442, the link Merch.-Squire *ibid.* 476, 478; the ending of the Merch. Tale *ibid.* 473, part of the Retractation *ibid.* 684. This MS was used by Tyrwhitt; it is described in Bernard 3360, B 30, as "Chaucer's Tales." Its contents were listed by Hearne, see his Remarks and Collections, II: 194 ff.

Order of Tales:—A E¹ D E² F¹ B¹ B² G C F² H I. The connection Clerk-Merchant is complete, although the tales are separated. The Merchant epilogue and Squire's prologue are as in modern eds., but there are no Words of the Franklin. The Squire's Tale has the eight spurious lines of conclusion after its part II, then the two lines of part III. The Man of Law endlink introduces the Shipman, as in no other known MS of the Cant. Tales; see p. 277 here for the adoption of this reading by the Chaucer Society, etc. The Monk's Tale has the modern instances last, and the endlink in the short form, see p. 242 here. There is a spurious link of 14 lines Canon's Yeoman-Doctor. The MS has the Retractation.

From the facts that B² has the short form of the Monk's endlink, that there are no Words of the Franklin, and two spurious passages, I cannot concede authority to this MS' connection Man of Law and Shipman.

(4) *In Oxford Colleges*

Descriptions of MSS in Oxford colleges may be found in: Catalogus codicum manuscriptorum qui in Collegiis Aulisque Oxoniensibus hodie adservantur. H. O. Coxe, 2 vols., Oxford, 1852. This omits the Christ Church MSS, which are listed in G. W. Kitchin's Catalogus codicum MSS qui in bibliotheca Aedis Christi apud Oxonienses adservantur, Oxford 1867. A suppl. to the Corpus catalogue was issued in 1887.

Christ Church 152:

The Pardoner's Tale is printed Ch. Soc. Specimens part I. The Nun's Priest's endlink is printed Six-Text p. 301.

Order of Tales:—A Gamelyn D E¹ C, Shipman-Second Nun, most of the rest of B², H F² B¹ E² F¹, a new Plowman's Tale, Prioress-Canon's Yeoman-Parson (imperfect). [From the Trial Tables.] This order is erroneously given, according to Beatty's introduction to A New Ploughman's Tale, Ch. Soc. 1902, pp. vii-viii. Order there given—A Gamelyn D E¹ C B² H F² B¹ E² F¹ Plowman G I. See also Zupitza in Ch. Soc. Specimens part I, p. xvi.

Folio 42 is reproduced Ch. Soc. Autotypes; there dated "second third of the XV century", or "1435-1465."

[I have not examined this MS].

Corpus Christi 196: "A handsome vellum folio in a clean, formal hand", says Furnivall, Temp. Pref. 59-60.

[I have not examined this MS.]

Printed entire by the Chaucer Society, in the Six-Text and separately, its gaps supplied by Selden and Royal 17. The tale of Gamelyn is printed in the Appendix to the Six-Text, Group A, and with the MS. The link Man of Law-Squire is printed Ch. Soc. Specimens of Moveable Prologues p. 4. Described in Bernard 1665.198 as "Sir Jeffrey Chaucer's Canterbury Tales. Fol. Membr."

Order of Tales:—A Gamelyn B¹ F¹ D E¹ E² F² G C B² H I. (This I take from the Ch. Soc. print.)

The Summoner's Tale is in the full form; there is a gap at end of Clerk and beginning of Merchant; the Merchant's Tale breaks off with line 1704, as do Sloane 1686 and Lansdowne 851; there are no Words of the Franklin; the Monk's endlink is in the short form (see p. 242 here). Seventy-two lines are lacking at the beginning of the MS; gaps are supplied in the Ch. Soc. print from the Selden MS.

An interesting feature of this codex is the presence of numbers to several of the Tales, also a feature of the Mm codex of the Cambridge University Library. The numbers in this MS are:— Reeve iii, Cook iiii, Man of Law v, Wife of Bath vii, Pardoner xvi, Shipman xvii, Sir Thopas xix, Melibeus xx, Monk xxi, Nun's Priest xxii, Manciple xxiii, Parson xxiv. Numbers iii, v, vii, xix and xxiv agree with the Mm markings, but Corpus' numbers iv, xvi, xvii, xx-xxiii are not in Mm, and Mm has three numberings not in Corpus. It is however important that, although neither MS agrees in existing order with the numberings, the two sets of numbers fit together, and unite in indicating a sequence A Gamelyn B¹ F¹ D E¹ E² F² G C B² H I. Folio 12b is reproduced Ch. Soc. Autotypes; there dated ca. 1430.

New College:

The Pardoner's Tale is printed Ch. Soc. Specimens part III. The MS is described in Bernard 1278.314 as "Chaucer's Works." Folio 12b is reproduced Ch. Soc. Autotypes; there dated ca. 1430.

Order of Tales:—A (Prologue imperfect) B¹ F¹ E² D E¹ F² G¹ C B² H I. [From the Trial Tables.]

The MS was used by Morell and by Tyrwhitt.

[I have not examined this MS].

Trinity College 49:

> The Pardoner's Tale is printed Ch. Soc. Specimens part IV.
> The MS is described in Bernard 1991.54 as "Jeffrey Chaucer's
> Works." It was used by Morell.
> Order of Tales:—A Gamelyn D E F¹ C¹ F² B² (two tales only)
> C² B¹ rest of B² G H I. [From the Trial Tables.]
> [I have not examined this MS].

(5) *In the University Library, Cambridge*

For descriptions of MSS, see the Catalogue of the Manuscripts in the
University Library, Cambridge, 7 vols., 1856-67. Now antiquated, but the only
available guide.

Dd iv, 24: "A Folio, chiefly on paper, 179 leaves, about 45 lines in
each page. The handwriting, which is uniform throughout,
belongs to the close of the 14th century; imperfect both at the
beginning and the end." [From the Univ. Libr. MSS Cat. I :
228. I have not examined this MS.]

> Printed entire by the Chaucer Society, issue for 1902, forewords
> dated Feb. 1903. Gaps supplied from Egerton 2726. An Appendix,
> pp. 679 ff., contains:—Lines and parts of lines from Skeat's edi-
> tion, left out of the MS.—The Hymn of Chaucer's Oxford clerk
> Nicholas . . . from Arundel MS 248, in English and Latin.—Wood-
> cuts of Paintings of the 23 Tellers of the Cant. Tales, copied from
> the Ellesmere MS and cut by Mr. W. H. Hooper.—Woodcuts of 6
> Tellers of 6 of the Cant. Tales, the Reeve, Cook, Wife of Bath,
> Pardoner, Monk, and Manciple,—and of 6 Allegorical Figures for
> the Parson's Tale—Envy and Charity, Gluttony and Abstinence,
> Lechery and Chastity,—copied from MS Gg iv, 27 in the Cambridge
> University Library and cut, by Mr. W. H. Hooper.
> Order of Tales:—A B¹ D E F C B² G H I. There is no
> Man of Law's endlink (Shipman's prologue). The Monk's Tale
> has the modern instances at the end. There is a Nun's Priest's end-
> link, without the six spurious lines; printed Six-Text p. 301.
> Used by Tyrwhitt, and by him classed as one of the best.

Ee ii, 15: Folio, paper, much mutilated, of 95 leaves, containing
eight articles; written late in the XV century. The second
entry is the Man of Law's Tale, imperfect and without heading.
See Univ. Libr. MSS Cat., II : 31-33.

Gg iv, 27: Vellum, of 516 leaves 12⅜ by 7⅜ inches, mainly in one
hand of the early XV century, well and strongly written.
After fol. 516 there are 35 leaves carrying transcriptions from
the printed eds., in two Jacobean hands. These leaves contain
the Retractation, a glossary, a table of contents, and three short
poems, viz., a stanza on humility, 7 lines of Chaucer's Purse,
and his Truth. The XIV century portion of the MS mentioned in the Univ. Libr. MSS Cat. has been removed and
bound separately.

A number of leaves have been cut out, and many of the
pictures of the pilgrims and of allegorical figures, with which
the MS was formerly enriched, have been cut away; twelve
such pictures are reproduced by the Chaucer Society in the
Appendix to its print of MS Cambridge Dd, and were announced by them as to be issued in 1884 with the Six-Text.
Nine pages are reproduced Ch. Soc. Autotypes, all but one
dated 1430-40; one is dated 1420-30. The MS was described
by Urry; by Hearne in his Remarks and Collections V : 7; it
was then (1712) already shorn of its pictures. Contents given
Temp. Pref. p. 7, see p. 51. See Skeat I : 55, II : lxx, III :
xlviii. Described in Camb. Univ. MSS Cat. III : 172-74.

Contents :—
　Four leaves gone at beginning.
　(1) Chaucer's ABC, headed in a Jacobean hand. Printed Ch.
Soc. PT p. 123. (2) Chaucer's Scogan; printed Ch. Soc. PT p.
419, OT 299. (3) Chaucer's Truth; printed Ch. Soc. PT p. 407.
(4) A Parliament of Birds, showing the influence of Chaucer. Fifteen stanzas of eight lines. Printed Jour. Gc. Phil. 7 : 105 ff., and
to be printed in vol. 18 of Section II of the Belles Lettres Series,
Boston. (5) Two macaronic poems between a lover and his lady.
(6) Troilus and Cressida, printed Ch. Soc. (7) The Cant. Tales,
printed Ch. Soc. in the Six-Text and separately, gaps supplied
from Harley 1758, Sloane 1685, and Royal 17. Order of Tales :—
A B¹ D E F C B² G H I. There is no Man of Law's endlink
(Shipman's prologue). Thirty-six lines are lost at the beginning.
(8) The Legend of Good Women, with the unique form of the
prologue as noted below. Printed Ch. Soc. PT pp. 243 ff.; the prologue is also printed OT pp. 23 ff.; and in One-Text Print the entire
Gg copy is reproduced, pp. 191 ff. The prologue was privately printed Cambridge 1864 by Bradshaw, who discovered
this text. (9) Chaucer's Parlement of Foules; printed Ch. Soc.
PT pp. 49 ff. and One-Text Print pp. 45 ff. (10) Lydgate's Temple
of Glass, ed. by Schick for the EETS, 1891. See ibid. pp. xxi,
xxii, xxx. Other copies are there listed.
　Bradshaw was especially proud and fond of this MS, see
Jusserand as cited in Prothero's memoir of Bradshaw, p. 357. The
peculiar textual conditions of the codex have called forth much
comment, but as yet no thorough investigation has been made.
Skeat, ed. LGW page x, remarked on the badness of this MS; Koch,
Chronology p. 82, said "It is by no means a trustworthy MS; it has
a good many acceptable readings indeed, but on the other hand
it often enough spoils the sense and the metre entirely." Furnivall in Macmillan's Magazine, 27 : 390 (1872-3) spoke of the
codex as "largely corrected by a contemporary reviser." Pollard,
Athenaeum 1901, II : 631-2, said "I have some doubts as to
whether in the Pardoner's Tale (on which the Zupitza classification
is based) the Gg scribe had got back to his usual text, from which
in the previous Tale he widely departs."
　An examination of the MS shows that from the beginning of
the Troilus to the close of the volume no poem ends with a
gathering; i. e., the work was practically continuous. It is curious,
to say the least, that so much of the contents should be, textually,
of composite origin. The version of the LGW is now plausibly

maintained to be Chaucer's revision of his earlier work, see
Section IV here. On the Troilus, McCormick remarks, p. xli-xlii
of the Globe Chaucer, that Gg and Harley 4912 are throughout
close together, and of a composite character, following a "revision"
to Books II-III, and showing thereafter the readings of the first
draft. On the Temple of Glass, Schick points out that Gg and
Adds. 16165 have the end of the poem wanting, and a "Compleynt"
of over 600 lines appended; from this and other data he considers
that they derive independently from a common original. He opines
page 1 that the Compleynt is not by Lydgate, but a bungling addition, while the Gg-Adds. text itself must not be taken as basis
of a critical edition. The Canterbury Tales appear in a form
which Bradshaw explained as due to "some editorial supervision
exercised after Chaucer's death"; but, as elsewhere remarked,
many peculiarities of this type of MSS have been adopted by
modern editors without demonstration of Bradshaw's possible
error in this opinion; and in its text of the Tales the Gg constantly varies for the worse as compared with the Ellesmere. For
reference on its Parl. of Foules text see under that heading here,
Section IV.

A careful evaluation of this codex as a whole, taking into consideration its occasional lack of phrases or half-lines, its un-
English miswritings (*mental* for *mantel*, *schekes* for *chekes*, *dedyr*
for *thider*, *fynelli* for *finally*, *cryatour* for *creature*, etc.), its suggestions of ear-error (*bakystere* for *beggestere*, *scole heye* for
scoleye, *wekedel* for *wikkedly*), and the far more frequent eye-
errors and wilful distortions (*semili kope* for *semycope*, *neuer* for
nowher, *strong* for *straunge*, *ffarwel* instead of *for wel*, *which was*
instead of *with wawes*, *vertu* for *venim*, *strenthe* for *trouthe*, *owene*
for *avow*, *tabbard* for *thombe*, *heye it was boughte* instead of *he
the hewes boughte*, *non other weye* instead of *no remedye*, *stylle
and sterne* for *stable is and eterne*, *rygh of his poyn devise* instead of *rytes of his payen wise*, etc.)—is a desideratum in Chaucer-
study.

Ii iii, 26: Described in the Camb. Univ. Libr. Cat. of MSS, III :
429. Contains the Canterbury Tales and "Bona Carta gloriose
Passionis Domini nostri Jesu Christi." Lacks lines 1-66 of the
Prologue.

The Pardoner's Tale is printed Ch. Soc. Specimens part III.
The link Man of Law-Squire is printed Ch. Soc. Specimens of
Moveable Prologues p. 17; the spurious link Pardoner-Shipman is
printed *ibid*. p. 29; the link Squire-Merchant is printed *ibid*. p. 44;
the link Merchant-Franklin *ibid*. p. 48. The MS was used by
Tyrwhitt, and was by him termed one of the best.
Order of Tales:—A Gamelyn B¹ F¹ E² F² D E¹ G C B² H I.
[I have not examined this MS].

Mm ii, 5: Vellum, 252 leaves, in eights, 45 lines to the page.
Lacks one leaf at beginning, and also leaf 76. Contains the
Canterbury Tales only. In four cases the booklets are not of
eights; the MS began on the first recto of the first gathering.
Described in the Camb. Univ. Libr. Cat. of MS IV : 128.
Used by Morell, his MS "M"; and collated by Wright as far as
the Wife of Bath's Tale.

The Pardoner's Tale is printed Ch. Soc. Specimens part IV.
The link Man of Law-Squire is printed Ch. Soc. Specimens of
Moveable Prologues p. 21; the link Shipman-Pardoner is printed
ibid. p. 29; the link Squire-Merchant is printed *ibid.* p. 43; the link
Merchant-Franklin is printed *ibid.* p. 50.

Order of Tales:—A Gamelyn B² impf., B¹ F¹ E² D E¹ F² Nun's
Priest G C Sir Thopas, Melibeus H I.

Fragment B² opens with the spurious link Pard.-Shipman, 12
lines, quite out of place in that connection. The Shipman and
the Prioress follow, and then the Monk, with his headlink beginning "When ended was the tale of Mellibe", but with Melibeus
out of place also. The Nun's Priest's headlink and that of Sir
Thopas are inappropriate to their positions. The Clerk's Tale does
not end ready for the Merchant, and there is no Merch. prologue;
the Merchant's epilogue appears after the Clerk's Tale, and introduces the Franklin.

A clue to the arrangement back of the confusion shown in Mm
is found in the existence here of a system of old numbering to
the Tales, appearing also in Corpus, *q. v.* These numbers are:—
Reeve iii, Man of Law v, Wife of Bath vii, Summoner ix, Franklin
xii, Prioress xviii, Sir Thopas xix, Parson xxiv. This is confirmed
by the Corpus markings, but does not at all fit the present order
of the codex. As noted under Corpus, the sequence indicated for
the archetype is A Gamelyn B¹ F¹ D E¹ E² F² G C B² H I. Note
the similar displacement of Shipman and Prioress in the Petworth MS.

(6) *In Cambridge Colleges*

Dr. Montague Rhodes James, Provost of King's College, Cambridge, has
compiled catalogues of many of the MS collections in Cambridge and elsewhere; see his book On the Abbey of S. Edmund at Bury, Cambridge, 1895,
and his study of The Ancient Libraries of Canterbury and Dover, London,
1904. His Cambridge catalogues include Jesus College (1895), King's (1895),
Sidney Sussex (1895), Peterhouse (1899), Emanuel, and, most extensive of
all, The Western Manuscripts in the Library of Trinity College, Cambridge,
1900-04, 4 vols. Dr. James is now engaged upon the MSS of Corpus Christi,
Cambridge. The long-needed catalogue of the Pepys collection is now planned;
see Nation 1907 II: 141.

Pepys 2006, Magdalen College: Described in Mod. Lang. Notes
19 : 196-98; contains Melibeus and the Parson's Tale, besides
minor poems by Chaucer, etc.

Trinity College, R 3, 3: Described in James as above, II : 50. On
vellum, in double columns, 42-46 lines to the column. Written
in a fine pointed book hand, neat and clear, beginning on 1a of
first booklet. Close of Parson's Tale lacking; other gaps, see
James.

The Pardoner's Tale is printed Ch. Soc. Specimens part II.
The link Man of Law-Squire is printed Ch. Soc. Specimens of
Moveable Prologues p. 23. The MS was used by Morell and by
Tyrwhitt; brief note in Skeat IV: xiii.

Order of Tales :—A B¹ F¹ E² E¹ D G C Nun's Priest H Sir
Thopas, Melibeus, Monk, Shipman, Prioress, F² I.

The Clerk's Tale ends ready for the Merchant, but there is no
Merchant's headlink. The headlink to the Nun's Priest is entirely
inappropriate to its position; it appears in the short form, see p. 242
here. There is a spurious prologue of four lines to Sir Thopas;
only 30 lines of that Tale are present, then comes the 48-line link
to Melibeus, with two more spurious lines added: "When ended
was the tale", etc. No headlink to Shipman. The Prioress has no
endlink introducing Sir Thopas. The word Manciple is altered
to Franklin in the Parson's headlink.

Trinity College R 3, 15 : Paper, XV century, of 316 leaves, 30 lines
to a page usually. Gaps here and there, see James II : 65;
lacks 56 lines at beginning of Prologue. Before the Canterbury
Tales are entered copies of the Eight Goodly Questions, To
the King, and Chaucer's Prophecy, in a hand later than the
body of the MS, "possibly after 1600." Hence these may be
copied from the prints. Piers Plowman's Crede, following the
Tales, is in this same hand.

The Pardoner's Tale is printed Ch. Soc. Specimens part III.
The link Man of Law-Squire is printed Ch. Soc. Specimens of
Moveable Prologues p. 17; six lines of the Verba Hospitis or com-
ment on the Clerk's Tale, treated by the MS as a link Pardoner-
Franklin, are printed *ibid*. p. 52.

The MS was used by Morell and by Tyrwhitt; brief note in
Skeat IV : xii. It is described in James II : 65, and by Todd, Illustrations pp. 119-121.

Order of Tales :—A B¹ F¹ E² D E¹ C² F² G¹ C¹ Shipman,
Melibeus, Monk, Nun's Priest, H I.

The Clerk does not end ready for the Merchant, but the
Merchant has his headlink,—no epilogue, no Squire's prologue.
There are no Words of the Franklin, no tales of Prioress or Sir
Thopas, and no link Shipman-Prioress. The interruption to the
Monk is in the short form, see p. 242 here. There is no Canon's
Yeoman's Tale.

Textual agreements between this MS and Caxton's first ed.
are very marked, so far as comparison has been made. Koch, in
his ed. of the Pard. Tale, pp. li, lii, notes this; and my comments
in Modern Philology 3 : 170, 171 have been confirmed, so far as
the Prologue and the coarse additions to the Merchant's Tale
are concerned, by examination of the MS, which agrees with
Caxton in those points.

(7) *In Private Possession, etc.*

Ashburnham : The four MSS of the Canterbury Tales belonging
to the late Earl of Ashburnham, and marked in his library
Ashburnham Appendix 124, 125, 126, 127, were sold by the
present Earl, with the entire Appendix collection, to Mr. Yates
Thompson, in 1899. Mr. Thompson, reserving such volumes
as he desired for his own library, put the rest into the market;

13

hence the sale of this part of the Ashburnham MSS is sometime spoken of as the Yates Thompson sale. The four MSS were purchased as follows: Ashburnham 124 by Mr. Lawrence Hodson, sold again in 1906 with Mr. Hodson's library, and purchased by Quaritch; Ashburnham 125 by the nation, now Brit. Mus. Adds. 35286, *q. v.;* Ashburnham 126 by Prof. McCormick of St. Andrews; Ashburnham 127 by Quaritch.

Ashburnham 124, see below under Hodson (2).

Ashburnham 126 is imperfect; its copy of the Clerk's Tale is printed Ch. Soc. Specimens part VI.

Ashburnham 127 is described by Quaritch, Catalogue No. 193, p. 17, as a small folio on vellum, of 576 pages if perfect. Mutilations are frequent; eight leaves are missing between Man of Law and Squire, eight in the tale of Melibeus, and six at the end of the MS. According to Quaritch, "a careful and excellent text, the orthography of which is so close to that of Chaucer's own that the versification runs smoothly, with very few traces of the metrical irregularities which are apparent in other MSS." The Pardoner's Tale is printed Ch. Soc. Specimens part V.

On the collection and the sale see: Hist. Comm. MSS Report VIII, Appendix 3, p. 106; Book Prices Current XIII : 559, XIV : 647; Fletcher, English Book Collectors, pp. 382 ff.; Ellis in Quaritch's Dict. of Eng. Book Collectors, pt. X; Zeitschr. f. Bücherfreunde I, pt. 1, p. 281; pt. 2, p. 590; II, pt. 1, p. 186. On the late Lord Ashburnham's refusal to allow transcription from his MSS see Temp. Pref. pp. 5-6.

Askew I and II: For descriptions of the MSS thus entitled by Tyrwhitt see under Adds. 5140 of the British Museum and Egerton 2864 of the same library, recently Hodson-Ingilby as described below.

Canby: Mentioned in Bernard 9185.6. Furnivall inquires regarding it in N. and Q. 1871 II : 526. Used by Urry.

Cardigan: A MS of the Tales belongs to Lady Cardigan, who, according to Furnivall, p. 8 of the Ch. Soc. Announcements, and to Koch, ed. of the Pard. Tales p. xxxiii, will not permit any one to examine it.

Chandos: Urry mentions a MS thus entitled, regarding which Furnivall inquires in N. and Q. 1871 II : 526.

Cholmondeley: Now belonging to Lord Delamere, see Delamere below.

Delamere: In the possession of Lord Delamere. Described by Furnivall, N. and Q. 1872 I : 353; Furnivall there says that this is Urry's Cholmondeley MS. Contains several articles other than the Cant. Tales, for which see ref. cited. On vellum, in double columns, date about 1450 according to Furnivall. The Cant. Tales has lost 22 leaves, comprising most of Fragment D and part of the Clerk's Tale, also lines 1-176 of the Prologue, etc. Order of Tales: A, Gamelyn (no link to A), Squire with link to Man of Law, Merchant, Man of Law, Wife of Bath impf., Clerk impf., no link to Merchant, spurious link, Franklin, G C B² H I. There are four spurious lines at the end of Thopas; there is no NP endlink; the Retractation is present.
(Description cited.)

Devonshire: In the possession of the Duke of Devonshire. According to the note, p. xvi of preface to the Ch. Soc. Specimens Part I, the order of Tales is A B¹ D E F C B² G H I.
The Pardoner's Tale is printed Ch. Soc. Specimens part I.

Ellesmere: In the possession of the Earl of Ellesmere. Printed entire by the Chaucer Society in its Six-Text, and also separately. See Flügel in Anglia 30 : 401-412, on A New Collation of the Ellesmere MS. Described by Todd, Illustrations p. 128 ff.; by Furnivall, Temp. Pref. pp. 44-50.

> Order of Tales:—A B¹ D E F C B² G H I.
> A page is reproduced Ch. Soc. Autotypes, and in Garnett and Gosse's Engl. Lit., vol. I, as frontispiece. Dated by the Ch. Soc. ca. 1420.
> The miniatures of the pilgrims with which this MS is ornamented are reprod. in color by the Ch. Soc. with the Six-Text and with each of the eight separate prints of Cant. Tales MSS issued by the Society.

Ely: Urry used a MS which he mentions under this title; Furnivall inquired regarding it in Notes and Queries 1871 II : 526.

Fenwick: See under Phillipps below.

Glasgow, the Hunterian Museum, V, i. 1: Written by Geoffrey Sparling of Norwich and his son in 1476; see Hist. MSS Comm., Report III : 424.
> The Pardoner's Tale is printed Ch. Soc. Specimens, Part II.
> Order of Tales:?

Haistwell: See Egerton 2726 of the British Museum, London.

Helmingham: In the possession of the Tollemache family, Helmingham Hall, Suffolk.

Order of Tales:?
The Pardoner's Tale is printed Ch. Soc. Specimens, Part III.

Hengwrt 154: In the possession of Mr. W. E. Wynne, Peniarth.

Printed in full by the Chaucer Society in their Six-Text, and separately. Described in Hist. MSS Comm. Report II, p. 106; Temp. Pref. pp. 50-51. Folio 204a is reprod. Ch. Soc. Autotypes; there dated ca. 1450.
The gaps in this MS are in the Ch. Soc. print supplied from Royal 18, Harley 1758, Adds. 5140. In the Athen. 1872 II : 208 ten Brink is cited as of the opinion that this MS is a hybrid, copied in general from an imperfect MS of the Ellesmere type, the missing pages supplied from a MS of the Harley 7334 type.

Hodson: Four MSS of the Canterbury Tales were until 1906 in the possession of Mr. Lawrence W. Hodson of Compton Hall, near Wolverhampton, England. In 1906 most of the Hodson library was sold at auction by Sotheby, and three of the MSS described below were purchased as follows: Hodson-Ingilby and Hodson-Norton for the British Museum, Hodson-Ashburnham 124 by Quaritch. In 1905 Mr. Hodson most kindly sent me notes and collations of his MSS, excerpts from which are here given.

(1) The Norton MS, No. 59 in Skeat's list, IV : xv, and not in Koch's list, see note to p. xxxi of his ed. of the Pard. Tale. This MS, Mr. Hodson says, is on vellum, of 214 leaves, 38 lines to the page, written in a very good court hand, and originally decorated with illuminated capitals and half-borders; but every illuminated page has been cut out, and it is only by an occasional "set-off" on a following page that it is possible to get any idea of the extent of the decoration. "It belongs to the Petworth group, and corresponds with the Petworth MS in many of its readings." Contains Gamelyn; the order of Tales is: A Gamelyn B^1 F^1 E^2 D E^1 F^2 G C B^2 H I.
It has one, and perhaps two, spurious prologues to the Doctor, and a spurious prologue to the Shipman; the Man of Law's endlink introduces the Squire; the Words of the Franklin are given to the Merchant; the end of the Clerk's Tale, as indeed the beginnings and ends of nearly all the Tales, has suffered mutilation as described, so that the MS has many gaps in the text.
Now MS Brit. Mus. Egerton 2863.

(2) The MS formerly Ashburnham Appendix 124; No. 49 in Skeat's list, IV : xiv; described in Quaritch's Catalogue

No. 193, Oct. 1899. On vellum, of 278 leaves, 38 lines to the page; "belongs to the Petworth group." The writing is poor, and the only decorations are rubrishings in red, very roughly done; there are a few rough pen-decorations to capitals. Order of the Tales: A Gamelyn B^1 F^1 E^2 D E^1 F^2 G C B^2 H I. The end of the Parson's Tale is missing, as is the end of the Man of Law's Tale and the beginning of the Squire's. The Words of the Franklin are given to the Merchant; the Tales of Doctor and of Shipman have spurious prologues; the pro- logue to Melibeus is missing. The MS has 3 flyleaves at the beginning and 4 at the end; part of the Pardoner's prologue is written on one of these, fol. 275.

The Pardoner's Tale is printed Ch. Soc. Specimens part V. MS now in the hands of Quaritch (1907).

(3) Hodson 39. This MS, says Mr. Hodson, was bought by Quaritch in the West of England, and was until then unknown; it is not in Skeat's list, and is No. 28 in Koch's list, see his ed. of the Pard. Tale pp. xxxviii-ix for notes on text of that Tale. On paper, of 195 folios, "probably not earlier than 1450." The writing is cramped and difficult to read; the MS is in its original binding of oak boards covered with sheep skin. The text is perfect, without gaps. The contents are given on pp. 73-75 of the 2d supplement to Ch. Soc. Specimens part V.

Order of Tales:—A B^1 D E F C B^2 G H I. Has the Re- tractation, headed "Here takith þe maker his leue." Below, "Explicit fabule cant.," and "Iste liber constat Johi Brode Iuniori." (Note the signature Edorb qd,=Brode? in MS Digby 181, see Section IV A here.) The MS has the six lines of the WBTale printed Skeat V : 292-3, accepted by him and by Tyrwhitt, but rejected by Furnivall as spurious, see Ch. Soc. print of the MS Dd, page v of introduction. It has the Verba Hospitis at the end of the Clerk's Tale; it omits the two lines of Squire's Tale, part III; it has the NP epilogue, with six spurious lines more introducing the Second Nun; the "modern instances" are at the end of the Monk's Tale. See below under Hodson-Ingilby.

The Pardoner's Tale is printed Ch. Soc. Specimens part V, supplement 2; and the gap in the Longleat copy of the Clerk's Tale is supplied from this text, see Ch. Soc. Specimens part VII, p. 82.

(4) Hodson-Ingilby, formerly Askew I, now Brit. Mus. Egerton 2864. Furnivall, Trial Tables, says that the Haistwell MS, now Egerton 2726 of the Brit. Mus., was Askew I; Skeat, IV : xiv-xv, mentions the Ingilby and the Askew I used by Tyrwhitt as two separate codices, Nos. 54 and 57 of his list; he says that he cannot trace the Askew I, and merely remarks of the Ingilby that it is of the A type, *i. e.,* of the Ellesmere group. Koch, in his ed. of the Pard. Tale, p. xxxii, marks the

Ingilby as identical with Tyrwhitt's Askew I, which is correct. Tyrwhitt, also correctly, had described Askew I (now Egerton 2864), Askew II (now Brit. Mus. Adds. 5140), and Haistwell (now Egerton 2726) as three separate MSS.

Mr. Hodson obtained the MS from its former owner, Sir Henry Ingilby of Ripley, Yorkshire. It is on paper, of 350 folios, very well written, without decoration, and perfect. Mr. Hodson dates it not later than 1450.

Order of Tales:—A B^1 D E F C B^2 G H I.
It has the ML endlink cut out, as in the Ellesmere group; the Verba Hospitis follow the Clerk's Tale; it has the eight-line Sq. prologue; the Monk's tragedies end with Ugolino; the interruption to the Monk is begun by the Host instead of the Knight, but is of the full 54 lines, like the other Askew MS, now Adds. 5140; the epilogue to the NPTale is in the MS, with six additional spurious lines as in Adds. 5140 and as in Hodson 39. As in Hodson 39, the introd. to the CYTale is headed Words of the Pilgrims; the Retractation is headed "Here takith the Maker his Leve."

Lydgate's Story of Thebes follows the Canterbury Tales, as in MS Adds. 5140.

Holkham: In the possession of the Earl of Leicester.

The Clerk's Tale is printed Ch. Soc. Specimens part VI.
Order of the Tales, according to the Trial Tables:
A (lacking 1 and with 2 imperfect), G (impf.), H, F^2, F^1 (impf.), B^1, D^1, E (impf.), D^2, D^3 (impf.), B^2 with its 1, 3, and 4 imperfect.

Ingilby: See Hodson-Ingilby above.

Kemble, afterwards Phillipps, see under Phillipps below.

Lestrange, in Urry's list, is now the Devonshire MS, *q. v.*

Lichfield Cathedral: Described in Bernard 1382.2, as "An ancient Chaucer, with gilt letters. Fol."

The Pardoner's Tale is printed Ch. Soc. Specimens part IV. The Canon's Yeoman's preamble and Tale are printed Six-Text to supply a gap in the Hengwrt MS.
Order of Tales, as given in the prefatory note to the Trial Tables: A B^1 F^1 E^2 D E^1 F^2 G C B^2 (lacking Melibeus) H I.

Lincoln Cathedral:

The Pardoner's Tale is printed Ch. Soc. Specimens part IV. Order of Tales:?

Longleat 257: In the possession of the Marquess of Bath, and at Longleat House, Warminster, Wiltshire. On vellum, of 212

leaves 12 by 8⅜ inches. A note states that Henry Bradshaw found the following leaves wanting: 28, 49, 50, 51, 52, 68,
82, 87, 88, 101, 106, 111, 112, 113, 114, 115, 116, 117, 145, 146,
147, 148, 151, 155; 108 is misplaced as flyleaf at the beginning,
before 1. Neatly and carefully executed in one very small
conventional XV century hand, capitals and running titles
colored, some large capitals with half borders, but those not
well done. A blank shield in the design on fol. 1, and several
others, also blank, later in the volume. On fol. 98b, at the foot
of a page of the Ipomedon, Richard of Gloucester, afterwards
Richard III, has written his name.

> Contents: Foll. 1a-48b, Lydgate's Siege of Thebes, imperfect.
> Foll. 53a-77a, "Arcite & Palomon."
> Foll. 77b-89b, running title "Grisild," colophon "Explicit Grisild
> full of Pacience."
> Foll. 90a-106b, Ipomedon, in prose. A copy in Harley 2252;
> see note in Ellis' Metrical Romances, III : 208.
> On 107, 109, 110, are later notes, rules for gentleman ushers,
> etc.
> Foll. 119a-end of MS, a series of Biblical paraphrases in long
> couplets, imperfect.

Described as Longleat 25 in Engl. Stud. 10 : 203-206; there
erroneously dated of XIV or beginning of XV century. Brief
note on the MS in Hist. MSS Comm. Report III, p. 188. Dated
in Ch. Soc. Specimens part VII p. 82 as about 1450, and termed
"Northern."

The Clerk's Tale is printed Ch. Soc. Specimens part VI.
(I am indebted to the kindness of Lord Bath for permission to
use this volume.)

Naples: See "Notice of an Old English MS in the Royal Library
at Naples", Reliquiae Antiquae II : 58 ff. Description and print
of a portion of contents, which include the Clerk's Tale and a
stanza of Doublenesse. Dated 1457. See also: "Die neapoli-
tanische Handschrift von Chaucer's Clerk's Tale", J. Koch in
Beiträge zur neueren Philologie, 1902, p. 257 ff. (the Schipper
Festschrift).

> The Clerk's Tale is printed Ch. Soc. Specimens part VI.

Northumberland: In the possession of the Duke of Northumberland. See Hist. MSS Comm. Report III, p. 112.

> Order of Tales, as given by Zupitza, Ch. Soc. Specimens part I,
> p. xvi: A B¹ F¹ E² D E¹ F² G¹ Prioress, Doctor, Shipman, Thopas,
> Pardoner, Canon's Yeoman, Beryn, Melibeus, Monk, Nun's Priest,
> H I.
> The Pardoner's Tale is printed Ch. Soc. Specimens part I.
> The unique Tale of Beryn, with its prologue, has been printed as
> noted Section V here.

Norton: See under Hodson MSS above. Now Brit. Mus. Egerton 2863.

Paris: In the National Library, fonds angl. 39. See Gesenius in Archiv 5 : 1-15 (1849) with print of 100 lines. See Raynaud, Catalogue des manuscrits anglais de la Bibliothèque Nationale, Paris 1884. See Halfmann, Das auf der Bibl. Nat. zu Paris befindliche MS der Canterbury Tales, diss. Kiel, 1898; rev. Koch, Engl. Stud. 29 : 116.

> The Pardoner's Tale is printed Ch. Soc. Specimens part II.
> Order of Tales, according to Raynaud, A B¹ E¹ D E² F C B²
> G H; the Parson's Tale is lacking.
> On paper, of 83 leaves, of the XV century. Furnivall says,
> Corrections and Additions to Temp. Pref., that the MS is by
> "Duxworth Scriptor" and seems by the hand to be about 1440-50.

Petworth: In the possession of Lord Leconfield. The text of the Canterbury Tales is printed entire by the Chaucer Society in the Six-Text and separately; its Tale of Gamelyn is printed in the Appendix to Part I of the Six-Text, and with the MS. Its gaps are supplied by Adds. 5140.

Idiosyncrasies of the MS are discussed Temp. Pref. pp. 60-62, with a note of description. Described in Todd's Illustrations, pp. 118-19.

A page is reprod. Ch. Soc. Autotypes; there dated of the second third of the XV century.

> Order of Tales: A, Gamelyn, Shipman, Prioress, B¹ F¹ E² D
> E¹ F² G C, rest of B², H I. The spurious link Pard.-Shipman
> is present in front of the Shipman, showing that the position of
> Shipman and Prioress here is due to accident; there is a spurious
> link Canon's Yeoman-Doctor; the Monk's endlink is in the short
> form (see p. 242 here).
> The MS bears the arms of the 4th Earl of Northumberland,
> says Furnivall. Other Percy MSS are: Selden B 10, see Section
> IV A (3) here, and Royal 18 D ii, see Ward's Catalogue I : 81.

Phillipps: The enormous collection of the late Sir Thomas Phillipps at Cheltenham is discussed in Fletcher's English Book Collectors, p. 367 ff., and in Madan's Books in Manuscript, p. 88. A catalogue of the MSS, unfinished and never formally published, was begun 1837, and is accessible in large libraries, says Madan as noted. The collection was bequeathed by Sir Thomas to his daughter Mrs. Fenwick and her husband; they have disposed of portions to foreign governments, and have from time to time sent parcels to Sotheby's auction-rooms; in this way Phillipps 9053 has passed into the British Museum as Adds. 34360; but four MSS of the Cant. Tales still remain in the Cheltenham library, viz., Nos. 6570, 8136, 8137, 8299. From the first three the Pardoner's Tale is printed, Ch. Soc. Specimens, part II, part IV, part IV; and from Phillipps 8299, a fragmentary copy, the Clerk's Tale is printed Ch. Soc. Specimens part VI. Phillipps 8299 is there dated about 1440.

Prynne: See under Canby above.

Spelman, in the Thomas-Urry list,=a Phillipps MS, see above.

Webb: See under Lansdowne 851 of the British Museum.

Worseley: Inquiry regarding this and four other MSS mentioned by Urry was made by Furnivall in Notes and Queries 1871 II : 526.

Yates Thompson: See under Ashburnham as above.

C. Editions of the Canterbury Tales
In Chronological Order

Caxton, about 1478? See Blades p. 193. According to Quaritch's
Catalogue No. 193, pp. 18-19, the typographical composition of
the book is inaccurately given by Blades. "Apparently it was
issued as 374 leaves, of which number leaves 1, 266, and 374
were blank; or, in other words, as 47 sheets of eight leaves
each, except the thirty-third which had ten, the fortieth which
had six and the forty-seventh which had six leaves." (Quaritch.) Without date, place, or printer's name. Blades knew
of nine copies existing; Quaritch says: "To the number we
must now add the above described example (his own copy,
priced for sale at £2500), and also the magnificent copy which
I bought at Sotheby's in February 1896, wanting seventeen
leaves, which is now in America."

For description earlier than Blades see Dibdin I : 291-295.
The order of Tales (A B¹ F¹ E² D E¹ F² G C B² H I),
etc., is discussed in Mod. Phil. 3 : 159 ff. The Pardoner's Tale
is printed Ch. Soc. Specimens part V.

For modern prices of Caxtons see Auction Prices; see Athen.
1896 I : 283, 346. An imperfect copy fetched £720 at the Ashburnham sale, see Athen. 1897 II : 67; a copy wanting 19 leaves
fetched £1020. In Athen. 1896 as above eleven copies are
specified of this work, and it is stated that five formerly known
are now unaccounted for.

Caxton, about 1484? See Blades, p. 290. No place or date, but
with a remarkable proheme signed by Caxton, for print of
which see Flügel, Neuenglisches Lesebuch, 1895. With woodcuts, see under H below. The only perfect copy known is in
the library of St. John's College, Oxford, from which Grenville
reproduced the missing leaves of his copy, now in the British
Museum. Blades says that eight copies are known.

Described in Dibdin I : 295-301. For order of Tales (A
B¹ F¹ E² F² D E¹ G C B² H I), etc., and comparison of the
two Caxtons, see my paper, Mod. Phil. 3 : 159 ff.

The Pardoner's Tale is printed Ch. Soc. Specimens part V.
Koch, in his ed. of the Tale, derives the second Caxton from
the first, allowing for corrections made by Caxton on the
authority of a MS of the Ellesmere-Dd type; for criticism of
this see Mod. Phil. as noted.

An imperfect copy fetched £300 at the Ashburnham (1897)
sale; see Athen. 1897 II : 67; also Auction Prices.

This ed. was censured by Thynne in his Animadversions, as
compared with the ed. of 1532 by Thynne's father; but Tyr-

whitt, in his Appendix to the Preface, thought that the latter's material variations from Caxton's second edition were all for the worse.

Pynson, about 1492. (See Handlists.) According to Tyrwhitt, Appendix to Preface, this is from Caxton's second ed.; Caxton's proheme is reprinted, with slight modifications, see preface to Urry, note 1. The Retractation is omitted from this edition.

Described in Dibdin II : 521-25; Dibdin and Lowndes mention copies in the library of the Royal Society and in the collection of Earl Spencer; the latter copy passed to the Rylands Library at Manchester, and is barrenly described in Gordon Duff's catalogue of the latter as "The Canterbury Tales. fol. [R. Pynson. London. 1490.]" According to the Athen. 1897 I : 85, this is the only perfect copy known. See *ibid.* p. 67 for sale of an Ashburnham copy for £233. There are two copies in the British Museum; one of them, the Grenville, has the two first and the last leaf supplied in facsimile; it is dated in the Brit. Mus. Cat. "1493?"

Facsimile of type in Gordon Duff, No. 20. For woodcuts see under H below.

[Wynkyn de Worde, 1495]. "Third impression, a reprint of Caxton's edition", says Lowndes, referring to Ritson's Bibliographia Poetica p. 20. Ritson, loc. cit. says merely "by Wynken de Worde in 1495." The report of an edition of this date, no copy of which has even been seen, comes apparently from a misprint in Ames; Tyrwhitt, Appendix to the Preface, cites Ames' mention of a 1495 folio edition, but remarks that Ames does not appear to have seen it himself, and that he has met with no other authority for its existence. Dibdin, II : 519, quotes Herbert as saying that the eds. of "1495, 1520 and 1522 are not found." Ames, following Bagford, had spoken of editions of 1520 and 1522; these, like the 1495, are unknown. For Bagford see Reference List.

Even Hain, †4924, has "Printed by Wynken de Worde at Westmestre 1495, f. g. ch." Copinger emends this by saying that 1495 should be 1498; he gives the collations from the Brit. Mus. copy; see below.

Wynkyn de Worde, 1498. The title of the British Museum (Grenville) copy is supplied in facsimile: "The boke of Chaucer named Caunterbury tales"; the colophon is: "Here endyth the boke of the tales | of Caunterbury Compiled by Geffray | Chaucer / of whoos Soule Criste haue | mercy. Emprynted At Westmestre by | Wynkin de Word þe yere of our lord M | C C C C. lxxxxviii." This copy has the first sheet supplied in facsimile.

The book was formerly erroneously described as of 1488. Brunet and Lowndes remark that a copy sold at auction in 1854 was then said to be of 1488; and the Athenaeum of July 10, 1897, in its account of the Ashburnham sale, says, "1488, perfect, sold for £1000." In Fletcher's notes on the Grenville collection, now in the British Museum (see p. 286 of his English Book Collectors), he says, quoting Panizzi, that the Grenville copy of this book is unique; on p. 301 he speaks of the Ashburnham copy, "believed to be the only copy extant."

The order of Tales in this print is: A B¹ D E F G C B² H I. There is a superficial resemblance here to Harley 7334; and the parts of E and F are fully joined. But at the end of the Merchant, connecting him with the Squire, is the Man of Law's endlink, used in one large class of MSS to bind Man of Law to the Squire. The Monk's endlink is in the short form, see p. 242 here; the Nun's Priest's epilogue, 16 lines, is present. The Tales end with the Retractation. The woodcuts of Caxton II are used. Lydgate's (?) Assembly of Gods follows the Canterbury Tales.

Collations in Copinger. See Dibdin II : 52; Maskell in N. and Q. 1884 I : 361-2.

For possible print of the Canterbury Tales by Hill see under Plowman's Tale in Section V here.

For the edition by Pynson in 1526, and all subsequent editions of the Canterbury Tales with Chaucer's Works or Poems, see above under Editions of the Works, Section II.

Morell. The Canterbury Tales of Chaucer, in the Original, from the Most Authentic Manuscripts; And as they are Turn'd into Modern Language by Mr. Dryden, Mr. Pope, and Other Eminent Hands. With References to Authors, Ancient and Modern; Various Readings, and Explanatory Notes. London. Printed by the Editor, &c. &c. 1737.

Edited by the Reverend Thomas Morell, whose name does not appear, except that occasional passages supplied in the modernizations are signed T. M. Only the Prologue and Knight's Tale are contained in this volume; no more published.

Contents: The dedication; Thynne's dedicatory letter to Henry VIII; Some Account of the Life of Chaucer, from Urry; a preface, an extract from which is printed below, Section VI, under Versification. There follow: the Prologue, in the Early English text, pp. 1-70; the Knight's Tale, in the Early English text, pp. 71-206; then, with a separate titlepage, Chaucer's Characters, or the Introduction to the Canterbury Tales, by Mr. Betterton, pp. 209-246.

Betterton's partial version is completed by the addition of Dryden's character of the Parson, and by passages signed T. M. Palamon and Arcite, or the Knight's Tale, by Mr. Dryden, follows, pp. 247-348. An appendix of annotations fills pp. 349-432; and ten pages following this are given up to MS variant readings. Morell used 13 MSS which he mentions separately, besides speaking in general of the Harley and the Trinity College MSS, see below.

Reprint of the above, London 1740; slight change in the title-page, which reads, ... by several Eminent Hands. Probably a mere attempt to work off unsold copies. The Brit. Mus. Cat. *s. v.* Pope says there are eds. of 1741, 1742.

Tyrwhitt in his edition acknowledges his debt to Morell; see under that ed. below and under Glossaries in Section VI for comment on the relation of the two pieces of work, a matter which deserves closer investigation. As the first edition of any portion of Chaucer which attempted to construct and to annotate the text, this work is of especial interest to students.

See Edinb. Review 1870, p. 1 ff. For a letter from Morell to Ames on his edition see MS Brit. Mus. Adds. 5151, fol. 249.

I have not succeeded in identifying all of Morell's MSS. I give his nomenclature (Bernard's) and the modern equivalents where possible.

Bodl. Libr. 3360=Selden B 14.
Mr. Slater Bacon's MS.
Univ. Libr. Cambr.
Cott. Libr. 18=Royal 18?
Cholmondeley=Cholmondeley.
Cott. Libr. 17=Royal 17?
Bodl. Libr. 2527. 32=Bodley 686.
Bodl. Libr. 1234=Laud 739.
The Earl of Oxford's MSS=The Harleian MSS of the Brit. Museum.
Hatton 4138. 1=Hatton Donat. 1.
Laud 1476=Laud 600.
Bishop More's at Cambridge=Univ. Libr. Mm ii, 5?
New Coll. Oxford=New College, Oxford.
The Trin. Coll. MSS at Cambridge=the two Trin. Coll. MSS of the Cant. Tales.
Trin. Coll. Oxford=Trinity 49.

Inasmuch as the Cotton and the Royal MSS were stored together in Ashburnham House in 1730 and for some time following, it is not improbable that Morell's "Cotton 17 and 18" mean Royal 17 D xv and Royal 18 C ii.

Tyrwhitt, 1775-8. The Canterbury Tales of Chaucer. To which are added an Essay on his Language and Versification, and an

Introductory Discourse, together with Notes and a Glossary.
By Thomas Tyrwhitt. London, 5 vols., 1775-8.

Vols. 1-4 appeared in 1775; the 5th, containing the Glossary,
followed in 1778. Second edition Oxford 1798, two vols.
quarto; a tribute of respect to Tyrwhitt's memory.

The work contains: The Preface; an Appendix to the Preface,
comprising (a) An Account of former editions of the Cant.
Tales, (b) A list of MSS collated or consulted, with the abbreviations by which they are cited, (c) An abstract of the historical
passages of the life of Chaucer. These are followed by "An
Essay on the Language and Versification of Chaucer", and "An
Introductory Discourse to the Canterbury Tales." The text of
the Tales then follows, with Notes, and a Glossary, to which is
prefixed an Account of the Works of Chaucer, dealing with the
question which are genuine and which spurious.

Tyrwhitt's text has been many times reissued since the two
authentic editions, viz., by Pickering, London 1822, 5 vols., again
1830; by Routledge frequently, and usually without date, but
approximately as follows: "The Canterbury Tales of Chaucer,
from the text and with the Notes and Glossary of Thomas Tyrwhitt,
condensed and arranged under the text", London 1853, small
octavo; in Routledge's British Poets 1854; again 1857, with illustrations by Corbould, reprinted 1863, 1868, and again [1878] as
part of the Standard Library, also [1882] as part of the Excelsior
Series. Also 1890 (no illustrations) as part of Routledge's Red
Line Poets, and 1892 as one of Sir John Lubbock's Hundred Best
Books. D. Appleton and Co. have a New York ed. of the Canterbury Tales, 1869, 1894, with titlepage like the 1853 Routledge.

Tyrwhitt's text was also used in eds. of Chaucer's works by
Bell (1782), Anderson (1793), Chalmers (1810), the Chiswick
(1822), Moxon (1843) and its reprints 1855 and by Routledge
1874; also in the Aldine of 1845. The revised Aldine of 1866
and the Bell of 1854-56 use Wright's text; the appearance of the
Six-Text Chaucer from 1868 on gives the foundation for later
semi-critical editions.

Tyrwhitt's Essay, Introd. Disc., Notes, and Glossary are in the
Gilfillan-Clarke modernization of the Tales, Edinb. 1860 and London 1875.

There was little recognition of the quality of Tyrwhitt's work
by his contemporaries or in the generation following his death.
His edition brought him no profit, see his letter in the Gent. Mag.
1783 I : 465; and it received slight notice from the reviews. See
the Monthly Review 1775, 53 : 26-27, the London Magazine 1775,
44 : 652-3, the Critical Review 1775, 40 : 205-7. To the two last
it is evidently a new notion that French was current in England
before Chaucer's time or that English was formerly pronounced
differently. The Monthly Reviewer asserts that Tyrwhitt's theories
are in accord with "the idea we ever entertained." All commend
him conventionally; the London Mag. alludes to his "good defence
of our old bard Chaucer as to his metre." His work was mentioned with great respect by Anderson, in the Life of Chaucer
prefixed to his 1793 ed. of the Works; also by Ellis in his Specimens of Early Eng. Poetry, 1790, I : 209; and see Gent. Mag.
1809 I : 512 and 1836 I : 501; further the opinions of Tyrwhitt's
classical fellow-scholars as referred to in the Dict. Nat. Biog.
article on Tyrwhitt. Ritson, in his Observations on Warton's His-

tory of English Poetry, London 1782, called Tyrwhitt's ed. of the
Cant. Tales "erudite, curious, and valuable", and urged Warton to
seek Tyrwhitt's advice and help.

But the later successors of Tyrwhitt in Chaucer-scholarship did
not look with due respect to his example. It is not the least of
the enormities of William Godwin, in his so-called Life of Chaucer,
that he repeatedly and energetically vilified the methods and
impugned the judgment of Tyrwhitt. See for example the 1803
ed. of Godwin I : x, xiv, 261-2, 269-70, 272, 275, 352, 357, 387,
441, 449 ; II : 158, 403-4. Wright, editor of the Cant. Tales in 1847-
51, and of much other Early Eng. work overrated in his time, also
attacked Tyrwhitt in his Anecdota Literaria, 1844, p. 23, and again
in the preface to his ed. of the Cant. Tales p. xxxiii ff. Hertzberg, p. 9 of the introd. to his translation of the Cant. Tales,
and Lounsbury, Studies I : 313 ff. censure Wright for this. Guest,
in his Hist. of Eng. Rhythms, 1838 and ed. by Skeat 1882, praises
Tyrwhitt's sagacity, but points out defects.

The Westminster Review of 1866, 86 : 199 gives Tyrwhitt a
mixture of censure and praise. The Retrospective Review of
1826, 14 : 307 intimates that he was conspicuously indebted to
Morell's notes and glossary; and this is repeated in the Bell
Chaucer of 1854, I : 59 and in Lowndes s. v. Chaucer. Lounsbury, Studies I : 297, disavows this, and says, p. 302: "What
Tyrwhitt did alone in this one matter has much surpassed the combined
labors of all who have since followed in his footsteps.
Many of the most loudly vaunted modern discoveries were anticipated a century ago by this quiet scholar."

Compare here the discussion over *Chaufecire,* chafewax, as
source and meaning of Chaucer's surname, Athenaeum 1899 I : 145,
210, 242, 274, 338, 435, 468, with Tyrwhitt's footnote (a) to part C of
the Appendix to the Preface. See the note from Lord Campbell's
Life, printed N. and Q. 1881 II : 512. Also, compare under
Craft of Lovers, Section V here, and observe that the displacement
of leaves in the MS of the Romaunt of the Rose (Skeat I : 12)
was remarked by Tyrwhitt in his concluding note on the Cant.
Tales; see N. and Q. 1894 I : 446.

See Nichols Literary Anecdotes III : 147-151 ; see the Aldine
ed. of Chaucer, I : 174; the advertisement to Gilman's ed.;
Corson's review of Gilman, Atlantic Mo. 45 : 110; Skeat, Athen.
1893 I : 765, Oxford Chaucer VI : xx, VII : lxxiii, Canon p. 23 ;
Lounsbury, Studies I : 300-313; cp. p. 306 on Tyrwhitt's mistakes
regarding Early English, already commented on by Ritson as
above cited.

The Text. For his text Tyrwhitt used 25 MSS, viz.:

Harley 1239	Bodley 686
Harley 1758	Laud 600
Harley 7333	Laud 739
Harley 7334	Selden B 14
Harley 7335	Hatton Donat. 1
Sloane 1685	New College, Oxford
Sloane 1686	Barlow 20
Royal 17 D xv	Univ. Libr. Cambr. Dd iv, 24
Royal 18 C ii	Univ. Libr. Cambr. Ii iii, 26

Trinity Coll. Cambr. R 3, 3
Trinity Coll. Cambr. R 3, 15

Askew I=Ingilby, later Hodson-Ingilby, now Brit. Mus. Egerton 2864.

Askew II=Brit. Mus. Adds. 5140.

Haistwell=Brit. Mus. Egerton 2726.

Webb=Brit. Mus. Lansdowne 851.

Cholmondeley-Norton collations made by Thomas for the Urry ed. Cholmondeley=Delamere. Norton=Hodson, now Brit. Mus. Egerton 2863.

The most credit is due, says Tyrwhitt, to Harley 7335, Dd, Ingilby, Adds. 5140, and Egerton 2726. Wright censured Tyrwhitt for not using Harley 7334. Professor Child said of Tyrwhitt's text:

"The first serious attempt to restore the genuine text of the Canterbury Tales was made by Tyrwhitt in 1775, three hundred years after they were first printed by Caxton. Tyrwhitt's edition of the Canterbury Tales has enjoyed the highest reputation, and the estimation in which it has been held is in great part deserved, and ought to be permanent. He 'collated or consulted' about twenty-five MSS, illustrated the Tales with many admirable notes, to which very little has since been added, and drew up a very good Glossary of the whole works of Chaucer. The weak point of Tyrwhitt's edition of the Canterbury Tales is the text, which was formed on a wrong principle, and without sufficient philological knowledge. Tyrwhitt, to be sure, made some attempt to ascertain the laws of Chaucer's language, and the comparative value of the MSS he employed, but the grammatical rules he has given us are both inadequate and inaccurate, while he put's at the head of the five MSS to which he ascribes most credit a very 'incorrect and carelessly written volume,' (Sir F. Madden) part vellum, part paper (Harl. MS 7335), and excludes from this list the very best MS in the Museum (Harleian 7334). We do not know on what principles the order of the MSS used was settled, but correct philological principles were certainly not the guide. One MS was taken for a standard for a time, then another, and then a third. The impropriety of such a procedure is obvious on a moment's reflection, and will be forcibly felt if the unsettled state of English at the end of the fourteenth century and the liberties taken by the copyists, is borne in mind. The natural result of an arbitrary compounding of a dozen MSS, representing the dialects of various dates and localities (not without an admixture of the idiosyncrasies of their respective writers), is an artificial text, conformable to the actual speech of no time, place, tribe, or individual. And this, so far as we can see, was the procedure of Tyrwhitt."

In a footnote is added:

"I have in my possession Tyrwhitt's original collations of

nearly all the MSS in the Museum at Cambridge mentioned in his list. The Oxford collations are not included. Tyrwhitt took an old printed copy, and corrected it minutely on the margin according to the various MSS which he adopted as authoritative, sometimes changing at an interval of less than a page, sometimes keeping on with one and the same for ten pages. He then entered the various readings of other MSS on blank leaves. Those marked in his list A, C, C¹, T, W, are most used. The marginal corrections are, more than half the time, made according to A, the inferior codex spoken of above; about one-third of the time according to C¹. C (the excellent Harleian MS 7334), is the guide for only the first two pages of the Prologue, but is collated throughout."

[F. J. Child: Observations on the Language of Chaucer, in Mem. of the Amer. Acad. of Arts and Sciences, n. s., vol. VIII, pp. 445-502 (1862). Pages 447-8 are above cited.]

Notwithstanding the justice of Child's animadversions upon the text offered by Tyrwhitt, it may be asserted that our progress beyond him has not been equal to our professions. The conception of a critical text, that is, a text constructed after determining the relations of all the authorities, and abiding impartially by the conditions which these relations indicate, had in Tyrwhitt's day not yet dawned in the minds of classical scholars. Tyrwhitt, like his immediate predecessor Morell, knew of no better method than the examination of a number of apparently good codices, and the selection from them of what seemed to him the "best" readings. The result was what we now call an "eclectic" text, a text which, however smooth its flow, however satisfactory its movement to the champion of Chaucer's metrical command, labors under the disadvantage of editorial subjectivity, of interpretation to us by a partial advocate, not transmission to us by an unbiased witness. But while we are obliged to agree with Professor Child's strictures, we must not forget two important facts. First, that in Tyrwhitt's day the modern "critical" theory of text-construction had not yet been formulated. Tyrwhitt belonged to the third of the post-Renaissance periods of scholarship, periods usually named from their founders or tendencies the age of Petrarch or of imitation mainly Italian, the age of Scaliger or of the French encyclopedic method, the Anglo-Dutch period dominated by Bentley, and the modern or German era which, as regards textual criticism, was inaugurated by Wolf and by Lachmann after the death of Tyrwhitt. Of the 18th century Tyrwhitt still remains, the age of cautious and thorough annotation, of eager search in original and recondite sources, of painstaking and enormous labor,—but not of modern critical method.

And secondly, after we have justified his procedure historically, let us remember how little Chaucer scholars have passed beyond him. The edition of Skeat in 1894 is still an edition of the 18th-century type; and although the term "critical" has been applied to the Globe Chaucer, it is undeserved. For a cardinal necessity in the erection of a critical text is the close examination of all the authorities; and to this, a century and a half after Tyrwhitt, we are not yet arrived. The Chaucer Society, by making accessible in printed form eight MSS of the Canterbury Tales and small portions of other MSS, has apparently encouraged editors to believe the labor of complete collation unnecessary.

Sources. Of the 23 Cant. Tales which exist in a finished or partly finished condition (the Cook's Tale being excluded), Tyrwhitt assigned those of Knight, Monk, Doctor, Nun's Priest, Second Nun, the Tale of Melibeus, and the Wife of Bath's prologue, to definite sources. He partially traced, or discussed in general terms, the Tales of Merchant, Reeve, Shipman, Pardoner, Franklin, Manciple, and Parson, and professed himself unable to identify those of Miller, Friar, Summoner, Prioress, and Squire. He considered Sir Thopas and the narrative of the Canon's Yeoman as having their sources in Chaucer's general experience rather than in any special book; and he erroneously derived the tales of Man of Law and of Wife of Bath from Gower, failing also to perceive clearly the alliance between the Clerk's Tale and the Latin of Petrarch.

The subsequent investigations of the Chaucer Society have accumulated a mass of analogues, largely French and Oriental, to some of the Tales; and the sources of the Clerk's and the Man of Law's Tales have been more exactly treated than by Tyrwhitt. But in the 160 years which have elapsed since he worked, no more definite source has been found for the stories of Merchant, Reeve, Miller, Shipman, Friar, Summoner, Manciple, Franklin, or Squire than was known to him; and while many details have been noted, *e. g.* regarding the tales of Melibeus and of the Second Nun, it is a striking fact that the investigation of the last ten years has done as much to modify the additions of Tyrwhitt's successors as to impugn the work of Tyrwhitt. Cp. the work of Miss Petersen on the Nun's Priest's Tale and the Parson's Tale, superseding the discussions by Skeat.

The Canon. It is perhaps upon the canon of Chaucer that the results of Tyrwhitt's labors are most conspicuous and most permanent. The last ed. of Chaucer previous to Tyrwhitt's, that of Urry in 1721, had added to its predecessor, the work of Speght, several poems not in Speght's collection; Speght in 1598 had added, though not largely, to the 1561 ed. by Stow; Stow had appended a mass of short poems to the ed. of Thynne; and Thynne himself, publishing the "First Folio" in 1532, had printed along with the 16 works which we still accept as Chaucerian some 22 pieces, occasionally marked with the name of Scogan, of Hoccleve, or of "Dan John", but more frequently without name, and therefore supposedly Chaucer's. Doubts had been expressed regarding a few of these poems by Francis Thynne, and by Thomas in his preface to Urry; but the first

thoroughgoing examination was made by Tyrwhitt. He formed
his judgments, it would appear, mainly upon his notions of
Chaucer's style. With this as a criterion, he rejected some 20
of the additions made by his predecessors, including the entire
mass of poems appended by Stow, all these, with the exception
of one or two in Stow's list, being still to-day regarded as
spurious; but he retained in the canon a half-dozen works
which have since been struck out by Hertzberg, ten Brink,
and Bradshaw. See under Testament of Love, Court of Love,
Complaint of the Black Knight, Chaucer's Dream (Isle of
Ladies), and Cuckoo and Nightingale, in Section V below.
And it should be remarked that, although Tyrwhitt failed to
push the process of censorship so far as subsequent editors
have pushed it, he suggested no additions to the canon.

Language and Versification, see Section VI here.

Glossary, see Section VI here.

Notes. Tyrwhitt's ripe classical scholarship was of great aid
in the compilation of his notes on the Canterbury Tales; but
his reading ranged over the medieval and modern fields as well,
witness his reference to Bernard's Megacosmos in his note on
line 4617, and his comparison of line 3880 to a passage of Gray's
Elegy.

Wright: The Canterbury Tales of Geoffrey Chaucer. A New
    Text with Illustrative Notes. Edited for the Percy Society by
    Thomas Wright, 3 vols. London, 1847-51.

Text from MSS Harley 7334; illustrative notes at the foot of
the page; no glossary. Introduction of 42 pages includes
abridgement of Nicolas' life of Chaucer, 14 pages; remarks on
the Tales 14-23; citation of Tyrwhitt's list of editions, to page
31; explanation of the plan of the present edition, censure of
Tyrwhitt's methods, and praise of MS Harley 7334, to p. 42.
Wright says of his own treatment of the text that he has made
comparatively few alterations, and only such as appeared absolutely necessary; he states that where the reading of the Harley
was plainly bad, he has corrected it by comparison with another
MS, usually Lansdowne 851, and that he has not loaded the
book with notes pointing out the alterations.

Child, who used this text of Wright's as the basis of his 1862
paper on Chaucer's language (see Section VI B here) was
confident of its accuracy; later criticism has been generally
severe. Cp. Skeat, Acad. 1890 I : 269; Athen. 1893 I : 765;
Canon pp. 23-25. Nor was the review in Athen. 1851, p. 294,
a laudatory one.

Wright's text was reprinted 1853 in Cooke's Universal Library, as No. 25.

Ellis, EEPron. I : 243 footnote, says that Wright's text has been reprinted, large octavo double columns, pubd. by R. Griffin & Co., Lond. and Glasgow, at half-a-crown. This ed. I have not seen; it suggests in style the Routledge reprint of the Moxon Chaucer of 1843, see Section II D here, while *Charles* Griffin was the publisher of the reprint of Robert Bell's 1854-56 Chaucer, see *ibid.*

Gilfillan-Clarke, 1860, see under Modernizations, Section **III E** below.

Parchment Library. Chaucer's Canterbury Tales, ed. A. W. Pollard, 2 vols. London, 1886-7.

Brief notice in Athenaeum 1886 II : 670 of vol. 1; of vol. 2 *ibid.* 1887 II : 892. Vol. 1 contains Prologue, Knight's Tale, Man of Law's Tale, Prioress' Tale, Clerk's Tale. Text treated according to "a somewhat eccentric procedure." "Students who wish to know what it is most probable that Chaucer actually wrote must seek other guidance." Vol. 2 contains "all the remaining Cant. Tales which are suitable for general readers." Observe that the arrangement of Tales in this selected edition is arbitrary.

Eversley Series. Chaucer's Canterbury Tales, ed. A. W. Pollard, 2 vols. London 1894.

Reviewed Anglia Beiblatt 5 : 281 (Andrae); Mod. Lang. Notes 10 : 177-180 (Hempl); Archiv 94 : 441-446 (Zupitza); Dial 17 : 260 (Corson).

Pollard's Canterbury Tales text is separately reprinted from the Globe Chaucer, London 1902. Rev. Hoops, Engl. Stud. 31 : 288. Same type, format, and paper as the Globe. No introduction.

Pollard's ed. of the Canterbury Tales. 2 vols. 12mo. Paul, Trübner & Co., 1905.

Editions of Portions for School Use

Of the Prologue.

A Specimen of Chaucer's Language. (The first 100 lines, with notes.)   L. Edman, Upsala, 1861.

Ed. by W. McLeod, Lond., 1871, with life, notes, glossary.

The Book of the Tales of Caunterbury. Prolog. Mit Varianten zum Gebrauch bei Vorlesungen herausgegeben. J. Zupitza, Marburg, 1871. Second ed. Berlin 1882, repr. 1896.
Rev. Koch in Anglia 5 : Anz. 138-9 and Littblatt 1885 p. 325; Foerster in Archiv 103 : 178; Wülker in Centrblatt 1883 p. 92.

Prolog zu den Canterbury Tales : Versuch einer Kritischen Ausgabe. Bernh. ten Brink, Marburg 1871 pp. viii, 29, quarto. [Beigabe der Marburger Universitätschrift, diem natalem . . . . imperatoris ac regis Guilielmi I.]

An Introduction to the Study of Chaucer. (The Prologue with notes). A. Monfries, Edinburgh, 1876.

The Prologue: the Text collated with the seven oldest MSS. With life, grammar, and notes. Ed. E. F. Willoughby, Lond. 1881 (Black's School Classics). Rev. Athen. 1881 II : 205.

The Prologue, with notes, examination papers, and glossary. Ed. J. M. D. Meiklejohn, Lond. 1882.

The Prologue. Ed. W. W. Skeat, Oxford, 1891.
Rev. Kölbing, Engl. Stud. 16 : 273-278; Zupitza, Archiv 86 : 428. Again issued Oxford 1900, 1903, 1906. Kölbing's review contains addit. notes, mainly from Early Eng. romances.

Ed. with introd. and notes, by A. W. Pollard, London 1903. Rev. Greg in Mod. Lang. Quart. 6 : 111; Athen. 1903 II : 153.

Ed. C. T. Onions, Lond. 1904, the Carmelite Classics.

Of the Prologue and Knight's Tale.

English of the Fourteenth Century, illustrated by Notes on Chaucer's Prologue and Knight's Tale. S. H. Carpenter, Boston, 1872. Again issued 1901.

Ed. A. J. Wyatt, Cambridge, 1895. (University Tutorial Series.) With a glossary by S. J. Evans. Again issued Lond. 1897, 1899, 1900.

Of the Prologue and Nun's Priest's Tale.
>   Ed. A. J. Wyatt, Lond. 1904. Rev. Greg, Mod. Lang. Quart. 6 : 111.

Of the Prologue and Squire's Tale.
>   Ed. A. J. Wyatt, Lond. 1903.

Of the Prologue, the Knight's Tale, the Nun's Priest's Tale.
>   Ed. R. Morris, Oxford 1867. Later eds. 1869, 1872, 1874, 1875, 1881, 1886. Re-ed. by Skeat, with new notes, Oxford 1889; rev. Mod. Lang. Notes 5 : 466-473 (A. H. Tolman) ; see *ibid.* 6 : 266-69, 8 : 57-9. Again issued 1903.

>   Ed. F. J. Mather, Boston 1898. Rev. Koch, Engl. Stud. 29 : 116; Root, Jour. Gc. Phil. 3 : 372-3; Nation 1901 II : 284; Schröer in Anglia Beibl. 13 : 259.

>   Ed. M. H. Liddell, New York, 1901, repr. 1902.
>   Also pub. in two parts, Part I comprising a Middle Eng. grammar, with introd. and notes, Part II the text. Professes to offer a critical text. Rev. Nation 1901 II : 284; see the Athen. 1901 II : 380, 597. Rev. Mod. Lang. Notes 17 : 382-86 (W. A. Read).

>   Ed. A. Ingraham, Lond. 1902. (Macmillan's Pocket Classics). With notes and glossary. See Athen. 1902 II : 851.

Of the Knight's Tale.
>   Pub. W. and R. Chambers, Edinb. and Lond. 1896. With life, grammar, notes, glossary, and exam. questions.

>   Ed. A. W. Pollard, Lond. 1903. Rev. Mod. Lang. Quart. 7 : 104; Athen. 1903 II : 753.

Of the Man of Law's Tale.
>   Pub. W. and R. Chambers, Edinb. and Lond. 1884. With life, grammar, notes, and glossary.
>   In Morris and Skeat's Specimens, revised ed., Oxford 1889.

Of the Clerk's Tale.
>   Pub. W. and R. Chambers, Edinb. and Lond. 1883, 1888.

>   In Sprague's Masterpieces in English Literature, N. Y. 1874.

>   Ed. R. S. Sheppard, Madras, 1900, with notes.

>   Ed. C. M. Barrow, Madras, 1900, with introd., notes, and questions.

>   Ed. E. Winckler, Madras, 1900, with introd. and notes.

Of the Squire's Tale.
> Pub. W. and R. Chambers, Edinb. and Lond. 1882.

> Ed. A. W. Pollard, Lond. 1899, with notes.

> Ed. W. J. Goodrich, Madras, 1899, with introd., notes, and appendices.

> Ed. A. D. Innes, in Blackie's English Classics, 1905.

Of the Pardoner's Tale.
> The Pardoner's Prologue and Tale. A critical edition. J. Koch, Berlin 1902, and for the Chaucer Society, 2d series No. 35. Reviewed DLZ 1902 p. 2023, Björkman in Engl. Stud. 32 : 275-77, Jespersen in Nord. Tidskr. 12 : 26. See comment by me in Mod. Phil. 3 : 166 ff.; trivial reference Acad. 1902 II : 101.

> In the 1867 ed. of Morris' Specimens. Not in the revised eds.

> In O. F. Emerson's Middle English Reader, Lond. and N. Y. 1905. Text from the Ellesmere MS. A few notes.

Of the Prioress' Tale.
> In the 1867 ed. of Morris' Specimens; not in later eds.

Of the Prioress' Tale, the Rime of Sir Thopas, the Monk's Tale, the Clerk's Tale, the Squire's Tale.
> Ed. Skeat, Oxford, 1874; again 1877, 1880, 1881, 1888, 1889, 1891, 1898 (seventh ed.).

Of the Man of Law's Tale, the Pardoner's Tale, the Second Nun's Tale, the Canon's Yeoman's Tale.
> Ed. Skeat, Oxford, 1877; revised 1889, 1897.

D. Editions of Selections, from the Works and from the Canterbury Tales

1790. Ellis, George. Specimens of the Early English Poets, etc. In 3 vols., third ed., Lond. 1803. Vol. I has extracts from Chaucer; brief passages and running comment. Notes on Chaucer's life; Doctor Johnson is quoted and reproved; Tyrwhitt's opinion as to Chaucer's versification is supported.

1819. Campbell, Thomas. Specimens of the British Poets; with Biographical and Critical Notices, and an Essay on English Poetry. Lond. 1810, 7 vols. 2d ed. Phila. 1869. The Essay fills vol. I; in vol. II are Chaucer's prologue (the characters only) and extracts from Gower and Lydgate.

1819. Sanford and Walsh. The Works of the British Poets, with Lives of the Authors. Phila. 1819. The series was projected for 50 vols., of which 25 were issued, down to Young. Vol. I contains selections from Chaucer, Gower, Skelton, Wyatt, Surrey, and Gascoigne. From Chaucer are printed the Prologue, the Miller's Tale, the Friar's prologue and Tale, the Clerk's prologue and Tale, the Doctor's prologue and Tale, the Pardoner's prologue and Tale, the Rime of Sir Thopas and its prologue, the Second Nun's Tale, the Canon's Yeoman's prologue and Tale, and the Flower and the Leaf.

The introduction to this work is cited above under Collections of British Poetry, p. 131.

1825. Hazlitt, William. Select Poets of Great Britain. Lond. 1825. The Prologue, the Squire's Tale, the Prioress' Tale, the Flower and the Leaf, part of the Knight's Tale, the Wife of Bath's prologue, "Similies from Chaucer", *i. e.,* three stanzas from Troilus and one from the Man of Law's Tale.

1827. John Johnstone. Specimens of Sacred and Serious Poetry, from Chaucer to the Present Day. Edinb., again Edinb. 1855. 12mo.

Includes the Prioress' Tale and the Character of a Good Parson; there is no statement of the text used.

1828. John Johnstone. Specimens of the Lyrical, Descriptive, and Narrative Poets of Great Britain, from Chaucer to the Present Day. Edinb., 12mo.

The "preliminary sketch of the history of Early English poetry" which forms the introd. to this volume contains passages from Troilus and Cressida. There are no selections from Chaucer in the text.

1831. Robert Southey. Select Works of the British Poets from Chaucer to Johnson. London. Contains the Prologue, the tales of Knight, Man of Law, Squire, the Parl. of Foules, the Cuckoo and Nightingale, the Flower and Leaf, Truth, Purse.

1833-35. For the work of Charles Cowden Clarke see under Modernizations below.

1846. Leigh Hunt. Wit and Humour, selected from the Old English Poets. London. A prose version into modern English is added, at the foot of the page, to the characters of the pilgrims from the Prologue, ending with the Shipman, the Friar's Tale, 20 lines describing the Pardoner's way of preaching, the Merchant's opinion of wives, the "Gallantry of Translation" from the NPTale, the "Disappearance of the Fairies" from the WBTale. For Leigh Hunt's other work in Chaucer, 1823 ff., see Section III E below.

1847. C. D. Deshler. Selections from the Poetical Works of Geoffrey Chaucer, with a concise Life. New York, again 1850, 1854. Brief passages and running analysis, somewhat like Saunders' (see under Modernizations below), but weakly literary. After the Life are remarks on Chaucer's poetry, an analysis of the Prologue, and then groups of passages classed as Rural Descriptions, Paintings of Female Characters, Paintings of Masculine Characters, Narrative Poetry, Miscellaneous. There is an appendix on Gower, Lydgate, Douglas, etc., defending Lydgate and giving extracts.

1856. James Parton. Humourous Poetry of the English Language. Boston. Contains Chaucer's Purse.

1867. Richard Morris. Specimens of Early English, vol. II, Oxford. Includes the tales of the Pardoner and the Prioress; the Morris and Skeat revised eds. of 1872, 1889, 1898 substituted for these the Man of Law's Tale, in part.

1867. E. Maetzner. Altenglische Sprachproben. Berlin. Includes the WBTale (400 lines), lines 2721-2966 of the Romaunt of the Rose, the Roundel, the tale of Melibeus.

1870. For the work of Purves see under Modernizations below.

1874. R. Wülker. Altenglisches Lesebuch. Halle, 2 vols. Vol. 2, 1879, includes the Squire's Tale, its text from Morris; an extract from Troilus, an extract from the Parson's Tale, and passages from Boethius.

1876-82. Morley. In Cassell's Library of English Literature, ed.
Henry Morley, vol. I includes the Clerk's Tale and Truth, vol.
V the General Prologue.

1880. T. H. Ward. Selections from the English Poets. London,
again 1891. 4 vols. Vol. I contains extracts from the Book
of the Duchess, from Troilus, from the Parl. of Foules, from
the House of Fame, the prologue to the LGW, part of the
Prologue to the Cant. Tales, extracts from the Man of Law's
tale, the envoy to the Clerk's tale, extracts from the tales of the
Franklin and the Knight, Truth. As "Poems commonly attributed to Chaucer" are printed extracts from the Romaunt of
the Rose, from the Flower and the Leaf, and from the Court
of Love. There are 14 pages of introd. by Ward.

1886. Henry Sweet. Second Middle English Primer. Oxford.
Extracts from the Book of the Duchess; Pity, Words to Adam,
the Parl. of Foules, the Former Age, Truth, the Prologue to
the Cant. Tales, a condensation of the Pard. Tale.
    Rev. Koch, Engl. Stud. 11 : 290-298.

1886-7. See "Parchment Library" Cant. Tales, under Editions
above.

1888. F. N. Paton. Selections from Chaucer. Lond., in the "Can-
terbury Poets." Pity, the Book of the Duchess, the Parl. of
Foules, Troilus and Cressida, Words to Adam, House of Fame,
Legend of Good Women, Selections from the Cant. Tales, =
Prologue, Man of Law's Tale, Wife of Bath's, Doctor's, Nun's
Priest's, Second Nun's, Canon's Yeoman's prologue. Truth,
Scogan, Bukton, Gentilesse, Purse, Stedfastnesse, Fortune. A
glossary.

1896. Hiram Corson. Selections from Chaucer's Canterbury Tales.
Lond. and N. Y. The Prologue, selections from the Knight's
Tale, from the Miller's Tale, headlink and selections from the
Reeve's Tale, the Cook's Tale, a bit of the Man of Law's headlink, selections from his Tale, address of the Host to the Monk,
bit from the Monk's Tale, the Nun's Priest's Tale, selections
from the Doctor's Tale, the Pardoner's Tale, selections from
the Wife of Bath's Tale, the Squire's Tale, the Canon's Yeoman's prologue and Tale.
    Rev. Klaeber, Anglia Beibl. 8 : 121.

1896. For Warner's Library of the World's Best Literature see
under Modernizations below.

1897. In the 5th ed. of Zupitza's Alt und Mittelenglisches Uebungs-buch, ed. by Schipper, are included Bukton and Stedfastnesse. Previous eds. contained no Chaucer.

1902. C. H. Herford. English Tales in Verse. London. The Squire's Tale, the Prioress' Tale, the Pardoner's Tale, the story of Ugolino from the Monk's Tale. Text of the Globe Chaucer, "with slight occasional divergences."

1902. J. L. Robertson. The Select Chaucer. Edinb. and London. Selections from the Cant. Tales Prologue,=The Pilgrims, Talk and Incident by the way; Tale of Knight, extracts from Miller and Reeve, Tale of the Man of Law, extracts from the Ship-man, Tales of Prioress, Monk, and Nun's Priest, extracts from Doctor, Tale of Pardoner, extracts from Wife of Bath and Summoner, Tale of Clerk, extracts from Merchant, Squire, Franklin, and Manciple. Part II contains the Minor Poems, = Romaunt of the Rose, Book of the Duchess, Parl. of Foules, House of Fame, Troilus, prol. to the Legend of Good Women, the legend of Ariadne, Former Age, Truth, Purse. A glossary.

1905. A. W. Pollard. The Canterbury Tales, selected. Lond., the Dryden Library. [Brit. Mus. Cat.]

1907. English Poetry, 1170-1892. John M. Manly. Boston. In-cludes selections from Troilus and Cressida, part of the Pro-logue to the Cant. Tales, the Squire's Tale and the Words of the Franklin, the Roundel from the Parlement of Foules, Truth, Purse, and Gentilesse.

E. Modernizations, Imitations, and Translations
Chronologically Arranged

The influence of Chaucer, both in narrative and in lyric, was felt already in his own time, and especially in the generation just following. A study of the effect exercised by his lyrical and semi-lyrical verse would, however, carry this bibliography too far afield, and include not merely a good share of the work of Lydgate, and much by the Scottish school of the fifteenth century, but anonymous medieval verse such as the bird-poem in MS Cambridge Gg iv, 27, or the charming Lover's Mass of MS Fairfax 16, both printed in the Journal of English and Germanic Philology, 7 :95 ff. The history could also with justice be extended to include some of the greatest names in English poetry of the succeeding centuries, from Spenser to William Morris. As such a study would be too ample for any general bibliography, the subject has here been limited mainly to Chaucer's narrative work, and to the acknowledged modernizations or imitations of such kind, with inclusion also of attempts at the writing of Chaucerian language. Poems in imitation of Chaucer which have at any time been printed with his works are not discussed here, but in Section V below; and the titles of some studies on the influence of Chaucer will be found in an Appendix to this section. For imitations of the framework-plan of the Canterbury Tales see p. 153; a most interesting essay on this whole subject is to be found in Lounsbury's Studies, vol. III, "Chaucer in Literary History."

Lydgate's Story of Thebes, written in continuation of the Canterbury Tales, was first printed with the works of Chaucer in 1561; see Section V here for notes upon it.

The Tale of Beryn, with its prologue The Mery Adventure of the Pardoner and the Tapster, was first printed by Urry in the 1721 Chaucer; see Section V here for further notes.

John Lane's continuation of the Squire's Tale, although licensed for the press in 1614-15, was not published until the Chaucer Society printed it in 1888; see under Squire's Tale in G below.

Spenser: On Spenser as a follower and imitator of Chaucer see:
> Warton. Observations on Spenser's Faery Queene, 1752, sect. 5.
> Wagner. On Spenser's Archaisms. diss. Halle 1879, 60 pp.
> Legouis, E. Quomodo Edmundus Spenserus ad Chaucerum se fingens in eclogis "The Shepheardes Calender" versum heroicum renovarit. Paris, 1896. 84 pp.
> Herford, C. H. Ed. of The Shepheard's Calender, Macmillan, 1897, introd. pp. xlviii ff.

In W. Bullein's Dialogue against the Fever Pestilence, 1564, 1573, 1578,—see reprint by EETS, 1888, pp. 16-17,—Chaucer is introduced; and six lines of verse which conclude his description are apparently intended to be in his "manner." The passage, with the lines, is also in Todd's Illustrations pp. xxix-xxx. This is accordingly an earlier "imitation" than that mentioned by Lounsbury as below.

The earliest effort to represent Chaucer's manner, according to Lounsbury, Studies III : 115, was by Francis James, in an encomium prefixed to Kynaston's Latin Troilus and Cressida of 1685. This short poem is reprinted under Troilus, Section IV here. See just above for an earlier imitation.

Lounsbury, Studies III : 154 footnote, says that he has seen in booksellers' catalogues "a book purporting to have been published in 1641, which is entitled Canterbury Tales, translated out of Chaucer's Old English into our usual Language"; but that he has never met with the book nor with any account of it; see his later note, *ibid.* 452; see N. and Q. 1892 I : 377, from which we may infer that the poem, of about 130 lines with alternate rimes, is no real attempt at modernizing Chaucer, but merely an attack on Laud disguised as literature. Livingston, Auction Prices *s. v.* Chaucer, mentions this work as by A. Brome; the Brit. Mus. Cat. gives the title as "A Canterbury Tale, translated out of Chaucer's Old English into our usuall Language. Whereunto is added the Scots Pedler. Newly enlarged by A. B." According to the Cat., of 1641, quarto.

One of the plays of William Cartwright, The Ordinary, written in 1643, in imitation of Jonson's Alchemist, introduces a character, Moth, speaking Chaucerian English. See Lounsbury, Studies III : 116-7.

The Musarum Deliciae of Sir John Mennis and others, published in 1656, contained two satiric pieces in imitation of Chaucer's style; see Lounsbury, Studies III : 118. The former of these is entitled Partus Chauceri Posthumus, Gulielmi Nelson, and is of 56 lines in heroic couplets; the latter, of 52 lines, is entitled Imitatio Chauceri altera, in eundem.

A collection entitled Choyce Drollery, which appeared in 1656, included an imitation of the tale of Sir Thopas; see Lounsbury, Studies, III : 118.

In 1672 appeared "Chaucer's Ghoast, or a Piece of Antiquity containing twelve Pleasant Fables of Ovid penn'd after the ancient manner of writing in England." See Lounsbury, Studies III : 118, where it is stated that the contents of this volume are taken bodily from Gower's Confessio Amantis. In Brit. Mus. Cat. under P. Ovidius Naso.

In the first part of the Return from Parnassus, Act IV, scene 1, is introduced a poem supposedly in Chaucer's "vein." It is of three seven-line stanzas (the second of six lines only). The last word is *jape,* and the hearer of the declaimed poem assures the author that his lady will not endure a word in the last "canto"; the author replies that the word as Chaucer uses it has no "unhonest meaning," but signifies a jest. For note on this word see p. 507 here. The three Parnassus plays were presented 1597-1601. See ed. by Macray, Oxford 1886.

Dryden: Dryden's modernizations of the Knight's Tale, the Nun's Priest's Tale, the Wife of Bath's Tale, the Character of a Good Parson, and the (spurious) Flower and Leaf, were first published in his Fables of 1700, and are printed in the eds. of his works from 1760 to that by Scott in 1808, its reissue in 1821, and the Scott-Saintsbury ed. of 1882 and following, where they are included in vol. 11, the original text (from Morris), being reprinted in vol. 12. They are also to be found in the eds. of the Fables separately, from 1700 to 1822. The Chaucerian text was also printed in the ed. of 1700. Ogle and Lipscomb as noted below, and Morell as noted under C above, reprinted Dryden's work in their collections, although Lipscomb did not include the Nun's Priest's Tale. For comment on Dryden's modernizations see:

Warton. Essay on the Genius and Writings of Pope. Ed. 1806, II : 11-16.

O. Schoepke. Dryden's Uebertragungen Chaucers im Verhältnis zu ihren Originalen. diss. Halle, 1878, pp. 44.

O. Schoepke. Dryden's Bearbeitungen Chaucerscher Gedichte. Anglia 2 : 314-353.

See Cornhill Magazine 82 : 545 for note on Leigh Hunt's opinion.

See:—Dryden and Speght's Chaucer. F. J. Tupper. Mod. Lang. Notes 12 : 347.

See Lounsbury, Studies III : 162-176.

A collection entitled "Chaucer's Whims, being some select Fables and Tales in Verse, very applicable to the Present Times", appeared London 1701, 8vo. They are political, in various measures; there is no attempt at imitating Chaucer.

Pope: Pope's "January and May: or the Merchant's Tale from Chaucer" appeared in part 6 of Tonson's Poetical Miscellany in 1709; his "The Wife of Bath: her Prologue, from Chaucer" was included in Steele's Poetical Miscellany of 1714, another ed. of which appeared in 1727; and his "Temple of Fame", a revision of the House of Fame, appeared in 1715. A brief "Imitation" of Chaucer, done in Pope's youth, is also included in the eds. of his Works, see Warton, Essay on the Genius and Writings of Pope, ed. 1806 II : 28. The modernizations are included in the eds. of Pope from 1751 to those of Murray in

1771, of Elwin and Courthope in 1870-1889, and that by Ward
in the Globe series, 1889. On Pope's modernizations see:
A. Schade. Ueber das Verhältnis von Popes 'January and
    May' und 'The Wife of Bath, Her Prologue' zu den ent-
    sprechenden Abschnitten von Chaucers Canterbury Tales.
    Engl. Stud. 25 : 1-130 and 26 : 161-228.
F. Uhlemann. Chaucer's Hous of Fame und Pope's Temple of
    Fame. Anglia 6 : 107 ff.
Warton. Essay on the Genius and Writings of Pope, section
    VII; Lounsbury, Studies III : 179-185.

Chaucer's Characters, or the Introduction to the Canterbury Tales,
    by T. Betterton. Reprinted in Morell's ed. of 1737, see under
    C above.
The Miller of Trompington, or the Reeve's Tale from Chaucer, by
    T. Betterton. London, 1712, in Lintot's Miscellany; again 1720,
    1722. Both reprinted, with augmentations to the introduction,
    in Ogle, in Lipscomb, see below. See Lounsbury, Studies III :
    186.

The Carpenter of Oxford; or the Miller's Tale from Chaucer,
    attempted in modern English by S. Cobb. To which are added
    two imitations of Chaucer, I. Susannah and the Two Elders.
    II. Earl Robert's Mice. By Mr. Prior. London 1712.
        The first of these bits by Prior is of eight lines, the second
    of 61 lines. They are reprinted in the eds. of his works, e. g.,
    the Aldine of 1885; and in Chalmers' British Poets, vol. 10,
    p. 187. Cobb's work is reprinted in Ogle, in Lipscomb, as
    below. On Prior see Lounsbury, Studies III : 188.

Brown Bread and Honour, a Tale Moderniz'd from an ancient
    Manuscript of Chaucer. London 1716.
        An allegorical satire, no trace of Chaucer's influence. Of
    8 pages, in 4-beat couplets. Begins:
        In Days of old, so Poets feign,
        Not quite so old as Saturn's reign,
        Honour was not an empty word,
        But rul'd the Court, and edg'd the Sword.   (etc.)

Gay, see under Summoner's Tale in G below.

A Tale devised in the plesaunt manner of Gentil Maister Geoffrey
    Chaucer. Elijah Fenton, 1717. Reprinted in Chalmers, 10 : 412.

Chaucer's Incensed Ghost, printed at pp. 542-44 of Morgan's Phoenix
    Britannica, London 1732, is no imitation, but a poem in 17
    seven-line stanzas written "on the Occasion of a Scurvy Piece

in Praise of Tobacco being impertinently fathered upon Chaucer." Begins :

> From the frequented Path, where Mortals tread
> Indignant Chaucer, having long retir'd,   (etc.)

Said to be from a 1618 MS.

The Whimsical Legacy (=the Summoner's Tale). By Grosvenor. In Budgell's Bee, 1733, II : 1020-25. Reprinted in Ogle, in Lipscomb, as below.

The Pardoner's Tale was modernized by Mrs. Elizabeth Cooper, in her Muses' Library, of which the first ed. appeared in 1737, again 1738 and 1741 with modified titlepages, which according to Lowndes were resorted to as a means of working off the impression. See Lounsbury, Studies III : 242.

Mrs. Cooper's sagacity and sense of humor may be estimated from her remark on Lydgate: "Many authors are so profuse in his praise as to rank him very little below his master, and often quote them together; which rais'd my Curiosity so high that I gave a considerable Price for his Works, and waded thro' a large Folio, hoping still to have my Expectation gratified. . . . . But I must either confess my own want of Penetration, or beg Leave to dissent from his Admirers."

Gualtherus and Griselda: or the Clerk of Oxford's Tale, from Boccace, Petrarch, and Chaucer. G. Ogle. London 1739.

The Canterbury Tales of Chaucer, Modernis'd by several Hands. Publish'd by Mr. Ogle. 3 vols., London, 1741.

Contents: Vol. I: Life of Chaucer, by Mr. Urry. Prologue to the Tales, by Mr. Ogle. The Characters of the Pilgrims, the Knight, the Squire, the Squire's Yeoman, the Prioress, the Monk, the Fryar, the Merchant, by Mr. Betterton; the Clerk of Oxford, by Mr. Ogle; the Man of Law, the Franklin, by Mr. Betterton; the Haberdasher, the Weaver, the Carpenter, the Dyer, the Tapestry-maker, the Cook, the Shipman, the Doctor of Physick, the Wife of Bath, by Mr. Betterton; the Parson, by Mr. Dryden; the Plow-man, the Miller, the Manciple, the Reve, the Sumner, the Pardoner, by Mr. Betterton. Prologue to the Knight's Tale, by Mr. Ogle. The Knight's Tale, by Mr. Dryden. Prologue to the Miller's Tale, by Mr. Ogle. The Miller's Tale, by Mr. Cobb. Prologue to the Reve's Tale, by Mr. Ogle. The Reve's Tale, by Mr. Betterton. Vol. II: Prologue to the Cook's Tale, by Mr. Ogle. The Cook's Tale, by Mr. Boyse. Prologue to the Man of Law's Tale, by Mr. Ogle. The Man of Law's Tale, by Mr. Brooke. Prologue to the Squire's Tale, by Mr. Ogle. The Squire's Tale, by Mr. Boyse. The Squire's Tale, continued, from Spenser, by Mr. Ogle. Vol. III: Prologue to the Merchant's Tale, by Mr. Ogle. The Merchant's Tale, by Mr. Pope. Prologue to the Wife of Bath's Tale, by Mr. Pope, continued by Mr. Ogle. The Wife of Bath's Tale, by Mr.

Dryden. Prologue to the Fryar's Tale, by Mr. Ogle. The Fryar's Tale, by Mr. Markland. Prologue to the Sumner's Tale, by Mr. Grosvenor. Prologue to the Clerk of Oxford's Tale, by Mr. Ogle. The Clerk of Oxford's Tale, by Mr. Ogle. The conclusion to the Clerk of Oxford's Tale, by Mr. Ogle.

In vol. II, the Cook's Tale is the Tale of Gamelyn, and the so-called Prologue to the Cook's Tale is Chaucer's Cook's Tale, patched to serve as preliminary to Gamelyn.

All in couplets of five-beat lines, even the Man of Law's Tale, with the sole exception of the Squire's Tale and its conclusion, which are in ten-line stanzas, Boyse 140 stanzas, Ogle 141-214 stanzas. Vol. III has at the beginning "A Letter to a Friend, with the Poem of Gualtherus and Griselda", signed George Ogle. In it Ogle discusses among other things the possible meeting of Chaucer and Petrarch in Italy, giving the Latin text of Petrarch's letter to Boccaccio. Ogle's version of the Clerk's Tale was reprinted in Angelica's Ladies' Library, 1794, see below. Ogle's work was reprinted entire by Lipscomb in 1795, see below.

Second edition, Dublin 1742, 2 vols. On Ogle see Lounsbury, Studies III : 186-197.

Andrew Jackson, a London bookseller of the 18th century, who published in 1740 a rimed version of Paradise Lost book I, issued in 1750, "with somewhat better success",—Matrimonial Scenes; consisting of the Seaman's Tale, the Manciple's Tale, the Character of the Wife at Bath, and her Five Husbands— all modernized from Chaucer; by A. Jackson. Lond. 1750 oct.

[Nichols, Literary Anecdotes of the 18th Century, 1812, III. 625-6. Not in Brit. Mus. Catalogue.]

Nichols cites 6 lines of verse, apparently Jackson on Chaucer.

William Mason published in 1747 his Musaeus, including an imitation of Chaucer's style; the poem is accessible in Chalmers' Poets, vol. 18, p. 323; also in Bell's Classical Arrangement of Fugitive Poetry, Lond. 1790, vol. 9.

On Mason's imitation see Lounsbury, Studies III : 127.

According to Lounsbury, Studies III : 125, William Thompson (died about 1766) has an imitation of Chaucer entitled "In Chaucer's Boure." Ibid. p. 201 is mentioned the Chaucer-imitation of William Dunkin, died 1765; and ibid. 125-6 that of Warton.

Thomas Chatterton, d. 1790. Author of the so-called Rowley poems, purporting to be of the fifteenth century, and written in presumably archaic language. The Rowley poems were ed. by Tyrwhitt in 1777, by Milles in 1782, by Southey and Cottle in

15

1803, by Willcox in 1842, by Skeat in 1871, 2d ed. Aldine Poets 1883, 2 vols. The last-named ed. has the Rowley poems in vol. 2, with prefatory essay by Skeat. Tyrwhitt argued the spuriousness of the poems in the Appendix to his 3d ed., 1778, and in his Vindication of his Appendix, 1782, a contribution to a mass of literature on the subject for which see *s. v.* Chatterton in Dict. Nat. Biog. According to Skeat, loc. cit., the influence of Chaucer upon Chatterton was very small, and his knowledge of Old English almost nil; his archaic vocabulary was derived in part from the words marked Obsolete in the dicts. of Kersey and of Bailey, in part from the distortion of such words and from sheer invention. Helene Richter, in Bausteine I : 29-67, 90-104, seeks to add to Kersey and Bailey as source the Gloucestershire dialect; she rates the actual derivation from the dictionaries as very small, much more being due to Chatterton's coinage.

Inasmuch as Skeat's ed. has a modernized text and scanty notes, the question of Chatterton's real sources has not yet been fully answered in the form of an annotated text; nor has the problem of his attempt to imitate Early English grammar received attention. Fraülein Richter, loc. cit. p. 58, calls his use of -en as the ending of the third singular of verbs an "arge Verwirrung"; but neither that nor the poet's -eth as ending of the first person singular has been treated as due to contemporary notions of Early Eng. grammatical forms, exemplified in the work of Mason and of Milles.

This incorrect use of -en in the singular has a long and curious history. It begins with the Court of Love, see Lounsbury, Studies I : 503, III : 125, flourishes in Urry, see op. cit. I : 288, is a characteristic of 18th century imitations, and reappears in our own time, *e. g.* in Carolyn Wells' pseudo-Chaucerian lines, Harper's Monthly, Oct. 1906.

Constantia, or the Man of Law's Tale. By H. Brooke, in his collection of pieces formerly published by himself, London, 1778, 4 vols. Previously appeared in Ogle, was printed again by Lipscomb as below, and is also accessible in Chalmers' English Poets, vol. 17, p. 382, with a reprint of Tyrwhitt's text at the foot of the page.

Cambuscan, or the Squire's Tale of Chaucer, modernized by Mr. Boyse; continued from Spenser's Fairy Queen by Mr. Ogle, and concluded by Mr. Sterling. Dublin, 1785. See the 1741 Ogle, above.

Anderson's Bee (an Edinburgh periodical of brief existence) has in IV : 182 (Aug. 1791) a ten-line "Imitation of Chaucer." On marriage; attempt at Chaucerian language.

Chaucer's Pardoner's Tale Modernized. By W. Lipscomb. 1792.
(Not in the Brit. Museum catalogue. I make this entry from
Lipscomb's own statement in the preface to his more extensive
work mentioned below, and from the brief review in the Gentleman's Magazine, 1792 II : 1022).

Gualtherus and Griselda, or Happiness Properly Estimated, a Tale,
fills pp. 73-104 of Angelica's Ladies' Library, sm. 4to Lond.
1794, with 8 plates by Angelica Kauffman and H. Bunbury.
Tale in 5-beat couplets, apparently Ogle's version, though his
name is not given. The plate is after Angelica Kauffman.

The Canterbury Tales of Chaucer: Completed in a Modern Version.
(Rev. William Lipscomb) Oxford, 1795, 3 vols.
    Lipscomb's name is not on the titlepage, but the dedication
is signed by him. "Completed" as compared with Ogle's work,
which Lipscomb reprinted, rearranging the tales to the order as
in Tyrwhitt's edition; he also reprinted the introductory discourse and life of Chaucer from Tyrwhitt. All indelicacies are
expurgated; the tales of the Miller and the Reeve are omitted
for this reason, that of the Parson because it is "dry and unentertaining." Lipscomb apologizes for printing his own version
of the Nun's Priest's Tale instead of Dryden's, saying that he
did not know of the existence of Dryden's work until too late.
He has added the Tales of the Franklin, Doctor, Pardoner,
Shipman, Prioress, Rime of Sir Thopas, Melibeus, Tales of
Monk, Nun's Priest, Second Nun, Canon's Yeoman, Manciple.
    For criticism of Lipscomb see introd. to Horne of 1841 as
below; see Blackwood's Mag. 58 : 114-128; see Lounsbury,
Studies III : 197-200.

In the Gent. Mag. for 1800, II : 1263, is a paraphrase of the description of the Parson, signed Trinitarius.

Wordsworth. According to Dowden, in the paper cited below,
    Wordsworth modernized the Prioress' Tale, passages from
    Book V of the Troilus, and the pseudo-Chaucerian Cuckoo and
    Nightingale; these were done in the winter of 1801. The
    Prioress' Tale was pubd. in 1820, in the Miscellaneous Poems
    of William Wordsworth, vol. 3; it, with the other renditions,
    is accessible, e. g., in the Macmillan 1 vol. ed. of Wordsworth,
    or in the Knight ed., vol. 2. The other poems were contributed
    to the Horne volume of 1841, see below. From a passage in a
    letter to Prof. Reed of Philadelphia, also cited by Dowden, it
    appears that Wordsworth modernized the Manciple's Tale, but
    considered it unfit for publication. See "Wordsworth's Modern-
    izations of Chaucer", by Dowden in Wordsworthiana, ed.

Wm. Knight, Lond. 1889, pp. 17-28, and digested as notes in Knight's ed. of Wordsworth, 1882.

See also on Wordsworth's work Lounsbury, Studies III : 208-217. According to Horne (see 1841 volume below), the rendering of the Flower and the Leaf in that collection was virtually Wordsworth's.

Cambuscan, an heroic poem in six books; founded upon and comprising a free imitation of Chaucer's fragments on that subject.
R. Wharton, in his "Fables, consisting of select parts from Dante, Berni, Chaucer, and Ariosto, imitated in English heroic verse." Lond. 1804, 1805. 2 vols. [From the Brit. Mus. Cat.]

The Squire's Tale, imitated from Chaucer.
In the Poetical Register and Repository of Fugitive Poetry, vol. IV, London, 1806, p. 275. No signature.

A note in the Acad. 1880 I : 472 says that Prof. Dowden has obtained a manuscript marked The Canterbury Tales Modernized, vol. II, containing also Gamelyn and Beryn. In verse. Watermark of the paper 1811.

Keats. The tinge of the archaic in Keats' vocabulary is derived not from Chaucer but from Chaucer's students, Spenser and Chatterton, for whom Keats felt deep admiration. The title of La Belle Dame sans Merci, the sonnet after reading the pseudo-Chaucerian Flower and Leaf, the motto to Sleep and Poetry, and the attempt at Early English inserted into the Eve of St. Mark (lines 99-114) are all which we can ascribe to the influence of Chaucer. Keats alludes to Chaucer in Endymion I : 134.
See de Sélincourt's ed. of Keats, N. Y. 1905; see W. A. Read on Keats and Spenser, diss. Heidelberg 1897, pp. 60.

Arcita and Palemon. Modernized by Lord Thurlow. Lond. 1822; 2d ed. in the same year, with the Flower and the Leaf. See Lounsbury, Studies III : 203-8.

Leigh Hunt. Hunt published in the Liberal, vol. II p. 317 (1823), a version of Part I of the Squire's Tale, entitled Cambus Khan, a Fragment. In his Stories in Verse, Lond. 1855, this reappears, and also a version of the Pardoner's Tale entitled Death and the Ruffians; both are reprinted with his Poetical Works, Boston 1855, Lond. 1860. The latter ed. also contains his poem The Tapiser's Tale, "attempted in the manner of Chaucer," first pubd. in Fraser's Mag. for 1859, 57 : 160-63. To the Horne vol. of 1841 Hunt contributed another version of the Squire's Tale, also versions of the Friar's Tale and Manciple's Tale; he appended to his Wit and Humour modernizations of the Chaucer selections, see p. 217 here. Hunt's interest in Chaucer was great; he frequently quotes him and discusses his verse. See Lounsbury, Studies III : 210-212.

H. W. Tytler, in his Miscellanies, Calcutta, 1828, included a mod. of the tale of Gamelyn, as "Sir John of Bounds", 449 stanzas in ballad measure; also "Walter and Grisild", in eight-line stanzas. Tytler censures Ogle's work as tedious and without humor.

Charles Cowden Clarke. Tales from Chaucer in Prose, designed chiefly for the use of Young Persons. Lond. 1833, 2d ed. 1870.
A paraphrase, containing the Prologue, tales of Knight, Man of Law, Wife of Bath, Clerk, Squire, Pardoner, Prioress, Nun's Priest, Canon's Yeoman, and Gamelyn.
Rev. Athen. 1834, p. 68; Gent. Mag. 1834 II : 173.

Charles Cowden Clarke. The Riches of Chaucer, in which his impurities have been expunged, his spelling modernized, his rhythm accentuated, and his obsolete terms explained. Also have been added a few explanatory notes and a new life of the poet. Lond. 1835, 2 vols. Again Lond. 1870, 1877, 1896 (this last announced as a stereotyped reprint from the ed. of 1870).
Rev. Gent. Mag. 1835 I : 288, 1836 II : 45; Athen. 1835 p. 104.

Contents: Vol. 1, Prologue, tales of Knight, Man of Law, Wife of Bath, Friar, Clerk, Squire, Franklin, Pardoner, Prioress, Nun's Priest, Canon's Yeoman. Vol. 2, Troilus and Cressida, five legends from the Legend of Good Women, two extracts from the prologue, Anelida, the Flower and Leaf, Chaucer's Dream (=Isle of Ladies), Black Knight, Book of the Duchess, extracts from House of Fame, Romaunt of the Rose, Parl. of Foules, Stedfastness, Go forth King, Purse, Gentilesse, Doubleness, Alone Walking, In Feuerere, Against Women Unconstant, Of their Nature, Words to Adam, Truth. This text is used in the Edinburgh 1860 ed. of the Cant. Tales, see below.

Griselda, the Clerk's Tale. Re-made from Chaucer. In Blackwood's Mag., May 1837, pp. 655-667. In five-beat couplets; no signature.

The Persoune of a Toun, 1370; his character from Chaucer, imitated and enlarged by Mr. Dryden, now again altered and abridged, together with the Persones prologue and tale. By the Persone of a toun, 1841. London, 1841.

Horne. The Poems of Chaucer Modernized. London, 1841.

Introd. by R. H. Horne. Life of Chaucer by Leonhard Schmitz. Eulogies on Chaucer by his Contemporaries and others. Prologue to the Canterbury Tales by R. H. Horne. The Cuckoo and the Nightingale by William Wordsworth. The Legends of Ariadne, Philomene, and Phillis by Thomas Powell. The Manciple's Tale by Leigh Hunt. The Rime of Sire Thopas by Z. A. Z. Extract from Troilus and Cresida by William Wordsworth. The Reve's Tale by R. H. Horne. The Flower and the Leaf by Thomas Powell. The Friar's Tale by Leigh Hunt. The Complaint of Mars and Venus by Robert Bell. Queen Annelida and False Arcite by Elizabeth B. Barrett. The Squire's Tale by Leigh Hunt. The Franklin's Tale by R. H. Horne.

The original metre is preserved, Thopas in six-line stanzas, the Cuckoo and Nightingale in five-line stanzas, Anelida in rime royal, etc.

Horne in his introd. discusses previous modernizations, censuring the "unceremonious paraphrases" of Dryden and Pope, denouncing Pope's brief youthful imitation of Chaucer as "rank offal", and a disgrace to Pope's reputation, condemning the "grossness and vulgarity" of Betterton and Cobb and the presumption of Lipscomb, treating Boyse with more leniency, praising Lord Thurlow, and still more Wordsworth; commending Cowden Clarke's efforts, and dismissing Markland, Grosvenor, and Brooke with contempt. English versification is then discussed, especially elision and the use of the hendecasyllabic line. Note pp. lxxvi and following. The literary qualities of Chaucer are also considered.

For Horne's 1878 modernizations see below.

Portions of this volume are reissued by Briscoe in the Bibelots, 1901, see below. On Horne's work see preface to vol. I of the 1854 Bell Chaucer; see Lounsbury, Studies III : 213 ff.; see under Hunt, Wordsworth, ante. Severe criticism Athen. 1841 p. 107.

In Thomas Wright's life of Walter Pater, 2 vols., Lond. 1907 (a book "too childish-foolish for this world"), it is related of Pater, at II : 268, that he took up the Horne modernization of Chaucer, and remarked that he had heard of the Canterbury Tales, but did not know that they were considered of sufficient importance to be modernized.

Eight lines in imitation of Chaucer, put into the poet's mouth, are in Punch for 1845, p. 185, "the Lament of the Statues." According to Spielmann (Portraits of Chaucer p. 17) these are by Percival Leigh.

Saunders. Canterbury Tales from Chaucer. London 1845, 2 vols., 2d ed. 1870. New and revised ed. Lond. 1889. 1 vol. revised 1894, 1896 as "Chaucer's Canterbury Tales annotated and accented, with Illustrations of English Life in Chaucer's Time."

The Illustrations were originally pubd. separately as "Cabinet Pictures of English Life", Lond. 1845.

See Athen. 1847 p. 950; Anglia 12 : 628; Dial 10 : 254.

Gilfillan-Clarke. In Nichol's Library Ed. of the Brit. Poets, Edinburgh 1860 ff., vols. 1-3 are Chaucer's Canterbury Tales, with Tyrwhitt's Essay, Introd. Disc., Notes, and Glossary, a Memoir and Critical Dissertation by George Gilfillan, and the text ed. by Charles Cowden Clarke, whose Riches of Chaucer is used in part. Marginal glosses; language kept for the most part. Vol. I, 1867, II, 1860, III, 1861. Reissued in Cassell's Library Ed. of the Brit. Poets. [1875.]

Purves, D. Laing. The Canterbury Tales and the Faerie Queene, with Other Poems by Chaucer and Spenser. Edited for popular perusal, with current illustrations and explanatory notes. Edinb. 1870, 1874, 1884, roy. octavo, double coll.

Contents: The Cant. Tales (Melibeus and the Parson's Tale condensed and partly summarized); the Court of Love, partly condensed in prose; the Cuckoo and Nightingale; the Assembly of Foules; the Flower and Leaf; the House of Fame; Troilus and Cressida (one-fourth of the work, the passages connected by prose condensations); Chaucer's Dream (the Isle of Ladies); the prologue to the Legend of Good Women; the ABC; the Mother of Nurture; Stedfastnesse; Bukton; Gentilesse; Purse; Truth; Proverbs; Virelay; "Since I from Love"; Words to Adam; Prophecy; Ora pro Anglia Sancta Maria. Introductory notices to each of the longer works, with many refs. to Bell's ed., and a life of Chaucer prefixed, of no value. Language partly modernized.

Frederick Clarke. The Canterbury Tales done into Modern English. Lond. 1870, vol. I. No more published. Includes the Prologue, the Knight's Tale, the Miller's headlink and Tale, the Reeve's headlink and Tale, the Cook's headlink and Tale, the Man of Law's headlink and Tale, the Wife of Bath's prologue and Tale.

Horne, R. H. Modernizations of Purse and of a bit of the Knight's Tale, by Horne, were published in Temple Bar 52 : 353; 54 : 196. See Lounsbury, Studies III : 225. See Horne's 1841 vol., above.

The Library of Choice Literature, ed. A. R. Spofford and C. Gibbon, Philadelphia 1881-1888, includes in vol. II pp. 237-9 a prose version of the Pardoner's Tale; in vol. V pp. 133-36 a version of the Knight's Tale, partly in verse, with connecting prose paragraphs.

Skeat, W. W. The Song of Emilye, 30 lines in heroic couplets, by Skeat, is printed Acad. 1884 II : 137. See also below, 1901.

Pitt-Taylor, Frank. The Canterbury Tales, being selections from the Tales of Geoffrey Chaucer rendered into modern English, with close adherence to the language of the poet. London 1884. In verse. Contains: Prologue, Tales of Knight, Man of Law, Prioress, Monk, Nun's Priest, Doctor, Pardoner, Wife of Bath, Clerk, Second Nun, Prologue to the Canon's Yeoman and his Tale, Tale of the Manciple.

Haweis, Mrs. H. R. Tales from Chaucer. Routledge's World's Library, 1887. See also under Versions for Children, below.

Calder, W. The Canterbury Pilgrimage Epitomized. Edinb. 1892. Contents: Prologue, Tales of Knight, Man of Law, Wife of Bath, Clerk, Squire, Franklin, Pardoner, Prioress, Nun's Priest, Manciple. Glossary. Only the prologue is printed in full; the remainder are paraphrases, with passages from the tales.

The story of Griselda is included in Corbet's Romantic Tales of the Olden Time.   1895.

Warner. The Library of the World's Best Literature, ed. C. D. Warner, N. Y., 1896, includes in vol. VI bits from the Prologue, the Knight's Tale, a bit from the Wife of Bath's Tale, most of the Pard. Tale, the Nun's Priest's Tale, Truth. Texts but slightly modernized, glossed for the untrained student. In verse.

Briscoe, J. P. Chaucer's Canterbury Tales. London, 1901, the Bibelots. A partial reprod. of the Horne collection of 1841, see ante. Contents: The description of the Pilgrims from the General Prologue, the Reeve's Tale, the Friar's Tale, the Squire's Tale, selections from the Franklin's Tale, an extract from Troilus, selections from the Flower and the Leaf and from the Cuckoo and Nightingale. The last four items are abridgments.

Skeat, W. W. To An English Miscellany, presented to Dr. Furnivall . . . . Oxford 1901, is prefixed a cento of Chaucerian lines, in part those descriptive of the Clerk, applied by Skeat to Furnivall.

Mackaye, Percy. The Canterbury Tales of Geoffrey Chaucer. A Modern Rendering into Prose of the Prologue and Ten Tales by Percy Mackaye . . . . with Pictures in Colour by Walter Appleton Clark. New York, 1904. Quarto.

The ten tales are those of Knight, Prioress, Nun's Priest, Doctor, Pardoner, Wife of Bath, Clerk, Squire, Franklin, Canon's Yeoman. Each has its prologue; there are four pages of brief notes and six illustrations. The envoy to the Clerk's Tale is in verse.

Darton, F. J. Harvey. Tales of the Canterbury Pilgrims, retold from Chaucer and others. London, 1904. In Darton's Fine Art Series. With an introduction by Furnivall, and numerous illustrations by Hugh Thomson. 1st ed. Sept. 1904, 2d ed. Dec. 1904. Noticed Athen. 1904 II : 873.

Contents, in prose: The Tales of Knight, Man of Law, Nun's Priest, Doctor, Pardoner, Clerk, Squire,—quite fully given; other Tales are reduced to a paragraph or a mention. The non-Chaucerian tales are Gamelyn, "The Story of Cambuscan Bold", from Spenser, the "Mery Adventure", under the title of "The Chequer of the Hoop", Beryn, and Lydgate's Story of Thebes.

Skeat, W. W. The Knight's Tale, or Palamon and Arcite, by Geoffrey Chaucer, done into modern English. London, 1904, the King's Classics. pp. xxv, 158. In verse. See Athen. 1904 II : 14, Engl. Stud. 36 : 145-149 (Koch).

The Man of Law's Tale, the Nun's Priest's Tale, the Squire's Tale, by Geoffrey Chaucer, done into modern English. Lond. 1904, the King's Classics. In verse; pp. xxii, 127.

The Prioress' Tale and four other Tales by Geoffrey Chaucer, done into modern English. Lond. 1904, the King's Classics, pp. xxv, 158. Contents: The Tales of Prioress, Pardoner, Clerk, Second Nun, Canon's Yeoman. In verse. See Athen. 1905 I : 143.

Eight lines of verse in imitation of Chaucer, by Carolyn Wells, are in Harper's Monthly for 1906, p. 803. Note her erroneous use of -en as the verbal ending of the third singular, a trick usual to imitators from Chatterton down.

Skeat, W. W. The Story of Patient Griselda, from the Clerk's Tale of Geoffrey Chaucer. Done into modern English with a few notes. Ill'd. with photogravures by Gilbert James. Lond., Routledge, 1906, the Photogravure Series. In verse.

The Legend of Good Women, by Geoffrey Chaucer, done into modern English. London, 1907, the King's Classics.

Versions for Children

See Cowden Clarke as ante under Modernizations, 1833.

Chaucer for Children, a Golden Key. Mrs. H. R. Haweis. London, 1876-77, second ed. 1882, again 1900.

A prose version, with extracts from the originals, of the Prologue, the tales of Knight, Friar, Clerk, Franklin, and Pardoner; also verse-renderings of Purse, Truth, and "Two Rondeaux"=Youre Eyen Two and Since I from Love. Illustrated with colored pictures and numerous woodcuts by the author. Notes and explanations of words.

Chaucer for Schools. Mrs. H. R. Haweis. London, 1881, again 1889, pp. xxiv, 184. Rev. Athen. 1881 I : 489.

Text and Modern English (rimed) parallel, interspersed with prose condensation; words explained in margin. Introduction. Contents: Prologue, Tales of Knight, Clerk, Monk, Nun's Priest, Man of Law, Pardoner. Also Truth, Gentilesse, Youre Eyen Two, Proverbs, Virelai, Purse, two bits from LGW and one from Parl. of Foules.

Canterbury Chimes; Chaucer Tales retold for Children. F. Storr and H. Turner. London 1878.

Chaucer's Stories Simply Told. Mary Seymour. London 1883. Ed. for Germany by F. Klopper, see Anglia Beiblatt 8 : 245, Archiv 101 : 207 (1898).

Tales from Chaucer. Told by Clara L. Thomson. Illustrations by Marion Thomson. Pp. vi, 216. London, Horace Marshall & Son, 1903. [Brit. Mus. Cat.]

Stories from Chaucer told to the Children. Janet Harvey Kelman. New York, n. d. (1905?), 114 pages, 12mo. With eight pictures by W. Heath Robinson. Four stories in prose, Franklin, Knight, Clerk, Man of Law.

The Canterbury Tales. (In the series: Old Stories Retold for Young Readers.) C. D. Wilson, with decorations by R. F. Seymour. Chicago 1906.

In prose; the Prologue, the Tales of Knight, Man of Law, and Clerk. The language closely follows the original.

Stories from Chaucer. J. Walker McSpadden. N. Y., Crowell, 1907.

    In N. Y. Times of Sept. 21 termed "literary Mellin's Food"; see McSpadden *ibid.* Oct. 5.

Birthday Books, etc.

Chaucer's Beads. (Birthday book, diary, and concordance of proverbs.) Mrs. H. R. Haweis. London 1884.

Chaucer Birthday Book. Harriet Waechter. London 1889. See Jahresber 1890, pp. 264-5.

Translations

Into German.

Kannegiesser, K. L. Gottfried Chaucers Canterburysche Erzählungen. 2 vols., 24mo., Zwickau 1827.
Vol. I, Prologue and Knight's Tale. Vol. II, Franklin's
prol. and tale, Pardoner's prol. and tale, Doctor's prol. and
tale, Cook's tale, *i. e.*, Gamelyn; real Cook's tale not included. In verse.

Fiedler, E. Canterburysche Erzählungen. Vol. I, no more
publ. Dessau, 1844.
With introd. and notes. Tales of Knight, Miller, Reeve,
Cook, Man of Law. In verse.

[Jacob, Chaucer Uebersetzt, Lübeck 1849, is mentioned by
Mayor, N. and Q. 1876 II : 530, but I can learn nothing of
the work.]

Hertzberg, W. Chaucers Canterbury-Geschichten.
Hildburghausen, 1866. Repr. by the Bibliographisches
Institut, Leipzig and Vienna, n. d.
In verse, with good introd. and notes. Rev. by Asher,
Blätter für litterarische Unterhaltung, May 2, 1867; brief
mention Asher in Archiv 43 : 477.

Von Düring, G. Geoffrey Chaucers Werke. 3 vols., Strassburg 1883-86.
Vol. I, House of Fame, Legend of Good Women, Parlement of Foules. Vols. II and III, the Canterbury Tales.
In verse, with some notes. Rev. by Würzner, Ztschr. f.
vergleich. Littgesch. 1 : 112. Rev. by Koch, Anglia 8 :
Anz. 1-8; by Rolfs in Littblatt 1884 p. 390.

Into French.

Gomont, H. Geoffrey Chaucer, poète anglais du xive siècle.
Analyses et fragments. Paris, 1847.

Chatelain, Chevalier de. Contes de Cantorbéry, traduits en
vers français. London, 1857-60, 3 vols.
Rev. Athen. 1857 p. 908, 1858 I : 272, 1861 I : 156.

Simond, Ch. Contes de Canterbury, traduits pour la première
fois en français, avec étude biographique et littéraire.
Angers 1869, Paris 1899. Nouvelle bibliothèque populaire
à 10 centimes. 32 pages.
The Brit. Mus. Cat. says that this=a selection from
Chatelain.

A transl. of the Cant. Tales by E. Legouis, J. Derocquigny, L. Morel, Ch. M. Garnier, L. Cazamian, A. Koszul, Ch. Petit, E. Bourgogne, J. Delcourt, is to appear. Paris, Alcan, 3 vols., in a limited number of copies.

Into Italian.

Chiarini, C. Dalle Novelle di Canterbury. Saggio di una prima traduzione italiana. Bologna 1897.
In prose. The Prologue, the tales of Knight, Man of Law, Clerk, Pardoner, the Rime of Sir Thopas. With a preface and some notes.

For Koch's translations of several of the Minor Poems into German see Section IV C below; for translations of the single works see under each separate heading.

Note on the Influence of Chaucer

A few references only are here given; for a summary of the subject see Lounsbury's Studies in Chaucer, chap. VII, "Chaucer in Literary History"; and for the influence of the Prologue to the Canterbury Tales upon some special works see Section III G below. For the framework idea before and since Chaucer, see Section III A above.

Chaucer's Influence upon King James I of Scotland as Poet. Henry Wood. diss. Leipzig, 1879, pp. 43. Also in Anglia 3 : 223-265.

Chaucer's Einfluss auf die Originaldichtungen des Schotten Gawain Douglas. P. Lange. diss. Leipzig, 1872, pp. 52. Also in Anglia 6 : 46-95.

Ueber die Sprache einiger nördlicher Chaucerschüler. H. Hagedorn. diss. Göttingen, 1892, pp. 38.

[Chaucer's influence upon Lydgate and Hoccleve is discussed in the EETS eds. of those poets, in Koeppel's monograph upon Lydgate's Falls of Princes, in Krausser's ed. of the Black Knight, in Schleich's ed. of the Fabula Duorum Mercatorum, and in ten Brink's History of English Literature. For his influence upon the Court of Love, the Flower and the Leaf, and other works formerly ascribed to him, see Section V here.]

Chaucer's Einfluss auf das englische Drama im Zeitalter der Königin Elisabeth und der beiden ersten Stuartkönige. O. Ballmann. diss. Strassburg, 1901, pp. 85. Also in Anglia 25 : 1-85.

The Relation of the Elizabethan Sonnet Sequence to Earlier English Verse, especially that of Chaucer. D. E. Owen. diss. Univ. of Pennsylvania, 1903, pp. 34.

Chaucer und Shakspere. G. Sarrazin. Anglia Beiblatt 7 : 265-269.
See also Quarterly Review 134 : 225-255 (1873) ; Ballmann as
above pp. 4-14; J. W. Hales in his Notes and Essays on
Shakspere; Sidney Lanier in his Music and Poetry, N. Y. 1898,
pp. 159-196; see under Troilus and Cressida, Section IV below.

[For Chaucer's influence upon Spenser and for direct imitations
subsequent to Spenser, see under Section III E above.]

Chaucer's Romaunt of the Rose and Sackville's Induction. E.
Koeppel, Archiv 101 : 145.

Chaucer and Milton. W. H. Hulme. (Publ. Mod. Lang. Assn.
17 : xxx.) Printed in the Western Reserve University Bulletin
for November, 1902.

Byron und Chaucer. Zupitza in Anglia 1 : 478; Kölbing in Engl.
Stud. 21 : 331.

Geoffrey Chaucer and William Morris. New Monthly Magazine,
149 : 280 (1871).

Chaucer and Balzac. Nation 1885 I : 417 (G. Norton).

The Influence of Chaucer upon the Language and Literature of
England. Dr. Phenè. Trans. Royal Society of Literature, 22 :
33-93 (1900-01).
    The title of this paper bears no relation whatever to its
contents, which are a copiously illustrated archaeological dissertation on pre-Roman influence upon Britain, especially as
seen in place-names. Chaucer is mentioned a half-dozen times,
but the allusion is always perfunctory.

F. The Dates of the Tales

Comment upon this point has been made by ten Brink, by Hales, by Koch, by Skeat, by Pollard, by Herford, with greater or less fullness. All students have recognized that some Tales were written before the idea of the Pilgrimage was conceived, also that some Tales were not at first intended for the pilgrims to whom they now belong. Lowell, in his essay on Chaucer, said, "These stories had been written, and some of them even published, at periods far asunder, and without any reference to connection among themselves. The prologues . . . . are in every way more mature, in knowledge of the world, in easy mastery of verse and language, and in the overpoise of sentiment by judgment." Ten Brink, in his Hist. Eng. Lit. II: 157-182, considers that Clerk, Merchant, Doctor, and Second Nun were earlier productions, that the Shipman's Tale was originally written for the Wife of Bath, that the Squire's Tale was written for that character, that the B² fragment belongs to the parts composed towards the end of the whole collection, that the Manciple's Tale was perhaps intended for the homeward journey, and that the Parson's Tale was written at a time when Chaucer no longer hoped to accompany his pilgrims back to Southwark.

Hales, in his Dict. Nat. Biog. article on Chaucer, dates the ML Tale, the Clerk's Tale, and the Prioress' Tale "many years before" the Canterbury Tales.

Koch, in his Chronology pp. 67-69, makes a few vague notes upon this point. He thinks that Chaucer began work upon the poem about 1386-87; that the Man of Law's prologue and Tale and the Tales of Doctor and Clerk may belong in the anxious years 1386-89, perhaps also the Tales of Melibeus and of the Monk. In 1389-91 he would perhaps place the prologues of Wife and of Pardoner, and the Merchant's Tale. The last tale was probably that of the Parson, written as Chaucer sank again into misery. The first version of the Knight's Tale Koch dates 1375-6 (p. 30), and the Life of St. Cecyle he puts about 1374 or soon after (p. 27).

Skeat, II : xxxvi-vii, considers the dates of the Canterbury Tales as compared with the translation of the Boethius. He thinks that the Tales of Second Nun, Clerk, and even Melibeus, may have been written before the Boethius, that the Knight's Tale, the Man of Law's Tale, and the Monk's Tale, as revised, were later than the Boethius; and that among the Tales latest written were the Nun's Priest's Tale, the three of Group D, those of Merchant, Squire, Franklin, Canon's Yeoman, and Manciple. In I: xxxi Skeat assigns to a place "amongst the earlier works"—"the original form of the Life of St. Cecily", "the original form of the Man of Lawes Tale, of the Clerkes Tale, and some parts of the Monkes Tale", also "the original Palamon and Arcite."

Pollard, introd. to the Globe Chaucer p. xxv ff., assigns the Second Nun's Tale, the Clerk's Tale, part of the Monk's Tale, and the Man of Law's Tale to a period anterior to the Canterbury Tales. The Prioress' Tale Pollard places later than the conception of the Pilgrimage; the Knight, the Franklin, and the Squire are dated near the period of the Troilus (1379-1385); and the tales of Doctor and of Manciple are relegated to a "less happy period of Chaucer's career." It is inconceivable, Pollard says, that Chaucer should have planned the Tales earlier than the end of 1385 or beginning of 1386, and he thinks it not unreasonable to suppose that when Chaucer conceived the plan he had already a considerable amount of material at his disposal. See also Pollard's Chaucer Primer, 1903, chap. VI.

Herford, English Tales in Verse, 1902, introd. p. xxvi, says that "the Tales of the Man of Law, the Physician, and the Second Nun, were all clearly composed before Chaucer had planned the Canterbury Tales, in which they were finally incorporated."

On the Relative Dates of the Canterbury Tales
With a Tentative Classification of the Manuscripts[1]

One of the most constant and most tempting problems of Chaucer's Canterbury Tales is that of the date and the dramatic intention of the separate pieces of work which compose the unfinished poem. Critics pounce upon the obvious stiffness of the Second Nun's Tale and, backed by the allusion in the prologue to the Legend of Good Women, class it confidently as ante-pilgrimage work. But with the Squire's Tale, the Man of Law's Tale, the Clerk's Tale (to take a few examples), we have no guide but our own desires in terming them early or late, personal or impersonal. We cannot prove that the Clerk's Tale was translated soon after Chaucer was in Italy, that the archaic plot of the Constance story is not as deliberate on Chaucer's part as the romantic extravaganza of Sir Thopas, or that the Nun's Priest's Tale was written for that pilgrim. No partial early sketch, no record of tentative assignments, exist to aid us in discussing the dates of the Tales and their artistic purpose.

It is therefore particularly interesting to find even a slight trace of revision by Chaucer within the Tales, and interesting moreover to find that revision in one of the Links. For it was long ago observed by Bradshaw that the state of the Links was the important factor in determining the relations of the MSS; and we cannot avoid noticing that the text of the Tales is relatively constant among the many MSS, while groups of codices vary with equal constancy in their treatment of certain Links.

This trace of revision is found at the abrupt ending of the Monk's Tale. In the usual modern text, which follows the latest version of the Tales, the Ellesmere,[2] the Knight begs the Monk to break off his chain of tragedies. He says that life has enough of heaviness, and it were better to speak of man's struggle upward than of his fall; in this he is promptly seconded by the Host, who declares that he was almost asleep for dullness, and that in such case no judgment of the Tale would have been possible, he being sole arbiter. He demands a different style of narration, is refused, and calls upon the Nun's Priest. This Link fills 54 lines, lines 1-13 belonging to the Knight, and the tone changing completely with the Host's appearance.

In a few MSS, however, another form of this Link is found. I subjoin a copy, from Brit. Mus. Harley 7333, the text which is transcribed from John Shirley.

> O quod the kny3t gode sir nomore of this
> Þat ye hane saide is ry3t Inow Iwis
> And moche more for litle heuynesse

[1] For preliminary discussion on this point, see above, pp. 167-172.
[2] The Ellesmere group of MSS is here treated as the representative of Chaucer's last retouchings; the reasons will appear below.

16

Is ryght Inow for moch folke I gesse
Your talis don vs no disport nor game   5
þerfor sir monke. o Dan pers by your name
I pray you hertli telle vs sumwhat eles
ffor sikirli nere for clynkyng of your bellis
þat on your bridel hongen on euery syde
Be hevene kyng that for vs al dide   10
I shulde er this have falen don for slepe
Al þow the snowe had neuere ben so depe
þan had your tale al be tolde in veyne
ffor certayne as þat þes clerkes seien
Wher as a man may have noon audience   15
Nou3t helpith to telle his sentence
And wel I wot þe substaunce is in me
Yf any thing shal wel reportid be
Sir seie sumwhat of huntyng I you praye
Nay quod this monke / I have no lust to plaie   20
Now late A noþer telle as I have tolde
þan spake our host with rude speche & bolde

(The remaining 12 lines are like the usual version)

A few notes on this text may be added before proceeding
further. Other MSS having this form of Link are Hengwrt,
Corpus, and Petworth (printed by the Chaucer Society),[1] Sloane
1686, Selden B 14, Trin. Coll. Cambr. R 3, 3 and R 3, 15, also the
prints by Caxton (first edition) and by de Worde in 1498. Among
these there is a distinction; Caxton and R 3, 15, copies of near
relation to one another,[2] have in the first line the word *hoste;* all
others read *Knight,* like Harley 7333.[3] On this variant reading it
may seem near to suggest that the debased ancestor of Caxton
and Trinity was quite capable of writing *Hoste* for uniformity's
sake; but in view of the fact that the wording of the shorter Link,
with its assumption of literary dictatorship, is suited only to the
Host, I would rather opine that in the archetype of all these copies
the word *Knight* had already been written above or beside *Host,*

[1] The editor-in-chief of the Society, Dr. Furnivall, apparently regarded
this form of Link as due to omission, since he inserted lines from other codices
to fill out the usual 54 verses.

[2] The resemblances of Caxton I and Trinity R 3, 15, hinted at by me in
Modern Philology 3: 170-171, have upon closer examination appeared still
more striking; the two copies are very clearly allied in corruptions.

[3] Except that Adds. 5140, a codex usually classed with the revised Ellesmere group of MSS, begins,
                    Ho qd our hoost sire nomore of this
and has as its fifth line— Your talis don vs— which is then crossed out,
the scribe continuing, for the full 54-line form,—
                    I sey for me hit is a gret disese
as in the more general form of the Link. Also, the other Askew MS, afterwards Ingilby, afterwards Hodson, now (1907) in the British Museum as Egerton 2864, begins in the same way and has 54 lines in the Link.

preparatory to the expansion of the Link which Chaucer almost immediately made. Some descendant may then have copied this before the revision was carried out, while the original of Caxton and R disregarded the marginal change.

It is more than likely that this double form of the Monk's end-link indicates a revision by Chaucer, and probably a revision following very closely upon the first form of the text, as the briefer version remains in so few manuscripts. We must feel it also plausible to suppose that when Chaucer put the Nun's Priest into connection with the fragment ending with Melibeus and the Monk, he may have recognized that an interruption to the Rime of Sir Thopas by the Host and an interruption to the Monk by the Host, separated only by one Tale, was an inartistic repetition; the transference to the Knight was accordingly planned at once, and very quickly carried out.

The evidence offered by this brief passage towards the chronology of the Canterbury Tales is of course infinitesimal; but when taken in conjunction with other evidence as to the arrangement of Tales in the MSS, and with facts drawn from comparison of Chaucer's own words, there results a theory regarding the relative dates of the Tales which will at least bear study. The discussion of these data and of their meaning obliges us, first, to present and prove certain assertions about the manuscripts.

(1) The Canterbury Tales was worked upon and first circulated in booklets which were separate or separable, making confusion possible. For note: (a) The systematic confusion seen in the MSS. (b) The distorted arrangement in several MSS by which a Tale *and its headlink* follow another Tale out of proper connection, *e. g.*, MS Hatton with Cook and Gamelyn between Man of Law and Squire, although a Link binds the two latter. Or Cambridge Mm with several of its Tales bearing numbers derived from its archetype and now manifestly arranged out of sequence, also with the Nun's Priest standing incongruously after the Pardoner, its headlink carrying the Monk-interruption as usual. (c) The fact that in existing MSS a Tale, or a headlink and Tale, still frequently begins a booklet, so that this confusion could arise if booklets were originally separate. Cp. Barlow 20, with the Man of Law endlink on the last verso of a gathering, and the Squire's Tale on the first recto of the next booklet; Laud 600 and Egerton 2726 with the Wife of Bath beginning a booklet; Hatton and Rawlinson 149 with the Merchant, Harley 7334 with the Squire, at the opening of a booklet. For a similar opinion see ten Brink as cited in Athen. 1872 II : 208.

(2) The scribes, who were often conscious of Chaucer's plan, could and did alter Links to fit conditions which arose by displacement. For compare (a) the existence of spurious Links

Pardoner-Shipman, Canon's Yeoman-Doctor, in one class of MSS; or (b) a note such as that in Harley 7335, in a blank space between Summoner and Second Nun, "Allocucio Hospitis desinit."

Upon these grounds I would explain the arrangement Man of Law, Squire, Merchant, Franklin which appears in one large class of MSS, a class also disfigured in many of its members by spurious additions to the Links. It is hardly necessary to remind the student that in only one MS, Selden B 14, does the Man of Law's endlink introduce the Shipman's Tale, but that in the Ellesmere class of MSS this Link does not exist, while in the group above mentioned it binds Man of Law and Squire. And in three texts the Summoner's name stands in the endlink, although his Tale does not follow. Now, I have suggested[1] in explanation that, as ten Brink judged from the context, the Summoner was intended to appear at this point; but that his name was deleted from the Link by Chaucer, perhaps when the group Wife-Friar-Summoner was planned; and in the remote ancestor of this one class of MSS the half-illegible word beginning with S was misread to *Squire*, the Squire's Tale being then brought up by scribes to follow the Man of Law.

This suggestion I would now carry further. And in the following argument, in which there is advanced an explanation of the Tale-confusion in one large class of MSS, as also a theory of MS-classification, I shall proceed upon the assumption that the scribes of the Canterbury Tales did not omit Links which they found in their originals, although they might alter them; rather did they accumulate all they could get. Although we hear Caxton, in the proheme to his second edition of the Tales, censure his first text for its preservation of words which Chaucer "never made ne set in his volume", we may justly believe that Caxton meant the coarse passages of some Tales as seen in the (late and debased) Trinity R 3, 15, or as added in the margin of Harley 1758 by its copyist. If then we make this assumption just formulated, we shall assert that the absence of certain Links from a MS or a group of MSS means (barring plain evidence of mutilation) that the archetype of those MSS was not possessed of those Links. And I continue by assuming that this absence of Links from some MSS means that Chaucer had not yet written the passages in question when their archetype was transcribed. Such an assumption of course leads direct to a chronological and genealogical tree of manuscripts.

The variation in Links is not so extensive or so complicated a question as this prelude would cause the student to infer. In the large group of codices which bring the Squire up to follow the Man of Law, as just described, there are but four divisions

[1] Mod. Phil. 3: 163-164.

according to the state of the Links. Two subclasses of this group have also carried up the Merchant to follow the Squire, using the altered Words of the Franklin to the Squire as a connective, and changing the word *Franklin* to *Merchant* to make that Link suitable. Inasmuch as another group of MSS, represented by Harley 7333, shows the sequence Man of Law-Squire-Merchant, without any false connective Squire-Merchant, and has otherwise the same order as these two subclasses, I would say that the same (accidental?) displacement of the Merchant was present in the archetype of the two subclasses; that one subclass (Harl. 1758) afterwards became possesed of a MS having the Words of the Franklin to the Squire, perhaps in their proper use; but having already misplaced the Squire and the Merchant, it added the Words at the close of the Squire, and altered *Franklin* to *Merchant,* to make the Link fit its false position. The blank space which many MSS leave at the close of the unfinished Squire's Tale would render this very easy.

Another peculiar variant in the treatment of the Links is the binding of Franklin to the misplaced Merchant by the regular Merchant endlink and the present eight-line Squire prologue, the word *Squire* in the latter being altered to Franklin. For this we may seek a similar explanation. The archetypal scribe became possessed, after his booklets were copied, of the Merchant-Squire link, and inserted it at the end of the Merchant's Tale; but as the Squire-lines closing that Link could not introduce the already displaced Squire, he altered the word *Squire* to *Franklin,* since the Franklin's Tale was lying next, after the removal of the Squire. The order of this MS-group (Hatton) is exactly like that of the Corpus class, except that Merchant-Franklin have in the Hatton been brought up to follow Squire, with the Words of the Franklin as a connective. These Words do not appear in the Corpus class, nor does the Link Merchant-Squire appear there, although Squire is displaced as is regular in this whole group; and I call attention to this in support of my conjecture that these two Links are later additions to an archetype which had already bound Squire to Man of Law, a step it would hardly have taken had the Links Merchant-Squire and Squire-Franklin been in place. Had such been the case, we would expect the procedure of the Selden, which has the link Merchant-Squire, and therefore substituted *Shipman* for *Sompnour* or *Squire* in its Man of Law endlink.

Apart from the creation of spurious Links between Canon's Yeoman and Doctor, Pardoner and Shipman, found in nearly all the MSS of the group which connects Man of Law and Squire; apart from the deletion of the Man of Law's endlink in the revised (?) Ellesmere type of codex; apart from the variant in the Monk's endlink above pointed out, there is but one special peculiarity of the Links requiring comment. That is the presence in one class of MSS of a Link between Clerk and Franklin; this class also forms part of the large group binding Man of Law and Squire together. The link between Clerk and Franklin looks like either a selection from the genuine Merchant-Squire connective, altered into stanzas, or the result of partial notes by Chaucer for his Link, garbled and "completed" by a scribe. In it there is no mention of the Merchant, and the word *Squire* is of course altered to *Franklin* in the latter part. It would seem as if this patchwork had been inserted in front of the Franklin instead of after the Merchant; but how the condensation or distortion arose I cannot pretend to explain. It may be remarked, however, that the same order of Tales, without such Links, and with the sequence Man of Law-Squire, exists in Harley 7333; that is, in the type of MSS opposed to that with which the Hatton degenerations are most nearly allied.

These peculiarities, so far as the MSS binding Man of Law and Squire are concerned, may be graphically expressed as below. The curved line of connection indicates the presence of a Link.

Classification of the MSS Connecting Man of Law and Squire[1]

The Corpus-7333 Group

(a) Harley 7333 and R 3, 15. Caxton I is allied here.
[A B^1 F^1 E^2 D E^1 F^2 G C B^2 H I.]

(b) Corpus, Sloane 1686, Lansdowne.[2]
[A Gam. B^1 F^1 D E^1 E^2 F^2 G C B^2 H I.]

(c) Harley 1758, Sloane 1685, Rawl. poet. 149, Lichfield, Hodson-Ashburnham, Egerton 2863, Royal 18, Laud 739, Barlow.   [A Gam. B^1 F^1 E^2 D E^1 F^2 G C B^2 H I.]

(d) Petworth, Mm. [A Gam. B^1 F^1 E^2 D E^1 F^2 G C B^2 H I.]
    Hatton, Ii.   [A Gam. B^1 F^1 E^2 F^2 D E^1 G C B^2 H I.]

Two of these MSS, Corpus and Mm, contribute interesting evidence in the form of a partial set of numbers prefixed to Tales, numbers which do not fit the Tale-sequence of either codex, but which agree with one another. They unite in numbering the Reeve as 3, the Man of Law as 5, the Wife of Bath as 7, Sir Thopas as 19, and the Parson as 24; in addition Corpus marks the Cook 4, the Pardoner 16, the Shipman 17, Melibeus 20, the Monk 21, the Nun's Priest 22, and the Manciple 23, while Mm numbers the Summoner 9, the Franklin 12, and the Prioress 18. The two codices thus join in indicating the sequence A, Gamelyn, Man of Law, Squire, D, Clerk, Merchant, Franklin, G, C, B^2, H, I. The

---

[1] In Northumberland and in New College the order is A B^1 F^1 E^2 D E^1 F^2 G C B^2 H I, according to the Trial Tables, but the state of their Links is unknown to me. Bodley 414 is probably an imperfect copy of this class, as is R 3, 3, which resembles Petworth in structure, but with some variants.

[2] Of these MSS only Lansdowne shows links G C B^2. Delamere, with these links, perhaps belongs here.

MS showing this sequence, which I shall call the Corpus-Mm
archetype, was antecedent to the (b) and (d) groups above listed,
groups which unite in their connection Man of Law-Squire and
their spurious bonds Canon's Yeoman-Doctor and Pardoner-Shipman, but which differ in that the (b) group has no bond Merchant-
Squire or Squire-Franklin, has but a partial connection Clerk-
Merchant (the Merch. headlink being absent), and shows a short
form of the Merchant's Tale. The (d) class, on the other hand,
has obtained the connectives Merchant-Squire and Squire-Franklin,
taking with them the liberties above described; there is a slight
difference among the four MSS of this class in that Petworth and
Mm, though copying the garbled Merchant-Franklin link to precede
the Franklin, do not move that Tale up to follow the Merchant
as do Hatton and Ii.

Groups (a) and (c) bear a superficial resemblance in Tale-
order, but the (c) group is much debased in its Links. It has the
spurious connectives GC and CB^2, like groups (b) and (d); it
has also a connective between the Clerk and the Franklin, which
may take several forms, the Verba Hospitis and the altered Squire
headlink, as in Laud 739; the Verba, seven lines of comment, and
the headlink, as in Harley 1758, Barlow, Royal 18; or the comment
and headlink without the Verba, as in Lichfield and Sloane 1685.
In none of these does the Clerk end ready for the Merchant; in
Barlow, Laud, and Royal a spurious connective E^2D has been
introduced. See Ch. Soc. Specimens pp. 51-56.

Group (a) has no connection E^2F^1 or F^1F^2, but it links Clerk
and Merchant, though displacing the latter to stand between Squire
and D. This displacement is particularly noticeable, because occur-
ing also in the (c) class of manuscripts, where, on the explanation
I have above advanced, it must have been made before the Squire-
Franklin link was appended to the misplaced Squire. That is,
there are two classes of MSS forcing the Merchant up before D;
in (c) it may seem accidental, but in (b) it happens in spite of the
full connective Clerk-Merchant. Shall we believe that one MS
could influence another as regards Tale-order alone?

The conditions in Royal 17 are here interesting. This MS has
the Summoner introduced by the Man of Law's endlink, like Harley
7334; but the Squire follows instead, as in the MSS just analyzed.
And the Squire's Tale has been brought up accompanied by its own
eight-line prologue and by the Merchant's endlink. A procedure
so contrary to sense can have been followed only by an unthinking
scribe, who blindly obeyed the numbering of booklets as dictated to
him by a MS other than that which he used for his B^1 text; unless,
indeed, his archetype was a composite in different hands from
different sources. The fact that the Nun's Priest's epilogue, a
characteristic of but five other MSS, all of late type, is also found
in this codex, indicates that at least three classes of texts con-

tributed to the formation of this; and when we observe that the hand of all of the MS after the Clerk's Tale is that of the MSS Harley 2251 and Adds. 34360, whose origin in a scriptorium and liability to contamination I have discussed (in Anglia 28), our suppositions are confirmed.

The de Worde print of 1498 shows superficially the same order as Harley 7334; and a student glancing at the volume and seeing no endlink following Man of Law might be tempted to ally the volume with the Ellesmere or the 7334 class. However, the Man of Law's endlink, with some verbal alterations, appears after the Merchant's Tale, and introduces the Squire, serving in lieu of the regular link Merchant-Squire, which is present neither here nor in the Caxtons. That is, the order E^1 E^2 F^1 F^2 has been re-imposed upon an arrangement of Tales in which the displacement of F^1 had previously happened. The Monk's endlink is in the short form, as in Caxton I; the Words of the Franklin are present, and also the Nun's Priest's epilogue, as in Caxton II.

From such facts and from the division and redivision in MS-alliances it is demonstrable that MSS could be influenced by other types of MSS during transcription, a fact which Moore has pointed out as true of the Divina Commedia codices to a most complicating extent. It might accordingly happen that a manuscript of fairly sound textual origin, so far as Tales went, added to itself spurious or distorted Links, an addition which could be made without any effect upon the Tales; and such a manuscript might then hand on to its descendants a mixture of excellence and impurity. The presence of spurious connectives in a codex is thus not *per se* an argument against the text of its Tales. Compare a minor point like the reading of Knight's Tale 1154, where R 3, 3 and Harley 7333, volumes free from spurious matter, have:

Armed Complyaunt Ooþes & ffiers Courrage   Harley

Armed compleint with othes and fers corage   Trinity

while Sloane 1685 and Royal 18, MSS charged with illegitimate additions to their Links, read:

Armed compleynt outhees and fires corage.

Therefore, as Moore has remarked for Dante, only an exhaustive comparison of the entire work can show us in which MSS a sound text remains untouched, in which it has been slightly obscured by spurious Links and verbal errors here and there, in which it presents a compound of early uncorrected work and continuation on a later plan, and in which it has been debased textually and distorted in connections so as to place it out of court in a genealogical study. The state of the Links and the arrangement of the Tales can at present give us no conclusive and detailed evidence towards a genealogy of the manuscripts, although it may suggest a tentative grouping and a line of investigation. This tentative grouping is, for the body of MSS above discussed:

THE CORPUS-7333 GROUP OF MANUSCRIPTS

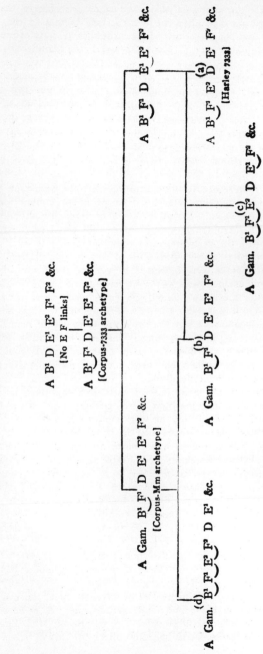

It will be seen that the remotest archetype here deduced does not differ, in the Tale-order A-F, from the two other main MS-types represented by the Ellesmere and by Harley 7334. This seems proven from the numberings in Corpus and Mm and from the sequence appearing when the misplaced Squire of this archetype and of the Harley 7333 archetype is returned to his proper place. Certainly, until evidence is forthcoming for another theory, we may argue that it was an order like that of Harley 7334, but without the E and F links there seen, which lay behind the Corpus-7333 group, and that it was the misreading of the deleted word *Sompnour*, still seen in Harley 7334's Man of Law endlink, which set on foot all the displacements characteristic of the Corpus-7333 line of descent.

We arrive therefore at the conclusion that the archetype of the Corpus-7333 group represents the most primitive known form of the Canterbury Tales, a form which went into circulation before Chaucer had written the E and F links, and which received those additions during the early stages of copying.

This conclusion also brings with it several corollaries. First, if the E and F links were indeed later written, the fusion of these four Tales into a whole was, as ten Brink affirmed, made by Chaucer some time after the completion of the Tales themselves, or of most of them. That it was later than the writing of the Clerk's envoy may be argued from the fact that in many Corpus-Mm manuscripts the Clerk's envoy, when existing, does not end ready for the Merchant; and when it does so end in other groups, I would suggest that its rearrangement had been made to meet the (therefore later written) Merchant headlink.

It follows that the conditions of the MSS can thus, in minor points at least, give us some light on the relative dates of the Links, perhaps of the Tales, and on the workings of Chaucer's mind. For is it not a plausible inference that in these later E and F links Chaucer was endeavoring to make more appropriate the telling of two of the Tales (Merchant and Franklin) by their narrators? The vividly autobiographical tone of these two introductions is of the same character as are the Wife of Bath's prologue and the Pardoner's exhortation, pieces of the framework which every student would assign to Chaucer's ripest maturity; and yet the Tales which they prelude are not in themselves so appropriate to their narrators as are those, *e. g.,* of Clerk and Squire.

This leads readily to the assertion that there are in the Canterbury Tales three sorts of Tales; those which Chaucer had previously written, assigned to a pilgrim whom he created later, after the idea of the pilgrimage had occurred to him; those written with the pilgrim in mind; and those written after the poem was in progress and forced upon a pilgrim. Cp. ten Brink, Hist. Eng. Lit. II : 149. The evidence which we can collect for this or any chronological division comes partly from our personal judgment as to plot and treatment in a Tale, partly from Chaucer's own allusions, lastly, from the manuscripts.

The first of these sources has hitherto received the most attention. Ten Brink did not deal minutely with the Canterbury Tales; but Skeat and Koch base their remarks sometimes upon their personal judgment regarding Tale-structure, sometimes upon a parallelization of the known facts of Chaucer's life which has led them to extremes. Thus, the one critic suggests that the coarser Tales were probably composed after Chaucer's loss of his wife; the other considers that the ponderous theological portions of the Tales were the expression of Chaucer's period of poverty and anxiety. As actual evidence, such opinions have no solid value.

Facts which do serve as basis for a chronological theory are to be found in the Chaucerian text. When in the Legend of Good Women prologue (of 1386?) Chaucer alludes to the stories of Palamon and Arcite and of St. Cecilia as in existence, this is a bit of definite evidence, already well used. When in the Gg text of the Legend of Good Women prologue and in the Tales of Wife, Merchant, and Franklin, Chaucer speaks of and uses a book unmentioned by him elsewhere, we may, with Professor Lowes,[1] argue that this group of work was of similar date, and subsequent to Chaucer's introduction to the material which he applies so lavishly and with such enjoyment.[2] Or when we find Chaucer, in the Monk's Tale, translating the story of Ugolino from the 33d canto of Dante's Inferno, while in the tragedy of Caesar (in the same Tale) he amalgamates Brutus and Cassius into one person, shall we not argue that the Caesar was written before he knew Dante? for in the 34th canto of the Inferno Brutus and Cassius are unmistakably separate persons. Compare the two translations of Virgil's "pernicibus alis", and the probability that the wrong one antedated the right, noted in Professor Lowes' paper, page 857.

Skeat's note on this amalgamation is entirely pointless; what the writer of the Serpent of Division blundered in throws no light upon Chaucer, from whom the later author (Lydgate?) probably obtained the error; and no remark is made upon the curious fact that the same mistake appears in King Aelfred's translation of Boethius. Add here also that a line in the tragedy of Nero (487) is from Dante, as noted by Cary, and we query whether we cannot safely date the four "modern instances" and Nero (at least) after Chaucer's acquaintance with Dante, the Caesar before that time. Should not the Croesus, moreover, be dated later than most of the tragedies, as the earlier form of the endlink (see above) makes no citation from it?

[1] Publ. Mod. Lang. Ass'n 20: 749 ff.
[2] See Tatlock in Mod. Phil. 3: 367.

Again, does not the miswriting *alto stilo* for Petrarch's *alio stilo*, translated by Chaucer as *high style* (Clerk's prol. 41, Tale 1092), make it probable that Chaucer executed that translation before he punned on "high style" in the Squire's Tale lines 105-6?[1] Similarly, might not the agreement in idea and wording between the "Verba Hospitis" and the Melibeus endlink lead us to believe that the former, perhaps the original endlink to the Clerk's Tale, was written earlier than the connective between Melibeus and the Tales of Monk and Nun's Priest? In which case we would surmise that the latter Tales were added to the B² fragment before the present Clerk-envoy was written, which again, as I argue, antedated the rearranging of that Envoy and the writing of the Merchant headlink which meets it.

Further, do not the lines of the Man of Law's headlink,

> But Chaucer, though he can but lewedly
> On metres and on ryming craftely

with their strong resemblance to the Host's comment upon the Rime of Sir Thopas, suggest to the student that that part of the headlink, at least, was once intended to come later than Chaucer's public failure as a doggerel romancer? For where is the point of the Man of Law's apology for Chaucer unless this apology followed Chaucer's public disgrace? Moreover, is it not possible that this headlink, with its conclusion promising a prose story, once introduced the Melibeus, which still follows Sir Thopas as Chaucer's second narrative? This latter has been suggested by Furnivall, and the only other conjecture regarding the original prose narrative has been that of Professor Lowes, see his paper already cited. It is especially interesting in this connection to find that Lounsbury, Studies I : 418, would date the Man of Law's headlink earlier than the Medea story of the Legend of Good Women; with this consideration and that above advanced, I would suggest for the ML headlink a date parallel not with the second, but with the first, period of work upon the Legend.

When discussing such a repetition as that just mentioned between the Man of Law's headlink and the Host's words interrupting Sir Thopas, it is necessary to decide first what view we shall take of Chaucer's tendency to repeat himself. Sometimes these echoes and agreements are of a character which indicate nearly contemporary composition; for instance, the description of the tournament encounter, lines 1745 ff. of the Knight's Tale, and of the seafight in the Cleopatra of the Legend, lines 56 ff.; compare also the refusal of the Knight to describe the wedding feast, lines 25-30, with lines 37-44 of the Cleopatra. Or we might parallel the

---

[1] See Professor G. L. Hendrickson's paper in Mod. Phil. 4: 190; to which I may add that the two MSS of Petrarch's Latin in the library of Corpus Christi College, Cambridge, show in one case *alio stilo*, in the other case *alto stilo*. Professor Hendrickson's conjecture is thus established as fact.

remarks of the onlooking common people in Knight's Tale 1655 ff. with the Squire's Tale 202 ff.; see moreover the notes by Lowes, loc. cit. page 791. But the case is not so clear in verbal echoes like the following:

Trouthe is the hyeste thing that man may kepe	Frankl. Tale 751
Trouthe is a thing that I wol ever kepe	Can. Yeo. Tale 491
Allone withouten any companye	Kn. Tale 1921
Allone withouten any companye	Mill. Tale 18
Allone withouten any companye	Melibeus 2749-50
That it is lyk an heven for to here	Sq. Tale 271
His maner was an heven for to see	Sq. Tale 558
It was an heven upon him for to see	Troil. II : 637
That ech hir lovede that loked on hir face	Clerk's Tale 413
That alle hir loven that loken on hir face	M L Tale 532
That ech him lovede that loked on his face	Troil. II : 1078
. . . . what eyleth thee to wryte	
The draf of stories and forgo the corn?	Prol. L G W 311-12
Let be the chaf and wryte wel of the corn	*Ibid.* 520
Me list nat of the chaf nor of the stree	
Maken so long a tale as of the corn.	M L Tale 603-4
Eek Plato seith, whoso that can him rede,	
The wordes mote be cosin to the dede.	Gen. Prol. 741-2
The wyse Plato seith, as ye may rede,	
The word mot nede accorde with the dede.	Manc. Tale 103-4
For pitee renneth sone in gentil herte	Kn. Tale 903
That pitee renneth sone in gentil herte	Sq. Tale 471
As gentil herte is fulfild of pitee	M L Tale 562
But pitee renneth sone in gentil herte	Prol. L G W 503
Lo, pitee renneth sone in gentil herte	Merch. Tale 742

    This line, according to Paget Toynbee, is from Dante, Inferno 5 : 100. Note also that Dante took it from Guido Guinicelli, see the Volgari Eloquio.

Our interpretation of these echoes can hardly be uniform. The last-mentioned group of lines must be due to conscious repetition on Chaucer's part; and the two parallels preceding it may well have seemed immaterial to him. But the first four cases have more the appearance of a sort of formula, repeated half-mechanically if the keyword came into Chaucer's memory. The second case of the list is particularly interesting from the fact that there occurs at the opening of the Miller's Tale almost a cento of echoes from the tales of Knight and Clerk, with one phrase reminding us of Sir Thopas; if my conjecture below be correct, that the group of tales including that of the Miller was added to an outline already containing Knight, Clerk, and Sir Thopas, then these echoes would be due to Chaucer's re-reading of his previous work before writing up his Miller-Fabliau.

What interpretation we should give to the similar stanzas of the Second Nun's Tale and the Prioress' Tale, or to the descriptions of the caged bird in Sq. Tale 602 ff. and in Manc. Tale 59 ff., pointed out by Tyrwhitt and by Koeppel, it is not our province to discuss here; but we surely have basis for asserting that in turn of phrase, as well as in the mode of approaching his subject, Chaucer tended to repeat himself. By the latter sort of repetition I mean the double use of the quarrel-motive in Miller and Reeve, Friar and Summoner, with the hinted third quarrel in Manciple and Cook; or we may point to the double interruption within the B² fragment, and the intrusion of both Miller and Summoner in front of more dignified characters, the Monk in one case, the Parson in the other.

Allusion has just been made to "the group of Tales including that of the Miller." By this I mean, roughly speaking, the Tales of that set of personages who appear in the Prologue at line 542. Chaucer, who has just finished a long catalogue of pilgrims, says at that point:

> There was also a Reeve and a Mellere,
> A Sompnour and a Pardoner also,
> A Maunciple and myself; ther were na mo.

This group is added in such a way that it suggests an afterthought on Chaucer's part, a piecing-on to the partially completed Prologue of some further characters whom he had decided to include. In support of this view we may consider the following.

First, with the Cook and the later added Canon's Yeoman, the characters in this small group are the lively members of the party. Their quarrels give the journey noise and movement; the dispute of Reeve and Miller, the attack of the Summoner upon the Friar, the audacity of the Pardoner, enliven the pilgrimage. The catalogue of characters enumerated by Chaucer had been up to this point more a deliberately conceived social panorama; Knight, Squire, and Yeoman are the first group; Monk, Prioress, and Friar are the following ecclesiastical types; then come single representative figures like Merchant, Clerk, Man of Law, and Franklin; the group of the Craftsmen with their Cook then appears, followed by Shipman, Doctor, Wife of Bath, and the paired Parson and Plowman. With the addition of the latter group above mentioned, and the creation of the links recounting their quarrels, however, the Pilgrimage becomes dynamic; the story-telling falls into dramatic groups instead of into pictorial ones.

Some objections may be raised to this supposition. First, the group of persons last added is merely parallel to the earlier group of Craftsmen, and is, as the lowest ranking of the Pilgrimage, properly brought in appendix-wise. But it must not be forgotten that every one of these added figures tells a Tale, while the earlier-mentioned Craftsmen do not; and especially must it be noted that in several cases the Tales of these pilgrims are the last of the Fragments in which they occur. Those of Miller and Reeve are followed in the A-fragment only by the hardly-begun Tale of the Cook; that of the Summoner closes the D-fragment, and that of the Pardoner ends the C-fragment. We should further remark that while the Tales of Miller, Reeve, Summoner, and Pardoner all bear the marks of mature and masterly narrative workmanship, the first Tale, in several of the Fragments, shows relatively earlier handling or may be argued of early date. The tales of Knight, Prioress, Clerk, Second Nun, are of this sort. Note also that as Miller and Reeve, Summoner and Friar, tell Tales at each other's expense, these Tales must have been conceived at the same time that the characters were created. The profession of carpenter was perhaps forced upon the Reeve to account for his anger at the Miller, since there was already a carpenter among the pilgrims.[1]

Another objection likely to be raised here is the disagreement of Chaucer's nine-and-twenty pilgrims, as announced at the beginning of the Prologue, with the number of the pilgrims remaining when this "subsidiary group" is treated as a later addition. On this point I would remark that the pilgrimage of thirty which Chaucer at first planned is pretty evidently an artificial number; it is a large number because Chaucer's plans were usually large, and its nine-and-twenty plus Chaucer is directly comparable to the nineteen ladies plus Alcestis of the Legend. But any pressing of the number as he first gave it into agreement with the never finished scheme is as certain to break down as the attempt to work out Spenser's Faerie Queene allegory or to reconcile Chaucer's list of good women in the Legend with the list in the Man of Law's headlink. In its present form the pilgrimage of the Tales does not agree in number with that of the Prologue; but instead of attempting to emend the "prestes thre" in order to obtain a more correct count, I would rather say that, Chaucer being Chaucer, he announced a round number of pilgrims and paid no further attention to numerical congruity. It is even possible that, when inserting his "added group" into the body of the Prologue, Chaucer noticed that his addition rendered his "wel nyne and twenty" very nearly correct; and this caused him to say, in his hurriedly patched connective, "ther wer na mo."

[1] Noted by Lounsbury, Studies in Chaucer III : 435.

There is yet a reason for believing that the General Prologue as it stands is not "aus einem Guss", and that is the correspondence of the Wife of Bath's portrait with her prologue, in which latter the deafness and the five husbands of the General Prologue are discussed in detail. That there was a woman something of her type in Chaucer's plan from the first we may believe from the feminine pronouns of the Shipman's Tale, which was probably composed earlier than the Tale of the Wife; but there is no obstacle to the theory that the Wife's portrait and her autobiography were done at much the same time, a time which also contained the writing of her Tale and the writing of the Friar-Summoner altercation at the end of her prologue, to which she alludes as she begins to narrate,—a time in which any idea of matching her and the Merchant as opponents, perhaps once in Chaucer's plan, was abandoned. In brief, Fragment D and the Wife's character were worked out at the same time; as were, earlier, the added group of pilgrims and the quarrel-idea; each of these sets of pilgrims, with the corresponding Tales, is the result of a fresh impulse to Chaucer's imagination, which at the outset of the pilgrimage was occupied with the single figure and with romantic-religious material.

Indeed, one of the more marked differences between the Tales of this added group and some of those Tales which stand at the beginning of Fragments is the conception of the former in pairs as contrasted with the conception by single figure. The Knight, the Squire, the Prioress, the Monk, the Clerk, the Parson,—many of Chaucer's first long list of pilgrims—are described and displayed as isolated figures, studies in portraiture complete in themselves, and narrating stories which illuminate themselves alone, stories either written or remodeled especially for them. Also, as said, these narratives are usually of a romantic or religious cast. On the other hand, the "fabliau" themes treated by Miller and Reeve, Summoner and Friar, (also Wife of Bath I, now Shipman), are intended partly as social satire, partly as attacks upon other members of the pilgrimage; and the command of dialogue in them is on a par with that displayed in the Links as a whole. Yet a third class of narratives in the Canterbury Tales is what I may term the Marriage Group, the mass of material suggested or enriched by Jerome Adversus Jovinianum, and developed in the Wife of Bath's prologue, the Merchant's Tale, and the inserted passage in the Franklin's romance, lines 639 ff. The strongly autobiographical character of the Merchant's and the Franklin's headlinks, of the framework of the Pardoner's Tale and of the Wife of Bath's prologue, opens the way to the suggestion that Chaucer's advanced maturity, with its natural tendency to autobiographical reflection, was the time in which these pieces of work originated, a time later than the development of the quarrel-motive above mentioned.

The rough and tentative chronology at which we have arrived is accordingly:

(1) The assignment or writing of Knight, Prioress, Monk, Clerk, Man of Law-Melibeus, Squire, Chaucer-Thopas, Doctor, Second Nun, Manciple, Parson. The partial arrangement of B², (say) Prioress-Thopas Melibeus-Monk.

(2) The writing and framing of Miller and Reeve; the writing of Cook, Summoner (?), Pardoner, the insertion of the "subsidiary group" of characters into the Prologue, the Summoner's Tale being intended to follow the Constance story, as in Harley 7334. At this time Constance was assigned to Man of Law, the ML endlink was written and the transfer of the Melibeus headlink was made, also possibly the writing of the Manciple's headlink.

(3) The idea of the Marriage Group; the transfer of Wife (?) to the Shipman and the placing of the Shipman in front of the Prioress; the writing and framing of D; the writing of the Merchant, and the writing or revision of the Franklin; the addition of the Clerk's Envoy. Observe that the Tales of Merchant and Franklin, written in Chaucer's third manner, are not intrinsically appropriate to their narrators, but forced upon them by the later-added headlinks.

(4) The rearrangement of the Clerk's envoy to meet the (new) Merchant's headlink; the addition of the Words of the Franklin and the revision of the Monk's endlink. These changes were not complete when the Tales went into circulation, as MS-conditions show.

In the threefold classification of Tales above made, the fragment B², the sequence Shipman-Prioress-Thopas-Melibeus-Monk-Nun's Priest, is not included. It is a sequence, not a series of detached studies; but it is a sequence not bound by unity of theme or by a quarrel-motive. Nevertheless, a bond it has, and a bond of the most subtle type existing in the Tales, the bond of literary contrast. Ten Brink long ago remarked upon the marvelous variety of form in this group of Tales; and we should remember also that this one fragment contains within itself Chaucer's two criticisms upon his own work, the censure upon Sir Thopas and that upon the Tragedies of the Monk. Nay, we might even go further. For if, as I have just queried, a part of the present Man of Law's headlink once followed Sir Thopas and introduced Melibeus (told by the Man of Law), there was at that time in the B² fragment a third criticism by Chaucer, that passed upon two common medieval stories told by Gower.

This suggestion is extreme. We should however observe the appropriateness of the headlink's wording when following the Thopas endlink, as above noted; the appropriateness of the Melibeus to the Man of Law and the harmony of its prose form with the announcement of the headlink; also the fact that in very many

17

early type MSS the Melibeus endlink begins "When ended was *the* tale of Melibe", instead of *my* tale of Melibe, as in the Ellesmere (revised) class of MSS. The deviation is suggestive from its very slightness; and if we argue from the earlier reading of the two that this endlink was originally written for the Melibeus when belonging to the Man of Law, not to Chaucer, we shall find ourselves opining that the B² fragment, with the possible exception of the Nun's Priest's Tale, was framed not far removed in time from the Verba Hospitis, or stanza of comment on the Clerk's Tale, originally intended to close it, and agreeing nearly in content with the Melibeus endlink. A reason for excepting the Nun's Priest's Tale from this suggestion may be found in the fact that in the Thopas endlink is contained the implication that no other pilgrim had yet been interrupted; hence the Monk endlink, even in the earlier form, was the later written of the two endlinks.

We may then for the present imagine that the B² fragment was originally composed of Prioress, Thopas, Man of Law-Melibeus, and Monk. When the Nun's Priest was added, and the Monk endlink written (in the short form), the double interruption by the Host and double summons to another pilgrim became noticeable, because separated by only one Tale; and a change was therefore made. The one pilgrim, Chaucer, was given a second opportunity by depriving the Man of Law of Melibeus; the Thopas endlink was rewritten accordingly, and the Man of Law-Melibeus headlink transferred to the unassigned Constance-story.[1] Later, the Monk's endlink was expanded; and, as above remarked, the allusion to the Croesus-tragedy was then inserted.

The question at once suggests itself: Why should Chaucer alone, of all the pilgrims, have a second opportunity? We must argue that the assignment of the Melibeus to him was rather early; for the assignment of the Constance story to the Man of Law antedated the writing of the present Constance endlink, as is seen from its "lerned men in lore" and its introduction of the Summoner as the pilgrim to follow, a plan not abandoned until the D group was conceived, but assuredly later than the addition of the Summoner and his fellows to the party. The transfer of Melibeus to Chaucer, we accordingly surmise, was earlier than the D-group of Tales and very near in time to the conception of the subsidiary group of pilgrims. At this stage of Chaucer's work, then, in what we are conjecturing to have been the first of his Tale-framing, may he not have attempted to finish some of his two-Tale arrangements, and remove both himself and the Monk from the competition? That

[1] When the Man of Law's headlink was expanded, by the addition of its first part, the date was added; which, I would say, with Koch, was probably the first day of the journey. The Cook's prologue and Tale, in which Chaucer's fabliau mood had run away with him, he may have intended to delete and let Man of Law follow Reeve after a halt.

he alone has in actuality two narratives merely shows the incompleteness of the poem, which was enlarged in scale by the creation of the subsidiary group of pilgrims very soon after the Melibeus had been given to Chaucer.

This subsidiary group was also, on this supposition, of later date than the Nun's Priest's Tale; and the shift of Chaucer's attention from the ecclesiastical members of the pilgrimage, the Prioress, the Monk, the Nun's Priest, to the group of coarse-tongued vulgarians, was complete; equally marked is the change in method, from the subtle literary criticism which reworked and combined medieval material in a framework of comment contrasting almost as sharply with the embodied Tales as do those Tales with one another, to the direct personal treatment of figures in pairs, the management of social satire and racy dialogue in the form of class-quarrels, from which all trace of conscious art has disappeared.

Assuming then that the framing of B^2 antedated the planning of the quarrel-groups, we shall be obliged to believe that the expansion of the Man of Law's headlink, with its fixing of the date, was after the writing of the Miller-Reeve-Cook bit. At the moment, we would say, when Chaucer realized the excess of this fabliau-material following closely upon the Knight's dignified narrative, he placed the equally long and dignified narrative of the Man of Law in its present position, enlarging the headlink to set it, I believe, after the first pause in the journey; and he also removed the Cook to the other end of the pilgrimage, bringing him into juxtaposition with his natural business rival, the Manciple, but, with habitual economy of material, leaving the fragmentary Cook's Tale standing for possible use later. This (conjectured) difference in time between the removal of the Man of Law-Melibeus headlink from its place and its expansion into the present Man of Law-Constance headlink merely by the addition of lines at its beginning may be offered as explanation of its incongruity. The story of Constance itself is of course not "dated" by any surmises regarding its present headlink; and although it has been suggested that the omission of this and the Griselda story from Chaucer's catalogue of works in the prologue to the Legend, where he is defended from the charge of slandering woman and Love, argues a later date for these Tales, this suggestion seems to me unnecessary. For, granting that they would be his strongest shield against such an accusation, far stronger than Palamon and Arcite or the Life of St. Cecile which are adduced, they might be withheld from mention from the simple desire not to make an impregnable defence of a poet whom a literary convention was compelling to a new piece of work. That the writing of the Constance story followed or closely preceded the publication of the Confessio Amantis in 1390 is not impossible. There is no evidence of its existence in an earlier form, which Skeat assumes in his desire to make Gower the borrower; and the

repetitions and medieval crudenesses of the plot afford no reason
for the modern critic's relegating it to Chaucer's immaturity.[1]
Chaucer is the last man of whom we can assert that what we call
the best is in every case the nearest our own time; he is nothing if
not inconsistent, surprising, a mixture of medieval convention and
modern insight, of energy and indolence, a workman as careless in
his carelessness, as powerful in his strength, as was Shakspere or
Thackeray.

From Lounsbury's suggestion above cited it would follow that
the first sketch of B[2], with the Prioress and Thopas and a part of
the present Man of Law's headlink, antedated part of the Legend
of Good Women, at least the Medea story. This would bring the
Man of Law's allusion to the Legend contemporaneous with the
first work upon the Legend. And if, as Lowes suggests, the
allusion to Jerome in the unique Gg version of the Legend-prologue
puts that version contemporary with the use of Jerome in the Canterbury Tales (Merchant, Wife of Bath), then both recensions of
the Legend were in hand at the same time as were the Tales. It
is interesting to observe that if both versions of the Legend accompanied the Tales, the Legend must probably have arisen in response
to some outside pressure, which was however insufficient to secure
its completion.

But while Lowes' connection between the Gg version of the
Legend, which alludes to Jerome, and the Tales using Jerome-

---

[1] The query suggests itself whether the fragmentary copies of the Tales
give clue to an earlier form of this or of any other Tale. These copies are:—

Sion College	Tales of Clerk, Wife, Friar, Summoner.
Harley 1239.	Tales of Knight, Man of Law, Wife, Clerk, part of Franklin.
Longleat 257.	Tales of Knight, Clerk.
Naples.	Tale of Clerk.
Phillipps 8299.	Tale of Clerk.
Cambridge Ee ii, 15.	Tale of Man of Law.
Harley 1704.	Tale of Prioress.
Harley 2251.	Tale of Prioress.
Harley 2382.	Tales of Prioress and Second Nun.
Rawlinson C 86.	Tale of Clerk, part of Prioress.

The appearance in this list of Tales to which an early origin has been
assigned is at first sight suggestive; but nothing definite regarding the circulation of single narratives before the entire work can be drawn from these
meagre data. All the codices are of the XV century, some later, and examination shows that Sion College is a fragment of the whole poem, Harley
1239 a selection; for e. g. the Clerk's headlink and the allusion to the Wife
of Bath in his Envoy both appear in the latter, and the allusion to the Wife
in the former. Naples is imperfect at the beginning, but has the envoy-
allusion. Longleat is also imperfect at the beginning, omits that allusive
stanza, and ends, "I yow counsaille"; its colophon is "Explicit Grisild full
of pacience." Phillipps omits that stanza and the one preceding, but has the
rest of the envoy ending "care . . . waille"; it has no headlink. The Cambridge copy of the Man of Law's Tale is imperfect at beginning; and the
copies of the Prioress' Tale are all poor. That in Harley 2382, a collection of medieval legends, is entitled "Fabula Monialis", which points to excerp-
tion from the Tales. Of the set, the Longleat is the most interesting; it is
described Section III B (7) here.

material, is tempting, we hesitate to assign that group positively to the vicinity of the year 1394. Lowes argues this partly on the ground that Gg, representing the "later" version, does not show the couplet requesting the poet to offer the finished work to the queen at Eltham or at Sheen. As the palace of Sheen was destroyed (?) in 1394, after the death of Queen Anne, Lowes finds in the removal of the Sheen couplet from the Gg version a strong argument for dating that recension later than the summer of 1394. But it should be remembered that the Gg is the only authority we have for this omission; that the excision of an allusion to a palace no longer in existence[1] might possibly be the work of an intelligent arbitrary scribe such as Gg or his source apparently was, or it might be the alteration of a scribe writing at a time when England had no queen, —1400-1403—who deleted the couplet as an impossibility. Whether this can be proven for the Gg or not, there is at any rate an element of insecurity in the treatment of the unique and often arbitrary Gg text as on a par with the other and well-attested recension.

We have therefore no certain date for the last of Chaucer's groups of Tales, any more than for the first; nor can we date the Squire's Tale, the Canon's Yeoman's Tale, the Nun's Priest's Tale. That the first-mentioned was nearly contemporary with one version of the Legend-prologue, as Lowes suggests (Publ. Mod. Lang. Assn. 20 : 797), is very probable; and that the Nun's Priest's Tale was added to B^2 at a relatively early time I have above argued. The assignment of this superlative bit of narrative to the obscure and almost unmentioned Nun's Priest may at first seem surprising, but it is at least possible that Chaucer emphasized the failure and public rebuke of the most prominent ecclesiastic in the company by giving to the insignificant priest a narrative triumph. Also, the gathering of the Church at this point,—Monk, Prioress, Nun's Priest,—is noteworthy as corresponding with their appearance in the Prologue together, and lends perhaps color to my suggestion that Chaucer's earlier work in assigning Tales was with the pilgrims at the head of his first long list. The literary perception which differentiated these ecclesiastics and nevertheless arranged this Fragment out of the most typical medieval material is a perception of the same subtleness as that which parodied the romance in the dancing mockery of Sir Thopas, escaped from suspicion of parody or of archaism behind the rebuke of the unlettered Host, and created the dialogue of the Cock and the Hen. The master of narration, the possible dramatist, and the founder of English literary criticism, all speak in this one Fragment, through the medium of religious legend, interminable didactics, degenerate romance, and beast-epic.

[1] It may be added that I do not as yet find proof of the destruction of Sheen. Froissart speaks of Richard's command to that effect, but Miss Strickland, in her life of Anne, remarks that although the rooms in which the queen died were dismantled, Henry V restored them.

The dating of the Man of Law's Tale is also at present impossible, as has been above remarked. Its stanzaic form does not warrant us in relegating it to Chaucer's earlier years, nor does its treatment of material used by Gower (taken in connection with the headlink's allusion to stories told by Gower) warrant us in arguing a date later than the "publication" of the Confessio. For we cannot assert that either poet was unaware of the plans and perhaps the details of the other's work; the relations between them, for aught we know, permitted an interchange of opinions and of manuscript.

That the Canterbury Tales was generally known before the Corpus-7333 type went into circulation is however unlikely. No evidence exists of the "publishing" of separate Tales, and the fact that this group contains the unrevised Gamelyn, misplaces the Squire, and is without the Links last written, leads me to argue that its archetypal copy was made without the consent of Chaucer. A conjecture which might plausibly be drawn from the variations in arrangement and Links within this large group, and only within this group, is that the stolen copying was done with one or two fascicules at a time in the hands of the scribes, not a complete text. It is of course important in this connection to inquire if the Retractation exists in this "pirated" version; for if the Retractation be indeed the work of the failing Chaucer, it can hardly appear in the original of a type of Tales published before the E and F Links, works of Chaucer's maturity, were written.

An examination of the manuscripts with this point in view reveals the interesting fact that in all types of text, even in the earliest, the Retractation is present wherever the MS is complete; no codex, so far as known, shows the entire Parson's Tale without this appended prayer. Only in the Thynne Chaucer of 1532 and its followers[1] does the Tale appear without the Retractation. Shall we accordingly think that the late-written Retractation was added with remarkable unanimity to all early copies? or that instead of being the work of the failing Chaucer it antedates the final arrangement of E and F? These are two possible suppositions in case we treat the prayer as genuine; if we view it as spurious we may argue that it was illegally added to the "pirated" copy, and transferred from that to the last or Ellesmere type of manuscript, which in this case we must assume was retouched after Chaucer's death.

One more possible explanation may be offered. If no long time separates the "pirated" and the Ellesmere recensions, if the mood of the E and F Links and the mood of the Retractation are not far apart in point of time, the existence of the Retractation in all types of the Tales may be accounted for. Let us suppose that the tran-

---

[1] What interpretation shall we put upon this fact? remembering, as we must, that for a long passage in the Book of the Duchess, Thynne is our only text, and that he had access to a better copy of the House of Fame than did Caxton.

scription of the Corpus-7333 archetype was made in parcels, that E and F were in that scribe's hands before their connectives were written by Chaucer, and that before the conclusion of the work was reached by the Corpus-7333 scribe the Retractation had been appended. This supposition may explain the presence of the Retractation in all types of MSS.

Should we refuse to explain the universal appearance of the Retractation on any of the above modes, we shall be obliged to assume one ultimate original for all surviving types of the Canterbury Tales, and to assume a kind of critical omission on the part of the scribes whose MSS show no E and F links, etc., which appears to me incredible. The theory which I offer is indeed complicated; but, as Hugh Miller long ago said, only the complicated explanation fits the complex phenomenon.

The contradictions which Chaucer never reconciled remain in his last work for our bewilderment; and though we may suggest explanations for some of them, there is one explanation to which we cannot attain. We cannot, peering through the tangle of Chaucer's partly cleared path and of officious copyists' guidance, see the clue which fits his Tales into an orderly scheme of hours and days and places along the Canterbury road. He possibly had a plan in mind at first, and returned to it once when he set the Man of Law in place; but the most rational thing which we can at present do for text or for arrangement of the Canterbury Tales is to take the latest version from his hand as represented *e. g.* in the Ellesmere, and forswear not only all readings of earlier MSS, but all attempt at changing the Tale-order dictated by that MS. (Cp. ten Brink, Hist. Eng. Lit. II : 150.) The sort of textual study which can give us most help at present is an endeavor to follow the movement of Chaucer's mind among his material. Of course the greatest of caution is needed for this study, which is almost as elusive as the attempt to trace the influence of one author upon another without external evidence. We have had the student who saw in Byron's use of *What ho!* evidence of the influence of Macbeth upon him, and we may yet have the student who will find in the cry of Thekla:

> Du Heilige, rufe Dein Kind zurück!
> Ich habe genossen das irdische Glück,
> Ich habe gelebt und geliebet!—

a proof that Schiller was familiar not only with the prayer of Chaucer's Dido,

> Tak now my soule, unbind me of this unreste,
> I have fulfild of fortune al the cours,

but also with the Wife of Bath's

> . . . . it dooth myn herte bote
> That I have had my world as in my time.

If a change in mood, in material, and in method of treatment separates two Tales, no mere verbal resemblances between them can prove their contemporaneous composition. It can prove only that in Chaucer's mind the same economy which borrowed every plot and six times reworked the Theseus-story led him also to re-employ a phrase or simile if the keyword came into his memory. Thus, in Manciple's Tale and Squire's Tale, the simile of the caged bird cannot of itself prove their like date, because of their difference in tone and material; but the recurrence of group scenes and festal scenes in the Legend, the Knight's Tale, the Squire's Tale, the use of similar material in a similar way, casts quite a different light upon their resemblances in phrasing. The poet's attitude in them is the same; and it is an attitude diametrically different from the attitude of the Wife's prologue, or the Rime of Sir Thopas, or the Reeve's Tale.

G. The Separate Tales

In Order as in the Oxford Chaucer

FRAGMENT A

The General Prologue; the Knight's Tale, the link between Knight and Miller; the Miller's Tale, the link between Miller and Reeve; the Reeve's Tale, the link between Reeve and Cook; the unfinished Cook's Tale. In many MSS there follows, connected with the Cook, the tale of Gamelyn. For note on this tale and on the spurious connectives between it and the Cook, see under Cook's Tale below; for note on different form of the Cook's Tale in one MS see *ibid.*

Skeat III : 380 considers that the Cook's Tale was "almost the last portion of his great work which the poet ever revised in its final form"; he emphasizes *ibid.* the admirable compactness and completeness of the fragment. But ten Brink, Hist. Eng. Lit. II : 150-156, does not so regard this fragment.

On the fragment see ten Brink as cited; Root, Poetry of Chaucer pp. 151-181.

General Prologue to the Canterbury Tales

MSS: See under MSS of the Cant. Tales, III B above. A leaf with a bit of the Prologue is marked Douce d. 4 in the Bodleian Library; see Madan, Summary Catal. IV : 622.

Prints and Editions: See under Editions of the Cant. Tales, Editions of Selections or Portions. Privately printed at the Ashendene Press, Hertfordshire, Engd., 1897, quarto, 38 pages, as "The Prologue to the Tales of Caunterbury."

A work entitled Chaucer's Prologue and Characters from the Canterbury Tales, 12mo. 1812, with frontispiece by William Blake, I have not seen. For Blake see Pictures of the Pilgrims, p. 324 below.

Date: Koch, Chronology p. 48, says that the first calculation of the date was made by Scherk at the request of Hertzberg, and printed in Hertzberg's Canterbury-Geschichten, pp. 666-67; Scherk and later students work upon the assumption that the supposed times mentioned in the Pilgrimage are real, and that the allusions of the Prologue, the Man of Law's headlink, the Parson's headlink, and the Knight's Tale lines 1413, 1509, indicate actual hours. Scherk accordingly decided for April 28, 1393, as the date of the Parson's headlink; his note was translated and printed Ch. Soc. Essays pp. 415-17, but with a postscript by Skeat combating its results and pointing out that the date mentioned in the Man of Law's headlink is April 18, not 28. Koch, Ausgew. Klein. Dicht., found by revising the calculation the date April 18, 1391; then Ehrhart in Engl. Stud. 12 : 469-70 argued for April 6, 1388, which Koch, Chronology 49-50, declines to admit as probable. Koch reasons *ibid.* from the state of Chaucer's personal circumstances that he must have formed the plan of the Cant. Tales between 1385 and 1391-2; on p. 54 Koch decides for 1385-86 as the most likely date. On p. 62-67 he argues that as the pilgrimage lasted three days, and as the date given in the Parson's headlink marks the time of full moon, only April 18-20, 1386, will do; the first day of the Pilgrimage is then the April 18 mentioned in the Man of Law's headlink. It is more probable that Chaucer would explicitly date the first day than the second, says Koch, Chronology p. 57.

A student accepting this supposition would not be obliged to doubt the theory on p. 252 here; for the first portion of the Man of Law's headlink may have been written when Chaucer determined to assign the Constance story to him and to connect it with the present A fragment,—a determination never fully carried out.

There are notes upon the date of the pilgrimage earlier than those discussed by Koch, especially Brae as below. Tyrwhitt, in § v of his Introd. Disc., errs in astrology and in the MS readings which he elects for the Man of Law's headlink; the date which he conjectures is accordingly April 28; the year he makes no attempt to reckon except by remarking that as the rebellion of 1381 is the latest date mentioned in the Tales (Nun's Priest's Tale), the Pilgrimage may be accordingly imagined as of about 1383. In his note on line 14709 (Monk's Tale) he apologizes for having forgotten the date of 1385 there implied, and alters his supposition to the year 1387. Brae, in N. and Q. 1851 I : 315, 345, 385, 419, 515, points out Tyrwhitt's errors, and after elaborate calculation dates the Prologue April 18, 1388. *Ibid.* 1868 II : 348 he protests against Skeat's claiming credit for refuting Tyrwhitt's errors; see Skeat *ibid.* II : 271-2, and Skeat's acknowledgement of Brae's work, Oxford Chaucer V : 132.

In the Athenaeum for 1893, I : 443, reprinted Folia Litteraria p. 99, J. W. Hales showed that line 277 of the Prologue was in all probability written between 1384 and 1388. Skeat III : 373, V : 1 considers that the Pilgrimage began upon April 17, and that the year "may be supposed to be 1387." Pollard, Globe Chaucer p. xxviii, accepts Skeat's dictum, and believes that 1387 is the most probable date for the beginning of the Tales. See Tatlock, Devel. and Chronol., Chap. V, § 2.

It is apparently assumed by students that the General Prologue is all of one date, one time of composition; for different view see under F above. For theories as to the duration of the pilgrimage see p. 161 above.

Imitations: The opening of Chaucer's Prologue found frequent imitation in the two centuries after his death. Lydgate's Prologue to the Story of Thebes, written as an additional Canterbury Tale, shows him, in ten Brink's opinion (Hist. Eng. Lit. II : 226) "almost as Chaucer's ape"; but Churton Collins, in a severe review of Jusserand (Ephemera Critica, 1901, p. 199), thinks that the pictures of contemporary life which this later prologue contains are as vivid as Chaucer's See Section V here for references on the Story of Thebes. Other of Lydgate's writings also show the opening temporal clause with a description of spring half "natural", half "astrological"; cp. his (?) Assembly of the Gods, his Complaint of the Black Knight (see Section V here). Stephen Hawes, in his Pastime of Pleasure (Percy Society, 1845) is, as an imitator of Lydgate instead of Chaucer, even more conventional in his use of the mannerism; but the writer of the Flower and the Leaf (Skeat VII), and the Scottish school of Chaucer's admirers, are much freer and more poetic in their management of a similar mode of opening a poem. Cp. Henryson's Testament of Cresseid, Dunbar's Thrissil and the Rois (both printed in vol. II of the Abbotsford Series of the Scottish Poets, Glasgow, 1892, and Henryson also in Skeat VII, Dunbar in the eds. of his works by Schipper, Vienna 1894 or by Small for the Scottish Text Soc. 1893). Other Scottish imitations are by Bellenden in the opening stanzas of his Banner of Pictie, and in the proheme prefixed to his translation of a history of Scotland. For these see vol. III of the Abbotsford Series, or see the Hunterian Club print of the Bannatyne MS, vol. I : 149, II : 621. Cp. the opening of the Quair of Jelusy, in the MS Selden B 24, printed in the Bannatyne Miscellany II : 161, by the Bannatyne Club; a few of the lines are given here, from the MS:

> This lusty may the quhich all tender floures
> By nature incrisith with hir hote schoures
> The felde oureclad hath with ye tender grene
> Quhich all depaynt with diuers hewis bene
> And euery thing makith to conuert
> Agayn the stroke of winter cold and smert
> The samyn moneth and the sevynt Ide
> The sonne the quhich yt likith not to hyde
> His courses ascending in the Orient
> From his first gree and forth his bemys sent

Throu quhich he maketh euery lusty hert
Out of thair slouth to walkyn and astert   etc.

One or two bits of unprinted poems may be added. A doggerel
poem in couplets, entitled How a Lover Prayseth hys Lady, in
MS Fairfax 16, begins:

When the son the laumpe of heuen ful lyght
Phebus with hys eye ful gret round and bryght
In the lyon rent yn hys domynacion
Boyling the herbes the rede. swart. white to brown
With hys coleryk hete and hys nature
Rypeth then euery vitatall creature
And diane echates bothe I here call
The cold mone the sonnes doghter royall
Verrey lady and goddes of the see
Of moystur and spirites that yn the eyr be
With her yong hornys shynyng on her fronte
Al with her tynnyd hiwe on our oryzonte
XXti degres was yn libra ful shene   etc.

A poem in the noble Chaucerian MS Gg iv, 27 of the University Library, Cambridge,[1] begins:

In may whan euery herte is ly3t
And flourys frosschely sprede & sprynge
And Phebus wt his bemys bry3hte
Was in þe Bole so cler schynynge   etc.

On the subject of Stories in a Framework, before and since
Chaucer, see ante under A. Lists of character-descriptions, in
some cases influenced by Chaucer, may be found in Thynne's
Pride and Lowliness, written probably before 1570, pubd. by
the Shakespeare Society in 1841; from this Greene plagiarized
his Quip for an Upstart Courtier, 1592. The character-writing
of the 17th century, with all its later development as seen in
the satires of Butler, Pope, etc., is more probably due to
classical and French tendencies; see Morley's Character Writings of the Seventeenth Century, London 1891. The subject
might repay investigation, with consideration of the influence,
if any, exerted by earlier processional poems and by allegorical
personifications upon Chaucer.

For lists of personages in works openly imitated from
Chaucer, see under Stories in a Framework, ante in A; and see
the list of Modernizations and Imitations printed in E above.

Source: In the Athen. 1893 II : 65 Skeat pointed out a close
resemblance between the opening of the Prologue and a passage
of Guido delle Colonne's Historia Trojana; see also Skeat
V : 2, where the passage is cited.

[1] Printed by me in Jour. Gc. Phil. 7: 105.

Several lines in the description of the Prioress, 127 ff., are imitated from Le Roman de la Rose, as Tyrwhitt pointed out in his note on the passage. The connection between the Parson and the Roman de Carité has been remarked by Kittredge, Mod. Lang. Notes 12:113-115. Bryant, *ibid.* 17:470-1, questions if the character of the Knight be not derived from Boccaccio. Mead, Publ. Mod. Lang. Assn. 16:388-404, thinks that the character of the Wife of Bath is derived from the Vieille of the Roman de la Rose.

Notes: With the date chosen by Chaucer for the Pilgrimage compare the opening of Dante's Comedy and the remark of his 14th century commentator Benvenuto da Imola that according to astronomers and theologians God in the beginning placed the sun in Aries, and that the time when the Sun begins gradually to ascend is good for the commencement of any undertaking, etc.; see Vernon, Readings on Dante's Inferno I : 19.

The number of pilgrims in the party, and the lack of accordance with the "Wel nyne and twenty", announced by Chaucer in line 24, have occasioned much discussion. See Thynne's Animadversions, ed. Furnivall, p. 11. Tyrwhitt, Introd. Disc. § vi, would emend the Prioress' three priests to permit of but one, and this suggestion has generally been followed, see notes on the Prioress below. Furnivall, who maintains that passage as it stands, Temp. Pref. 92, implies *ibid.* pp. 10, 11 and note, that Chaucer may merely have failed to carry out his first plan. See also p. 255 above.

For notes on the separate pilgrims see in each case under the corresponding Tale here. For the identification of the Host see N. and Q. 1857 I:228 and 1902 I:97; also W. Rendle and P. Norman, The Inns of Old Southwark and their Associations, Lond. 1888.

On the shrine of St. Thomas, the pilgrimage, and the road, see Weever's introd. to his Ancient Funeral Monuments, Lond. 1631, chap. 17; see Erasmus' dialogue entitled Peregrinatio religionis ergo Todd, Illustrations p. 355, cites from a MS in the Cathedral Library at Canterbury to show the immense popularity of St. Thomas. See Saunders, and Jusserand's English Wayfaring Life, for descriptions of pilgrimages and pilgrims; see Rodenberg's Kent and the Canterbury Tales, in his England Literary and Social, 1875, pp. 1-77; see Dean Stanley's Historical Memorials of Canterbury. For discussion of the road see H. Littlehales' Some Notes on the Road from London to Canterbury in the Middle Ages, Ch. Soc. 2d Series No. 30; see J. and E. Pennell, The Pilgrimage to Canterbury, London 1885; see H. Belloc, The Old Road, London 1904, reviewed Athen. 1904 II : 837; see The Canterbury Pilgrimages, by H.

Snowden Ward and C. M. Barnes Ward, London and Phila. 1904, with 50 fullpage plates from photographs and three maps, reviewed Dial 1906 I : 268.

Notes on the Prologue, see the eds. of Tyrwhitt and of Skeat; Todd's Illustrations; Warton-Hazlitt II : 363-379; Godwin's Life chap. 51; Morley's Eng. Writers V : 276-347; and collections of notes on the text by Flügel in Anglia 24 : 437-508, Jour. Gc. Phil. 1 : 118-135. See H. B. Hinckley's Notes on Chaucer, Northampton, 1907.

Knight's Tale

MSS, Prints, and Editions: See under Cant. Tales, Editions of Works, Editions of the Cant. Tales. A copy of this Tale and of the Clerk's Tale are in MS Longleat 257. The Tale is in the Selections of Hazlitt (part), of Southey, of Ward, of Corson (part) ; of Warner (part) ; in Robertson. See under E above.

Modernizations and Translations: Modernized by Dryden, 1700; by Lord Thurlow, 1822; a bit of the Tale is rewritten in Gent. Mag. 1818 II : 293; the "Temple of Mars" is done into verse by R. H. Horne in Temple Bar 54 : 196. Modernized by Cowden Clarke, by Purves in 1870, by F. Clarke, by Pitt-Taylor, by Darton, by Mackaye, by Skeat; see under E above.

For 30 lines in Chaucerian English, "The Song of Emilye", see Skeat in Acad. 1884 II : 137.

Transl. into German by Kannegiesser, by Fiedler, by Hertzberg, by von Düring; into French by Chatelain; into Italian prose by Chiarini. See under E above. A transl. into Persian is mentioned Acad. 1879 I : 95.

Source: Already Francis Thynne, in his Animadversions, pointed out that this Tale was taken from Boccaccio's Teseide; and Warton, in his Essay on the Genius and Writings of Pope, ed. 1806 I : 335, says that Niceron, in his Memoirs (1736) II : 44, gives an abstract of Boccaccio and remarks, "G. Chaucer, l'Homère de son pays, a mis l'ouvrage de Boccace en vers anglais." On Boccaccio's poem see under Section II C (3) here. A collation of the Italian and the English was made by Ward, and is printed Temp. Pref. pp. 104-5; beside the Cambridge and the Lansdowne texts, in the Six-Text, are printed marks indicating the relation of the English to the Italian; cp Skeat V : 60 for summary. Skeat III : 392 ff. reprints the analysis of the Teseide made by Tyrwhitt in his Introd. Disc. § ix; a fuller summary is in Koerting, Boccaccio's Leben und Werke, pp. 594-615. Mather, in the introd. to his school ed., compares the two narratives. A detailed study is still lacking, but is preparing for the Chaucer Society.

See Koeppel in Anglia 14 : 239-40; see Rodeffer in Mod. Lang. Notes 17 : 471 against Constans' assertion that Chaucer used the Roman de Thèbes

Date: This question is complicated with that of a possible version of the Tale earlier than the plan of the Cant. Tales. In the prol. to the Legend, line 420, Chaucer speaks of a "Palamon and Arcite" as his; Tyrwhitt, Introd. Disc. § ix, remarked that it was "not impossible that at first it was a mere translation of the Theseida of Boccace, and that its present form was given it when Chaucer determined to assign it the first place among his Canterbury Tales." See Godwin, Life, chaps. 14, 18. Sandras, Étude p. 51, considered that the present Tale was little different from the earlier version; Ebert, reviewing Sandras in Jahrbuch 1862 p. 85, transl. Ch. Soc. Essays, opined that the earlier version was more literal than the Tale; Kissner p. 59 agreed with Ebert; Hertzberg, reviewing Kissner in Jahrbuch 1867 p. 153, seems to agree with Sandras.

Ten Brink, in his Studien pp. 47 ff., gave the question fuller argument than it had yet received; he considered that the original Palamon and Arcite was written in seven-line stanzas, and was pitched in a higher and more epic key than the later Tale. He dated the Palamon and Arcite after 1373. Koch, in Engl. Stud. 1 : 249, transl. Ch. Soc. Essays p. 359 ff., accepts ten Brink's theory and adds other proofs; see his summary *ibid.* He dates the Palamon and Arcite about 1374-6, a date which he retains in his Chronology as 1375-6. Kölbing, Engl. Stud. 2 : 523, made a few additional notes. Skeat ranges himself with ten Brink and Koch; see his ed. of the Prioress' Tale etc. in 1874, his postscript to the revision of Morris' ed. of the Prologue in 1888, his Oxford Chaucer I : 529, III : 306, 381, 389-90. He dates the Palamon and Arcite in 1372-3, see Oxford Chaucer I : lxiii. As for the date of the Tale itself, Skeat argues that the fictitious time, as given in lines 605 ff. of the Tale, is the real time; he decides for 1387. (See N. and Q. 1868 II : 243, repr. in Temp. Pref. p. 103.) In his notes V : 70 Skeat seems to decide for 1386.

Pollard, in the Globe Chaucer pp. xxvi-vii, expresses an opinion contrary to that of previous critics; he regards the theory of a lost seven-line version of Palamon and Arcite "as a needless hypothesis." He dates the Palamon and Arcite in 1383 or 1384. See his introd. to the Knight's Tale, Lond. 1903, p. xvi. Pollard is disputed by Koch in Engl. Stud. 27 : 2.

George Hempl, in a paper read before the Modern Language Association of America in 1897, and noticed in their Publ. 1898

p. lviii as The Relation of the Knight's Tale to Palamon and Arcite, argued that the earlier poem was in couplets.

F. J. Mather, Jr., writing On the Date of the Knight's Tale, in Eng. Misc., 1901, pp. 301 ff., agrees with Pollard as to the "needless hypothesis"; he dates the Tale 1381.

G. L. Kittredge, Chaucer and Some of his Friends, in Mod. Phil. 1 : 1 ff., shows that the Tale was quoted by Clanvowe in a poem written before 1392, possibly before 1391.

Lowes, in Publ. Mod. Lang. Assn. 20 : 841 ff., argues the existence of an earlier form of the present Tale. For his relative dating of this, the House of Fame, the Legend and its prologue, and the Troilus, see *ibid*. In Mod. Lang. Notes 19 : 240 Lowes argues from line 26 of the Tale to the date 1382. Tatlock, Devel. and Chronol., chap. III § 3, argues for a date about 1385; *ibid*. pp. 45-70, he argues that the Palamon and Arcite was not stanzaic, and was but slightly revised for its place in the Tales, into which it was put about 1388-90.

Other Versions: Fragments of a Palamon and Arcite in MS are found in a Dublin MS, printed Reliquiae Antiquae II : 11, repr. Ch. Soc. Essays p. 418; and in a MS at Stockholm, see Skeat III : 504. For Lydgate's Story of Thebes see Section V here. Richard Edwards' Palamon and Arcite was produced at Oxford in 1566; see Nicholls' Progresses of Queen Elizabeth, ed. 1788, I : 44, cp. Hales in Athen. 1902 II : 684; see Publ. Mod. Lang. Assn. 20 : 502 ff. Henslowe mentions a play of that name in his Diary, 1594; see ed. of the Diary by Collier, Shaks. Soc. vol. VII (1845) pp. 43-44; new ed. of the Diary by Greg, vol. I 1904, vol. II to appear. Beaumont and Fletcher's Two Noble Kinsmen was printed 1634; see Herford's introd. to his ed. in the Temple Dramatists, 1897, and see Leuschner, Ueber das Verhältnis von The Two Noble Kinsmen und Chaucer's Knightes Tale, diss. Halle 1903, pp. 45. See also Th. Bierfreund, Palemon og Arcite: en literaturhistorisk undersøgelse som bidrag til Shakespearekritiken, Copenhagen, 1891, pp. 79.

Notes: See Dr. Johnson in his Life of Dryden; Scott in his Life of Dryden; cp. Lounsbury, Studies III : 160; Warton-Hazlitt II : 298-317; Godwin chap. 18; Sandras, Étude pp. 50-56; Hertzberg p. 63, p. 594 ff.; Morley, Eng. Writers V : 312 ff.; Furnivall, Temp. Pref. p. 104; ten Brink, Studien pp. 39-69, Hist. Eng. Lit. II : 63-72; Saunders p. 223; Skeat III : 389 ff., V : 60 ff.; the introd. by Mather to his school ed.

On the Knight see Todd, Illustrations pp. 227-9; Toulmin Smith's ed. of Expeditions to Prussia and the Holy Land made by Henry Earl of Derby, afterwards King Henry IV, in the years 1390-91 and 1392-3 (Camden Society, 1894). See Saunders, pp. 30 ff.; Flügel in Anglia 24 : 440-448; Stevens in Mod. Lang. Notes 18 : 140-41; Cook in Jour. Gc. Phil. 4 : 50-54. Bryant in Mod. Lang. Notes 17 : 470 suggests that the source of the description of the Knight may be Boccaccio's Teseide VI : 40.

Most modern students are of the opinion that Chaucer's treatment of the story, though based upon Boccaccio, surpasses the Italian in poetic fitness and in narrative power; cp. Tyrwhitt, Introd. Disc. note 10; Schlegel, in his Charakteristiken und Kritiken, II : 371, thought that Chaucer treated the tale better than did Boccaccio; W. P. Ker, in his Epic and Romance, Lond. 1897, pp. 416-17, says "Chaucer's modifications of Boccaccio here are a lesson in the art of narrative which can hardly be overvalued by students of that mystery." See also his remarks on the Troilus, Section IV here.

But the contrary opinion has its supporters, e. g., Sandras, Étude pp. 51 ff.; Hortis op. cit. pp. 579-80; Ebert, Jahrbuch 1862 pp. 85 ff., transl. in Ch. Soc. Essays pp. 14-22. And see under discussion of Stories in a Framework, Section III A here.

Chaucer's Knightes Tale, with an Abstract of the Poet's Life, by C. Wihlidahl, programm, Budweiser, 1882, pp. 27, is severely criticised by Koch, Anglia 6: Anz. 51, Littblatt 1885 p. 325.

Minor notes Acad. 1874 I : 65, 1889 II : 87; N. and Q. 1851 I : 131, 201, 252.

On line 60 of the General Prologue, *ariue* or *armee:* The MS readings are not yet collected. Caxton ed. I has aryue, ed. II arme; Thynne has armye; Speght army; Urry army; Morell aryve; Tyrwhitt armee. Skeat prints aryve, with condemnation of armee as giving no good sense, and due probably to misreading of the spelling ariue. Skeat is criticised by Flügel, Jour. Gc. Phil. 1 : 124-5, Anglia 24 : 443-6, with citations for armee, in the sense of "military expedition." The New Eng. Dict. takes Tyrwhitt's reading, not Skeat's, for annotation.

Line 26 of the Tale, "And of the tempest at hir hoomcominge", is discussed by Lowes, Mod. Lang. Notes 19: 240-242.

Line 1036 of the Tale, "Westward right swich another in the opposit", is by Saintsbury, Hist. Eng. Prosody I: 175 note, termed an Alexandrine; but see McKerrow, Mod. Lang. Review, 2 : 69 note.

Line 1159 of the Tale, *shippes hoppesteres.* The readings of the MSS are: shippes (shippis) hoppesteres (hoppesteris) ap-

18

pears in Ellesmere, Hengwrt, Sloane 1685, Laud 600, Laud 739,
Egerton 2726, Harley 7335, Royal 18, Selden, Petworth; the
same, with the variant schippes or -is, appears in Sloane 1686,
Harley 1758; Lansdowne writes schippes hoppesters; Barlow,
shippes hopsters; Harley 7333, shippes hoppesters; Corpus,
schippes hoppestereres; Trinity R 3, 3, shippes hopstores;
Rawlinson 149 has shippus vppe sterys; Hatton, shippes
vppesteris; Adds. 5140, shipes vp the steris; Royal 17 reads
schypen hopstarys; Cambridge Gg, schepis hospesterys. The
passage is not in Harley 7334, Trinity R 3, 15, nor Trinity's
close ally Caxton I. Caxton II reads shippes hoppesteris, the
de Worde of 1498 shyppes hoppesteris.

The word was included in the glossary to the 1598 Speght,
but a space left blank, without attempt at explanation. In the
1602 Speght it was annotated "(Gubernaculum tenentes)
pilotes"; possibly this comment is due to Francis Thynne, see
p. 125 here. In the 1721 Urry, Thomas' note, citing Speght,
prefers the reading of the Cholmondeley MS, "ships upon the
steries", interpreted to mean "as they steered or sailed along",
and favored as "a much more terrible image." Morell in 1737
printed "Schepys Hyposterys", giving variant readings and his
predecessors' notes; observe his spelling. Tyrwhitt printed
hoppesteres, and interpreted it to mean "dancers"; he cited
the "navi bellatrici" of the Teseide, and remarked that Chaucer's
adjective was less appropriate than the Italian. Bell in 1854
gave the phrase from Statius, and cited Speght and Tyrwhitt.
Hertzberg in 1866 translated the line "Ich sah das Schiff
verbrannt im Meere schwanken." Skeat, in 1904, rendered
the line "Next saw I tossing ships, that blazed amain."

In 1867 the Athen. II : 688 cited a suggestion by Brae that
the word was to be interpreted as related to the verb *oppose*,
with a feminine suffix, see Brae's ed. of the Astrolabe, 1870,
pp. 105-8. This is referred to, without Brae's name, in the eds.
of the Tale by Morris and by Skeat. Skeat rejects the possibility of such a formation, and conjectures a misunderstanding
on Chaucer's part, or a miswriting by his original, of *bellatrici*
into *ballatrici;* this was previously suggested in N. and Q.
1850 II : 31 and *ibid.* 1869 II : 114; the former was cited Athen.
1867 II : 688, the latter in Warton-Hazlitt II : 311 note. The
same explanation was offered by ten Brink, Athen. 1871 II : 317.
Brae, ed. Astrolabe, replied to Skeat's dismissal of the formation from *oppose* as impossible by asking explanation of the
form *divinistre*, Kn. Tale 1953. (Cp. also *chydestere,* Merch.
Tale 291.) Pollard, ed. Knight's Tale, 1903 p. 100, adopts the
"ballatrici" conjecture.

Surmises more or less groundless are printed in N. and Q.
1857 II : 407-8, 1860 II : 227, 1877 II : 301-3.

Miller's Tale

MSS, Prints, and Editions: See under Cant. Tales, eds. of Cant. Tales, eds. of Works. In the Selections of Sanford and Walsh; portions in Corson; in Robertson.

Modernizations and Translations: Modernized by Cobb in 1712, reprinted in Ogle, omitted from Lipscomb; modernized in Saunders, in Purves, in F. Clarke. Translated into German by Fiedler, by Hertzberg, by von Düring; into French by Chatelain. See Section III E here.

Source, Analogues, etc.: See Koehler in Anglia 1 : 38, 186, 2 : 135; see Varnhagen in Anglia 7 : Anz. 81; Proescholdt in Anglia 7 : 116; Fraenkel in Anglia 16 : 261; Coote in Athen. 1880 II : 64; Wlislocki in Ztschr. f. vergl. Littgesch. 2 : 191; Bolte's ed. of Schumann's Nachtbüchlein, Littver. Stuttgart. 1893; Müllenhoff, Sagen, Märchen, und Lieder, p. 589; Kölbing in Ztschr. f. vergl. Littgesch. 12 : 448; summary, and genealogy of the story by Zupitza, Archiv 94 : 444-45; Skeat III : 395-6.

Date:

Notes: A comment on this Tale and that of the Wife of Bath was published by R. Brathwait in 1665, discussed in Corser's Collectanea II : 447-9; Brathwait was ed. for the Ch. Soc. by Spurgeon in 1901, rev. Koch, Engl. Stud. 30 : 458; see Lounsbury, Studies III : 90. See Acad. 1881 II : 327, 365; Athen. 1887 II : 54, 84; N. and Q. 1849 I : 229, 281; 1871, II : 22; Warton-Hazlitt II : 356-61; Saunders pp. 137, 438; Todd's Illustrations p. 257; Thorold Rogers' Six Centuries of Work and Wages p. 65; Skeat V : 47-49, 96-112.

Reeve's Tale

MSS, Prints, and Editions: See under Cant. Tales, Eds. of Works, Eds. of Cant. Tales. Portions are in Corson, see Section III D here.

Modernizations and Translations: Modernized by Betterton in 1712, reprinted by Ogle, not by Lipscomb; modernized by Horne in his 1841 vol., by Saunders, by Purves, by F. Clarke. The Miller of Abingdon, an imit., according to Warton-Hazlitt II : 362 note, is printed Wright, Anecd. Lit. Translated into German by Fiedler, by Hertzberg, by von Düring; into French by Chatelain; see Section III E here.

Source, Analogues, etc.: See Ch. Soc. Orig. and Anal. pp. 85, 93;
see Engl. Stud. 9 : 240 (Varnhagen); Koeppel in Anglia 14 :
249.

Notes: See N. and Q. 1871, II : 144, 202. Warton-Hazlitt II :
361-2 mentions "an old English poem on the same plan", see
above. On the Reeve see Todd, Illustrations p. 259; Saunders
p. 140; Thorold Rogers, Six Centuries of Work and Wages,
pp. 48 ff.; Skeat V : 50-51, 112-128.

Cook's Tale

MSS, Prints, and Editions: See under the Canterbury Tales above.
Ashmole's copy of this Tale and of that of Gamelyn are in MS
Ashmole 45.

Modernizations and Translations: See under Gamelyn, Section V
here; see the work of F. Clarke, of Darton, in Section III E
above.

Date: This Tale was left unfinished by Chaucer. See ten Brink,
Hist. Eng. Lit. II : 155-156, for the view that Chaucer abandoned
this Tale, realizing that three stories of the same stamp in succession would be too much; see on the relative date under F
above.

Notes: On the last page of the 1687 Chaucer appears the following
"Advertisement." "Whilst this work was just finishing, we
hapned to meet with a Manuscript, wherein we found the Conclusion of the *Cook's Tale,* and also of the *Squire's Tale* (which
in the Printed Books are said to be lost, or never finish'd by the
Author,) but coming so late to our hands, they could not be ·
inserted in their proper places, therefore the Reader is desir'd
to add them, as here directed. Immediately after what you find
of the Cook's Tale, add this:

What thorow himself & his felaw þt fought
Unto a mischief both they were brought,
The tone ydamned to prison perpetually,
The tother to deth, for he couth not of clergy,
And therefore yong men learne while ye may,
That with many diverse thoughts beth pricked all the day,
Remembre you what mischief cometh of misgouernaunce,
Thus mowe ye learn worschip and come to substaunce:
Think how grace and governaunce hath brought aboune
Many a poore man'ys Son chefe state of the Town,
Euer rule thee after the best man of name,
And God may grace thee to come to þe same."

For the remainder of the Advertisement see under the Squire's Tale. The twelve lines above printed are found in MS Bodley 686. Thomas, in the preface to the Urry Chaucer, printed both these conclusions, repudiating them. Tyrwhitt, Appendix to the Preface, note m, refers to them as spurious, and says that the conclusion to the Cook's Tale is in Bodley 686, which has also "at least thirty more lines" inserted in different parts of the Tale.

In MS Rawl. 141 this Tale has a 4-line conclusion; there is no tale of Gamelyn. A link Cook-Gamelyn of 4 lines is in Lansd. 851, printed Ch. Soc. Six-Text, Appendix to Group A. and with the Lansd. MS; a link of 2 lines is in Royal 18, Sloane 1685, Barlow, Laud 739, Petworth, Mm, Hatton; see Six-Text p. 129.

On the Cook see Saunders, p. 161 ff.; Todd's Illustrations pp. 251-3; Skeat V : 37, 128-131.

FRAGMENT B¹

The Man of Law's Tale, with headlink, prologue, and endlink.

There are several difficulties connected with this group, viz.: (1) That of the endlink, and the differences existing among the MSS as to the Tale next following. In one large group of MSS line 17 of the endlink contains the name of the Squire, and the Squire's Tale follows; see under F here, and Mod. Phil. 3 : 163, for attempted explanation. In the important group of MSS headed by the Ellesmere the endlink is not present; according to Bradshaw, it was cut out of that type of MSS, perhaps by a reviser after Chaucer's death. In Harley 7334 and at least two other MSS (see Mod. Phil. 3 : 164) the word *Sompnour,* instead of *Squire,* appears in line 17 of the endlink; but the D fragment, not the Sompnour's Tale, follows, as is the case in the Ellesmere group. Note the opinion of ten Brink, Hist. Eng. Lit. II : 160, that Chaucer had the Sompnour in view at this point. In one MS only, the Selden, the word *Shipman* appears in line 17 of the endlink, and the Shipman's Tale follows. This arrangement recommended itself to Bradshaw and to the Chaucer Society, largely because the sequence of Tales appearing when Bradshaw "lifted" the fragment headed by the Shipman up to follow the Man of Law corresponded more nearly to the geography of the pilgrims' road; for the allusion to Rochester which the Monk's headlink (in the B² fragment) contains, was thereby made to precede the allusion to Sittingbourne, ten miles further from London, which is found in the Sompnour's headlink, in the D fragment. See Temp. Pref. pp. 21-22. It should however be noted that although the Selden MS joins B¹ and B², it does not move B² up to follow B¹, as Bradshaw and modern editors arrange the Tales, but moves B¹ down to meet B², late in the Tales. (Its archetype, of course, may have had the two parts of B connected and following A, while the confusion reflected in the Selden may have arisen later.) In the de Worde print of 1498 this endlink connects Merchant and Squire.

In consequence of the arrangement adopted by Bradshaw, Furnivall, and Skeat, as above mentioned, the Man of Law's endlink is usually spoken of as the Shipman's prologue; but see Mod. Phil. 3 : 164.

Another difficulty, or group of difficulties, is (2) that of the headlink. This contains an allusion to Chaucer and to some of his work, a censure of two narratives which are related by Gower in the Confessio Amantis, and a statement by the Man of Law that he will speak in prose, although the tale which follows is in verse, and is, moreover, based on the same original as is one of the longest narratives of Gower in the Confessio Amantis. Our lack of definite knowledge as to the personal relations of Chaucer and Gower or as to the relative dates of Chaucer's and Gower's stories adds to the puzzle. So far as known, the relations of the two poets were as follows: When Chaucer was sent on a mission abroad in 1378, he appointed Gower one of his attorneys during his absence, see Life-Records IV : 216; Chaucer dedicated the Troilus to Gower and to Strode; and Gower has in his epilogue to the first recension of the Confessio Amantis a passage alluding to Chaucer, Venus speaking of him as her disciple, and bidding him set an end of all his work with a testament of love; this passage does not appear in later recensions of the Confessio, not even in that which, according to Macaulay (Works of John Gower II : xxii) was issued a few months after completion of the first version.

Many students, viewing the facts above given, have seen in them material for a theory of strained relations or actual quarrel between the two poets. Thus Tyrwhitt, in his Introd. Disc. § xiv, said that Chaucer's allusions to Canace and to Apollonius, in the headlink, were "unlucky" if Chaucer "really did not mean to reflect upon his old friend." Godwin, giving the rein to his imagination, described the quarrel, see his Life of Chaucer, chaps. 17 and 51. Todd, p. xxvii note, seems to agree with Tyrwhitt; Hertzberg, p. 613, is convinced that the sharpness of Chaucer's censure must have caused feeling upon Gower's part; Maetzner, Altengl. Sprachpr. I : 348, thinks that undisturbed friendship between two poets who were unequal rivals in ability needs positive proof; Simon, Ch. Soc. Essays, part III p. 291, thinks that their estrangement may have been due to religious differences, Chaucer inclining to Wicliffite doctrines; Bell, in his Chaucer ed. of 1854, II : 9-10, says that Tyrwhitt's conjecture has not yet been satisfactorily disproved; ten Brink, Hist. Eng. Lit. II : 159, considers that Chaucer refers to Gower in the Man of Law's headlink, and in a way which shows

that "the old friendship of the two poets was now somewhat
cooled"; *ibid.* p. 196 he says that Gower certainly omitted the compliment to Chaucer from his epilogue on personal and not political
grounds. Previous comment was reviewed by Meyer, in John
Gower's Beziehungen zu Chaucer und König Richard II, diss. Bonn,
1889, pp. 73. Meyer, pp. 10-12, thinks that Chaucer merely intended
to tease Gower by his words in the ML headlink, but the irascible
Gower took offence, and removed Chaucer's name from the Confessio; that this removal was deliberate, and not due to scribal
omission, is shown by the exact agreement in number of lines
removed and lines inserted in the revision. (See Macaulay as cited
below.)   Skeat, III: 413-17, decides that the asperity of Chaucer's
references to Gower's tales was deliberate, and that in consequence
Gower may well have thought fit to omit the allusion to Chaucer
from the Confessio. Kittredge, Nation 1895 I : 240, regards this
view as without ground. Lowes, Publ. Mod. Lang. Assn., 20 : 789-
90 note, speaks of Chaucer's allusions to the two objectionable tales
as "generally conceded to be a goodnatured fling at Gower."

On the other hand, Sir Harris Nicolas, in his Life of Chaucer,
considered that Gower's excision of Chaucer's name was after the
latter's death, and not prompted by any feelings of anger; upon
which Hertzberg remarks that if Chaucer were no longer living,
this was all the more reason for a complimentary reference to him
by his surviving friend. Wright, in his ed. of the CT, I : 204 note,
says that there is no foundation for believing that Chaucer in the
ML headlink was censuring Gower for "cursed stories", since one
of them at least was very common in the Middle Ages. Pauli, in
his 1857 ed. of the Confessio Amantis, I : xv, thought that the
"timid and obsequious" Gower omitted the verses referring to
Chaucer because Chaucer was then in trouble with the government,
and that neither this omission nor Chaucer's words in the headlink
were intended as any disrespect to a friend. Ward, Life of Chaucer,
p. 83, and Morley, Eng. Writers V : 325, think there is no reason
for believing that Chaucer intended a reflection on Gower. Bech,
Anglia 5 : 376, thinks that the two narratives censured by the Man
of Law are censured because of the criminal illegality upon which
they turn, not because of any reflection by Chaucer upon Gower.
Macaulay, ed. of Gower, II : xxviii, considers that the omission of
Chaucer's name from the epilogue may have been accidental, and
devoid of any personal intent. (See Meyer as cited above.) Root,
Poetry of Chaucer, p. 184 note 2, dismisses the quarrel-theory as
false. Tatlock, Devel. and Chronol. p. 173 note 2, rejects Macaulay's
suggestion, and thinks that we cannot deny the existence of some
ill-feeling between Chaucer and Gower.

Regarding the commonness of the story of Canace, observe
that Rymer, Short View of Tragedy pp. 76-77, says that
Suetonius mentions *Canace parturiens* among the plays in which

Nero performed. Sperone Speroni composed a tragedy of
Canace after the model of the ancients. Lydgate narrates the
story at the end of Book I of the Falls of Princes.

Of the two other, and lesser, difficulties in the headlink, the
closing sentence "I speke in prose", introducing not a prose, but a
verse tale, has occasioned some comment. Furnivall, cited by Skeat
V : 141, thought that the Tale of Melibeus was originally intended
to follow instead of the story of Constance; Skeat III : 406 thinks
that the sentence is to be taken as meaning "I usually speak in
prose", a view which is opposed by Lounsbury, Studies III : 436.
Lowes, Publ. Mod. Lang. Assn. 20 : 795 ff., suggests that a prose
Tale was originally intended to follow, a rendering of part of Pope
Innocent's De Contemptu Mundi, but that Chaucer wearied of the
work and discarded all but the verse-prologue on poverty, which is
from the Contemptu, and which still precedes the Tale. Additional
ground for this hypothesis is found in the time-connection which
Lowes *ibid.* has argued between the Man of Law's headlink and the
revision of the prol. LGW; in the A-version of this prol. (according to Lowes the later of the two) there are added two lines which
include a translation of Pope Innocent among Chaucer's works.
On either this hypothesis or that of Furnivall, the "I speke in prose"
would represent one of Chaucer's oversights, failures to correct
details after alteration of his first plan. And see under F above.

The third of the difficulties in this headlink, the allusion to
Chaucer and his work, has troubled commentators mainly because
of the non-agreement between the contents of the LGW as here
given and as actually existing. See ten Brink, Studien p. 123;
Hertzberg p. 611; Bech, Anglia 5 : 371 ff.; Lounsbury, Studies
I : 416-18; Skeat III : xxvi ff.; Lowes, Publ. Mod. Lang. Assn. 20 :
817-19 note.

The headlink is connected in date with the A-version of the
LGW prologue, ca. 1394, by Lowes as cited 20 : 863. If its allusions
to Canace and to Apollonius are understood as meaning Gower's
versions of those stories, it is probably to be dated later than 1390,
the year in which the first recension of the Confessio was completed, see Macaulay loc. cit. II : xxi ff. All earlier commentators
on the relations between Chaucer and Gower, including Skeat, have
supposed a date anterior to 1390, see Pauli, Hales, etc., as cited by
Macaulay; and the arguments as to Chaucer's influencing Gower,
or vice versa, have been biased by this belief. See below under
Date of the Tale.

Lounsbury, Studies I : 416-418, has notes on the headlink. On
p. 418 he says that it must antedate the Medea of the Legend of
Good Women, because of the difference in the treatment of Medea's
story. It may be queried, see under F above, whether the lines in
the ML headlink,

> But Chaucer, though he can but lewedly
> On metres and on ryming craftely

do not argue a date for the headlink later than the assignment of the Rime of Sir Thopas to Chaucer, and later than the writing of the Host's interruption to that Tale, in which the language is closely similar to that of this Link; the allusion to Chaucer here loses its point unless his public failure as a narrator in verse had already been made.

Tatlock, Devel. and Chronol. chap. V § 6, dates the Man of Law's headlink after the first prologue to the Legend, and before the assignment of the Constance story to the Man of Law. For view that the headlink is a composite written at two different dates, see under F above.

The headlink contains an astrological statement of the day and hour of the pilgrimage. The MSS differ in their readings; see Skeat V : 132-4. Furnivall, Temp. Pref. pp. 20, 42, thinks that the Tale falls on the second day of the pilgrimage; Skeat, V : 132, seems to think the first day possible; see Koch, Chronology pp. 56-57, for advocacy of this theory, doubted by Tatlock, Publ. Mod. Lang. Assn. 21 : 478 ff., and supported p. 258 above.

Lounsbury, Nation 1889 II : 10-11, Studies I : 426, II : 329-334, first pointed out the source of parts of the prologue to the ML Tale in Pope Innocent's De Contemptu Mundi, and suggested that these passages were the remains of the transl. of the "Wrecched Engendrynge of Mankind" mentioned by Chaucer among his works in the A-version of the prol. to the LGW. See Koeppel in Archiv 84 : 405-13. For further conjecture as to this translation see Lowes, Publ. Mod. Lang. Assn. 20 : 795-6.

The Man of Law's Tale

MSS, Prints, and Editions: See under MSS of the Cant. Tales, Eds. of Works, Eds. of Cant. Tales. A copy of this Tale is listed in the Cambridge University Library Catalogue of MSS II : 31-33, under Ee ii, 15.

In the Selections of Southey; extracts in Ward; the Tale in Paton, in Robertson, selections in Corson; see Section III D here.

Modernizations and Translations: Modernized by Brooke, printed in Ogle, separately in 1778, repr. in Lipscomb, and in Chalmers vol. 17 p. 382. By Cowden Clarke, by Saunders, by Purves, by F. Clarke, by Pitt-Taylor, by Calder, by Darton, by Skeat.

Translated into German by Fiedler, by Hertzberg, by von Düring; into French by Chatelain; into Italian by Chiarini; see Section III E here.

Source, Analogues, etc.: Tyrwhitt thought that Chaucer took the story, with very little variation, from Gower, see Introd. Disc.

§ xv. The derivation of Gower's story from Trivet's French prose Chronicles was first shown by Wright, in his ed. of the CT, I : 206; he supposed that Chaucer's original was a French romance, see *ibid.* p. 205 footnote. In 1872 Trivet's Chronicles (the portion of them in question here) were ed. for the Ch. Soc. Orig. and Anal. (pp. 1 ff.) by Mr. Edmund Brock, who in his introd. pointed out that Chaucer also derived the story from Trivet. See, earlier, Athen. 1869 II : 873. See:

Das Leben der Constanze bei Trivet, Gower, und Chaucer. E. Lücke. Anglia 14 : 77-122 and 147-185 (1892).

Lücke considers that Chaucer used both Trivet and Gower. Skeat III : 415 ff. and Macaulay, ed. of Gower II : 483-4, both restate Lücke's results, but Skeat arrives at a different conclusion, that Gower used Chaucer's work. To this he is apparently led by his assumption of a first form of the Man of Law's Tale, seen by Gower while he was working on his story of Constance; he stated his theory in a paper before the Cambridge Philological Society, reported in abstract Acad. 1893 I : 246. Kittredge, Nation 1895 I : 240, considers Skeat's arguments for revision "not at all convincing." Tatlock, Devel. and Chronol., chap. V § 6, dates Chaucer later than Gower and thinks that Chaucer had read Gower's work.

Other analogues of the Constance story are printed in Ch. Soc. Orig. and Anal. pp. 57-70, 71-84, 221-250, 365-414. For a discussion of the cycle of stories to which the Tale belongs see Suchier, Oeuvres poétiques de Philippe de Rémi, Sire de Beaumanoir, Paris, 2 vols., 1884-5, vol. 1, pp. xxiii ff. See also: The Constance Saga. A. B. Gough. Berlin, 1902, 84 pp. (vol. 23 of Palaestra), reviewed Archiv 111 : 453, Centrbl. 1902 p. 1433, Engl. Stud. 32 : 110-13. See: Der Konstanze-Griseldistypus in der engl. Literatur bis auf Shakspere. O. Siefken. Rathenow, 1902, 110 pp. (Beilage zum Jahresber. des Progymnasiums zu Rathenow), also Siefken's diss. (Leipzig) on Das geduldige Weib in der engl. Literatur bis auf Shakspere. Teil I. Der Konstanzetypus, Rathenow. 1903, pp. 77. In the Archiv 84 : 406-13 Koeppel shows traces of Innocent's influence on Chaucer.

Date: Skeat III : 408-9 posits an earlier version, about 1380, which was revised and added to the Tales about 1387. Herford, Eng. Tales in Verse, p. xxvi note, Pollard, Primer p. 70, Globe Chaucer p. xxvi, date the Tale as early work, Pollard putting it just anterior to 1380. Tatlock, Devel. and Chronol. chap. V § 6, dates the tale very probably after 1390, after the appearance of Gower's Confessio Amantis.

Notes: The inappropriateness of this Tale to the Man of Law was remarked by Lounsbury, Studies III : 436 and Nation 1889 II : 10-11; also by Pollard, Globe Chaucer p. xxvi. Ten Brink, Hist. Eng. Lit. II : 157-9, thinks that Chaucer may have meant to relate the Tale himself; so Siefken as above. Brandl in Paul's Grdr. II : 679 sees satirical intent in the assignment of the Tale. See Lowes, Publ. Mod. Lang. Assn. 20 : 796; and see under F above.

On the Tale see Lounsbury, Studies II : 489-90; Skeat III : 405 ff., V : 132 ff. On the Man of Law see Fortescue's De Laudibus Legum Angliae, chaps. 50, 51; Todd's Illustrations p. 244; Saunders pp. 100 ff.; Flügel, Anglia 24 : 484-96.

In the painting of Ford Madox Brown, "Chaucer at the Court of King Edward III", Chaucer is supposed to be reading aloud from the story of Constance. This painting, executed in 1851, hangs in the Municipal Gallery, Sydney, Australia; it is reprod. in Hueffer's 1896 life of the artist pp. 71-2, in Bryan's Dictionary of Painters and Engravers I : 202, in Hunt's Preraphaelitism I : to face p. 124.

FRAGMENT B²

In the opinion of students such as Bradshaw, Furnivall, and Skeat, the Tale of the Shipman, with which this Fragment opens, is bound to the Man of Law's Tale by the Link which these scholars term the "Shipman's prologue", but which is here spoken of as the Man of Law's endlink. The Fragment is otherwise composed of the Shipman's Tale, the Link to the Prioress, her Tale, the Link connecting that to the Rime of Sir Thopas, the Rime, its interruption by the Host, the prose Tale of Melibeus, the Link between that and the Monk, the latter's Tale and its interruption by Knight and Host, the Tale of the Nun's Priest. Six MSS, Caxton's second ed. of the Tales, and de Worde's ed. of 1498, have after the Nun's Priest's Tale an epilogue of 16 lines, the last line of which is, in three MSS and the two prints, "Said to another as ye shall hear", no definite pilgrim being introduced. But in the other three MSS this line has been altered to read "Said to the Nun" etc., with an addition of six spurious lines and the placing of the Second Nun's Tale next. The MSS are Adds. 5140 and Egerton 2864, formerly the two Askew MSS discussed by Tyrwhitt in his note on line 15468, where he prints the six spurious lines from them; the other codex showing the additional lines is Hodson 39, whence the lines are printed Ch. Soc. Specimens part V, 2nd Suppl. p. 75. The genuine Link exists in Cambridge Dd, Christ Church, and Royal 17, whence it is printed in the Six-Text p. 301, along with the Chaucerian portion of the Adds. MS epilogue.[1]

There is a spurious link of 12 lines Pardoner-Shipman in Rawl.

[1] My note in Modern Philology 3 : 174 should be emended by the above.

poet. 149, Harley 1758, Sloane 1685, Egerton 2863, Barlow, Laud 739, Royal 18, Petworth, Mm, Hatton, Ii; it would accordingly seem that this addition is characteristic of the groups IV (c) and (d) of the classification on p. 172 here. Specimens of this Link, excepting Rawlinson and Harley 1758, are printed Ch. Soc. Specimens of Moveable Prologues pp. 26-30. A spurious headlink of six lines introduces the Shipman's Tale in the Lansdowne MS; it is printed in Wright's 1847 Chaucer, II : 283 note, and in the Ch. Soc. separate print of Lansdowne, p. 456.

There is in Trin. Coll. Cambr. R 3, 3 a spurious prologue to the Rime of Sir Thopas, viz.:

> Whan Chaucers be oure oost was praide
> To telle a tale he is nat withsaid
> But beningly and with gode chere
> Began his tale and saide as folwith hiere.

The same MS adds to the 48 lines of the Thopas-Melibeus link,

> Wich anon in prose I wol telle in this presence
> Of Melibe & his wif & there dougter Sapience.

According to Furnivall, N. and Q. 1872 I : 353, the Delamere MS has four spurious lines at the end of Sir Thopas.

The interruption by the Host to the Rime of Sir Thopas has been discussed by Saintsbury, Hist. of Criticism I : 450-52, as the typical example of Chaucer's critical ability.

The link at the close of the Monk's Tale has in some MSS, Caxton II, and the 1498 de Worde a different (and briefer) form from that seen in the generality of MSS; see p. 242 ante.

On the fragment see ten Brink, Hist. Eng. Lit. II : 172-179, III : 268-70; Root, Poetry of Chaucer pp. 187-218.

Shipman's Tale

MSS, Prints, and Editions: See under MSS of Cant. Tales, Editions of Cant. Tales. This Tale is lacking, with the link Shipman-Prioress, in MS Harley 7333. Extracts are in Robertson, see Section III D here.

Modernizations and Translations: Mod. by Jackson in 1750; by Lipscomb, by Saunders.

Translated into German by Hertzberg, by von Düring; into French by Chatelain; see Section III E here.

Originals and Analogues: Tyrwhitt said, Introd. Disc. § xxxi, that "this tale is generally supósed to be taken from the Decameron, Day 8, Novella 1, but I should rather believe that Chaucer was obliged to some old French Fableour, from whom Boccace had also borrowed the groundwork of his Novel." Ten Brink, Hist. Eng. Lit. II : 172, Skeat III : 420, agree.

Date: Koch, Chronology p. 79, puts this Tale, with others, in 1389-90. See Tatlock, Devel. and Chronol., chap. V, § 8.

Notes: It was first remarked by Tyrwhitt, in his note on line 12942, that the pronouns here "would lead one to suspect that this Tale was originally intended for a female character." Bell, in his ed. of 1854, III : 92 note, considers Tyrwhitt's suggestion "scarcely credible." Hertzberg, p. 643-4, is of the same opinion as Tyrwhitt; von Düring, III : 427-8, cites ten Brink as suggesting that this Tale was once a woman's; von Düring adds, perhaps the Wife of Bath's, though the matter is not fully decided, and it may even be that Chaucer would allow himself the liberty of varying his pronouns in a Tale which presents now the views of one sex, now those of another. Ten Brink himself, Hist. Eng. Lit. II : 172, says the Tale "was originally written for the Wife of Bath." See Skeat III : 421. See under F above.

On the Shipman and the barge "Maudelayne" see Karkeek in Ch. Soc. Essays part V; a paper on medieval shipping is in Barnard's Companion to Eng. Hist., Oxford 1902. See Saunders p. 151 ff.; Skeat V : 38-39, 168-173; Todd's Illustrations p. 253.

Prioress' Tale

MSS, Prints, and Editions: See under Cant. Tales, Eds. of Works, Eds. of Cant. Tales. A copy of this Tale and of the Second Nun's Tale, without other of the Tales, are found in MS Harley 2382; a copy of this Tale alone is found in MS Harley 2251; the first 180 lines are in Rawlinson C 86. This Tale is printed, with that of the Pardoner, in Morris' Specimens, Oxford 1867, from Harley 7334; in Skeat's revision of Morris' work, 1872, 1889, these Tales are not reprinted, but the Man of Law's Tale is used instead. Privately printed Guilford 1902. In the Selections of Johnstone of 1855, of Herford 1902, of Robertson 1902; see Section III D here.

Modernizations and Translations: By Lipscomb; by Wordsworth, printed in 1820 and following eds. of his poems; by Cowden Clarke, 1835; by Saunders; by Purves in 1870; by Pitt-Taylor; by Calder; by Skeat; by Mackaye; see Section III E here.

Translated into German by Hertzberg, by von Düring; into French by Chatelain; see Section III E here.

Originals and Analogues: See Ch. Soc. Orig. and Anal. pp. 107, 251, 273; see Foerster in Archiv 110 : 427; see Child, English and Scottish Ballads, vol. III : 233 ff.; see Life and Miracles of St. William of Norwich, ed. Jessopp and James, Cambridge, 1896; see C. F. Brown, Chaucer's Prioress' Tale and its

Analogues, in Publ. Mod. Lang. Assn. 21 : 486-518. Regarding lines in the description of the Prioress from the Roman de la Rose, see under the Sources of the General Prologue, ante. See Skeat III : 421.

Date: "Probably belongs to the later period", Skeat III : 421; "written after the conception of the plan of the Cant. Tales", Pollard, Globe Chaucer xxvi; "certainly late", Lowes, Publ. Mod. Lang. Assn. 20 : 848; "probably later" than Troilus, Saintsbury, Hist. Eng. Prosody, I : 157. See under F above.

Notes: Several cruces are found in the description of the Prioress, viz.:

(1) Her greatest oath, by Saint Loy, Prol. line 120.

See Todd's Illustrations p. 234; Acad. 1880 II: 64, 137; Furnivall in Anglia 4: 238; Hertzberg p. 581; Hales in Athen. 1891 I: 54, Ellis and Belinfante ibid. 1892 I: 150, 214. Hales is repr. Folia Litteraria p. 102-5. Warton, in his Hist. Eng. Poetry, thought that Loy was a corruption of Louis; this opinion is cited by Skeat V : 14, but excised from the ed. of Warton by Hazlitt and others, III : 364. Skeat loc. cit. refers to Hales' theory, that Chaucer means us to understand that the Prioress never swore at all, as interesting, but apparently does not wish to settle the question. See Mod. Lang. Notes 22: 51.

(2) Her French of Stratford atte Bowe, Prol. line 125.

Tyrwhitt, in his note on this line and in note 55 of his Essay, advanced the theory that Chaucer "thought but meanly of the English-French spoken in his time." This opinion was later disputed: N. and Q. 1870 II: 386, 465; 1890 I: 305, 414, 497, II: 57, 98, 298, 392; 1904 I: 122. See Mod. Lang. Notes 8: 57, 19: 62; Lounsbury, Studies II: 457. Kittredge in Nation 1895 I : 240 says that Skeat's note V : 15 is "the very worst note ever written on a passage of Chaucer." Minor note N. and Q. 1906 II : 326.

(3) Her nun-chaplain and three priests, Prol. line 164.

Tyrwhitt, Introd. Disc. § vi, considered the text here as due to interpolation, and believed that Chaucer had cut out a portion, which was patched up by some one else. Bradshaw, Coll. Papers p. 110, agreed with Tyrwhitt, and suggested as a probable reading:

Another Nonne with hire had she certeyn
And eke a Prest that was here chapelleyn.

Hertzberg p. 581 would emend, and offers:

Than was her chapellein, a preest, thes thre.

Furnivall, Acad. 1874 I : 89 and Ch. Soc. Essays pt. III, shows that in medieval abbeys women could hold chaplaincies; he defends the passage as it stands. Hales, Acad. 1874 I : 121, repr. Folia Litteria 106-7, accepts the chaplain, but agrees with Tyrwhitt otherwise. See N. and Q. 1888 II : 485, Acad. 1890 II : 152, 1894 II : 86. Skeat III : 380, cp. V : 19, accepts the nun-chaplain, but agrees with Tyrwhitt in rejecting "and prestes thre." The suggestion was made by ten Brink that "& prestes þre" was misread by scribes from "a prest parde." In Athen. 1906 I : 231, 265, 299, 329 is a correspondence over the suggestion of Kastner, "a prest estré."

For the Jews in England see refs. given by Gross, Sources and Literature of English History, p. 510, especially Jacobs' Jews of Angevin England, Lond. 1893.

On the "little clergeon" of the Tale see C. F. Brown in Mod. Phil. 3 : 467-491. See Todd, Illustrations p. 233; Saunders, pp. 369-376; Lounsbury, Studies II : 490-91; Skeat V : 13-19, 173-182.

Brandl, Grdr. II : 680, terms the Prioress' Tale a "Verspottung kindischer Legenden."

Rime of Sir Thopas

MSS, Prints, and Editions: See under MSS of the Cant. Tales, Eds. of the Cant. Tales, Eds. of Works. Included in the selections of Sanford and Walsh, 1819, see Section III D here; in Burlesque Plays and Poems, ed. Morley, Lond. 1885.

Modernizations and Translations: In Lipscomb of 1795; in Horne of 1841, by "Z. A. Z."; in Purves of 1870, see Section III E here.
    Transl. into German by Hertzberg, by von Düring; into French by Chatelain; into Italian prose by Chiarini; see Section III E here. In Choyce Drollery, 1656, is an imitation, according to Lounsbury, Studies III : 118. Dunbar's burlesque Sir Thomas Norray is in the same stanza; see also Drayton's ballad of Dowsabell, in his 8th Eclogue.

Date: Skeat III : 423 says of the headlink that it "evidently belongs to the late period; we recognize here some of the author's best work"; of the Tale he says ibid.: "Judging by the rhythm-test, this might be of early workmanship; but judging by the language, it is late." See also under F above.

Title: According to Skeat, V : 183, this Tale is called "The ryme of Sir Thopas" in the blackletter editions, a title not found in the seven best MSS. The Caxtons mark it "Ryme of sir Topas", "Ryme of Syr Thopas"; Thynne of 1532 agrees with

Caxton II. Of the printed MSS, Ellesmere and Hengwrt mark
it "Chaucers tale of Thopas", Gg "Chaucers tale of sere
Thopas", Corpus "þe tale of Chaucer of sire Thopas", Petworth
"Sire Thopace."

Relation to Medieval Romance Literature: The burlesque character
of this poem was first discussed by Bishop Hurd, in his Letters
on Chivalry and Romance, pubd. in 1762, and included in vol. 4
of the 1811 ed. of his works, pp. 335 ff. Hurd quotes "a curious
Observer", and does not apparently make the statement on his
own responsibility; he is cited by Warton, in his Observations
on Spenser's Faery Queene, sect. V, and Hist. Eng. Poetry;
Tyrwhitt, in his notes on lines 13692, 13739, also cites Hurd.
In the latter passage Tyrwhitt refers to Hurd the opinion that
the story of the giant Olyphaunt and Chylde Thopas was not a
fiction of Chaucer's own, but "a story of antique fame." This
opinion is apparently favored by Thomas Wright, see his ed. of
the Cant. Tales, vol. II, p. 311 note, a view denied by Hertzberg,
p. 49, pp. 646 ff.

On the Tale as an imitation of the Romances see: Chaucers
Sir Thopas. J. Bennewitz, diss. Halle, 1879. Rev. Lindner,
Engl. Stud. 4 : 339-40, and discussed at length, with additional
matter, by Kölbing, Engl. Stud. 11 : 495-511.

Early English romances to be compared with Sir Thopas are:
Sir Isumbras, Sir Perceval of Galles, Sir Eglamour, all ed. by
Halliwell in the Thornton Romances; Sir Bevis of Hamtoun,
ed. Kölbing, EETS; Sir Guy of Warwick, ed. Zupitza, EETS;
Li Beaus Desconus, ed. Kaluza, Leipzig, 1890; Sir Tristrem, ed.
Kölbing, Heilbronn, 1878-82; Sir Orfeo, ed. Zielke, Breslau,
1879; Richard Coer de Lion, ed. Weber, Metrical Romances,
vol. III; Horn Childe, ed. Ritson, Ancient Metr. Romances;
Octavian, ed. Sarrazin, Heilbronn, 1885; Squyr of Lowe Degre,
ed. Mead, Boston, 1904.

Notes: On this Tale and its interruption see Courthope, Hist. Eng.
Poetry I : 259, "Here we see the germs of literary criticism."
See Saintsbury, Hist. of Criticism, I : 451-2, for insufficient
comment.

With regard to the metre of the Tale, Urry's ed. heads the
poem with the statement that it was "purposely utter'd by
Chaucer in a Rime and Style differing from the rest, as though
he himself were not the Author, but only the Reporter of the
other Tales." To this interpretation Bennewitz as above pp. 24-
25 objects, and follows Hertzberg p. 646, von Düring III : 433,
Schipper Engl. Metrik I : 286 in thinking that Chaucer varied
his metre in imitation of the wavering methods of the ro-
mancers. On the other hand, Tyrwhitt opined that some lines

were lost; and Kölbing, in his review of Bennewitz as above, considers that the variations are due to bad scribal transmission.

The lax rime *chivalrye: Gy* in lines 188-191, pointed out by Bradshaw, has never been regarded as evidence against the authenticity of the poem, cp. Saintsbury, Hist. of Criticism I : 450 footnote, and Hist. Eng. Prosody I : 145 footnote. See Skeat V : 199, Lounsbury, Studies I : 388.

Others of the Cant. Tales which have been treated as of satirical intent are: the Monk's Tale (by Lowell), Melibeus (by Ker); and Brandl, Grdr. II : 680, views the Prioress' Tale and the Man of Law's Tale as of such purpose.

Sir Thomas Wyatt, in his epistle to Poines, mentions this Tale as one which he cannot prefer to that of the Knight. Godwin, chap. 55, remarks that in this Tale Chaucer declared open war against the romance manner. See Hertzberg as cited above; Lounsbury, Studies II : 201; Skeat II : 423 ff., V : 183 ff.; Herford, Eng. Tales in Verse, p. xxv; Ker in Quart. Review April 1903, p. 447, repr. Essays in Medieval Literature.

Tale of Melibeus

MSS, Prints, and Editions: See under MSS of the Cant. Tales, Eds. of Works, Eds. of the Cant. Tales.

A copy of this Tale and of the Parson's Tale are in Pepys 2006, without other of the Canterbury Tales. According to Report II of the Hist. MSS Commission, p. 145, there is a copy of the Tale of Melibeus in a MS at Stonehurst College; according to Ward's Catalogue II : 224 there is a copy in MS Arundel 140; according to Bernard there was a copy among the Norfolk MSS at Gresham College, London. Bernard also mentions, as 5264.32, "Melibeus, sive Moralia Praecepta rythmis. Lingua Belgica"; in the Bodleian, given by Mareschall.

The Tale is printed separately in Maetzner's Altenglische Sprachproben, from Morris' text of 1866. For note on a lost print, see under Plowman's Tale in Section V here.

Modernizations and Translations: In the Lipscomb of 1795; a condensed mod. in Purves of 1870. See under III E above.

Source, Analogues, etc.: Tyrwhitt, in his Introd. Disc. § xxxiv, gave "Le Livre de Melibee et de Dame Prudence" as the source, mentioning no author, but referring to MS copies in French prose. Brock, in N. and Q. 1869 I : 30, shows the connection of this narrative with Albertanus Brixiensis' Liber Consolationis, which latter has been ed. for the Ch. Soc. by Thor

19

Sundby, 1875; see under Albertanus in Section II C (4) here. Echoes in Melibeus from older "wisdom" collections are pointed out by Knust, Mitteilungen aus dem Escurial, Litt. Verein Stuttgart, vol. 141, 1879; see Boll in Anglia 21 : 228-9.

Date: Koch, Chronology p. 79, places the Melibeus, with other Tales, in 1386-7; Skeat II : xxxvii notes that the absence of any influence of Boethius upon it may place it anterior to that translation. For possible transfer of this earlier-written Tale from the Man of Law to Chaucer see under F above. See Tatlock, Devel. and Chronol. chap. V § 7.

The connection of this Tale with that of the Merchant is remarked by Koeppel, Archiv 86 : 34.

Notes: Thomas, in his MS notes to the Urry Chaucer, observed a blank verse movement in the flow of this Tale; see Tyrwhitt, who in his note on the Tale agrees with Thomas so far as the first part of the Tale is concerned. Guest, in his Hist. of Eng. Rhythms, ed. Skeat pp. 542-544, points out blank verse in the Tale.

On Chaucer's prose see Heussler, Die Stellung von Subjekt und Prädikat in der Erzählung des Melibeus und in der des Pfarrers in Chaucers Canterbury Tales, diss. Wesel, 1888, pp. 28.

Ker, in the introd. to the Chaucerian selections in vol. I of Craik's English Prose, says of the Melibeus, "perhaps the worst example that could be found of all the intellectual and literary vices of the Middle Ages, bathos, forced allegory, spiritless and interminable moralising." He remarks that its faults are so great that we are tempted to think the Tale a "mischievous companion to the Rime of Sir Thopas", but adds that this is however "a desperate suggestion." And again: this Tale is "beyond rivalry for its enjoyment of the weakest common-places" . . . . there is "a glow and unction about its medi-ocrity" . . . . "the intolerable arguments of Dame Prudence are a masterpiece, as though written in an orgy and enthusiasm of flatness and insipidity." Again, in his Essays on Medieval Literature, Ker calls this Tale a "thing incapable of life, ... a lump of the most inert first matter of medieval pedantry."

Without controverting Ker's strictures, it may not be out of place to remark that the average class of college students is more disposed to accept the Melibeus than to berate it; and that such denunciation as that of Professor Ker is the opinion of the highly trained modern literary critic. See Tatlock, Devel. and Chronol. p. 189. See Skeat V : 201-224.

Monk's Tale

MSS, Prints, and Editions: See under MSS of the Cant. Tales, Editions of Works, Editions of the Cant. Tales.

The Tale is copied in MS Trin. Coll. Cambr. R 3, 19, fol. 170b; see MacCracken in Mod. Lang. Notes 23 : 93.

The tale of Ugolino is in Herford, the Monk's Tale in Robertson, a bit in Corson; see Section III D here.

Modernizations and Translations: By Lipscomb, by Pitt-Taylor, by Purves. Translated into German by Hertzberg, by von Düring; into French by Chatelain; see Section III E here.

Source, Analogues, etc.: Plan from Boccaccio's De Casibus, the separate tragedies from various writers, as was pointed out by Tyrwhitt in his Introd. Disc. § xxxv. For Boccaccio see Section II C (3) here; and for the single stories see Skeat V : 227 ff., although Skeat has not sufficiently discussed the influence of Boccaccio.

Traces of the reading of Seneca's tragedies may be seen here, says Peiper in Fleckeisen's Jahrbuch für Philologie u. Pädagogik, 87 : 65 (1868).

See, for the influence of Innocent III, Koeppel in Archiv 84 : 416; for echo of the Roman de la Rose see Koeppel in Anglia 14 : 260.

For influence of the mythographers on the Croesus story see Gelbach in Jour. Gc. Phil. 6 : 657-660.

Date, and Order of Tragedies: The date 1385, alluded to in the tragedy of Barnabo, and the latest date thus far known to be indicated in the CT, need not be assumed as that at which the entire Monk's Tale was composed. The tragedy of Barnabo, with those of Peter of Spain and Peter of Cyprus which precede it and that of Ugolino following it, are not always found in the same position in the MSS; Tyrwhitt, who puts all these "modern instances" last, remarks, in his note on line 14685, that "in several MSS" they appear between the tragedies of Zenobia and of Nero. Modern eds., *e. g.* Skeat, Pollard, put them after Zenobia, in order to obtain clear connection with line 16 of the NP headlink. The variation in order of tragedies in this respect, although emphasized by Bradshaw as one of the tests necessary for classification of the MSS, has never been worked out. Note, as under F above, that the earlier form of the NP headlink has not the allusion to the Croesus tragedy.

With or without these modern instances, the Monk's Tale has been dated as follows; by Koch, Chronology p. 79, in 1386-7; by Skeat II : xxxvii as later than Boece, in its revised form;

in II : lvi Skeat seems to suggest that "the former part" of the Tale is earlier than the Troilus. See Tatlock, Devel. and Chronol. chap. V § 5, for opinion of relatively late date; see under F above for suggestion that the modern instances and the tragedy of Nero postdated Chaucer's knowledge of Dante, while the tragedy of Caesar preceded it.

Notes: On the Monk as described in the Prologue, and on passages there, see Flügel in Anglia 24 : 448 ff.

Chaucer's treatment of Brutus and Cassius as one person, line 707, is inadequately annotated by Skeat V : 245. Note that in the old English translation of the Consolatione, ch. xix, occurs "se waes haten brutus, oþre naman Cassius." This does not appear in the verse-rendering of the Metra, and is not annotated in even the most recent ed. of the Old English by Sedgefield, Oxford 1899; nor is it discussed by Schepss, Archiv 94 : 149-160, see p. 154. In Chaucer's own Boethius-rendering the error does not appear, see Skeat II : 49.

Lowell said: "In the Monk's Tale [Chaucer] slyly satirizes the longwinded morality of Gower." (Essay on Chaucer, in My Study Windows.)

For the several English versions of the tragedy of Ugolino (from Dante), see Toynbee, Mod. Lang. Rev. 1 : 9 ff. The story does not seem to have impressed Lydgate sufficiently to cause him to expand Boccaccio's two lines of Latin. (De Casibus bk. 9, Falls of Princes bk. 9 cap. 28.) In N. and Q. 1897 I : 205, 369, it is stated that Chaucer used Villani's chronicle for his Ugolino, as well as Dante.

On some of the lines in the Monk see O. F. Emerson, Mod. Phil. 1 : 105-115, Flügel, Jour. Gc. Phil. 1 : 126-155 and as above.   Minor refs. N. and Q. 1871 II : 449.

See Todd, Illustrations p. 237; Saunders p. 67; Skeat V : 19-24, 224-247.

For the persistence of this type of narrative see Lydgate's Falls of Princes, the Mirrour for Magistrates, Drayton's tragedy-poems, etc.

Nun's Priest's Tale

MSS, Prints, and Editions: See under MSS of the Cant. Tales, Eds. of the Cant. Tales, Eds. of Works.

In the selections of Paton, of Corson, of Warner; see under D above.

Separately ed. by W. C. Bamburgh, N. Y., 1902, the Grafton Press, blackletter.

Modernizations, Imitations, Translations: Imit. by Henryson, The

Taill of Schir Chantecleir and the Foxe, see ed. of Henryson
by G. Gregory Smith, vol. II of Henryson's Works, Scottish
Text Society 1906. Mod. by Dryden, The Cock and the Fox,
e. g., in the Scott-Saintsbury ed. of Dryden, III : 206 ff. Mod.
by Lipscomb, by Cowden Clarke, by Saunders, by Purves, by
Pitt-Taylor, by Calder, by Darton, by Skeat, by Mackaye; see
under III E above.

Transl. into German by Hertzberg, by von Düring; into
French by Chatelain; into Italian by Chiarini; see under E
above.

Source, Analogues, etc.: Tyrwhitt, Introd. Disc. § xxxvi, derived
this Tale from a Lai by Marie de France; see Ch. Soc. Orig.
and Anal. p. iii. Wright, in his ed. of the Cant. Tales, pointed
out the Roman de Renart as the more immediate source; see
Ch. Soc. Orig. and Anal. p. 333 ff., Skeat, Acad. 1887 I : 56,
Oxford Chaucer III : 431-3, VI : c. See in full:
On the Sources of the Nonne Prestes Tale. Kate O. Petersen.
Boston, 1898. Rev. Foulet, Romania 28 : 296; Koeppel, Engl.
Stud. 30 : 464.
See also: Cock and Fox: a critical Study of the History and
Sources of the Medieval Fable. E. P. Dargan, Mod. Phil.
4 : 39-65.

Date:

Notes: See Warton-Hazlitt II : 351-53, Petersen op. cit. pp. 94 ff.;
Quart. Rev. 1888 II : 340 ff.; Mather's ed. lxxiv ff.; Skeat in
Athen. 1896 II : 566, 677, Oxford Chaucer III : 431 ff., V : 247
ff.; ten Brink, Hist. Eng. Lit. II: 178; Saunders pp. 377-393.

Minor notes by Koeppel, Anglia 14 : 260. On the assignment
of this Tale see under F above.

Fragment C

The Doctor's Tale, without a (genuine) headlink; a link from
Doctor to Pardoner, and the Tale of the Pardoner, which has a
prologue by the Pardoner, and is followed by a sermon preached in
his characteristic manner; this latter provokes the Host's wrath,
and the fragment closes with his angry words and with peace-
making by the Knight. There is no clue as to the next speaker.
This fragment occupies three different positions in MSS and eds.
(1) after Fragment F, as in the Ellesmere group of MSS, in Harley
7335, and in Tyrwhitt and the eds. based upon his down to the work
of the Chaucer Society. (2) After Fragment G, as in most other
MSS, and in the Caxtons and the prints down to and including

Urry. (3) After B² as advocated by the Chaucer Society and adopted by subsequent eds.; although Skeat III : 434, calls the Ch. Soc. order arbitrary, and considers that this group should follow F. See Furnivall in Acad. 1894 II : 86.

Three forms of spurious prologue are found to this fragment. In Harley 7335 is one of six lines, which Tyrwhitt printed, though doubting the authenticity of all but its first line; this was reprinted by eds. using his text, and may be seen in a footnote to Skeat IV : 289, in Wright's ed. of 1847, II : 245-6, and in the Bell ed. of 1854, III : 56. Another prologue, of 16 lines, is found in MS Lansd. 851, and is printed by Wright, vol. II of the 1847 Chaucer, p. 245; it is also printed by Skeat III : 435. The third of these spurious prologues is found, according to Skeat, in the blackletter eds.; he reprints it, from the ed. of 1532, in III : 434; it is of 14 lines, and may be seen in the ed. by Morris, as well as in the eds. from 1532 down to and including Urry. It is found in MSS Selden, Rawl. poet. 149, Hatton, Sloane 1685, Barlow, Laud 739, Royal 17, Royal 18, Petworth, Mm; as Harley 1758 has a gap at this point, and the Ii conditions are unknown to me, it is possible that this link was a characteristic of the MS-groups IV (c) and (d) in my classification, p. 172 above.

Doctor's Tale

MSS, Prints, and Editions: See under MSS of the Cant. Tales, Eds. of the Cant. Tales, Eds. of the Works.
     In Sanford and Walsh, in Paton, in Corson; see above under D.

Modernizations and Translations: Mod. by Lipscomb, by Saunders, by Purves, by Pitt-Taylor, by Darton, by Mackaye; see under E here.
     Transl. into German by Hertzberg, by von Düring; into French by Chatelain; see under E here.

Source, Analogues, etc.: Tyrwhitt, in his Introd. Disc. § xxix, accepted Chaucer's statement regarding Livy as his authority, and thought that Chaucer might also have been indebted to Gower in some particulars, see the Confessio Amantis bk. VII. In his note on line 12074 Tyrwhitt adds the Roman de la Rose, as Chaucer's principal source. See Skeat III : 435-7, Lounsbury, Studies II : 279-284. Root, Poetry of Chaucer p. 221 ff., has transl. the French. See O. Rumbauer, Die Geschichte von Appius und Virginia in der engl. Literatur, diss. Breslau 1890, pp. 49. Note in Anglia 14 : 259-60 by Koeppel.

Date: "The Tales of the Man of Law, the Physician, and the

Second Nun, were all clearly composed before Chaucer had planned the Canterbury Tales, in which they were finally incorporated." Herford, Eng. Tales in Verse, p. xxvi note. See Tatlock, Devel. and Chronol. chap. V § 3. Ten Brink as below connects the close of the Tale with 1388.

Notes: Root, Poetry of Chaucer p. 219, thinks that this Tale was perhaps written for the Legend of Good Women, and that it does not fit the Doctor as he is described in the Prologue, because he is ignorant of the Bible, and this Tale contains the story of Jephthah's daughter. But note that the latter story is told by Gower in the Confessio. Kittredge, Mod. Phil. 1 : 5, connects lines 72 ff. with the third Duchess of Lancaster; compare ten Brink's view of the same passage, as below. On the Tale see ten Brink, Hist. Eng. Lit. II : 120-21. On the Doctor see Morris, The Physician in Chaucer, Eng. Misc. pp. 338-347; Saunders p. 111 ff.; Flügel in Anglia 24 : 496-98. See English Medicine in the Anglo-Saxon Times, J. F. Payne, Oxford 1904; Skeat III : 434-8, V : 260 ff.

Pardoner's Tale

MSS, Prints, and Editions: See under Cant. Tales, Eds. of Works and of the Cant. Tales. Specimens of variant line-readings are printed Ch. Soc. Specimens of Moveable Prologues, etc. pp. 58-69.

In Morris' Specimens of Early English, Oxford 1867; not included in Skeat's revision of the volume, Oxford 1872, 1889. In Sanford and Walsh, in Sweet's Second Mid. Eng. Primer, in Corson, in Herford, in Robertson, in Manly. In Emerson's Mid. Eng. Reader. See under D above.

This Tale and its prologue are printed by the Ch. Soc. from 45 MSS and 3 prints, in their 1st Series Nos. LXXXI, LXXXV, LXXXVI, XC, XCI, and its Suppls. 1 and 2. A critical ed. by Koch, Berlin 1902 and adopted as a publ. by the Ch. Soc., 2nd Series No. 35, is based upon these prints. Koch is rev. by Björkman in Engl. Stud. 32 : 275-77; and see Mod. Phil. 3 : 159 ff.

Modernizations and Translations: Modernized by Mrs. Cooper; by Lipscomb; by Leigh Hunt; by Cowden Clarke, by Saunders, Purves, Pitt-Taylor, Calder, Spofford, Warner, Darton, Skeat, Mackaye; see under E above.

Translated into German by Kannegiesser, by Hertzberg, by von Düring; into French by Chatelain; into Italian by Chiarini; see under E above.

A dramatization of this Tale, by H. D. Wescott, was presented at New Haven in 1900 by the Yale University Dramatic Association.

Source, Analogues, etc.: Tyrwhitt remarked that the "mere outline" of this narrative was to be found in the Cento Novelle
Antiche. For fuller identification and discussion see D'Ancona
in Romania 3 : 182-3 (1874) ; Morris in Contemp. Rev. May
1881, p. 738; Francis in Acad. 1883 II : 416, cp. *ibid.* 1884 I : 30;
Tawney in Jour. of Philol. 12 : 203; Ch. Soc. Orig. and Anal.
pp. 129, 415, 544; Kittredge in Amer. Jour. Phil. 9 : 84 and
Mod. Lang. Notes 15 : 385-7; Koeppel in Archiv 84 : 411-13;
Canby in Mod. Phil. 2 : 477-487; Petersen as below.

A parallel is contained in the Decameron, Day 6, Novel 10.
In modern literature cp. Kipling's story of the King's Ankus,
in his Jungle Book.

The Pardoner's prologue and epilogue, and his presentation
of his narrative as a sermon, give it the character of an "exemplum." See Miss Petersen's monograph on the NPTale, pp.
98 ff.

Date: Koch, in his Chronology p. 79, dates this and other Tales
in 1389-90; Skeat II : xxxvii puts this, with many other Tales,
as among the latest written. See under F above.

Notes: See Chaucer's Pardoner and the Pope's Pardoners. J. J.
Jusserand, Ch. Soc. Essays, part V.—English Popular Preaching
in the 14th Century. L. Toulmin Smith, Eng. Hist. Rev., 7 : 25
(1892).—Chaucer's Pardoner. G. L. Kittredge, Atl. My., 72:
829-33 (1893). See Todd, Illustrations pp. 262-5; Saunders p.
87; Jusserand, Eng. Wayfaring Life pp. 309 ff.; Skeat III : 438-
445, V : 269 ff. Other descriptions of pardoners are in Piers
Plowman, see B text 66 and Skeat's notes, Heywood's Foure Ps,
Sir David Lyndesay's Satire of the Three Estates.

FRAGMENT D

This Fragment has no headlink. It is composed of the Wife's
prologue, with an altercation between the Friar and Summoner at
its close, the Tale of the Wife, the link from that to the Friar's
Tale related at the expense of the Summoner, and the Summoner's
retaliation. No endlink.

Ten Brink, Hist. Eng. Lit. II : 126, III : 267, considers that the
Wife's prologue was once a separate narrative, and that the sketch
of the Wife in the General Prologue is a résumé of the WBprol.
The relations of this prologue, the Wife's Tale, and the description
in the General Prologue, form an interesting question. If the
present Shipman's Tale was written for the Wife, as its tone and
its feminine pronouns seem to indicate, was the description of the
Wife in the General Prologue written before the Shipman's Tale?
It would seem that the WBprologue, with its explanation of her five

husbands and of her deafness, must have been written after or with
the description in the General Prologue. Again, the opening of the
Wife's Tale, with its sly dig at friars, was probably written after
the Friar's interruption to her reminiscences had been planned, and
thus presumably after the Friar-Summoner strife was arranged by
Chaucer. Are we to suppose that the entire D fragment and the
description of the Wife, in its present form, are of the same date?
See Tatlock, Devel. and Chronol. chap. V § 8, for date of WBprol.
before Melibeus.

In MSS Barlow, Laud 739, Royal 18, there is a spurious link
of 16 lines connecting Merchant and Wife; in Lansdowne 851 four
lines introducing the Wife are appended to the eight spurious verses
at the end of the Squire's Tale. The latter are printed Six-Text, p.
334; the former link reads, in Royal 18 C ii:

> Oure oost gan tho to loke vp anon
> Gode men quod he herkeneth euerichon
> As euere mote I drynke wyn or ale
> This marchande hath Itolde a mery tale
> How Januarye hadde a lither Jape
> His wyf put in his hood an ape
> But here of I wil leue of as now
> Dame wyf of Bathe quod he I pray 3ow
> Telle vs a tale now next after þis
> Sire oost qd she so god my soule blis
> As I fully therto wil consente
> And also it is myn hole entente
> To done 3ow alle disporte as þat I can
> But holde me excused I am a woman
> I can not reherse as these clerkes kune
> And ri3t anon she hath hir tale bygunne

For the shorter form of the Summoner's Tale see below under
that heading.

On the D fragment see ten Brink, Hist. Eng. Lit. II : 160-64;
Root, Poetry of Chaucer pp. 231-252; Skeat V : 291 ff.

Wife of Bath's Tale

MSS, Prints, and Editions: See under MSS of the Cant. Tales,
    Eds of Works, Eds. of the Cant. Tales. In Maetzner's Altengl.
    Sprachproben I : 338 ff. are printed 400 lines, text from Wright's
    ed. of 1847-51. In Hazlitt's Selections (the prologue); in Leigh
    Hunt's Wit and Humour (a bit); in Paton, in Corson, in War-
    ner. See under D above.

Modernizations, Translations, etc.: The prologue was modernized
    by Pope, the Tale by Dryden; Pope's version of the prologue,
    continued by Ogle, and Dryden's version of the Tale, are in

Ogle and in Lipscomb. Jackson made a version of the prologue and Tale, 1750; the Tale is in Cowden Clarke, in Saunders, in Purves, in F. Clarke (with the prologue), in Pitt-Taylor, in Calder, in Mackaye. See under E above.

Translated into German by Hertzberg, by von Düring; into French by Chatelain; see under E above.

The Brit. Mus. Cat. notes "The Wife of Beith, by Chaucer", an anonymous poem suggested by this Tale. Glasgow, 1785? (a penny chapbook). Other eds. of this, according to the Catalogue, are entitled "The New Wife of Beith." Also, "The Old Wife of Beith, by Chaucer", a chapbook in verse, Edinburgh, 1778. This, according to the Catalogue, is another ed. of The New Wife of Beith. None of these has any connection with the Tale; the verse represents the Wife as applying at heaven's gate for admission, and defeating with her ready tongue every patriarch who attempts to refuse her. That there was an earlier ballad is possible. Horace Walpole, in a letter to Horace Mann of July 29, 1742, said: "They have given Mrs. Pulteney an admirable name, and one that is likely to stick by her; instead of Lady Bath, they call her the Wife of Bath." On this Walpole notes, "In allusion to the old ballad"; his editor, Peter Cunningham, adds, "Rather to Chaucer's Canterbury Tales." Note the theory of ten Brink, Hist. Eng. Lit. II : 126, that the Wife's name was probably a sort of proverb before Chaucer undertook to make it immortal.

Gay has two versions of a comedy entitled The Wife of Bath. The first appeared in 1713, and was unsuccessful; a revision by the author in 1730 was not more popular. Both are printed in vol. III of his Miscellaneous Works, Lond. 1772-3. In the earlier version Chaucer appears as a character, and four amorous couples, with a monk and "Doctor Astrolabe", walk through a tangle of vulgar intrigue and broad dialogue, alike without complication and without wit. The revision removed Chaucer from the list of characters and substituted "Sir Harry Gauntlet", but made no essential changes in text or motives. In this version the Miller and Shipman appear as minor characters, and both plots are supposedly laid during the Pilgrimage, but there is not the slightest trace of the medieval. See Lounsbury, Studies III : 234.

Another and very interesting use of this motive is in:

The Riddle; a pleasant pastoral comedy adapted from the Wife of Bath's Tale as it is set forth in the works of Master Geoffrey Chaucer. By Walter Raleigh. Liverpool, 1895, 400 copies, printed for the author.

Presented at Otterspool on Midsummer Eve, 1895. In 5-beat rimed couplets, with songs interspersed; the jester and Eglamour, a foppish knight, speak in prose. At the opening the knights of Arthur's court discuss the plight of Pharamond; he appears and tells of his ill-success in obtaining an answer to the fateful question; it is remarked that they are on fairy ground and that the time is one of special fairy meaning. Pharamond is left alone; the Old Woman appears, summons the fairies, and a dance follows, which Pharamond interrupts, and the fairies flee. He and the Old Woman converse, and she promises him aid in return for his pledge of obedience. Exeunt. The Court convenes for the trial; Pharamond gives the answer, and the Old Woman claims his promise. A scene between them follows, ending with her transformation and the joy of all.

Source, Analogues, etc.: See Child, Eng. and Scott. Ballads, I : 288 ff., and refs. there given; see Görbing in Anglia 23 : 405-423.

See Ch. Soc. Orig. and Anal. pp. 481, 546. See Woollcombe in Ch. Soc. Essays part III, pp. 298-306, where various passages of Jerome's Latin are translated; Koeppel, Archiv 84 : 413-416 and Anglia 14 : 250 ff., adds to Woollcombe. Flügel, Anglia 18 : 133-140, pointed out the genuineness of the Wife of Bath's citations of Ptolemy, which had been regarded by Tyrwhitt as apocryphal (see his note on line 5764) and emphatically dismissed by Skeat as such, see V : 295, 300. Boll in Anglia 21 : 222-230 somewhat modifies Flügel's results.

See Mead, Publ. Mod. Lang. Assn. 16 : 388-404, rev. Koch in Littblatt 1903, p. 157. See: The Wife of Bath's Tale, its Sources and Analogues. G. H. Maynadier. Lond. 1901. Rev. Athen. 1901 II : 274, Engl. Stud. 30 : 460 (Koch), Folklore 12 : 373 (J. L. Weston), Nation 1901 II : 284, N. and Q. 1901 II : 135, Revue Celtique 22 : 349, Mod. Lang. Quart. 5 : 76-79 (W. W. Greg), Littblatt 1903, 153-55 (Koch). Cp. Rajna in Romania 32 : 233.

On the use of Dante and of the Roman de la Rose in the Wife of Bath's discussion of gentility see Child in Athen. 1870 II : 721. The passage on "gentilesse" is cited in Bossewell's Workes of Armorie, Lond. 1572, as is the poem of Gentilesse. Rajna, in Romania 32 : 248, says there are echoes of Boccaccio's Corbaccio in the WBprol. Among the doctorate dissertations of Harvard University, 1907, is The Loathly Lady: a Study in the Popular Elements of the Wife of Bath's Tale. By J. W. Beach. (Unpublished.)

Date: Earlier than Bukton, as the latter poem contains an allusion to the Wife of Bath; perhaps sent to Bukton with the Envoy. Dated by Koch, Chronology p. 79, in 1389-90. Skeat II : xxvii puts it among the Tales "latest written." See under the Shipman's Tale above for critical opinions as to the original assignment of that Tale to the Wife; see under F above; see Tatlock, Devel. and Chronol., chap. V § 8.

Notes: This Tale begins *Experiment* (instead of *Experience*) in MSS Corpus, Sloane 1686, Barlow, Laud 600, Lansdowne; it begins *Eryment* in Rawl. 149.

According to Furnivall, pref. to Ch. Soc. print of Dd MS, p. vi, this Tale was to have been used for the Ch. Soc. Specimens of all Unprinted MSS, etc., but Zupitza, editor of the work, disliked the subject, and the Pardoner's Tale was taken instead. The greatest number of variants are shown in the WBTale.

The six lines printed by Skeat V : 292-3 are by him and by Tyrwhitt considered genuine; Furnivall, pref. to Ch. Soc. print of Dd MS, page v, says they are spurious.

See Brathwait's Comments (1665) upon this Tale and that of the Miller, printed Ch. Soc. 2d Series No. 33. See, in Brunet's Manuel du Libraire, *s. v.* Evangiles, a bibliographical account of the French Evangiles des Conoilles, first printed ca. 1475 at Bruges, and ed. from MSS etc., and with notes, Paris 1855. In Dibdin, Typogr. Antiq. II : 332, is an account of the English transl. of this, printed by de Worde as the Gospelles of Distaues; cp. the resemblance between Dame Isengrim and the Wife, as on p. 333.

Ten Brink, Hist. Eng. Lit. II : 127, considers that the original introduction to this Tale was omitted when the story was incorporated into the Cant. Tales, and that possibly the intention was to have different persons relate in succession their views of marriage. (Cp. the plan of the Evangiles as above mentioned.)

Brandl in Grdr. II : 681 says that the WBprol. was sent with the Envoy to Scogan to deter him from marriage.

Root p. 238 says the Tale was chosen with direct reference to the teller. On the relative date of prologue, description in Gen. Prol., and Tale, see ante under F, and Tatlock, Devel. and Chronol., chap. V § 8.

Remarks are in Warton's Essay on the Genius and Writings of Pope, II : 7-11. Koch, Anglia 6 : 105-6, cites an allusion to the Wife in a Latin work pub. 1691; the author is quoting Selden's Uxor Hebraica, of 1646. The influence of this prologue is strongly marked on Dunbar's Twa Mariit Wemen and the Wedo, see ed. of Dunbar STS 1893. On "Trotula" of line 677 of the prol. see Hamilton in Mod. Phil. 4 : 377. See Todd's Illustrations p. 255; Saunders p. 167 ff.; ten Brink as cited above; Skeat V : 291 ff.; Root, Poetry of Chaucer pp. 231 ff.

Friar's Tale

MSS, Prints, and Editions: See under MSS of the Cant. Tales, Eds. of Works, Eds. of the Cant. Tales. In Sanford and Walsh; see under D above.

Modernizations and Translations: Modernized by Markland in Ogle; for criticism see Horne's pref. of 1841. Mod. by Leigh Hunt, by Cowden Clarke, by Saunders, by Purves; see under E above.

Transl. into German by Hertzberg, by von Düring; into French by Chatelain; see under E above.

Source, Analogues, etc.: Tyrwhitt, Introd. Disc. § xix, professed himself unable to trace this or the next Tale to any writer older than Chaucer; he conjectured that both might have been built upon "traditional pleasantries." See Ch. Soc. Orig. and Anal. p. 103; this parallel Latin story was earlier printed by Wright in Archaeologia vol. 32. See Skeat III : 450-52, Foerster in Archiv 110 : 427, Vetter in Anglia Beibl. 13 : 180, Koeppel in Anglia 14 : 256.

Date: Koch, Chronology p. 79, gives no conjectural date; Skeat II : xxxvii puts the whole of this group among the Tales latest written.

Notes: On the Friar see Todd p. 239: Flügel, Jour. Gc. Phil. I : 133-5, Anglia 23 : 225-233 and 24 : 460-72. See Brewer, Monumenta Franciscana, Rolls Series, introd. See ten Brink, Hist. Eng. Lit. III : 267-8; Saunders pp. 75 ff.; Skeat V : 24, 322-330.

Summoner's Tale

MSS, Prints, and Editions: See under MSS of Cant. Tales, Eds. of Works, Eds. of Cant. Tales. In MS Petworth this Tale stops abruptly, lacking lines 2159 to close of D fragment, and substituting for them four lines which Furnivall, Six-Text p. 397, terms a spurious ending. Other copies of this ending are in Sloane 1685, Royal 18, Rawl. poet. 149, and Laud 739. See Lounsbury, Studies I : 249-50.

Modernizations and Translations: By Grosvenor in Budgell's Bee, II : 1020-25 (1733), and in Ogle; this was reprinted in Lipscomb, see under E above.

Translated into German by Hertzberg, by von Düring; into French by Chatelain. See under E above.

Source, Analogues, etc.: See Legrand d'Aussy, Fables et Contes; see Ch. Soc. Orig. and Anal. p. 135. See Skeat III : 452, Koeppel in Anglia 14 : 256.

Date: Koch, Chronology p. 79, dates this Tale in 1389-90; Skeat

II : xxxvii, puts this entire group among the tales latest written. See under F above.

Notes: The poet Gay wrote, An Answer to the Sompner's Prologue of Chaucer, in Imitation of Chaucer's Style, published in
Lintot's Miscellany of 1717, and in eds. of Gay, e. g., Chalmers'
Poets, 10 : 504. It is of 70 lines. See Lounsbury, Studies III :
125.
  On the Summoner see Todd p. 260; see Flügel in Anglia
24: 505 ff.; Ramsay in Acad. 1880 I: 160; Saunders pp. 82 ff.;
Skeat V : 51-54, 330-341.
  On Chaucer's possible first intention to place the Summoner
next after the Man of Law see ten Brink, Hist. Eng. Lit. II :
160, III : 268, Hammond in Mod. Phil. 3 : 163-4, and above
under F.

FRAGMENT E

  The Clerk's headlink, prologue, Tale, and Envoy; the headlink
of the Merchant, who catches up the last line of the Clerk's envoy
and proceeds at once to his own Tale. His Tale is followed by a
comment from the Host (22 lines), not in all MSS, and which in
the Ellesmere group and Harley 7334 passes immediately into the
eight-line headlink of the Squire. Ten Brink considered (see Hist.
Eng. Lit. II : 165, III : 268) that the four Tales of this and the F
fragment were originally all single, and at a later date fused into a
whole; he regarded it as a mistake to separate the E and F fragments. Skeat III : 462 sees no reason in ten Brink's view. But see
under F ante.
  The E fragment occupies differing positions in the MSS. In the
Ellesmere group and in Harley 7334 this fragment is composed as
above described, and lies between D and F. But in the Corpus-
7333 group, as discussed p. 246 above, the Tales of Clerk and Merchant are without their full set of connectives in some cases, and in
some cases have those connectives distorted to serve as bonds to
other Tales. Thus, in the (a) branch of that group the two Tales
of this fragment are separated, though their connective is present
in part; in the (b) branch the Tales lie together, but are only
partially connected; in the (c) and (d) branches the Tale of the
Merchant has been carried up to follow that of the Squire, to which
it is connected by the (altered) Words of the Franklin; while the
Clerk's Tale, remaining after Fragment D, has in (c) a garbled
bond to the Tale of the Franklin next following. This bond does
not appear in the (d) branch, in which the Franklin also is carried
up with the Merchant, the Clerk remaining after Fragment D. In
the de Worde print of 1498 the Tales of Merchant and Squire are
connected by the ML endlink.

The last three stanzas of the Clerk's Envoy, which is a tour de force in riming, quite different in tone from the Tale, and probably written later, are not arranged identically in all MSS. This was pointed out by Tyrwhitt, Introd. Disc. § xxi; and Tyrwhitt first adopted for these stanzas an order, found in some MSS, which brought the first line of the Merchant's headlink into immediate echo with the last line of the Clerk's envoy. Bradshaw noted this variant as one of his tests. Of the eight MSS reproduced by the Chaucer Society, Petworth alone departs from this order.

Immediately following the Clerk's Envoy there occurs in many MSS a 7-line stanza of comment by the Host, which we may for convenience call the Verba Hospitis. This stanza is in MSS Ellesmere, Hengwrt, Gg, Dd, Egerton 2726, Adds. 5140, Egerton 2864, Selden, Harley 7333, Harley 1758, Trin. Coll. R 3, 15, Royal 18, New College, Laud 739, Barlow. Tyrwhitt printed the stanza in his note on line 9088, remarking that it was probably a bit of an unfinished connective with the Merchant's Tale, left uncancelled by Chaucer when he decided to unite the two Tales in the present manner. Tyrwhitt notes that the idea, and part of the phrasing, of the stanza are used in the link between the Monk's Tale and Melibeus. Skeat prints the stanza in a footnote IV : 424, remarking that it was originally intended to conclude the Tale; neither he nor Furnivall, in his brief headings to the Ch. Soc. prints of the lines, discusses this stanza in connection with the probable chronology of Chaucer's revision of his framework.

An interesting fact in relation to Tyrwhitt's theory is that the stanza is present in MSS of the Ellesmere or revised group, in Selden, and in the (a) and (c) branches of the Corpus-7333 type. Selden and the (c) group MSS are hybrid in character, but the stanza thus exists in both the earliest and the latest recension of the Tales.

In MS Rawlinson C 86 the Envoy ends " . . . . I you counsell", and is followed by:

> But yet god graunte vs grace to make good ende
> And brynge vs oute of euery bale
> And euer to have pacience in oure mynde
> ffinis Gryseld

On the Fragment see Root, Poetry of Chaucer, pp. 253-266.

Clerk's Tale

MSS, Prints, and Editions: See under MSS of the Cant. Tales, Eds. of the Cant. Tales, Eds. of Works.

The Clerk's Tale and the D fragment only are contained in the Sion College MS; the Tales of the Clerk and the Knight are contained in the MS Longleat 257; the Clerk's Tale and part of the Prioress' in Rawlinson C 86; the Clerk's Tale only, of the CT, is in Phillipps 8299 and in the Naples MS. This Tale is printed by the Chaucer Society, in its Specimens, from eight MSS; see their First Series Nos. XCII, XCIII. The introd. by Koch is pubd. as No. XCVII.

Privately printed by W. A. Wright, Cambridge 1867, from MS Dd iv, 24. In the Tauchnitz Library collection entitled Five Centuries of the English Language and Literature, Leipzig 1860. In Sprague's Masterpieces of English Literature, N. Y. 1874. Included in the Selections of Sanford and Walsh; envoy in Ward; in Morley; see under D above.

Modernizations and Translations: Modernized by Ogle, 1739, and in his coll. of 1741, reprinted by Lipscomb in 1795; by Tytler in 1828; in Blackwood's Mag. for May 1837; by Cowden Clarke, by Saunders, by Purves, by Pitt-Taylor, by Calder, by Corbet (?), by Darton, by Skeat, by Mackaye; see under E above.

Translated into German by Hertzberg, by von Düring; into French by Chatelain; into French prose in vol. I of Les deux Griselidis, Paris 1813, 2 vols. 12mo. (the other tale from Maria Edgeworth); into Italian by Chiarini; see under E above.

Source: Translated from Petrarch's Latinizing of Boccaccio's tenth story of the tenth day in the Decameron, as De obedientia et fide uxoria Mythologia. The translation was sent by Petrarch to Boccaccio in 1374, but may have been executed a year earlier, see Mather as cited below. Petrarch's Latin is accessible in Ch. Soc. Orig. and Anal., pp. 151-172, where the letter of Petrarch which accompanied the translation is also printed. Boccaccio's Italian had been in circulation since 1353; cp. Petrarch's having heard it "ante multos annos." Clouston thinks (Orig. and Anal. pp. 527-536) that a French fabliau may have antedated the Italian rendering of the story. That Chaucer had Petrarch's Latin before him is evident from the closeness of his rendering. A critical text of the Latin and detailed study of Chaucer's treatment of it are desiderata. The Chaucer Society has regrettably printed the text not from a MS, but from the Basel ed. of 1581, which is of ill repute for accuracy. For interesting divergences in Chaucer's probable original see Hendrickson's paper on Chaucer and Petrarch: Two Notes on the Clerkes Tale, in Mod. Phil. 4 : 179-192; and add that Hendrickson's surmise regarding *alio* or *alto,* on p. 190, is borne out by the two texts of Petrarch in Corpus Christi College Library, Cambridge, one of which has the first reading, the other the second.

Date: The Clerk's Tale must therefore postdate 1373; and the linking Prologue was written after Petrarch's death in 1374. The fact that Chaucer was himself in Italy in 1373 has led to the conjecture that he may have met Petrarch and obtained from him the story, as he makes his Clerk assert.

Did Chaucer Meet Petrarch?

In the life of Chaucer prefixed to the Speght Chaucer of 1598 we find: "Some write that he with Petrarke was present at the marriage of Lionell Duke of Clarence with Violant daughter of Galeasius, Duke of Millaine: yet Paulus Iouius nameth not Chaucer, but Petrarke he saith, was there." Tyrwhitt, in his Introd. Disc., quotes this, and observes that Chaucer is not mentioned in English records as of Clarence's retinue at this time; and he further remarks that it is uncertain if Chaucer went upon the Italian embassy to which he was appointed in 1372. We now know that Chaucer did visit Italy in 1372-3; and the question of his meeting with Petrarch has been extensively discussed.

The preface to Urry's Chaucer and the Life of Chaucer by Godwin both assume the meeting of Chaucer and Petrarch, which is also argued by Ogle, op. cit. vol. III; Godwin, chap. 35, summing up an account in which is given even the tenor of the conversation between the two poets, says: "A man must have Mr. Tyrwhitt's appetite for the fascinating charms of a barren page and a meagre collection of dates, not to perceive that the various coincidences enumerated,—Chaucer representing the speaker as having learned his tale from Petrarca at Padua, though it was previously the property of Boccaccio; Padua being then Petrarca's actual residence; the embassy of Chaucer to Genoa in 1373; and Petrarca having in that very year translated the tale into Latin prose;—not to perceive, I say, that these coincidences furnish a basis of historical probability seldom to be met with in points of this nature."

Godwin, despite the frequent exaggeration and untrustworthiness of his biography, discovered and used some original documents; the letters of protection for Chaucer and his fellow-ambassadors to Genoa were printed by him; and Nicolas, in his Life of Chaucer, pubd. in 1844-45, credits Godwin with this, and discusses at some length the possible meeting of the two poets; he considers that it must remain among the doubtful circumstances. The accurate Nicolas overlooks in his sketch one fact of which Godwin had taken note (see Anglia 21 : 252); he speaks of the length of Chaucer's stay in Italy as "not quite twelve months." Inasmuch as the possibility of the two poets' meeting must depend somewhat on the amount of time which Chaucer had for traveling, the question of the length of Chaucer's stay abroad in 1373 is important.

20

Ten Brink, Studien p. 37 (1870), says that the journey lasted in all probability eleven months; he reckons from the date of the letters of protection, Dec. 1372, to the date at which Chaucer received his pension in England, Nov. 1373.

But in 1873 (Trial Forewords, p. 130) Furnivall mentioned that Chaucer's accounts for his journey closed on May 23, 1373, and gave reference; this would reduce the poet's stay abroad to about six months, and lessen the probability of any detours in Italy. In his note (1875-6) to the EETS edition of Thynne's Animadversions, p. 22, Furnivall repeated the fact, which was again emphasized by Flügel in his review of Skeat, Dial 1896 vol. 18 : 116, and in Anglia 21 : 252 (1899). Cp. also Flügel in Nation 1896 II : 365. Notwithstanding this, the eleven months' stay continued to be assumed by students of Chaucer; see Flügel in Anglia as above for review of the history of the error.

Relying upon the supposed longer duration of Chaucer's first visit to Italy, critics argued the likelihood of his meeting with Petrarch. Thus, Hales in Dict. Nat. Biog. (1887) says, "The probability is that Chaucer got the Latin (of the Clerk's Tale) from either Petrarch or Boccaccio, probably Boccaccio. But who introduced him to Petrarch? Likely enough Petrarch's friend. For many years Boccaccio had been living at Florence. . . . . It is conceivable that Chaucer may have been present at his first Dante lecture at Florence, 3 August, 1373."

Upon this Paget Toynbee, Athen. 1905 I : 210, points out that Boccaccio did not enter upon his Dante lectureship until October 23, 1373, and that Hales' suggestion is therefore impossible. The October date was noted already by Brandl in Paul's Grundr. II : 674 and by Cochin in Revue des Deux Mondes, July 15, 1888.

It should also be pointed out that the existence of a miswriting like *alto* for *alio* in the Latin before Chaucer would militate somewhat against the notion that Chaucer got his copy direct from the author. See Hendrickson's paper as cited above.

Lounsbury, Studies I : 68, thinks that with the knowledge we at present possess we cannot assert a meeting between Chaucer and Petrarch. But Furnivall, Trial Forew. p. 20, calls the meeting "probable." Skeat I : xxiv says Chaucer must have returned before Nov. 22, 1373, and gives the May date in a footnote *ibid.;* on p. xxv he opines that the poets must have met; Kittredge, Nation 1894 II : 309, regrets that Skeat should do this, considering "the ambiguous and nugatory character of the evidence."

Jusserand, Did Chaucer Meet Petrarch? pubd. in Nineteenth Century, June 1896, answers the question in the affirmative.

Bellezza, Chaucer s'e trovato col Petrarca, in Engl. Stud. 23 : 335 (1897) combats Jusserand.

Mather, in the Nation 1896 II : 269, writes on Chaucer's first Italian journey; in Mod. Lang. Notes 11 : 419 he prints the official documents, already referred to by Furnivall and Skeat as above; and *ibid.* 12 : 1-21 he argues that the meeting of the two poets is unlikely; he adds that the Tale must postdate the Legend of Good Women, because if then in existence Chaucer could not have been so severely blamed for his writing about women.

> Siefken in his book cited below has made a similar (later) observation. But consider the remark under F above that literary convention might restrain Chaucer from making adequate defence in his prologue.

Flügel, Nation 1896 II : 365, shows that the documents were already known; Mather *ibid.* 385 and Mod. Lang. Notes 11 : 510 explains.

In the Athen. 1898 II : 388, 419, 643, 716, 791 are printed long letters from C. H. Bromby and St. Clair Baddeley on Chaucer's Italian journeys and meeting with Petrarch. Of little value.

See Hendrickson's argument, in the paper above cited, against an interpretation of Chaucer's vivid language regarding Petrarch to mean personal contact.

Segrè's paper on Chaucer e Petrarca, reprinted in his Studi Petrarcheschi, Milan 1903, I have not seen.

Tatlock, Devel. and Chronol., chap. V § 4, argues against the meeting, pointing out, p. 160, that had Chaucer met Petrarch he could not have failed to learn who was the author of the Griselda-story and of the De Casibus.

There is a general tendency among students to date the translating of Petrarch's Latin soon after Chaucer's return from Italy; an exception to this is the remark of Mather above cited.

Ten Brink, Hist. Eng. Lit. II : 123, quotes the stanza of the Tale reproaching popular fickleness, and is inclined to connect it with events late in 1387; Skeat III : 454 thinks that the main body of the story was written 1373 or early in 1374, and that when revised the prologue, two stanzas at the close, and lines 995-1008, as well as the envoy, were added. See also V : 349, 351.

Koch, Beiträge zur neueren Philologie 1902, 257 ff., thinks lines 1170-1212 were added later to make better connection with the Merchant.

See Tatlock, Devel. and Chronol., chap. V § 4.

Analogues, Later Versions, etc.: See R. Koehler in Ersch & Grüber's Allgemeine Encyclopedie, art. *Griseldis,* and his paper in Archiv 1870; both are repr. in his Kleinere Schriften (1898) vol. 2. See Die Griseldissage in der Literaturgeschichte, von Westenholz, Heidelberg, 1888; rev. Ztsch. f. vergl. Littgesch. 2 : 112.

See Die Griseldissage auf der iberischen Halbinsel, by Wannenmacher. diss. Strassburg, 1894; rev. Ztsch. f. vergl. Littgesch. 9 : 142.

See Der Konstanze-Griseldistypus in der engl. Literatur bis auf Shakspere. O. Siefken. Rathenow 1902. 110 pp. (Beilage zum Jahresber. des Progymnasiums zu Rathenow.)

For dramatic and ballad versions see Warton-Hazlitt II : 226, 350; Hazlitt, Handbook p. 245; Chambers, Medieval Stage, II : 205; Skeat's refs. III : 455-57; Koehler's refs. as above cited.

Edwin Arnold's tragedy of 1856 and a four-act drama by Miss M. E. Braddon in 1873 (see Athen. 1873 II : 669) are probably the most recent dramatic treatments of the subject; the earliest are probably those of Ralph Radcliff, and of Chettle, Dekker and Haughton; see reprod. of the 1603 ed. of the latter in Erlanger Beiträge zur englischen Philologie, 1893. See the 1619 Patient Grissill printed by Collier for the Percy Soc. in 1842; see the chapbook history of 1703. The poem *Griseldis,* by Eleanora L. Hervey, in Athen. 1850 I : 583-4, is not an imitation, but a modern lyrical treatment of the theme. See the opera by Scarlatti (1721) and the French drama by Ostrowski, as cited Ztsch. f. vergl. Littgesch. 2 : 112.

For transference of the story to Queen Katharine of Arragon see Warton-Hazlitt IV : 229 and Athen. 1876 II : 686.

Notes: On the Clerk and his Tale see Todd p. 243; Flügel in Anglia 24 : 476-84; see Lowes, Publ. Mod. Lang. Assn. 19 : 641 note; see Saunders pp. 126, 308; ten Brink, Hist. Eng. Lit. II : 121-3; Hales in ed. Percy Folio MS III : 421; Warton-Hazlitt II : 349-51; Skeat V : 31, 342-353. On the word *aventaille* in the Envoy see Hamilton in Mod. Phil. 3 : 541.

Pictures treating the Griselda-story are: Skeat III : 457 mentions one by Pinturicchio; there is a series of three, by an unknown artist of the Umbrian school, in the National Gallery, London, nos. 912-14. Angelica Kauffman's painting is engraved as noted p. 227 here. C. W. Cope's Griselda's First Trial of Patience, painted ca. 1848 on the wall of the upper waiting hall of the House of Lords, is now in ruins, according to the Dict. Nat. Biog., *art.* Cope. Another "Marriage of Griselda" by the same artist was painted for private possession, see *ibid.*

Cp. the remark in WB prol. lines 688-91.

On the attribution of the story to Petrarch and not Boccaccio see Lydgate in the prologue to Book IV of the Falls of Princes, where the catalogue of Petrarch's works ends:

> Of famous weomen he wrote the excellence,
> Gresild preferryng for her great pacience.

Landau, Beiträge zur Geschichte der italienischen Novella, Vienna 1875, says p. 47 that it is more than probable that Chaucer very well knew the real writer of the Griselda-story, but preferred to parade before the English public the more famous poet. See under Lollius in II C (4) above.

Merchant's Tale

MSS, Prints, and Editions: See under MSS of the Cant. Tales, Eds. of Cant. Tales, Eds. of Works.

In MSS Corpus, Lansdowne, Sloane 1686 this Tale breaks off with line 1074. Harley 7333 lacks a still longer passage, but in this MS the gap is due to loss of a gathering from the codex.

For spurious lines inserted into this Tale in Caxton I and its followers see Tyrwhitt's note on line 10227 and my note in Mod. Phil. 3 : 173. The lines are in Harley 1758, inserted on the margins by the scribe of the MS; they are printed thence in the Ch. Soc. Six-Text pp. 474-75.

Modernizations and Translations: Modernized by Pope, see ante under E for refs.; on the relation of Pope's work to the original see *ibid.* Pope was reprinted in Ogle, in Lipscomb. Paraphrase in Saunders; in Purves; see under E above.

Translated into German by Hertzberg, by von Düring; into French by Chatelain; see under E above.

Source, Analogues, etc.: See Ch. Soc. Orig. and Anal. pp. 177, 341, 544; see Varnhagen in Anglia 7 : Anz. 155-165; see Koeppel *ibid.* 14 : 257. Skeat, III : 458-462, points out that this Tale really falls into three parts; the Ch. Soc. analogues are of the third part, which was traced already by Tyrwhitt, see his Introd. Disc. § xxii, cited by Skeat as above.

Date: Koch, Chronology p. 79, puts this Tale, with others, in 1389-90; Skeat, II : xxxvii, "among the latest written"; III : 458-9, "later than Melibeus, Troilus, Boethius, or the Wife of Bath's Tale." See ante under F; see Tatlock, Devel. and Chronol., chap. V § 8.

Notes: On the Merchant see Todd p. 242; Saunders pp. 146-150; Flügel in Anglia 24 : 472-76. Ten Brink, Hist. Eng. Lit. III :

267, thinks this story "can scarcely have been written with regard to the Canterbury Tales." See *ibid.* II : 130-32; Warton-Hazlitt II : 353-55.

For influence of this Tale see Shackerley Marmion's play of The Antiquary, 1641.

FRAGMENT F

The Tale of the Squire, with a headlink of eight lines; his unfinished Tale is followed by the "Words of the Franklin to the Squire", 36 lines; the Franklin's prologue, 20 lines, and his Tale, with no endlink, then follow. For ten Brink's opinion on the unity of Fragments E and F, see Hist. Eng. Lit. II : 165, III : 268.

The Squire's Tale occupies one of two positions in the MSS. (1) It follows immediately after the Man of Law's Tale, with which it is connected by the Man of Law's endlink, now called the Shipman's prologue, and editorially treated (Skeat, Pollard) as the bond between Man of Law and Shipman; line 17 of this Link contains in such texts the word *Squire* instead of *Shipman* (or *Sompnour*). This displacement of the Squire, an explanation of which was suggested Mod. Phil. 3 : 163 ff., is found in twenty and more MSS, classed under F above as the Corpus-7333 group. Manuscripts showing this displacement do not connect the Franklin with the Squire; instead, they frequently place the Merchant's Tale next after the misplaced Squire, transferring the "Words of the Franklin" to the Merchant by altering the name *Franklin* in line 2 of the Words to *Merchant*. This additional distortion appears in the MSS classed under (c) and (d) of the above mentioned group. The use of the ML endlink to bind Merchant and Squire is found in the de Worde print of 1498, *q. v.* (2) The other and normal position occupied by the Squire's Tale is between the Tales of Merchant and of Franklin. This is its place in Harley 7334 and in the Ellesmere group of MSS. In this position it is bound to the following Franklin's Tale by the "Words of the Franklin." This arrangement was adopted by Tyrwhitt, by the Chaucer Society, and by modern editors generally, in contradistinction to the sequence Squire-Merchant of the more debased Corpus-7333 texts, seen in the eds. down to that of Urry.

The Franklin's Tale occupies one of four positions in the MSS. (1) After the Squire's Tale, and connected with it by the Words. This is the normal arrangement just mentioned.

(2) After the Merchant's Tale, and united to it by a fusion of the Merchant's endlink and the Squire's eight-line prologue, the latter altered in its first line to introduce the Franklin. Seen in MSS Hatton, Ii, and Hengwrt, and arising from the acquirement, by

the (d) ancestor, of the eight-line prologue and the Merchant's epilogue after the Squire's Tale had been carried up to follow the Man of Law, and after the Words of the Franklin, acquired a little earlier, had been appended to the Squire and adapted to the already displaced Merchant. See discussion under F ante.

(3) After the Clerk's Tale, and preceded:

—by the fusion just described, with no real connection to the Clerk. In MSS Petworth, Mm. The difference of these MSS from their nearest relatives in arrangement, Hatton and Ii, may be due either to the accidental moving down of the Franklin booklet and its Merchant-links away from their position as in Hatton, or to the moving up of the Merchant, in Petworth and Mm, from a position between Clerk and Franklin as in the (b) type MSS. The former seems more possible.

—by two seven-line stanzas, of which the first is extracted from the Merchant's endlink, the second is the (garbled) Squire's prologue less one line, assigned to the Franklin. In MSS Lichfield, Sloane 1686, Laud 739.

—by the same two stanzas, preceded by the Verba Hospitis. In MS Harley 7333. There is no Squire's headlink in this MS.

(4) After the Pardoner's Tale, with its own prologue, but no Words of the Franklin. In Selden B 14, Trinity R 3, 3.

The inappropriateness of the union Man of Law-Squire was seen by Tyrwhitt, cp. his Introductory Discourse § xxxi; he also first printed the eight-line Squire's prologue. This prologue is found in MSS of the Ellesmere type, in Harley 7334, in Selden, in Laud 600 (a MS which must have been originally of the Ellesmere type), in the hybrid Royal 17, in Harley 7335. It is not in the (a) or (b) MSS of the Corpus-7333 group; but it appears, as above noted, in the (d) MSS of that group, and in a garbled form in such of the (c) MSS as are complete at this point.

The varying treatments of the E and F fragments were among the points listed by Bradshaw as tests for the classification of the Canterbury Tales MSS.

Squire's Tale

MSS, Prints, and Editions: See under MSS of the Cant. Tales, Eds. of Works, Eds. of Cant. Tales. This Tale is included in the Selections of Hazlitt, of Southey, of Corson, of Herford, of Robertson, of Manly; it is in Wülker's Altenglisches Lesebuch, Halle 1874, text from Morris.

Continuations, Modernizations, and Translations: The Squire's Tale was left unfinished by Chaucer. Parts I and II are followed, in many MSS, by two lines of a third part; these were considered spurious by Tyrwhitt, see his note on line 10984. The MSS in which these two lines appear are: Rawl. 149, Harley 1758, Sloane 1686, Corpus, Laud 600, Harley 7333, Barlow, Laud 739, Royal 17, Royal 18, Hatton, Egerton 2863, Hodson-Ashburnham, Petworth (there marked vacat), Hengwrt, Ellesmere. They are also in the second Caxton and the de Worde of 1498. Caxton notes after them "There is no more of the Squyeres Tale"; de Worde says: "There can be fownde no more of this forsayd tale, whyche I have right dilygently serchyd in many dyuers scopyes." Warton, Observations on Spenser's Faery Queene, ed. 1807, p. 213, says that Lydgate, in the Temple of Glass, speaks as if he had seen more of this Tale. See Schick's note on Lydgate, lines 137-42, where a similar opinion held by Waldron is doubted.

Spenser continued one thread of the story in Book IV of the Faery Queene; see Warton's Observations, Sect. 5; John Lane's continuation of the tale, though licensed in 1614-15, was first printed by the Chaucer Society in 1888, 2d Series, Nos. 23, 26. Lane's copy is now MS Douce 170 of the Bodleian; see Madan's Summary Catalogue IV : 543.

At the end of the Speght Chaucer of 1687, headed "Advertisement," are the newly-found "conclusions" to this Tale and to that of the Cook. The latter is reprinted ante under the Cook's Tale, with the introductory part of the advertisement, the remainder of which is:

"Immediately after these words, at the end of the Squire's Tale,

> Apollo whirleth up his chare so hie,
> Untill the God Mercurius house he flie.

Let this be added,

> But I here now maken a knotte,
> To the time it come next to my lotte,
> For here ben felawes behind, an hepe truly,
> That wolden talk full besily,
> And have here sport as well as I.
> And the day passeth certainly,
> So on this mattere I may no lenger dwell,
> But stint my clack, and let the other tell,
> Therefore ost taketh now good hede
> Who shall next tell, and late him spede."

As is noted under the Cook's Tale above, both these "conclusions" were rejected by Thomas and by Tyrwhitt. Tyrwhitt, in the Appendix to his preface, note m, says that this conclusion is found in MS Selden B 14, and that Hearne printed it from that MS in his Letter to Bagford "as a choice discovery." Eight lines of it are in the Lansdowne MS, printed Six-Text p. 497. See Lounsbury, Studies I : 446.

In the modernizations pubd. by Ogle, the prologue to this Tale, now treated as the Shipman's prologue, was done by Ogle, the Tale by Boyse, and Spenser's continuation by Ogle; all was reprinted by Lipscomb. In 1785 was pubd. the work of Boyse and Ogle, "concluded by Mr. Sterling." Other modernizations are by Wharton, by Cowden Clarke, by an anonymous writer in the Poetical Register, by Leigh Hunt, by Saunders, by Calder, by Darton, by Skeat, and by Mackaye, see under E above. Leigh Hunt once thought of writing a continuation, see Lounsbury, Studies III : 211.

Translated into German by Hertzberg, by von Düring; into French by Chatelain; see under E above.

Source, Analogues, etc.: Tyrwhitt, Introd. Disc. § xxiv, professed his inability to discover the original of this Tale, but said that he should with difficulty believe that it was of Chaucer's invention. See Warton-Hazlitt II : 337 ff., reprinted by Skeat III : 464 ff. Keightley, Tales and Popular Fictions, ed. 1834 p. 477, thought that Chaucer invented the story. Skeat, III : 470 ff., gives evidence that Chaucer used the travels of Marco Polo as a source book, controverted by Manly, Marco Polo and the Squire's Tale, in Publ. Mod. Lang. Assn. 11 : 349-362. (For review of this last paper see Nation 1896 I : 455.)

The magical elements of the Tale are discussed by Clouston in the Ch. Soc. ed. of Lane's continuation, part II, where analogues are also given. (Ch. Soc. 2d Series No. 26.) See also Warton-Hazlitt II : 336-348. See H. S. V. Jones, Publ. Mod. Lang. Assn. 20: 346-359, for the possible influence of Froissart's Cléomades upon this tale, remarked upon by Keightley as above pp. 41 ff., see 75-77 (chap. II). Cp. also Jones' paper in Jour. Gc. Phil. 6 : 221-243. See Koeppel in Anglia 14 : 257-8.

Date: See:—On the Historical Personages of Chaucer's Squyeres Tale, and of the spurious Chaucer's Dream. A. Brandl, Engl. Stud. 12: 161-186, and in Ch. Soc. Essays part VI. Overthrown by Kittredge, Supposed Historical Allusions in the Squire's Tale. Engl. Stud. 13 : 1-25.

Koch, Chronology p. 79, does not date this Tale. Skeat, II : xxxvii, places it among the latest written. In I : 534 and V : 385 he points out the resemblance of the falcon-episode in this Tale to the tone and situation of Anelida. Wülker in his print says "about 1393." For a date earlier than the "latest" Tales, see under F here.

Notes: On the Squire see Saunders pp. 39 ff.; on his duties and education see EETS Boke of Nurture (1868), Household Ordinances of Edward II, etc., in Ch. Soc. Life Records.

See N. and Q. 1864 II : 40, 200; 1904 I : 123. A few notes suggested by Wülker's text are in Engl. Stud. 4 : 503-6.

Franklin's Tale

MSS, Prints, and Editions: See under MSS of the Cant. Tales, Eds. of Works, Eds. of Cant. Tales.

Modernizations and Translations: Modernized by Lipscomb, by Cowden Clarke, by Horne in his 1841 vol., by Saunders, by Purves, by Calder, by Mackaye; see under E above.

Translated into German by Kannegiesser, by Hertzberg, by von Düring; into French by Chatelain; see under E above.

Source, Analogues, etc.: Tyrwhitt, Introd. Disc. § xxvi, was unable to trace the source further than Chaucer's own statement that he was following "a British lay." He pointed out that the list of virtuous women cited by Dorigen was copied from Jerome against Jovinian. See Ch. Soc. Orig. and Anal. p. 289; see :—

Chaucer's Franklin's Tale. W. H. Schofield. Publ. Mod. Lang. Assn. 16: 405-449. Reviewed Anglia Beibl. 14: 368-70 (Binz); Littblatt 1903, p. 155 (Koch); Moyen Age 1902, pp. 109-112; Nation 1901 II: 284. Replied to in: Le origini della novella narrata dal 'Frankeleyn' nei Canterbury Tales del Chaucer. P Rajna. Romania 32 : 204-267 (1903).

See also: Le prologue du Franklin's Tale et les lais bretons. L. Foulet. Ztschr. f. roman. Phil. 30 : 698-711.

Skeat III : 484-5 goes no further than the material offered by Tyrwhitt and by the Ch. Soc. He notes the dramatization by Beaumont and Fletcher as The Triumph of Honour; and also a comedy of the Two Merry Milkmaids, 1620. Boccaccio has narrated a similar story as the tenth novel of the fifth day. See Kittredge on Sir Orfeo in Am. Jour. Phil. 7 : 176-202; see Koeppel, Anglia 14 : 258.

Date: Koch, Chronology, gives none; Skeat II : xxxvii puts this Tale "among the latest written." See under F above

Notes: See Fortescue, De Laudibus Legum Angliae, ch. 29; Spelman's Glossarium under *Vavasour;* Todd p. 247; Saunders p. 133 ff.; Skeat V: 32-35, 388-400.

A water color by Burne Jones, "Dorigen of Bretaigne", is in the Victoria and Albert Museum, London.

The Tale of the Second Nun, with a prologue but no headlink; the tale of the Canon's Yeoman, with a headlink mentioning that of the Second Nun as just ended.

The G fragment occupies usually one of two places in the MSS. (1) It follows the Franklin and is followed by the C fragment; or, (2) it follows the B² fragment and is followed by Manciple and by Parson. The second of these positions is that assigned it by the Chaucer Society and by subsequent editors, although the "pushing of the G fragment down late" was according to Bradshaw one of the characteristics of the text edited after Chaucer's death. But inasmuch as the addition of the Canon's Yeoman's Tale, with a prologue which places the pilgrims within five miles of Canterbury, seems to require the position of this fragment near the close of the CT, the order B² G H I, as in the Ellesmere group, has been adopted by modern editors as Chaucerian.

Tyrwhitt, note on line 16023, is not certain whether the pilgrims, in this Fragment, were riding to or from Canterbury. But see Skeat V : 415.

Second Nun's Tale

MSS, Prints, and Editions: See under MSS of the Cant. Tales, Eds. of Works, Eds. of Cant. Tales. A copy of this Tale and of that of the Prioress are in Harley 2382. In the Selections of Paton; see under D above.

Modernizations and Translations: Modernized by Lipscomb, by Pitt-Taylor, by Saunders, by Purves, by Skeat; see under E above.

    Translated into German by Hertzberg, by von Düring; into French by Chatelain; see under E above.

Source, Analogues, etc : Tyrwhitt, Introd. Disc. § xxxvii, remarked that this Tale was almost literally translated from the Life of St. Cecilia in the Legenda Aurea. Hertzberg p. 660 and ten Brink, Studien p. 130, repeat this: ten Brink shows that a part of the introductory stanzas to the Tale are from Dante, see p. 131 ff. Kölbing, Engl. Stud. 1 : 215 ff., showed that Tyrwhitt's account was but partially correct. See Ch. Soc. Orig. and Anal. pp. 189 ff.; Holthausen, Archiv 1887 pp. 32-54; Skeat, Acad. 1889 I : 133, 222, Oxford Chaucer III : 485 ff.

Date: This Tale was probably a separate and early piece of work; Chaucer refers to it, prol. LGW line 426, as the Lyf of Seint Cecyle. Furnivall, Trial Forewords p. 16, dates it 1373; ten

Brink, Studien p. 138-9, says not before 1373 or after June 8, 1374; Koch, Chronology 27-28, dates it "after Pite, in the spring of 1374"; Koeppel, Anglia 14 : 227, dates it later, after the Troilus; this is disputed by ten Brink, Engl. Stud. 17 : 1-22, cp. Koeppel *ibid*. 189-200. Koeppel's view is also rejected by Skeat III : 485 footnote, and by Kittredge, Nation 1894 II : 309.

Notes: Lines 62 and 78, with their phrases "unworthy sone of Eve", and "yow that reden that I wryte", show that Chaucer had not revised this Tale for its place. See Tyrwhitt, Introd. Disc., note 30. On the Second Nun, or Nun-Chaplain, see under the Prioress, ante.

Kölbing, Engl. Stud. 1 : 240, points out that the prose of the Cecilia-legend in Caxton's Golden Legend shows a resemblance to the Chaucerian story. Compare here the Lydgatian phrasings in Caxton's prohemye to the second ed. of the CT.

See ten Brink, Studien pp. 130-139, Hist. Eng. Lit. II : 57-60; Lounsbury, Studies II : 486-89; Skeat V : 401-414.

Canon's Yeoman's Tale

MSS, Prints, and Editions: See under MSS of the Cant. Tales, Eds. of Works, Eds. of Cant. Tales. This Tale is printed in Ashmole's Theatrum Chemicum Britannicum; for a description and list of contents of this curious alchemical volume see Corser's Collectanea I : 63-66.

Printed in Corson's Selections; the prol. is printed in Paton; see under D above.

Modernizations and Translations: Modernized by Lipscomb, by Cowden Clarke, by Saunders, by Purves, by Pitt-Taylor, by Skeat, by Mackaye; see under E above.

Translated into German by Hertzberg, by von Düring; into French by Chatelain; see under E above.

Source, Analogues, etc.: The source of this Tale, as of Ben Jonson's Alchemist, is to be sought in the author's personal knowledge, see Tyrwhitt and ten Brink as cited below. On alchemy see the introd. to C. M. Hathaway's ed. of Jonson's Alchemist, diss. Yale, pub. N. Y. 1903, and The Story of Alchemy, by Muir, N. Y. 1903; both of these are later than Prof. Skeat's notes, and present the subject more historically and clearly.

Date: Placed by Skeat, II : xxxvii, III : 492-3, among the Tales latest written.

Notes: Skeat III : 493 notes the haste with which this Tale is written, and yet the maturity of style and command of rhythm which it shows. Ten Brink, Hist. Eng. Lit. II : 180-81, points out that this Tale is in substance from real life, and queries whether Chaucer himself, toward the close of his life, was swindled by an alchemical impostor. Tyrwhitt, Introd. Disc. § xxxviii, had already remarked that "some sudden resentment" apparently determined Chaucer to introduce this Tale. See Saunders pp. 120 ff., Skeat V : 414-434.

FRAGMENT H

The Tale of the Manciple, with a headlink of 104 lines. In the Ch. Soc. Trial Tables Furnivall treated this Tale and that of the Parson as constituting one fragment; but in his Temp. Pref. p. 37 he explains his reason for altering his opinion, and for considering the Tales of Manciple and of Parson as two separate fragments.

Ten Brink, Hist. Eng. Lit. II : 182, thought that this Tale was intended for the return journey; doubted by Skeat, V : 415. Furnivall, Temp. Pref. pp. 31 ff. (see p. 36), remarks that Lydgate wrote his story of Thebes as the first Tale of the Canterbury pilgrims' return journey, which he would not have done had Chaucer written his Manciple's Tale for the same position. Here, however, we must observe that Lydgate read Chaucer's work so carelessly that in the prologue to the same Story of Thebes he alludes to the quarrel of the Pardoner with the Friar.

In the headlink to this Tale the Host first calls upon the Cook to narrate, although that pilgrim had already begun a Tale, see end of Fragment A. On this point see under F here.

In Caxton's first ed. of the Tales there is no epilogue to the NPTale; in his second ed. this epilogue appears, but is printed continuous with the Manciple's prologue, and under the heading of the Manciple's prologue. Hence the treatment in the blackletter eds. mentioned by Skeat III : 501.

Manciple's Tale

MSS, Prints, and Editions: See under MSS of the Cant. Tales, Eds. of Works, Eds. of Cant. Tales.

Modernizations and Translations: Modernized by Wordsworth, who however considered it unfit for publication, see p. 227 here. Modernized by Jackson, by Lipscomb, by Leigh Hunt, by

Saunders, by Purves, by Pitt-Taylor, by Calder; see under E above.

Translated into German by Hertzberg, by von Düring; into French by Chatelain; see under E above.

Source, Analogues, etc.: Tyrwhitt, Introd. Disc. § xxxix, remarked that this fable had been related by so many narrators, from Ovid to Gower, that it was impossible to say whom Chaucer principally followed. See Ch. Soc. Orig. and Anal. pp. 437-480, 545, Koeppel in Anglia 13 : 181, 14 : 261-2, Archiv 86 : 44 ff., Skeat III : 501. The story is in Gower's Confessio Amantis, book 3.

Date: Furnivall, Athen. 1871 II : 495, says this Tale "must be late"; Koeppel, Anglia 14 : 261-2, says this Tale must have been written before that of the Squire. See under F here.

Notes: See Saunders p. 108; Skeat V : 50, 439-443.

FRAGMENT I

The Parson's headlink and Tale.

The opening line of this headlink contains the Manciple's name. Furnivall, p. 589 of the Six-Text, says that there was originally a blank at that point, into which the Manciple's name was put by the scribes; note the erasure in the Hengwrt MS, over which the name is written. MS Christ Church, in which the Canon's Yeoman precedes the Parson, has the name Yeoman in line 1 of the Parson's headlink. At first Furnivall treated this Fragment and the Manciple's Tale as one, see Trial Tables; but the realization of the above probability caused him to separate them, see Forewords to Trial Tables, and Temp. Pref. p. 37.

The allusion to the exaltation of the moon in line 10 of the headlink has occasioned difficulty to commentators. See Brae, N. and Q. 1851 I : 419-21, and for the most recent note Garnett in Athen. 1902 I : 625.

Parson's Tale

MSS, Prints, and Editions: See under MSS of Cant. Tales, Eds. of Works, Eds. of Cant. Tales. Fragments are in a Longleat MS, see Hist. MSS Comm. Report III, p. 181. In Pepys 2006, with the Tale of Melibeus.

Modernizations and Translations: Lipscomb omitted this Tale from his modernizations because of its "dry and unentertaining" character. An abridgment appeared Lond. 1841. The

Tale is condensed and partly summarized in the work of Purves, 1870. Translated into German by von Düring, though not by Hertzberg. See under E above.

Title: Marked in the Longleat MS "The Three Parties of Penaunce."

Authenticity: Doubt as to Chaucer's authorship of the Tale in its present form was expressed by Simon in—Chaucer a Wicliffite. An Essay on Chaucer's Parson and Parson's Tale. Ch. Soc. Essays, part III. Previously published, "Chaucer ein Wicliffit" in a programme, Schmalkalden, 1876. Simon argues (1) that Chaucer was a Wicliffite. (2) That consequently the Catholic parts of the Parson's Tale, which are also the dryer and poorly written parts, were not his, but interpolations into his treatise De Poenitentia. He discovers three separate hands in the Tale, which was interpolated at Westminster, in the first decennium of the XV century.

Reviewed Koch, Anglia 2 : 540-44, adversely.

The theory of interpolation by another hand was also advocated in Die Erzählung des Pfarrers in Chaucers Canterbury-geschichten und die Somme de Vices et de Vertus des Frère Lorens. W. Eilers, diss. Erlangen, 1882, pp. 66. Transl. and printed Ch. Soc. Essays, part V. Reviewed Koch, Anglia 5: Anz. 130-34; Archiv 69: 464; Littblatt 1885, p. 326.

Eilers' main discussion is on the source; but he agrees with Simon as to the composite character of the treatise, though denying the possibility of separating the Chaucerian parts from the spurious.

Lowell, in his essay on Chaucer (My Study Windows), doubts the authenticity of this Tale.

Morley, Eng. Writers V: 346, agrees with Eilers that the Pars. Tale is longer than Chaucer made it.

Ten Brink, Hist. Eng. Lit. II : 183, says that "different hands, whose work is badly matched, may be distinctly seen."

The opposite view, that of the genuineness of the Tale as it stands, has been maintained by Furnivall, Trial Forewords p. 113; by Koch in his reviews of Simon and of Eilers as above cited; by von Düring in his transl. of the CT, III : 467; by Koeppel in Ueber das Verhältniss von Chaucers Prosawerken zu seinen Dichtungen, und die Echtheit der Parsons Tale, Archiv 87 : 33-54 (1891). Koeppel shows that many passages of the Pars. Tale appear, in a slightly modified form, in other parts of the CT. Skeat III : 504 supports Koeppel's view. Similarly Root, Poetry of Chaucer p. 287.

Source: Morris, in his ed. of Chaucer, 1866, first suggested as source the Somme de Vices et de Vertus of Frère Lorens. Detailed comparison of the two works was made by Eilers in the monograph above mentioned. Suggestions were added by Koeppel, Archiv 84 : 417 (1890). Liddell, in a paper entitled A New Source of the Parson's Tale, pubd. in An English Mis-cellany, pp. 255-278, suggested The Clensyng of Mannes Sowl_t as well as Lorens. But

The Sources of the Parson's Tale, Kate O. Petersen, Boston, 1901, rev. Spies, Archiv 108 : 430; Koeppel, Engl. Stud. 30 : 464; Nation 1901 II : 284; Koch in Littblatt 1903 p. 156; Romania 31 : 641—has put an entirely new face on the matter. Miss Petersen argues that the immediate source of the Tale is not yet known, but that the sources of that source were Latin treatises by Pennaforte and by Peraldus. Her monograph is, of course, later than Skeat's Oxford Chaucer, in which, III : 502-4, are found the theories of Morris and of Eilers.

Maetzner, Altengl. Sprachproben II : 56, notes correspond-ences between this Tale and the Ayenbite of Inwit.

Date: Hertzberg, p. 670, considered this one of the Tales written before Chaucer conceived the plan of the CT, and assigned to the Parson as the character best suited. Furnivall, Athen. 1871 II : 495, Trial Forewords pp. 9, 28, and Koch, Chronology p. 79, put this Tale at the end of Chaucer's life, in his period of decline. Koeppel, Archiv 87 : 50, says it was done in Chaucer's last years. Ten Brink, Hist. Eng. Lit. II : 182, thinks that it was composed at a time when the poet no longer hoped to accompany the pilgrims back to Southwark, at the time when he gave the final touches to his work. Skeat III : 503 says that the Tale was probably written before 1380, at much the same time as the Melibeus, but that a few paragraphs near the end were later insertions.

Notes: On the Parson see Todd p. 256; Saunders pp. 94 ff.; Skeat V : 45-47; the Tale is annotated *ibid.* 444 ff.; Anglia 24 : 498-503. On the prose of the Tale see the dissertation of Heussler cited under Melibeus above.

See ten Brink as cited; Root, Poetry of Chaucer pp. 284-88.

The "Retractation"

MSS: Some MSS of the Canterbury Tales are defective at close, or lack a portion of the Tales, so that the existence of the Parson's Tale or of the Retractation in them is doubtful. Such MSS are: Hengwrt, Dd, Trinity R 3, 3, Sloane 1685, Laud 739, Harley 7335, Corpus, Egerton 2863, Laud 600 (whose gaps, including this portion, are supplied in a Jacobean hand). Sloane 1686 and

Barlow end with the Manciple's Tale; Harley 7333 ceases copying, with space left blank, before the end of the Parson's Tale is reached.

The Retractation exists in Harley 7334, Selden, Ellesmere, Adds. 5140, Gg, Egerton 2726, Egerton 2864, Hodson 39, Harley 1758, Royal 18, Mm, Petworth, Lansdowne 851, Rawlinson 149, Trinity R 3, 15.

Prints and Editions: In both eds. by Caxton, and in the blackletter eds. down to 1532, when Thynne did not print it; it did not reappear until the Urry of 1721; regularly printed since then.

Title: Marked in Harley 7334 "Preces de Chauceres", in the Ellesmere "Here taketh the makere of this book his leve", in Adds 5140, "Hic capit Autor licenciam", in Selden "Here endeth the tales of Caunterbury And next thautour taketh leve." Harley 1758 supplies the Retractation in the Ch. Soc. print of the Gg MS, but the heading is still in the Gg, "Here takyt the makere of this bok his leue." Egerton 2726 reads "Here the maker taketh His leue." Most of the Retractation in this MS is in a late 18th century hand; Furnivall notes, p. 677 of the Ch. Soc. print of Dd, that this transcription is perhaps from Laud K. 50 (Laud 600), which the same 18th century hand has used for the Gamelyn it has copied into the Egerton. The Petworth heads the Retractation "Here takeþ þe maker of þis booke his leue." Lansdowne 851 has "Composito huius libri hic capit licenciam suam."

Caxton's second ed. heads it "The Prayer"; the de Worde of 1498 marks it "Here takyth the maker of this boke his leue." The title "Retractation" is due to Urry, and is probably derived from the wording of the text, "my retraccions."

Authenticity: Gascoigne, in his Dictionarium Theologicum, of the 15th century, cited by Hales, Athen. 1888 I : 404, and printed Ch. Soc. Life Records part IV, p. 332, refers to the Retractation in terms which imply his acceptance of it as genuine.

Hearne, in his Remarks and Collections II : 200, says that he believes the Revocation genuine; in his Letter to Bagford he says: "I begin to think that the Revocation is not genuine, but that it was made by the monks." The reasons Hearne gives are that the copies differ, and that the scribe includes himself in the petition.

Tyrwhitt, in his Notes, will not go quite so far as Hearne, but he considers that the middle part of the Recantation may be an interpolation. Dibdin, Typographical Antiq. I : 294, "The whole of this passage is now allowed to be surreptitious, it having been foisted in by the zeal of some pious monk."

21

Nicolas, Life of Chaucer: "If the authenticity of this were unimpeachable, it would be one of the most interesting passages Chaucer ever wrote." . . . . "unsafe to reject it as a forgery." . . . . "great hesitation in accepting it."

Wright, 1847 ed. of the Cant. Tales, introd. p. xxii, thinks that the Retractation was "perhaps introduced by the person who arranged the text after Chaucer's death."

Hertzberg, p. 672 of his Canterbury Geschichten, "work of a wellmeaning but clumsy zealot" . . . . "spurious."

Simon as cited above, 1876, says, "He who adulterated the Parson's Tale crowned his ignoble work by adding the Retractation." Ward, Life of Chaucer, p. 56, "The extraordinary tag (if it may be called by so irreverent a name) to the extant Canterbury Tales." Morley, Eng. Writers V: 346, "fabulous."

Hales, Dict. Nat. Biog., *art.* Chaucer, "One would rejoice if this morbid passage . . . . could be shown to be the interpolation of some monk, but as it is, we must suppose that to Chaucer there came an hour of reaction and weakness." Hales thinks we cannot blink the evidence of Gascoigne.

Lounsbury, Studies I : 413-15, III : 40, holds opinion similar to Hales.

Skeat, III : 503, V : 475, thinks that the Retractation was interpolated, as Tyrwhitt suggested, but by Chaucer himself. Pollard, Chaucer Primer, pp. 125-126, "has a genuine ring." Liddell, Acad. 1896 II: 116, is against its genuineness. Kittredge, Mod. Phil. I : 13, notes a parallel case against those who consider the Retractation incredible. Tatlock, Devel. and Chronol. p. 25 note, terms it "certainly genuine."

Notes: For a fantasy suggested by the Retractation, see Dum Regnat Dolor. A Legend of Geoffrey Chaucer. By Layton Crippen. New York, 1895.

Privately printed, on vellum, 50 copies only; very wide margins, and fanciful letterpress. A prose narrative of an interview between Chaucer and a priest, who reproves him for lustful language, and proffers him the Retractation to sign, threatening him with the pains of hell if he refuses. This document is left with Chaucer, and he muses wearily over it; in his sleep that night he dies, and the Retractation is found unsigned beside his bed.

H. Pictures of the Pilgrims

The illustrations of the Ellesmere MS of the Canterbury Tales, and what remain of the illuminations of the Cambridge Gg MS are reproduced by the Chaucer Society with the Six-Text. The Ellesmere pictures are also reproduced in each of the separate prints of the six texts, and with the prints of Harley 7334 and Cambridge Dd; the two latter contain the Gg pictures as well. All these are drawn by W. H. Hooper. They are also reproduced in Saunders' Canterbury Tales, in Mrs. Haweis' Chaucer for Schools, and in Garnett and Gosse's English Literature, vol. I.

An illumination of the pilgrims leaving Canterbury on the return journey is in MS Royal 18 D ii, a copy of Lydgate's Story of Thebes; it is reproduced by T. Wright in his 1847 Canterbury Tales vol. I, in Wülker's Gesch. der engl. Lit. (after p. 155), in Garnett and Gosse's Engl. Lit. vol. I to face p. 150, and as frontispiece to Skeat's 1904 modernization of the Knight's Tale. A photographic plate from the original is also in my possession.

In MS Rawlinson poet. 223 there are figures of the Friar and of Melibeus.

Caxton's second ed. of the Tales, ca. 1484, contains woodcuts of the pilgrims; that of the Shipman, with a few lines of text, is reprod. in the Bibliographical Society's Transactions vol. VI to face p. 38. Gordon Duff, in his William Caxton, has reprod. the cut of the Squire; in Pollard's Early Illustrated Books p. 222 and in Garnett and Gosse's English Literature I: 152 is reprod. the page bearing the cut of the Canon's Yeoman. The cut of the pilgrims all seated at table is reprod. by de Worde in his print of Lydgate's Assembly of the Gods, facsimiled by the Cambridge University Press, 1906; in Simonds' Student's Hist. of Eng. Lit., in Mather's ed. of the Prologue, and in Jusserand's English Novel in the Time of Shakespeare, the same cut is reproduced. See Dibdin, Typogr. Antiq. I: 300.

The woodcuts of the second Caxton are used in the Pynson Canterbury Tales of 1492, also in the de Worde of 1498; and there are woodcuts in the Thynne ed. of the Works of 1542. The undated Thynne has however but two cuts, differing from those of 1542. The cuts of the 1484 Caxton also appear in one of the issues of the Works of 1561, q. v. See Quaritch, Catalogue No. 234.

Other eds. illustrated with pictures of the pilgrims are: the Urry Chaucer of 1721; the Bell of 1782, with its vignette frontispieces drawn by Stothard, also in the Cooke of 1798; the Cumberland Chaucer, q. v.; and several of the Routledge Chaucers, by Corbould. See also in especial the Kelmscott Chaucer.

Pictures of the pilgrims are to be found in the various Chaucers for Children, see under that heading; and note especially those drawn for the Mackaye modernization of the Canterbury Tales by the late Walter Appleton Clark, which were also reprod. by Fox, Duffield and Co. on a calendar for 1907.

J. H. Mortimer's Chaucer Drawings were published in 1787, see Furnivall in N. and Q. 1880 II : 325, cp. 355. The original drawings are in the Victoria and Albert Museum, South Kensington; according to information kindly furnished me by Mr. H. M. Cundall of the Board of Education, these drawings and the engravings from them include: January and May; The Sompnour, the Devil, and an Old Woman; The Three Gamblers and Time; The Coke and Perkin; The Frere and Thomas; The Miller of Trumpington and Two Scholars; Palamon and Arcite; Nicholas the Carpenter and Robin; The Departure of the Canterbury Pilgrims. The engravers were J. K. Sherwin, E. Williams, Sharp, and Jacob Hogg.

In 1806 Thomas Stothard received from R. H. Cromek a commission to paint the Canterbury Pilgrims. Cromek had previously seen a design by William Blake on the subject, for which he had unsuccessfully negotiated; Stothard accepted the commission in ignorance of Blake's work, but the result was a rupture between Stothard and Blake, who had until then been friends and occasional collaborators. Stothard's work was exhibited in 1807 and was a decided success; an elaborate critical description of it by W. Carey was pubd. in 1808. Blake laid the matter before the public in an exhibition of his own work, for which he wrote a descriptive catalogue, Oct. 1809; this catalogue is reprinted in Gilchrist's Life of Blake, 1880, II : 137 ff.; the picture follows, p. 144. See also Chaucer's Prologue and Characters from the Canterbury Tales, Lond. 1812, 12mo., with Blake's picture as frontispiece. The engraving from Stothard's picture, done by the Schiavonettis, by Engleheart, and by Heath, was pubd. October 1817. Stothard's picture is reprod. in Garnett and Gosse's Engl. Lit. vol. I, in Robertson Nicoll's Bookman Illustrated Hist. of Eng. Lit., vol. I, to face p. 12 (part of the picture only).

Edward Corbould, who illustrated the Routledge Chaucer, q. v., also painted The Pilgrims Leaving the Tabard Inn; this was engraved by Wagstaffe, and forms a picture 32 by 22½ inches.

Wall paintings are in Eaton Hall, the seat of the Duke of Westminster, painted by H. S. Marks, R. A.; in Mr. George Gould's summer home at Lakewood, N. J., painted by Robert Van Vorst Sewell, reprods. obtainable through Klackner of New York City.

In 1900 was unveiled the stained glass window in St. Saviour's, Southwark. For description of the window in Westminster Abbey see Temp. Pref. pp. 133-36.

A drawing of the Pilgrims by Paul Hardy was published by the Chaucer Society with No. XCI supplement of their 1st Series, q. v.

See also under Man of Law's Tale, Clerk's Tale, Franklin's Tale, above.

SECTION IV

WORKS OTHER THAN THE CANTERBURY TALES

THE LEGEND OF GOOD WOMEN, THE TROILUS AND CRESSIDA, THE ASTROLABE, THE BOETHIUS, THE MINOR POEMS

In Alphabetical Order

According to Furnivall, PT p. 407, Bradshaw used the term Minor Poems to mean those of one movement,—the ABC, the Former Age, Words to Adam, Mother of God, Proverbs, Truth, Complaint of Venus, Scogan, Bukton, Gentilesse, Stedfastnesse, Fortune, Purse. The others Bradshaw classed as Stories and Complaints, that is, Pity, the Mars with the complaint of Mars, Anelida and Arcite with its complaint of Anelida; or as Narrative Poems,—the Duchesse, the Troilus, the Parlement of Foules, the House of Fame, the Legend of Good Women.

Furnivall himself uses the term Minor Poems in a wider sense, to include all of Chaucer but the Canterbury Tales. See PT p. 407. On the Contents leaf of the PT, dated October 1879, he says, speaking of his arrangement of the Minor Poems: "The Poems not in chronological order are the englisht ABC, which may be Chaucer's earliest work, and is certainly of his First Period; the Complaint to Pite, which is assuredly Chaucer's first original Minor Poem, and before his Blaunche of 1369, and the Parlement of Foules, which Dr. John Koch has well argued to be of the year 1381. . . . If we put the ABC, Pity, and Mars in Chaucer's First Period, the Mother of God, Anelida, Former Age, and Adam in the Second; the Parlement, Fame, and Legend in the third, and the remaining Ballads and Poems of Reflection and Later Age in the fourth, we shall have as good a classification of the Minor Poems as I can at present get at."

Skeat, in his revised ed. of the Minor Poems, p. vii, says that he includes all of Chaucer's genuine poetical works with the exception of . . . . the Canterbury Tales, Troilus and Cressida, and the Legend of Good Women. He does not there print any part of the Romaunt of the Rose; but on pp. xxiv-xxv he first rejects it, and then, in his revised ed., adds a sentence accepting lines 1-1705.

In the Globe Chaucer there are classed as Earlier Minor Poems: the Book of the Duchesse, Pity, the ABC, Mars, the Complaint to his Lady, Anelida, and the Parlement of Foules. As Later Minor Poems are printed: To Rosemounde, Former Age, Fortune, Truth, Gentilesse, Stedfastnesse, Scogan, Bukton, Venus, Purse, Proverbs. Five Doubtful Minor Poems are also included in the volume. The Words to Adam are placed separately, following Troilus and Boece.

325

A. The Manuscripts

In the following list the manuscripts of all the poems other than the Cant. Tales are mentioned or described, but not manuscripts of the Astrolabe or the Boethius; for MSS of those works see under their respective headings. Descriptions printed in Anglia, Englische Studien, or Modern Language Notes, are not here reproduced. The descriptions of editors have been meagre. Thomas, in his preface to the Urry Chaucer, mentioned briefly some MSS; and Bell, in the 1854 Chaucer, alluded occasionally to peculiarities in a codex. Skeat, I : 48-58 and Minor Poems xl ff., is very unsatisfactory in his hasty and summary remarks, which called forth from Flügel, Anglia 22 : 510 ff. (1899), a censure accompanied by a collection of facts from the pages of the Chaucer Society prints, etc. A list of MSS, but without annotation, had previously been made by Koch, Anglia 4 : Anz. 112-117 (1881).

Catalogues of the British Museum MSS, the Oxford MSS, the Cambridge MSS, may be found as referred to in Section III B here.

In the lists of contents of the separate MSS, the Chaucerian minor poems may be found discussed, in alphabetical order, in Section IV here; the non-Chaucerian works which have at any time been printed as genuine are discussed, in alphabetical order, in Section V here.

For a note on the Editing of the Minor Poems, see Mod. Lang. Notes 23 : 20.

(1) *In the British Museum*

Additionals 9832: See Catalogue of Additions . . . . etc., and Skeat III : xlix. An incomplete copy of the Legend of Good Women; printed Ch. Soc. SPT pp. 59 ff.

Additionals 10340: A copy of Chaucer's Boece, on vellum, in double columns, written in a small, conventional hand, with archaic characters, and very dark ink. Of 40 leaves, with fly-leaves at end which contain, in another and more current hand,, also early XV century,—Chaucer's Truth. Printed Athen. 1867 II : 333; in Ch. Soc. PT p. 407, One-Text Print p. 293. In the Appendix to Morris' revision of the Aldine Chaucer; see notes on the poem below. The second column of the same page contains the description of the Parson, from the Gen. Prol.; the verso and the other flyleaves are scribbled. This page is reprod. Ch. Soc. Autotypes; there dated of the first third of the XV century.

Note on the MS in Skeat I : 57, II : xlii-iii. The entire MS was ed. by Morris, EETS. Furnivall, in Forewords to Ch. Soc. Autotypes, says that the existence of the additional stanza to Truth in this MS makes it "one of the greatest Chaucer treasures in Great Britain"; but see under the discussion of the poem below.

Additionals 12044: A Troilus MS; see Skeat II : lxxiv.

Additionals 12524: Contains the Legend of Good Women; see Skeat III : xlix. Printed Ch. Soc. First Series No. LIX, SPT pp. 59 ff.

Additionals 16165: Described and contents listed Mod. Lang. Notes 19 : 35-38. In the hand of John Shirley. The Chaucerian entries are Boece, Anelida; also a balade headed by Shirley as Chaucer's, which is printed Mod. Lang. Notes as above, with refs. to earlier prints. A page is reprod. Ch. Soc. Autotypes; there dated ca. 1450. On Shirley see Section VII B below, and Anglia 30 : 320-348.

Additionals 22139: A copy of Gower's Confessio Amantis, well written on vellum in double columns in two early XV century hands, with rubrics and colored caps., but much mutilated. Of 138 leaves about 14 by 10¼ inches. The poem ends on fol. 137b with the usual Latin colophon; on 138a the same scribe has copied Purse, Gentilesse, Stedfastnesse, and Truth, without any note. The date 1432 appears on fol. 1. Observe the grouping of these poems in this MS, Cotton Cleop. D vii, and Harley 7578.

See Macaulay, Works of John Gower, II : cxlvi; Meyer, John Gower's Beziehungen, pp. 50-51; Skeat I : 57.

Additionals 28617: A fragment of the Legend of Good Women, printed Ch. Soc. SPT pp. 59 ff. Note in Skeat III : l.

Additionals 34360: Described and contents listed Anglia 28 : 1 ff. Its Chaucerian entries are Purse and Pity; it has also the Ballad of Pity, and Womanly Noblesse, see Section V here.

Cotton Cleopatra D vii: On vellum, of 192 leaves about 9¾ by 6½ inches, irregularly cut. In several hands of the XV century, square and archaic. The last scribe took up the work on fol. 140a, in the middle of a French prose chronicle which ends abruptly fol. 182b, at anno 6 of Edward III. From 183a to 187b the same writer copies a prose Life of Our Lady, then a brief prose bit on tribulation, then, on foll. 188b and 189a, Chaucer's Gentilesse, printed Ch. Soc. PT p. 427; Chaucer's Stedfastnesse, printed Ch. Soc. PT p. 433; Chaucer's Truth, printed Ch. Soc. PT p. 407; Newfanglenesse, see Section V below.

On fol. 190 continues a Latin coronation order which was art. 1 of the volume, and had been broken off at foot of 5a. Note on the volume in Skeat I : 57.

Cotton Otho A xviii: See Flügel in Anglia 22 : 512-514 for full account of this non-existent MS and of the erroneous statements made concerning it.

Harley 78: An entirely miscellaneous codex, its contents thrown arbitrarily together by the binder, and of various sizes, dates and tenor. Skeat I : 58 speaks carelessly of it as "one of Shirley's MSS." Four leaves only, now numbered 80-83, are in the hand of Shirley, and contain the bits printed in the supplem. volume of the Ballad Society, p. 39, by Furnivall; Chaucer's Pity; and, with no complete break, the poem printed Ch. Soc. OT pp. ii-v as the Ballad of Pity, also printed by Skeat I : 360 and Minor Poems as Chaucer's. Nothing else in the volume concerns Chaucer students; much of the contents is of the XVI century. Gaertner, in his diss. on John Shirley, p. 18, enumerates its articles, but fails to perceive its composite character. Dated by the Ch. Soc. 1460-70. Note in Skeat I : 58.

Harley 372: On paper, of 114 leaves 11⅞ by 8⅜ inches. Written in a clean, clear hand, by one scribe up to fol. 71, after which the verse is by Hoccleve; anterior to that point by Lydgate and Chaucer, *viz.*:

(1) foll. 1a-25a. Lydgate's St. Edmund.

(2) foll. 25a-43b. His St. Fremund.

(3) foll. 43b-44b. The prologue to St. Edmund, nine stanzas of eight lines. These poems are printed from Harley 2278 by Horstmann, Altengl. Legenden, pp. 376 ff., with variants from Ashmole 46.

(4) foll. 45a-51a. Poem on marriage, printed from this MS by Halliwell, Minor Poems of Lydgate, p. 27.

(5) foll. 51a-53b. Lydgate's Verses on English Kings, Henry VI last. See note in Anglia 28 : 6-7.
The date 1422 is twice written.

(6) foll. 54b-55a. "An exhortation of the crucifix." Fifteen stanzas of eight lines, beginning "Man to refourme thyn exil & thi los." Copies also in Harley 7333, Laud 683, R 3, 21, Kk i, 6. [The Complaint of Christ.]

(7) foll. 55a-55b. A Gaude. Eight stanzas of seven lines. Not the same as that in Lambeth 306, printed Pol. Rel. and Love Poems, p. 145.

(8) fol. 56a. A prayer to St. Sebastian, Latin and English, in parallel cols., both texts crossed out.
Fol. 56b is blank except that a later hand has noted the preceding contents.

(9) foll. 57a-60b. Anelida and Arcite. Printed Ch. Soc. PT pp. 145 ff.

(10) foll. 61a-69b. La Belle Dame sans Mercy. See Section V here. This text is printed Pol. Rel. and Love Poems pp. 52 ff.
At the end of the poem, foot of fol. 69b, the scribe has written, Qui legit emendat scriptorem non reprehendat.

(11) fol. 70a-b. In another hand, seven seven-line stanzas beginning O sterr of Jacob glorye of Israell. Also in Laud 683.

On fol. 71a begins, imperfect, Hoccleve's De Regimine Principum, in the hand of another scribe, and with a much later heading. At the end of the volume are, in later and very small hands, six quatrains against dress, accompanied by the Latin; also the Ballad of Little John Nobody.

A close investigation will perhaps bring out relations between this MS and Harley 7333 on the one hand, Fairfax 16 on the other. Note the agreements in contents with the Harley 7333 codex, and the presence in the Fairfax of La Belle Dame (not in its sister Bodley 638) and of a copy of the Anelida which shares with this MS certain textual peculiarities not seen in other MSS.

Harley 1239: See ante under MSS of the Canterbury Tales, Section III B (1).

Harley 2251: On paper, 293 leaves 11⅝ by 8¼ inches. The Harleian Catalogue ascribes the codex to Shirley, an error which is repeated by Skeat I : 57 and by the Dict. Nat. Biog. s. v. Shirley. Foerster, Archiv 103 : 149-151 (1899), pointed out the impossibility. List of contents in the Harleian Catalogue; note by Flügel in Anglia 22 : 511; full description of this volume and its partial sister Adds. 34360 in Anglia 28 : 1 ff. The Chaucerian entries are Purse, Fortune, Gentilesse, the ABC, and the Prioress' Tale.

Harley 2280: Described in the Harleian Catalogue as "A parchment Book reduced by the plough of a knavish Binder from a folio to a 4to, containing Geffrey Chaucers Poem of 'Troilus & Criseida' in five books." Printed in full Ch. Soc. First Series Nos. LXIII, LXIV. Note by Skeat II : lxix.

Harley 2392: Described in the Harleian Cat. as "A Book in 4to, written partly upon Parchement, but mostly upon Paper; wherein is contained Geffrey Chaucers Poem of Troilus & Cresseida."
Note by Skeat II : lxxii.

Harley 3943: Described in the Harleian Cat. as "Chaucer's Loves of Troilus & Cresseide, in five books. An old Copy, on vellum. Bought at Mr. Rawlinson's Sale of MSS, 1734. 'This has been collated by Wm. Thomas, Esq.'"
Printed in full by the Ch. Soc., First Series Nos. XLIV, LXV, with Rossetti's collation of the Italian, literally translated. Note by Skeat II : lxxi.

Harley 4912: Described in the Harleian Cat. as "A vellum MS

marked on the first leaf 'Petri Le Neve Norroy, pr. 1 lb. 01
sh. 00 d.' The writing throughout distinct, but not elegant.
It contains the chief part of Chaucer's Troilus & Cresseyde,
from the beginning to the end of the 98th stanza of Book IV.
The second book begins at fol. 15, the third at fol. 40, the
fourth at fol. 66. The whole number of leaves at present is
75." Note by Skeat II : lxxiv.

Harley 7333: See ante under MSS of the Canterbury Tales, Section III B (1).

Harley 7578: Like Harley 78, a miscellaneous volume, papers of
different sizes, dates, and nature, bound together subsequently.
Leaves 2 to 20 are vellum, rubbed in places, written over in a
small, cramped late XV century (or later) hand, and about
11¼ by 7⅞ inches in size. Contents:

(1) Lydgate's Summum Sapientiae, marked "Liber Proverbiorum."
Other texts in Harley 2251, Ashmole 59. See Foerster in
Archiv 104: 304-309; also Anglia 28: 22.

(2) Four stanzas of eight lines, beginning "Al holly youres withouten others parte." Printed by Skeat, Athen. 1894 II : 98
as Chaucer's. Also in his revised ed. of Minor Poems p. 468,
Oxford Chaucer IV : xxvii. Entitled by him "Complaint to
my Mortal Foe"; see Section V here.

(3) Three stanzas of seven lines, beginning "It is no right alle
other lustes to lese." Printed in part by Furnivall, Athen.
1871 I : 210, from Adds. 16165, where Shirley marks the
page as by Chaucer. Printed complete, with another poem
from the same MS, by Furnivall in the supplem. vol. of the
Ballad Society, pp. 34-36; again printed Mod. Lang. Notes
19 : 35-38, q. v.

(4), (5) The next 16 stanzas are apparently two poems. The word
"Balade" is written in the margin beside the first, and also
beside the 10th stanza; the first nine stanzas are of seven
lines, the remaining seven of eight lines. Skeat has printed
the first seven stanzas as "Complaint to my Lodesterre",
Athen. 1894 II : 162, Oxford Chaucer IV : xxix, Minor
Poems p. 470. The poem written in strophes of eight lines
begins: "Burgeys thou haste so blowen atte the Cole"; it
is exceedingly coarse in character.

(6) Chaucer's Gentilesse, without any break, not even a capital
letter. Printed Ch. Soc. PT p. 427.

(7) Chaucer's Stedfastnesse; "Balade" written in the margin, but
no capital letter. Printed Ch. Soc. PT p. 433.

(8) Newfanglenesse, see Section V here. Three stanzas of seven
lines.

(9) Lydgate's Doublenesse, 13 stanzas of eight lines. See Section V here.

(10) At the foot of fol. 18b is a stanza of the Latin headings
belonging to the next poem, which begins, on 19a, "Most
soueraine lord o blessith crist Jesu." Twelve stanzas of
seven lines; copies also in Fairfax 16, Trin. Coll. Cambr.
R 3, 21, Harley 2251, Adds. 34360; see Anglia 28 : 8. This
text is printed Reliq. Antiq. I : 227.

(11) One stanza of seven lines, beginning, "Desceit descayuable";

also in Fairfax 16, Hatton 73, Trin. Coll. Cambr. R 3, 20. See Anglia 28 : 9.

(12) One stanza of seven lines, beginning "Worship women wyne vnweldy age"; for note on which see Anglia 28 : 21.

(13) "Prouerbe of Chaucers" written in four long lines; printed Ch. Soc. PT p. 431.

(14) Followed without space by the two stanzas beginning respectively "The more I go" and "The world so wide." See Anglia 28 : 4.

(15) Chaucer's ABC, without heading, six stanzas only. Printed Ch. Soc. SPT p. 27. Note that the Pepys 2006 fragment is of the same length.

A brief note on this MS is in Mod. Lang. Notes 19 : 38; comment in Skeat, I : 58. Dated PT p. 432 as about 1450.

The agreements between this MS and Fairfax 16 in the texts and grouping of a number of these poems are too close to be fortuitous.

Lansdowne 699: Part vellum, part paper, of 176 leaves 7⅜ by 5⅜ inches; imperfect at beginning and end; written in one small current hand of the latter XV century. The poems usually begin on a recto, with titles entered at foot of the preceding verso; the stanzas are spaced, and small, roughly colored caps. are frequent. The codex once belonged to William Browne, who has twice written his name; other MSS formerly his are listed Anglia 30 : 321. Margins much scribbled by later owners; contents mainly by Lydgate. The codex Leyden Vossius 9, which is a close duplicate of this, is described by Robinson, Harvard Studies V : 186 ff. Brief note on this MS in Skeat I : 59. Contents:

(1) foll. 1a-2b. Lydgate's St. Giles, defective at beginning. A copy in Harley 2255 is printed by Horstmann, Altengl. Legenden, p. 371.

(2) foll. 3a-18a. Lydgate's Fabula Duorum Mercatorum. Ed. by Zupitza-Schleich, Strassburg 1897, from six MSS.

(3) foll. 18b-27b. Lydgate's Guy of Warwick. The text in Laud 683 was ed. by Zupitza, Vienna 1873; list of variants in Lansdowne was pubd. Germania 25 : 365. Other MSS are Harley 7333, R 3, 21, and the Leyden and Harvard University codices described by Robinson as above.

(4) foll. 27b-34b. Lydgate's Churl and Bird. Other MSS are the Leyden, Harley 116, R 3, 19, Hh iv, 12 and Kk i, 6, Cotton Caligula A ii, Longleat 258 (imperfect). The Harley copy was printed Halliwell, Minor Poems of Lydgate, p. 179. The poem was twice printed by Caxton, see Blades pp. 201, 210; by Pynson about 1490; by de Worde; by John Mychell about 1540; by W. Copland about 1550; by Elias Ashmole in his Theatrum Chemicum Britannicum, 1652; and by Sykes for the Roxburghe Club 1818, from Caxton's second ed. Ashmole entitles the poem Hermes Bird, and says that "the whole Work is Parabolicall and allusive, yet truly Philosophical, and the Bird the Mercury of the Philosophers." A fragment of six stanzas is printed in Corser's Collectanea, VIII : 381.

(5) foll. 35a-41b. Lydgate's St. Austin at Compton. In MS
Leyden; another copy, in Harley 2255, was printed by Halliwell, Minor Poems of Lydgate, p. 135. An imperfect copy is
in Hh iv, 12. The Latin prose story is in Cotton Vespasian
A ix.

(6) foll. 41b-50b. Lydgate's Dance Macabre. There are 11 known
copies of this poem, representing two main recensions: the
Ellesmere, Harley 116, Selden 53, Bodley 221, Laud 735, R 3,
21; the Bodley 686, Corpus Christi College Oxford 237, Lans-
downe, Leyden, and an imperfect copy in Cotton Vespasian
A xxv. The Coventry School MS, which contained the poem,
has disappeared. Printed at the end of the 1554 print of
Lydgate's Falls of Princes; by Dugdale in his Monasticon
Anglicanum, 1673; by Douce as appendix to his Holbein's
Dance of Death, London 1790; in Holbein's Alphabet of
Death, ed. Montaiglon, Paris 1846, cp. Nichols, Lit. Anecd.
IV : 704. An ed. of the Ellesmere and Lansdowne texts is in
prep. for the EETS by Miss Florence Warren; the Selden
text is to be printed in vol. 18 of Section II of the Belles
Lettres Series, Boston.

(7) foll. 51a-61a. Lydgate's "Arthurus Conquestor." 79 stanzas
of seven lines. From the Falls of Princes, book VIII, caps.
24, 25. Ritson's No. 37, in his Bibl. Poet. catalogue of Lydgate's works, perhaps means this extract. In MS Leyden, in
MSS of the Falls.

(8) foll. 61b-66b. The Legend of Constantine, 42 stanzas of
seven lines. I do not identify this with Book VIII chap. 12
of the Falls of Princes, although the subject is similar. In
MS Leyden.

(9) foll. 67a-78b. Lydgate's Horse, Goose, and Sheep. Ed. by
Degenhart, Berlin 1900, from eight MSS; he did not use the
copy in Adds. 34360. A fragment is in Laud 598.

(10) foll. 79a-80b. Lydgate's Verses on English Kings. See
Anglia 28 : 6-7, and Robinson as cited p. 191.

(11) foll. 81a-83a. Chaucer's Fortune. The heading, written as
usual in this MS at the foot of the preceding page, is not
reprod. by the Chaucer Society; see under Fortune below.
Text printed Ch. Soc. SPT p. 167. The Leyden copy of
Fortune is as yet unprinted.

(12) As if continuous with Fortune there is written below, "La bon
conseil de le Auctour." Chaucer's Truth follows, with colophon "Explicit optimus tractatus de ffortuna." Printed Ch.
Soc. SPT p. 153.

(13) foll. 83b-85a. Lydgate's Stans Puer ad Mensam. For note
see Anglia 28 : 20.

(14) foll. 85b-88a. Dietary. For note see Anglia 28 : 7, and especially Robinson as cited above, p. 192 note.

(15) foll. 88b-89b. "Incipit descripcio garcionis." See Anglia 28 :
15. This copy is printed by Halliwell, Minor Poems of Lydgate p. 52.

(16) foll. 90a-91a. Lydgate's Letter to Gloucester. See Anglia
28 : 7.

(17) foll. 91b-94b. "Compilacio sancta contra gulosos &c." Twen-
ty-six stanzas of seven lines, beginning, "The . . . . whan
Saturn was first kyng." The second word is erased. According to Robinson loc. cit. p. 192, from Falls of Princes book
VII, chap. 10. A copy is in Leyden.

A torn white page follows, bearing Browne's name, and a few
lines in his hand, from the beginning of his Britannia's Pastorals.
The rest of the codex is filled by Lydgate's Life of St. Albon,
imperfect.

(2) *Other MSS in London*

Sion College L 40. 2a , Sion College, Victoria Embankment, London.
       3

A copy by John Shirley of the prose translation of De Guileville's Pélérinage de la Vie Humaine, into which is inserted the ABC of Chaucer. A description of the codex may be found in the Gent. Mag. 1860, pt. II, pp. 642-6, signed J. C. J(eaffreson?). Variae lectiones are there printed; there is no mention of the name of Shirley, whose handwriting was not recognized until Furnivall noted the fact, Acad. 1877 II : 551. Previous to that he had discussed the MS on pp. 65 and 78 of Ch. Soc. Odd Texts.

On paper, 93 leaves 10¾ by 7½ inches; imperfect at beginning and end, and heavily cropped and trimmed. In the Acad. as cited it is said that the MS has lost the first two leaves and the last one; this however does not forbid the theory that there were other fascicules preceding or following; see Anglia 28 : 14. The MS shows the injuries which it received by fire and water in the great fire of London.

The leaf bearing the ABC is reproduced Ch. Soc. Autotypes; there dated 1440.

Another Sion College MS, a fragment of the Canterbury Tales not in Shirley's hand, is sometimes mentioned in such a way as to be confused with this; see Dict. Nat. Biog. *s. v.* Shirley, where the "Sion MS of Chaucer" is classed as Shirley's.

(3) *In the Bodleian Library, Oxford*

Ashmole 59: Described in detail, with comparison of other Shirley MSS, in Anglia 30 : 320-348. Already in Anglia 27 : 381-98 the date post 1447 for this MS was argued, a date only a few years before the death of Shirley at ninety; his great age at the time of its transcription is to be recollected in considering the numerous errors and licences which mar this codex, licences which should exclude the volume from any share in the formation of a critical text. The only Chaucerian contents are Gentilesse (included in Scogan's Moral Balade), Fortune, Venus.

Bodley 638: See below, p. 335.

Digby 181: See below, p. 339.

Fairfax 16: A stout vellum volume of 336 leaves 9⅛ by 6⅝ inches, in eights. Written almost entirely in one hand, a clear, firm professional script of the first half of the XV century; the date 1450 is on the flyleaf in a hand apparently contemporary. For

facsimile of the script see Skeat, Twelve Facsimiles, and Oxford
Chaucer, front. to vol. III. Notes by Fairfax on the flyleaf
are mentioned by Schick, Temple of Glass p. xix, and by Simmons, Lay Folks' Mass Book, EETS, p. 389, note. Schick
remarks that John Stow, to whom the MS at one time perhaps
belonged, has inserted some missing lines and made corrections.
Another Jacobean hand is also to be seen in the codex, which
has not only filled the gap in the Book of the Duchess, but has
inserted the Ten Commandments of Love upon leaves left blank
by the scribe. (Skeat is therefore incorrect in his supposition,
Canon p. 122, that the Commandments must be as early as 1450
because of their appearance in this MS.) This same hand has
added to the House of Fame the Caxton-Thynne conclusion.
The last three leaves of the codex are in another hand than that
of the usual scribe.

A contemporary table of contents fills fol. 2; from there to
the beginning of Mars on fol. 15a the leaves are blank except
for a faded sketch on 9a, and for an elaborate illumination on
14b, representing Mars, Venus, and Jupiter. This is very
briefly described PT p. 100, where no mention is made of the
coat of arms below, blended with the border of the illumination,
and therefore of the same date. This coat is: Quarterly, first
and fourth argent, on a bend azure three stags' heads caboched
or; second and third argent, on a bend azure three mullets or.
Above, a helmet surmounted by a holly tree eradicated vert.
Except for one detail, this is the coat of Stanley-Storeton-
Hooton, a family with principal seats in Cheshire; and this
detail, that the mullets should appear on a bend vert, is probably
a mistake of the illuminator. The uniform orthography and
high standard of accuracy of this codex, which was apparently
executed for a Lord Stanley by a well-trained scribe, give it
great value.

Notes on the MS are in Hearne's Remarks and Collections
II : 198, and in his Letter to Bagford; in the Bell Chaucer of
1854, VI : 192; in Warton-Hazlitt III : 61; in Schick, Temple
of Glass, p. xix; in Skeat I : 51.

The first 29 entries of this MS are given in sequence in the
table printed below; these articles are discussed either under
the head of MS Tanner 346 or in other parts of this work, with
the exception of the stanza called Deceit, a note upon which is
in Anglia 28 : 9, and the Complaint against Hope, which is
mentioned Section V here and also under the description of
MS Harley 7333, Section III B (1) here. Other contents are:

(30) foll. 198b-199a. A ballad by Hoccleve, printed in Furnivall's
     ed. of H.'s Minor Poems, EETS, p. 62, from Phillipps 8151.
(31) foll. 199a-199xb. Doublenesse. See Section V here.
(32) foll. 199xb-200b. Prayer for king, queen, and people; see
     Anglia 28 : 8.

(33) fol. 201a. Truth, second copy in this MS. Printed Ch. Soc. SPT p. 153. 201b is blank. In the lower part of 201a is written in red, "Qui legit emendat scriptorem non reprehendat."

(34) foll. 202a-300a. Lydgate's Reson and Sensuallyte. Ed. for the EETS by Sieper, 1901. Pages ruled but blank to 306a.

(35) foll. 306a-312b. "How a loucr prayseth hys lady." In rough doggerel couplets. To be printed. Fol. 313 is blank.

(36) foll. 314a-316a. The Solemn Service, or Lover's Mass. Printed by Simmons, Lay Folks' Mass Book, EETS, pp. 389 ff. Printed Jour. Gc. Phil. 7 : 95 ff.; and to be printed in vol. 18 of Section II, Belles Lettres Series, Boston.

(37) foll. 318a-329a. A series of ballads, letters, and complaints, 19 in all, usually of three or four stanzas, except that No. 18 is of 17 and No. 19 of 16 stanzas. The last is headed Parlement. Several of these are to be printed in the Belles Lettres volume as above.

(38) The articles pertaining to the order of Heraults, seven paragraphs in prose. This and the next are in a hand other than the body of the codex.

(39) Lydgate's Verses on English Kings, see Anglia 28 : 6-7.

A noticeable feature of this MS is the frequency of blank leaves. La Belle Dame sans Mercy ends with a gathering, on a verso, the Temple of Glass beginning on the next recto. The House of Fame ends on the first verso of a gathering composed of only four leaves, the three remaining leaves being blank; then the sequence of eights again begins with Chaucer's Pity, and a blank leaf which follows the second copy of Truth is the last of a fascicule. Lydgate's Reson and Sensuallyte begins on the next recto; and from 300b through 305b is again blank, the last leaves of a fascicule; on 306a is How a Lover Prayseth His Lady, and the last leaf of that fascicule is blank. These and other considerations suggest to the student that several codices were used by the Fairfax scribe in the compilation of his volume. We note for instance that the parallel with Bodley 638 (see table following) extends only to fol. 201b or a little earlier; and at this point, as above mentioned, the scribe has written a formula which implies that he was closing his work. And, except for the blank leaves which the scribe left for the remainder of the House of Fame, the codex is continuous and largely Chaucerian up to this point; the work was resumed with Lydgate's Reson and Sensuallyte, which may therefore have been derived from some volume other than that previously used by Fairfax (and Bodley); and for the completion of this poem several blank leaves were left. The next article, the very different doggerel poem, is in its turn set off by a gap of one leaf from the far superior love-poems which follow.

Bodley 638: Paper quires in vellum covers, 219 leaves about 8 by 5⅜ inches, in eights. Imperfect at beginning and end, pages spotted, margins scribbled by various owners. In more than one hand, or by the same hand at different times; if the book be opened at any two places the pages will often vary in size of script, but it is not possible to say where the change comes. Written loosely, coarsely, unevenly, and in a very untidy manner as compared with the Fairfax; straggling red lines are drawn to separate stanzas of poems; running titles in red. Trimming has cut away some of the old margins; modern pagination. Catchwords on 16b, 36b, 52b, 97b, 191b, with similar scroll borders; the rubricator, Lity or Lyty, has put his name into the pattern of the colophon on 4b, 7a, 38a, 45b, 141a, 209b. Notwithstanding the slovenly appearance of the codex, it is occasionally better textually than its handsomer sister the Fairfax, with which it closely agrees in contents, see diagram following. For notes on its texts see below. The MS has been briefly described by Schick, ed. of the Temple of Glass, p. xx, and Skeat I : 53.

Mutilations of the Bodley are: Seven quires lack each a leaf, while two have eight paper leaves instead of six; these latter are the 3d and 4th of the codex, between 16b and 36b. The quires which contain but 5 paper leaves are: (1) and (2) in the Legend of Good Women, (7) near the end of the MS; but no textual gaps are here visible in the work. Possibly the scribe, writing on sheets already sewed, spoiled a page and cut it out without loosening the booklet. Other losses are plain; a leaf is gone at the beginning of the Parl. of Foules, and another in that poem between foll. 110 and 111, with lines 157-199 of the text; a blank leaf is perhaps gone near the beginning of the Book of the Duchess, see below; and a leaf is missing from the Chance of the Dice, between 200 and 201. As in the Fairfax, space has been left for the continuation of the House of Fame; part of 193b and all of 194 are thus blank.

The facts regarding the Book of the Duchess are: The Fairfax and the Bodley texts of this poem are sisters except that both show a gap preceding line 97; but Fairfax begins the poem on a recto, stopping at line 30 with the page not full, has a blank verso, and resumes with line 97 at the top of the next recto. The small Jacobean hand has with difficulty squeezed in the 66 missing lines, for which Fairfax did not allow nearly enough space at his own scale of writing. Bodley begins the poem on a verso, has there but 23 lines, which just fill it, and continues on the next recto with line 97, like Fairfax; but it has seven lines less than appear in Fairfax. As 73 lines are missing from its text, the theory of loss of a leaf after transcription will not explain the gap of 27 lines more than a leaf would carry. Nevertheless, the gathering which contains this passage is of but five paper leaves, and the running titles at this point show the full heading on the verso and but the latter part of the title on the recto facing. I would therefore argue that a leaf *was* lost after transcription, but that that leaf carried only the seven lines (24-30) which are present in the Fairfax, the rest of the leaf being blank; *i. e.*, in this poem, as in the House of Fame, the Bodley followed the same procedure as its sister the Fairfax, and left space for completion; like the Fairfax, again, it did not here allow sufficient space. We may remark that Tanner 346, a MS closely allied to Fairfax and Bodley, and with them the only volumes possessing the poem, has the same number of lines as the Fairfax, but leaves no space. This is not surprising, since Tanner is much inferior in scrupulousness to the other two MSS; and it indicates that the common ancestor of all three, which I shall call Oxford, has not only lost a leaf at this point, but that it carried about 33 lines to the page. (I may add that the copy of the Letter of Cupid which appears in these three MSS presents a confusion of stanzas by tens which shows that the archetype had five seven-line stanzas on a page.) Also note that the archetype began this poem on a verso, and Fairfax's niggardly allowance of space is due to his beginning the poem on a recto; further, that the archetype had its heading and 30 lines on that verso, the next leaf perhaps mutilated or so torn away that the careful Fairfax-Bodley could see that one leaf was gone. This MS, the immediate ancestor of Fairfax and Bodley, transcribed the 30 lines seen in Fairfax and left a space; Bodley as well as Fairfax copied the 30 lines, but Bodley has lost the almost blank leaf carrying lines 24-30, and has, with its smaller pages, too little space for completion.

Tanner 346: On vellum, 132 leaves about 9 by 6½ inches. In several hands of the XV century, but with borders and initials apparently by one workman; perhaps therefore executed at a dealer's, as compared with Fairfax 16, which was executed for private ownership. Contents:

(1) foll. 1a-40b. Legend of Good Women. Printed Ch. Soc. PT pp. 243 ff.
(2) foll. 41a-48b. Letter of Cupid. See Section V here.
(3) foll. 48b-59a. Complaint of the Black Knight. See Section V here.
(4) foll. 59b-65a. Anelida. Printed Ch. Soc. PT pp. 145 ff. Not displaced as in Fairfax and Bodley, but with the Complaint following the body of the poem.
(5) foll. 65a-71a. Mars. Printed Ch. Soc. PT pp. 100 ff.
(6) The Complaint of Venus follows at once, headed by the Jacobean hand; a separating horizontal border has been drawn, while there is no separation of the complaint of Mars from the body of the poem other than the leaving of a space. Venus is printed Ch. Soc. PT pp. 411 ff.
(-) foll. 71a-73a. Pity. Printed Ch. Soc. PT pp. 39 ff.
(8) foll. 73a-74b. No heading. Begins "As ofte as syghes ben in herte trewe"; theme "So ofte and ofter I sygh for youre sake." To be printed in vol. 18, Section II, Belles Lettres Series, Boston.
(9) foll. 74b-75b. Begins "For lak of sighte grete cause haue I to pleyne", eight stanzas of eight lines and an envoy of four. The second, third, and fourth entries of the MS Ff 1, 6 at Cambridge are Chaucer's Pity and these two laments, all copied in one hand.
(10) foll. 76a-97a. Lydgate's Temple of Glass. Ed. Schick for the EETS, 1891. See Section V here.
(11) foll. 97a-101b. The Cuckoo and the Nightingale. See Section V here. Followed by
(12) the envoy to Alison, without break except that "Explicit" precedes it. See Section V here under Alison.
(13) foll. 102a-119b. Book of the Duchesse. Printed Ch. Soc. PT pp. 1 ff.
(14) foll. 120a-131a. Parlement of Foules. Trimming has cut away nearly all of the old heading, which apparently was The Parlement of Briddis. Printed Ch. Soc. SPT pp. 1 ff.

Notes on the MS see Schick, loc. cit. pp. xvii-xviii; Krausser, Anglia 19; Skeat I : 54.

Contents of Three Oxford MSS

Fairfax 16	Bodley 638	Tanner 346
(1) Mars	[MS defective at beginning]	Mars (5)
(2) Venus		Venus (6)
(3) The Black Knight	The Black Knight (1)	The Black Knight (3)
(4) Anelida	Anelida (2)	Anelida (4)
(5) Cuckoo and Night.	Cuckoo and Night. (3)	Cuckoo and Night. (11)
(6) Truth		
(7) Letter of Cupid	Letter of Cupid (5)	Letter of Cupid (2)
(8) Ragman Roll	Ragman Roll (16)	
(9) La Belle Dame		
(10) Temple of Glass	Temple of Glass (4)	Temple of Glass (10)
(11) Legend of G. W.	Legend of G. W. (7)	Legend of G. W. (1)
(12) Parl. of Foules	Parl. of Foules (8)	Parl. of Foules (14)
(13) Book of Duchesse	Book of Duchesse (9)	Book of Duchesse (13)
(14) Envoy to Alison		Envoy to Alison (12)
(15) Chance of the Dice	Chance of the Dice (11)	
(16) House of Fame	House of Fame (10)	
(17) Pity	Pity (6)	Pity (7)
		[8 and 9 not in Fairfax or Bodley]
(18) A B C	A B C (12)	
(19) Fortune	Fortune (13)	end of MS.
(20) Scogan, Purse, Bukton, Stedfastnesse, Newfangleness, Deceit, Quatuor infatuant,		
(27) Proverbs		
(28) Complaint-Hope	Complaint against Hope (14)	
(29) Complaint d'Amours &c., &c.	Complaint d'Amours (15)	
	Order of Fools (17)	
	end of MS.	

In the foregoing table the contents of the Fairfax are enumerated in order so far as that large MS is listed; it contains ten more entries, which are noted above. The entire contents of the Tanner (14 entries), and of the Bodley (17 entries), are placed parallel with those of the Fairfax, a numeral denoting the position of each extract in its own codex. It will be seen that, except Nos. 8 and 9, the entire contents of the Tanner are to be found in the Fairfax, and that the entire contents of the Bodley are also duplicated in the Fairfax, with the exception of Bodley's last article. Fairfax possesses several poems not in either of the smaller codices.

Editors discussing texts found in these MSS have observed that the ultimate origin of the three is identical, and that while Fairfax and Bodley are undoubtedly sisters, the source of the Tanner is a MS other than the immediate original of Fairfax and Bodley, probably the next ancestor of that original.

It is evident that the lost archetype of these codices, which we may call Oxford, included all the poems copied in Tanner; and since that catalogue comprises the Black Knight, the Cuckoo, the Letter of Cupid, and the Temple of Glass, as well as Chaucerian poems, Oxford cannot very well date earlier than ?1415. The source of Fairfax and Bodley, which we may call FB, received most of its texts from Oxford, adding four non-Chaucerian poems, Nos. 8, 15, 28, 29, of the Fairfax, and also the House of Fame, the ABC, and Fortune. It is interesting to observe that our knowledge of the House of Fame comes only from FB and from a fragment in Pepys 2006, our knowledge of the Book of the Duchesse only from Oxford. There is, of course, the possibility that the additional poems of FB were also in Oxford, and that the Tanner merely did not transcribe them; but as other MSS allied to this group, Digby 181 and Longleat 258, show no House of Fame, no ABC, and no Fortune, it is more probable that FB had a second source other than Oxford.

The value of this "Oxford Group" consists in the simplicity and definiteness of its main relations; in the sober accuracy of the FB, the Fairfax, and the Bodley; in the preservation by the group of the House of Fame and the Book of the Duchesse; in the remote possibility that its Anelida may represent a retouching by Chaucer, see under Anelida here. Its less valuable features are the fact that Oxford itself was a XV century composite, containing Lydgate and Hoccleve, etc., as well as Chaucer; and the presence of various errors,—the displacement of stanzas above noted, the lost leaf in the Book of the Duchesse, and the faults in the Parlement of Foules text mentioned in Decennial Publ. of the Univ. of Chicago, VII : 1-22. For brief remarks on the "Oxford Group" see Mod. Lang. Notes 23 : 20.

Digby 181: Paper, 93 leaves 11 by 8 inches. In perhaps three hands; script generally small, narrow, and high, but not stiff. Imperfect at the beginning; few headings, and none in red. No running titles; very wide margins up to Troilus, wide also there. Vellum flyleaves at front and end; recto of the first front leaf *Peter Idywerte* written large. Catchwords on 17b and 37b; blank spaces of half a page sometimes at ends of poems, *e. g.*, 3, 4, 5, 6, 8.

Contents:

(1) foll. 1a-6b. Letter of Cupid, see Section V here.
(2) foll. 7a-8b. A poem against marriage, printed from this MS by Wright in the Appendix to his 1841 ed. of Map, Camden Soc., p. 295. The 1509 print by de Worde was repr. by Collier for the Percy Society, 1840. Twenty-two stanzas of seven lines; fragments are in Harley 2251 and in Ff 1, 6. See Anglia 28 : 21.
(3) foll. 8b-10a. A poem on the deceit of women, 15 stanzas of seven lines, beginning, "To Adam and Eue Crist gaue the souereinte." I do not find the lines in Lydgate's Falls of Princes.
(4) foll. 10b-40b. "Formula honestae vitae." An English poem in seven-line stanzas, with Latin prologues to the several sections; headed "Ego Petrus Idyllearte filium meum Thomam bonis operibus ac moribus conformare ac de amore dei . . . . sic Incipio." See Miessner's diss. on "Peter Idle's Instructions to his Son", Greisswald 1903, 50 pages; see Foerster, Archiv 104 : 293. Other MSS are: Harley 172, Univ. Libr. Cambr. Ee iv, 37, Trin. Coll. Dublin D 2, 7.
(5) foll. 31a-39a. Lydgate's Complaint of the Black Knight. See Section V here. At the close is written "Explicit Edorb qd"; see note on MS Hodson 39, Section III B (7) here.

(6) foll. 39b-43b. Chaucer's Anelida. Text printed Ch. Soc. PT 145.

(7) foll. 44a-52a. Chaucer's Parlement of Foules. Text printed Ch. Soc. SPT p. 1.

(8) foll. 52a-53b. An extract from Lydgate's Falls of Princes, I : 13, beginning "All though so be in euery maner age." Nineteen stanzas of seven lines.

(9) foll. 54a-close. In another hand, an incomplete copy of the Troilus. See Skeat II : lxxv.

The relation of this codex, a partial descendant of Oxford, to Fairfax, Bodley, and Tanner, is undergoing investigation.

Hatton 73: Vellum, 122 leaves 11⅜ by 8 inches. On verso of first flyleaf at end is the name Margaret More, below it in later hand (?) the name Elizabeth Windsor; on the recto opposite is an inscription stating that the latter died Jan. 18, 1531. On the recto of the next leaf preceding (the last of the MS proper) is the name Elizabeth Windsor again, with date Dec. 14 in the fourth year of Henry VIII; on the lower part of fol. 121b, below the last poem of the MS, is "This is my lady more book And sumtyme it was Quene margarete boke." Written in neat, clear XV century hands, stanzas spaced, some colored caps. Contents almost entirely by Lydgate, and of a religious nature; his Life of Our Lady, wrongly headed in a later hand as Gower's Confessio Amantis; this ends on 118b, and is followed, in another hand, by Chaucer's Truth and Stedfastnesse. The second of the scribes who copied the Life of Our Lady then copies the poem beginning "Quene of heuen of helle ek emperesse"; this is followed by another short religious poem.

Laud 416: Paper, 289 leaves 12 by 8½ inches, imperfect at beginning and end; of the XV century. There is some similarity between the rubricking of this MS and that of Tanner 346. On fol. 226b is written "Scripsit Rhodo per Iohannem Newton die 25 Octobris 1459." Contents religious; also Lydgate's Story of Thebes, Hoccleve's De Regimine Principum, and a copy of the Parlement of Foules imperfect because of the MS' mutilation at close.

Laud 740: Vellum, 10⅜ by 7½ inches, of 109 leaves, heavily trimmed at top. A copy of the English prose transl. of De Guileville's Pélérinage de l'Homme, with pictures, colored caps., and illuminated borders; well written in a firm, square XV century hand, with notes and summaries by other hands. Chaucer's ABC is inserted into the text on 103b-106b; no mark of authorship.

Rawlinson C 86: Described among the MSS of the Canterbury Tales, Section III B (3) here.

Rawlinson Poetry 163: Contains the Troilus, etc. Note in Madan's Summary Catalogue III : 318. Fol. 39 is reprod. with McCormick's paper on Troilus in An English Miscellany, pp. 296 ff.; the leaf containing To Rosemounde is reprod. in Skeat's Twelve Facsimiles. For the Troilus text of this MS see McCormick as cited, and Skeat II : lxxiv.

Arch. Selden B 10: A solid and handsome MS on vellum, containing Harding's Chronicle; of 209 leaves 13⅛ by 9¾ inches. At the end of the Chronicle are the arms of Percy Earl of Northumberland, apparently a Percy later than 1474; the Chronicle comes down to Edward IV, ending on fol. 195 of the MS. On fol. 197a, with a huge capital containing later Percy arms, begin, according to the rubric, "The Prouerbes of Lydgate." The miscellaneous collection which follows is in the same hand (not that of the Chronicle) which has made additions to another Percy MS, Royal 18 D ii of the British Museum; see Ward's Catalogue I : 81, where that hand is dated 1520. This collection of "Proverbs" is a mixture of envoys from Lydgate's Falls of Princes, didactic poems by Lydgate, and Chaucer's Fortune and Truth. The colophon at the end reads "Empryntede at london in fletestret at the sygne of the sonne by Wynkyn Worde."

As this MS copy is evidently derived from a de Worde print, its texts have but a very secondary value; Dibdin's query Typogr. Antiq. II : 360 should be reversed. It is worth remark that not only here, but in the Lydgate MSS Lansdowne 699 and its sister Leyden Vossius 9, these two poems by Chaucer, and no others, are entered. In this case the copy is clearly from a print; what is the connection among the three MSS and de Worde's text?

On this MS see Warton-Hazlitt III : 124, Macray, Annals p. 123; the de Worde colophon is noted in Bernard 3356.26.

Arch. Selden B 24: On paper, of 228 leaves 10¼ by 6⅝ inches, trimmed in binding. Up to fol. 209b, within one copy of the Kingis Quair, apparently in one hand, late XV century, slovenly and scrawling. Date after 1486, see Liddell, Athen. 1895 II : 902; Skeat's 1475, in his ed. as below p. xxxvii, is incorrect. On fol. 118b, at the end of the Troilus, is a small coat of arms, that of the Scottish lords Sinclair, whose name the MS also contains on one of the flyleaves. A correspondence in the Athen. 1899 II : 835, 898, shows that the scribe of the codex was the Scotchman James Gray, a protégé of Lord Sinclair. Macaulay, Acad. 1895 I : 338, praises the copy of the Troilus as "by an intelligent and careful scribe from an excellent MS"; but its text of the Parlement of Foules, besides carrying a

conclusion written by some one other than Chaucer, is arbitrary
and careless throughout. The unique copy of the Kingis Quair
which it contains was ed. by Skeat STS 1884; see the work of
J. T. T. Brown, Glasgow 1895, on the Authorship of the Kingis
Quair, pp. 5, 9, and appendix pp. 70 ff., for full description and
list of contents. See also Athen. 1896 II : 66, 128, 164, 193, 225,
291; 1897 II : 674; and Brandl's review of Brown, Archiv
99 : 167-170. Notes on the MS Skeat I : 47, II : lxxiv.

Contents:

(1) foll. 1a-118b. Troilus and Cressida, no heading.
(2) fol. 118b. One stanza, bidding the book wear black and
grieve. Printed by Brown as cited, p. 72.
(3) fol. 119a. Truth. Printed Ch. Soc. OT p. 289.
(4) One stanza of 8 lines, no heading. See under Prosperity,
Section V here.
(5) foll. 119b-120a. No heading, seven stanzas of seven lines,
beginning "Deuise prowes and eke humylitee." Colophon
"Qd Chaucere quhen he was ry auisit." Not by Chaucer; see
Brown loc. cit.
(6) foll. 120b-129b. Complaint of the Black Knight; see Section V here. Colophon "Here endith the mayng and disport
of Chaucere."
(7) foll. 130a-131b. Hoccleve's Mother of God; see Section V
here. Printed Ch. Soc. PT pp. 137 ff.
(8) foll. 132a-137a. Mars. Printed Ch. Soc. PT pp. 100 ff. On
the inner side of 134a is a border, and after a separation,
with a capital, "The Compleynt of Mars."
(9) foll. 136a-137a. "The compleynt of venus folowith." No
border or special cap. to separate from the preceding.
Colophon "Qd Galfridus Chaucere." Printed Ch. Soc. PT
pp. 411 ff.
(10) foll. 137b-138a. No heading; six stanzas of eight lines,
beginning "O hie Emperesse and quene celestial." Colophon
"Qd Chaucere."
(11) fol. 138a. "Leaulte vault richesse." See Section V here.
(12) foll. 138b-141b. The Cuckoo and Nightingale; see Section V
here.
(13) foll. 142a-152a. Parlement of Foules, printed Ch. Soc. SPT
pp. 1 ff.
(14) foll. 152b-191b. Legend of Good Women. Printed Ch. Soc.
PT pp. 243 ff.
(15) foll. 192a-211a. The Kingis Quair. The hand which has
copied thus far in the MS changes on fol. 209a to a small,
square script. For the poem see Skeat and Brown as above.
(16) fol. 211b-217a. The Letter of Cupid. See Section V here.
(17) foll. 217a-219a. No heading. Twenty-one stanzas, usually
of nine lines, but the 8th, 9th, and 14th are of eight lines,
the 20th of seven, and the 21st of ten. Begins: "Befor my
deth this lay of sorow I sing." Rime scheme in nines is
aabaabbab; in the eights is aaabaaab; in the sevens is
aabaaab; in the ten-line is aabaabbaab.
(18) foll. 219a-221b. No heading. A prol. of eight seven-line
stanzas beginning "Be cause that teres waymenting and
playntes." The poem following begins: "Quho may com-
pleyne my langour & distresse." Twelve stanzas of varying
lengths, first of eight lines, next four of nine, sixth of 16

fourbeat lines, rest of nine lines. Colophon "Here endis the
lufaris complaynt &c."

(19) foll. 221b-228b. Heading inserted in another hand, "Here
beginith ye quare of Ielusy a Vise ye gudely folkes and sue."
The first 16 lines are an imitation of Chaucer's Prologue;
the poem is of 607 lines, partly in couplets, partly in stanzas
of varying lengths. Printed in Bannatyne Miscellany II :
161. Brown, loc. cit., misrepresents the heading.
     The next two leaves are much repaired and rubbed, scrib-
bled in later hands.

(20) fol. 229a. No heading. Begins "My frende gif thou will be
a seruitur." Four stanzas of eight lines.

(21) fol. 229b. Two seven-line stanzas condemning the world.

Arch. Selden supra 56: Contains the Troilus. Note in Skeat
II : lxxiv.

(4) *Other Oxford MSS*

Corpus Christi College 203: Tiny vellum MS of 14 leaves 5¼ by
3¾ inches. Described by Glauning in his ed. of Lydgate's Two
Nightingale Poems, EETS. Contains one of those poems,
Chaucer's Truth, headed "Prouerbium Scogan" (see Flügel,
Anglia 21 : 258), and three stanzas of "proverbs" by "R.
Stokys", beginning "Se meche sey lytyll and lerne to suffre in
tyme."

St. John's College, 57: Paper, 244 leaves 11⅞ by 8 inches. Written
in one large, inelegant but legible XV century hand. On 186a
is the name John Davenant and the date 1516. Contains only
4 items,—the Prick of Conscience, a prose chronicle from Richard I to tenth Henry VI, the Parlement of Foules, and the
army regulations of Henry V, prose.

(5) *In the University Library, Cambridge*

Ff i, 6: Paper, now of 185 leaves; formerly of 159 leaves, as
described in the old catalogue, but rebound under the supervision of the late Henry Bradshaw, when blank leaves were
inserted and numbered to represent the original condition of
the codex. The description of the volume here given follows
Bradshaw's paging. About 8¾ by 6 inches in size, but pages
irregular. In many hands, all latter XV century if not later,
and all slovenly, current, and untidy; inks of different shades,
no running titles, catchwords, or bookmakers' marks of any
kind. Some entries appear to have been crowded in later,
and the MS is much scribbled. Imperfect at beginning and end,
and otherwise damaged. Several scribes have signed their
names, Lewestoun, Calverley, Nicholas "plenus amoris", and
the man who uses a rebus of a tun, below which is a scroll

with two pendent fishes, and the motto "A God when." This is perhaps the rebus of Lewestoun (luce-tun), although the hand does not seem the same as that of Chaucer's Purse, which is signed Lewestoun. But the remark in Reliq. Antiq. I : 27 as to the English poet "Godwhen" is of no meaning. Most of the extracts in the MS are brief and lyrical, and a number of the poems are in short stanzas with rime couée; to these the scribes have drawn lines and brackets to show the rime-connection, but as the drawing is untidily and coarsely done, the appearance of the codex is not improved.

The codex was dated by Furnivall 1460-70, by Bradshaw some 20 years earlier, see Trial Forew. p. 53 footnote. Eight of the shorter poems were printed in Reliq. Antiq., 1843, vol. I; the Chaucerian contents are Purse, Pity, the Parl. of Foules, a bit from Troilus, one from the LGW, and Anelida; all printed Ch. Soc. as noted below. Two extracts are printed Pol. Rel. and Love Poems as noted. Chaucer's Pity and the two poems following are in MS Tanner 346 in the same order, and it is to be noted that ten Brink considered the Ff text of Pity as derived from that of Tanner. See Ch. Soc. Essays, part II.

Brief notes on the MS are in Skeat I : 55, Macaulay's Gower II : clxvi. For a note on "plenus amoris" as a scribal surname see Macray, Annals of the Bodleian Library, p. 21 footnote.

Contents:

(1) foll. 3a-7a. Two tales from the Confessio Amantis, see Macaulay as cited.
(2) foll. 15a-17a. Chaucer's Pity. Printed Ch. Soc. PT pp. 39 ff.
(3) foll. 17a-18b. A love-lament, beginn. "As ofte as syghes ben in herte trewe", 13 stanzas of eight lines; transcribed for publication.
(4) fol. 19a-b. Another, beginn. "For lac of sight grete cause I haue to pleyne", 7 stanzas of eight lines and a four-line envoy. This copy omits a stanza in the Tanner MS. Transcribed for publication.

   Nos. 2, 3, and 4, as noted above, are also in the MS Tanner 346, in the same order. All are, in this codex, in one hand, not that of No. 1.

(5) fol. 20a-b. Another lament, beginn. "I may well sygh for greuous is my payne." Five stanzas of seven lines and four lines of another, MS defective. In a hand different from that preceding.
(6) foll. 22a-28a. The Cuckoo and Nightingale. For ed. and notes see Section V here. In another hand.
(7) foll. 29a-42b. Chaucer's Parlement of Foules, in two hands different from the preceding. Printed Ch. Soc. PT pp. 49 ff.
(8) foll. 45a-51a. Story from Confessio Amantis, see Macaulay as cited. In another hand.
(9) foll. 51a-53a. The Parliament of Love. Printed Pol. Rel. and Love Poems, p. 48. See Neilson, Court of Love, p. 158. Perhaps in two hands.
(10) fol. 53b. Roundel on Fortune. Printed Ritson, Ancient Songs and Ballads, ed. 1877, I : 111.

(11) Below, proverb, in another hand, printed Reliq. Antiq. I : 315, from Douce 15 and Harley 629; this copy imperfect. Printed by Ritson, Ancient Songs I : 129.

(12) fol. 56a. A lyrical poem printed Reliq. Antiq. I : 23. In another hand.

(13) foll. 56b-58b. The Seven Deadly Sins, printed Pol. Rel. and Love Poems p. 215, from this MS. See Brydges' Censura Literaria 8 : 77-81 for copy apparently in MS in the "Hawkins library at Nash Court, near Canterbury." Cp. *ibid.* 7 : 344.
At close, "Quod Lewestoun."

(14) fol. 59a. Chaucer's Purse. Printed Ch. Soc. PT p. 447. A "rekenyng" is scribbled in.

(15) foll. 61a-63b. Chaucer's Anelida. In another hand, very loose and bad. Printed Ch. Soc. SPT p. 47.

(16) foll. 64a-67b. Bit from Chaucer's LGW, printed Ch. Soc. OT p. 139. In another hand, signed "Nomen scriptoris Nicholaus plenus amoris."

(17) foll. 68a-69b. Chaucer's Venus, printed Ch. Soc. PT pp. 411 ff. In another hand.

(18) fol. 69b. A love-song printed Reliq. Antiq. I : 169, with several misprints. An inventory of clothes, etc., at "Fyn-dyrne" is noted.

(19) foll. 71a-76b. The Letter of Cupid, by Hoccleve, see Section V here. Incomplete, but from the heading and the dis-arrangement of the stanzas transcribed an alliance with the Oxford Group of MSS is probable. In still another hand.

(20) foll. 81a-84a. A poem beginn. "I rede þat þou do right so", which I have not identified.

(21) foll. 84b-95a. Story of King Antiochus, from the Conf. Amantis.

(22) foll. 96a-109b. "Sir Degrevaunt." Written in double col., in different hands. Printed by Halliwell among the Thorn-ton Romances, 1844. The names Elisabet Koton, Elisabet Frauncys, are appended.

(23) foll. 110a-113b. "The Cronekelys of Seynts and Kyngs of Yngelond." See Bradshaw's note, Trial Forew. p. 53 foot.

(24) foll. 117a-134b. La Belle Dame sans Mercy. See Section V here. In another hand.

(25) There follow, foll. 135a-145a, a number of short poems and roundels, often in 3-line or 5-line stanzas. The first line of each is here given: (a) Welcome be ye my souereine. (b) Come home dere hert your tarieng. (c) To you my Ioye and my wordly plesaunce. (d) There may areste me no plesaunce. (e) Wo so list to loue. Printed Reliq. Antiq. I : 24, and Ritson, Ancient Songs, I : 111-13. (f) Now wold I fayne sum myrthis make. Printed Reliq. Antiq. I : 25. (g) Alas alas and alas why. (h) Alas what planet was y born vndir. (i) Continuance   Of remembraunce. Printed Reliq. Antiq. I : 25-26. (k) Myself walkyng all alone. Printed Reliq. Antiq. I : 26. (l) Vp son and mery wether. Printed Reliq. Antiq. I : 202. (m) ffor to pente And affter repente Hyt were ffoly. (n) In ful gret hevenesse myn hert ys puyght.

(26) fol. 146a-b. Prayer to the Virgin, beginn. "Most glorius quene regnyng yn hevene."

(27) foll. 147a-150a. Lydgate's Wicked Tongue, see Section V here.

(28) foll. 150a-151a. An extract from the Falls of Princes, bk. I, chap. 13, combined with three stanzas from Chaucer's Troilus; printed Ch. Soc. OT p. xi, without identification of the stanzas as by Lydgate.

(29) fol. 151a. One stanza beginn. "The mor I goo the further I am behynde", see Anglia 28 : 16-17.

(30) foll. 151a-152a. Seven wise Counsels to a Prince, see Anglia 28 : 22 and ref. *ibid.* to Foerster, Archiv 104 : 297.

(31) foll. 152b-155a are filled with short lyrical bits, sometimes of one stanza only.

(32) fol. 156a-b. A portion of the poem against marriage copied in Digby 181, and printed by de Worde, and by Wright in appendix to his Poems of Walter Mapes, Camden Soc., 1841 p. 295. For note see Anglia 28 : 21; and cp. the Latin stanzas printed by Du Méril, Poésies populaires Latines, II : 179 ff. This fragmentary copy begins like the de Worde print.

(33) foll. 156b-159b. "How myschaunce regnyth in Ingleland." Printed Wright, Polit. Poems II : 238.

(34) foll. 159b-161b. "A Compleint on to dame ffortune Capto xxviij."

(35) fol. 162b. On the four complexions.

(36) fol. 164a. Treatise for Lavandres. Printed Reliq. Antiq. I : 26. See Anglia 28 : 9.

(37) foll. 166a-177b. Imperfect at beginn. "Cassamus roos after this talkynge", 71 stanzas of eight lines. Probably part of transl. of Les Voeux du Paon, see Madan's Summary Catal. IV : 588, under MS Douce 308, and Ward, Catal. of Romances I : 146 ff.

(38) fol. 178a. Three stanzas to Fortune.

(39) foll. 181a-close. A mutilated copy of Burgh's Cato. See Anglia 28 : 22 and ref. to Foerster, Archiv 101 : 45, also *ibid.* 115 : 298-323, 116 : 25-40.

Ff v, 30: Contains the ABC. I have not examined this MS. See under ABC below.

Gg iv, 27: For description see under MSS of the Canterbury Tales, Section III B (5) here.

Hh iv, 12: Paper and vellum, of 99 leaves 8¼ by 5½ inches, somewhat irregular in size; volume shabby and worn, imperfect at close. In three hands of the XV century; no headings, running titles, or authors' names. The hands are all small, clear, and somewhat current. Caps. and half-borders by several hands. Contents:

(1) foll. 1a-31a. Burgh's Cato; ed. by Foerster, Archiv 115 : 298-323, 116 : 25-40. Twenty-five MSS are there listed.

(2) foll. 31b-33b. Lydgate's Stans Puer ad Mensam. Caps. colored, stanzas spaced. Fourteen stanzas of seven lines. Other texts, see Anglia 28 : 20.
Below is written, in another hand, "This boke was made in ye yer of our lord & god 1500 as for the kyng*es* name of this lord I cannot say for her wher . . . . are non."

(3) foll. 35a-40a. Lydgate's St. Austin at Compton. Another

hand, large colored capital. Forty-three stanzas of eight lines; eight stanzas are lost with a missing leaf. Copies in Lansdowne 699, Leyden Voss. 9; that in Harley 2255 is printed by Halliwell, Minor Poems of Lydgate p. 135.

(4) foll. 40b-41a. Chaucer's Former Age; printed Ch. Soc. PT p. 173.

(5) foll. 41b-44a. The Complaint of the Virgin, with refrain "Quia amore langueo." Sixteen stanzas of eight lines. See Anglia 30 : 330.

On 44b are scrawled some lines from the Dietary, and the date of the 22d year of Henry VIII's reign. 45b is also scribbled; John Yarrade's name appears.

(6) foll. 46a-57b. Lydgate's Horse, Goose, and Sheep. Ed. by Degenhart, Leipzig, 1900, from eight MSS.

(7) foll. 58a-74a. Lydgate's Fabula Duorum Mercatorum. Ed. Zupitza-Schleich, Strassburg 1897, from six MSS.

(8) foll. 74b-81a. Lydgate's Churl and Bird. Other MSS, see under description of Lansdowne 699 in this section.

(9) foll. 82a-83b. Lydgate's Utter thy Language. See Section V here.

(10) foll. 84a-85a. Lydgate's Horns Away. See Anglia 28 : 9, *ibid.* 30 : 336 note, and p. 343.

(11) fol. 85a-b. "Upon a cros nayled I was for thee." Five stanzas of eight lines. Copies in Harley 2255, Laud 683, Univ. Libr. Cambr. Kk i, 6, Jesus Coll. Cambr. 56, Cotton Calig. A ii, Rawl. poet. 32, Adds. 29729. This text printed Polit. Rel. and Love Poems, p. 111.

(12) foll. 86a-87b. Midsummer Rose. See Anglia 28 : 15.

(13) fol. 88a-b. "The world so wyde the ayer so remoueable." Seven stanzas of eight lines, the second of six lines. See Anglia 28 : 4.

(14) foll. 89a-91a. "Thorow out a palys as I gan passe"; refrain "All women may be ware by me." Printed from MS Balliol College 354 by Wright, Polit. Songs, Rolls Series, II : 205 as the Lament of the Duchess of Gloucester (Eleanor Cobham). Seventeen stanzas of eight lines.

(15) foll. 91a-93b. "Quid eligam ignoro." Twenty-one stanzas of eight lines.

(16) foll. 94a-99. Chaucer's Parlement of Foules, defective at close. Printed Ch. Soc. OT p. 1 ff.

Apparently the same hand made the copies from Utter thy Language through the MS. The Parlement of Foules is either in two hands or written at different times by the same copyist.

Ii iii, 21 : On vellum, 298 leaves 12⅝ by 8⅝ inches. A copy of Chaucer's Boece and of "Theutonicius'" exposition of it. Of the XIV century, according to the catalogue. On fol. 52b begins the Former Age, headed as described under the poem, Section IV D below; on 53a, at the close of the Former Age, follows Fortune, headed "Causer / Balades de vilage sanz peinture." A folio is reprod. Ch. Soc. Autotypes; there dated 1420-30, and dated in the Forewords *ibid.* "of the first third of the XV century." See Skeat II : xxxvii-xli.

Kk i, 5 : Described by Lumby, preface to EETS ed. of Ratis

Raving, 1870, as a volume of eight parts; part 6, in one hand
of the XV century, is in the Lowland Scots dialect, and comprises 11 items. The third of these is Chaucer's Truth. The
entire contents of this part are printed by Lumby; Truth is upon
his pp. 9-10.

(6) *In Cambridge Colleges*

Trinity College: MSS R 3, 19, R 3, 20, R 3, 21, and R 14, 51 are
described by James in volume II of his Catalogue of Western
Manuscripts in the Library of Trinity College, Cambridge,
4 vols., 1900-1903. See also notes on R 3, 20 in Anglia 22 : 364
ff., 27 : 381-398, 28 : 1-28, 30 : 320-348; and Brotanek, Die engl.
Maskenspiele, Vienna and Leipzig, 1902.

St. John's College: G 21 contains the ABC; I have not seen this
MS. L 1 contains the Troilus; I have not seen this MS; see
Skeat II : lxxv.

Magdalen College Pepys 2006: Description in Mod. Lang. Notes
19 : 196-198. List of contents in Todd's Illustrations, p. 116.

Corpus Christi College: Number 61 contains the Troilus; I have
not seen this MS; see Skeat II : lxix.

(7) *In Private Possession, etc.*

Bannatyne: In the Advocates' Library, Edinburgh. Printed, with
introductions, for the Hunterian Club, 1873-1880, 3 vols. The
MS was compiled by George Bannatyne, a Scotchman, in 1568,
as a collection of Scottish poetry. Its texts are Scottish or
Scottified, and frequently corrupt.

Bedford: Described by Furnivall, Athen. 1876 II : 623-24.

Campsall: In the possession of Mr. Bacon Frank. A copy of the
Troilus, executed for Henry V while he was Prince of Wales,
before 1415. Printed for the Chaucer Society, First Series
Nos. LXIII, LXIV, and separately as No. LXXIX. See Hist.
MSS Comm. Report VI, p. 464-5; Skeat II : lxvii-ix. Two
pages are reprod. Ch. Soc. Autotypes.

Durham V ii, 13. Contains the Troilus. See Skeat II : lxxv; see
Catalogi Veteres Librorum Ecclesiae Cathedralis Dunelm.,
Surtees Soc., 1838, pp. 154-55.

Glasgow, Hunterian Museum Q, 2, 25 contains the ABC. The

manuscript V, 3, 7 is described by Skeat I : 13; see under Romaunt of the Rose, Section V below.

Leyden, Vossius 9: See Robinson in Harvard Studies V : 187 ff. Contains Fortune and Truth, the texts unprinted, but probably sisters to those in Lansdowne 699.

Longleat 258: In the possession of the Marquess of Bath, and at Longleat House, Warminster, Wiltshire. List of contents given Ch. Soc. Odd Texts p. 251; contents and descriptions in Mod. Lang. Notes 20 : 77-79. See Schick, Temple of Glass, pp. xxiv-xxv, Hist. MSS Comm. Report III : 188-9.

The Chaucerian contents are: Mars, Pity, Anelida, Parlement of Foules.

Phillipps 8252: Contains the Troilus. See Skeat II : lxxv.

B. Prints and Editions of the Minor Poems

Caxton: Caxton printed, without date, these minor poems as by
Chaucer: the Parlement of Foules, Scogan unto the Lords,
Gentilesse, a stanza beginning "With empty hand man may no
hawkes lure", Truth, Fortune, Scogan, Mars, Anelida, Purse,
and the couplets printed by Thynne just after his table of contents described here (Section V) under Prophecy and It Falleth;
these, as the second and fourth bits above named, are non-
Chaucerian. All the Chaucerian texts are printed by the
Chaucer Society; see under each heading below. The texts
are described by Blades, see his pp. 202, 211, 212; Blades gives
the Parlement of Foules the title Temple of Bras, as in Caxton.
The copy of the Anelida, in the Cambridge University Library,
is unique, and a facsimile has been issued by the University
Press, 1906. The volume as described by Dibdin I : 306-311
was bound in separate parts under Bradshaw's direction, cp.
Blades p. 201.

Caxton also printed two eds. of the Canterbury Tales, see
Section III C ante, and the House of Fame, the Boethius, the
Troilus; see under each heading here.

No collection, even partial, of the Minor Poems was brought
together until the ed. by Pynson in 1526, see Section II D here.
In subsequent prints of the Works or Poems the minor poems
are included.

Pickering: The Romaunt of the Rose, Troilus and Cressida, and
the Minor Poems. With a life of Chaucer by Sir Harris
Nicolas. London, Pickering, 1846, 3 vols.

Here are included, under the title Minor Poems: Legend of
Good Women, a *Goodly Balade of Chaucer (*Mother of
Nurture), Book of the Duchess, Assembly of Foules, Anelida
and Arcite, *Complaint of the Black Knight, *Praise of Women,
House of Fame, Mars and Venus, *Cuckoo and Nightingale,
*Court of Love, *Chaucer's Dream (*Isle of Ladies), *Flower
and Leaf, ABC, Balade sent to King Richard (Stedfastnesse),
Good Counseil of Chaucer (Truth), Ballade of the Village
without Painting (Fortune), Lenvoy de Chaucer (Scogan),
*Go forth King, To his empty Purse, A ballad (Gentilesse),
*Proverb against Covetise and Negligence, Pity, *Virelai,
*Chaucer's Prophecy, Chaucer's Words unto his own Scrivener.
The Prophecy has Singer's note, with his initials, see Section V
here; the texts are thus probably from the Pickering ed. of
1822, the Chiswick Chaucer, see Section II D. Bukton, as in
the Chiswick, follows the Book of the Duchesse, with no heading; its first line reads "My master, Bukton . . . . ", see below.

Starred works are discussed in Section V, others below under D.

Skeat: Chaucer. The Minor Poems. W. W. Skeat, Oxford 1888. Second and enlarged ed. Oxford 1896. Contents: ABC, Pity, Book of the Duchesse, Mars, Parlement of Foules, Merciles Beaute, Anelida, Words to Adam, House of Fame, Former Age, Fortune, Truth, Gentilesse, Lak of Stedfastnesse, Against Women Unconstant, Scogan, Bukton, Venus, Purse, Proverbs. An appendix contains: Compleint to his Lady, Amorous Compleint, Balade of Compleint; and the Supplement to the second ed. adds: To Rosemounde, Womanly Noblesse, Complaint to my Mortal Foe, and Complaint to my Lodesterre.

Reviewed Athen. 1889 I: 466; Acad. 1889 I: 178, 222 (Pollard); see Skeat *ibid.* 205; Anglia 11 : 641-2 (Wülker); Amer. Jour. Phil. 10: 97-8 (Garnett); Dial 10: 107; Engl. Stud. 15: 399-418 (Koch); Mod. Lang. Notes 4: 359-363 (Bright); Nation 1889 I: 527-29 (Lounsbury); Sat. Review 67: 712.

Skeat's additions to the Chaucer Society list are, in his first ed., Merciles Beaute, Against Women Unconstant, and the three poems of the Appendix; in his second ed. he further added the poems of the Supplement. See under each poem in Section V here.

C. Editions of Selections: Translations, etc.

Koch: A Critical Edition of Some of Chaucer's Minor Poems.
J. Koch, Berlin, 1883. Pp. 26. Contents: the ABC, Words to
Adam, Former Age, Fortune, Truth, Gentilesse, Stedfastnesse,
Bukton, Scogan, Purse.

> Reviewed unfavorably by ten Brink, Littblatt 1883, pp. 420-
427, to which Koch replied *ibid*. 1884 pp. 42-43. Reviewed by
von Düring, Anglia 8 : Anz. 1 ff.

Bilderbeck: Selections from the Minor Poems of Chaucer. With
introduction, notes, and glossary. Ed. J. B. Bilderbeck. London 1895. Pp. 31, 146. In Bell's English Classics.

> Contents: Seys and Alcyone (from the Book of the
Duchesse), the Parlement of Foules, Anelida, Fortune, Former
Age, Truth, Gentilesse, Stedfastnesse, Purse. Text based on
the Ch. Soc. prints. Introd. on pronunciation, language, and
versification.

Koch, J.: Ausgewählte Kleinere Dichtungen Chaucers. Im vers-
maasse des Originals in das Deutsche uebertragen und mit
Erörterungen versehen. Leipzig, 1880, pp. 66.

> Includes: Pity, Words to Adam, Parlement of Foules,
Truth, Gentilesse, Stedfastnesse, Fortune, Bukton, Scogan,
Purse.

> Reviewed Anglia 4: Anz. 47-49 (Schröer); Archiv 66: 230, 68:
426; Engl. Stud. 4 : 339 (Lindner); Academy 1880 II : 289
(Furnivall). In the Anglia review are reprinted bits from the
Parlement of Foules.

> Out of print, and difficult to obtain.

For modernizations and translations of the separate poems
see under each heading in D below.

Notes

Furnivall, F. J.: Trial Forewords to my Parallel-Text Edition of
Chaucer's Minor Poems, Part I. Chaucer Society, 1871, 2d
Series No. 6. Discusses Pity, Book of the Duchesse, Parlement
of Foules, Mars.

Würzner, A. Ueber Chaucers Lyrische Gedichte. Steyr, 1879,
pp. 19.

> Discusses ABC, Pity, Former Age, Mars, Venus, Words to
Adam, Truth, Mother of God, Scogan, Bukton, Prosperity,
Gentilesse, Stedfastnesse, Fortune, Purse.

Reviewed Littbl. 1880, pp. 383-5 (Koch); Engl. Stud. 4 : 461
(Lindner); Anglia 4: Anz. 44-47 (Schröer).
Capone, G. I poemi minori di Chaucer. Saggio critico. Modica,
1900, pp. 24.

Discusses the Court of Love, the Complaint of the Black
Knight, Flower and Leaf, Testament of Love, Cuckoo and
Nightingale.

The antiquated point of view of this work is plain from its
treatment of these spurious works as Chaucer's. Capone says
that the most recent and the most philologically trustworthy
edition of Chaucer is that of London 1859 with Tyrwhitt's
introduction.

D. The Separate Works
In Alphabetical Order.

ABC

MSS: Ff v, 30 of the Univ. Libr. Cambr., G 21 of St. John's Coll. Cambr., Hunterian Museum Glasgow Q 2, 25, Laud 740, Univ. Libr. Cambr. Gg iv, 27, Fairfax 16; printed Ch. Soc. PT p. 123 ff. Harley 2251, Bedford, two fragments from Pepys 2006, and a fragment from Harley 7578 are printed Ch. Soc. SPT p. 27. Sion College and Bodley 638 are printed Ch. Soc. OT p. 65 ff. The Ff v, 30 text is also printed in One-Text Print, p. 83, with the French on opposite pages, and in the EETS ed. of Lydgate as below.

Another copy, in a MS at King Henry VIII School, Coventry, mentioned by Bernard, Catalogus 1457.12, has now disappeared with the MS volume. The library of this school has suffered shocking neglect and injury; but the recently appointed master is doing his utmost to preserve what remains of the collection.

In the first four MSS above mentioned, and in the Sion College MS, the poem is inserted into a prose Englishing of De Guileville's Pélérinage de la Vie Humaine; see Furnivall's note, PT p. 123. In the verse-translation of De Guileville's work by Lydgate, a space is left for the hymn, but it is not transcribed; see Trial Forew. pp. 13-15, Skeat I : 59-60, and the EETS print of Lydgate's transl. p. 528, where the text is inserted from the Ff MS.

Textual Notes, see Koch, Anglia 3 : 182-3 and 4 : Anz. 100, also Engl. Stud. 15 : 401, 27 : 38-39. Heath in Globe Chaucer xxxiv agrees with Koch, and gives diagram. Koch's paper in Anglia 4 is criticised by ten Brink in Littblatt 4 : 420-27.

Prints and Editions: By Speght in 1602; in the subsequent eds. of the Works; in the eds. of the Minor Poems by Pickering and by Skeat. Critical ed. by Koch, see ante under C. Speght's text is reprinted Ch. Soc. SPT p. 27.

Modernizations and Translations: Mod. by Purves in 1870, see Section III E here.

Title and Authenticity: Headed in MSS Ff, Bedford, and Sion College "Incipit carmen secundum ordinem Litterarum alphabeti"; the two Pepys copies have "Pryer (Prier) A nostre Dame . . . per Chaucer." Shirley's copy, which is marked *Chaucer* in the margin in his hand (see reproduction in Ch. Soc. Autotypes), has as running title "the Devoute dytee of oure Ladye" in various wordings. For Lydgate's evidence see

Skeat I : 59-60. Speght in the 1602 Chaucer headed the poem "Chaucers ABC, called *La Priere de Nostre Dame:* made, as some say, at the Request of Blanch, Duchesse of Lancaster, as a praier for her priuat vse, being a woman in her religion very deuout." (This Skeat I : 59 terms "probably a mere guess.") In the Urry Chaucer of 1721 headed "Chaucer's A. B. C. called *La Priere de nostre Dame"*, with Speght's heading below; later editions as in Urry, without Speght's title. Marked by the Chaucer Society "An ABC, or Alphabetic Hymn to the Virgin"; Skeat, An ABC.

Source : The French of De Guileville, printed in One-Text Print as above noted, and reprinted thence by Skeat, I : 261 ff., below the Chaucerian text.

Date : Furnivall, Trial Forew. p. 19 dates the poem 1367? ; Skeat I : 59 says that a probable date is 1366. Koch, Anglia 3 : 182-3, is not entirely agreed that the poem is of Chaucer's first period ; in Chronology p. 7 he would date it close before, or even after the Book of the Duchesse, written 1369.

Notes : See Sandras, p. 106 ; Furnivall, Trial Forew. pp. 13-15 ; ten Brink, Hist. Eng. Lit. II : 60-61 ; Skeat I : xxx, 58-61, 452-7 ; Root, Poetry of Chaucer pp. 57-58. For other ABC poems see Polit. Rel. and Love Poems 1866, p. 244, and Jubinal's Nouveau Recueil, II : 245-90.

Adam Scrivener, *see* Words to Adam.

Aetas Prima, *see* Former Age.

ANELIDA AND ARCITE

MSS : Harley 7333, Fairfax 16, Tanner 346, Harley 372, Digby 181, printed Ch. Soc. PT pp. 145 ff. ; Adds. 16165, Bodley 638, Longleat 258, and three MSS of the Complaint only, Trin. Coll. Cambr. R 3, 20, Univ. Libr. Cambr. Ff i, 6, Pepys 2006, printed Ch. Soc. SPT pp. 37 ff. ; the Complaint from Phillipps 8299, printed Ch. Soc. MOT pp. 17 ff. The Harley 7333 text is printed Ch. Soc. One-Text pp. 109 ff.

Genealogy of the texts, see Koch, Anglia 3 : 184 ; enlarged tree *ibid.* 4 : Anz. 102 ; tree also in Globe Chaucer p. xxxviii.

Textual notes, see Koch, Engl. Stud. 15 : 408-9 and 27 : 43-47.

The Complaint of Anelida, vv. 211 to close, is by MSS Fairfax and Bodley placed as if the first part of the poem; four
copies, one a Shirley, are of the Complaint only; and Adds.
16165, another Shirley MS, transcribes the Complaint at foll.
241b-243b, the rest of the poem at the end of the volume, foll.
256b-258b. The independence of the Complaint, originally, thus
becomes a possible question.

The copy of the Complaint in MSS Fairfax and Harley 372
shows a body of variants which impress the student as perhaps
due to Chaucer himself.

Prints and Editions: By Caxton, see Bradshaw in Trial Forew.
p. 118, and Blades p. 212, cp. 201. Caxton is repr. Ch. Soc. PT
pp. 145 ff., and a photographic facsimile was issued by Macmillan and Bowes, Cambridge, 1906. Printed by Thynne in the
1532 Chaucer, and in subsequent eds. of the Works, and of the
Minor Poems by Pickering, Skeat, Bilderbeck.

Modernizations and Translations: Mod. by Cowden Clarke in his
Riches of Chaucer, 1835; by Elizabeth Barrett (Browning) in
the Horne volume of 1841; see Section III E here.
Transl.

Title: Headed by the copyist of Shirley in Harley 7333 "Lo my
lordis and ladyes Here folowyng may ye see the maner of the
lovyng bytwene Arcite of Thebes and Anelida the faire Quene
of Hermony which with his feyned chere doublenesse and
flateryng disceiued her wtouten cause / she beyng than oon of
þe trewest gentilwomen that bere lyf compleyneth her I beseche
you"; above the Complaint is written "The Compleynte of
Anelida þe Quene of Hermonye vpon arcyte borne of þe blode
Riall of Thebes for his Doublenesse." Headed by Shirley himself in R 3, 20, "þe Compleynte of Anelida", and below, "Takeþe
heed sirs I prey yowe of þis compleynt of Anelyda Qweene of
Cartage Roote of trouthe and stedfastnesse þat pytously com-
pleyneþe / vpon þe varyance of Daun Arcyte lord borne of þe
blood Royal of Thebes englisshed by Geffrey Chaucier / In
þe best wyse and moost Rethoricyous þe moost vnkouþe /
metre coloures and Rymes þt euer was sayde to fore þis Day /
redeþe and preveþe þe sooþe." Shirley's other heading, in
Adds. 16165, is "Balade of Anelyda Qwene of Cartage / made
by Geffrey Chaucyer / "; the Complaint, in the same MSS, is
headed "Here endiþe þe Dreme and þe compleynt of þe
desyrous seruant in loue / and filowing begynneþe þe compleint of Anelyda þe feyre Qweene of Cartage vpon þe Chiual-
rous Arcyte of þe royal blode of Thebes descend." [The
"dreme and compleynt" refer to the Temple of Glass, which

precedes in the MS.] The colophon in Adds. 16165 is "And
þus endiþe here þe compleynt of Anelyda." Fairfax's heading
is "The compleynt of feire Anelida and fals Arcite", and for the
complaint "The compleynt of Analida the quene vpon fals
Arcite." Bodley has in the same way "The complaynt of feyre
Anelida on fals Arcyte &", and "The boke of feyre Anelida &
fals Arcyte." Digby heads the poem "litera Annelide Regine";
its colophon is "Explicit lamentacio Annelide Regine Ermonie."
Harley 372 heads the poem "Here begynneth the Compleynt of
faire Anelida & fals Arcite"; and marks the complaint "The
compleynt of faire Anelida vpon fals Arcyte." Longleat has
no heading; its colophon is "Here endith the complaint of
Annelade the quene ayeinst fals Arcite the Theban knyght."
Pepys heads its complaint "The Complaint of Anelida quene of
Hermenye vpon false Arcite of Thebes." Phillipps has as
colophon "Here endeth the compleynt of Anelida the Quene of
Hermenye vpon fals Arcite of Thebees." Tanner has no
markings.

Caxton has as colophon "Thus endeth the compleynt of
anelida." The blackletter prints head the poem "Of Quene
Annelida and fals Arcyte", marking the Complaint separately;
so Urry, the Bell of 1782, Bell of 1854, Aldine, etc.; Skeat,
"Anelida and Arcite."

Bale in his 1548 list of Chaucer's works calls the poem "De
Augea et Telepho"; in the later list he terms it "De Anelida et
Arcyto"; this later list contains both titles, thus duplicating the
poem, and also adds an entry of the "Broche of Vulcan", from
Lydgate's list of Chaucer's works (see Section II A here)
which probably means the Anelida. Leland did not include the
work.

Authenticity: Marked as Chaucer's by two Shirley MSS, the Adds.
and the Trinity; also by Harley 372. Not mentioned in
Chaucer's own lists, but in Lydgate's, as above noted.

Date: Tyrwhitt, in his Account of the Works of Chaucer, says:
"The Arcite whose infidelity is here complained of, is quite a
different person from the Arcite of the Knightes Tale; from
which circumstance we may perhaps be allowed to infer, that
this poem was written before Chaucer had met with the
Theseida." Hertzberg p. 61 dates the poem earlier than the
first form of the Knight's Tale; ten Brink, Hist. Eng. Lit.
II:189, places this poem before the completion of the Knight's
Tale, not far from 1390; Koch, Engl. Stud. 1:289, transl. Ch.
Soc. Essays 409-11, says between 1382-1385. Furnivall, Trial
Forew. p. 10, says "poor enough for Chaucer's decline, yet I put
it soon after the Mars"; on p. 21 he dates it 1375-6?. In Par.

Texts p. 145 he says "I cannot agree with Prof. ten Brink's late date . . . . . and I put it even earlier than Dr. Koch's 1382"; in his note on Koch as above he says "before 1382, I think." Koch gives date 1383? in his Chronology pp. 46-48, Skeat I : 77 says that the poem is difficult to date, but must be placed after 1373; *ibid.* xxxi he calls it "somewhat early." Bilderbeck, N. and Q. 1896 I: 301-2, discusses the historical basis and conjectures date 1386. Mather, Eng. Misc. p. 311, thinks Chaucer began Anelida as a pendant to Troilus, but relinquished this plan and suppressed the poem, not mentioning it in either LGW prol. or Retractation. Lowes, Publ. Mod. Lang. Assn. 20 : 860 ff. see note *i* on p. 861, considers Mather's view untenable, and dates Anelida before Palamon and before Troilus. Tatlock, Devel. and Chronol. chap. III, § 4, opposes Bilderbeck as to the historical basis; he considers that Chaucer could not treat de Vere, the petitioner for Chaucer's deputy in the Customs, so harshly as the language of the Anelida does, on Bilderbeck's interpretation.

But perhaps compare Lydgate's adulation of Gloucester, in the Falls of Princes, etc., with the tone of the same poet's Complaint for my Lady of Gloucester (Anglia 27 : 381-98).

Source: Ten Brink, Studien pp. 49 ff., points out Chaucer's indebtedness to Boccaccio's Teseide, correcting Tyrwhitt; he mentions also Statius as Chaucer's source. According to Skeat, Oxford Chaucer I : 77, the source of lines 71-210 is at present unknown. Lines 211-350 are by Skeat I : 78 given a partial source in the Balade of Pite, see Section V here. Note also Skeat's remark on the relation between this poem and the SqTale, I : 534. See Koeppel, Anglia 14 : 239.

Notes: On the name Anelida and the word Ermony see: Cowell, Ch. Soc. Essays pp. 617-621; Koeppel, Engl. Stud. 20 : 156-158; Schick, EETS ed. of the Temple of Glass, p. cxx note; Skeat I : 77; Bilderbeck, N. and Q. 1896 I : 302.

On the poem see Sandras, Étude, pp. 111-112; ten Brink, Hist. Eng. Lit. II : 189-193; Morley, Eng. Writers V : 152-154; Skeat I : 76-78, 529 ff.; Root, Poetry of Chaucer, pp. 68-9.

The relation between this poem and the Knight's Tale is an enduring Chaucer-crux.

Assembly of Foules, Assembly of Fowls, *see* Parlement of Foules.

Astrolabe

MSS: Skeat, III: lvii ff., lists 22; in his note III: 233 he speaks of 18; Liddell, Globe Chaucer p. liv, says "18 are now known." Skeat enumerates: At Cambridge, Univ. Libr. Dd. iii, 53; Dd. xii, 51; Corpus Christi Coll. 424; Trin. Coll. R 15, 18; St. John's Coll. E 2. At Oxford, Bodl. e Musaeo 54, e Museo 116, Ashmole 360, Ashmole 391, Ashmole 393, Bodley 68, Bodley 619, Digby 72, Rawl. Misc. 3, Rawl. Misc. 1262. In London, Adds. 23002, Adds. 29250, Egerton 2622, Sloane 261, Sloane 314. Others are Phillipps 11955, and a MS at Brussels, "No. 1591." Bernard has mentioned, of these, the Digby, the Corpus, a "MS of Bishop More's" (Cambr. Univ. Libr.), and a Hatton MS which does not appear in Skeat's list. Todd, Illustrations p. 125, mentions four Cambridge MSS; James, in his Cat. of the Trin. Coll. MSS, II : 356-7, describes the Trin. Coll. MS. In the Athen. 1868 II : 370 is a letter calling attention to the corrections in the Cambr. Dd iii, 53 MS as possibly by Chaucer's own hand. According to Skeat, III : lxi, Brae in his ed. described but three MSS.

Prints and Editions: First printed in the Thynne of 1532; in the reprints of this, in Stow, in the Speghts, in Urry. Not in the 1782 Bell or in Anderson, these being collections of poetry only. In Chalmers among the prose works; not in the Chiswick, Moxon, Aldine of 1845, Bell of 1854, or Gilman. The work was ed. by A. E. Brae, Lond. 1870, and by Skeat for the EETS in 1872, rev. Athen. 1872 I : 746. It is included in Skeat vol. III, and in the Globe Chaucer, ed. by Liddell. That Skeat used his own earlier work without careful revision may be surmised from his terming Brae's ed. "recent." (III : lxxi.) The prologue was printed by Mone, Quellen und Forschungen, 1830, from the Brussels MS, without knowledge of its authorship. See Acad. 1878 I : 118.

Title: Chaucer in his prologue calls the work the "Tretys of the Astrelabie." He first describes the instrument, and then gives the "conclusions of the Astrolabe." The Corpus MS marks the work Tractatus Astrolabii, see Skeat III : 233; some other MSS mark it "Brede and Mylke for children", see Globe Chaucer p. 638 note. The early prints head the work "Conclusions of the Astrolabe"; Skeat entitles it "Treatise on the Astrolabe." Leland and Bale term it "De Astrolabio", "De Astrolabii ratione."

Authenticity: Skeat, Canon p. 61, says there is MS authority for assigning the work to Chaucer; at the end of his text, which is from MS Dd iii, 53, is printed a colophon from MS, ascribing the work to Chaucer. Lydgate's list (see Section II A here) refers to this work as a treatise to his "sonne Lowys."

Source: Skeat III : lxix points out as source the Compositio et Operatio Astrolabii, by Messahala, an Arabian astronomer of the 8th century; the second part of this is printed in full in Skeat's EETS ed. of the Astrolabe. Skeat, in a footnote III : lxx, says that Bradshaw gave him the hint, and mentions Selden's reference to the source, in his preface to Drayton's Polyolbion. Liddell, Globe Chaucer p. liii, says that the definitions and descriptive astronomy are from John de Sacrobosco's De Sphera.

Date: Furnivall in Athen. 1871 II : 495 says 1391; Skeat, III : lxiv mentions 1391; Liddell, Globe Chaucer, p. liii, "a late period of Chaucer's life."

Notes: This work was left unfinished by Chaucer. It is discussed by Godwin in chap. 51; by Brae as above; by Morley, Eng. Writers V : 268-71; by Root, Poetry of Chaucer, pp. 85-87; by Skeat in vol. III of Oxford Chaucer and in his 1872 ed. as above.

BOETHIUS' DE CONSOLATIONE PHILOSOPHIAE

MSS: Brit. Mus. Adds. 10340; printed EETS, ed. Morris, 1868, with collations from the MS next named. See Skeat II : xlii. —Univ. Libr. Cambr. Ii iii, 21; printed by the Ch. Soc., ed. Furnivall, 1886. See Skeat II : xxxvii-xli.—Of the same library, Ii iii, 38, see Skeat II : xli-xlii.—Brit. Mus. Adds. 16165, a codex written by John Shirley, see Skeat I : 56, and Section IV B (1) here.—Brit. Mus. Harley 2421, see Skeat II : xliii.—The Hengwrt MS of the CT contains a part of the Boethius, see Skeat II : xliii, and the Hist. Comm. of MSS, 2d Report p. 106. (It may be noted that in this report the MS of the CT is numbered 184, in the Ch. Soc. Autotypes 154.) See also Furnivall, Temp. Pref. 50-51.—A MS in Salisbury Cathedral, found by Wülker, see Academy 1878 II : 337, and a bit printed by him in Anglia 2 : 372.—Bodley 797, see Liddell in Academy 1896 I : 529.—Phillipps 9472, mentioned by Skeat II : xliv, no description.—Auct. F. 3, 5 of the Bodleian Library is mentioned by Skeat II : xviii as containing a prose translation not that of Chaucer. Liddell, Academy 1896 I : 199, says that the translation is Chaucer's, "disguised to a certain extent." It is of Book I only.—See Blades' Caxton p. 214 for mention of a MS in Bruges.

Prints and Editions: For diplomatic prints of the MSS see above. Printed by Caxton, before 1479, see Blades p. 213. A collation of this print with the Adds. 10340 and Ii iii, 21 readings was printed by Kellner in Engl. Stud. 14 : 1-53; see Skeat, II : xliv. Printed by Thynne in the 1532 Chaucer, a facsimile of which appeared from the Oxford University Press in 1905.

The Consolatio was included in subsequent eds. of the complete works. Two extracts are printed by Wülker, Altengl. Lesebuch II : 188-191 (Morris' text).

Authenticity and Title: That Chaucer made a translation of Boethius is apparent from the Words to Adam, "Boece or Troilus for to writen newe"; also from the Retractation and from LGW prol. 425, where the work is said to be in prose. The heading in Shirley's MS Adds 16165 is "Boicius de consolacone prosed in Englisshe by Chaucier"; neither MS printed by the Chaucer Society has a heading. Blades, in his Caxton p. 214, quotes Dibdin, Typograph. Antiq. I : 306, as doubting Chaucer's authorship of the translation; but the constant evidence of Chaucer's familiarity with the Consolatio and the note of Shirley prove the contrary.

The title in the Thynne ed. of 1532 is "Boetius de consolatione philosophie"; Chaucer himelf calls it "Boece" in the Words to Adam and the LGW prologue, "Boece de consolacione" in the Retractation.

Date: Ten Brink, in his Studien p. 142, placed this work and the Troilus in close conjunction, partly because the influence of the former is so evident upon the Troilus and other poems of that period, partly because of Chaucer's mention of the two works together in the Words to Adam. He dates them between 1373 and 1384, nearer the latter date. Koch, in his Chronology of Chaucer's Writings dates the Boethius 1377-8. Skeat considers between 1373 and 1384 sufficient, but in I : 78 he says "somewhere about 1380"; see II : xxxvii for a grouping of the Canterbury Tales as compared with the date of the Boethius.

Source: Primarily, the Latin of Boethius, on whom see Section II C (4) here.

For a mass of notes on the popularity and influence of the Consolatio, see H. F. Stewart's Boethius: an Essay, London 1891. Stewart, p. 204, suggested as a secondary source of Chaucer's translation the French version made by Jean de Meung; Skeat II : xiv dismissed this suggestion as "improbable and unnecessary." See Liddell in the Acad. 1895 II : 227, and in the Nation 1897 I : 125, on this point and that of the influence of the "Pseudo-Aquinas" commentary upon Chaucer.

Miss Kate Petersen, in the Publ. Mod. Lang. Assn. 18 : 1 ff.
(1903) brings evidence to show that a commentary by Trivet
"was the single source of this material in Chaucer's Boethius."
On Trivet and his commentary see Jourdain: Excursions his-
toriques et philosophiques à travers le moyen-âge, Paris 1880;
and see Section II C (4) here for note on Trivet.

Other Versions: See Stewart, op. cit., chapter on Some Ancient
Translations; see Sedgefield's introd. to his ed., Oxford 1899,
of the Old Eng. Boethius; see, for Eng. translations, later than
Chaucer's, Skeat II : xv-xix, but note that the version in Auct.
F 3, 5, contrary to Skeat, is by Chaucer, see above under MSS.
Note also that of Bracegirdle's transl., mentioned by Skeat II :
xix, there is an extract printed by Flügel, Anglia 14 : 499-501;
also that Walton's 1410 version, discussed Warton-Hazlitt III :
39-40 and Skeat II : xv-xviii, is to be ed. for the EETS by
Liddell; extracts will be included in vol. 18 of Section II of the
Belles Lettres Series, Boston. Letters on the subject of an ed.
of Walton are in Athen. 1892 I : 565, 600, 1895 II : 902-3, with
a list of 14 MSS.

There is a modern Eng. transl. by James, Lond. 1897, easily
accessible in Routledge's New Universal Library.

Notes: Passages in Chaucer showing the influence of Boethius
are listed by Stewart, op. cit., appendix B; see also Skeat II :
xxviii ff., Koeppel in Archiv 87 : 33 ff. Mistranslations by
Chaucer are listed by Stewart pp. 222 ff., see Skeat II : xxiv ff.

See Morris' introd. to the print of MS Adds. 10340; Blades
pp. 213-15; Morley, Eng. Writers V : 144-146; ten Brink,
Studien 139-142, Hist. Eng. Lit. II : 78-81; Lounsbury, Studies
II : 265-267; Skeat ?I; Root, Poetry of Chaucer pp. 80-85.

BOOK OF THE DUCHESSE

MSS: Fairfax 16, Bodley 638, Tanner 346. Printed by the
Chaucer Society (Fairfax and Tanner) PT p. 1 ff.; the Bodley
is in OT p. 213 ff. The Fairfax text is also in One-Text
Print p. 1 ff.

Textual Notes, see Max Lange, Untersuchungen über
Chaucers Boke of the Duchesse, diss. Halle, 1883, 34 pages;
reviewed by Koch, Anglia 6 : Anz. 91-100, Littblatt 1885, p. 236.
Lange's paper comprises, pp. 1-12, notes on text-relations;
pp. 13-20 emendations, etc.; pp. 20-34, French influence on the
poem.

See also for textual notes Koch as above and in Anglia 4:
Anz. 95, Engl. Stud. 11 : 294, 15 : 403-6, 27 : 32-37. The tree
of MSS is given, after Koch and Lange, by Skeat I : 64, and

in Globe Chaucer p. xxxiii. Skeat's statement I : 64 that the lines 31-96 are missing from the three MSS is insufficient; Bodley lacks still more,—lines 24 to 31,—a fact which, in view of the constant and intimate alliance of texts between this MS and Fairfax, requires explanation. See under Bodley 638, p. 335 ante.

Prints and Editions: By Thynne in the 1532 Chaucer; reprinted Ch. Soc. PT p. 1 ff., and in the facsimile of this Chaucer, 1905. In the subsequent eds. of the Works, and of the Minor Poems; in the selections of Ward (extract), of Sweet (extracts), of Paton, of Robertson. See Section III D here.

Modernizations and Translations: Modernized by Cowden Clarke in his Riches of Chaucer; by Purves in 1870; see Section III E here.

Title: In Fairfax and Bodley, "The booke of the Duchesse", Fairfax with an additional historical note in a hand perhaps Stow's. In Tanner 346, in a later hand, "Chaucer's Dream." In Thynne "The Dreame of Chaucer." Stow, in 1561, headed the poem "The dream of Chaucer otherwise called the book of the Duchesse or Seys and Alcione with a balade to his master Bucton"; Speght copies this in his 1598 table of contents, and when printing the Isle of Ladies for the first time, in the same volume, prefixed a note entitling that poem Chaucers Dreame, and saying "that which heretofore hath gone vnder the name of his dreame is the book of the Duchesse: or the death of Blanch, duchesse of Lancaster."

Francis Thynne, in his Animadversions, combated Speght's change of title. Urry, in 1721, followed Speght; but the 1782 Bell and Anderson printed in immediate sequence Chaucer's Dream (the Isle of Ladies), and the Dream of Chaucer (this poem). Chalmers separates the two poems, copying Speght's heading for the former, and marking this poem "the book commonly entitled Chaucer's Dream"; Singer, separating the two poems, marks this "The Book of the Duchess or the Death of Blanche, commonly entitled Chaucer's Dream." Moxon, the Aldine of 1845, etc., continue the title "Book of the Duchess."

Bale, in both eds., has "De Ceyce et Halcyona", followed by "In obitum Blanchiae ducissae"; he and Leland also give it as "Somnium Chauceri", following Thynne as above.

Authenticity: "There is no assignment of the Dethe of Blaunche to Chaucer in any of our three MSS of it; but as he names a Dethe of Blaunche the Duchesse as his, and Lydgate does so too; as the Blaunche we have is found in volumes containing other acknowledged poems of Chaucer, and as this Blaunche conforms to Chaucer's ryme-laws, and has the run of his lines, we count the external evidence for it fairly complete." (Furnivall in Trial Forew. p. 128.)

Date: Stow's (?) marginal note in the Fairfax MS identifies the mourning knight of this poem as John of Gaunt, lamenting the death of Blanche. The note was appended to the heading of the poem in Stow's and later eds., and Tyrwhitt, in his comment on CT line 4477, says he believes "John is very right in his conjecture." As the Duchess Blanche of Lancaster died in 1369, and the Duke of Lancaster married again in 1372, the poem was probably composed near the former date; ten Brink, Studien p. 6, Hertzberg p. 61, Skeat I : 63, etc.

In Acad. 1894 I : 191 Skeat prints the Bishop of Oxford's interpretation of lines 1318-19.

Source: Sandras, in his Étude, first pointed out the connection between this poem and Froissart's Paradys d'Amour; but it was long supposed that the French poet was the borrower. See list of critics holding this opinion in Engl. Stud. 26 : 322 note, i. e., ten Brink, Studien p. 175 note 7, Furnivall in Trial Forew. pp. 51-52, Hales in Athen. 1882 I : 444 repr. Folia Litteraria pp. 83 ff., Skeat ed. Minor Poems (1888) pp. 234, 242, Oxford Chaucer I : 462, 468, Lounsbury, Studies I : 245, III : 13, Lange, Book of the Duchess pp. 14-16, Koch, Anglia 6: Anz. 97, Morley in Engl. Writers, Ward in his life of Chaucer. Rossetti in Athen. 1882 I : 568 seems to assume that Chaucer was the borrower, but the question was not fully examined until Macaulay, in Macmillan's Magazine 1895 I : 230, and Bradley in Acad. 1895 I : 125-6 pointed out that Chaucer was the borrower. The full proof was presented by Kittredge in Engl. Stud. 26 : 321-336.

The crux Eclympasteyre in this poem, line 167, thus becomes a problem for French rather than for English students; for various suggestions, all assuming Chaucer's use of the word earlier than Froissart, see N. and Q. 1858 I : 229, Sandras' Étude pp. 90, 295 note (see Trial Forew. p. 52), Hertzberg p. 42, Bell's 1854 Chaucer VI : 141, ten Brink's Studien pp. 11-12, Athen. 1882 I : 444, 508, 568, Acad. 1889 I : 10. Tyrwhitt included the word in his list of Words and Phrases not Understood, at the end of his Glossary.

The influence of Machault is evident upon this poem, see Sandras, Étude, pp. 90, 290 ff.

See Klaeber, Mod. Lang. Notes 12 : 378-80, on the Traces of the Canticum and of Boetius' De Consolatione Philosophiae in Chaucer's Book of the Duchesse.

See Koeppel, Anglia, 14: 238-9, Engl. Stud. 20: 154.

Notes: It is apparent from Stow's heading,—see ante under Title, —that he identified this poem with the "Ceys and Alcion" mentioned by Chaucer ML headlink line 54 as his youthful work. Furnivall, Trial Forew. p. 36 and Skeat I: 63, consider that the Ceyx and Alcyone episode was originally a piece of work separate from and earlier than the Book of the Duchesse. Ten Brink, Studien pp. 6-8, Hist. Eng. Lit. II: 42 ff., seems to identify the poems. Lydgate possibly regarded the poems as separate works, see his list, Section II A here, although, in spite of Hertzberg's reference to him (p. 44 note 71, p. 36) as well-informed and exact, his words can never be treated as conclusive evidence, partly because he sometimes merely restates Chaucer, partly because his mode of expression is too confused and uncertain to serve as basis for argument. See on the point also Lounsbury, Studies I : 424.

A discrepancy appears in line 455, where the mourning knight is alluded to as 24 years old, although in 1369 John of Gaunt was 29. Francis Thynne, in his Animadversions, attacked Speght's (Stow's) note as to the hero and title of this poem, on this account; Tyrwhitt, in his comment on CT line 4477, thought that Chaucer might be designedly misrepresenting; ten Brink, Studien p. 5, suggests that Chaucer was not aiming at exactness; Skeat I : 476 gives Brock's suggestion of scribal error.

In the Jour. Compar. Lit. I : 82-84 Torraca argues that lines 1024 ff. of this poem, alluding to "the Carrenare", show a reminiscence of Dante, Inferno 9 : 113-14, in which case Chaucer must have known Dante's text before his first journey to Italy.

Godwin, in his life of Chaucer chaps. 20, 29, discusses this poem, censuring faults of taste; Furnivall as cited above pp. 33-63, criticises the ending, p. 42; see ten Brink, Hist. Eng. Lit. II: 44. Sandras, Étude pp. 89 ff., is also severe on the poem, a judgment which Ward, Life of Chaucer p. 72, tries to mitigate. Courthope, Hist. Eng. Poetry I: 267, considers the "design singularly barren of genuine invention." See also Morley, Eng. Writers V : 180-186, Root, Poetry of Chaucer pp. 59-63. The poem is discussed by ten Brink, Studien pp. 3-14, Hist. Eng. Lit. II: 42-48; Skeat I: 63-64, 462-495.

On the lay woven into this poem, lines 475-486, see Trial Forew. pp. 33, 114; Koch in Anglia 6 : Anz. 98; ten Brink, Sprache u. Versk. § 346.

Lines 405 ff. are annotated by Klaeber, Mod. Lang. Notes 17: 323-324; lines 1028-29 by Lowes, Mod. Phil. 3: 1 ff.

See: Die Verwendung des Traummotivs in der englischen Dichtung bis auf Chaucer. W. Baake. diss. Halle 1906. Pp. 58.

See: W. O. Sypherd, Studies in Chaucer's House of Fame. Ch. Soc. 1907.

Book of Fame, *see* House of Fame.

BUKTON

MS: Fairfax 16, printed Ch. Soc. PT p. 428 and One-Text Print p. 303.
  Textual Notes, see Koch, Anglia 4 : 107-8, Engl. Stud. 15 : 417.

Prints and Editions: By Notary, 1499-1501, repr. Ch. Soc. PT p. 423. By Thynne in 1532, repr. Ch. Soc. *ibid.,* and in the facsimile of the Thynne Chaucer. In the subsequent black-letter eds., in Urry, and in later eds. of the Works or Poems. In Paton; in the 5th ed. of Zupitza's Uebungsbuch, 1897. Critical ed. by Koch, Berlin 1883.

Modernizations and Translations : Transl. into German by Koch, see Section IV C here; mod. by Purves in 1870, see Section III E here.

Authenticity: Marked as Chaucer's by the MS.

Title: In the MS, "Lenvoy de Chaucer A Bukton"; in Notary, "Here foloweth the counceyll of Chaucer touchyng Maryag &c. whiche was sen te te Bucketon &c." No heading in Thynne. Thynne printed the poem immediately after the Dream of Chaucer (Book of the Duchess), noting it in the table of contents as the "Dreme of Chaucer with a balade", and putting no separate heading to Bukton in the text. Stow, in 1561, placed it similarly, marking it in the table of contents "The dream of Chaucer otherwise called the Book of the Duchesse or Seys and Alcione with a balade to his master Bucton", no heading to Bukton in the text. Speght copied Stow. Urry, putting the ballad in the same position, headed it "This seems an Envoy to the Duke of Lancaster after his Loss of Blanch"; he was imitated by the Bell Chaucer of 1782 and by Anderson, although Tyrwhitt had termed the note "unaccountable." Chalmers, who went back to the blackletter eds. for his texts, put no heading to the poem, placing it after the Book of the Duchess; the Chiswick editor followed suit. Moxon relegated Bukton to a place among the Minor Poems; the Aldine of 1845 and

Pickering of 1846, which copied the Chiswick, moved it back to follow the Duchess; the Bell of 1854 and subsequent eds. print it among the Minor Poems.

From Thynne of 1532 to the Chiswick all eds. printed the first line as:

> My master &c. when of Christ our king

with an &c instead of the name Bukton; this is not seen in the MS or in Notary, which write Bucton, Bucketon. Even Stow, despite his correct marking in his table of contents, writes &c. Singer, the editor of the Chiswick Chaucer, took Tyrwhitt's information and corrected the reading. Furnivall thus erred in saying, p. 423 of the Par. Texts, that the Moxon first made the emendation; he corrected himself in a slip issued with the Odd Texts. The title as in the MS was first printed in Bell of 1854. Furnivall, Par. Texts p. 423, and One-Text Print, entitles the poem Marriage, or Bukton.

Date: Furnivall, Trial Forew. p. 8, cp. 17, says about the same time as Scogan. Koch, Chronology pp. 72-73, says end of 1396. Skeat, Acad. 1888 I : 257, says the winter of 1396 is meant in the poem.

Notes: The letter printed N. and Q. 1870 I : 28 is entirely without foundation. On the poem see Morley, Eng. Writers. V : 274; ten Brink, Hist. Eng. Lit. II : 193-4; Root, Poetry of Chaucer, 76-7; Skeat I : 85, 558-9.

Chaucer's Dream, *see* Book of the Duchesse.

Chaucer unto the King, *see under* Purse.

Complaints, *see* Fortune, Mars, Pity, Purse, Venus.

"Dant in English", *see under* House of Fame.

Death of Blanche, *see* Book of the Duchesse.

Envoy to Bukton, Envoy to Scogan, *see* Bukton, Scogan.

FORMER AGE

MSS: Univ. Libr. Cambr. Ii iii, 21, Hh iv, 12. Both printed Ch. Soc. PT p. 173 ff. The Ii text is also in One-Text Print p. 123, and at pp. 180-2 of Ch. Soc. First Series No. LXXVI. Skeat

I : 539 says: "Both MSS are poor, and omit a whole line
(line 56), which has to be supplied by conjecture." This he
does; the Globe Chaucer leaves a gap. Observe the rime-error
line 47. Textual notes by Koch, Engl. Stud. 11 : 293, 15 : 417.

Prints and Editions: Discovered by Henry Bradshaw, says Fur-
nivall PT p. 173. First printed by Morris in the Aldine
Chaucer of 1866, and since included in eds. of the Works. In
the eds. of the Minor Poems by Skeat and by Bilderbeck.
Crit. ed. by Koch, 1883. In Sweet's Primer; in Robertson's
Select Chaucer; see Section III D here.

Modernizations and Translations:

Authenticity and Title: Headed in the Ii MS,—a copy of the
Boethius,—"Chawcer vp on this fyfte met*ur* of the second
book." See note on the MS, Section IV A (5) here. No
heading in Hh; colophon "Finit Etas prima Chaucers." Morris
entitled the poem Aetas Prima; it was termed Former Age in
the Ch. Soc. prints.

Source: Bradshaw, in 1867 (Memoir p. 212) discovered the source
of this poem in Boethius; stanzas 1-4 are translated from the
De Consol. Phil., bk. II metre 5. Cp. Chaucer's prose transl.
of the same passage. For stanzas 5-8 no original has yet been
noted, though Skeat refers to Jerome (or John of Salisbury),
and to the Roman de la Rose, see Skeat I : 539 ff. See Petersen
on Chaucer and Trivet, in the Publ. Mod. Lang. Assn. 18 : 190
ff. for French, Latin, and Mid. Eng. of the Boethius bit parallel.
See Moore, Studies in Dante, I : 217; Koeppel, Anglia 14 : 247.

Date: Schröer, Anglia 4: Anz. p. 45, says that the somewhat
awkward *usage* of line 4, as compared with the prose, indicates
that it was chosen to rime with *outrage,* already in the prose;
hence the prose is earlier. Skeat I : 78 says probably later than
the prose transl. of Boethius by Chaucer; *ibid.* he considers it
likely that the five poems (named below under Notes) were all
written at about the same period. Heath, Globe Chaucer, prints
them in sequence, and says p. xlvii that they were written after
1382, and probably before 1390. Koch, Chronology p. 74 ff.,
thinks the five poems were written either in 1386-9 or after
1397; on p. 78 he would put them 1393-99.

Notes: Koch, Crit. Ed. p. 22, thinks that this poem, Fortune, Truth,
Gentilesse, and Stedfastnesse form a cyclus, being free tran-
scriptions of passages in Boethius.
    On the work see Skeat I : 78-9, 539-42; Root, Poetry of
Chaucer pp. 70-71.

FORTUNE

MSS: Univ. Libr. Cambr. Ii iii, 21, Ashmole 59, Trin. Coll. Cambr. R 3, 20, Fairfax 16, Bodley 638, Harley 2251, printed Ch. Soc. PT 439-445. Pepys 2006, Lansd. 699, and Caxton's print, are printed Ch. Soc. SPT 167-170; Selden B 10 is reprod. MOT 35. The copy in Leyden Voss. 9, which is probably sister to the Lansd., has not been printed; for note on the MS see Robinson, Harvard Studies V : 187. The Ii text is in One-Text Print p. 315, and at pp. 182-4 of Ch. Soc. First Series No. LXXVI. Textual notes see Koch, Anglia 4 : Anz. 110, Engl. Stud. 15 : 416, 27 : 57. Koch's conclusions are schematized Globe Chaucer p. xlvii; note that Heath there mentions eight MSS instead of ten.

Prints and Editions: By Caxton, see Bradshaw in Trial Forew. p. 116 ff. Caxton is reproduced Ch. Soc. as above. By Thynne in 1532, and in subsequent eds. of the Works. In eds. of the Minor Poems,—Pickering of 1846, Skeat, Bilderbeck. Crit. ed. by Koch, Berlin 1883. In the Selections of Paton.

Modernizations and Translations: Transl. into German by Koch, see Section IV C here.

Authenticity: Marked as Chaucer's by two Shirley MSS, Ashmole 59 and R 3, 20; also by Ii iii, 21 and Fairfax 16.

Title: Shirley heads the poem in Ashmole 59, "Here foloweþe nowe a compleynte of þe Pleintyff ageinst fortune translated oute of ffrenshe in-to Englisshe by þat famous Rethorissyen / Geffrey Chaucier / ." In his Cambr. MS he marks it "a balade made by Chaucier of þe louer and of Dame ffortune." Fairfax, Bodley, and the Ii codex head it "Balade (s) de vilage saunz peynture"; Fairfax adds "Par Chaucer." Selden writes "Paupertas conqueritur super fortunam." Lansd.'s heading, not reprod. by the Ch. Soc., and appearing at the foot of the preceding page, is "Incipit quedam disputacio inter conquerilatorem & ffortunam." Harley and Pepys use the poem's own phrase "(Le) pleyntyf (en)countre fortune." Caxton has "Balade of the vilage without peyntyng." Caxton's heading was reprod. from Thynne, 1532, to the Bell of 1854, which latter, using the MSS, printed the title as in Fairfax. The error of *vilage* for *visage* appears in all MSS and prints using that form of title; see Chaucer's transl. of Boethius, bk. II, prose 1, for the origin of the title. The Bell Chaucer of 1854, vol. VIII : 125, says that "the title bears no relation whatever to the subject"; the error was pointed out by Bradshaw, according

24

to Trial. Forew. p. 8 footnote. The Globe Chaucer p. xlvii incorrectly says that the MSS entitle this poem "Balades de visage sanz peinture."

Source: Skeat I : 543 says the foundation is Boethius' De Consolatione bk. II, prose 1, 2, 3, 4, 5, 8, and metre 1; also the Roman de la Rose, 4853-4944 of the French text. The origin of the poem in Boethius was pointed out by Bradshaw, see Memoir, p. 212. For the Roman see Koeppel in Anglia 14 : 248.

Date: In Athen. 1871 II : 495 and Trial Forew. p. 7, cp. p. 17, Furnivall assigns the date 1398. Skeat as above under Former Age dates the group of five poems there mentioned later than the Boethius, i. e., probably after 1380. Koch, Chronology p. 79, puts them between 1394 and 1398. Heath, Globe Chaucer xlvii, thinks the five poems were written between 1382 and 1390. Bilderbeck, in Athen. 1902 I : 82, places this poem in 1391-4.

Notes: Gaston Paris, in his *Villon*, Paris 1901 pp. 95-96, has commented admirably upon the constant reappearance of Fortune and Death, as terrible unescapable powers, in late medieval literature. The conception of Fortune as a deity is Greek, and especially Roman; allusions in classical Roman lit. are frequent, cp. Ovid, Tristia V : 8, 15, and Horace, Odes I : 35, III : 29, lines 49 ff. With the establishment of Christianity the difficulty of defining her power as compared with the Divine became a constant problem, and as interesting to the medieval mind as was the relation between freewill and foreknowledge to Milton, or to Boethius and Chaucer, see Tatlock in Mod. Phil. 3 : 370. The subject was treated now seriously by the Christian mind such as Boethius', see his De Consolatione bk. II, and now in a purely literary manner, as by Alanus in his Anticlaudianus, Book VIII, or by Boccaccio in his De Casibus Virorum Illustrium. The discussion of Fortune in this latter and in Petrarch's De Remediis utriusque Fortunae contributed to the influence exerted by Boethius in making the topic a commonplace of the fourteenth and fifteenth centuries.

Cp. also Dante, Inferno 7 : 64 ff., where Dante is under the influence of Boethius, see Moore, Studies in Dante, I : 285. See the passages in Boccaccio used by Chaucer, Troilus bk. IV opening, Knight's Tale 67-68. See Guido Cavalcanti's Song of Fortune, printed in Poeti del primo secolo, 1816, II : 326, and transl. in Rossetti's Dante and His Circle, p. 151. See Vernon's Readings on Dante's Inferno, 2d ed. I : 246, for notes on the pavement wheels of Fortune in Sienese and Veronese churches. See the poems of the de Condé, ed. Scheler, Bruxelles 1866, III : 15, for a Dis de Fortune.

On the poem see Sandras, Étude, pp. 106-107; Morley, Eng. Writers V : 272; ten Brink, Hist. Eng. Lit. II : 194-5; Root, Poetry of Chaucer pp. 71-2; Skeat I : 79-80, 542-47.

GENTILESSE

MSS: Ashmole 59, Trin. Coll. Cambr. R 3, 20, Harley 7333, Cotton Cleop. D vii, Harley 7578, Adds. 22139, printed Ch. Soc. PT p. 427; Harley 2251, Trin. Coll. Cambr. R 14, 51, and the Caxton print, printed Ch. Soc. SPT p. 161. The Ashmole copy is also in One-Text Print p. 307.

Ashmole's copy of the poem is included in its transcription of Scogan's Moral Balade, which is printed Ch. Soc. PT 427, 430.

Textual Notes, see Koch in Anglia 4: Anz. p. 108, Engl. Stud. 15 : 416 and 27 : 58.

Prints and Editions: Caxton printed Scogan's Moral Balade, which cites the entire text of Gentilesse; see Blades' Caxton, p. 202. Thynne also included the Moral Balade in his 1532 Chaucer, reprinted 1542. Stow, in the 1561 Chaucer, not only printed the Scogan poem, but placed first in the list of his additions to previous editions this poem, as "A balade made by Chaucer teching what is gentilness, or whom is worthy to be caled gentil." In the same way, Speght and Urry give two copies of the Chaucerian text, as did the Bell of 1782, though the Scogan poem was there relegated to the end of the collection. Anderson, in 1793, discarded Scogan's poem, giving only one text of the Chaucerian stanzas. Chalmers prints the poem three times, on p. 403, p. 553, p. 557; Chiswick, Moxon, and later eds. give the one Chaucerian text. In the eds. of the Minor Poems by Pickering, by Skeat, and by Bilderbeck. Critical ed. by Koch. In the Selections of Paton, of Manly; see Section III D here. For Scogan's poem see Section V here.

The poem is cited entire in Bossewell's Workes of Armorie, 1572, pp. 13b-14a, as is also an extract from the WBTale on "gentilesse."

Modernizations and Translations: In Cowden Clarke's Riches of Chaucer; in the 1870 Purves; see Section III E. Transl. into German by Koch, see Section IV C here.

Title and Authenticity: Scogan, in his Moral Balade, says that the stanzas which he quotes are by Chaucer; accordingly Shirley, in his Ashmole 59 copy of Scogan, writes in the margin by these stanzas "Geffrey Chaucier made þeos thre balades nexst þat folowen"; R 3, 20, also a Shirley copy, heads the poem

"Balade by Chaucier"; Harley 7333 (from Shirley) marks it "Moral Balade of Chaucier." No ascription elsewhere, and no heading except that R 14, 51, a fragment of one stanza, writes "Balade."

Speght, Urry, the 1782 Bell, Chalmers, and Chiswick retain Stow's title as above under Prints, the two latter capitalizing A Ballade; Bell, in 1854, headed it "A Ballade", as did Morris. The Chaucer Society, followed by Skeat, has used the title Gentilesse.

Date: Trial Forew. p. 12, "certainly not of Chaucer's best time,— after 1390." *Ibid.* p. 17 "near 1397". Koch, Chronology p. 79, dates this and the other poems from Boethius in 1394-98.

Source: Skeat I : 553 gives as groundwork Boethius bk. III prose 6; cp. Roman de la Rose 18807 ff.; see WBTale 253 ff., Dante, Purgatorio 7 : 121, Convito IV canzone 3. These refs. were pointed out by F. J. Child in Athen. 1870 II : 721, with mention also of Gower, Conf. Amantis IV : 2200 ff., and the note that Tyrwhitt remarked on Boethius as the source.

A Dis de Gentilesse is in the works of de Condé III : 97, see ref. above under Fortune.

On the poem see Morley, Eng. Writers V : 273; Skeat I : 82-84, 553-5; Root, Poetry of Chaucer p. 74.

HOUSE OF FAME

MSS: Fairfax 16 and Bodley 638, sister texts of 2158 lines each, printed Ch. Soc. PT p. 179 ff.; Pepys 2006, of 1843 lines only, printed Ch. Soc. OT p. 79 ff. The Fairfax text is also in One-Text Print p. 129 ff.

Both Fairfax and Bodley break off suddenly, apparently as Chaucer left the poem; a Jacobean hand has copied into Fairfax the 12-line conclusion written by Caxton and Thynne, see below. The original scribe of the Fairfax stopped on a verso with only 23 lines written; the 12 added lines fill out the page. The next three leaves were left blank by the scribe, but the same later hand has inserted into part of this space the Ten Commandments of Love, see Section V here. The Bodley MS stops with the same line as the Fairfax, halfway down a verso, and leaves the next leaf blank; later owners have scribbled in the space, but the Caxton-Thynne conclusion is not transcribed.

Textual Notes, see Koch, Anglia 3 : 186, 4 : Anz. 102-3, Engl. Stud. 15 : 409-15, 27 : 53-57. And see Willert as below.

Prints and Editions: By Caxton, *n. d.*, see Dibdin, Typogr. Antiq. I : 311, Blades p. 292, where Caxton's prose epilogue is re-printed; it is also in Ch. Soc. PT p. 241. Blades' statement that the verse-conclusion, also written by Caxton to close the poem, was of 2 lines, is incorrect; it is of 12, see Furnivall in Acad. 1878 I: 52, Skeat III: 287, and the reprint in PT p. 179 ff. Cp. Willert p. 34 of his 1883 monograph, Koch in Anglia 4: Anz. 103, 7: Anz. 24-30, 203, 208. The MS used by Caxton broke off with line 2094, at which point he appended his conclusion.

Printed by Thynne, in the 1532 Chaucer; his text is reproduced Ch. Soc. PT p. 179 ff., and also in the 1905 facsimile of his volume. Thynne printed 2158 lines of the poem (all now known) and altered the first two and one-half lines of Caxton's conclusion to make better connection. The spuriousness of these lines was not recognized until the work of Bradshaw and the Chaucer Society.

Printed in the Pynson Chaucer of 1526, and in subsequent eds. of the Works; in the eds. of the Minor Poems by Pickering, by Skeat; selections in Ward; in Paton, in Robertson. Lowndes says, *s. v.* Chaucer, "Chaucer's Book of Fame was printed also at Edinburgh by Walter Chepman in 1508, in the Scottish dialect or orthography, under the title of 'The Maying or Disport of Chaucer.'" This statement, taken from Ritson, Bibliographia Poetica, 1802, and repeated in the Bell Chaucer of 1854, is erroneous; the poem thus entitled and printed was Lydgate's Complaint of the Black Knight, which is marked as above in the Scottish MS Selden B 24. See Krausser in Anglia 19 : 213, 215, and the description of the Selden MS in Section IV A (3) here.

Poem separately ed. by Skeat, Oxford 1893, 1896, 136 pages. Crit. ed. by Willert, The Hous of Fame: Einleitung und Textverhältniss, diss. Berlin 1883, pp. 34; The Hous of Fame: Text, Varianten, Anmerkungen, Berlin 1888, pp. 45. Reviewed by Koch Anglia 7: Anz. 24-30, 208; see Willert *ibid.* p. 203-7. Koch also notes the work Engl. Stud. 15 : 409-15, Littblatt 1885 p. 361.

Modernizations and Translations: Rewritten by Pope as the Temple of Fame; see p. 222 here. Modernized by Purves in 1870; extracts in Cowden Clarke; see Section III E here.

Transl. into German by von Düring, see Section III E here.

Title and Authenticity: No mark of authorship in the MSS, and no heading in Pepys; Fairfax and Bodley head it "The House of ffame." In the LGW prol. line 405 Chaucer mentions a "House of Fame" as his; in the poem itself the eagle addresses the narrator as "Geffrey"; and in the Retractation the "Book of Fame" is mentioned among the works of the author of the Canterbury Tales. That the poem was known to Shirley, as the House of Fame, is evident from his heading to the Temple of Glass in MS Adds. 16165, see Schick p. xxiii. Cax-

ton entitled it "The Book of Fame"; Leland and Bale term it
"De Fama", "De Fama et ejus domicilio."

The omission of the poem from the list of Chaucer's works
given by Lydgate has occasioned comment. Skeat, I : 22-25,
considers it perfectly clear that in the lines of Lydgate (printed
Section II A here)

> He wrote also ful many day agone
> Daunt in English him self so doth expresse
> The pitous storye of Ceis and Alcion . . . .

the phrase "Daunt in English" refers to the House of Fame,
because of the strong influence of Dante upon the poem.
Kittredge, Nation 1894 II : 310, says that this explanation does
not carry conviction, and terms Lydgate's phrase "maddening."
Koeppel, in his 1885 monograph p. 82 (see Reference List)
interpreted the passage to mean that Lydgate praises Chaucer
by declaring that he wrote as Dante would have written in
English. In Anglia 13 : 186 Koeppel repeats his opinion; see
Hupe *ibid.* p. 363, Koeppel *ibid.* p. 363-4, and Kaluza in Engl.
Stud. 22 : 278.

It may be noted in this connection that, as Blades remarks in
his work on Caxton p. 295, manuscripts of the House of Fame
were difficult to get already in the fifteenth century, and that Lydgate perhaps did not know the poem, or know it as Chaucer's.
Cp. ten Brink's comment, Studien p. 54, that Lydgate is much
better informed about Chaucer's later works than about his earlier.
Skeat, in support of his suggestion, calls attention to Lydgate's
frequent allusions to Fame's palace or house; these allusions may
however be to the supposed house itself, the idea of which Lydgate could get from either Virgil or Ovid. Cp. the remark concerning Petrarch, in the prologue to Book IV of Lydgate's Falls of
Princes, that he is "set and registred in the house of fame",
by which Chaucer's poem is not meant, unless we assert that
Lydgate understood Lollius, in line 1468, to mean Petrarch.

The difficulty in accepting Lydgate's statement as a bit of
literary criticism, with Koeppel, is that Lydgate is not capable of
any such critical utterance; nor can we yet feel that the comparison would have found recognition in the England of his time,
although among the books given by Humphrey of Gloucester to
Oxford, in 1443, were "Librum Dantes" and "Commentaria
Dantes"; and it may have been through his connection with
Gloucester that Lydgate obtained the meagre knowledge of the
Commedia which he sums up in two lines of the prologue to
Book IV of the Falls of Princes, giving in the same passage an
elaborate catalogue of Petrarch's Latin works.

The difficulty in accepting Skeat's interpretation of the passage
is the unlikelihood of Lydgate's perceiving an analogy between a
poem in short couplets and one in eleven-syllabled lines in terza
rima. Moreover, such correspondences as Rambeau has asserted
(see below) between the Commedia and the House of Fame not
only do not meet the endorsement of most modern scholars, but
are manifestly outside the ken of a medieval monk unacquainted
with Italian. If Lydgate spoke from his own knowledge, which is
by no means certain, he is more likely to have referred to the

tale of Ugolino, at the close of which Chaucer says "expresse" that the story has been told by Dante; but upon this suggestion I would lay no stress.

See Lounsbury, Studies I : 425, II : 236; Godwin, Life, chap. 18. Bale, in making up his list of Chaucer's works, probably got his "Dantem Italum transtulit" from Lydgate's ambiguous phrase. He terms Gower "alter Dantes ac Petrarcha."

Source: Pope, in a note to the first ed. of his Temple of Fame, 1715, said, speaking of allegory, "Almost all the poems in the old Provençal had this turn, and from these it was that Petrarch took the idea of his poetry. We have his Trionfi in this kind, and Boccaccio pursued in the same track. Soon after Chaucer introduced it here, whose Romaunt of the Rose, Court of Love, Flower and the Leaf, House of Fame, and some others of his writings are masterpieces of this sort." In this passage the examples are apparently Pope's, but the general statement is from Rymer, who was followed also by Dryden. It is probable that this passage furnished the starting-point for the assertions of Provençal influence upon the House of Fame, made by both Warton (Warton-Hazlitt II : 331) and Sandras (Étude p. 122). Tyrwhitt, Appendix to Preface, criticised Warton, to which Warton replied, see Warton-Hazlitt II : 298 note. The theory has been rejected by critics from Tyrwhitt and Godwin to Skeat, III : viii. Sandras says, p. 122, "Pope a vu un rapport de filiation entre ce poème et le Trionfo della Fama de Petrarque"; and Kissner p. 68 quotes Pope for the same statement, which Pope did not make. Ten Brink, Studien p. 185 note 52, was unable to find the passage in Pope; Asher, Archiv 47 : 318, gives the passage.

Both Sandras, Étude p. 117, and Kissner, op. cit., recognize the influence of Dante upon the poem; this influence was discussed by ten Brink, Studien p. 88 ff. The point has been elaborately treated in:

Chaucers Hous of Fame in seinem Verhältnis zu Dantes Divina Commedia. A. Rambeau, Engl. Stud. 3 : 209-268, and separately Heilbronn 1880.

Reviewed in Jahresbericht 1880 p. 231 and Littblatt 1882 p. 225 (Koch) as mainly a restatement of others' work. Willert, p. 12 of his 1883 monograph (see above) says that Rambeau's main thesis is correct, but that in detail he goes too far. Rambeau's view is apparently accepted by Skeat III : vii ff. and Minor Poems p. lxx, but is protested against by Lounsbury, Studies II : 242 ff. and by Robinson in his review of Chiarini as below; also disputed in detail by Sypherd as below. See Lowes in Publ. Mod. Lang. Assn. 20 : 854 note 2.

Other sources pointed out by ten Brink as above are the Somnium Scipionis, the Aeneid, Ovid, the Anticlaudianus of

Alanus, Machault's Fontaine Amoureuse, Boethius. See also
Sandras, Étude p. 118. Willert p. 13 notes that single person-
ages are from the Ecloga of Theodulus and from Josephus
Iscanus' De Bello Trojano. Later studies are:

Chaucer's House of Fame and Boccaccio's Amorosa Visione.
C. G. Child. Mod. Lang. Notes 10: 379-384.

Studies on Chaucer's House of Fame. A. C. Garrett. Harvard Studies V : 151-175 (1896).

Chaucer and the Italian Renaissance. F. T. Palgrave. Nineteenth Century, 1888 II : 340-359.

Letters by F. T. Palgrave and C. H. Herford in Acad. 1889
I : 305, 342, 379, 413.

Di una imitazione inglese della Divinia Commedia, la Casa
della Fama di G. Chaucer. C. Chiarini. Bari, 1892.

Reviewed by F. N. Robinson, Jour. Compar. Lit. I : 292-297,
as a popular exposition of the theory that the House of Fame
is essentially an imitation of the Divine Comedy. Robinson
protests: "Intelligent appreciation of Chaucer and his work is
not served by such comparisons as Rambeau and Chiarini have
tried to make between two incomparable poets."

Chaucer und Theodulus. F. Holthausen. Anglia 16 : 264-66.

Studies in Chaucer's Hous of Fame. W. O. Sypherd. London, Chaucer Society, 1907, pp. 185.

Minor notes are: Ker in Mod. Lang. Quart. 1899, p. 38; Bright
in Mod. Lang. Notes 9 : 481; Koeppel in Anglia 14 : 245-7.

Date: Ten Brink, Studien pp. 114-16, 122-24, 150-51, gives arguments for 1383-4, which are repeated by Koch, Chronology p.
42-43, and Skeat III : xi. Brandl in Paul's Grundriss II : 677
says that the date can be exactly determined, December 10,
1383; this is disputed by von Westenholz, Anglia Beibl. 12:170-
72. Lowes, Publ. Mod. Lang. Assn. 20 : 854-61, suggests that
the Fame preceded the Troilus, and dates it "in the very late
seventies." Tatlock, Devel. and Chronol., chap. II, § 1, argues
that the Fame followed the Troilus, and dates the former
"about 1379."

Heath, Globe Chaucer pp. xliii-iv, and von Westenholz, Anglia
Beibl. 12 : 170-72, suggest that part III of this poem was written
later; this is endorsed by Pollard, Globe Chaucer p. xxiv and
in Garnett and Gosse I : 146, but denied by Lowes, Publ. Mod.
Lang. Assn. 20 : 860 note 1.

Furnivall, Athen. 1871 II : 494, Koch in Chronology p. 43,
and Skeat III : xi, all say, discussing date of this poem, that
Chaucer here "complains of the burden of his official duties";

Pollard, Globe Chaucer p. xxvii increases this to "complains bitterly." But the passage of the House of Fame upon which these inferences are based, lines 652-660, gives no ground for such statement. See Kittredge in Nation 1894 II : 309; Tatlock in Mod. Phil. I : 326 ff.

Notes: On the language see: Observations on the Language of Chaucer's House of Fame. H. C. Ford. diss. Univ. of Virginia, 1899, pp. 90.

Von Westenholz, Anglia Beibl. 12 : 170-72, thinks that the man introduced at the close of the poem is Thomas of Gloucester.

The House of Fame, and Fame herself, appear in Ben Jonson's Masque of Queens, 1609. Part of the House of Fame is prosed in the Testament of Love, q. v. in Section V here.

See Godwin, chap. 37; Warton-Hazlitt II : 331-336; Sandras, Étude pp. 116-127; ten Brink, Studien pp. 88-114, 150, Hist. Eng. Lit. II : 104-8, III : 267; Morley, Eng. Writers V : 217-233; Root, Poetry of Chaucer pp. 123-134; Skeat III : introd.

Minor Notes: Skeat, Athen. 1902 I : 274 (lines 1208, 1228); Bradley, Athen. 1902 I : 563 (line 1124).

King Richard, Balade to, *see* Stedfastnesse.

Lack of Stedfastnesse, *see* Stedfastnesse.

LEGEND OF GOOD WOMEN

MSS: Univ. Libr. Cambr. Gg iv, 27, Fairfax 16, Tanner 346, Trin.
Coll. Cambr. R 3, 19, Selden B 24; printed Ch. Soc. PT p. 243
ff. Bodley 638, and incomplete copies in Adds. 9832, Pepys
2006, Adds. 12524, are printed Ch. Soc. SPT p. 59 ff. Adds.
28617 and single legends from Univ. Libr. Cambr. Ff i, 6 and
Rawl. C 86 are printed Ch. Soc. OT p. 133 ff.

The differing prologues from the Gg MS and from the type
represented by the Fairfax are printed on opposite pages in
Ch. Soc. OT p. 23 ff. and on p. 191 ff. of the One-Text Print,
where the entire text of the Gg MS is reproduced.

For studies in the MSS and their relations see:

Das Verhältniss der Handschriften von Chaucers Legend of
Good Women. S. Kunz, diss. Breslau, 1889, pp. 36; rev. Koch,
Engl. Stud. 15:422-4.

Chaucer's Legend of Good Women: The Character and Relations of the Manuscripts. The Prologues. Some Doubtful
Readings. J. B. Bilderbeck. London, 1902; rev. Koch, Engl.
Stud. 36 : 133-139 (1905), as well-meaning but not well-con-
sidered.

Textual Notes by Koch, Anglia 4: Anz. 104-5, Engl. Stud.
15 : 418-22, 27 : 25-29.

Prints and Editions: In the eds. of the Works from the 1532
Thynne to date. Thynne's text is reprinted Ch. Soc. PT p.
243 ff., and is also in the facsimile of that edition issued Oxford
1905.

The prologue is included in the Selections of Ward, of
Robertson; the latter also contains the Legend of Ariadne.
Selections are in Paton. The prologue was privately printed
from the Gg MS by Henry Bradshaw, Cambridge 1864. First
edited as a separate poem by Corson, Phila. 1864; then by
Skeat, Oxford, 1889. Skeat is reviewed: Athen. 1889 II :414;
Acad. 1889 II:95 (Pollard); Dial 10:254 (Anderson); Engl.
Stud. 15:418-22 (Koch).

Modernizations and Translations: Three legends are in Horne of
1841, repr. in Briscoe; five legends are in Clarke's Riches of
Chaucer; see Section III E here. Modernized by Skeat, London 1907 (King's Classics).

Transl. into German by von Düring, see Section III E here.

Title: Called in the poem itself, prol. 483-4, the "Legend of Good
Women"; in MSS Fairfax and Bodley marked "The Prologe
of ix goode Wymmen"; in R 3, 19 entitled "Here begynneth
the Boke called the legend of ladyes"; in Selden, "Here
begynnis the legendis of ladyes"; the colophon in Adds. 12524

is printed below under Mars. In the Retractation at the end of the CT the poem is spoken of, so far as printed MSS testify, as The book of the xxv ladies; (Skeat alters this to "nynetene", see his note V : 475). In the prol. to the Man of Law's Tale it is termed "the Seintes Legende of Cupyde"; in Hoccleve's Letter of Cupid, line 316, Cupid calls it "my Legende of Martres"; Lydgate, Falls of Princes, ed. 1554, fol. 164b, mentions it as "the Legend of Cupide"; and in his list printed ante Section II A he terms it a "legende of parfite holines"; in the poem called Venus' Mass, printed Lay Folks' Mass Book, EETS, p. 389 ff., and Jour. Gc. Phil. 7 : 95, it is spoken of as "The holy legende of martyrs of Cupydo"; in the Master of Game, by Edward Duke of York, who was killed at Agincourt in 1415, it is alluded to as "the prolog of xxv good wymmen."

The Master of Game is preserved in MSS Adds. 16165 (Shirley), Douce 335, Bodley 546, Digby 182, Royal 17 B ii, 17 B xli, 17 A lv, 17 D iv, 17 D xii, 18 C xviii, Harley 6824 (impf.). See descript. in Gent. Mag. 1827 I : 309 ff. It is about to be published (Quaritch) with reproductions of the Bodley MS drawings.

Title in Thynne "The Legende of good women." Leland rendered this "Amores Heroidum", placing that title next after "Testamentum Chrysidis"; Bale in 1548 did not include the Leland title, but mentioned after the Test. Chrys. "Laudes bonarum mulierum"; in 1557 he gave both titles, as two separate works. Lounsbury, Studies III : 336 and Skeat, Acad. 1893 I : 246, suggest that Gower, in the epilogue to the Confessio Amantis, may have meant this poem when he makes Venus bid Chaucer execute "his testament of love."

Authenticity: The prologue to the poem itself gives a list of works, recognizable as Chaucer's, which are there attributed to the author of the poem; mentioned in the prol. to the Man of Law's Tale as Chaucer's; in Lydgate's list, see Section II A here.

Date: Tyrwhitt, Introd. Disc. note 3, and Hertzberg, introd. to his Canterbury-Geschichten p. 61, pointed out that this poem must have been written after Richard II married Anne of Bohemia in 1382; ten Brink, Studien p. 147 ff., added that the prol. must have been written in gratitude to that queen for the poet's release from official duties, that is, not before Feb. 1385, when his deputy was appointed. Furnivall, Trial Forew. p. 25, says that the prol. was written in 1385, "the rest probably at different times." Koch, Chronology pp. 43, 45, and Appendix, decides on 1384-5; Skeat III : xvi ff., fixes on the spring of 1385.

The theory of ten Brink is somewhat damaged by the publication, Athen. 1888 I : 116, Life Records, Ch. Soc. pt. IV, p. 251, of the text of the petition to Richard on Chaucer's behalf. This petition was signed by "Oxen", *i. e.*, by Robert de Vere, Earl of Oxford and Duke of Ireland, the king's favorite, and a man of no good repute with posterity. The queen's intervention, upon which have been based arguments as to date and occasion, does not appear, although her real influence in the matter is not thereby precluded. For Oxford see Tait in the Dict. Nat. Biog., *art.* Vere; and cp. among other contemporary documents a passage in Walsingham's Historia Anglicana, ed. Riley, Rolls Series, 1864, II : 160: "Accidit his diebus (1387) ut Robertus de Veer, elatus de honoribus quos Rex impendebat eidem, jugiter suam repudiat uxorem, juvenculam nobilem atque pulchram, genitam de illustri Edwardi regis filia, Isabella; et aliam duceret, quae cum Regina Anna venerat de Boemia, ut fertur, cujusdam sellarii filiam, ignobilem prorsus atque foedam; ob quam causam magna surrepsit occasio scandalorum; cujus nomen erat, in vulgari idiomate, 'Launcecrona.' Favebat sibi in hiis omnibus ipse Rex"   etc.

> This passage is cited by Bilderbeck, N. and Q. 1896 I: 301-2, to elucidate Chaucer's Anelida. Vere's wife was Philippa de Coucy. See also the story in Froissart.

Cp. here the curious fact that in the Ellesmere MS of the CT there is contained, anterior to the copy of the Tales, a poem in praise of Vere. Its text is printed in Todd's Illustrations pp. 302-9; Todd considered it Chaucer's; Furnivall, Temp. Pref. p. 45, says "certainly not Chaucers"; Skeat, IV : xiii, calls Todd's supposition absurd. See Section V here under Poems . . . . written during . . . . Imprisonment.

Speght, in his 1598 Chaucer, has as "Argument" to the LGW "For that some Ladies in the Court tooke offence at Chaucers large speeches against the vntruth of women, the Queene enioyned him to compile this booke in the commendation of sundry maydens and wiues, who shewed themselues faithfull to faithlesse men." Lydgate also says, see Section II A, that Chaucer wrote at the request of the queen. It may be questioned, however, whether either had any more knowledge of the matter than was afforded him by Chaucer's own ambiguous words in the poem.

Bech, Anglia 5 : 379, and Bilderbeck, op. cit. p. 89, have suggested that Chaucer perhaps wrote a legend each year, say for the queen's birthday. But see Lowes, Publ. Mod. Lang. Assn. 20 : 802 note.

Recent papers are:

Chaucer and Some of his Friends. G. L. Kittredge. Mod. Phil. 1 : 1 ff. (1903)

> Arguing that the prol. LGW perhaps alludes to a poem

composed by Deschamps before 1386, and may have been written not very long after that poem.

The Dates of Chaucer's Troilus and Criseyde and Legend of Good Women. J. S. P. Tatlock. Mod. Phil. 1 : 317 ff. (1903).

> Arguing that there is no connection between the LGW and the date 1385. Revd. Koch, Engl. Stud. 36 : 139-142 (1905).

The Two Prologues: The question of the date of the poem is interwoven with the problem of the two forms of the prologue. Until 1864 the only form of the prologue known to students was that contained in the majority of the MSS; and as the print of the differing and unique Gg text issued in that year by Henry Bradshaw was private, little publicity was given to Bradshaw's discovery until 1871, when Furnivall announced it in Athen. I : 754, following this *ibid.* II : 528 by a note on the two forms of the prologue, in which he said that "it can hardly be doubted that Gg is the earlier version." Similarly in Trial Forew. p. 104, Odd Texts p. 23. His view was accepted by Bech, op. cit. below under Sources, by Kunz. op. cit. above, by Skeat in his ed. of LGW, 1889.

In Engl. Stud. 17 : 13-23, (1892), ten Brink questioned this view, and dated the Gg version of the prol. later, not before 1393. This was attacked by Koch, Chronology (Appendix), but endorsed by Koeppel, Engl. Stud. 17 : 196, and by Kaluza, *ibid.* 22 : 281. See also Koeppel, Littblatt 1893 pp. 51-53. Skeat, III : xxi, remains in ignorance of ten Brink's theory and the consequent discussion, as does Pollard, Globe Chaucer xliii-iv. But Mather, in his ed. of the Prologue, etc., 1899, p. xxiii, accepted ten Brink's hypothesis as proven.

Detailed discussion of the question began with:

Quel fut le premier composé par Chaucer des deux prologues de la Légende des Femmes Exemplaires? E. Légouis, Le Havre, 1900, pp. 20.

In this Légouis maintains the priority of the Gg version. He was reviewed by Koch, Engl. Stud. 30 : 456-58, and by Binz, Anglia Beiblatt 11 : 231-37. Binz presents the counter-arguments in his review.

Next followed a discussion by Bilderbeck, in his monograph cited above under MSS. He agrees with Légouis, having arrived at that result independently; he considers that the two prols. were separated by about five years.

The opposed view was then argued by John L. Lowes, in two very important papers:

The Prologue to the Legend of Good Women as related to the French Marguerite Poems and to the Filostrato. Publ.

Mod. Lang. Assn. 19: 593 ff.; revd. Koch, Engl. Stud. 36: 142-
145.

The Prologue to the Legend of Good Women considered in its
Chronological Relations. Publ. Mod. Lang. Assn. 20 : 794 ff.

Both papers discussed by Pollard in Acad. 1906 I : 61, 227.

Lowes attempted to demonstrate the later writing of the Gg
version, which he dated about the middle of 1394, some seven
or eight years after the more widely circulated earlier recension.
His opinion was opposed:

The Problem of the Two Prologues to Chaucer's Legend of
Good Women. John C. French. diss. Johns Hopkins Univ.,
1905, pp. 100.

French was reviewed, with censure or with counter-argument,
by Lowes in a long footnote at the opening of his second paper,
and by Tatlock in Mod. Lang. Notes 21 : 58-62 (1906).

See further Tatlock, Development and Chronology of Chaucer's Works, Ch. Soc. 1907, chap. IV.

A question which lies back of the problem of dates here is,
Why should Chaucer revise the poem? Two classes of reasons
are offered in answer, reasons political or personal on the one
hand, explaining the textual changes as due to Chaucer's relations
with the Court; and on the other hand, reasons purely literary,
explaining the revision as due to the poet's wish to improve his
work. The difficulty with the former theory is our ignorance of
English court life at that time, and the difficulty with the latter is
the immediate intrusion of our personal judgment in the attempt
to decide what are improvements. Students of Chaucer are agreed
that he was prone to plan largely and to leave incomplete that of
which he wearied, also that he was notably economical in his use
and re-use of material, his distribution of a translation, *e. g.*,
among various of his poems. Also, it is true of Chaucer that a
large number of his poems, this among them, bear the stamp of
"occasional" work. It can be plausibly argued that some strong
external pressure, some impulse other than the critical, must have
been upon Chaucer in order to induce him to take up again a
work of which he had evidently wearied. And it might also be
argued that if this work was in hand at the time of the writing
of the present Man of Law's headlink,—if that headlink (as I
conjecture p. 257 here) was originally in B^2 between Thopas and
Melibeus,—it was written at a time when Chaucer had not yet
devised the quarrel-motive nor received his Marriage Group in-
spiration, but was handling and adapting medieval material to his
Tales somewhat slowly, and with a strong critical bias. Despite
the asserted unlikelihood that Chaucer should return from the
Tales to the Legend, see Koeppel, Littblatt 1893, p. 52, we cannot
deny that that is possible, provided there were enough external
pressure. Whether some complication between Oxford and the
Ccurt ladies, some breach in the circle of flower-worshippers or
revival of the cult, be responsible for the changes in the prologue,
we do not know. Nor do we know whether Gower also may have
urged the resumption of a work so much to his taste, cp. Lounsbury's suggestion cited above under Title.

Sources: See:

Quellen und Plan der Legend of Good Women und ihr Verhältniss zur Confessio Amantis. M. Bech. Anglia 5 : 313-383 (1872). Reviewed Koch, Littblatt 1885, p. 326.

Chaucer's Legend of Good Women and Boccaccio's De Genealogia Deorum. C. G. Child. Mod. Lang. Notes, 11 : 476-490 (1896).

Chaucer and Froissart. G. L. Kittredge. Engl. Stud. 26 : 336 note.

The Prologue to the Legend of Good Women as related to the French Marguerite Poems and to the Filostrato. John L. Lowes. Publ. Mod. Lang. Assn. 19 : 593-683. Reviews noted ante.

Koeppel in Anglia 14 : 248-9.

Notes: On the language of the poem see:

Observations on the Language of Chaucer's Legend of Good Women. John M. Manly. Harvard Studies II : 1-120 (1893). Based on MS Cambridge Gg.

On the word *lavender* of prol. line 353 see the rectification of Skeat by Krapp in Mod. Lang. Notes 17 : 204-6. On the word *Agaton* of prol. 526 see, in addition to Skeat, Toynbee in Mod. Lang. Quart. 1 : 5 (1897) and, previously, Sandras, Étude p. 115.

Koeppel thought the revision might be intended as a Canterbury Tale, see Littblatt 1893 p. 51, Engl. Stud. 30 : 467.

Douglas' Palice of Honour is an imitation of the prologue to the Legend; see Lounsbury, Studies III : 21. Note Tennyson's Dream of Fair Women.

See Godwin, Life, chap. 44; Sandras, Étude, pp. 113-116; ten Brink, Studien, pp. 143-149, Hist. Eng. Lit. II : 108-116; Morley, Eng. Writers V : 234-241; Lounsbury, Studies II : 185, 220 ff., III : 335 ff.; Skeat III : xvi ff., 288 ff.; Root, Poetry of Chaucer pp. 135-150.

Marriage, *see* Bukton.

MARS

MSS: Fairfax 16, Tanner 346, Harley 7333, Trin. Coll. Cambr. R 3, 20, Selden B 24, printed Ch. Soc. PT p. 100 ff. Pepys 2006 (two copies), and Longleat 258 are printed Ch. Soc. SPT p. 141 ff. There was once a copy in Adds. 12524 (not 12254 as in Trial Forew. p. 78) ; this is seen from the colophon to the LGW in that MS, "Here endyth the legend of ladyes and begynneth the compleynte of Mars and Venus." No more of the MS. The Fairfax text is also in One-Text Print p. 71.

Textual Notes, see Koch, Anglia 4 : Anz. 99, Engl. Stud. 15 : 406-7 and 27 : 39-41. Scheme of MS relations in the Globe Chaucer p. xxxvi.

Prints and Editions: By Notary, 1499-1502, reprinted Ch. Soc. PT p. 100; see Dibdin, Typogr. Antiq. II : 585-6. In the Thynne Chaucer of 1532, and in subsequent eds. of the Works. In the Pickering and the Skeat eds. of the Minor Poems.

Title and Authenticity: Connection of the Mars with the Complaint of Venus: In Shirley's MS R 3, 20 the sequence of poems is Mars, Venus, Fortune. The Mars is headed, "Loo yee louers gladeþe and comforteþe you of þallyance entrayted bytwene / þe hardy and furyous Mars þe god of armes and Venus þe double goddesse of loue made by Geffrey Chaucier at þe comandement of þe renomed and excellent Prynce my lord þe Duc Iohn of Lancastre." At close of the poem, "þus eondeþe here þis complaint whiche some men sayne / was made by my lady of York doughter to þe kyng of Spaygne / and my lord of Huntyngdoun some tyme duc of Excestre. and filowing begynneþe a balade translated out of frenshe in to englisshe / by Chaucier Geffrey þe frenshe made sir Otes de Grauntsomme knight Savosyen." At the end of this poem (the Venus) Shirley has written "Hit is sayde þat Graunsomme made þis last balade for Venus resembled to my lady of York. aunswering þe complaynt of Mars / and here filoweþe a balade made by Chaucier of þe louer / and of Dame ffortune." (Fortune follows.)

In Harley 7333, probably copied from Shirley, the Mars is transcribed in double columns, and breaks off unfinished, the second column not full. Two leaves following have been cut from the MS, which does not contain the Venus. The heading is "The Broche of Thebes as of the love of mars and venus"; as remarked in Mod. Lang. Notes 19 : 196, this heading was apparently once above the first Pepys copy, the second being without title. Of the two occurrences of these poems in the Pepys codex, the earlier is a group,—Mars, Venus, Fortune,—and the second is Mars, Venus, Anelida, etc. There is no break between the Venus and the Mars in either transcription, but while the second scribe marked neither poem, the first wrote in the margin of p. 119 and p. 122 "The compleynt of Mars", and "The compleynt of Venus"; the latter heading is almost completely trimmed away, and filled out in the hand of Pepys. The two poems were thus regarded by this copyist as two parts of one work, and the same appears in the Fairfax MS, which writes as heading "Complaynt of Mars and Venus", on fol. 15a; on 17a, in margin, is "The copleynt of Mars", and on 19a "The copleynt of Venus." The contemporary table of contents writes "The complaynt of Mars and Venus", "The complaynt of Mars by him self", "The complaynt of Venus by hir self."

The Tanner MS, in which the headings are entered by a Jacobean hand, has a capital and side-border on 65a, at the opening of the Mars; on 67b, with a space, there is again a capital and border for Mars' complaint; much less space is left on 69b, where the Venus follows, but a separating horizontal line has been drawn, as well as a capital and border.

In the Selden MS the Venus follows the Mars without border or separation; it is marked "The compleynt of venus folowith", and although there is no heading on fol. 132a, at the opening of the poem, the inner side of 134a has a border and "The Compleynt of Mars" is separately headed. Longleat 258, imperfect at beginning, has as colophon "Here endith the Complaint of Mars." Chaucer's Pity follows.

It thus appears that, with the exception of Shirley, the copyists of these poems regarded them as constituting a three-part whole,—a narrative proem followed by two complaints. The Complaint of Venus occurs without the Mars in two MSS, Shirley's Ashmole 59 and Trin. Coll. Cambr. Ff 1, 6. Mars without Venus occurs only in Longleat 258.

Julian Notary, the first printer of the poem, headed it "The loue and complayntes bytwene Mars and Venus." Above the Venus, which follows, is "The compleynt of Venus for Mars", and the colophon is "Explicit the compleyces of Maris and Venus / and of the broche of Thebes." Thynne, in 1532, headed the poem "The complaynt of mars & venus", marking off in smaller type "The complaynt of Mars" and "The complaynt of Venus."

Leland and Bale listed the poem as "Querela Martis et Veneris."

Thynne's procedure was followed by editors until Furnivall, in his Trial Forew., separated the Mars and the Venus by nearly twenty years in time of composition, and printed the two, for the Chaucer Society, distinct from one another. The discovery of a French original for Venus, and not for the Mars,

25

has confirmed modern editors in the separation of the two poems.

Chaucer's authorship of the Mars rests upon the testimony of Shirley, see above.

Modernizations and Translations: Mod. by Robert Bell, in Horne of 1841, see Section III E here.

Source, Occasion, Date: The date of the Mars has been variously argued, from historical evidence, from astrological allusions, from stylistic peculiarities. Shirley's statements, in MS R 3, 20, are discussed by Furnivall, Trial Forew. p. 80 ff., with suggestion of 1374, perhaps 1377-79. *Ibid.* p. 12 Furnivall says "The Mars links itself by its opening lines to the Parl. of Foules, and follows rather than precedes it." Brae, N. and Q. 1851 I : 235, 258, discusses the astronomical allegory, which he says was unnoted by Tyrwhitt, but offers no conjecture as to the date. Sandras, in his Étude p. 109, has nothing; Morley, Eng. Writers V : 150-1, dates the poem "about 1374." Koch, Anglia 9 : 582-4, reprints Thurein's computations published Berlin 1886, and dates the poem 1379; in his Chronology pp. 30-33 he decides for 1380. Ten Brink, Hist. Eng. Lit. II : 74 and III : 266, develops the information given by Shirley, and assigns the incidents described in the poem to the spring of 1379. Manly, On the Date and Interpretation of Chaucer's Complaint of Mars, in Harvard Studies V : 107 ff., says that the poem is a mere exercise of ingenuity in the description of a supposed astronomical event in terms of human action and emotion. "To draw from the astronomical data any inference as to the year in which the poem was composed would be, to say the least, hazardous." Skeat I : 64-66 refers to Furnivall, to Koch's paper in Anglia, and says "The date 1373-9 is near enough." Mather, ed. of Prologue, etc., p. xxxiii, terms the poem "only a *jeu d'esprit* in versified astrology."

Notes: See ten Brink, Studien 152-54; Morley and Skeat as above; Root, Poetry of Chaucer, p. 63; Furnivall, Trial Forew. pp. 78-92.

PARLEMENT OF FOULES

MSS: University Library Cambridge Gg iv, 27, Trin. Coll. Cambr. R 3, 19, Harley 7333, St. John's Coll. Oxford 57, Univ. Libr. Cambr. Ff 1, 6, printed Ch. Soc. PT pp. 49 ff.; Tanner 346, Digby 181, Selden B 24, Fairfax 16, Bodley 638, Longleat 258, printed Ch. Soc. SPT pp. 1 ff.; Pepys 2006, in OT pp. 263 ff.; Univ. Libr. Cambr. Hh iv, 12 and Laud 416 (fragments) in Ch. Soc. OT pp. 1 ff. The Gg text is also in One-Text Print p. 45 ff.

The six MSS in the SPT prints are not arranged in six parallel columns, as are those in the PT prints, but three and three; see note on No. XXII of the Ch. Soc. First Series, Section VII here.

Bell, in his ed. of 1854, mentioned but two MSS of this poem, the Ff and the Fairfax.

Textual Notes, see Koch, Anglia 4 : Anz. p. 100, Engl. Stud. 11 : 294-97 and 27 : 47-53; Hammond, Univ. of Chicago Decennial Publ. VII : 1-22, rev. Kaluza, DLZ Jan. 31, 1903, Spies, Engl. Stud. 35 : 111, Koch, Littbl. 1903, p. 158, Root, Jour. Gc. Phil. 5 : 189; this last is criticised by Tatlock, Devel. and Chronol. p. 44 note 2. See further Koch, Archiv 111 : 64, 299, and 112 : 46. Tree *ibid.* 112 : 69. Crit. note of censure on this last by Foerster, Archiv 115 : 301. The Globe Chaucer p. xxxix prints a MSS-tree in which the editor says that he agrees with Koch, *i. e.*, with Koch's Anglia notes.

Prints and Editions: By Caxton, see Trial Forew. p. 116 and Blades p. 211; Caxton is reprinted Ch. Soc. PT p. 49 ff. By de Worde in 1530. By Rastell, *n. d.*, fragment in the Bodleian Library; for these last two refs. see Handlists. For account of the de Worde with its curious verse-address to "newfanglers", mentioning Chaucer, see Dibdin II : 278-80. In the Pynson Chaucer of 1526, the Thynne of 1532, and subsequent eds. of the Works. In the eds. of the Minor Poems by Pickering, by Skeat, by Bilderbeck. In the Selections of Southey, of Ward, of Sweet, of Paton, of Robertson. Printed for Houghton, Mifflin and Co. in Gothic letters on handmade paper, thin octavo, Boston 1904, 325 copies. Text from Gilman's 1880 ed. of Works, see Section II D here. For critical ed. see Koch: Versuch einer kritischen Ausgabe von Chaucers Parlament of Foules, issued as Beilage zum Jahresbericht des Dorotheenstädtischen Realgymnasiums zu Berlin. 1904. 36 pp.; reviewed by Glöde, Engl. Stud. 35 : 403.

Modernizations and Translations: Partially modernized version in Clarke's Riches of Chaucer; in Purves, see Section III E here.

A passage was imitated by Thomas Warton, senior, 1748; see Lounsbury, Studies III : 125-6.

Transl. into German by Koch, see Section IV C here; by von Düring, see Section III E here.

Analyzed, with verse-transl. of passages interspersed, by Schipper in Oesterreichische Rundschau 1883 heft 6.

Authenticity and Title: The Gg heading is "Here begynyth the parlement of ffoulys"; its colopon "Explicit parliamentum Auium In die sancti Valentini tentum secundum Galfridum Chaucer. Deo gracias." The Ff copy has as colophon "Explicit Parliamentum Anium Quod W. Caluerley." Fairfax, Bodley, and Tanner have the colophon "Explicit tractatus de Congregacione Volucrum die sancti Valentini." Tanner and Fairfax head the poem "The Parlement of Briddis"; Bodley is imperfect at beginning. Longleat has as colophon "Here endith the Parlement of foules"; Digby heads the poem. "the parlement of Fowlis"; Harley 7333 has "The Parlament of Foules." Both this Harley MS and the copy in R 3, 19 have at the close a spurious stanza beginning "Maister gefferey chaucer that now lyth in graue," which is separately printed in the Stow Chaucer of 1561, see Section II D here. The R 3, 19 heading is "Here foloweth the parlement of Byrdes reducyd to loue &c." Laud 416 has in the margin "Of þe assemble of þe byrdis on Seint Volantins day." Caxton's colophon is "Explicit the temple of bras"; see Schick op. cit. p. xvii, Blades p. 211. Entitled in the Pynson of 1526 "The Assemble of Foules"; so in the de Worde print of 1530, the Thynne of 1532 and later, down to the Aldine, which entitled the poem "The Parlement of Briddes, or the Assembly of Foules." Headed by the Chaucer Society The Parlament of Foules. In the prol. LGW, A-version line 407, it is called by Chaucer "The Parlement of Foules"; in the Retractation at the end of the CT it is mentioned as the "Book of seint Valentynes day of the Parlement of Briddes"; and in Lydgate's list (see Section II A here) it is termed "of foules .... the parliament." Leland and Bale call the poem "Chorus avium", "Volucrum conglobatio."

Date: Tyrwhitt thought that the poem alluded to the intended marriage of John of Gaunt and Blanche of Lancaster, which took place in 1359; see his Appendix to the Preface, C, note e, and note on CT line 1920. Godwin accordingly dated the poem 1358. The Saturday Review of April 15, 1871, cited in Trial Forew. pp. 69 ff., gives the date 1345; Furnivall loc. cit. castigates the error, and says "Who will unriddle the persons" of this poem. Koch, Engl. Stud. 1 : 288, transl. Ch. Soc. Essays pp. 406-7, connected the poem with the marriage of Richard II;

this he again points out Chronology pp. 37-40 and Engl. Stud.
15 : 399. The conjectured date is about a year before the
marriage. Ward, Life of Chaucer pp. 86-87 and ten Brink,
Hist. Eng. Lit. II : 83-4, adopt Koch's explanation; ten Brink
dates the poem 1382. Koch, who in Ausgew. Dicht. thought
1380 a more likely date, ultimately agreed with ten Brink;
Mather, Eng. Misc. p. 305, agrees in date 1382. Morley, Eng.
Writers V : 154 (1890), agrees with Tyrwhitt and disputes ten
Brink. Von Westenholz, Anglia Beibl 12 : 169-70, is not convinced by Koch as to date. See Tatlock, Devel. and Chronol.
of Chaucer's Works, chap. II § 2.

Source: Tyrwhitt, Account of the Works, and note on line 1920,
first remarked that 15 stanzas of this poem, lines 183-287, are
from Boccaccio's Teseide; see Trial Forew. pp. 59 ff. for
Chaucer's text parallel with Rossetti's transl. of the Italian,
also printed in Skeat, Minor Poems pp. lxii ff. and I : 68-73.
Later criticism adds a few more lines to those discussed by
Tyrwhitt. Tyrwhitt also pointed out *ibid.* that the opening of
the poem "is built upon the Somnium Scipionis of Cicero." In
Acad. 1881 II : 384 Hales remarked that Alanus de Insulis' De
Planctu Naturae is the source of much of the description of
Nature in lines 295ff.; Koch, Littbl. 1885 p. 326 note, says that
he anticipated Hales in this, in his Ausgew. Dicht. p. 61. The
Alanus passage is printed Skeat I : 74 and MP lxv. The
parallels with Dante which occur in lines 85 ff., 169, were
remarked by Cary in his transl. of the Divine Comedy, 1805.
Cary also noted lines 201 ff. as parallel with Purgatorio 28 : 9
ff.; he omitted to remark on the parallel between line 109 and
Inferno 1 : 83, which was pointed out by ten Brink, Studien
p. 125, or between lines 127 ff. and Inferno 3 : 1 ff., which was
noted by Sandras, Étude pp. 67-68; this latter passage is by
Koeppel, Anglia 13 : 233, connected with Boccaccio's Amorosa
Visione. The derivation of lines 99-105 from Claudian was
pointed out by Lounsbury, Studies II : 256-57. Note by Koeppel
in Anglia 14 : 244-5. See on the subject W. O. Sypherd,
Studies in Chaucer's House of Fame, Ch. Soc. 1907.

Notes: Seelmann, Ueber Vogelsprachen und Vogelparlamente, in
Jahrb. d. Vereins f. niederd. Sprachforschung 14 : 101 ff. (1888),
discusses mainly the proverbial and didactic sayings put into the
mouth of birds; he points out that Chaucer's poem and two
other bird-parliaments (the Pavo of the mid-thirteenth century
and the Parlement of Byrdes of the latter fifteenth) are in a
class by themselves.
    Comment on the poem in Godwin, Life, chap. 21; Morley,
Eng. Writers V : 154-165; Sandras, Étude pp. 65-73; Trial

Forew. 53 ff.; ten Brink, Studien 124-29, Hist. Eng. Lit. II :
84-85; Root, Poetry of Chaucer 63-68; Courthope, Hist. Eng.
Poetry I : 270; Skeat I : 66-75, 505 ff.

Notes on line 65, see p. 109 here; on line 353, see p. 111 here;
on line 243, see p. 519 here.

PITY

MSS: Fairfax 16, Bodley 638, Tanner 346, Harley 78, Univ. Libr.
Cambr. Ff 1, 6, Trin. Coll. Cambr. R 3, 19; printed Ch. Soc.
PT p. 39 ff. Harley 7578 and Longleat 258 are printed Ch. Soc.
OT p. 251 ff. Adds 34360 (formerly Phillipps 9053) is printed
MOT p. 9. The Fairfax text is also in One-Text Print p. 39.
For the Balade of Pity which follows this poem in two MSS,
the Harley 78 and the Adds., see Section V here.
Textual Notes, see Koch, Anglia 4: Anz. 96, Engl. Stud.
11 : 293, 15 : 403 and 27 : 6, 37. See Flügel, Anglia 23 : 195 ff.,
for notes on the Adds. text of the poem, which is not con-
sidered by Heath, Globe Chaucer p. xxxvi.

Prints and Editions: First printed by Thynne in the 1532 Chaucer,
and in subsequent blackletter eds. of the Works. In Urry; in
the 1782 Bell; by Chalmers placed among the Poems Imputed
to Chaucer. In subsequent eds. of the Works, and in the eds.
of the Minor Poems by Pickering, by Skeat, and by Bilderbeck,
see Section IV B here. Crit. ed. by ten Brink from six MSS,
Ch. Soc. Essays pt. II, and by Koch, see Section IV C here.
In Sweet's Primer, in Paton; see Section III D here.

Authenticity and Title: Shirley in Harley 78 heads the poem "And
nowe here filowing / begynneþe a complaint of Pitee made by
Geffrey Chaucier þe aureat Poete þat euer was fonde in oure
vulgare to fore hees dayes." Adds. 34360, copied from Shirley,
has "And now here folwith A complaynt of pite made bi Geffray
Chaucier the Aureat Poete that euer was founde in oure vulgar
to fore his dayes." The title in Fairfax was entered later, in
a hand perhaps that of John Stow, "Complainte of the deathe
of pitie"; Bodley has "The complaynte vnto Pyte", with the
same in colophon; the Trin. Coll. MS has in its colophon "Here
endeth the exclamacion of the Deth of Pyte." The Longleat
copy has the same colophon, and the table of contents of the
MS has "Exclamacio de morte pietatis." The Ff copy is
headed with the name of *Jesus*.
The 1532 Chaucer gave the poem a special titlepage, "Howe
pite is ded and beried in a gentyll hert", and this name was
retained until the Chiswick, which headed the poem "The Complaint of Pitie", with the old title as subtitle. The Bell of

1854 marked it "The Compleynte of the Dethe of Pite", with
the old title as subtitle; the Aldine followed the Bell. Entitled
by the Chaucer Society "The Compleynte to Pite"; by Skeat
"Compleynte unto Pite." Bale noted it as "De misericordia
sepultura", and as "De pietate mortua"; Leland used the latter
title.

Modernizations and Translations: Transl. into German by Koch,
see Section IV C here.

Date: Furnivall, in Trial Forew. p. 31, says "The Pity is, I have
now no question, the earliest original work of Chaucer, say
1366-8, the first in date of his four linkt-together early works,
the Pity, Blaunche, Parlement, and Mars." Ibid. p. 12 he remarks that the Pity is the awkwardest of all the poems to deal
with, and that it contains the key to Chaucer's life. (See
notes below.) Ten Brink, Sprache und Versk. § 305, Hist.
Eng. Lit. II : 48 dates the poem 1370-72; see Schipper, Engl.
Metrik I : 427. Koch, Chronology p. 7, argues after 1372; in
the introd. to his Ausgew. Dichtungen he said 1373. Skeat
I : 62 says a probable conjectural date is about 1367; ibid. xxxi
he thinks it belongs rather after than before the Book of the
Duchesse, and may be of the beginning of the period following
1373.

Notes: See Sandras, Étude p. 107; Furnivall, Trial Forew. pp. 35
ff.; ten Brink, Hist. Eng. Lit. II : 48-49; Morley, Eng. Writers
V : 146-7; Lounsbury, Atlantic Monthly 40 : 592, Studies I : 221
ff.; Skeat I : 61, 457-61; Root, Poetry of Chaucer 58-9.

Minor note by Bright, Mod. Lang. Notes 17 : 278.

Furnivall and ten Brink find in this poem Chaucer's declaration of a long and hopeless love; this theory is contested by
Lounsbury, and by W. O. Sypherd, Mod. Lang. Notes 20 : 240-
43. See Section I here, Appendix (b).

Proverbs, see Section V here.

PURSE

MSS: Fairfax 16, Harley 7333, Univ. Libr. Cambr. Ff 1, 6, Pepys
2006, Adds. 22139, Harley 2251, printed Ch. Soc. PT pp. 447 ff.;
Phillipps 9053, now Adds. 34360, printed MOT p. 41. The
Fairfax text is also in One-Text Print p. 319.

    Textual Notes, see Koch, Anglia 4: Anz. p. 110-11, Engl.
Stud. 15 : 417-18. The poem occurs in three forms: as three
seven-line stanzas with a five-line envoy; similarly without the
envoy; without the envoy and having continuous with it a
series of seven-line stanzas on imprisonment. This last is the
case in MSS Harley 2251 and its partial sister Adds. 34360; see
Anglia 28 : 3-4. In Ch. Soc. MOT p. 43 this continuation is
ascribed to Lydgate; see the remark of Speght in his life of
Chaucer, Section I here, and the note by Hearne cited in Anglia
as above. Envoyless copies of the poem are these two MSS
and Adds. 22139. The "continuation" appears separately in
Harley 7333.

Prints and Editions: By Caxton, reprod. OT p. 295. In the
Thynne Chaucer of 1532, and subsequent eds. of the Works.
In eds. of the Minor Poems by Pickering, by Skeat, by Bilder-
beck. Critical ed. by Koch, see Section IV C here. In the
Selections of Southey, of Parton, of Paton, of Robertson, of
Manly; see Section III D here.

Modernizations and Translations: Mod. by Clarke in his Riches
of Chaucer; by Horne in Temple Bar 52 : 353 (1878); Furnivall *ibid.* 54 : 144 added the envoy. Mod. by Purves in 1870;
see Section III E here.

    Transl. into German by Koch, see Section IV C here.

Title and Authenticity: Headed in the Fairfax MS "The complaynt of Chaucer to his Purse"; in Harley 7333 "A supplicacion
to Kyng Richard by chaucier"; in Pepys "La Compleint de
chaucer A sa Bourse Voide"; colophon in Ff "Explicit quod
leweston" (the name of the scribe). Thynne and Stow head
the envoy separately; the 1602 and 1687 Speghts mark both
poem and envoy as by Hoccleve. Godwin II : 547 doubts the
genuineness of the envoy, or even of the poem; ten Brink, Hist.
Eng. Lit. II : 205, Littblatt 1883 pp. 426-7, thinks the envoy may
have been written later; so Hales in Dict. Nat. Biog. *art.*
Chaucer, and Skeat I : 88, 563.

Date: Furnivall, Athen. 1871 II : 495, Trial Forew. p. 7, thinks
1399; in PT p. 447 he says "Except the Recantation at the end
of the Parson's Tale and (no doubt) the englishing of the latter
part of that Tale, this *Purse* is the last bit of Chaucer that we

have." Ten Brink, Hist. Eng. Lit. II: 205, thought that the envoy was added for King Henry IV, in late 1399; Skeat I : 562 dates the envoy on Sept. 30 or Oct. 1-2, 1399, placing the rest of the poem "some time beforehand." He considers the envoy as "almost certainly Chaucer's latest extant composition." Koch, Chronology p. 73, dates the poem 1399.

Notes: See ten Brink, Hist. Eng. Lit. II : 199, 205; Morley, Eng. Writers V : 274; Skeat I : 87-88, 562-4; Root, Poetry of Chaucer p. 78.

SCOGAN

MSS: Univ. Libr. Cambr. Gg iv, 27, Fairfax 16, Magd. Coll. Cambr. Pepys 2006. Printed Ch. Soc. PT p. 419-20; the Gg copy is also in One-Text Print p. 299.
　　Textual Notes by Koch, Anglia 4: 107, Engl. Stud. 15: 417.

Prints and Editions: By Caxton, reprod. Ch. Soc. OT p. 293. By Thynne in the 1532 Chaucer, and in subsequent eds. of the Works. In Skeat's ed. of the Minor Poems; in the Selections of Paton. Critical ed. by Koch, 1883.

Modernizations and Translations: Transl. into German by Koch, see Section IV C here.

Authenticity and Title: Fairfax and Pepys head it "Lenuoy de Chaucer A Scogan"; Gg heads it "Litera directa de Scogon per G. C." The early eds. mark it merely "Lenuoye"; the Chiswick, following Tyrwhitt's note (in his Account of the Works), headed the poem "Lenuoy de Chaucer a Scogan", and this has since been retained.

Date: Furnivall, in Athen. 1871 II: 495 and in Trial Forew. p. 8, p. 17, said "perhaps 1393." Koch, Ausgew. Dicht., 1880, introd., said that a very wet year between 1391-99 must be meant; in Littblatt 1880 p. 385 he gives information received from Furnivall regarding 1393, and decides for that year; in Anglia 4: Anz. 49, he says that in Littblatt as cited he had exactly dated Scogan; so in his Chronology pp. 70-71.

Notes: See ten Brink, Hist. Eng. Lit. II : 195; Morley, Eng. Writers V: 274; Root, Poetry of Chaucer pp. 75-6; Skeat I: 85, 556-8.

STEDFASTNESSE

MSS: Harley 7333, Trin. Coll. Cambr. R 3, 20, Cotton Cleop. D vii, Fairfax 16, Adds. 22139, Harley 7578, printed Ch. Soc. PT pp. 433-37; Trin. Coll. Cambr. R 14, 51, the Bannatyne MS copy, and Thynne's print, are in SPT p. 163; Hatton is printed MOT p. 31. The Harley 7333 copy is also in One-Text Print p. 311.
Textual Notes, see Koch, Anglia 4 : Anz. 109, Engl. Stud. 15 : 416, 27 : 5-6; Holt in ed. below cited.

Prints and Editions: First printed by Thynne in the 1532 **Chaucer,** pubd. 1905 in photographic facsimile. In the subsequent eds. of the Works. In the eds. of the Minor Poems by Pickering, 1846, by Skeat, by Bilderbeck; in the 5th ed. of Zupitza's Uebungsbuch, 1897. Crit. ed. by Koch, Berlin, 1883; by Holt in Jour. Gc. Phil. 6 : 419-431. In the Selections of Paton.

Modernizations and Translations: Mod. by Cowden Clarke, by Wordsworth in the Horne of 1841, by Purves in 1870; see Section III E here.
Transl. into German by Koch, see Section IV C here.

Title and Authenticity: Harley 7333 marks the poem "This balade made Geffrey Chaunciers the Laureall Poete of Albion and sente it to his souerain lorde kynge Richarde the secounde þane being / in his Castell of Windesore." Trin. Coll. R 3, 20 has "Balade Royal made by oure Laureal poete of Albyon in hees laste yeeres." Hatton heads it "These baladdis were send to the kyng"; Fairfax, Harley 7578, and R 14, head it "Balade." Thynne gave the poem no heading; neither did Stow, Speght, Urry, the 1782 Bell, Anderson, or Chalmers; all printed it immediately following Scogan unto the Lords. The Chiswick editor marks the poem "Ballad sent to King Richard"; he was followed by the Moxon, the Aldine, and the 1854 Bell; the present title (Lack of Stedfastness) is due to the Chaucer Society.

Date: Furnivall, in Athen. 1871 II : 495 and Trial Forew. p. 8, p. 27, says "probably 1397"; in Par. Texts p. 433 he says 1397-99. Ten Brink, Hist. Eng. Lit. II : 198, says perhaps at the beginning of 1398. Skeat, Minor Poems lxxvii, Oxf. Chaucer I : 84, says 1393-99; Koch, Chronology p. 77, agrees.

Source:

Notes: Ten Brink as above; Root, Poetry of Chaucer 74-5; Skeat I : 84, 555-6.

———

Temple of Bras = Caxton's title for the Parlement of Foules, *q. v.*

MSS: Campsall, Harley 2280, Univ. Libr. Cambr. Gg iv, 27, St. John's Coll. Cambr., Corpus Christi Coll. Cambr. 61, Harley 1239, Harley 3943, Harley 2392, Harley 4912, Adds. 12044, Selden B 24, Selden supra 56, Digby 181, Rawlinson Poetry 163, Durham V ii, 13, Phillipps 8252. Fragments are in Trin. Coll. Cambr. R 3, 20 and Univ. Libr. Cambr. Ff 1, 6; these are printed Ch. Soc. OT Appendix p. ix ff. The Chaucer Society has printed seven of the above-mentioned MSS; the first three in First Series Nos. LXIII and LXIV; the next three in First Series Nos. LXXXVI and LXXXVIII; Harley 3943 is printed with Rossetti's transl. of the Italian in Nos. XLIV and LXV; and the Campsall text is also separately printed, Ch. Soc. First Series No. LXXIX.

Textual Notes, see Koch, Anglia 6 : Anz. 80-91; see McCormick's introd. note, Globe Chaucer, p. xli; in An English Miscellany McCormick says that he has failed to make out any satisfactory pedigree of the Troilus text; his introd. to the Troilus, announced by the Chaucer Society for 1896, is to appear. Report of a paper by him before the Philological Society is in Acad. 1895 II : 552

On the Selden text see Macaulay, Acad. 1895 I : 338. On the probability of two recensions of the poem see also Tatlock, Devel. and Chronol. chap. I § 1.

Skeat, Acad. 1890 I : 82, discusses a "lost MS" of Troilus at Copenhagen.

Prints and Editions: By Caxton, *n. d.;* see Blades, p. 297. See Dibdin, I : 313. By de Worde, 1517, "a reprint of Caxton's text" (Globe Chaucer p. xlii). See Dibdin II : 212-14.

The Brit. Mus. catal. has "1482? fol." and "1486? fol."

In the Pynson of 1526, also "a reprint of Caxton's text" (Globe Chaucer p. xlii). In the Thynne Chaucer of 1532, and in subsequent eds. of the Works. Pubd. with the Romaunt of the Rose and the Minor Poems by Pickering in 1846. A page of the Kelmscott Press print is reprod. in Garnett and Gosse's Engl. Lit. I : 145.

Bits are in Hazlitt, in Wülker, in Ward. In Paton, in Robertson. Selections in Manly. See Section III D here.

Modernizations and Translations: In Hazlitt's Collections and Notes, 1867-76, under Chaucer, is mentioned:

"A Paraphrase upon the three first Bookes of Chaucer's Troilus and Cresida. Translated into our Modern English for the satisfaction of those, who either cannot, or will not, take the paines to vnderstand the Excellent Authors Farr more

exquisite and significant Expressions, though now growen
obsolete, and out of vse. By J(onathan) S(idnam)." Circa
1630. An unpublished MS, folio, 70 leaves, in seven-line
stanzas; no introductory matter. Sold at Puttick and Simpson's
in June, 1893.

Modernized by Clarke, Riches of Chaucer; by Wordsworth
in the Horne of 1841, repr. by Briscoe; by Purves in 1870.
Analyzed, with verse-transls. interspersed, by Schipper in
Osterreichische Rundschau 1883, hefte 10, 12.

Translated into Latin by Sir Francis Kynaston, and the two
first books published in 1635, with the English (from Thynne)
on opposite pages. The titlepage and specimens are given
below.

See Retrospective Review, 12 : 106-123 (1825), with extracts.
See Corser's Collectanea, IV : 334-39; see Ellis, Specimens of
Early English Poetry, III : 265; Lounsbury, Studies III : 77, 81.

Kynaston had prepared notes for his transl., which was never
pubd. in full. When Urry compiled the glossary for his 1721
Chaucer, he had the use of some excerpts from the MS of
Kynaston, which was then in the possession of Henry Aldrich,
Dean of Christ Church College, Oxford; so we are told by
Thomas in the preface to the Urry Chaucer; but Thomas did
not know what had become of the MS, though he expresses his
hope of its ultimate recovery and publication, emphasizing its
probable value. In 1796 the MS was in the possession of F. G.
Waldron, who published:

The Loves of Troilus and Creseid, written by Chaucer; with
a Commentary, by Sir Francis Kinaston; never before published. London, 1796, 26 leaves. (The first 12 stanzas only,
intended as a specimen. See Lounsbury, Studies III : 77, 81.)

Singer, in the Chiswick Chaucer, 1822, II : xx, says that the
MS is then in his possession. It was bought at his death by
James Crossley, president of the Chetham Society; he died in
1884, and his library was sold, the first portion at Manchester,
by Thompson and Son, in May, 1884, and the remainder in two
portions by Sotheby in London, July 1884 and June 1885. In
the Athen. 1884 II : 147 is noticed the former of the London
sales, with remark on the "wretched condition" of many of the
books; the second sale is not discussed, though it is advertised
ibid. 1885 I : 714. The Manchester attorneys in charge of the
library are named loc. cit. p. 714.

In the Biographia Britannica s. v. Chaucer, p. 1307 footnote,
the MS is alluded to as missing and its loss deplored; see also
J. W. Bright, Acad. 1896 II : 50, Lounsbury, Studies III : 81.
Present whereabouts of the MS unknown; a letter to N. and
Q. 1905 II : 109 elicited no response.

(Titlepage and extracts are given below.)
Amorum | Troili | et | Creseidae | Libri duo priores | Anglico-
Latini
(woodcut device)
Oxoniae | Excudebat Iohannes Lichfield | Anno Domini | 1635 |

Latin dedication to Junius by Kynaston; preface *Candido
Lectori* by Kynaston, telling of his difficulties; a number of short
poems and commendatory stanzas, in Latin and in English, by
various writers, praising Kynaston for his rescue of Chaucer from
oblivion. The English (in blackletter) and the Latin of Kynaston
are printed on opposite pages. The Latin is in seven-lined stanzas,
rimed; the first is:

> Dolorem *Troili* duplicem narrare
> Qui Priami Regis Trojae fuit gnatus,
> Vt primùm illi contigit amare,
> Vt miser, felix, & infortunatus
> Erat, decessum ante sum conatus.
> Tisiphone fer opem recensere
> Hos versus, qui, dum scribo, visi flere.

The commendatory stanzas are signed by Art. Ionstonvs Med.
Reg., by Guil. Strode, by Tho. Lloyd, by Dudleius Digges, etc.
The poem of Guil. Barker includes these lines:

> "I'me glad the stomacke of the time's so good,
> That it can relish, can digest strong food:
> That Learning's not absurd; and men dare know,
> How Poets spake three hundred yeares agoe.
> Like trauellors, we had bin out so long,
> Our Natiue was become an vnknowne tongue,
> And homebred *Chaucer* vnto vs was such,
> As if he had bin written in High Dutch:
> Till thou the Height didst Leuéll, and didst Pierce
> The depth of his vnimitable verse.
> Let others praise thy how; I admire thy what.
> Twas Noble, the adventure; to Translate
> A booke, not tractable to every hand,
> And such as few presum'd to vnderstand:
> Those vpstart verse-wrights, that first steale his wit,
> And then pronounce him Dull: or those that sit
> In judgement of the Language they nere view'd,
> And because they are lazie, *Chaucer's* Rude:" etc.

The last of these commendatory poems, by Fr. James, of New
College, Oxford, printed in blackletter, is as follows:

> "Certes, yt is a thinge right hard to done
> Thee myckel Prayse, o doughtie KYNASTONE,
> I peyne me sore to done Thee grace, for here
> I Thee alowth there no wight nys thy peere,
> And who that saith it nat he is right nice,
> I dare well wage, tho mote mine hert agrise
> In bytter stound, all were my life etern,
> Bote if I should thee prayse both late and yern.
> There nas none wight couth wryte more thriftely
> Ne eke more bet, ne eke more Clerkly,

There nyst none speken bet of Troilus,
Ne of dame Creseid ne of Pandarus.
For that thy boke beareth alder prize,
That I nat how vnneth thou couth devise,
To maken Chaucer so right wise and sage
Who couth all craft in werkes, take pilgrimage
To Rome, and sothly there lerne Latine verse
In little throwe, so seemelyche to reherse.
With sythes of connyng thou hast mowen clean
Toforne thee great Reekes: that I but glean
Fro the great shefes of wytt, with boystous worde
In lewdnes fro thilk wrytings that afforde
Swylke goodlyhede, tho stant I evyll apayd,
Whan men me iape and moughten me vpbrayd.
Withouten maugre, thou hast mowen the flower
Fulfilled of all Courtship and all honour,
Farced with pleasaunce and all goodlyhede
That deyntie is to see: Thee thus I reade,
    Faire mought thee fall, who are the second Poet
    Fro Brittons Homer nephew to Payne Roet."

Lounsbury, Studies III : 115-6, says that this is the first attempt at writing Chaucerian English which is known to him, although the passages in the Return from Parnassus may be earlier. But see Bullein's Dialogue against the Fever Pestilence, 1564.

Source: It was pointed out by Trywhitt, Essay § ix, note 62, and in a note on the Retractation, that the source of this poem was Boccaccio's Filostrato. (This was scouted by Godwin, Life, ch. xiv.) In 1867 Kissner partly demonstrated this indebtedness; and his work was minutely completed by W. M. Rossetti:
Chaucer's Troylus and Cryseyde compared with Boccaccio's Filostrato. Chaucer Society, 1875. (The Chaucerian text is printed from MS Harley 3943, in columns parallel to Rossetti's literal transl. of the corresponding passages of the Italian; Rossetti follows the Moutier ed. of Boccaccio.) See Savi-Lopez on the Filostrato in Romania 27 : 442-479.
Sandras, in his Étude, 1859, suggested that Chaucer was also indebted to Benôit de Sainte-More's Roman de Troie; and it was argued by Hertzberg, Die Quellen der Troilus-Sage, Shakspere Jahrbuch (1871) 6 : 169-225, that Chaucer used Benôit as a subsidiary source. But in 1862, in his review of Sandras (Jahrbuch 4 : 85) Ebert had asserted that it was an open question whether Chaucer's secondary source was Benôit or Guido delle Colonne's Historia Trojana.
Already Tyrwhitt, note on CT line 15147, had remarked that Guido only translated the work of Benôit, a comment which was repeated by Douce, Illustrations of Shakspere.
Ten Brink, Studien p. 85, did not discuss the point; in his Hist. Eng. Lit. II : 92, 113, he intimates that Chaucer used Benôit; Lounsbury, Studies II : 309, cp. 313-315, disavows any knowledge of Benôit on Chaucer's part, while affirming that

Chaucer knew Guido; Skeat, II: liii ff., lays stress on Chaucer's indebtedness to Guido; Macaulay, in his review of Skeat, Acad. 1895 I : 297, insists that Guido was not Chaucer's source, and urges the claims of Benôit; and Furnivall, in Three More Parallel Texts of Chaucer's Troilus and Cryseyde, Ch. Soc., note in introd., pointed out traces of Benôit's influence in Chaucer's Book V. See:

The Indebtedness of Chaucer's Troilus to Benôit's Roman. J. W. Broatch. Jour. Gc. Phil. 2 : 14-29 (1898).

Broatch contends that all the passages adduced by Skeat as from Guido might equally well have come from Benôit, and that some passages occur in Benôit and not in Guido.

See further:

The Indebtedness of Chaucer's Troilus and Criseyde to Guido delle Colonne's Historia Trojana. G. L. Hamilton. Columbia Univ. Studies, 1900. Disparagingly reviewed by W. A. Neilson, Jour. Compar. Lit. 1 : 292 (1903). Rev. by Spies in Engl. Stud. 35 : 110, by Koch in Anglia Beibl. 14 : 321-4.

See also McCormick in Globe Chaucer, p. xli, and notes on pp. 543, 546, 553 ibid.

Koeppel, Engl. Stud. 20 : 156-58, points out that the passage beginning "Ek though I speke of love unfelingly", Troilus II : 19 ff., is from the Intelligenza, see Section II C (3) here. Skeat I : liv is therefore unguarded in putting this passage among Chaucer's personal allusions.

Karl Young, in Mod. Phil. 4 : 169, discusses "Chaucer's Use of Boccaccio's Filocolo" in the Troilus III : 512-1190. A dissertation (Harvard Univ. 1907) by the same author on the origin and development of the Troilus-story is as yet unpublished. Koeppel, Anglia 14 : 241-44, has some notes.

For discussion of the Troy-saga see Section II C (4) here for refs.

Other Versions of the Story: See Lydgate's Troy Book, Henryson, the Gest Hystoriale; for Nicholas Grimoald's play, and that acted at the English court in 1516 see Creizenach's Geschichte des neueren Dramas, III : 570. For Shakspere's play of the same name and its possible relation to Chaucer see eds. of Shakspere, Lloyd's Essays on Shakspere, Hales' Essays and Notes on Shakspere, Godwin's Life of Chaucer, Hertzberg in Shakspere Jahrbuch 1871 pp. 169-225, Eitner ibid. 1867 pp. 252-300; see:

Das Verhältniss von Shakspere's Troilus and Cressida zu Chaucer's gleichnamigen Gedicht. E. Stache. progr. Nordhausen, 1893. Rev. Anglia Beibl. 1894, p. 264.

For the use of Chaucer by the author of Sir Gyles Goosecappe
see Kittredge in Jour. Gc. Phil. 2 : 10. For Dryden's treatment
of Shakspere's play see eds. of Dryden.

Date: Ten Brink, Studien pp. 123, 172, suggested a date shortly
before 1384; Furnivall, Trial Forew. p. 24, conjectured that the
poem was finished in 1382; Morley, Eng. Writers V : 189, says
possibly a little after 1380; Koch, Chronology p. 79, dated it 1380-
81; Hales in the Dict. Nat. Biog. said about 1380; Pollard, Chaucer
Primer p. 58, said 1380-83; Skeat, II : xlix, about 1380-82.
Mather, in his ed. of the Prologue, etc., put this poem between
1378 and 1381. Tatlock, Mod. Phil. 1 : 317-324, argued that
"we must accept 1376 as the latest possible date for Chaucer's
Troilus and Criseyde." This is combated by Lowes, Publ.
Mod. Lang. Assn. 20 : 823 ff., summed up p. 860-64 with "per-
haps 1383-85" as date for the poem. Root, Poetry of Chaucer,
p. 91, calls Tatlock's argument "not convincing." See further
Tatlock, Devel. and Chronol. chap. I § 2. Lowes, Publ. Mod.
Lang. Assn. 23 : 285 ff., argues for 1382.

Notes: The language of the poem is analyzed by Kittredge:
Observations on the Language of Chaucer's Troilus. Chaucer
Society, 2d Series, No. 28. Revd. Nation 1896 I : 492.
See also: The Coördinate and Subordinate Conjunctions in
Chaucer's Troilus and Cressida, with a comparison of the
Romaunt of the Rose. Helen I. Whiton, diss. Columbia Univ.
1898.
On the poem see: Zu den Kunstformen des mittelalterlichen
Epos (Hartmann's Iwein, das Nibelungenlied, Boccaccio's Filo-
strato, und Chaucer's Troilus and Cressida). R. Fischer.
Vienna 1899. Rev. Archiv 103 : 162 (Meyer); Zeitschrift für
Bücherfreunde 4 : 112-114 (Landau).
See: Troilus and Criseyde: a Study in Chaucer's Method of
Narrative Construction. T. R. Price. Publ. Mod. Lang. Assn.
11 : 307-322.
Opinion of the poem has varied widely. Sidney in his
Apologie for Poetrie, ed. Arber p. 62 said, "Chaucer vndoubtedly did excellently in his *Troilus and Cresseid,* of whom truly,
I know not, whether to meruaile more, either that he in that
mistie time could see so clearly, or that wee in this cleare age,
walke so stumblingly after him." Sir Walter Scott, in his
prefatory note to Dryden's Troilus and Cressida (Scott-Saintsbury ed. vol. 6) called Chaucer's work "a long and somewhat
dull poem." Marsh in his Origin and Hist. of the English
Language, 1862, revised ed. 1892, says p. 413 that "it cannot be
said that the poem is essentially improved by the changes of
the translator." Ebert, in Ch. Soc. Essays part I, p. 14, transl.

from Jahrbuch 1862, says that Chaucer's poem is far behind the Filostrato in an esthetical sense, and that Chaucer is wanting in unity. Minto, in his Encycl. Brit. article on Chaucer, can trace no change in method or spirit attributable to Italian influence, in comparing Chaucer's Troilus with his Romaunt of the Rose. But Rossetti, in the brief introd. to his Ch. Soc. comparison of the Filostrato and the Troilus, calls the Troilus "perhaps the most beautiful narrative poem of considerable length in the English language"; and Ker, Essays on Medieval Literature (repr. from Quart. Review 1895 p. 539), says that "no other poem of Chaucer's has the same dignity and the same commanding beauty." In his Epic and Romance p. 420 Ker calls the Troilus "the poem in which medieval romance passes out of itself into the form of the modern novel."

See for discussion: Warton-Hazlitt II : 327-331; Godwin, Life, chaps. 14-16; Blackwood's Magazine 10 : 295 ff.; Sandras, Étude, pp. 41-50, and the reviews of Sandras as given here; Quarterly Review 134 : 225-255; Morley, Eng. Writers V : 187-216; ten Brink, Studien pp. 71-85, Hist. Eng. Lit. II : 87-96; Jusserand, Lit. Hist. Eng. People, I : 300-311; Root, Poetry of Chaucer pp. 87-122; Skeat, II : introd. Skeat is criticised Dial 18 : 119, Nation 1894 II : 329-30, Acad. 1895 I : 297, 338 (Macaulay).

Minor Notes in Mod. Lang. Notes 19 : 235; 20 : 80. Cressida's character is discussed by Cook in Publ. Mod. Lang. Assn. 22 : 531-547.

For the application of the term *Trophee* to the original of the Troilus (cp. Lydgate's list of Chaucer's works, printed in Section II A here) see note at end of *Lollius* in Section II C (4) here.

TRUTH

MSS: Adds. 10340, Univ. Libr. Cambr. Gg iv, 27, Ellesmere, Cotton Cleop. D vii, two copies in Trin. Coll. Cambr. R 3, 20; printed in Ch. Soc. PT p. 407 ff. Harley 7333, two copies in Fairfax 16, Adds. 22139, Lansd. 699, and the print by Caxton are reprod. SPT p. 153 ff. Selden B 24, Univ. Libr. Cambr. Kk i, 5, and Corpus Christi Coll. Oxon 203 are in OT p. 289 ff.; Phillipps 8299, Hatton 73, Selden B 10 are reprod. MOT p. 25 ff. The Adds. 10340 text is also in One-Text Print p. 293, in Athen. 1867 II : 333 and in Morris' Appendix to the revised Aldine Chaucer. The Leyden Vossius 9 copy, unprinted, but probably sister to the Lansd. copy, is mentioned Harvard Studies V : 187. Kk is also printed in Lumby's EETS ed. of Ratis Raving, pp. 9-10.

26

Textual Notes, see Koch, Anglia 4 : Anz. 105-6, Engl. Stud.
11 : 294, 15 : 416, and especially 24 : 13-16; Flügel in Anglia
23 : 209-224. Heath, in the Globe Chaucer p. xlviii, gives tree
of MSS, but mentions only 13, instead of 18. Flügel, loc. cit.,
censures Skeat's use of only seven texts.

Prints and Editions: By Caxton, see Bradshaw in Trial Forew.
pp. 116-118 for description, also Blades pp. 201-2. In the
Pynson of 1526; in the Thynne Chaucer of 1532, and in subsequent eds. of the works. In Tottel's Miscellany, ed. Arber,
pp. 194-95, among lyrics by uncertain authors, see McClumpha
in Mod. Lang. Notes 6 : 205 (1891). In eds. of Minor Poems
by Pickering (1846), Skeat, Bilderbeck; see Section IV B here.
Critical ed. by Koch. Printed by Todd in his Illustrations, pp.
131-2, from the Ellesmere MS; Skeat's note I : 82 that Todd
used Cotton Otho A xviii is incorrect; on this MS see Section
IV A (1) here. In the Selections of Southey, of Morley, of
Ward, in Sweet's Primer, in Paton, Warner, Robertson, Manly;
see Section III D here.

Modernizations and Translations: Modernized by Harte, as *To
my Soul*, 3 stanzas of 6 lines, in Chalmers 16 : 348; in the
Biographia Britannica, *s. v.* Chaucer, II : 1304, 3 stanzas of
10 lines; in Blackwood's Mag. for 1838, p. 455. Modernized by
Clarke in his Riches of Chaucer; by Purves in 1870.
Translated into German by Koch, see Section IV C here.

Authenticity and Title: Marked in the Gg MS "Balade de bone
conseyl"; the first copy in R 3, 20 is marked "Balade þat
Chaucier made on his deeth bedde", the second copy "Balade
by Chaucier", Stow adding the words "on his dethe bede."
Harley 7333 heads it "Moral balade of Chaucyre"; the first copy
in Fairfax has as colophon "Explicit Le bone counseill de
G. Chaucer", while the second is headed "Balade." Lansdowne
transcribes the poem as if it were part of Fortune, marking it
"La bon Counseil de le Auctour", and writing as colophon
"Explicit optimus tractatus de ffortuna." Caxton heads it "The
good counceyl of chawcer." The Corpus copy heads it "Pro-
uerbium Scogan"; the Selden B 24 colophon is "Explicit
Chauceres counsaling"; the Hatton MS heads the poem "Good
conseylle", the Selden B 10 "Ecce bonum consilium galfridi
Chaucers contra fortunam." The Pynson Chaucer of 1526
headed the poem as did the Selden B 10 MS; note that the
Selden copy was probably derived from a de Worde print,
which may have been the source of Pynson's text, or vice versa.
Thynne, in 1532, marked the poem "Good counsayle of
Chaucer"; in this he was followed by Speght, Urry, the 1782

Bell, the Chiswick, the 1854 Bell, and the Aldine. In all these
it is of 3 stanzas. In the Athen. of 1867, II : 333, Furnivall
printed the Adds. 10340 copy, which has an additional envoy-
stanza; and in the Ch. Soc. prints of the PT etc., he entitled
the poem *Truth*.

Bale included the poem under "Epigrammata quoque."

Date: The truth of Shirley's heading, that the poem was written
on Chaucer's deathbed, was questioned already by Tyrwhitt,
who said, in his Account of the Works of Chaucer, that "of
such a circumstance some further proof should be required."
Also doubted by Furnivall, PT p. 407, and treated by Skeat,
I : 550 as "probably no better than a bad guess." But ten
Brink, Hist. Eng. Lit. II : 205, says "Why should we refuse to
admit a credible nucleus to a well-accredited tradition?"

That the poem was written late in Chaucer's life is usually
held; ten Brink, loc. cit., considers it his "latest poetical utterance." But Furnivall, Athen. 1871 II : 495, said 1386-7, and in
Trial Forew. pp. 8-9 said 1386 or 1388.

Source: There is some resemblance to a passage in Boethius, bk.
III, metre 11, which is regarded by Koch as the source; but
see Skeat I : 550 ff.

Notes: It is possibly the mistaken heading in the Corpus MS,
repeated by Ritson, Bibliographia Poetica, 1802, p. 97-98, cp.
p. 22, which led the writer of the life of Henry Scogan in the
Dict. Nat. Biog. to the error pointed out by Furnivall at Prof.
Lounsbury's request, N. and Q. 1898 II : 423, and castigated by
Flügel, Anglia 21 : 258.

For correction of Skeat's inaccurate note I : 552 as to the MS
Cotton Otho A xviii, see Flügel in Anglia 22 : 512-514.

The envoy is regarded as genuine by Furnivall, see his high
valuation of it in Athen. as above noted; and Skeat I : 553 sees
no reason for considering it spurious. But Koch in his crit. ed.
p. 24 and Anglia 4 : Anz. p. 106 thinks the envoy spurious, while
ten Brink, Hist. Eng. Lit. II : 206, leaves the envoy out of
consideration. Also Kittredge, reviewing Skeat, Nation 1894
II : 310, regrets Skeat's retention of a spurious stanza. Flügel,
Anglia 23 : 222-3, thinks the envoy was perhaps written when
Chaucer was dying.

Lounsbury discusses the poem Studies I : 362-4; he thinks
it has received undue praise. See also ten Brink as cited;
Root, Poetry of Chaucer, pp. 73-4; Skeat I : 82, 550-553.

The word *press* is mistakenly treated N. and Q. 1858 II : 371,
Acad. 1878 I : 35, see *ibid.* p. 55.

Venus

MSS: Trin. Coll. Cambr. R 3, 20, Ashmole 59, Tanner 346, Fairfax 16, Univ. Libr. Cambr. Ff i, 6, Selden B 24, printed Ch. Soc. PT p. 411 ff. Two copies in Pepys 2006 and Notary's print are in Ch. Soc. SPT p. 157. The R 3, 20 text is also in One-Text Print p. 295.

Textual Notes, see Koch, Anglia 4 : Anz. 106-7, Engl. Stud. 27 : 59. Diagram of MS relations in Globe Chaucer page 1.

Prints and Editions: See ante under Mars.

Modernizations and Translations: Mod. by Robert Bell in Horne of 1841; see Section III E here. Cp. Lounsbury, Studies III : 220.

Title and Authenticity: Connection with the Mars: For the latter point see under Mars here. There are but two MS copies of the Venus separately, that in Ashmole 59 (Shirley), and one in Ff i, 6. The Ashmole is headed "Here begynneþe a balade made by þat worþy Knight of Savoye in frenshe calde sir Otes Graunson, translated by Chauciers." The Ff text has no heading. In Acad. 1891 I : 442 Paget Toynbee remarks that the title of the poem, as suggested by the colophon in R 3, 20, is a misnomer for which Shirley is responsible.

In Ashmole 59 there is in the margin beside the envoy "Lenvoye by Thomas Chaucier to alle pryncis and princessis of þis translacon of þis complaynte and laye." This ten-line envoy is also copied earlier in the MS, as a tag to Chaucer's Fortune; it is there marked in the margin "Envoy by Chaucyer." The many slovenlinesses and errors of this MS may perhaps be ascribed to Shirley's great age, see Anglia 27 : 397-8, 30 : 320-348. But compare the curious assertion in vol. VIII p. 130 of the Bell Chaucer of 1854 as to Thomas Chaucer's poetical work.

Source: In Romania 19 : 411-416, s. v. Oton de Granson et ses Poésies, Piaget printed the ballades transl. by Chaucer; repr. Skeat I : 400 ff

Date: Trial Forew p. 17, see p. 8, says 1392. Skeat I : 86 "about 1393"

Notes: See Sandras, Étude p. 109; ten Brink, Hist. Eng. Lit. II : 193; Morley, Eng. Writers V : 151-2; Skeat I : 86, 559-562; Root, Poetry of Chaucer, p. 77.

WORDS TO ADAM

MSS: One copy only, in Shirley's codex Trin. Coll. Cambr. R 3, 20; reproduced Ch. Soc. PT p. 177, One-Text Print p. 127. A late copy is in MS Gg iv, 27.

Textual Notes, see Koch, Anglia 3 : 186, Engl. Stud. 11 : 294; Flügel in Anglia 23 : 207-9.

Prints and **Editions:** First printed by Stow in the 1561 Chaucer; in the subsequent eds. of the Works. In the eds. of the Minor Poems by Pickering, by Skeat. Crit. ed. by Koch. In the Selections of Sweet, of Paton, see Section III D here.

Modernizations and **Translations:** Mod. by Clarke in Riches of Chaucer; by Purves in 1870, see Section III E here.

Transl. into German by Hertzberg, Canterbury Geschichten p. 47 footnote; by Koch, see Section IV C here.

Authenticity and **Title:** Shirley heads the stanza: "Chauciers wordes. a. Geffrey vn-to Adame his owen scryveyne." Stow marks it "Chaucers woordes vnto his owne Scriuener."

In the margin by the stanza is written in Shirley's hand "lachares", as is pointed out in Mod. Lang. Notes 19 : 36 (1904). Qy., whether a miswriting of *lachesce*, sloth, or intended as a proper name?

Date: Because of its mention of "Boece or Troilus" in its second line, the Words to Adam has been generally assigned a date immediately following those works.

Notes: For particulars as to medieval scribes and their methods of work see Wattenbach, Schriftwesen des Mittelalters, 3d ed. pp. 467 ff.; Hardy, Descriptive Catalogue, Rolls Series, preface to vol. III; Le Clerc and Renan, Histoire littéraire de la France au XIVme siècle, ed. 1865, vol. I, pp. 303-363; Kirchhoff, Die Handschriftenhändler des Mittelalters; Madan, Books in Manuscript, London, 1893; Putnam, Books and Their Makers in the Middle Ages, 2 vols., N. Y. 1896-7.

See Root, Poetry of Chaucer, pp. 69-70.

SECTION V.

VERSE AND PROSE PRINTED WITH THE WORKS OF CHAUCER

In Alphabetical Order.

Against Women Unconstaunt, *see* Newfangleness.

ALISON

MSS: Fairfax 16, in which Alison follows the Book of the Duchess without a break; not in Bodley 638, a codex closely related to the Fairfax; in Tanner 346, a codex somewhat less closely allied to Fairfax, this poem follows the Cuckoo and Nightingale. The MS Ff i, 6, though it has the Cuckoo, has not Alison; the Selden copy of the Cuckoo is mutilated at close.

Liddell in Academy 1896 II : 116 erroneously says not in Fairfax.

For description of these MSS see Section IV A (3) and (5) here.

Prints and Editions: In the Thynne Chaucer of 1532, following the Cuckoo and Nightingale as an envoy, without any separate title. In all subsequent editions of Chaucer, even the Chiswick departing from Tyrwhitt's verdict, until the revised Bell of 1878 relegated the poem, with the Cuckoo, to the Works Attributed to Chaucer. Printed by Skeat VII : 359, from the Fairfax; his statement *ibid.* lxii is misleading; he partly corrects it in his Canon p. 113. Vollmer, in his edition of the Boke of Cupid (see Cuckoo and Nightingale here), prints the Tanner text of Alison on pp. 46-47. Also printed, at the close of the Cuckoo and Nightingale, Kelmscott Press 1896, with the Flower and the Leaf; and included with the Cuckoo and Nightingale in the undated editions and the eds. of selections mentioned under heading of that poem, *q. v.* below.

406

Authenticity: Doubted by Tyrwhitt, who accepted the Cuckoo and Nightingale; see his Account of the Works of Chaucer.

Title: The acrostic *Alison* formed by the last six lines was pointed out by Liddell, Academy 1896 II : 116. Skeat, Canon 113, says "The title is mine."

Modernized by Wordsworth, along with the Cuckoo and Nightingale, in the Horne volume of 1841, see Section III E here; Wordsworth did not keep the acrostic.

Notes: See Skeat VII : lxii, 529.

All thyng ys ordaynyd, *see* Poems . . . during his Imprisonment.

Alone Walking, *see* Virelay.

Amorous Complaint, *see* Complaint d'Amours.

ASSEMBLY OF GODS
(by John Lydgate?)

MSS: Trin. Coll. Cambr. R 3, 19; Brit. Mus. Royal 18 D ii.

Prints and Editions: By Wynken de Worde, 1498, with his print of the Canterbury Tales. Again by de Worde, no date, with the Temple of Glass and Story of Thebes; description in Schick's ed. of the former poem, p. xxvi. Pynson also printed the poem, separately, and there are two prints by Redman, of 1540 and of *n. d.* (Lowndes).

Edited by O. L. Triggs, University of Chicago Press and EETS, 1895.

Authenticity and Title: Assigned to Lydgate in the colophon of de Worde's 1498 print, not elsewhere. This colophon gives the work no title; de Worde's second print was termed in the colophon "Le assemble de dyeus." Redman marked it "The Assemble of goddis and goddesses." Stow, in his list of Lydgate's works for the 1598 Chaucer, includes the "Banket of Gods and Goddesses with a discourse of Reason and Sensualitie."

To the Trinity MS and the 1498 de Worde print is prefixed an "Interpretacon of the names of goddis and goddesses of this treatyse folowynge as Poetes wryte." From this, which is merely a list of dramatis personae for the work itself, Bale has drawn, for his catalogue of Lydgate's works, "De Nominibus Deorum"; Ritson, in his Bibliographia Poetica, *art.* Lydgate, assigns to Lydgate both the Banket of gods and goddesses as in Stow, and the Interpretation (etc.), as if the latter title represented a separate work.

It will appear from the above that the ascription of the poem to Lydgate rests upon de Worde, with perhaps the support of Stow. Schick, ed. Temple of Glass, EETS, p. cix, remarks that Lydgate's authorship is not absolutely certain.

Date: Triggs, loc. cit., suggests 1420 or 1422, possibly "even later."

Notes:

ASSEMBLY OF LADIES

MSS: Trin. Coll. Cambr. R. 3, 19; Brit. Mus. Adds. 34360; Longleat 258; this last is not mentioned by Skeat. The Trinity MS is described in vol. II of James' Western MSS in the Library of Trinity College, Cambridge; for the Adds. MS see Anglia 28 : 1 ff., and for the Longleat see Mod. Lang. Notes 20 : 77-79.

Prints and Editions: Printed by Thynne in his 1532 Chaucer; in the subsequent blackletter editions, in Urry, in the 1782 Bell, in Anderson, in Chalmers (under the heading of Poems Imputed to Chaucer); not in Chiswick, Moxon, the 1845 Aldine, or the 1854 Bell, etc.

Thynne's text is reprinted, with comparison of two MSS, by Skeat, VII : 380.

Authenticity: A Stuart hand has marked the Trinity copy "By Chaucer." Rejected from the canon by Tyrwhitt in his Account of the Works of Chaucer. Bell and Anderson paid no heed to Tyrwhitt's opinion, but Chalmers removed the poem as above noted.

Title: Marked in the Trinity MS, "Here begynneth the Boke callyd Assemble de Damys"; Adds. has no heading, but Stow has written it in the margin; Longleat has no heading, but a colophon "Here endith the boke of Assemble de dames." Trinity's colophon is the same. The title is given in the last stanza of the poem as "Lassemble de dames" (Longleat MS). Thynne's title, "The assemble of ladies", has been used by subsequent editors. Leland and Bale rendered it "Chorus Heroidum"; "Choream dominarum."

Source and Date: Not yet investigated. Skeat, VII : lxii-lxx, Canon 139 ff. and 110, argues that this poem and the Flower and the Leaf are by the same author, that that author was a woman, and that she was well acquainted with the LGW prol. and with the Confessio Amantis, and may have written her work in the last quarter of the XV century. See also refs. under Flower and Leaf below.

Notes: See Skeat VII : lxix, 535.

———

Balade: *See* Against Women Unconstant, Beware, Chastity, Doublenesse, *Gentilesse, "I have a Lady", "In the season", Mother of Nurture, Newfanglenesse, "Of their Nature", "O Mercifull", "O Mossie Quince."

Balade de bon Consail, *see* "If it befalle."

Balade of Compleynt, *see* Ballad of Complaint.

Balade of Good Counsel, *see* *Truth.

Balade of Good Counsaile by dan John Lydgate, *see* Wicked Tongue.

Balade in Commendation of Our Lady, *see* under that heading.

Balade in the Praise and Commendation of Geffrey Chaucer, *see* Praise and Commendation, etc.

Balade sent to King Richard, *see* *Stedfastnesse.

Balade de Vilage sans Peinture, *see* *Fortune.

Balade Plesaunte, *see* "I have a Lady."

Balade Symple, *see* Flower of Courtesy, the envoy.

Balade Warnyng Men, etc., *see* under Beware.

Balade that Chaucier made, *see* Womanly Noblesse.

*The starred references are to genuine poems, discussed in Section IV; others are found in this Section.

For a ballad (or two?) marked as Chaucer's in Shirley's MS Adds. 16165, printed by Furnivall in the Supplementary Volume of the Ballad Society, and discussed Mod. Lang. Notes 19 : 35-38, see closing paragraph of Section II A (4) here.

BALLAD OF COMPLAINT

MSS: Brit. Mus. Adds. 16165 (Shirley). The MS is briefly described in Mod. Phil. 1 : 331, Mod. Lang. Notes 19 : 35-38.

Prints and Editions: Discovered, and printed by Skeat in the Academy for 1888 I : 292; in his Minor Poems p. 222, Oxford Chaucer I : 415, see introduction p. 90. Printed in the Globe Chaucer among the Doubtful Minor Poems.

Authenticity: No mark of authorship in the MS. Pollard, Academy 1889 I : 178-9, says that Prof. Skeat is "laying down a new and very dangerous canon" by claiming these and other poems for Chaucer because of metrical smoothness. The poems are in a Shirley MS but not by him attributed to Chaucer; "a fact alone almost sufficient to condemn them." Skeat himself, Canon pp. 63-4 and 147, now rejects this poem from the list of Chaucer's works. It was disavowed earlier by Furnivall, MOT p. 6, by Koch, Chronology p. 21 and also Engl. Stud. 27 : 60.

Title: Marked in the MS "Balade of compleynt."

Notes:

BALLAD IN COMMENDATION OF OUR LADY

MSS: Ashmole 59 (Shirley); Sloane 1212 according to Skeat as below. The Ashmole is described Anglia 30 : 320-348.

Prints and Editions: By Thynne in the 1532 Chaucer; in the subsequent blackletter editions, in Urry, in the 1782 Bell, in Anderson, in Chalmers under the heading Poems Imputed to Chaucer; not in Chiswick or subsequent editions. Printed by Skeat VII : 275 ff. as two distinct poems, the second of which he entitles "To my Sovereign Lady", q. v.

Authenticity: Rejected from the canon by Tyrwhitt, Account of the Works of Chaucer; he suggested Lydgate's authorship, following Tanner. Skeat ascribes the poems to Lydgate, Canon 103-4, VII : xlvi, following the Ashmole MS, see Anglia 30 : 326.

Title: For the Ashmole MS see as above; title in Thynne ". . . . a balade in commendation of our Lady." Leland entitles it "Cantiones"; Bale, in his 1557 list of Chaucer's works, marks it "Cantiones quoque."

Notes: See Skeat VII : xlvi, 511.

BALLAD OF PITY, OR, COMPLAINT TO HIS LADY

MSS: Harley 78, Adds. 34360. The Harley text is printed Ch.
Soc. Odd Texts, Appendix pp. ii, v; the Adds. text is printed
MOT pp. 46 ff. The Adds. text, discovered by Furnivall, was
partly printed Academy 1889 II : 24 by Skeat; it has one more
stanza than the copy in the Harley MS, first printed by Skeat
as noted below. The Harley MS is noted Anglia 28 : 2 footnote; the Adds. is described *ibid.* in full.

Textual Notes, see Koch, Engl. Stud. 27 : 41-43.

Prints and Editions: By Stow in the 1561 Chaucer; in the Speghts,
in Urry, in the 1782 Bell (there printed immediately following
Pity), in Anderson in the same position, in Chalmers in the
group of poems added by Stow; not in the Chiswick or in subsequent editions until Skeat included it in the Oxford Chaucer
I : 360; and see his ed. of the Minor Poems p. 213. The Kelmscott follows Skeat's authority in reprinting the poem, which
the Globe also includes in the canon.

Authenticity: In Harley 78 this poem follows immediately upon
Chaucer's Pity, with a horizontal dividing line drawn between
by Shirley, and a sort of asterisk in the margin, a mark which
he frequently uses to denote the beginning of stanzas or poems.
Running title to both poems, "þe balade of Pytee By Chauciers."
In Adds. 34360, where the text is apparently derived from the
Shirley MS (see Skeat I : 360 footnote), there is a colophon
which the Chaucer Society prints "dan Chaucer lauceire",
and which is probably . . . *lautour,* as Skeat says Academy
1889 II : 24. It may be remarked that if the Adds. text is
derived from the Shirley, and is written a generation later than
that MS (see Anglia 28 : 1 ff.), this colophon, which furthermore is in script smaller than that regularly used by the scribe,
may be a fifteenth century interpretation of Shirley's markings,
and not a piece of independent testimony. Skeat, Minor Poems
lxxxi, 398, Oxford Chaucer I : 76, Canon p. 60, maintains its
genuineness; Koch, Chronology p. 21, concedes it; Furnivall,
Trial Forewords pp. 95-6, 120, opposes its inclusion in the canon.
The most weighty external evidence for Chaucerian authorship
is the continuing of Shirley's running title to include this poem
as well as the Pity; weighty internal evidence is the use in the
poem of terza rima, an Italian verse-form presumably unknown
to any fourteenth-century English poet but Chaucer.

Title: Stow heads the poem: "These verses next folowing were
compiled by Geffray Chauser and in the writen copies foloweth
at the ende of the complainte of petee." Later editions copy

Stow. The Chaucer Society uses the title Balade of Pite, Skeat, A Compleint to his Lady.

Date, Notes, etc.: Koch, Chronology pp. 25 ff., discusses the relations of this poem, the Amorous Complaint, and Balade of Complaint. See Skeat as cited; ten Brink, Hist. Eng. Lit. II : 211-12; Morley, Eng. Writers V : 147-8; Root, Poetry of Chaucer p. 68.

BERYN

MSS: The Tale of Beryn, with its prologue The Mery Adventure of the Pardonere and Tapstere at the Inn at Canterbury, exists in but one MS, the Northumberland MS of the Canterbury Tales, see Section III B (7) here.

Prints and Editions: First printed by Urry in the 1721 Chaucer; reprinted by Bell in 1782, by Anderson (with a disclaimer of its genuineness), by Chalmers in the section Poems Imputed to Chaucer. Edited for the Chaucer Society by Furnivall, 1876, as No. 17 of the 2d series. Urry's text, corrected, is printed by Wright in his 1847 ed. of the Canterbury Tales III : 191 ff.

Authenticity: Doubted by Thomas, preface to Urry; Tyrwhitt, Account of the Works of Chaucer, excludes it from the canon; note Anderson and Chalmers as above. The MS has as colophon (see p. 120 of Ch. Soc. edition) . . .
> Nomen autoris presentis Cronica Rome
> Et translatoris / Filius ecclesie Thome
Furnivall, op. cit., thinks the author was probably a monk.

Modernizations and Translations: See MS belonging to Prof. Dowden, mentioned p. 228 here; see Darton under Section III E above.

Date and Source: An abstract of the source, the French Histoire du Chevalier Berinus, is printed by Clouston, pp. 121 ff. of Ch. Soc. ed., with versions of the Asiatic parallel stories.

Notes: See Ch. Soc. ed. as above.

BEWARE

MSS: Trin. Coll. Cambr. R 3, 19, and O 9, 38; Harley 2251. For descriptions of MSS see Section IV A (6); Section III B (6) and Anglia 28 : 1 ff.

Prints and Editions: By Stow in the 1561 Chaucer; in the subsequent blackletter editions, in Urry, in the 1782 Bell, in Anderson, in Chalmers among Stow's additions; not in the Chiswick or subsequent editions. Printed by Skeat VII : 295, text from the Trinity R MS.

Title: No heading in Harley or Trinity R. Headed in the black-letter eds., etc., "A ballad warning men to beware of deceitful women"; so headed by Skeat.

Authenticity: The R MS has "Chaucer" lettered in the margin in a large print-like script; it is not certain whether Stow relied upon the frequent occurrence of this marking in the R MS for his transference of so many of its poems to the 1561 edition, or whether he is responsible for the insertion of the supposed author's name into the codex. The poem was rejected from the canon by Tyrwhitt in his Account of the Works of Chaucer, along with the rest of Stow's "heap of rubbish." Tyrwhitt loc. cit. ascribed it to Lydgate, relying upon MS Harley 2251; but the poem has no mark of authorship in that MS. See Skeat, Canon 124.

Notes: See Skeat VII : 1, 516.

———

Beware of Doubleness, *see* Doubleness.

———

BLACK KNIGHT
(By John Lydgate)

MSS: Fairfax 16, Bodley 638, Tanner 346, Digby 181, Selden B 24, Adds. 16165, Magd. Coll. Cambr. Pepys 2006, Asloan. The first five of these MSS are described under Section IV A (3) above; the Adds. is described Mod. Phil. 1 : 331, Mod. Lang. Notes 19 : 35-38; the Pepys is described Mod. Lang. Notes 19: 196-98; for comments on the Asloan see Athen. 1906 I : 422, 482, 516, 671.

Prints and Editions: By Wynkyn de Worde, *n. d.*, reprinted for the Roxburghe Club in 1818; by Chepman and Myllar, Edinburgh, 1508, in a collection of poems entitled The knightly Tale of Golagrus and Gawane and other Ancient Poems; the Black Knight appears there with the heading The Maying and Disport of Chaucer; see under House of Fame, Section IV here, for correction of Ritson's and Lowndes' attribution of this title and print to the House of Fame. A facsimile of the Chepman and Myllar print was edited by Laing, Edinburgh, 1827.

Printed by Thynne in the 1532 Chaucer; in the Speghts, in Urry, in the 1782 Bell, in Anderson, in Chalmers, in Chiswick, Moxon, the 1845 Aldine, the 1854 Bell, the revised Aldine; in the revised Bell of 1878 (Skeat) relegated to the section Poems Attributed to Chaucer. Printed by Skeat VII : 245, text from Thynne, collated with the MSS. Critical edition by Krausser, Anglia 19 : 211 ff. (1896).

Authenticity: According to Krausser, loc. cit. p. 238, the attribution to Chaucer by the Selden MS and by the Chepman and Myllar print (which go back to a common original), possibly caused Thynne to include the poem in his collection; accepted by Tyrwhitt, Account of the Works of Chaucer. First impugned by Bradshaw, partly on account of faulty rimes, and partly on the strength of Shirley's marking in Adds. 16165; see Krausser as cited.

Date: Tyrwhitt, who did not doubt Chaucer's authorship, suggested in his Appendix to the Preface, C, note e, that this poem might have been written for John of Gaunt's courtship of Blanche of Lancaster; though at the close of his work, in his Account of the Works of Chaucer, he partly cancelled this conjecture. Such a connection would place the Black Knight before 1359, when Gaunt and Blanche were married. Krausser, op. cit. above, pp. 240-42, dates the poem 1402-3, dismissing the date 1430 (Dict. Nat. Biog., art. Lydgate) as far too late. He argues from internal evidence.

Title: Headed by Shirley in Adds. 16165, "And here filowyng begynneþe a right lusty amerous balade made in wyse of complaynt of a right worshipfull knyght þat truly euer serued his lady enduryng grete disese by fals envye and malebouche / made by Lydgate." The running title is "A complaynte of An amorous knyght." In the Fairfax and Bodley MSS the heading is "Complaynte of a louers Lyfe"; the Tanner has no heading except by a later, Jacobean hand, which has written "The Complaint of þe black knight"; a Jacobean hand (Stow's?) has also written beside the rubric of Fairfax "or of the blake knight." Digby 181 has no title by the scribe, but a hand perhaps contemporary has written in, very small, "The man in þe erber." The Selden MS has no heading, but a colophon "Here endith the maying and disport of Chaucere." Pepys is headed in a hand later than the scribe's, "The complaynt of ye blak Knyght."

The de Worde print marked the poem "Complaynt of a loveres lyfe"; Thynne of 1532 headed it "The complaynt of the blacke knyght"; and this title was retained until the 1854 Bell, returning to the MSS for texts, marked it the "Complaynte of a Loveres Lyfe, or, the Complaint of the Black Knight." This heading was also used by Morris, in the revised Aldine; the title as in Thynne is used by Krausser and by Skeat. Leland and Bale term the poem "Querela equitis nigri", "Querimonia nigri militis." On the Digby MS title it may be remarked that the Flower and the Leaf is in Dryden's version subtitled "The Lady in the Arbour"; see Speght's explanatory heading and Godwin, Life II : 350.

Modernizations, etc.: By John Dart, 1718, as "The Complaint of the Black Knight, from Chaucer. By Mr. Dart." (Brit. Mus. Cat.) By Clarke in his Riches of Chaucer.

Notes: See Skeat and Krausser as cited; Godwin, Life chap. 42; ten Brink, Hist. Eng. Lit. II : 229, Studien pp. 170-171.

Book of Cupid, *see* Cuckoo and Nightingale.

CHASTITY

MSS: Trin. Coll. Cambr. R 3, 19; described in James as cited.

Prints and Editions: By Stow in the 1561 Chaucer; in the Speghts, in Urry, in the 1782 Bell, in Anderson, in Chalmers in the section reprinted from Stow. Not in Chiswick or subsequent editions.

Authenticity: Rejected from the canon by Tyrwhitt, Account of the Works of Chaucer, along with the rest of Stow's "heap of rubbish."

Modernizations and Translations: Mod. in Gent. Mag. 1737, p. 118, as "A Sonnet of Chaucer." No signature.

Notes: See Skeat, Canon 119-20. The Cambridge MS has 10 stanzas, the last of which has no connection with the rest, but is from Lydgate's thanks to Gloucester for a gift of money, prologue to Book III of the Falls of Princes.

Chaucer's Dream, *see* Book of the Duchesse, Section IV here, and Isle of Ladies, below.

Chaucer's Prophecy, *see* Prophecy.

CHRONICLE MADE BY CHAUCER

MSS: Ashmole 59 (Shirley); described in Anglia 30 : 320-348.

Prints and Editions: Printed from this MS by the Chaucer Society, OT Appendix p. vi ff.; also in Gaertner's John Shirley, sein Leben und Wirken, diss. Halle 1904, p. 66.

Authenticity, etc.: Headed by Shirley "þe Cronycle made by Chaucier. Here nowe foloweþe þe names of þe nyene worshipfullest Ladyes þt in alle cronycles and storyal bokes haue beo founden of trouþe of constance and vertuous or reproched womanhede by Chaucier."
Furnivall, Trial Forewords p. 97, says that the poem cannot possibly be by Chaucer; ten Brink, Hist. Eng. Lit. III : 272, censures Shirley for marking the poem as by Chaucer; Skeat I : 53 explains that Shirley does not actually attribute the stanzas to Chaucer.
See also Skeat, Oxford Chaucer III : lv.

Complaints, *see* Ballad of Complaint, Ballad of Pity, Black Knight, Complaint d'Amours, Complaint of a Lover's Life *under* Black Knight, Complaint to his Lady *under* Ballad of Pity, Complaint to my Mortal Foe, Complaint to my Lodesterre, Lamentation of Mary Magdalen.

COMPLAINT D'AMOURS

MSS: Fairfax 16, Bodley 638, Harley 7333; described Section IV A (3) and (1) here

Prints and Editions: Printed by Skeat, Academy 1888 I : 307; also in Minor Poems p. 218, Oxford Chaucer I : 411. Not in the Kelmscott; printed by the Globe Chaucer among the Doubtful Minor Poems.

Authenticity: Furnivall, MOT p 6, will not acknowledge this poem as genuine; Koch, Chronology p. 21, is inclined to concede it, though in Engl. Stud. 15 · 418 he cast suspicion on its genuineness; in Engl. Stud. 27 : 60 he says it is, if Chaucerian, a first effort in the seven-line stanza. See Lounsbury as below.
In all three MSS this poem is preceded by one markedly similar in tone, headed in the Fairfax "Complaynt ageyne hope", 15 stanzas of eight lines.

Title: Fairfax heads the poem "Complaynt damours"; Bodley "Complaynt Damowre"; Harley "And next folowyng begynneth an amerowse compleynte made at wyndesore in the last may tofore nouembre." Entitled by Skeat "An Amorous Complaint", by the Globe "Compleynt Damours."

Date, Notes, etc.: Koch, Chronology p. 26, conjectures 1374; on pp. 25 ff. he discusses the relations of this poem, the Balade of Complaint, and the Complaint to his Lady.

See Skeat, Minor Poems p. lxxxi, Lounsbury, Studies I: 452-3. See Bright, Mod. Lang. Notes 17 : 278; Root, Poetry of Chaucer p. 79.

Consider well with every circumstance, *see* Wicked Tongue.

COMPLAINT TO MY MORTAL FOE

MSS: Harley 7578; described Section IV A (1) here.

Prints and Editions: Discovered in Harley 7578 by Skeat, and printed by him Athen. 1894 II : 98, Oxford Chaucer IV : xxvii, Minor Poems (revised ed.) suppl. p. 468. Not printed in the Globe Chaucer.

Authenticity and Title: Title in MS, "Balade"; no mark of authorship. Skeat, Minor Poems p. 463, believes this and the poem here following are by Chaucer; Kittredge, Nation 1895 I: 240, says "more than doubtful." And see Skeat, Canon p. 64.

Notes: Skeat as cited and Canon p. 148.

COMPLAINT TO MY LODESTERRE

MSS: Harley 7578; described Section IV A (1) here.

Prints and Editions: Discovered in Harley 7578 by Skeat and printed by him Athen. 1894 II : 162, Oxford Chaucer IV : xxix, Minor Poems (revised ed.). suppl. p. 470. Not in the Globe Chaucer.

Authenticity and Title: Marked in the MS, "Balade"; no author's name. Ascribed by Skeat to Chaucer, see above; but cp. his later note in Canon p. 64. Title given by Skeat.

Notes: Skeat as cited and Canon p. 148.

Concords of Company, *see* Utter thy Language.

27

Court of Love

MSS: Trinity Coll. Cambr. R 3, 19; described in James as cited. See Skeat VII: lxxiv note for note on age of this fascicule of the MS.

Prints and Editions: By Stow in the 1561 Chaucer; in the subsequent blackletter eds., in Urry, in the 1782 Bell, in Anderson, in Chalmers, in Chiswick, Moxon, the 1845 Aldine, the 1854 Bell, the revised Aldine. In the revised Bell relegated to the section Poems Attributed to Chaucer. Printed by Skeat VII : 409, from the Trinity MS.

Title: Marked by the MS, by Stow, and in following eds., as above.

Authenticity: Accepted by Tyrwhitt, Account of the Works of Chaucer; and asserted to be Chaucer's by Godwin, Life I : 205. Rejected from the canon by Bradshaw as cited Temp. Pref. 107-8, by ten Brink, Studien p. 168. The reviewer of the Studien, Acad. 1870-71, defended some of the poems pronounced spurious by ten Brink, this among them; Furnivall replied, Acad. *ibid.* p. 60; in N. and Q. 1872 I : 32, 70, 110, 156, is a correspondence on the subject.

In Athen. 1876 II : 592 Skeat again attacked the genuineness of the poem; Furnivall *ibid.* p. 658 repeated that Bradshaw had rejected it; the article on Chaucer in the Encycl. Brit., by Minto, which recognized the poem as Chaucerian, called out censure from Furnivall, Athen. 1877 I : 417, to which Minto replied *ibid.* p. 447, quoting the opinion of Swinburne. Swinburne himself wrote an exceedingly characteristic letter, *ibid.* p. 481; and see p. 512. In the Acad. 1878 I: 365 Furnivall praised Skeat's revision of the Bell Chaucer for its removal of the spurious poems to a separate volume; T. Arnold, *ibid.* p. 489, protested in favor of the Court of Love; Skeat replied *ibid.* p. 512, see also 1878 II : 66, 116; 1889 I : 431.

Morley, Eng. Writers V : 125-144, queries if we have in this poem a late transcript of a work by Chaucer, accommodated to the ears of later readers. Cp. Lounsbury on the poem as an imitation with impossible linguistic forms, Studies I : 503.

Brandl, in Paul's Grundriss II : 684, suggested that the poem might be by Henry Scogan; Kittredge, Harvard Studies I : 109 ff., discredited this theory, defended by Brandl, Archiv 106 : 390-401. The author is not known, says Skeat VII : lxxv; Lange, Archiv 110: 104, hints at Lydgate's authorship.

See Lounsbury, Studies I : 496 ff.; Skeat, Canon chap. 12.

Modernizations and Translations: By A. Maynwaring, in Ovid's

Art of Love. Together with his Remedy of Love. Translated into English Verse by several Eminent Hands (Dryden, W. Congreve, and N. Tate). To which are added The Court of Love, a Tale from Chaucer (by A. Maynwaring), and the History of Love (by C. Hopkins). London, Tonson, 1709, 1712, 1719, 1735, 1776, 1782, 1791; also London (1850?), (1884?), 1888?).—From the Brit. Mus. Cat.—I find also London 1757 and London 1803.

By Alexander Stopford Catcott, Oxford 1717; in heroic couplets, 32 pages.

A print in partially modernized language, with 83 of the 206 stanzas represented by a prose abridgment, is included in Purves, see under III E here, p. 231.

Date: The New Eng. Dict. dates the poem 1450; Skeat, Acad. 1889 I : 431, says this is too early; 1500 is better.

Notes: A diss. on the language of the poem, by K. F. R. Hochdörfer, Harvard University, 1888, 144 pages, is in manuscript in the library of that institution.

Notes on the language of the poem by Skeat, Canon chap. 12, VII : lxxii, 540; according to Brandl these are to be taken with great caution.

See Godwin Life I : 205-245, chap. 11; see ten Brink, Studien 168-70; Sandras pp. 56-65; Schick, introd. to EETS ed. of the Temple of Glass, p. cxxix; Lange, Archiv 110 : 104; J. T. T. Brown on the Authorship of the Kingis Quair, pp. 31-48 and 84-89, criticised by Brandl, Archiv 99 : 167; Lounsbury, Studies I : 496 ff.; Morley, Eng. Writers V : 125, reproved by Skeat, Acad 1891 II : 56; Piaget in Romania 20 : 417 ff.; Lowes, Publ. Mod. Lang. Assn. 20 : 754-6 note.

In general see Neilson, Origins and Sources of the Court of Love, Harvard Studies vol. VI; P. Rajna, Le Corti d'Amore, Milan 1890; J. F. Rowbotham, The Troubadours and Courts of Love, London 1895; L. F. Mott, System of Courtly Love, Boston, 1896. Neilson is reviewed Archiv 106 : 390-401 (Brandl), Anglia Beibl. 14 : 364-8 (Binz), Jour. Gc. Phil. 5 : 112-16 (Root).

Court of Venus, *see* under Pilgrim's Tale, below.

CRAFT OF LOVERS

MSS: Adds. 34360 and Harley 2251; for study of these see Anglia 28 : 1 ff. Also in Trin. Coll. Cambr. R 3, 19, described in James, op. cit.

Prints and Editions: By Stow in the 1561 Chaucer, probably from the Cambridge MS; in the subsequent blackletter editions, in Urry, in the 1782 Bell, in Anderson, in Chalmers among Stow's additions. Not in Chiswick, Moxon, or subsequent editions.

Authenticity and Title: Rejected from the canon by Tyrwhitt, Account of the Works of Chaucer. He gives the true date of the poem, from the Harley MS; this was announced as a discovery by Skeat, Acad. 1888 I : 152, from the Cambridge MS. In the last stanza of Trinity the date 1448 is given; Stow has scribbled in the margin, "Chaucer died 1400." A Tudor or Jacobean hand has written in the corner of the page "The Craft of Lovers. Chaucer." No heading in Harley; in Adds. Stow has written "The Crafte of Love."

Lowell in his essay on Chaucer notes that this poem is by Ritson attributed to Lydgate, but says that it is "too bad even for him."

Notes: See Skeat, Canon p. 120.

CUCKOO AND NIGHTINGALE
(By Clanvowe)

MSS: Fairfax 16, Bodley 638, Tanner 346, Selden B 24, Univ. Libr. Cambr. Ff i, 6. Described Section IV A (3) and (5) here.

The short poem called by Skeat Envoy to Alison is in MS Tanner copied immediately after this poem; it does not appear in either the Cambridge or the Bodley MS, nor in the Selden, which is imperfect at close; in Fairfax 16, contrary to Skeat's statement VII : lxii, it follows the Book of the Duchesse. See under Alison above.

Prints and Editions: By Thynne in the 1532 Chaucer; in the subsequent blackletter eds., in Urry, in the 1782 Bell, in Anderson, in Chalmers, in Chiswick, Moxon, the 1845 Aldine, the 1854 Bell, the revised Aldine. In the revised Bell (1878) relegated to the section Poems Attributed to Chaucer.

In Southey's selections, see Section III D here. In the undated eds. by Blackwood and by Crowell, see p. 143 here. Printed by Ellis at the Kelmscott Press, 1896, with the Flower

and the Leaf. (Three hundred copies pubd. at 10 shillings.)
Printed by Skeat, VII : 347 ff., from Thynne, with MS collations. Critical ed. by Vollmer, Berlin 1898, under the title Das
mittelenglische Gedicht The Boke of Cupide (The Cuckow and
the Nyghtyngale). Reviewed Archiv 103 : 179.

Authenticity: Accepted by Tyrwhitt, Account of the Works of
Chaucer; Bradshaw seems to have been the first to doubt its
genuineness, see Temp. Pref. pp. 107-8. Skeat in ed. of the
Minor Poems p. xxviii suggested Hoccleve as the author;
Furnivall in Dict. Nat. Biog. *s. v.* Hoccleve said "Very doubt-
ful." Relegated to a place among the spurious poems by Skeat
in his revision of Bell; see his letter Acad. 1894 II : 67. The
Ff colophon giving Clanvowe's name was pointed out by Skeat
Acad. 1896 I : 365; on Clanvowe see Skeat VII : lvii, but cp.
Kittredge in Mod. Phil. 1 : 1 ff.

Title: In the Fairfax and Bodley MSS "The boke of Cupid god
of loue." No heading in the Selden or the Ff MS; the Tanner
has, in a later hand, "Of ye Cuckow & ye Nightingale." The
Ff MS has as colophon "Explicit Clanvowe." The title Cuckoo
and Nightingale appears in Thynne, and was followed by editors
until Morris, in the Aldine of 1866, used the MSS and printed
both titles. Bale mentioned the poem as "De cuculo et
philomela."

Modernizations, etc.: By Wordsworth in Horne; reprinted,
abridged, by Briscoe, see under Section III E above. See
Brydges' Restituta II : 1 ff. for a version of Cuckoo and
Philomela by Richard Nicols in 1607.

Notes: See Lounsbury, Studies I : 486; Skeat VII : lvii, 526,
Canon 107-8; Vollmer as cited above.

DOUBLENESS
(By John Lydgate)

MSS: Fairfax 16, Harley 7578, Adds. 16165, Ashmole 59 (much
altered). The first two MSS are described Section IV A (3)
and (1) here; the Adds. MS is described Mod. Phil 1 : 331,
Mod. Lang. Notes 19 : 35-38; the Ashmole is discussed in
Anglia 30 : 320-348. A stanza is in the Naples MS, see Section III B (7) here.

Prints and Editions: Printed by Stow in the 1561 Chaucer; in the
subsequent blackletter editions, in Urry, in the 1782 Bell, in
Anderson, in Chalmers. Not in Chiswick, Moxon, nor the

Aldine; printed in the 1854 Bell under the heading Poems Attributed to Chaucer, and relegated to that section in the revision by Skeat (1878). Printed by Skeat in VII : 291, from Fairfax 16, collated with Stow.

Authenticity and Title: No heading in MSS Fairfax or Harley, where the poem is of 13 stanzas; entitled in Shirley's Adds. 16165 "Balade of wymen constaunce", with "Balade made by Lydegate" in margin, and of 12 stanzas only. Heading in Ashmole (Shirley) "Nowe here foloweþ a balade made by Lidegate of wymen for desporte and game per Antyfrasim", 11 stanzas only, a garbled version. Entitled by Stow, "A balade which Chaucer made in the praise or rather dispraise of women for their doubleness." Rejected from the canon by Tyrwhitt, Account of the Works of Chaucer, who pointed out that "Ashmole 6943" ascribed it to Lydgate.

Modernized by Clarke in his Riches of Chaucer.

Dream of Chaucer, *see* Book of Duchesse, Section IV here.

Eight Goodly Questions with Their Answers

MSS: Trin. Coll. Cambr. R 3, 15; the Bannatyne MS. The Trinity MS is described Section III B (6) here; the Bannatyne is described and printed as noted Section IV A (7) here.

Prints and Editions: By Thynne in the 1532 Chaucer; this and three other short bits appear at the end of his table of contents. Printed in the same position by the succeeding blackletter editions, by Urry, and by the 1782 Bell; omitted by Anderson and by Chalmers, also by the Chiswick and by Moxon; printed by the 1854 Bell among the poems attributed to Chaucer; not in subsequent editions.

Authenticity and Title: No mark of authorship in the MSS or in Thynne. Skeat, Canon p 115, thinks it may be by Lydgate. Bale listed it under Chaucer's works as "Octo Questiones", the prints head it as above.

Notes: On the source see Skeat VII : xv, Canon 115.

Envoy to Alison, to Bukton, to Scogan, see under Alison, in this section, under Bukton and Scogan among the genuine works of Chaucer.

FAIREST OF FAIR

At the close of Chaucer's Dream (=Isle of Ladies) there follow, without break, 27 lines of verse, beginning as above. The first six lines seem to be separate from those which follow; the next twenty-one lines are arranged in three stanzas, with the refrain, "the bliss that thou desirest oft." The two closing lines are apparently mere doggerel, without any visible connection with what precedes.

For MSS and prints of these bits, see under Isle of Ladies in this Section; for discussion see Skeat, Canon pp. 138-9. Skeat thinks that the three seven-line stanzas are of the early part of the fifteenth century, and "almost certainly by Lydgate."

FLOWER AND LEAF

MSS: None known; the poem was once in Longleat 258, see Ch. Soc. OT p. 251 and Mod. Lang. Notes 20 : 77-79. Cp. Lounsbury, Studies I : 489.

Prints and Editions: By Speght in the 1598 Chaucer; in the subsequent blackletter eds., in Urry, in the 1782 Bell, in Anderson, in Chalmers, Chiswick, Moxon, the 1845 Aldine, the 1854 Bell, the revised Aldine. In the revised Bell (1878) relegated to the section Poems Attributed to Chaucer.

Printed by Todd, Illustrations p. 203, from Speght; by Skeat VII : 361 from Speght; ed. by Ellis at the Kelmscott Press, with the Cuckoo and Nightingale, 1896, (300 copies pubd. at 10 shil.) ; pubd. Essex House Press, under care of C. R. Ashbee, Lond. and N. Y. 1902, 8vo.

In the Selections of Sanford and Walsh, of Hazlitt, of Southey; see Section III D here. In the Book of Celebrated Poems, Lond. 1854 (Brit. Mus. Cat.). In Campbell's British Poets; in the Pickering Chaucer of 1846, see Section IV B here.

Modernizations and Translations: Mod. by Dryden, see Section III E for eds. and notes; on Dryden's work see Godwin, Life, II : 342; Schoepke in Anglia 3 : 35-58; Lounsbury, Studies III : 162-175. Mod. in 1822 by Lord Thurlow; by Clarke in his Riches of Chaucer; by Powell in Horne; selections from Powell are reprinted by Briscoe; see Section III E here.

Translated into French verse by Chatelain, with the Eng. text on opposite pages, Lond. 1855, second ed. 1857.

Dryden entitled his work "The Flower and the Leaf: or, The Lady in the Arbour." Note that in MS Digby the Black Knight is subtitled "þe man in þe erber."

Authenticity: First doubted by Tyrwhitt, Account of the Works of

Chaucer; treated as Chaucer's in the eds. above mentioned
and by Sandras, Étude p. 96; ten Brink, Studien p. 156,
argued that the language was too late for Chaucer; Hall, N.
and Q. 1872 I : 109, defended Chaucer's authorship; Furnivall
ibid. p. 156, Athen. 1872 II : 49, asserted its spuriousness, as did
Bradshaw, see Temp. Pref. p. 107; cp. Hall, Athen. 1872 II :
82, N. and Q. 1887 II : 167. See also Skeat in the introd. to
his revision of Bell, and often, *e. g.,* VII : lxii, Canon p. 139;
see Lounsbury, Studies I : 489 ff. Marsh, Origin and History
of the Eng. Lang., 1862, and revised ed. 1892, discussed the
poem as Chaucer's; Morley, Eng. Writers V : 249-61, said "no
evidence for or against Chaucer's authorship"; still claimed
for Chaucer by Saintsbury, Short Hist. of Eng. Lit. pp. 119, 126.

In the Acad. 1878 I : 9 is a note saying that the fifteenth
century date of the work is now confirmed by an observation
of Bradshaw's on line 519, and that the poem is by a lady.
For theory of a woman's authorship, first advanced by Godwin,
see further Skeat, Acad. 1889 I : 448, refs. above cited, Athen.
1903 I : 340, and Mod. Lang. Quart. 1900, III : 111. Hales,
Athen. 1903 I : 403, opposes this view, as does G. L. Marsh,
Jour. Gc. Phil. 6 : 373-394; Marsh would ascribe the poem to
Lydgate.

Probably ascribed to Chaucer because of the passage in the
prol. to the LGW, lines 72, 189, etc. See Lowes as below.
Treated as Chaucer's by Godwin chap. 44; by Hazlitt in his
Farewell to Essay-Writing; by Keats in his sonnet (1817).

Source: See McClumpha, Mod. Lang. Notes 4 : 402-6 (1889);
   Kittredge, Mod. Phil. 1 : 1 ff.; Lowes, Publ. Mod. Lang. Assn.
   19 : 593 ff.; in full by G. L. Marsh, Sources and Analogues of
   the Flower and the Leaf, Mod. Phil. 4 : 121-167, 281-327.

Notes: On the vogue of the poem see G. L. Marsh's note, loc. cit.
   p. 121. Comments of less value than those above are: Dryden
   in Preface to Fables; Tyrwhitt in Appendix to Preface;
   Godwin chap. 44; Todd, Illustrations pp. 275 ff.; Sandras,
   Étude pp. 95-106; ten Brink, Studien 156-64; Skeat VII :
   lxii ff., 529 ff., Canon 139 ff. See Acad. 1878 I : 35, 55.

FLOWER OF COURTESY
(By John Lydgate)

MS: None known, according to Skeat, Canon p. 102.

Prints and Editions: By Thynne in the 1532 Chaucer; in the subsequent blackletter eds., in Urry; but not in later eds. Printed
   by Skeat VII : 266 from Thynne.

Authenticity and Title: Already Leland, in his list of Chaucer's works, appended to this title: "qui libellulus a multis, tanquam nothus, rejicitur." It appears however in the lists of Bale and Pits. Thynne headed the poem "The Floure of Curtesy", which Leland rendered "Flos Humanitatis", Bale "Urbanitatis florem." Stow marked it "The Floure of Curtesie made by Iohn Lidgate." Tyrwhitt, in his Account of the Works of Chaucer, pointed out that the title in Stow mentioned Lydgate as author.

Date: See Schick, Temple of Glass, page c; Skeat, Canon p. 102.

Notes: The "Argument" prefixed in the Speght Chaucer is: "In this booke is set foorth the rare vertues of a certaine Lady: made by Iohn Lidgate, as some thinke, in the behalfe of some gentlewoman in the Court."

The envoy is separately marked "Balade symple."

See Skeat VII : xlv, 509.

GAMELYN

MSS: Harley 1758, Sloane 1685, Royal 17, Royal 18, Barlow 20, Petworth, Mm, Rawlinson 149, Ii, Lansdowne 851, Sloane 1686, Harley 7334, Laud 600, Trinity 49, Corpus, Christ Church, Egerton 2726 (inserted in later hand), Ashmole 45. All but the last are described under the Cant. Tales MSS here; Ashmole 45 is Ashmole's own copy of the fragmentary Cook's Tale and of Gamelyn, 16 leaves in all, being the third of four MSS bound together as Ashmole 45.

Tyrwhitt said, Introd. Disc. § xiii, that this Tale was not found in any MS of the first authority, for which he is censured by Morley, Eng. Writers V : 320-23.

Prints and Editions: By Urry in the 1721 Chaucer; in the 1782 Bell, in Anderson (with a disclaimer of its genuineness), in Chalmers. Not in Chiswick or subsequent eds. of the Works. Printed by Wright in his 1847 ed. of the Cant. Tales, from Harley 7334; printed by Bell 1854 from Wright. Printed by the Chaucer Society, in Appendix to Fragment A of the Six-Text, from six MSS, viz.: Royal 18, Harley 1758, Sloane 1685, Corpus, Petworth, Lansdowne 851. Also printed as Appendices to Ch. Soc. separate issues of the six MSS of the Six-Text, viz.: with the Ellesmere from Royal 18, with the Hengwrt from Harley 1758, with the Cambridge from Sloane 1685, with the Lansdowne, Corpus, and Petworth texts from those MSS. The Society's print of Harley 7334 has the Tale as in that MS; its print of Dd iv, 24 has no Gamelyn.

Printed by Skeat, Oxford Chaucer, Appendix to vol. IV, pp. 645 ff., and separately ed. by him, Oxford 1884, re-ed. 1893; the 1884 ed. is rev. Lindner, Engl. Stud. 9 : 111.

Modernizations and Translations: Mod. by Boyse in Ogle; see the MS owned by Dowden, p. 228 here; by Tytler; by Clarke; see under Section III E here.

Transl. into German by Kannegiesser, see Section III E here.

Authenticity: Doubted by Thomas, preface to Urry; rejected from the canon by Tyrwhitt, Introd. Disc. § xiii; not since printed as Chaucer's, though critics generally feel that the Tale is of Chaucer's age, and was perhaps included among his papers as the raw material to be worked over and assigned (possibly) to the Squire's Yeoman. See the Bell of 1854; Morley, Eng. Writers V : 320; Skeat III : 399. Morley however suggested that the Tale was intended for the Cook.

Notes: See Delius' ed. of Shakspere II : 347 (1872); Zupitza in Jahrbuch der deutschen Shakspere-Gesellschaft, 21 : 69 (1886); Lindner, The Tale of Gamelyn, in Engl. Stud. 2 : 94-114, 321-343, cp. Skeat III : 403; Skeat III : 399 ff., Canon 143; Morley, Eng. Writers V : 321-3 for analysis of Tale; see ten Brink, Hist. Eng. Lit. II : 183-9, III : 271.

On the verse of the Tale see Saintsbury, Hist. Eng. Prosody I : 195, Cambridge Hist. Eng. Lit. II : 221-24.

Go Forth, King

MSS:

Prints and Editions : "First printed by Wynkyn de Worde about 1498, at the end of Lydgate's Temple of Glass", Skeat, Canon, p. 105. See Dibdin II : 303-5, where the de Worde is undated. In the Thynne of 1532 and the subsequent blackletter eds., in Urry, in Anderson, in Chalmers, Chiswick, Moxon, the 1845 Aldine, and the 1846 Pickering; in the 1854 Bell and the revised Bell of 1878 relegated to the section Poems attributed to Chaucer. Printed by Skeat VII : 408 from Thynne. In Dibdin loc. cit. from de Worde.

Modernizations: By Clarke in his Riches of Chaucer; in Blackwood's Magazine, 1838 p. 455.

Authenticity : See note on eds. above. Skeat, Minor Poems p. xxix, VII : lxxi, etc., ascribes the lines to Lydgate; he is followed by Schick, Temple of Glass p. 68.

Source: Dibdin loc. cit. remarked that the stanzas were a para-
phrastical translation of "Duodecim Abusiones", a series of
Latin phrases occurring with them in de Worde, and printed
by Dibdin ioc. cit.; also printed Schick p. 68, and by Skeat
VII : 408.

Notes: Note on the source in Schick page clx, repr. by Skeat
VII : lxxii, cp. 540.

Go forth mine own true heart, *see* Fairest of Fair.

Goodly Balade, *see* Mother of Nurture.

"Halfe in dede sclepe, not fully revyved", *see* Poems . . . . during
Imprisonment.

How Mercurie with Pallas Venus and Minarva appered to Paris of Troie, he slepyng by a fountain.

MSS: Trin. Coll. Cambr. R 3, 19, whence Stow probably obtained
his text. MS described in James as cited.

Prints and Editions: By Stow in 1561; in the Speghts, in Urry, in
the 1782 Bell, in Anderson, in Chalmers under the heading of
Stow's additions; not again printed with Chaucer's Works.

Authenticity and Title: Rejected from the canon by Tyrwhitt,
along with the rest of Stow's "heap of rubbish." Headed by
Stow as above; called by Skeat, Canon p. 123, the Judgment of
Paris. In the 1782 Bell the error of *Minerva* was corrected,
and the word *Juno* substituted.

Notes: See Skeat, Canon p. 123.

If it befall

MSS: Skeat, Canon p. 117, knows of no MS copy; the lines are in
Trin. Coll. Cambr. R 3, 20, whence Stow probably obtained his
text. MS described in James as cited.

Prints and Editions: By Stow in the 1561 Chaucer; in the
Speghts, in Urry, in the 1782 Bell, in Anderson, in Chalmers
among Poems Imputed to Chaucer; not again printed with
Chaucer. In Skeat VII : 297, from Stow.

Authenticity and Title: Rejected from the canon by Tyrwhitt along with the rest of Stow's "heap of rubbish." Marked by Stow "Balade de bon consail."

Notes: See Skeat, Canon p. 117.

I HAVE A LADY

MSS: Trin. Coll. Cambr. R 3, 19, whence Stow probably obtained his text. MS described in James as cited.

Prints and Editions: By Stow in 1561; in the Speghts, in Urry, in the 1782 Bell, in Anderson, in Chalmers under the heading of Stow's additions; not again printed with Chaucer.

Authenticity and Title: Rejected from the canon already by Francis Thynne, in his Animadversions; also by Thomas, the editor of Urry; disavowed by Tyrwhitt, Account of the Works of Chaucer, along with the rest of Stow's "heap of rubbish." Headed by Stow "A balade plesaunte."

Date: See Skeat, Canon pp. 123-4.

IN FEUERERE

MSS: Trin. Coll. Cambr. R 3, 19, whence Stow probably obtained his text. MS described in James as cited.

Prints and Editions: By Stow in 1561; in the Speghts, in Urry, in the 1782 Bell, in Anderson, in Chalmers under the head of Stow's additions; not again printed with Chaucer.

Modernization by Clarke in his Riches of Chaucer.

Authenticity and Title: Rejected from the canon by Tyrwhitt, along with the rest of Stow's "heap of rubbish." Headed by Stow "A Ballade."

Notes: See Skeat, Canon p. 123.

"In wommanhede" etc., *see* Chastity.

Isle of Ladies

MSS: Brit. Mus. Adds. 10303 and Longleat 256. Morris, when editing the 1866 Aldine, said no MS known. Bradshaw, in a note p. 30 of Furnivall's ed. of Thynne's Animadversions, speaks of the Longleat as the only MS known, dating it as of Edward VI's time. The Adds. MS was pointed out by "T. N." in N. and Q. 1892 I : 467, also by Zupitza in Archiv 92 : 68-9 (1894). For notes on MSS see Sherzer as below.

Prints and Editions: By Speght in 1598, with the heading "Chaucers dreame, neuer before the yeare 1597 Printed. That which heretofore hath gone vnder the name of his dreame, is the book of the Duchesse: or the death of Blanch, Duchesse of Lancaster." Included in the Speghts, in Urry, the 1782 Bell, in Anderson, in Chalmers, Chiswick, Moxon, the 1845 and 1866 Aldine, and the 1854 Bell. In the revised Bell of 1878 relegated to the section Poems Attributed to Chaucer.

Edited from the MSS by Jane B. Sherzer, diss. Berlin 1905; rev. Fehr, Engl. Stud. 34 : 295.

Modernizations and Translations: Mod. by Clarke in his Riches of Chaucer; in Purves; see under III E here.

Title: Speght's title is used by subsequent prints, though censured by Thynne in his Animadversions; Thynne remarked that the MS (the Longleat) marked it "The Temple of Glasse". Skeat's connection of Bale's title "De Castello dominarum" with this work (*Index* ed. Poole p. 78) can hardly be correct. The present title is probably due to Henry Bradshaw, see Sherzer op. cit. p. 1 note.

Authenticity: Ascribed in the Longleat MS to Chaucer; accepted by Tyrwhitt, Account of the Works of Chaucer, by Godwin, Life chap. 22. Rejected from the canon, on account of impure rimes, by Hertzberg, Jahrbuch 8 : 133, by Ellis, EEPron. I : 251, and by ten Brink, Studien p. 165. See in detail McClumpha, Mod. Lang. Notes 4 : 129-133.

Date: It was supposed by Speght that the poem was a "covert report" of the marriage of John of Gaunt with Blanche of Lancaster; this was repudiated by Tyrwhitt. Hertzberg as above thought that the event alluded to might be the alliance of John of Gaunt with Katharine Swynford. Brandl, Engl. Stud. 12 : 175, argues that the marriage of Henry V with Katharine of France is meant; but see Kittredge, Engl. Stud. 13 : 24, McClumpha in Mod. Lang. Notes 4 : 129. See Sherzer as above.

Source, Analogues: Connected with the cycle represented by Marie de France's Lai d'Eliduc (Nation 1897 II : 303).

Notes: The twenty-seven lines of verse which follow after the "Amen, amen" of this poem, at the close, are discussed under *Fairest of Fair*, above.

See Godwin II : 576; Sandras, Étude, pp. 81-89; ten Brink, Studien 165-7; Morley, Eng. Writers, V : 166-80; Lounsbury, Studies I : 483; Skeat, Canon p. 137.

It Cometh by Kynde

This is the opening of the second of the two quatrains described below under "It Falleth for a Gentleman."

It Falleth For a Gentleman

Eight lines, placed by Thynne (1532) at the end of his table of contents, along with several other pieces of verse; these lines are the last of the four non-Chaucerian bits thus inserted. Thynne doubtless obtained them, with the "Prophecy" which precedes them, from the print by Caxton of a few of Chaucer's shorter poems; see Trial Forewords p. 118. Caxton does not there ascribe the lines to Chaucer, and probably printed them only to fill up a blank space; see Skeat, Canon p. 116.

MSS: Ashmole 781, Trin. Coll. Cambr. R 3, 15 (copied in by a XVI century hand). The Trinity MS is described Section III B (6) here.

Prints and Editions: See above. Also in 1561, in Speght's editions, in Urry, in the 1782 Bell; not in any subsequent edition until the 1854 Bell included them in the appendix of poems attributed to Chaucer. Printed by Skeat I : 46 and VII : 450, from Caxton; by Dibdin, Typogr. Antiq. II : 514-15 note, from the Ashmole MS (formerly 6986). According to the Ashmole catalogue, these bits were written between 1620 and 1631.

Authenticity: See above.

Jack Upland

MSS: Skeat says, Canon p. 142, "I have not succeeded in finding any MS copy." The preface to Urry speaks of a MS loaned the editor by T. Rawlinson, which is quoted in the Glossary, *e. g.*, see *underneme*. The Catal. of MSS in the Cambridge University Library lists a copy in Ff vi, 2; Bernard's Catalogus mentions a copy as 1642.41, among the Digby MSS; and Harley 6641 is the MS described in the Urry preface as belonging to Thomas Rawlinson.

Prints and Editions: "Usually said to have been first printed by Speght in 1602". Skeat VII : xxxv. Skeat gives a better text printed separately by John Gough, *n. d.* (1536?); this copy was already noted by Hazlitt, Handbook p. 148. Speght reprinted the tract in 1687, and Urry in 1721; but already in the latter edition the writer of the Life of Chaucer rejected it from the canon. The 1782 Bell, and Anderson, collections of poems only, printed the four-line Motto of the work; the tract was not again printed with Chaucer, though defended by Cowden Clarke in 1835; but it was printed in Foxe's Acts and Monuments, *e. g.*, in the ed. London 1843 II : 357-363, and by Wright, Polit. Poems, Rolls Series, 1861, II : 16-39, as alliterative verse. Wright took his text "from early blackletter prints." Printed by Skeat VII : 191 from the 1536 text.

Date: See Wright as cited, where the work is dated 1401; see Skeat as cited and Canon pp. 141-2.

JOHN GOWER UNTO THE WORTHY AND NOBLE KING HENRY IV

MSS: The "Trentham" MS, see Skeat VII : xxxviii; the MS is mentioned by Todd p. 95, described by Wright, Polit. Poems and Songs II : 4 ff.; see Warton-Hazlitt III : 33 ff.; and especially Macaulay, Works of John Gower I : lxxix ff.

Prints and Editions: By Thynne in the 1532 Chaucer; in the subsequent blackletter editions, in Urry; relegated by the 1782 Bell to a place near the close of the collection, and omitted by Anderson; printed by Chalmers among the Poems Imputed to Chaucer; not in the Chiswick or any succeeding edition of Chaucer.

Printed by Wright as cited above; by Skeat VII : 205; by Macaulay, Works of John Gower, III : 481 ff.

Title: The title "The Praise of Peace" was given to the poem by Mr. Nicholson, Bodley's librarian, see Skeat VII : xxxviii. Colophon in MS, "Carmen de pacis commendacione". Thynne's title (as heading here) was adopted by subsequent editors.

Date: According to Skeat, VII : 498, Canon p. 100, is of 1399.

Judgment of Paris, *see* How Mercurie.

LA BELLE DAME SANS MERCY
(By Sir Richard Ros)

MSS: Fairfax 16, Harley 372, Univ. Libr. Cambr. Ff 1, 6, Trin. Coll. Cambr. R 3, 19, Longleat 258. The first three MSS are described Section IV A (3), (1), and (5) here, the Trinity MS in James as cited, and the Longleat in Mod. Lang. Notes 20 : 77-79.

For a note on the transposition of stanzas in some of these copies see Skeat VII : liv.

Prints and Editions: First printed by Pynson in the 1526 Chaucer; Skeat VII : li says first printed in 1532; in his Canon p. 106 he emends this statement.

For variant in Pynson's copy see below.

In the subsequent blackletter editions, in Urry, in the 1782 Bell, in Anderson, in Chalmers under the head of Poems Imputed to Chaucer. Not in the later eds. of Chaucer.

Printed from Harley 372 by Furnivall in Polit., Relig. and Love Poems, EETS 1866 pp. 52 ff. Gröhler, Ueber Richard Ros' mittelengl. Uebersetzung des gedichtes von Alain Chartiers La Belle Dame sans Mercy, diss. Breslau 1886, knew only the Harley MS of the poem, and his text is therefore uncritical.

Printed by Skeat in VII : 299, from Thynne of 1532, collated with the Fairfax and Harley MSS. The re-edition of Polit., Relig. and Love Poems, EETS 1903, gives the Ff text of La Belle Dame, collated with the Harley and Trinity MSS.

Authenticity and Title: Rejected from the canon by Tyrwhitt, who called attention to the ascription to Sir Richard Ros in MS Harley 372. Marked by Bale (1548) "Carmen Facetum", (1557) "Super impia domina."

Notes, etc. See Piaget, La Belle Dame sans Merci et ses Imitations, in Romania 30 : 22-48, 317-351; 31 : 315-349; 33 : 179-208; 34 : 375-428, 559-602.

In the Pynson Chaucer of 1526 the six closing stanzas of La Belle Dame (incorrectly printed by Dibdin, II : 517-18 note) are:

> Lenvoy de limprimeur
> O ye lusty galondes of hote corage
> Put nat this example in oblyvion
> In love beware / vse nat to great outrage
> But moderate your desyres by discresion
> Els wyll it tourne to your owne confusyon
> & than *your* frendes shall have cause to morne
> Your enemyes you mocke / & faugh to scorne

And ye ladyes / endued with hye prudence
Whan these disceitfull louers labour styll
With their fayned and paynted eloquence
Their carnall lustus / to cause you to fulfyll
Many a huge othe / depose they wyll
Yet for all that / take hede above all thyng
It is no love they shewe / but blandysshyng

For very love is that / that dothe covete
His owne labour / his owne thing to dispende
To another persons pleasure and profete
His owne pleasure / in no wyse to attende
But he that woyng a lady dothe entende
Taccomplysshe his owne voluptuousnesse
Loveth nat her / but loveth him selfe doutlesse

For he that by wordes / or gifts doth pursue
To deprive a woman her best iewell
As her good name & fame / & chast vertue
Is signe of no good love / but hate cruell
Wherfore in reason / I may conclude well
Who loveth his lady after such rate
Sheweth her no true love / but most deedly hate

And he that consydreth the necessitees
Longyng to love / as attendance / thoght / & care
Labour / cost / and other incommoditees
Prudently ought / to take hede and beware
He finally shall fynde / none other welfare
But for the atchyveng of one plesaunce
To be sure to suffre / treble penaunce

Wherefore / ye gentyll people yong and olde
Men or women / what soever ye be
To love / I counsayle you be nat to bolde
Excepte it be ordred to suche degre
As concerneth spousayle / in honeste
Yet / if ye wyll in fervent love excell
Love god above althing / & than do ye well

LAMENTATION OF MARY MAGDALEN

MSS: None known, says Skeat, Canon pp. 112-13.

Prints and Editions: By Pynson in the 1526 Chaucer; in the blackletter eds. of Thynne and Speght, in Urry, in the 1782 Bell, in
Anderson, in Chalmers among the Poems Imputed to Chaucer;
28

not in Chiswick; in the 1854 Bell among Poems Attributed to Chaucer; not in subsequent editions. Edited by Bertha M. Skeat, diss. Zürich, 1897; pubd. Cambridge, Engd.; rev. W. E. Mead, Jour. Gc. Phil. 3 : 125-6.

Authenticity: Rejected from the canon by Tyrwhitt, see his Glossary s. v. *Origenes*. The work was probably included among those of Chaucer because of the "Origenes upon the Maudelayne" mentioned in the prol. LGW line 418, and now considered as lost. See Leland's remark, p. 5 here.

Title: Marked by Pynson, Thynne, etc. as at present. Leland and Bale entitle it "Threni Magdalenae."

Source, Date, etc.: Miss Skeat considers that the author was a nun, and suggests 1460-80 as the approximate date.

Notes: See Lounsbury, Studies I : 478, Skeat, Canon p. 112.

LEAULTE VAULT RICHESSE

MSS: Selden B 24; described Section IV A (3) here.

Prints and Editions: Printed by Pinkerton, Ancient Scotish Poems, Lond. & Edinb. 1786, II : 243, under the heading "Poemes be Unknawin Makars", as Pious Lines; printed by Morris in the Aldine Chaucer of 1866. Not in later eds. of Chaucer. Printed by Skeat VII : 449, from the MS.

Authenticity: Rejected by Bradshaw, see Temp. Pref. pp. 107-8. Skeat I : 48 suggests King James I as author.

Title: The colophon of the MS reads "Leaulte vault richesse"; this title used by Morris and by Skeat. For Pinkerton's title see above.

Notes: Skeat, Canon p. 147; VII : lxxxi, 554.

LETTER OF CUPID
(By Thomas Hoccleve)

MSS: Fairfax 16, Bodley 638, Tanner 346, Digby 181, Arch. Selden B 24, Univ. Libr. Cambr. Ff 1, 6, Trin. Coll. Cambr. R 3, 20; the "autograph" Hoccleve MS formerly belonging to Lord Ashburnham, and undergoing editing for the EETS by Gollancz; and a poor copy in the Bannatyne MS, printed by the Hunterian Club, 1879, p. 783. The poem was also once in Longleat 258, with a heading similar to that of the Oxford

MSS, see Ch. Soc. OT p. 251, Mod. Lang. Notes 20 : 77-79.

The four MSS first named above (the Oxford Group) show a marked disarrangement of stanzas by tens, indicating misplaced leaves in their common original; this is shared by Ff 1, 6 so far as that imperfect copy goes. Furnivall, printing the poem from Fairfax in vol. I of his EETS ed. of Hoccleve's Minor Poems, discovered this only in time to impose the "autograph Ashburnham" order upon the Fairfax text. Collations of the Ashburnham and Trin. Coll. MSS are printed *ibid.* 249-253. The first five MSS are described under Section IV (3) here, the Trinity in James as cited, the Ff in Section IV (5) above.

Prints and Editions: First printed by Thynne in the 1532 Chaucer; in the subsequent blackletter eds., in Urry, but not in the 1782 Bell nor in Anderson; in Chalmers under Poems Imputed to Chaucer, but not in any following edition. Printed from Fairfax 16, with some collation of other MSS, by Skeat, VII : 217. Printed from Urry by Arber in his English Garner, 1879 ff., and revised from this, "with the aid of the collations published by Professor Skeat", by A. W. Pollard, in Fifteenth Century Prose and Verse, Westminster, 1903. Printed from the Fairfax MS as above, and to be printed from the Ashburnham, by the EETS.

Modernizations and Translations: "The Proclamation of Cupid: or, a Defence of Women. A Poem from Chaucer [or rather imitated from T Occleve's Letter of Cupid] by Mr. Sewell." Lond. 1718, 20 pages. [Brit. Mus. Cat.]

Authenticity and Title: Headed in the Oxford Group MSS "Litera Cupidinis dei amoris directa subditis suis amatoribus"; in the Trinity MS "Nowe here filowing beginneþe a lytel traytis made and compyled by Thomas Occleue of þoffice of þe priue seel specifying þe maners and þe conuersacons beoþe of men and wymmen conuersantes in þis lytell yle of Albyone." Entitled from Thynne to Urry "The Letter of Cupid", Leland and Bale rendered this "Epistola Cupidinis."

Speght said, in the Life prefixed to his edition, that the poem was "none of Chaucer's doing", but was by Hoccleve; and also in the text he states, as heading, the fact of Hoccleve's authorship. Francis Thynne, in his Animadversions, thought that this and other poems ought to be separated from Chaucer's. Tyrwhitt, Account of the Works of Chaucer, again pointed out that the poem was not Chaucer's.

Source, Date, Notes: Translated, with adaptations, from Christine de Pisan's L'Epistre au Dieu d'Amours, printed in the ed. of Christine's works by Roy, Paris 1891; on pp. 243-248 of Furnivall's EETS ed. of Hoccleve's Minor Poems, vol. I, are printed extracts. On Christine see note below under Moral Proverbs. Her poem is dated in its last stanza 1399, which Hoccleve changes to 1402, thus fixing the date of his work.

See ten Brink, Hist. Eng. Lit. II : 216; Skeat VII : xl, 499-501; introd. to EETS edition.

LETTER OF DIDO TO AENEAS

MSS:

Prints and Editions: Printed by Pynson, in the 1526 Chaucer. The poem follows the Lamentation of Mary Magdalen, and the heading is: "Thus endeth the coplaynt of Mary Magdaleyn / and hereafter foloweth the letter of Dydo to Eneas: and fyrst the prologue of the translatour." This prologue is in nine stanzas of seven lines, beginning
"Folke disconforted / bere hevy countenaunce"
The letter itself is preceded by a woodcut, and consists of 242 lines in riming couplets, beginning
"Right (as ye swan) whan her dethe is nye"
Following it is "Lenvoy of the translatour", two seven-line stanzas beginning
"Ye good ladyes / whiche be of tender age"
The colophon is: "Thus endeth ye letter of Dydo to Eneas and here foloweth a lytell exortacion / howe folke shulde behave them selfe in all companyes" (=Lydgate's Utter thy Language, q. v.).

The style of this poem resembles that of Lydgate; his narrative of the death of Dido, Falls of Princes Book II, chap. 12 is, however, quite a different thing. He gives the story of Dido's killing herself rather than yield to the king "of Musitans"; the narrative is followed by an envoy of four seven-line stanzas, and this by a translator's envoy "direct to widows", of five stanzas. Near the close of the narrative itself Lydgate takes occasion to say that he is following Boccaccio, and not Ovid, and "the contrary I have set aside"; he censures the "large language" of those who found fault with Dido's conduct towards Aeneas.

"Maister Geffrey Chaucer", see Praise and Commendation of Geffrey Chaucer.

Maying and Disport of Chaucer, see Black Knight.

MERCILES BEAUTE

MS: Unique copy in Magd. Coll. Cambr. MS Pepys 2006. Printed by the Chaucer Society, MOT p. 51. MS described Mod. Lang. Notes 19 : 196-8.
Textual emendation suggested by Skeat, Mod. Quart. 2 : 38.

Prints and Editions: By Percy in his Reliques, see second edition, 1767, vol. 2, p. 11, as "An Original Ballad by Chaucer." Percy says in an introductory note, "This little sonnet, which hath escaped all the editors of Chaucer's works, is now printed for the first time from an ancient MS in the Pepysian library, that contains many other poems of its venerable author."

Not printed with the works of Chaucer until the Bell Chaucer of 1854, when the text was given from Percy, the title altered to "Roundel" as appropriate to the form of the poem. In Morris' revision of the Aldine Chaucer, 1866, from Percy, with title as in Bell. In Maetzner, Altenglische Sprachproben (1867) I : 347, text from Morris; entitled, 'Roundel.' Printed by Skeat, Minor Poems of Chaucer, p. 100 of 1896 edition, entitled Merciles Beaute; this title was previously used by Todd, in giving the contents of the Pepys MS, Illustrations, p. 116, and was assigned to the poem in Pepys' own table of contents of the MS. Printed by Skeat, Oxford Chaucer I : 387. Placed by the Globe Chaucer, p. 634, among the doubtful minor poems. Printed in Scribner's Mag. 1906, vol. 40, to face p. 350, as a decorated page; entitled "Chaucer's Roundel."

Authenticity: No mark in the MS. Ascribed by Bishop Percy to Chaucer, probably because of the markedly Chaucerian contents of the MS. Genuineness maintained by Skeat as cited, conceded somewhat doubtfully by Furnivall, MOT pp. 6, 51-52, by Koch, Chronology p. 40; Koch, Engl. Stud. 27 : 60, accepts the poem. Morley, Eng. Writers V : 271, says "undoubtedly Chaucer's."

Modernizations and Translations: About one-third of the poem is modernized by Purves (1870) under the title "Since I from Love." See Section III E here.

Date: Koch, Chronology p. 40, says "about the same time" as the Parl. of Foules, after the Troilus.

Mery Adventure of the Pardoner and the Tapster, *see under* Beryn above.

Moral Balade by Scogan, *see* Scogan unto the Lords, below.

MORAL PROVERBS OF CHRISTINE

MSS:

Prints and Editions: By Caxton in 1478, with an epilogue stating
that they were translated from the French by Earl Rivers; see
Blades p. 194, Dibdin I : 72 ff. In the Pynson Chaucer of 1526,
but not in any subsequent edition of Chaucer; see Lounsbury,
Studies I : 435-6.

Title: This poem is marked Moral Proverbes of Chaucer in the
1526 colophon of the article there preceding; the error reappears
in Ames, see Canon p. 160 footnote, where Skeat is unaware of
its origin; the preface to Urry gives the author correctly as
Christine, although Lounsbury, op. cit., gives the incorrect title,
and says that he obtains it from Urry.

Notes: On Christine de Pisan see Blades p. 195, pp. 336-8; Dibdin
as cited; Koch, Leben und Werke Christine de Pisan, Zeitschrift für Sprache und Litteratur 8 : 251. Works edited by
Roy, Paris 1886-96, 3 vols.; see proverbs in vol. III : 45 ff.

MOTHER OF GOD
(By Thomas Hoccleve)

MSS: Phillipps 8151 (a volume of the minor poems of Hoccleve),
Selden B 24, and Advocates' Library Edinburgh 18, 2, 8; the
two latter are Scottish texts. The three are printed Ch. Soc. PT
p. 137 ff.; Phillipps 8151 is also printed One-Text Print p. 101.
Notes on the MSS see Ross as below. See under Source for
note on an unknown text.

Prints and Editions: Printed from the Edinburgh MS by John
Leyden in the preliminary dissertation to his ed. of the Complaynt of Scotland, Edinburgh 1801, re-ed. EETS 1872. The
text of the Edinb. MS, collated with Leyden, was printed N.
and Q. 1855 II : 140; and this latter text was used in the Bell
Chaucer of 1854, the first ed. of Chaucer to include the poem.
Morris, in his revision of the Aldine Chaucer, 1866, printed the
Selden text of the poem, which he had discovered. Gilman also
printed the poem, using the Ch. Soc.'s texts above noted. After
the authorship of Hoccleve was ascertained (see below), Furnivall published the Phillipps text in vol. I of Hoccleve's Minor
Poems, EETS 1892, p. 52. It was not included in Mason's
print, 1796, of several of Hoccleve's poems; see Ross as below.

Authenticity and Title: Both Scottish MSS ascribe the poem to
Chaucer. The Edinburgh volume, which is a MS copy of John

de Irlandia's System of Theology, 1490, has the poem inserted, with a statement by Irlandia that it is by Chaucer, and the heading "Incipit Oratio Galfridi Chaucer." See Hist. MSS Comm. Report I, p. 125. The colophon in the Selden MS is "Explicit or*acio* Galfridi Chaucere." (Ross thinks that very likely Irlandia had the Selden MS to copy.) In the Phillipps MS the heading is "Ad beatam virginem", and the poem, with the rest of those in the MS, was listed by Ritson, Bibliographia Poetica 1802, as Hoccleve's; Bell heads it "Incipit Oratio Gelfridi Chauncer", and below "Orisoune to the Holy Virgin." Morris also uses the double title. The Chaucer Society takes the title "Moder of God" from the first line of the poem. The poem was included in the Society's list of genuine works (1869) in Trial Forewords p. 17, but was questioned by Koch, Anglia 3 : 183 (1880), and *ibid.* Anz. 4 : 101, 6 : 104. The Acad. 1880 II : 221 remarks on this doubt and the refusal of English scholars to entertain it. After the re-discovery of the Phillipps MS (see Ritson above) with the poem among the works of Hoccleve, Furnivall said, PT p. 137, "No one can suppose that poor Hoccleve had the power of writing his Master's Moder of God"; but upon seeing the volume himself, in 1882, Furnivall retracted his previous opinion, and considered the poem as Hoccleve's; see MOT pp. 6-7. Ten Brink, Hist. Eng. Lit. III : 272, was somewhat unwillingly convinced of Hoccleve's authorship. Lounsbury, Studies III : 25, does not consider Hoccleve's authorship as certain. The evidence is reviewed by Ross, Mod. Lang. Notes 6 : 385-389 (1891).

Date: See Furnivall's introd. to EETS ed. of Hoccleve as cited above, p. xxxix and passim.

Source: The Latin hymn O Intemerata which is the original of the last 6 stanzas is printed PT p. 138. It should be noted that the table of contents prefixed to MS Ashmole 59, but apparently belonging to some other Shirley MS (see Anglia 30 : 320 ff.), includes "An Invocacon of O Intemerata."

Notes: See Lounsbury, Studies I : 449-50, III : 25; ten Brink, Hist. Eng. Lit. II : 216.

MOTHER OF NURTURE

MSS: None known. (Canon p. 109.)

Prints and Editions: By Thynne in the 1532 Chaucer; in the subsequent blackletter editions, in Urry, in the 1782 Bell, in Anderson, in Chalmers, in Chiswick, but not in Moxon; in the 1845 Aldine, in the 1854 Bell, the revised Aldine. In Gilman relegated to the section Poems Attributed to Chaucer.
Printed by Skeat VII : 405, from Thynne.

Authenticity and Title: Thynne heads the poem "A goodlie Balade of Chaucer"; headed by Bale "Carmen Chaucer"; Thynne's title was used by subsequent editors, Skeat changing to "A Goodly Balade" and attributing the poem to Lydgate, VII : lxx, 539. The title here is given by me for clearness' sake, and is taken from the opening words of the poem.

Notes: See Skeat VII : lxx, Canon p. 109; Lounsbury, Studies I : 479.

NEWFANGLENESS

MSS: Fairfax 16, Cotton Cleopatra D vii, Harley 7578; described Section IV A (3) and (1) here.
The Cotton text is printed MOT flyleaf, with a denial of its authenticity by Furnivall, dated 1879.

Prints and Editions: First printed by Stow in the 1561 Chaucer; in the subsequent blackletter editions, in Urry, in the 1782 Bell, in Anderson; two copies in Chalmers, pp. 403 and 557; not in Chiswick, Moxon, the 1845 Aldine, the 1854 Bell, the revised Aldine, or Gilman.
Printed by Skeat, Minor Poems p. 199 (revised ed.), Oxford Chaucer I : 409. Not in the Kelmscott; the Globe includes it among the Doubtful Minor Poems.

Modernized by Clarke in his Riches of Chaucer.

Authenticity: No mark of authorship in the MSS; Stow heads the poem "A balade which Chaucer made agaynst women vnconstaunt." His source of information is unknown; and as Tyrwhitt in his Account of the Works of Chaucer did not exclude this poem from the sweeping condemnation which he passed upon Stow's "heap of rubbish", the editor of the Chiswick Chaucer, and those who followed him, did not reprint the poem.

Skeat, Minor Poems p. lxxvii, Oxford Chaucer I : 88, Canon
pp. 62-3 gives arguments for retaining the poem in the canon.
Koch, Chronology p. 41, favors its genuineness, somewhat
dubiously; in Engl. Stud. 27 : 60 he accepts it; Furnivall rejected
this, the Ballad of Complaint, and the Amorous Complaint, see
MOT p. 6; cp. also *ibid.*, flyleaf.

Title: Skeat follows Stow as above, and heads the poem "Against
Women Unconstant"; Furnivall, in the Chaucer Society prints,
calls it "Newfangelnesse", a name approved by Koch, Chronology p. 40. The MSS have no title, except that Fairfax marks
it "Balade."

Date: Koch, Chronology p. 42, dates it about 1380-4, along with
Merciles Beaute and To Rosemounde.

Source: See Skeat I : 88.

NINE LADIES WORTHY

MSS: Trin. Coll. Cambr. R 3, 19; described in James as cited.

Prints and Editions: By Stow in the 1561 Chaucer, probably from
the Trinity MS; in the subsequent blackletter eds., in Urry, in
the 1782 Bell, in Anderson, in Chalmers among the additions
of Stow; not in later eds. of Chaucer.

Authenticity and Title: Rejected by Tyrwhitt, Account of the
Works of Chaucer. Headed by Stow and subsequent editors
"The ix Ladies worthie."

Notes: See Skeat VII : xii, Canon p. 122.

OF THEIR NATURE

MSS: Trin. Coll. Cambr. R 3, 19; described in James as cited.

Prints and Editions: By Stow in the 1561 Chaucer, probably from
the Trinity MS; in the subsequent blackletter eds., in Urry, in
the 1782 Bell, in Anderson, in Chalmers among the poems added
by Stow; not in later eds. of Chaucer.

Modernized by Clarke in his Riches of Chaucer.

Authenticity and Title: Rejected by Tyrwhitt, Account of the
Works of Chaucer. Headed by Stow and later eds. "A Balade."

Notes: See Skeat VII : xii, Canon p. 122.

O Merciful

MSS: Trin. Coll. Cambr. R 3, 19; described in James as cited.

Prints and Editions: By Stow in the 1561 Chaucer, probably from
the Trinity MS; in the subsequent blackletter eds., in Urry, in
the 1782 Bell, in Anderson, in Chalmers among the additions of
Stow; not in later eds. of Chaucer.

Authenticity and Title: Rejected by Tyrwhitt, Account of the
Works of Chaucer. Headed by Stow and later eds. "A Ballade."

Notes: On the composite character of the poem see Tyrwhitt as
cited. See Skeat VII : xiii, Canon p. 123.

O Mossie Quince

MSS: Trin. Coll. Cambr. R 3, 19; described in James as cited.

Prints and Editions: By Stow in the 1561 Chaucer; in the Speghts,
in Urry, in the 1782 Bell, in Anderson, in Chalmers among the
additions made by Stow; not in later editions.

Authenticity and Title: At the end of the life of Chaucer prefixed
to the Urry ed. this poem is rejected; rejected by Tyrwhitt as
cited above. Headed by Stow and later eds. "An other Balade."

Notes: Stow and all later editors omit the second stanza of the
poem as contained in the Trinity MS; see Skeat, Canon p. 124,
p. 118.

————

Ora pro Anglia Sancta Maria quod Thomas Cantuaria: This line
appears above four brief verses which in the Chiswick, Bell,
and Aldine Chaucers are appended to Prophecy, q. v. Skeat,
Canon p. 115-16, says that the Aldine, etc., took their version of
Prophecy from a MS whose copy he prints *ibid.;* but he does
not print the four brief lines, only the line of heading or of
colophon as cited above. Purves (1870) prints the lines with
the Prophecy, see under III E here.

Oft Desired Bliss, *see* Fairest of Fair.

Oratio Galfridi Chaucer, *see* Mother of God.

Orisoune to the Holy Virgin, *see* Mother of God.

PILGRIM'S TALE

MSS: None known.

Prints and Editions: Only one fragment of the Pilgrim's Tale exists, a print in the Douce collection of the Bodleian Library. This fragment contained also the Courte of Venus, and of the Courte of Venus another fragment exists, among the books of Mr. Christie Miller at Britwell, Burnham, Buckinghamshire. Furnivall has reprinted the Pilgrim's Tale from the Douce fragment in his ed. of Francis Thynne's Animadversions for the Ch. Soc. as Appendix I, pp. 77 ff., and has discussed on pp. 138 ff. *ibid.* the Courte of Venus belonging to Mr. Christie Miller.

On the Courte of Venus see also Charlotte C. Stopes in Athen. 1899 I : 784-6, II : 38. In the latter note Sir Thomas Wyat the elder's authorship is suggested.

Authenticity: Francis Thynne, in his Animadversions, states that his father, editor of the 1532 Chaucer, prepared a printed book of Chaucer's works with one column on a side, in which was a tale called the Pilgrim's Tale; he gives the opening lines; see citation from the 1602 Speght, Section II D here, and the Animadversions, p. 12 of Todd's ed., p. 8 of Furnivall's ed. As Francis Thynne was but an infant at the time of his father's death, and as no edition of Chaucer containing the Pilgrim's Tale has ever been heard of, this story is generally disbelieved; see Bradshaw's presentation of the arguments against it in Furnivall's ed. of the Animadversions, pp. 75-76. Bradshaw, writing after the discovery of the Douce fragment of the Courte of Venus, in which the colophon is "And here follows the pilgrimes tale", thinks that "the one-column edition of Chaucer with the Pilgrim's Tale can only mean the quarto *Courte of Venus*, &c., printed between 1536 and 1540, which Bale saw." Bale, as may be seen, Section II A here, added to the list of Chaucer's works "De curia Veneris", giving its first line as "In Maio cum virescerent." The Britwell copy of the Courte of Venus begins:

> In the moneth of May, when the new tender grene
> Hath smothely couered the ground that was bare

Furnivall, loc. cit. p. xliii, is inclined to demur to Bradshaw's positive denial of Thynne's story. See Stopes as above.

Date: Tyrwhitt, Appendix to Preface, note e, pointed out that the allusion in the Pilgrim's Tale to Chaucer's Romaunt of the Rose, worded as if to a printed copy, must refer to the 1532

Chaucer, in which the Romaunt was first printed as Chaucer's; and that allusion must then have been written later than 1532. To this Lounsbury added (Studies I : 465) that in the 1532 Chaucer the lines cited by the Pilgrim's Tale are found in the place indicated by that Tale, viz., on the second page of the third leaf from the end. Also, the political references, as Tyrwhitt pointed out, mark a date after 1536.

Notes: The Advertisement to the Speght Chaucer of 1687 expressed the editor's regret at his inability to discover a copy of this Tale; see under Section II D here.

See Lounsbury, Studies I : 462 ff.

Pious Lines, *see* Leaulte vault Richesse.

Plowman's Tale

Two pieces of work bear this title. One is of unknown authorship, and was first printed with the works of Chaucer in the 1542 Thynne; the other is by Hoccleve, and is thus far known in two MS copies. Hoccleve's stanzaic poem exists in the Christ Church MS of the Canterbury Tales, and in the Ashburnham MS of Hoccleve's minor poems now editing for the EETS by I. Gollancz. It is printed from these two MSS, with a brief introduction, as

A New Ploughman's Tale. Thomas Hoccleve's Legend of the Virgin and her Sleeveless Garment, with a spurious Link. Ed. by A. Beatty for the Chaucer Society, 1902.

The Link, existing in MS Christ Church alone, is meant to connect the poem into the Canterbury Tales. See description of this MS in Section III B (4) ante.

Of the Plowman's Tale printed in 1542 as Chaucer's no MS is as yet known. Previous to 1542 the poem had been printed by Godfray, folio, *n. d.*, but "about 1532-5"—see Skeat, Canon p. 99 footnote; only one copy of this is known. It was again printed, by Powell, about 1547-8. Todd, in the introd. to his Illustrations, p. xxxix note, mentions "a very curious edition, hitherto unnoticed, of the poem falsely attributed to Chaucer. It is of the duodecimo size, in the black letter, without date, and imprinted at London in Paules churche yarde at the sygne of the Hyll by Wyllyam Hyll. . . The colophon of this book is, *Thus endeth the boke of Chaunterburye Tales.* This rarity belongs to the Rev. Mr. Conybeare, the present Professor of the Saxon language in the University of Oxford." Observe that Bale, in the notes printed in his *Index* ed. R. L. Poole,

p. 75, gives separately from the rest of Chaucer's works—"De
Meliboeo ac Thopa" and "Narrationem Agricole"—as "ex officina
Guilhelmi Hylle." From the colophon to Hill's print as cited by
Todd we may infer that Hill issued a part at least of the Tales
in duodecimo, copying even the colophon of the edition from which
he selected, and which was possibly that of 1542; for Hill's dated
works are of 1548-9, and it is only in the 1542 Chaucer that this
Tale stands last.

In the preface to the 1721 Urry, Thomas says that the description
of the Plowman and his Tale were "printed in 1606 in 4to with
notes which are thought by some to be Mr. Francis Thynne's." A
bookseller's catalogue of 1905 has this entry: The Ploughmans
Tale. Shewing by the doctrine and lives of the Romish Clergie
that the Pope is Antichrist and they his ministers; written by Sir
Geffrey Chaucer amongst his Canterburie Tales, and now set out
apart, with a short exposition of the words and matters, for the
capacitie and understanding of the simpler sort of readers. 4to.
1606. For Samuel Macham and Matthew Cooke. [Priced by the
dealer at £7, 10 shil.] The Brit. Mus. Cat. says "rather perhaps by
T. Brampton." See Corser, Collectanea IV : 330.

In the Thynne Chaucer of 1542 the tale of the Plowman was
appended after that of the Parson; the undated later ed. inserted
the Plowman in front of the Parson, and this procedure was imitated
by Stow, Speght, and Urry, although Francis Thynne, in his
Animadversions, censured the arrangement; see ed. by Furnivall
p. 69, ed. by Todd p. 77. Later eds. are noted just below.

Authenticity: Speght, in the Argument of this tale in his 1598
Chaucer, says: "A complaint against the pride and couetous-
ness of the cleargie: made no doubt by Chaucer with the rest
of the Tales. For I haue seene it in writen hand in Iohn
Stowes library in a booke of suche antiquity, as seemeth to
haue beene written neare to Chaucers time." (Nothing is
known of this MS.) The authenticity of the work was first
doubted by Dart in the life of Chaucer prefixed to the Urry
Chaucer of 1721, also in his Westmonasterium. But the tale
was regularly alluded to as Chaucer's—see Lounsbury, Studies
I : 469-473—until Tyrwhitt rejected it from the canon. The
Bell of 1782, Anderson, and Chalmers, printed the Tale, relegating it however to a position among the less certain works;
but Cowden Clarke, in 1835, still defended the Chaucerian
authorship. The tale was not printed again with the works
of Chaucer; it is printed by Wright, Polit. Poems I : 304, from
Speght, and by Skeat VII : 147 from the 1542 text. Skeat
attributes the poem to the author of Pierce the Ploughman's
Crede, but see Lounsbury, Studies I : 460-461 note. Thynne, in
his Animadversions, ed. Furnivall p. 10, says that this Tale was

wrongly supposed to be by "old Sir Thomas Wyat"; see Brit. Mus. Cat. above cited. And see under Pilgrim's Tale ante.

Date: Perhaps later than October 1396, says Skeat VII : xxxiv footnote. Bradley, Athen. 1902 II : 62, considers that a Lollard piece of the fourteenth century was much expanded during the sixteenth to its present form.

Notes: See Hearne's Letter to Bagford, pp. 605-6; see Todd, Illustrations, introd. p. xxxix; see N. and Q. 1873 I : 280; see Skeat VII : xxxi-xxxv, 484 ff.

POEMS SUPPOSED TO BE WRITTEN BY CHAUCER DURING HIS IMPRISONMENT

This title was given by Todd to two poems found at the beginning of the Ellesmere MS of the Canterbury Tales, on two leaves before the Prologue, and written in a hand coeval, though not the same as that of the CT, according to Todd, Illustrations p. 295. Todd there prints the poems, which he considered to be by Chaucer; for comment on his opinion see p. 380 here.

The first of these poems begins "Halfe in dede sclepe, not fully revyved"; its resemblance to the opening of La Belle Dame sans Mercy should be noted. The second poem begins "All thyng ys ordaynyd by Goddys provysyon"; it is written in compliment to Vere, probably the Earl of Oxford. At the close is written Amen per Rotheley; Todd considers that Rotheley was the scribe; Nicolas, in his life of Chaucer, note 81, says that it is nearly certain that this poem was written by Rotheley, and not by Chaucer.

The belief in Chaucer's "imprisonment" arose from the attribution of the Testament of Love to him, see Lounsbury, Studies I : 189 ff., and his remarks on the poems *ibid.* I : 454-5.

Praise of Peace, *see* John Gower unto . . . . Henry the Fourth.

PRAISE AND COMMENDATION OF GEFFREY CHAUCER

MSS: Copied at the close of the Parlement of Foules in MSS Harley 7333 and R 3, 19; the former is described Section IV A (1) here, the latter in James as cited.

Prints and Editions: By Stow in the 1561 Chaucer; in the Speghts, in Urry; not in the 1782 Bell nor in Anderson; printed by Chalmers among the Poems Imputed to Chaucer. Not again printed with Chaucer's works. In Skeat VII : 450, from the Trinity MS.

PRAISE OF WOMEN

MSS: Skeat, Canon p. 111, says the only MS copy is the Bannatyne. This MS is printed by the Hunterian Club; the poem is on p. 799.

Prints and Editions: By Thynne in 1532; in the succeeding black-letter editions, in Urry, in the 1782 Bell, in Anderson, in Chalmers, in the Chiswick despite Tyrwhitt's verdict; not in the Moxon, but in the 1845 Aldine, which went to the Chiswick for its texts; included in the revised Aldine; printed by the 1854 Bell and by Gilman among the poems attributed to Chaucer. Not printed by Skeat VII; by the Hunterian Club as above.

Authenticity and Title: Rejected from the canon by Tyrwhitt, Account of the Works of Chaucer. Entitled by Thynne, "A Preyse of Women"; this was rendered by Leland and Bale "Encomium mulierum", "Foeminarum encomion." Skeat, loc. cit., says the poem is probably by Lydgate.

Modernizations: By Cowden Clarke in his Riches of Chaucer.

Notes:

PROPHECY

MSS: Ashmole 59 (Shirley) has 4 couplets headed "Profecia Merlini"; the cataloguer of the Ashmole MSS remarks that this is perhaps the correct form. In Ashmole 781 is a copy of 3 couplets, written between 1620 and 1631, according to the catalogue. In R 3, 15 of Trin. Coll. Cambr. are entered, before the XV century copy of the Canterbury Tales, this Prophecy and the three other bits printed by Thynne at the end of his table of contents, all in a hand of the XVI century, according to James. These bits were described, with the MS, by Todd, Illustrations pp. 119-20. See Dibdin, Typogr. Antiq. I : 311. In Brydges' Restituta II : 200 is described a copy as "on the flyleaf of a missal illuminated on vellum"; dated on verso "M CCC xlxxj." Skeat, Canon p. 115, gives a variation on an odd detached flyleaf of a MS lent him; and on p. 116 he says that the Aldine edition's copy is from the same flyleaf; also that there is another version in MS Trin. Coll. Dublin E, 5, 10. Dibdin II : 514 mentions a copy on a spare leaf of a book in Herbert's library; he gives the text in a note; it is apparently from a print, as it is marked "Geffrey Chaucer cum privilegio ad imprimend. solum."

Prints and Editions: By Caxton, see Trial Forewords p. 118, Blades p. 212; in the Thynne Chaucer of 1532 inserted, with three other bits, at the end of the table of contents. Reprinted by Stow, Speght, Urry, and the 1782 Bell in similar position; not in Anderson or Chalmers; reappears in the Chiswick, at the end of the edition, from MS, with a note by Singer stating where he found it. Not in Moxon, but in the Aldine from Chiswick, see note on the Aldine ed. here. In the 1854 Bell, in which the other three bits first put together by Thynne are printed at the end of vol. 8 as Poems Attributed to Chaucer. In Gilman. Printed by Skeat I : 46, VII : 450 from Caxton; and he also prints the Ashmole version in Athen. 1896 II : 874, Oxford Chaucer VII : lxxxi; as stated above, another variation is printed Canon 115-16. Printed by Dibdin II : 514-15 from MS, and I : 311 from Caxton.

Authenticity: Not discussed by Tyrwhitt. Caxton did not ascribe the lines to Chaucer, and their inclusion in editions of Chaucer is due to Thynne, though he does not directly say that the short poems at the end of his table of contents are by Chaucer. Note that Shirley's copy is headed "Profecia Merlini"; there was no heading in the prints until Urry, in 1721, entitled it Chaucers Prophecie, noting that he took his authority from MS Ashmole 781.

Notes: Lounsbury, Studies I : 435. See the incorrect note on this "Prophecy" in the "First Folio" ed. of King Lear by Porter and Clarke (New York 1906), Act III, Scene ii, lines 83-6. The "Prophecy" is quoted in Puttenham's Arte of English Poesie, 1589.

PROSPERITY
(By John Walton)

MSS: Selden B 24, described Section IV A (3) here. Also copied in Harley 2251 as if the last stanza of Lydgate's Wicked Tongue; my note in Anglia 28 : 21 should be emended to recognize this, and to read 19 stanzas instead of 20 in the poem.

Prints and Editions: By Morris in the revised Aldine, 1866 etc.; in Skeat VII : 449.

Authenticity:—Marked in the MS, after the stanza, "Qd Chaucere." It was pointed out by Liddell, Athenaeum 1895 II : 902, that this stanza is from Walton's translation of Boethius; see Brown's ed. of the Kingis Quair p. 71, and Skeat VII : lxxxi, though in the Canon p. 147 Skeat does not give Liddell the credit, and in I : 48 had suggested King James I as author.

Notes: On John Walton see Warton-Hazlitt III : 39-40; Athenaeum 1892 I : 565, 600; 1895 II : 902. Liddell is to edit Walton's
translation of Boethius for the EETS. Some of the MSS containing this translation are Balliol Coll. Oxford 316 A, Bodl.
Rawl. 151 (imperfect), Trinity Coll. Oxford 75, Brit. Mus.
Royal 18 A xiii, Harley 44, Sloane 554, Univ. Lib. Cambr. Gg
iv, 18; copies are at Cheltenham (Phillips 1099), and Copenhagen. There is an extract from the prologue in Blades'
Caxton II : 68 (quarto ed.), and in Skeat II : xvii-xviii; see bits
in Wülker's Altengl. Lesebuch II : 56, and a fragment in Todd
p. xxxii; selections from the work are to be included in vol. 18,
section II, of the Belles Lettres Series, Boston.

In one MS of the translation which I have examined, the
Royal, this stanza is marked in the margin, "nota per exemplum", a fact which may explain its inclusion in the commonplace book of a later scribe.

PROVERBS

MSS: Adds. 16165 (Shirley), Harley 7578, Fairfax 16; printed
Ch. Soc. PT p. 431. The Adds. text is also in One-Text Print
p. 309. For descriptions of the MSS see Section IV A (1)
and (3) here.

Prints and Editions: By Stow in the 1561 Chaucer; in the subsequent eds. of the Works. There are two copies in Chalmers,
p. 403, p. 557.

Bell, in the 1854 Chaucer, vol. 8, p. 149, prints continuous
with the 8 lines of the Proverbs two seven-line stanzas found in
MSS Fairfax and Harley just after the Proverbs; these were
also included in the Aldine Chaucer, and are discussed Anglia
28 : 4, where other MSS and prints of these stanzas are mentioned. See Skeat, Canon pp. 145-6.

Modernizations and Translations: Mod. by Purves in 1870; see
under III E above.

Authenticity and Title: Shirley does not mark the poem as by
Chaucer; he heads it Prouerbe; Fairfax and Harley head it
Proverbe of Chaucer, Prouerbe of Chaucers. Stow marked it
Prouerbe against couetise and negligence; he was followed by
later eds. until Bell, 1854, who marked it Proverbes of Chaucer,
the revised Aldine doing the same. Skeat and the Globe
Chaucer entitle it Proverbs, Proverbe of Chaucer. Bradshaw
doubted the Chaucerian authorship of the lines, see Temp. Pref.
pp. 107-8. Koch, Chronology p. 78, Engl. Stud. 27 : 60, also
doubts. Skeat, Canon p. 145, says that they are genuine. The
lack of marking by Shirley and the opinion of Bradshaw have
led me to include the lines in this Section.

Date and Source: Furnivall, Athen. 1871 II : 495, dated the lines
about 1386-7; he remarked that a part of them corresponded to
a line in Melibeus. See Trial Forew. p. 17 note; Skeat I : 88,
564.

Notes: See as above; Morley, Eng. Writers V : 275; Root, Poetry
of Chaucer p. 78.

Quatuor infatuant, *see* Sayings of Dan John, above.

REMEDY OF LOVE

MSS: None known, see Skeat, Canon p. 113.

Prints and Editions: By Thynne in 1532; in the subsequent blackletter editions, in Urry, in the 1782 Bell, in Anderson, in
Chalmers. Not in Chiswick or in later editions of the Works.

Authenticity: Rejected from the canon by Tyrwhitt, Account of
the Works; see his glossary under *Cokewold*.
    Entitled by Leland and Bale "De Remedio Amoris."

Notes:

ROMAUNT OF THE ROSE

MSS: Unique copy in the Hunterian Museum, Glasgow, marked
V, 3, 7; described by Skeat I : 13; see *ibid*. p. 12 for note on
displacement of leaves in the MS; Skeat is however wrong in
claiming to be the first who observed this, as it was remarked
by Tyrwhitt at the close of his Notes on the Cant. Tales, and
corrected by the Bell of 1782. See Notes and Queries 1804
I : 446.

Prints and Editions: First printed in Thynne's 1532 Chaucer; in
the subsequent blackletter editions, in Urry, and in all editions
of the Works to date. Also in The Romaunt of the Rose,
Troilus and Cressida, and the Minor Poems, with life by Sir
Harris Nicolas, London, 1846. Edited by Kaluza for the
Chaucer Society, as follows:
    The Romaunt of the Rose, from the unique Glasgow MS,
parallel with its original, Le Roman de la Rose. Part I. The
Texts. 1891.
    The French original is mainly from Michel's edition of 1864,

collated with several MSS. Not a critical text, but an attempt at restoring the text that was in the hands of the Englisher or Englishers. Noticed briefly Nation 1893 II : 47.

Lines 2721-2966 are included in Maetzner's Altengl. Sprachproben, from Morris' text of 1866.

Modernizations and Translations: Extracts are in vol. II of Clarke's Riches of Chaucer.

Authenticity: This poem was long accepted and included in eds. of Chaucer, on the strength of Chaucer's own statement, in the prol. to the Legend of Good Women, that he had translated the Romaunt of the Rose. The single existing copy of such a translation in Middle English was accordingly treated as Chaucer's, although the MS, which lacks the first leaf, does not bear his name, and although, as Skeat has pointed out in Ch. Soc. Essays part V, there may be, and often are, several medieval versions or translations of the same earlier work.

Ten Brink, Jahrbuch 8 : 306 (1867), discussed the incompleteness of the existing text, which he attributed to scribal carelessness. The list of works rejected by Bradshaw from the canon, printed Temp. Pref. pp. 107-8, includes the Romaunt; this was pubd. in 1868. Bradshaw, see Prothero's Memoir p. 353, wrote to ten Brink in 1870 that we have no authority whatever for considering the existing version as Chaucer's, and that the onus probandi lies with those who maintain Chaucerian authorship. In the Athen. for 1870 II : 721, Professor Child pointed out the break in treatment at about line 5814, and expressed his opinion that this indicated different handling, "perhaps a different version."

Skeat, N. and Q. 1874 I : 185, cast doubt on the authenticity of the Romaunt, and in his revision of Bell's Chaucer, 1878, relegated this and other poems of dubious authenticity to a volume by themselves. For this he was commended by Furnivall, Acad. 1878 I : 365, but some protest was made, see ibid. I : 489, 512, II : 66, 143.

In his Trial Forewords, 1871, p. 7, Furnivall had remarked that ten Brink "is now inclined to give up" his position, i. e., that of regarding the Romaunt as Chaucer's. In Anglia 1 : 533 (1878) ten Brink declared that he no longer considered the Romaunt genuine; in his Chaucers Sprache und Verskunst, 1884, he accordingly did not include the work in the discussion, and in his Hist. Eng. Lit. II : 77 he asserted that the Glasgow fragment was not the translation by Chaucer, which was unfortunately lost to us. In his last published utterance, Engl. Stud. 17 : 9, ten Brink repeated this.

Skeat, in Ch. Soc. Essays part V, and in his third ed. of the Prioress' Tale, 1880, continued to argue against Chaucer's authorship. One of his arguments, based upon vocabulary, was attacked by Cook, Mod. Lang. Notes 1887, pp. 285-291. Furnivall, in an appendix "On the Genuineness of the Romaunt of the Rose", added to the second ed. of Morris' Aldine Chaucer, 1870, said that he was "not prepared to give up the Romaunt without a fight." In 1886 Fick, Engl. Stud. 9 : 161, appeared as the defender of Chaucer's authorship; see Skeat and Fick *ibid.* p. 506. Lindner, Engl. Stud. 11 : 163-173 (1887), elaborated what Child had already suggested, that the handling of the poem before and after line 5814 is different. The discussion was now taken up on that point, the two parts being termed A and B. Skeat, Acad. 1888 II : 153, declared that Chaucer could not have written part A; and in the introd. to his first ed. of the Minor Poems, 1888, he opined that Chaucer might have written part B.

In 1888 Kaluza undertook the editing of the unique MS of the Romaunt for the Chaucer Society; and he soon recognized a division into three parts instead of two, on the basis of the different treatment of the French original. Furnivall and Kaluza reported this conclusion in Acad. 1890 II : 11; Skeat *ibid.* p. 51 thought it possible that Chaucer had written fragment A, by which is now meant lines 1704-5. In the same journal 1891 II : 137 Skeat added line 1705 to fragment "A"; and definitely accepted fragment A as Chaucer's, a position which he has since maintained.

Kaluza's book on the subject, Chaucer und der Rosenroman, Berlin 1893, was reviewed: Anglia Beibl. 1893, p. 337 (Wülker); Engl. Stud. 18 : 104 (Lindner); both think that Kaluza has proved his point; Logeman, Museum 2 : 97, Schick, DLZ 1893 pp. 680-684, give Kaluza high praise. Kaluza maintains not only the division of the poem into three parts, but also the possibility of Chaucer's having written part C as well as part A. Skeat does not accept this second thesis. Schick, in the review just cited, and Sieper, Les Echecs Amoureux p. 244, note that Lydgate uses only the first 1700 lines of the Romaunt, from which they infer that Chaucer's transl. went no further. Cp. Skeat in Athen. 1896 I : 747. Note the remark, Nation 1900 I : 443, that it is but natural to suppose that the work as it stands is an attempt to combine A and C by filling the gap.

A second theory with regard to the poem is that of Koch, Chronology pp. 7-15, restated Engl. Stud. 27 : 61-73, 227-234, 30 : 450-456. Koch denies Chaucer's authorship of any part of the poem. In his Canon of 1900 Skeat devoted a chapter to

Koch's arguments as stated Engl. Stud. 27. Kaluza, reviewing the Canon, DLZ 1901 pp. 863 ff., decided in favor of Skeat, to which Koch replied Engl. Stud. 30, in his review of the Canon.

Luick, Untersuchungen zur engl. Lautgeschichte, 1896 pp. 268 ff., considers that the rime *love: behove* in lines 1091-2 renders the authorship of fragment A doubtful; he is opposed by Kaluza, Engl. Stud. 23 : 336.

The third theory as to the authenticity of the poem is that of Lounsbury, who in his Studies Vol. II chap. 1 asserts Chaucer's execution of the entire translation. Lounsbury has been very generally criticised for this, see Skeat, Acad. 1892 I : 206, 230, Kittredge on the authorship of the Romaunt in Harvard Studies I : 1 ff. (1892). Kittredge in closing says that the Romaunt is not Chaucer's with the possible exception of the first 1700 lines. The same criticism and conclusion were stated in the review of Lounsbury, Nation 1892 I : 214, 231. Lounsbury, N. Y. Tribune May 6, 1894, refused to consider himself defeated; see the Manchester (Eng.) Guardian of Feb. 27, March 5, March 7, April 18, 1894, and Lounsbury in N. Y. Tribune of Feb. 24 and March 3, 1895. See Kaluza in Engl. Stud. 20 : 338; Skeat in Ch. Soc. Essays part VI.

The only published attempt to support Lounsbury's view of the Romaunt is that of Louise Pound, Mod. Lang. Notes 11 : 193-204 (1896), in which data regarding sentence-length are adduced as evidence.

[Miss Pound no longer maintains the thesis of this paper.]

Lindner, in Engl. Stud. 11 : 172, suggested that the writer of the Testament of Love was one of the translators of the Romaunt. In the Athen. 1899 II : 66, 129, Skeat began discussion of the possible translator, and suggested King James I of Scotland as the author of fragment B; this theory he elaborated in his Canon as cited. J. H. Lange, Engl. Stud. 29 : 397, cp. *ibid.* 31 : 159-162, argued that the writer of fragment B was John Lydgate. Koch, Engl. Stud. 27 : 61-73, 227-234, would consider Lydgate the translator of fragment A also.

A. D. Schoch, The Differences in the Middle English Romaunt of the Rose and their Bearing upon Chaucer's Authorship (Mod. Phil. 3 : 339-358), recapitulates the evidence and emphasizes the unlikelihood of any settlement of the question without further external evidence.

Title: In the MS, which is defective at beginning, there is no mark; mentioned in the Legend of Good Women, prol., line 329, as "Thow hast translated the Romaunt of the Rose"; termed by Leland and Bale, De Arte Amandi; entitled in the black-letter and in subsequent eds., The Romaunt of the Rose.

Date:

Notes: On the French Roman de la Rose see in Section II D (2) above.

Axel Klint's paper on Chaucer's translation of the Roman de la Rose, 25 pp., no place or date, is rev. Lindner, Engl. Stud. 4 : 340 (1881) as "durchaus oberflächlich." A paper by Koeppel on Chaucer's Romaunt of the Rose and Sackville's Induction, is in Archiv 101 : 145. The careless notes of Courthope, Hist. Eng. Poetry I : 252, are censured by Kaluza, Engl. Stud. 22 : 276, and see Reference List here also, s. v. Courthope.

See: Godwin, chaps. 24, 25, 26; Warton-Hazlitt II : 317-327; ten Brink, Studien pp. 14-32, Hist. Eng. Lit. II : 77-78; Sandras, Étude pp. 31-40; Morley, Eng. Writers V : 116-123; Lounsbury, Studies II, chap. 1; Root, Poetry of Chaucer pp. 45-56; Cipriani in Publ. Mod. Lang. Assn. 22 : 552-595.

To My Sovereign Lady, see Ballad in Commendation of Our Lady.

SAYINGS OF DAN JOHN
(By John Lydgate)

MSS: These two seven-line stanzas exist in MS in the codex Trin. Coll. Cambr. R 3, 20, p. 8, a volume in the hand of Shirley. Skeat knew of no MS copy, Canon p. 117. On the MS see James as cited.

Prints and Editions: By Stow in the 1561 Chaucer; as the Cambridge codex was for some time in his possession, while he made from it the numerous copies preserved in Brit. Mus. Adds. 29729 (see Anglia 28 : 13), it is probable that this MS is the direct source of the print. Reprinted in the subsequent blackletter editions, in Urry, in the 1782 Bell, in Anderson, in Chalmers under the heading of Poems Imputed to Chaucer; not in later editions.
    Printed by Skeat VII : 297, from Stow.

Authenticity: Tyrwhitt, Account of the Works of Chaucer, pointed out that these bits were by Lydgate.

Title: Headed by Shirley in the MS, "A seying of daun Johan", and "Yit of þe same."

Notes: See Skeat VII : 1-li and Canon p. 117. Each of the two stanzas is perhaps a rewriting of that which I have termed "Quatuor infatuant", and which begins "Worship wymmen wyne vnweldy age;" see Anglia 28 : 4, 21; see Skeat, Canon p. 124; see Anglia 30 : 331.

SCOGAN UNTO THE LORDS AND GENTLEMEN OF THE KING'S HOUSE

(By Henry Scogan)

MSS: Ashmole 59, printed PT pp. 427, 430; MS described Anglia 30 : 320-348. In Harley 2251, see description of MS in Anglia 28 : 1 ff.

Prints and Editions: In Thynne of 1532; in the subsequent black-letter editions; in Urry; in the 1782 Bell, where it is relegated to the end of the collection; not in Anderson; printed by Chalmers among the Poems Imputed to Chaucer; not in Chiswick, Moxon, or any subsequent edition of Chaucer.

Printed by Caxton, see Blades p. 202. Printed by Skeat VII : 237 ff., from the 1542 Thynne.

Authenticity: The poem was perhaps printed by Thynne because of its citation of Chaucer's Gentilesse; since Urry it has been regarded as non-Chaucerian, which its title makes clear.

Title: Shirley, in MS Ashmole 59, marks the poem "Here foloweþe nexst a moral balade. to my lord þe Prince. to my lord of Clarence / to my lord of Bedford and to my lord of Gloucestre. by Henry Scogan. at a souper of feorþe merchande in þe vyntre in london. at þe hous of Lowys Iohan."

For note by Kittredge on Lewis Johan see Publ. Mod. Lang. Assn. 16 : 450-52 (1901).

Date and Notes: Skeat VII : xli-xliii, 502-3, I : 83. Skeat conjectures 1407 as date, see VII : xlii.

SINCE I FROM LOVE

Under this title Purves (1870) modernized the third portion of the roundel Merciless Beaute, see above.

STORY OF THEBES, OR, SIEGE OF THEBES

(By John Lydgate)

MSS: Arundel 119, Adds. 5140, Adds. 18632, Royal 18 D ii, Cotton Appendix 27; for notes on which see Ward's Catalogue of Romances I : 87-91; and see Ch. Soc. Life-Records pt. IV p. 152 note for comment upon Adds. 18632, a MS carrying on its fly-leaves the earliest record of Chaucer's connection with the English court. MSS Trinity College Cambridge R 4, 20 and O 5, 2, see James' catalogue as cited. MSS Bodley 776, Laud 416, Laud 557, Digby 230, Rawlinson C 48. MSS Mostyn 258, Longleat 257, see Hist. Comm. MSS Reports, IV : 361, III : 189, VI : 360; description of the Longleat MS and of Egerton 2864 (formerly Ingilby) under Section III B (7) and (1) above. Also in a Gurney MS, see Hist. MSS Comm. vol. XII, Appendix 9, p. 164. . . . A fragment is in the MS Christ Church Oxford 152 (of the Cant. Tales), see Section III B (4) here.

Of these MSS, the Adds. 5140, the Egerton, and the Christ Church contain the Canterbury Tales; Longleat 257 contains two of the Tales.

Also in Lambeth Palace Library MS 742; in a MS of the Tixall Library sold by Sotheby Nov. 6, 1899 (see Archiv 104 : 361). This last is probably identical with the "Story of Oedipus" recorded in the Zeitschr. f. Bücherfreunde III : 2 : 405 as sold at the Tixall sale; for Pits' confusion of titles (see Section II A here) shows that the poem might bear other names. Copied by Stow in Adds. 29729, perhaps from Laud 557, which once belonged to him; he first printed the poem with the works of Chaucer, though expressly assigning it to Lydgate. Bernard's Catalogus of 1697 also mentions a copy among the Denbigh MSS, one among the Pepys MSS, and one at Coventry School; the last-named MS has now disappeared.

Prints and Editions: By Wynken de Worde, n. d. quarto. First printed with the works of Chaucer by Stow, in the 1561 Chaucer; in the subsequent blackletter editions; in Urry; not in Anderson; in Chalmers with the poems added by Stow; not since printed with the works of Chaucer. The prologue was reprinted, from the 1561 text, by Wülker in his Altenglisches Lesebuch, 1879, II : 105 ff. An edition by Dr. Erdmann is long announced by the Early English Text Society. The prologue is to be printed in vol. 18 of Section II of the Belles Lettres Series, Boston.

Modernized in prose by Darton, see under III E here.

Notes: Discussed by the poet Gray, see Gosse's ed. of his Works, 1890, I : 387 ff.; see Warton-Hazlitt, III : 74 ff.; ten Brink, Hist. Eng. Lit. II : 225-6; see E. Koeppel, Lydgate's Story of Thebes: eine Quellenuntersuchung, Munich 1884.

TEN COMMANDMENTS OF LOVE

MSS: Trin. Coll. Cambr. R 3, 19; and a copy, in a Jacobean hand, into some of the blank leaves of Fairfax 16. As this latter hand is not contemporary with the rest of the Fairfax MS, Professor Skeat is not justified in his note, p. 122 of the Chaucer Canon, that the poem is at least as old as the Fairfax MS. The Trinity MS is described in James as cited, the Fairfax under Section IV A (3) above.

Prints and Editions: First printed by Stow, in the 1561 Chaucer; in the subsequent blackletter editions; in Urry; in the 1782 Bell; in Anderson; in Chalmers with Poems Imputed to Chaucer. Not again printed with Chaucer's works.

Authenticity: Rejected from the canon by Tyrwhitt, Account of the Works of Chaucer, in his sweeping condemnation of Stow's additions, cited under Stow in Section II D here.

TESTAMENT OF CRESSIDA
(By Robert Henryson)

MSS: The poem was in the Asloan MS, see Schipper's ed. of Dunbar, Vienna 1894, pp. 5 ff., p. 7; see Athen. 1906 I : 422, 482, 516, 671.

Prints and Editions: In the Thynne Chaucer of 1532; in the subsequent blackletter editions; in Urry; in the 1782 Bell; in Anderson; in Chalmers in the section Poems Imputed to Chaucer. Not again printed with Chaucer's works. The poem may be read in the Abbotsford Series of the Scottish Poets, volume on Medieval Scottish Poetry, or in Laing's ed. of Henryson, 1865. First printed as Henryson's by Charteris in 1593; this text repr. for the Bannatyne Club by Chalmers in 1824. Charteris' text is printed by Skeat VII : 327. Poem to appear in vol. III of the Works of Henryson, ed. G. Gregory Smith for the Scottish Text Society.

Authenticity: It was pointed out already by Francis Thynne, in his Animadversions, that this poem, the Letter of Cupid, and "I have a Lady", were not by Chaucer, and ought to be distinguished from the genuine works. In the 1602 Speght this suggestion was not adopted, but in the Urry of 1721 there is an introductory note to the poem stating that the editor has been informed by "Sir James Eriskin" that the author was "one Mr. Robert Henderson" etc. Kynaston, in his Latin translation of the Troilus, 1635, made the same statement on the authority of "Sir Thomas Erskine and divers aged scholars of the Scottish nation"; the wording of Kynaston is apparently copied in part by Urry, who speaks however as if he had received the information direct. As he was allowed the use of the Kynaston MS, see under Troilus ante, his independent knowledge may be doubted. Tyrwhitt quotes Urry's note, and supposes that Robert Henryson is meant.

Entitled by Leland and Bale "Testamentum Chrysidis."

Date, Notes, etc.: Henryson died before 1506, and was perhaps born about 1425. His poem was written as sequel to Troilus and Cressida, and was accordingly treated by Sir Francis Kynaston as the sixth book of the story. See Godwin, Life, chap. 16; Morley, Eng. Writers VI : 250; Skeat VII : lv, 520-525.

TESTAMENT OF LOVE
(By Thomas Usk)

MSS: None known, says Skeat, Canon p. 97.

Prints and Editions: By Thynne in the 1532 Chaucer; in the Speghts and in Urry; not in the 1782 Bell nor in Anderson; in Chalmers among the Prose Works; not in succeeding eds. Skeat VII : 1 ff. reprints Thynne's text, also now accessible in the facsimile of the 1532 edition.

The omission of this work from the 1782 Bell and from Anderson was more probably because of the professedly poetical character of those collections than because of any scruples as to authenticity.

Authenticity: Accepted by Tyrwhitt, Account of the Works of Chaucer. First questioned in print by Hertzberg, in the introd. to his Canterbury-Geschichten, 1866; also by ten Brink, Studien p. 155. Furnivall says, Athen. 1869 I : 606, that Bradshaw doubted Chaucer's authorship as early as 1863-5. See N. and Q. 1867 II : 303; Athen. 1868 II : 499, 611; 1869 I : 377, 410, 438, 541, 638; 1870 II : 211, 243, 462, for letters on the subject. J. P. Collier there insists on his priority in doubting Chaucer's authorship, he having raised the question in 1867; he nowhere alludes to Hertzberg, despite Asher's letter, Athen. p. 611 as cited. Cp. especially Furnivall's letter, Athen. 1870 II : 211; and see Bradshaw to Collier, Memoir, p. 355. Morley, Eng. Writers V : 268, says "surely not by Chaucer."

Skeat noticed that the initial letters of the chapters were intended to form an acrostic; this he read Tsknvi, and suggested one Kitsun as the author, see Acad. 1893 I : 222 and Oxford Chaucer V : xii note. In the Athen. 1897 I : 184, see Engl. Stud. 23 : 437, Henry Bradley showed that the leaves of the Testament had been displaced, and that if they were rightly arranged, the acrostic gave "thin Usk" as the author; he then identified Usk with Thomas Usk, executed in 1388. Cp. Skeat, Athen. 1897 I : 215.

The treatise was long used as a source of material for Chaucer's biography, and from it was derived the story as to his imprisonment for political reasons, etc. See the lives in the Urry Chaucer and by Godwin, Todd, etc.; cp. Lounsbury, Studies I : 181 ff., Skeat VII : xxii ff.

The ascription of the work to Chaucer perhaps came from the line in Gower's epilogue to the Confessio Amantis, where Venus bids Chaucer make his testament of love. Lounsbury and Skeat suggest that by this Gower may have meant the Legend of Good Women, see Studies, III : 336 and Acad. 1893 I : 246. Morley, Eng. Writers V : 261, says that Gower's words mean a witnessing of Divine love.

Entitled by Leland and Bale "Testamentum amoris."

Date: Brae, Athen. 1870 II : 462, said of Edward III's reign. Bradley as cited and Skeat VII : xx, Canon p. 97, say 1387.

Notes: Observe the prosing of part of the House of Fame, book II, chap. 2. See Godwin, Life, chap. 50; Morley, Eng. Writers V : 261-68; Skeat VII : xviii-xxxi, 451-484.

> THE MORE I GO . . . .
> THE WORLD SO WIDE . . . .

For note on these two stanzas, printed in the Bell Chaucer of 1854 as a continuation of Chaucer's Proverbs, see Anglia 28 : 4; Skeat, Canon p. 145.

TO THE KINGS MOST NOBLE GRACE AND TO THE LORDS AND KNIGHTS OF THE GARTER
(By Thomas Hoccleve)

MSS: Phillips 8151, see Furnivall as below. Copied into Trin. Coll. Cambr. R 3, 15, see James as cited, probably from a printed edition.

Prints and Editions: By Thynne in the 1532 Chaucer; in the sub-

sequent blackletter eds.; in Urry; in the Bell of 1782; not in
Anderson; the poem does not again appear with the works of
Chaucer until the 1854 Bell, when it was included among those
attributed to Chaucer. Printed with the Minor Poems of Hoccleve by Furnivall, EETS 1892. Printed by Skeat, VII : 233,
from the Phillipps MS.

Authenticity: In Acad. 1888 I : 325 Skeat says of Bell's text that
the poem must be by Hoccleve; see *ibid.* 361, where Skeat finds
that Mason had said so in his 1796 ed. of Hoccleve's poems.

Date, Notes, etc.: See Furnivall as cited; Skeat VII : xl, 501-2.

To My Sovereign Lady

See under Ballad in Commendation of Our Lady, above. The
latter part of the poem thus styled by Thynne in the 1532 Chaucer
is separated by Skeat VII : 281; see *ibid.* xlvii, 513.

Three Sayings, *see under* Sayings of Dan John.

To Rosemounde

MS: Rawlinson Poet. 163. The page containing the poem is
reproduced in Skeat's Twelve Facsimiles. Note on MS in
Section IV A (3) here.

Prints and Editions: By Skeat in the Athenaeum, April 4, 1891,
I : 440, see 472 and Hart at p. 667; privately printed by Skeat
in double leaflet, entitled A Poem by Chaucer, about April 8,
1891. Both these prints, as compared with MS facsimile, show
two errors, *Tristram* for *Tristam* and *secounde* for *secunde*.
    Text in Garnett and Gosse, Engl. Lit. I : 170. In Skeat's
Minor Poems, p. 464 (revised ed.); in the Oxford Chaucer
I : 389; in the Globe Chaucer p. 627.

Authenticity: The MS, which also contains the Troilus, writes
below the poem "Tregentil. Chaucer," the two names "a considerable distance apart", Oxford Chaucer I : 81. This poem
appears on a flyleaf of the MS, and the Troilus has, according
to Skeat, the same two names written, one just before, the
other just after, the colophon. Skeat considers that by
"Tregentil" is meant the scribe. Accepted by Koch as genuine,
p. 41 of Chronology.

Title: Given by Skeat.

Date: Koch, Chronology p. 42, places this poem, with Merciles Beaute and Newfangleness, about 1380-84.

Notes: See Skeat I : 549; Root, Poetry of Chaucer pp. 72-3.

Roundel, *see* Merciless Beaute.

UTTER THY LANGUAGE
(By John Lydgate)

MSS: Harley 2251, Adds. 34360, Harley 2255, Ashmole 59, Selden B 10, Univ. Libr. Cambr. Hh iv, 12, Trin. Coll. Cambr. R 3, 21, Jesus Coll. Cambr. 56.
    The Hh copy is printed Polit., Rel. and Love Poems p. 25, and the MS is described in Section IV A (5) above; the Selden MS is described in Section IV A (3) above, the Trinity and Jesus MSS in James as cited. For discussion of the two MSS first mentioned above see Anglia 28 : 1 ff., for Harley 2255 p. 24 *ibid.* The Ashmole codex is described in Anglia 30 : 320-348.

Prints and Editions: Printed in Pynson's 1526 Chaucer as noted Section II D here. The Hh copy is printed as above; the Harley 2255 copy is printed in Halliwell's Minor Poems of Dan John Lydgate, p. 173 ff., under the title of "The Concords of Company."

Title and Authenticity: This poem is the first entry in MS Harley 2255, and, as mentioned Anglia 28 : 24, has in its opening capital a small coat of arms; it has there no ascription, and there is none in any MS except Shirley's Ashmole 59, where it is marked. " . . . a poetycal balade of wysdame made by þe munke of Bury cleped Johan Lidegate." For the heading in Pynson see Section II D here. The title here given is taken from the poem's refrain "Lyke the audience so utter thy language."

Date, Notes, etc.:

VIRELAY

MSS: Trin. Coll. Cambr. R 3, 19; described by James op. cit.

Prints and Editions: First printed by Stow in the 1561 Chaucer; in the subsequent blackletter eds., in Urry, in the 1782 Bell, in Anderson, in Chalmers, Chiswick, Moxon, the 1845 Aldine, the 1854 Bell; in the revised Bell of 1878 (Skeat) relegated to the section Poems Attributed to Chaucer. Printed by Godwin in his Life of Chaucer, II : 356, with comments; printed by Skeat VII : 448, from the MS.

Modernizations: By Cowden Clarke in his Riches of Chaucer; by Purves in 1870.

Authenticity and Title: The long retention of this poem in the canon was doubtless due to the half-acceptance of it by Tyrwhitt in his Account of the Works of Chaucer. Tyrwhitt there spoke of it as "perhaps by Chaucer", and said that it came "nearer to the description of a Virelay than anything else of his that has been preserved." The piece was accordingly spoken of as a virelay. No title in the MS, where the word *Chaucer* is in the margin; whether it was written earlier or later than the printing of this and other bits by Stow as Chaucer's is not to be decided. Bradshaw rejected the poem from the canon.

Notes: See Morley, Eng. Writers V : 271; Skeat VII : lxxx, 554, Canon p. 122; Godwin as above.

When Faith Faileth, *see* Prophecy.

WICKED TONGUE
(By John Lydgate)

MSS: Skeat, Canon p. 105, mentions two; I have noted five: Harley 2251, Bodley 686, Adds. 29729 (Stow), Trin. Coll. Cambr. R 3, 20, Univ. Libr. Cambr. Ff 1, 6. The Harley MS is described Anglia 28 : 1 ff., the Bodley MS under III B (3) above, the Ff MS under IV A (5) above, the Adds. codex by Sieper in his EETS ed. of Lydgate's Reson and Sensuallyte, the (Shirley) Trinity MS in James *op. cit.* and in Anglia refs. as given in Section IV A (6) here.

Prints and Editions: In the Thynne Chaucer of 1532, and in subsequent blackletter eds.; in Urry, in the 1782 Bell, in Anderson; in Chalmers among the Poems Imputed to Chaucer; not in Chiswick or later eds. Printed by Skeat VII : 285 from Thynne, collated with the Ff MS.

Title and Authenticity: Stow headed the poem "A Balade of good counsaile translated out of Latine verses into Englishe by Dan John Lidgate cleped the monke of Burie." He probably took his information from the Trinity MS, a Shirley codex, which was for some time in his hands, and which shows this heading. The poem is evidently Lydgate's; and Tyrwhitt emphasized this in his Account of the Works of Chaucer.

Title: Marked by Shirley and Stow as above cited; Skeat entitles it "Ballad of Good Counsel"; the heading is here taken from the refrain, "A wicked tongue will alway deem amiss."

Notes: See Skeat VII : xlix, 514, Canon as above. My note in Anglia 28 : 21 should be emended by the statement that the last stanza of the poem as in Harley 2251, which apparently makes the copy there longer than other texts, is in reality the lines entitled Prosperity, see above.

WOMANLY NOBLESSE

MSS: Adds. 34360, described Anglia 28 : 1 ff.

Prints and Editions: By Skeat, Athen. 1894 I : 742; issued by Skeat as a leaflet in 1894; in the Oxford Chaucer IV : xxv, Minor Poems (revised ed.) p. 466. Included in the Kelmscott Chaucer; in the Globe Chaucer, p. 637.

In his letter to the Athen. Skeat announced the ballad as his discovery; Pollard *ibid.* p. 773 wrote that its existence was known to the Museum before purchase of the MS; see *ibid.* pp. 805, 837.

Authenticity: In the Canon p. 147 Skeat says "Attributed to Chaucer by Shirley in the MS copy." This is misleading. Adds. 34360 is not in Shirley's hand, and though the text and the heading, "Balade that Chauncier made" are perhaps derived by the scribe from a Shirley copy, the matter is not certain; see Anglia as above. Kittredge in Nation 1895 I : 240 opines that this poem is probably Chaucer's. Koch, Engl. Stud. 27 : 60; 30 : 450, refuses to accept it as Chaucerian.

Title: The title as above is given by Skeat; the Globe Chaucer uses the MS marking as cited.

Notes: See Skeat as cited; Root, Poetry of Chaucer p. 79.

Yet of the Same, *see* the second of the two stanzas discussed under Sayings of Dan John above.

Youre Eyen Two, *see* Merciles Beaute.

SECTION VI.

LINGUISTICS AND VERSIFICATION

A. Chaucer's Verse and Language: Comment, 1575-1847

1575

"Also our father Chaucer hath vsed the same libertie in feete and measures that the Latinists do vse; and who so euer do peruse and well consider his workes, he shall finde that although his lines are not alwayes of one selfe same number of Syllables, yet beyng redde by one that hath vnderstanding, the longest verse and that which hath most Syllables in it, will fall (to the eare) correspondent vnto that whiche hath fewest sillables in it; and likewise that whiche hath in it fewest syllables, shalbe founde yet to consist of woordes that haue suche naturall sounde, as may seeme equall in length to a verse which hath many moe sillables of lighter accents."

Gascoigne: Certayne Notes of Instruction concerning the making of Verse or Ryme in English.

1586

"*Chawcer,* who for that excellent fame which hee obtayned in his Poetry, was always accounted the God of English Poets (such a tytle for honours sake hath beene giuen him) was next after, if not equall in time to Gower, and hath left many workes, both for delight and profitable knowledge, farre exceeding any other that as yet euer since hys time directed theyr studies that way. Though the manner of hys stile may seeme blunte & course to many fine English eares at these dayes, yet in trueth, if it be equally pondered, and with good iudgment aduised, and confirmed with the time wherein he wrote, a man shall perceiue thereby euen a true picture or perfect shape of a right Poet. . . . for who could with more delight, prescribe such wholsome counsaile and sage aduise, where he seemeth onelie to respect the profitte of his lessons and instructions? or who coulde with greater wisedome, or more pithie skill, vnfold such

464

pleasant and delightsome matters of mirth, as though they respected nothing, but the telling of a merry tale?"

Webbe: A Discourse of English Poetrie.

1589

"Chaucer, Lydgate and others vsed *Cesures* either very seldome, or not at all, or else very licentiously; and many times made their meetres . . . of such vnshapely wordes as would allow no conuenient *cesure;* and therefore did let their rymes runne out at length, and neuer stayd till they came to the end." (etc.)

Puttenham: Arte of English Poesie, lib. 2, ch. 4.

1602

"And for his [Chaucer's] verses, although in divers places they seem to us to stand of unequal measures, yet a skilful reader, who can scan them in their nature, shall find it otherwise. And if a verse, here and there, fal out a syllable shorter or longer than another, I rather aret it to the negligence and rape of Adam Scrivener (that I may speake as Chaucer doth) than to any unconning or oversight in the author; for how fearful he was to have his works miswritten, or his verse mismeasured, may appeare in the end of his fift booke of 'Troylus and Creseide,' where he writeth thus:

> And for there is so great diversitie
> In English and in writing of our tongue,
> So pray I God that none miswrite thee,
> Ne thee mismetre for defaute of tongue.

Speght's second ed. of Chaucer's Works, 1602; perhaps due to the influence of Francis Thynne, see Lounsbury, Studies III : 51.

1634

"Some few ages after [the Norman Conquest] came the Poet *Geffery Chaucer,* who writing his Poesies in *English,* is of some called the first illuminator of the *English* tongue: of their opinion I am not (though I reverence *Chaucer,* as an excellent Poet for his time). He was indeed a great mingler of *English* with *French,* unto which language by like for that hee was decended of *French* or rather Wallon race, hee carried a great affection."

Verstegan: Restitution of Decayed Intelligence, pp. 203-4.

1640

In Ben Jonson's Grammar, first printed 1640, Chaucer is cited 25 times, principally from the House of Fame, Troilus, and the Man of Law's Tale; Gower is cited 27 times, Lydgate 14 times.

30

1668

"The English language has been hitherto too carelessly handled,
and I think has had less labour spent about its polishing than it
deserves; till the time of King Henry the Eighth there was scarce
any man regarded it but Chaucer, and nothing was written inn it
which one would be willing to read twice but some of his poetry;
but then it began to raise itself a little, and to sound tolerably well."

Sprat, Bishop of Rochester, in his History of the Royal Society.

1671

"*Chaucerus* poeta, pessimo exemplo, integris vocum plaustris ex
eadem Gallia in nostram Linguam invectis, eam, nimis antea à
Normannorum victoria adulteratam, omni fere nativa gratia & nitore
spoliavit, pro genuinis coloribus fucum illinens, pro vera facie
larvam induens."

Skinner: preface to the Etymologicon Linguae Anglicanae.

1691-2

"As to the poetry of the age, the beauty of speech, and the graces
of measure and numbers, which are the inseparable ornaments of a
good poem, are not to be expected in a rude and unsettled language;
and though Chaucer, the father of our poets, had not taken equal
care of the force of expression, as of the greatness of thought;
yet the refining of a tongue is such a work as never was begun,
and finish'd by the same hand. . . . And as in clothes, so in words,
at first usually they broke in unalter'd upon us from abroad; and
consequently, as in Chaucer's time, come not over like captives, but
invaders."

Preface to vol. ii of Antony à Wood's Athenae Oxonienses, by
James Harrington.

1693

"The Italian Authors acknowledge that the best part of their
Language, and of their Poetry is drawn from that of *Provence,* as,
indeed, is also that of the Spanish, and other Modern Languages.
It is certain that *Petrarch* (the Poet that the Italians brag most on
to this day) wou'd show very empty, if the *Provencial* Poets had
from him, all their own again.   And, in truth, all our *Modern* Poetry
comes from them.

But they who attempted verse in English, down till *Chaucers*
time, made an heavy pudder, and are always miserably put to't for
a word to clink: which commonly fall so awkard, and unexpectedly
as dropping from the Clouds by some Machine or Miracle.

Chaucer found an Herculean labour on his Hands; and did perform to Admiration.   He seizes all Provencal, French, or Latin that came in his way, gives them a new garb and livery, and mingles them amongst our English; turns out English, gowty, or super-annuated, to place in their room the foreigners, fit for service, train'd and accustomed to Poetical Discipline.

But tho' the Italian Reformation was begun and finished well nigh at the same time by *Boccace, Dante,* and *Petrarch.*   Our language retain'd something of the churl; something of the Stiff and Gothish did stick upon it, till long after *Chaucer.*

Chaucer threw in Latin, French, Provencial, and other Languages, like new Stum to raise a Fermentation; In Queen *Elizabeth's* time it grew fine, but came not to an Head and Spirit, did not shine and sparkle till Mr. *Waller* set it a running.   And one may observe by his Poem on the Navy, *An.* 1632, that Not the language only, but His Poetry then distinguish'd him from all his contemporaries, both in *England* and in other Nations; And from all before him upwards to *Horace* and *Virgil."*

Rymer: Short View of Tragedy, chaps. vi, vii.

This passage was referred to, approvingly, by Dryden, Preface to Fables, as below.

1700

"The Verse of *Chaucer,* I confess, is not Harmonious to us. . . . They who liv'd with him, and some time after him, thought it Musical; and it continues so even in our Judgment, if compar'd with the Numbers of *Lidgate* and *Gower* his Contemporaries: . . . There is the rude Sweetness of a *Scotch* Tune in it, which is natural and pleasing, though not perfect.   'Tis true, I cannot go so far as he who publish'd the last Edition of him; for he would make us believe the Fault is in our Ears, and that there were really Ten Syllables in a Verse where we find but Nine; But this Opinion is not worth confuting; 'tis so gross and obvious an Errour, that common Sense . . . must convince the Reader, that Equality of Numbers in every Verse which we call Heroick was either not known, or not always practis'd in *Chaucer's* age.   It were an easie Matter to produce some thousands of his Verses, which are lame for want of half a Foot, and some times a whole one, and which no Pronunciation can make otherwise."

From the Preface to Fables, Ancient and Modern.   Translated into Verse from Homer, Ovid, Boccace, and Chaucer.   With **Original Poems.** By Mr. Dryden.   London, 1700.

1721

"It is thought by some that his Verses every where consist of an equal number of feet, and that if read with a right accent, are no where deficient; but those nice discerning Persons would find it difficult, with all their straining and working, to spin out some of his Verses into a measure of ten Syllables. [Footnote refers to Dryden, Preface to Fables.] He was not altogether regardless of his Numbers; but his thoughts were more intent upon solid sense than gingle, and he tells us plainly that we must not expect regularity in all his Verses." [reference to the passage in the House of Fame, Book III, see citation ante from the 1602 Chaucer.]
From the Life of Chaucer by John Dart, revised by William Thomas, prefixed to Urry's Chaucer.

1721

Thomas, in his Preface to Urry's Chaucer, says of Urry's unfinished work: "His chief business was to make the Text more correct and compleat than before. He found it was the opinion of some learned Men that *Chaucer's* Verses originally consisted of an equal number of Feet; and he himself was perswaded that *Chaucer* made them exact Metre." ... "He had observed that several Initial and Final Syllables in use in *Chaucer's* time, and since, had been omitted or added at pleasure in the MSS by unskilful Transcribers, from whence the same Errors crept into the Printed Editions, whereby many Verses were rendered unjust in their Measure." ... "The Final Syllables were for the most part such as might be said rather to be added in the Pronunciation, than by Writing: The chiefest of which, and the most frequently made use of to help out a Verse otherwise deficient, was the Final *e*, which he always marked with an accent when he judged it necessary to pronounce it." ... "The next thing to be taken notice of as used for lengthening of words, is the distinct pronouncing of the Termination *ed* or *id* in the Preter Tenses of Verbs, and in Participles." ... "Another help he saw might be gained by making a discreet use of *en,* or *in,* a Termination of Verbs, Nouns, and Adverbs, but most frequently of Verbs." ... "And again the pronouncing of *es* or *is,* the Plural Termination of Substantives, and sometimes of Adverbs, and also of *is* the Termination of the Genitive Case Singular has contributed no small assistance towards the supply of a Foot to many Verses, which must otherwise have halted." ... "And here likewise it must be observed, that these Terminations are not always to be pronounced, but only where the Metre is deficient without it."

The different opinion of Dart, in the Life prefixed to the Urry Chaucer, may be seen just ante. See also glossary to Urry, s. v. *missemetre.*

1737

"'Tis true, Mr. *Speght,* in his Edition 1602 affirms, that Chaucer wrote in equal measure; but of other learned Men know I none of the same Opinion; I am sure, none that I have had the Honour particularly to converse with on this Occasion. (Morell quotes Dryden, the Life in Urry's Chaucer, and the eight lines from the *House of Fame* ending "though som verse faile in a sillable.") "From this last Line, I conclude, that an exact Numerosity (as Bishop Sprat expresses it in his Life of Cowley . . .) was not Chaucer's main Care; but that he had sometimes a greater Regard for the Sense than the Metre; His Numbers however, are by no Means so rough and inharmonious as some People imagine; there is a charming Simplicity in them, and they are always musical, whether they want or exceed their Complement: The former Case, I have observed, where it happens, is generally at the Beginning of a Verse, where a Pause is to be made, or rather two Times to be given to the first Syllable, as v. 368

Not in Purgatory, but in Hell

Mr. *Urry,* to make out his ten Syllables, reads it, *right* in Hell, which *right,* tho' I am no great Admirer of a Pun, is *Wrong,* as it renders the Verse very harsh and dissonant: But this is only one Verse among hundreds that are false accented in Mr. *Urry's* Edition, as may be seen by any one that thinks it worth while to consult the various Readings annexed to this."

"Some Verses are charg'd with an additional Syllable that were full before, as v. 1050, 1537, &c. others are as unnecessarily curtailed, for want of knowing, that as *Chaucer* sometimes gives two Times to one long Syllable, so he often uses two short Syllables, I mean, such as do not require a strong Accent, instead of one, v. 734, 309, 1219, 2056. In others, the *Apostrophe* or *Elision* is not observed, when it is necessarily required, v. 214, &c. But what I am more surpriz'd at is, that Mr. *Urry* very often disallows, the double *Rhime,* as v. 804, 325, &c. than which nothing can be more absurd."

Morell then says that the final *e* was anciently pronounced in feminine adjectives and in substantives which from Saxon have been made English by changing *a* into *e*, e. g., *nama.* "However, our author seems to have taken the liberty to use it or not, as it best suited his Metre":

Hickes' Thesaurus is quoted: "Non constat quomodo voces in *E* foeminino vel obscuro terminatae pronunciandae sunt in carmine: quae metrice forsan, nunc ut monosyllaba, nunc ut disyllaba edenda sunt."

"But give me leave to observe, that he has never used it in any even Place, except the 2d, where it is allowable, especially if the accent be strong upon the 4th."

Morell assures his readers that he keeps strictly to the orthography of the oldest MSS. He presents some general observations on Chaucer's language, which are in part notes upon medieval orthography. He quotes two passages from Hickes in reproof of Speght, see under Speght's 1602 edition of the Works, Section II D here; and concludes:

"This, then has been my Amusement for some Time, and I hope with no great Detriment to the more severe and decent Studies required by my Place and Character: I believe many a leisure Hour might have been spent worse."

From Thomas Morell's preface to his ed. of the Canterbury Tales.

Upon the line discussed by Urry and by Morell as above it may be noted that Tyrwhitt thought this could "never pass for a verse in any form", and said that Chaucer wrote, according to the best MSS, "Not only in purgatory, but in helle." See Skeat in the revision of Tyrwhitt's Essay for the Aldine Chaucer, note 65.

1755

"Chaucer . . . may perhaps, with great justice, be stiled the first of our versifyers who wrote poetically. He does not however appear to have deserved all the praise which he has received, or all the censure that he has suffered. *Dryden,* who mistakes genius for learning, and, in confidence of his abilities, ventured to write of what he had not examined, ascribes to *Chaucer* the first refinement of our numbers, the first production of easy and natural rhymes, and the improvement of our language, by words borrowed from the more polished languages of the continent. *Skinner* contrarily blames him in harsh terms for having vitiated his native speech by *whole cartloads of foreign words.* But he that reads the works of *Gower* will find smooth numbers and easy rhymes, of which *Chaucer* is supposed to have been the inventor, and the *French* words, whether good or bad, of which *Chaucer* is charged as the importer. Some innovations he might probably make, like others, in the infancy of our poetry, which the paucity of books does [not] allow us to discover with particular exactness; but the works of *Gower* and *Lydgate* sufficiently evince, that his diction was in general like that of his contemporaries: and some improvements he undoubtedly made by the various disposition of his rhymes, and by the mixture of different numbers, in which he seems to have been happy and judicious." &c.

From Dr. Johnson's history of the English language, prefixed to his Dictionary.

Johnson has previously referred to "Sir John Gower, who calls Chaucer his disciple, and may therefore be considered as the father of our poetry." In this he misquotes the epilogue to the Confessio Amantis, where Gower makes Venus term Chaucer her disciple.

Johnson was censured by Ellis, in his Specimens of the Early English Poets, 1790.

1760-61

"Though I would not with Mr. Urry, the Editor of Chaucer, insert words and syllables, unauthorized by the oldest manuscripts, to help out what seems lame and defective in the measure of our ancient writers, yet as I see those manuscripts, and the first printed editions, so extremely inconstant in their manner of spelling one and the same word as to vary continually, and often in the compass of two lines, and seem to have no fixed orthography, I cannot help thinking it probable, that many great inequalities in the metre are owing to the neglect of transcribers, or that the manner of reading made up for the defects which appear in the writing." (Gray then points out that the prefix y- is derived from the Old English prefix ge-, and that the final syllable of verbs, from the Saxon -an, -en, might also survive in pronunciation.) . . . "Our writers inserted these initial and final letters, or omitted them; and, where we see them written, we do not doubt that they were meant to fill up the measure; it follows, that these Poets had an ear not insensible to defects in metre; and where the verse seems to halt, it is very probably occasioned by the transcriber's neglect." . . . "This was commonly done, too, I imagine, in Chaucer's and Lydgate's time; but, in verse, they took the liberty either to follow the old language in pronouncing the final syllable, or to sink the vowel and abridge it, as was usual, according to the necessity of their versification; . . . and though in time the *e* mute was quite dropped in conversation, yet when the poet thought fit to make a syllable of it, it no more offended their ears than it now offends those of a Frenchman to hear it so pronounced, in verse."

> From Gray's Observations on English Metre, written, Gosse conjectures, at the date above given, printed by Mathias in 1814, and here quoted from Gosse's edition of Gray in four vols., N. Y. 1890, vol. I.

1775

Tyrwhitt, in the Essay on the Language and Versification of Chaucer, prefixed to his edition of the Canterbury Tales, endeavored to prove:

(1) That the admixture of French in Chaucer's vocabulary was not of his introduction, but represents the normal state of XIV century English.

(2) That the English language was in Chaucer's time a mixture of matter largely French, and of Saxon forms. He rapidly discusses these latter (inflexional endings, etc.), with a number of errors due to his treatment of the language by eye and not by ear, and to his ignorance of dialectal differences in Middle English.

(3) That rime, not a characteristic of Saxon poetry, was es-

tablished from foreign sources in Chaucer's time, and used in four principal forms, the septenar, the Alexandrine, the octosyllabic couplet, and the six-line stanza. That Chaucer used the last in the Rime of Sir Thopas, the third in several poems, but employed mainly the heroic line, in couplet or in stanza, which he seems to have introduced. That in adapting his language to this last form, Chaucer might err either in number of syllables, or in placing of accents. This he however did not do; the recognition of the inflectional syllables as an independent element, and of the French accentuation of borrowed words, rescues Chaucer's verse from imputations of roughness. "We may reasonably presume that our ancestors first passed from the broader sound of *a* to the thinner sound of *e* feminine, and not at once from *a* to *e* mute."

Tyrwhitt recognizes that Urry held this same opinion, and cites also Wallis' Grammatica Linguae Anglicanae, 1653, for the opinion that *e* (final or medial) could be pronounced or not, according as the metre required. See his notes 71 and 72. See Lounsbury, Studies I: 300-313. See censure of Tyrwhitt's linguistic ignorance in the preface to Wright's 1847 ed. of the Cant. Tales, cited in Skeat, Canon p. 23. On Tyrwhitt see under note of his edition in Section III C here.

1803

"Another obstacle which has prevented the general study and reading of Chaucer, is the real or supposed defects of his versification. [Dryden is censured.] Languages vary, in different periods of their history, as to the fashion of their pronunciation. Many letters are pronounced at first, which afterward by a sort of tacit consent are dropped in speech. Thus it was in French. . . . Chaucer has done nothing more in this respect than was done by the early French poets . . . [but] Chaucer on the contrary [from their regularity] preserves or sinks the sound of his syllables arbitrarily to suit his own convenience; the reader is frequently unable at a glance to discover his scheme of harmony" [etc.]

William Godwin in his Life of Chaucer, chap. 12.

1807

"It is not easy to understand Chaucer's system of versification, whether it was metrical or rhythmical; to speak plainer, whether he intended that his verses should consist of a certain number of feet, or like the modern *Improvisatori* was satisfied, so they were melodious, without restricting himself to any laws, either of length or cadence. I am inclined to think that this was his system, because upon this system, he is more melodious, and the pronunciation which otherwise is required is so variable, that it seems as if it must always have appeared ridiculous. Be that as it may, it is evident that he had well weighed the subject of versification."

From Robert Southey's Preface to his Specimens of the Later English Poets.

1815

Nott considers Tyrwhitt's "system respecting Chaucer's versification", and raises objections to it. He says that Tyrwhitt proposes three "expedients" for making each verse "a just Hendecasyllable", the principal of these "expedients" being the recognition of the final -e feminine as sounded separately. "These three expedients failing, it is then proposed to consult manuscripts and see whether some one manuscript may not afford a reading which would enable us to complete the measure; . . . All these means of filling up the measure failing, the verse which still continues defective is to be considered corrupt."

Nott declares against the recognition of such "Saxon terminations" as the -e feminine in Chaucer. "Chaucer's object was to polish the language of his day. To do this he would naturally reject all words of an obsolete form, and all vulgar modes of pronunciation." The sounding of the -e feminine "would be in direct opposition to the nature and genius of our language, which, instead of dilating words, . . . tends to contract." Nott scouts the idea of Chaucer's introducing "a novel mode of pronunciation." He says that Tyrwhitt admits that we have no specimens of any such sort of verse in our language previous to this supposed introduction of it by Chaucer.

What then, Nott asks, were the improvements made by Chaucer in our versification? He lists: (1) the rejection of alliteration. (2) The establishment of the practice of always changing the rime with the couplet. (3) The introduction of the heroic stanza of seven lines. (4) The dropping of the Alexandrine, and the substitution of the line of ten syllables. But he denies metrical movement; he insists that Chaucer's verse, like all English verse anterior to his, was rhythmical, not metrical; to be recited with a certain rhythmical cadence; "for which reason they seem to have been called 'verses of cadence.'" He admits that there are many iambic lines in Chaucer, but thinks that such lines were not intentional on Chaucer's part. He insists upon the marking of the cesural dot and upon the frequent dotting at the end of the line by the scribes of the manuscripts as proof that Chaucer "designed his lines to be read with a caesura and rhythmical cadence." The caution against "mismetring verse", at the close of the Troilus, means that the cesural dot must be carefully marked.

From "A Dissertation on the State of English Poetry before the Sixteenth Century", prefixed to vol. I of "The Works of Henry Howard Earl of Surrey and of Sir Thomas Wyatt the Elder. Edited by George Frederick Nott, D. D., F. S. A.' London, 1815, 2 vols. For summary and comment on this work see also Lounsbury, Studies I : 331 ff.; see Blackw. Mag. 57 : 700; Edinb. Review 27 : 390-422.

1838

Guest's History of English Rhythms, pubd. 1838, re-edited in 1882 by Skeat, is discussed by Gayley and Scott, Introduction to the Methods and Materials of Literary Criticism, Boston 1899, p. 466; also by Omond, English Metrists in the Eighteenth and Nineteenth Centuries, Oxford 1907.

Guest's remarks upon Chaucer, as upon later English poets, are invalidated by his theory as to the unvarying structure of the English line. See Omond as cited, pp. 125-131, for notes.

1841

"Our position is, that Chaucer was a most harmonious and melodious poet, and that he was a perfect master of the various forms of versification in which he wrote; that the principle on which his rhythm is founded fuses and subjects within itself all the minor details of metre; that this principle, though it has been understood only by the few, and never systematically explained, is, more or less, inseparable from the composition of an harmonious versification in the English language; and that he, the first man, if not unrivalled in the varied music of his verse, has scarcely been surpassed by any succeeding poet."

[Tyrwhitt's citation of Dryden's opinion is then quoted, in which, as can be seen ante, Dryden maintains that there are not ten syllables in each of Chaucer's heroic lines. Horne concedes this at once, and then proceeds to argue that the verse of nine and that of eleven syllables are indispensable as variants. A full discussion of "superfluous syllables" follows, with examples from modern poets; little is said of the nine-syllabled line, and that dubiously, see pp. lvi-lvii. Elision is explained.]

"Of the occasional deficiencies or 'lameness' in his verse, of which Chaucer has been accused, it is hoped that little need now be said. In the first place, we are to allow for his quantities, so far as we know them, or can feasibly conjecture what they were. In the second place, we are to give to a great poet who has accomplished so much harmony which *is* manifest, due credit for many instances where we are unable to perceive it, from our deficiency of knowledge. Thirdly, we are to allow for the errors of copyists, of whose ungodly pens Chaucer shows himself to be in much dread . . . It might be suggested, fifthly, that something should be allowed for the unsettled condition of the English language at his time, and that it was accounted an accomplishment for a man to be able to write even his own name. But this consideration I do not care to dwell upon in the case of one who shows such mastery. The main ground of defence consists in the examples given from modern poets—whose rich and harmonious versification is fully recognized

—demonstrating that the occasional introduction of lines which are short by half a foot, or more (as well as those which pass the common bounds of length), of the regular quantity of a particular metre, may enhance the power or beauty of the rhythm."

> From R. H. Horne's introduction to the volume of modernizations of Chaucer edited by him. On Horne see Omond, English Metrists, 1907, p. 136.

B. Studies in Chaucer's Language and Verse

1847. F. W. Gesenius. De Lingua Chauceri. diss. Bonn pp. 87.
> Commended by Child as below. A summary is in Ellis, EEPron. III : 664-671.

1859. Moritz Rapp, in his Vergleichende Grammatik, vol. III : 166-179.
> Abridged by Ellis, EEPron. III : 672-77.

1862. Francis James Child. Observations on the Language of Chaucer.
> In the Memoirs of the American Academy, *n. s.* vol. VIII : 445 ff.; separate prints are difficult to obtain. Condensed and reprinted in Ellis, EEPron. I : 342-397. Based on Wright's ed. of the Cant. Tales from MS Harley 7334, a text which Child somewhat overrated. Child, and Wright's text, were discussed by Herrig before the Berliner Gesellschaft, Jan. 6, 1863; see Archiv 32 : 386. The debt of students to this first methodical and scholarly analysis of Chaucer's language is in no wise lessened by the progress of study since the day of Child. See p. 521 below.

1867-1871. Alexander J. Ellis, On Early English Pronunciation, with especial Reference to Shakspere and Chaucer, 5 vols., 1867-1888. Published jointly by the Early English Text and Chaucer Societies.
> Of this comprehensive and most valuable piece of investigation Parts I and III are of especial importance to students of Chaucer. Vol. I p. 241 ff. deals with the rimes of Chaucer and Gower and the evidence as to pronunciation to be deduced from them; on p. 318 ff. Ellis takes up the question of -e final and its treatment by Chaucer, giving abstracts of Child's papers on Chaucer and Gower pp. 342-397, and commending most warmly Child's investigations. The accentuation of French words and its double treatment by Chaucer is

discussed p. 331 (see III : 650) and in the abstract of Child p. 369. Some other points may be mentioned: the opinion that scribes of Chaucerian MSS were uncertain as to the -e final, owing to the rapid change in English speech which had begun already in Chaucer's time, p. 330; the remarks on headless lines, p. 333, cited below under E (4) ; and that on trisyllabic measure pp. 334-5, see also III : 648. In vol. III are found illustrations of the pronunciation of Chaucer and Gower, in especial a phonetic transcription of the Prologue to the Cant. Tales, pp. 680-725, and abstracts of the papers of Gesenius and of Rapp as above. Ellis' opinion is frequently cited below. Ellis is reviewed Athen 1871 II : 393.

1872. Carl Isberg. Grammatical Studies of Chaucer's Language. diss. Upsala, pp. 38.

1874. Joseph Payne. On the Use of final -e in Early English, and especially in Chaucer's Canterbury Tales. Chaucer Society Essays, part II.

1873-4. Henry Sweet. History of English Sounds. In the Transactions of the Philological Society; again, revised, Oxford 1888.

1878. R. F. Weymouth. On *here* and *there* in Chaucer. In the Transactions of the Philological Society, 1877-9; in Chaucer Society Essays part IV.

1880. K. A. Schrader. Das altenglische Relativpronomen, mit besonderer Berücksichtigung der Sprache Chaucers. diss. Kiel, pp. 45.

1881-1888. J. Schipper. Englische Metrik in historischer und systematischer Entwickelung dargestellt. 3 vols., Bonn; also revised and condensed, 1 vol., as Grundriss der englischen Metrik, Leipzig, 1895. Reviewed Anglia 5 : Anz. 30, 139 (Einenkel) ; Nation 1890 I : 355-57; Mod. Lang. Notes 4 : 290-94 (Gummere). Schipper answers the American reviews in Anglia Beibl. 1891 pp. 36 ff.

[Schipper is also the author of the section on *Fremde Metra* in Paul's Grundriss der germanischen Philologie, art. *Englische Metrik.*]

The 3-vol. work discusses Chaucer in I : 442 ff. The texts of Morris and of the Morris and Skeat eds. of separate Cant. Tales for school use are the basis of discussion. On the five-beat line the points considered are: hovering accent, accent transposition, headless lines, double upbeat and dissyllabic thesis, slurring, elision, the cesura.

Schipper subjects the verse of Chaucer to a most mechanical and obdurate analysis. True, he repeats now and then that the variety of Chaucer's verseflow is beautiful and marvelous; but the appreciation is so formula-like in character and so surrounded by masses of unrelenting fruitless line-dissection that its effect is lost. The term "fruitless" is applied with intent. It appears to me that no more is gained for understanding of Chaucer's prosody by classing his "cesuras" as (1) masculine after the second foot, (2) feminine after the second foot, (3) lyric within the third foot, (4) masculine after the third foot, (5) feminine after the third foot, etc., than would be gained by classing the poet's lines as those beginning with a noun, those ending with a noun, those containing a noun in the second foot, those containing two nouns, etc. Indeed, the entire basis of Schipper's analysis is questionable, assuming and asserting as it does that Chaucer is to be treated line by line like an Anglo-Saxon versewriter, and that every one of his lines is divided by a cesura into two portions, each with one principal stress. To such excess of archaism does Schipper push this theory that he even treats lines like

He sette nat | his benefice to hyre   Prol. 507
That I was of | hir felawshipe anon   Prol. 32
By forward and | by composicioun   Prol. 848

as showing an almost imperceptible ("verwischte") cesura, which according to Schipper falls where I have drawn the bar.[1] In the face of the long recognition given to Schipper's bulky treatise, I would insist that for Chaucer at least the "cesura" and the "hovering accent" are fabrications of a mind which must name before it can see or feel, a mind which when confronted with a group of lines like:

Or like the snowfall in the river,
A moment white, then gone forever
                    Burns, Tam O' Shanter.

Like the foam on the river,
Thou art gone, and forever
                    Scott, Lady of the Lake.

To join the brimming river,
For men may come and men may go,
But I go on forever.
                    Tennyson, The Brook.

would find in the rime-divergence *ever: river* not an instance of sound-variety in sound-unity, peculiarly pleasing to the musical ear, but rather material for a theory of Gaelic influence upon Lowland Scottish short *e,* and the literary transfer of the resultant hybrid to the poetic dialect of the South of England a generation later.

This same anxious analytic insistence has led Schipper to dicta like the following: In the line

And held after the newe world the space   Prol. 176

it is uncertain whether *after* is to be considered a substituted trochee or a case of hovering accent; but in line 195,

And for to festne his hood under his chyn

[1] Ten Brink, Sprache und Verskunst, § 313, will not accept this.

the word *under* is possibly a trochee, because after a cesura such a reversal of accent is not disturbing.

Schipper would probably refuse the suggestion that in Chaucer, as in modern poets, there are two sorts of rhythmic variation: (1) that which is deliberate and emphatic, arranged by the poet to attract the ear of the reader and thus enhance the force or the beauty of the line-content for the mind. An example of one sort of such emphasis is

That if gold ruste, what shall iren do?

(2) And secondly, that which is unconscious on the poet's part, merely the expression of the inevitable tendency to vary which must be at work in rhythmic unity if monotony is to be avoided, and of the equally inevitable conflict between word-accent and verse-accent. Through analysis of deliberate variation we may better appreciate the verse and the poet; it is a misfortune, and a barrier to the development of prosodic study, that scholars have addressed themselves as much or more to the examination of unconscious variations.

Perhaps it is the mysterious power exerted by Schipper's array of categories which has prevented the placing of Chaucer's five-beat verse in comparison with its nearest of kin, the eleven-syllabled line of Boccaccio and Dante.

1883. A. Baret. Étude sur la langue anglaise au xivme siècle. Paris. Reviewed Littblatt 5 : 358, 6 : 330 as valueless.

1884. Bernhard ten Brink. Chaucers Sprache und Verskunst. Strassburg. Reviewed Anglia 7 : Anz. 141-43 (Wülker); Littblatt 1885 p. 187 (Einenkel); DLZ 1885, p. 607 ff. (Zupitza); Engl. Stud. 10 : 114-117 (Koch). Second ed. by Kluge, Leipzig 1899; rev. Anglia Beibl. 12 : 237-240 (Holthausen). Transl. into English by M. B. Smith, London 1901, as The Language and Versification of Chaucer.

See Smith, Some Remarks on Chapter III of ten Brink's Sprache und Verskunst, in Mod. Lang. Quart. 5 : 13-20 (1902), reviewed by Koch, Engl. Stud. 36 : 131-133, somewhat curtly; Koch says the point was already settled by Bischoff, see below under 1897.

1887. E. Einenkel. Streifzüge durch die mittelenglische Syntax. Reviewed Archiv 82 : 226 (Trautmann), Engl. Stud. 12 : 283-96 (Bülbring), Littblatt 1889 pp. 12-15, Acad. 1889 I : 327. Einenkel's references are to the Aldine Chaucer, by volume and page.

1888. A. Graef. Das perfektum bei Chaucer. diss. Kiel 1887, pp. 96, pubd. Frankenhausen 1888, pp. 102. Reviewed Anglia 11 : 326 (Wülker).

1890. C. W. Kent. On the Use of the Negative by Chaucer, with particular reference to the particle *ne*. Publ. Mod. Lang. Assn. 5 : 109-147.

1889. M. Freudenberger. Ueber das Fehlen des Auftakts in Chau-

cer's heroischem Verse. Leipzig. Reviewed Anglia Beibl.
I : 88-90 (Koeppel). See under E (4) below.

1891. A Graef. Die präsentischen Tempora bei Chaucer. Anglia
12 : 532-577.

1891. E. Gasner. Beiträge zum Entwicklungsgang der neuengl.
Schriftsprache. diss. Göttingen. pubd. Nürnberg, pp. 144.

1892. W. W. Skeat. Chaucer's Use of the Kentish Dialect. Chaucer Society Essays, part VI.

1893. G. Graef. Das futurum und die entwicklung von schal und
wil zu futurischen tempusbildnern bei Chaucer. Flensburg,
pp. 52. In Jahresbericht der Flensburger Handelsschule.

1893. In Paul's Grundriss der germanischen Philologie, the articles
on Englische Metrik are by K. Luick (Heimische Metra) and
J. Schipper (Fremde Metra).

1893. George Hempl. Chaucer's Pronunciation and the Spelling
of the Ellesmere Manuscript. Boston.

1893. John M. Manly. Observations on the Language of Chaucer's
Legend of Good Women. Harvard Studies, II : 1-120.

1894. G. L. Kittredge. Observations on the Language of Chaucer's
Troilus. Chaucer Society; and Harvard Studies, vol. III.

1894 ff. W. W. Skeat, in his ed. of Chaucer, vol. VI : xxiii ff.,
discusses the dialect of Chaucer, his pronunciations, his rimes,
Lounsbury's views on Chaucer's rimes, metres and forms of
verse, grammar, and versification. Skeat's dicta upon pronunciation, rime, and grammar are those generally accepted
in the present state of our textual knowledge; they are based
upon the text constructed by himself. His treatment of the
versification, similarly based, is very unsatisfying; the scheme
of scansion which he adopts is more inadequate than those
which he rejects.

1896. L. Morsbach. Mittelenglische Grammatik. Part I. Halle.

1897. O. Bischoff. Ueber zweisilbige Senkung und epische Cäsur
bei Chaucer. diss. Königsberg. Pubd. Engl. Stud. 24 : 353
ff., and 25 : 339-398. (See below, p. 499.)

1898. E. Hampel. Die silbenmessung in Chaucer's fünftaktigem
Verse. Teil I. diss Halle, pp. 45.

1899. H. C. Ford. Observations on the Language of Chaucer's House of Fame. diss. Univ. of Virginia, pp. 90.

1900. M. Kaluza. Historische Grammatik der englischen Sprache. Part I. Berlin.

1903. H. Remus. Untersuchungen über den romanischen Wortschatz Chaucers. diss. Göttingen, pubd. Halle, pp. 38.

1904. R. D. Miller. Secondary Accent in Modern English Verse (Chaucer to Dryden). diss. Johns Hopkins Univ.

1905. A. G. Kennedy. On the Substantivation of Adjectives in Chaucer. Univ. of Nebraska Studies, vol. 5, pp. 251-269.

1906. George Saintsbury. History of English Prosody. Part I. Lond. and N. Y. Reviewed Mod. Lang. Review 2 : 65-70 (McKerrow); Nation 1906 II : 189; Mod. Lang. Notes 22 : 122-124 (W. Hand Browne). See Omond, English Metrists, 1907, p. 239.

Chapter IV of Book II is devoted to Chaucer. Saintsbury takes the stand that we do not know what Chaucer wrote, and accordingly are in no position to discuss line-structure. His remarks are therefore general; but the student would have been more materially aided by a larger body of examples and a more thorough treatment of Chaucer as a poet, at the expense of the autobiographical comment, excess of literary allusion, and somewhat flippant gibe which appear in these pages. In this essay we have the complete opposite of Schipper's laborious technical analysis.

1906. Louis Round Wilson. Chaucer's Relative Constructions. diss. Univ. of North Carolina, pp. 60.

1906. H. Remus. Die kirchlichen und speziell-wissenschaftlichen romanischen Lehnworte Chaucers. Halle, pp. xii, 154.
See Remus' other work, 1903 above.

C. On the Language and Verse of Chaucer

Several considerations have created, and still keep alive, the feeling that Chaucer's verse, despite the imperfect copies which have come down to us, was in its original form smooth and beautiful. These considerations are: our knowledge that these copies are often careless "mismetred" renderings, marred as Chaucer himself deplored in his Words to Adam and at the close of his Troilus. Secondly, the fact that, in spite of this frequent injury, so large a proportion of his lines, as pointed out by Tyrwhitt, Essay part II, § xii, "sound complete to our ears." Thirdly, the superiority of any really critical text to even the best existing MS copy. And lastly, the instinctive inference of his readers that a man so greatly the master of structure, of character drawing, of selective art, of narrative power, must have been master also of verse-technique.

These arguments still hold. The danger in using them is one of detail rather than one of general principle. Pollard's remark, Athenaeum 1901 II : 631, that it is not likely that future editions of the Canterbury Tales will materially alter the reading of any twenty lines in that work, is in all probability true. But the advocate of the critical text, as defined by Liddell, ibid. p. 598, while reasonably assured of the poet's verse-command, desires in the first place to arrive at that assurance by sound methods, and in the second place to learn what licences or liberties Chaucer, the first master of the decasyllabic line in English, may have permitted himself in that form. Many critics, convinced of Chaucer's impeccability, attempt to force upon him verse-perfection according to modern notions, without regard to any metrical licences of his own which he may have originated. Thus, ten Brink disavowed the headless line now accepted as Chaucerian by all scholars, see below; Lowell also declined to credit the theory that Chaucer could have used it; and most authorities still refuse to accept the existence in Chaucer of the so-called "Lydgate line", i. e., the line in which a pause falls between two accented syllables. But we have not yet made that thorough and unbiassed examination of the texts which alone will enable us to say what variants Chaucer permitted himself on the analogy of the substituted anapest in Tennyson or the wrenched accent so frequent in Swinburne. Even among modern students there is found the tendency to reason in a circle, to start from the assumption that Chaucer is "impeccable", and, after constructing a body of texts on that hypothesis, by eliminating or altering whatever seems incompatible, to deduce from them the original assumption of the impeccability of Chaucer. The circle is then complete.

As the smoothness of Chaucer's verse is dependent primarily upon the number of its syllables and the position of the accents, the partial establishment of fourteenth-century syntax is a necessary prelude to the discussion of Chaucerian lines. Upon the sounding

31

or not sounding of the inflexional syllable must depend the number
of syllables in a given line, and, in consequence, its flow. It was in
part ignorance of Early English syntax which led Dryden, Johnson,
and other critics to consider Chaucer's verse as "often lame for want
of half a foot" etc.; see above under A.

The eighteenth century witnessed, as students of the Romantic
period have often emphasized, a wave of interest in the Teutonic
and Celtic past of England. Beside the revival of the ballad and of
the Norse saga there went a spirit of scientific investigation into
the past of the language. The seventeenth century lexicographers
Junius, Spelman, and Somner, the antiquarians Camden, Selden,
and Hearne, were followed by the investigators of Early English
grammar, the students of MSS, like Rawlinson and Hickes. The
first Anglo-Saxon grammar, Oxford 1689, was the work of Hickes,
who in 1705 published his larger work, the Thesaurus Grammatico-
criticus. In Hickes' time, says Mores in his Dissertation on English
Typographical Founders, London 1778, there was a "profluvium
of Saxonists" at Oxford; Hickes' nephew and niece, William and
Elizabeth Elstob, followed in his steps, the latter being the author
of the first Anglo-Saxon grammar composed in English (London
1715); and Edward Thwaites, another of the group, published in
1711 a brief abstract of Hickes in English for general use. Wotton's
"Conspectus Brevis" of Hickes appeared in 1708, and a "Short View"
of the Thesaurus, by Shelton, was published in 1735. Others of the
"profluvium" were Bishops Tanner and Nicolson, Mathew Gibson,
Humfrey Wanley, and T. Benson, author of a Vocabularium
Anglosaxonicum based on Somner and published at Oxford in 1701.
Lye's edition of Junius was in 1743.

Hickes, although demonstrating the derivation of English "ex
Anglosaxonica corruptione", made but passing comment upon the
relation between Middle English inflexion and Middle English verse
which necessarily followed from his proofs; but the little-known
Morell used Hickes' remark in his defence of Chaucer's verse, and
the opinion was also held by the poet Gray, see p. 471 here. Tyrwhitt, writing fifteen years after Gray, presented in his Essay the
first detailed historical argument for the verse-command of Chaucer;
his failure to conquer the 17th century tradition of Chaucer's halting
numbers is illustrated by the citations of opinion given above.

Following closely the arguments advanced by Tyrwhitt, we may
say that our grounds for belief in Chaucer's conscious adaptation of
his verse and his language, of his recognition and management of
the inflexional syllable, are:

(1) The history of word-endings in the language. If the Old
English inflexional syllables -a, -as, -an, etc., change in Middle
English to a nearly uniform -e, -es, -en, etc., and are in Modern English reduced to a silent -e or to an -s not separately sounded, and
if the development of our language has been gradual, then there

must have been a period when these syllables were sounded separately, though without the Old English full vowel-quality -a.

(2) The word-forms of a painstaking phonetician like Orm, early in the 13th century, writing in the septenar, show by their spelling and their verse-treatment that inflexional syllables were sounded by Orm.

> The unique and probably autograph manuscript of his *Orrmulum,* a barren paraphrase of parts of the Old Testament, is in the Bodleian Library, märked Junius I. It was edited in 1852 by White, revised in 1878 by Holt; extracts are in Morris and Skeat's Specimens of Early English, I : 39, and in the readingbooks of Maetzner, Sweet, and Zupitza. The work has no literary value, but its importance for English phonetics is very great. Orm attempted to indicate the quantity of vowels by doubling the consonant after a short vowel, provided that the consonant was final or was followed by another consonant. Thus, *was* is in his rendition *wass; folkes* is *follkess; turned* is *turrnedd.* But if the short vowel is followed by a consonant and then by another vowel, Orm does not double the consonant; *e. g.,* the k in *mikell.* He has thus no means of discriminating between such a short vowel and a long vowel, except that in his MS he has often put a mark above the long vowels. It has further been pointed out by Prof. Napier, Academy 1890 I : 188 cp. 133, that Orm has three different g-forms, according as the sound was g as in *good,* g as in *bridge,* or the y-sound. From the work of a man writing with such care and in a foreign metre we deduce that in his time the inflexional syllables were sounded separately. On Orm see Skeat, Canon, chap. I.
>
> The statement regarding Orm in Saintsbury's Flourishing of Romance, 1897 p. 198, is inaccurate. Orm does not double the consonant after every short vowel "without exception."

(3) The treatment of the French octosyllabic couplet by Chaucer's contemporary Gower shows that to Gower inflexional syllables were usually a separate element; see Macaulay's ed. of the Works of John Gower, II : cxx ff.

> On Chaucer's use of the four-beat couplet and the difficulty of judging it see below, p. 491.

(4) Double rimes, and rimes with proper names, in Chaucer's own work, often show the separate treatment of the inflexional syllable, thus: harmed, harm hid, BoDuch. 931-2; divynis, pyne is, Kn. Tale 465-6; blame, ba me, Mill. Tale 523-4; talis, Alis, WBprol. 547-8; preye, sey ye, Friar's Tale 157-8; youthe, alow the, Words of the Franklin, 3-4; sothe, to the, CYProl. 109-10; time, by me, CYTale, 651-2; swythe, hy the, CYTale, 741-2; and less conclusive instances like Dante, wante, LGWprol. 336-7; Lete, unswete, HoFame 71-2; Lyde, dyde, HoFame 105-6; Itaile, saile, HoFame 433-4.

For other cases see the Ryme Indexes pubd. by the Chaucer Society, and Ellis, EEPron. I : 318 ff.

It might seem that we have here an ample body of evidence for any deductions; but there are difficulties in the way of using it. Orm's testimony is clear, and the fact of linguistic evolution is clear; but neither proves for us at just what stage the development of English pronunciation and syntax had arrived in Chaucer's time. Nor does either answer the very important question how far Chaucer's scribes, through whom alone do we know Chaucer's syntax, agreed or disagreed with him in the linguistic forms which they used.

The conclusion to which scholars have come upon the former point is thus expressed by Skeat VI:lxv, "Chaucer's language is archaic; the use of the final -e was fast disappearing, and he probably was anxious to retain it for the sake of metrical effect." This conclusion meets with general acceptance, but there is however still uncertainty as to Chaucer's language and versification in matters of detail. To the body of rules drawn up for his rime-use, his treatment of the "dative", his management of inflexional -e, there are in each case exceptions; and this affects the scansion of many of his lines. We have:

Men moot yeue siluer to the poure freres   Prol. 232

and also

And pynnes for to yeuen faire wyues   Prol. 234

If we argue that such an infinitive as *yeue(n)* is invariably dissyllabic, we must recognize a slightly aberrant form of line in 232,— a form by no means disagreeable to the lover of English verse, but a stumbling block to some philologists. Again, if we view the adverb *sore* as a disyllable, and read,

He may not wepe al-thogh him sore smerte   Prol. 230

we might find some difficulty in Prol. 148,

But sore weep sche if oon of hem were deed

(On this line see p. 500 here.)

This possibly Chaucerian variation in the treatment of final -e is however but a trivial divergence compared with the variations plainly scribal—the writing not only of e. g., *fallethe* and *hathe,* but of *itte* and *frome,* which appear in the later MSS so frequently as to arouse the suspicion of students. The illogical and uncomprehending treatment of -e final by many fifteenth century scribes drives us to the conclusion that for them the -e's they wrote or omitted were largely conventional. Also, the autograph Chaucer-copies of John Shirley, in the first half of the fifteenth century, and the halting verse-imitations of Chaucer's admirer Lydgate at the same period, show an attempt to add expletives and a crudity of line-structure which argue that for both these lovers of Chaucer his verse had not the sound which it has after the revival of Early

English knowledge. From such facts we draw the conclusion that the change in English speech at the end of the fourteenth century was so great that the younger generation of scribes and writers failed to comprehend the verse system of a somewhat strict adherent to full linguistic forms such as was Chaucer.

We ought, therefore, before determining the kinds of lines and variants used by Chaucer, to work out the linguistic idiosyncrasies of his principal scribes,—of the ancestor of the Oxford Group (see Section IV A (3) here), of the MS Cambridge Gg, of the Ellesmere, the Campsall, etc.; from a comparison of these we can arrive with more than our present certainty at a conception of the difference between Chaucer and his best-known scribes. Certainly, until this analysis and comparison are made, we reason without one important source of evidence as to Chaucerian prosody; for our arguments for Chaucer's syntax and Chaucer's verse cannot be based upon the texts as they stand.

There remain to us at present the evidence of rimes, and in especial the sort of evidence last mentioned above, the instinctive deduction of Chaucer's poetic technique from his narrative technique. And here we are confronted by the question whether Chaucer was indeed a conscious artist in verse, as he was in the treatment of his literary material.

When we reach the Elizabethan age, we can say of the men of that period, and all succeeding periods of English poetry, that they were conscious artists. Criticism, often self-criticism, was accompanying their work. The air was full of discussion of language, of quantity, of epithet, of choice of line and movement. But in the middle of the fourteenth century, as Saintsbury has pointed out in his History of English Prosody, England was speaking a language not yet conscious of itself, a language in which no great poet or prose-writer had yet arisen, of which there were neither grammars nor dictionaries, a language which had not only no literature and no critic, but no tradition and no standards. We must, if we are to discuss Chaucer's technique, work out on the one hand the conditions of contemporary English, French, Italian, and Latin verse; and on the other hand we must collect from Chaucer's own text every critical remark, every trace of alteration of an original, every indication of phrase-lengthening or shortening, line-weighting or lightening, to accord with the movement of the thought, every case of repetition, of onomatopoeia, or of word-arrangement for the sake of emphasis. From these two bodies of facts we may, in default even of the critical text, deduce much as to Chaucer's prosody in general.

The first of these analyses is particularly necessary for a poet occupying, as Chaucer occupies, the position of a pioneer in English verse. With him the five-beat line appears in English; we have not in this case, as in that of blank verse or the sonnet, a period of tentative treatment and a gradual development of the form to high perfection. The ten-syllabled couplet has never been used in narrative verse with greater freedom and mastery than by Chaucer; and though his management of the same line in stanzas is less adroit and more slowly acquired, its flow in the Troilus has not since been surpassed by a poet working in strophes. It is therefore of especial interest to study Chaucer's handling of this lineform; the study of his four-beat line, as remarked below, is attended with peculiar textual difficulties.

Students have thus far traced the Chaucerian decasyllabic line to one of three sources; as noted below, Schipper derives it from thirteenth century English, Skeat from an isolated example in Machault; while ten Brink, in his Sprache und Versk. § 305 says, without discussion, that the heroic verse of Chaucer comes as near the verse of Dante and Boccaccio as the metre of a Germanic tongue can come to a Romance metre. (See also Tyrwhitt in his Essay, § ix and note 61.)

It is this last suggestion that I would emphasize. Far from regarding Chaucer's line, with Schipper, as the descendant of the Old English bipartite, heavily stressed verse; far from regarding it as akin to the French syllable-counting movement; far even from regarding it as the struggle and compromise of these two systems, I would see in Boccaccio and in Dante the true instructors of Chaucer. The briefest dip into Boccaccio's Filostrato will reveal the overrunning lines and the varying length of phrase which we class among Chaucer's most admirable freedoms, will show us the reversal of rhythm (or substituted trochee), and the skilful use of rhythmic emphasis to support idea-emphasis. Compare for instance Chaucer's rendition of

Tu savio, tu amico, tu sai tutto   Filostr. II, st. 33

into

But thou wys, thou wost, thou mayst, thou art al

Troilus I : 1052

and observe his recognition and accentuation of the Italian's stresses; compare the movement at the beginning of III, stanza 78 of the Filostrato,

Tu in unita le case e le cittadi,
Li regni, e le provincie, e'l mondo tutto
Tien, bella dea . . .

with a Chaucerian flow like

O tonge, allas ! so often here-biforn
Hastow made many a lady bright of hewe
Seyd, welawey ! the day . . .   Troilus III : 302 ff.

or with Milton's

> Seasons return, but not to me returns
> *Day,* nor the sweet approach . . . Par. Lost, III : 40 ff.

Different as often is the swifter, simpler flow of the purely narrative verse of Chaucer, solidly English though the movement may be of such a monosyllabic line as

> A knight ther was, and that a worthy man,

there can be little question but that he learned from the great Italians the essentials of his art. Could he fail to perceive, at the opening of the Inferno, the effect of the double reversal of stress in

> Questa selva selvaggia ed aspra e forte ?

Could it escape him that his translation

> The day gan failen, and the derke night   PoFoules 85

followed with fidelity the movement of Dante's

> Lo giorno andava, e l'aer bruno ?

It must of course be recognized that in Chaucer's hands any Romance original will become more strongly accentual. Indeed, it is a question if, with all his knowledge of Italian poetry, Chaucer did not grasp it more by eye than by ear; if he did not impose upon it, as any purely bookish English student to-day imposes upon his Dante, the Germanic rhythm. Consider the shortness of Chaucer's first visit to Italy, January to May, and his mature age at the time; also that, although his second visit extended over double the time of the first, it was made after six years, and when Chaucer was more than forty years old. But even with such limitations, I would suggest that Chaucer probably took from Italy his idea of the decasyllabic line, and took also, it may well be, his idea of the freedom possible in the number and position of its accented syllables.

To this last attention may be called. Our prosodic theories provide for the existence in English of "iambic pentameter" lines; it is incumbent upon the individual student to realize that this theoretical type is the rarest of all forms in the actual rhythm; that what we term the ten-syllabled line ranges from nine to twelve syllables; that what we term the five-beat line has more frequently four grammatical stresses, or three and a secondary; and that what we call "iambic" requires the constant presence of "trochees", "spondees", and "anapests" to satisfy our ear. It is the distinction of Chaucer, and a distinction probably arising under Italian influence, to have planted these standards of variation at the very opening of the course of English heroic verse; to have established once and for all the fact that

> Or breke it at a renning with his heed

has as much right in "five-beat iambic" context as

But thou wys, thou wost, thou mayst, thou art al.

Retaining as we do in our prosody the nomenclature of a poetry whose prime characteristic is its regularity, we find it hard to express the quality of a poet who took from Continental prosodies their liberties, and united them in the earliest modern English poetry. But because this freedom of flow is Chaucer's great contribution to English verse, it is before all things necessary that we study his variations from the theoretical verse-scheme.

The extreme refinement of vocalic and rhythmic effects we do not expect to find in a poet of Chaucer's early date; we do not seek in his verse for the artful opening and shutting of sound in imitation of air-effects, as in Milton's

Swinging slow with sullen roar

nor the dragging sweetness of Keats'

And no birds sing.

For when we speak of Chaucer's freshness and simplicity, it is his freedom from just such beautiful sophistications that we mean,—a freedom which befits the man who was first, last, and always the storyteller, and but incidentally the singer. We mean such contrasts as this:

For Cristes lore and his apostles twelve
He taughte, and first he folwed it himselve.

Prologue 527-8 (of the Parson)

Do not, as some ungracious pastors do,
Show me the steep and thorny way to heaven,
Whiles, like a puffed and reckless libertine,
Himself the primrose path of dalliance treads
And recks not his own rede.

Hamlet I, 3.

Or this:

As doon thise loveres in hir queynte geres,
Now in the croppe, now doun in the breres,
Now up, now doun, as boket in a welle.
Right as the Friday, sothly for to telle,
Now it shyneth, now it reyneth faste.
Right so can gery Venus overcaste
The hertes of hir folk. . . .

Knight's Tale, 673 ff.

O how this spring of love resembleth
The uncertain glory of an April day:
Which now shows all the beauty of the sun,
And by and by a cloud takes all away.

Two Gent. Verona I, 3.

But there is in Chaucer, notwithstanding his characteristically simple diction, ample evidence of conscious artistic intent. Not often do we find the device for attracting the ear to important words, such as Milton uses when he makes an expected light syllable heavy,

> Shoots far into the bosom of dim Night   Par. Lost I : 1036,

a device whose emphasis is still more clearly seen when misused as by Cowper,

> To adjust the fragrant charge of a short tube
> That fumes beneath his nose . . .   Task, V : 55-56.

Yet similar cases do occur in Chaucer. Compare for instance the line describing the Parson and his conception of duty,

> That if gold ruste what shal iren do

with the unexpected weight on *gold*. Other and more striking examples of artistic intent are easily found; Mather, in his edition of the Prologue, etc., p. xxxvi, points out several; note the rapid and hardbreathing movement of the preparations for the tournament, Knight's Tale 1636 ff., or the still more forcible and powerfully alliterative descriptions of the tournament itself and of the seafight in the Cleopatra story of the Legend of Good Women. Mather also cites single expressive lines like

> He was shortsholdred, brood, a thikke knarre

in the portrait of the Miller. To this, it seems to me, we may well add the two lines following in the Prologue,

> Ther nas no dore that he nolde heve of harre
> Or breke it at a renning with his heed.

The former of these is not so obvious as Pope's

> Up the high hill he heaved a huge round stone,

nor is the latter so marked as Tennyson's

> And flashing round and round and whirled in an arch,

but the two first of Chaucer's three lines are as certainly over-weighted with intent as is the last line underweighted to an almost imitative swiftness of motion.

To turn to another artistic possibility, that of vocalic tone-coloring, we may see, with Mather, conscious art in the line

> Ginglen in a whistling wind as clere   Prol. 170,

and recognize the "harsh and angular" adjectives of Knight's Tale 1117; or we may agree with Saintsbury as to the melodic effect of Troilus' song,

> If no love is, O God, what fele I so,
> And if love is, what thing and which is he?

But we shall not expect to find the oppressive richness of lines such as Tennyson's "Lit by a low large moon", or the intellectual melancholy of Arnold's "unplumb'd, salt, estranging sea." There, again, is the modern refinement of sensation developed since Chaucer's day. Even the farewell cry of Arcite, "Allone withouten any companye", we hesitate to accept at the full pathetic value accorded it by Mather when we see it used of the clerk Nicholas at the opening of the Miller's Tale, closely following the description of Arcite's death.

The collection of such observations upon the rhythmical and melodic effects of Chaucer has however formed no part of the work of prosodists. Schipper, upon whose methods are based the verse-analyses of subsequent Middle English students, has treated Chaucer as one treats the line-by-line workmen of earlier ages, and has erected (working with the uncritical text of Morris) a set of line-types and variants which are still accepted. It may however be questioned if a discussion of Chaucer's melody which proceeds on such methods alone can make that melody apparent. For it is based, in the first place, upon a text uncertain in those very matters of detail to which Schipper limits his analysis; in the second place, it ignores the general esthetic considerations which we can reach with even our present text, and which will at least give us a better conception of Chaucer's artistic power than will Schipper's classification of his cesuras. We can, for instance, note that the presence of the inflexional -e in Chaucer's language adds to his line a larger amount of open vocalic sound than our choked consonantal utterance permits, although the monotony of this recurring vowel sound makes the Englishman's line less intrinsically melodious than that of the Italian. The existence of this vowel sound, moreover, enabled Chaucer to manage the transitional parts of his narrative with a smaller proportion of the partially stressed pronouns and connectives than is possible to us when we try to modernize him. We must in rendering him either increase the amount of such words,—words rarely in themselves musical,—or increase his emphasis by using adjectives and adverbs not in his swift fluid narrative. Look, for example, at the opening of the Knight's Tale:

> Whilom, as olde stories tellen us,
> Ther was a duk that highte Theseus.   Chaucer.

> In days of old there liv'd, of mighty fame,
> A valiant Prince, and Theseus was his name.   Dryden.

> Whilom, as olden tales record for us,
> There lived a duke whose name was Thesëus.   Skeat.

Chaucer, working up to his principal idea, *Theseus,* the final rime-word of his couplet, reaches it with but four words on which emphatic utterance is necessary to our comprehension,—whilom, olde, stories, duke; the rest of his words are subsidiary, and three of his unaccented syllables are inflexional, making no tax upon enunciation or mind. Dryden not only loses the rise of the couplet to Theseus, and makes three pauses where Chaucer made two, but he adds two adjectival ideas, *mighty* and *valiant,* which are not expressed by Chaucer; his verse paces where Chaucer's springs. Comparisons between Chaucer and Dryden, at all moments when Dryden does not deliberately expand his original, reveal interesting divergences of this same sort. Dryden is almost invariably heavier than Chaucer, besides failing constantly to reproduce the reserve, the sparing use of epithet, so characteristic of the older poet.

A comparison of the two poets in this aspect of their work alone expresses the personalities of their geniuses as clearly as does a comparison of their lives and their entire literary production. In a poet, the verse is the man.

D. Chaucer's Line- and Strophe-Forms

Chaucer's line- and strophe-forms have been discussed in general by Tyrwhitt, by Schipper, by ten Brink, and by Skeat, as above referred to. Tyrwhitt and Skeat based their conclusions upon their own editions; ten Brink used the Chaucer Society's Six-Text and the prints of Harley 7334 and Dd by Morris and by Wright. Schipper used the eds. of Morris.

The Four-beat Line.

None of these students gives much attention to the four-beat line; see ten Brink, Sprache und Versk. §§ 297-303, Schipper, Engl. Metrik I : 280, Skeat VI : xcvii. See also: Zur Geschichte des kurzen Reimpaars im Mittelenglischen. C. L. Crow. diss. Göttingen, 1892, pp. 63, reviewed Anglia Beibl. 3 : 303 (Dieter), Engl. Stud. 18 : 225 (Kaluza). See also the eds. of the Book of the Duchesse and of the House of Fame by Lange and by Willert.

The study of this line is for Chaucer subject to peculiar limitations, which perhaps have not been sufficiently recognized by editors. The translation of the Roman de la Rose is not with certainty to be termed Chaucer's; the BoDuchesse is preserved in but three texts, and those all of one family, so that a critical text is not possible; while of the HoFame also but three copies remain, two of them sisters (and the same MSS which preserve the BoDuchesse), the third a very corrupt and untrustworthy codex. Our dicta regarding Chaucer's four-beat line are thus exceedingly tentative.

Any student devoting himself to an analysis of Chaucer's short couplet has first to reconstruct the Fairfax-Bodley text of the two poems above-mentioned, and then reconstruct from Fairfax-Bodley and Tanner the text of the BoDuchesse as it stood in Oxford (see p. 338 here). He will then have the readings of Fairfax-Bodley for one poem, the readings of the Oxford archetype for the other; and from notes on the kinds of error peculiar to each of these types (notes drawn from study of all the texts contained in them) he would then be able to introduce conjectural emendation of the "Oxford" type of error, to which he has in these cases no external MS evidence as check. See Mod. Lang. Notes 23 : 20-21.

The four-beat line is used by Chaucer in couplets in these two poems, and in other metres only in stanzas inserted into the BoDuchesse, lines 475-485, on which see under that poem, Section IV here; also, combined with shorter lines, in the Rime of Sir Thopas, six-line stanzas; also, combined with five-beat lines, in the fifth stanza of both strophe and antistrophe of the complaint of Anelida.

Licences or variants are discussed by Schipper, Engl. Metrik I : 280-82. See Saintsbury, Hist. Eng. Prosody I : 146.

The Five-beat Line.

Prototypes of Chaucer's five-beat line have been found by Schipper in thirteenth century English verse; see his Engl. Metrik I : 436, his Grundriss p. 207. Skeat III : 383 finds prototypes of Chaucer's five-beat couplet in the French of Machault, see Schipper, Engl. Metrik I : 453; Skeat VI : lxxxix says that Chaucer learned from Italian to vary the place of his pause, but lays no stress on Boccaccio and Dante as the possible inspirers of this form of verse. Ten Brink, Sprache und Versk. § 305 (note), hesitates to follow Schipper in identifying certain Middle English lines as the earliest examples of Chaucer's heroic verse; Schipper, Grundriss p. 207, comments on this. For ten Brink's recognition of Italian influence, and Tyrwhitt's remark, see p. 486 above.

The five-beat line is used by Chaucer in couplets, as in the Legend of Good Women and in most of the Canterbury Tales. It is combined in the Troilus into seven-line stanzas, a form borrowed from Old French poetry, see Schipper, Engl. Metrik I : 426. It is combined into eight-line stanzas in the Monk's Tale, the Former Age, etc.; this also is a form common in French, see Schipper, Engl. Metrik I : 428. The eight-line stanza with rime-arrangement as in the Italian ottava rima does not appear in Chaucer. The decasyllabic line also appears in nine-line stanzas rarely, two cases in the complaint of Anelida and one in the Mars; once it is found in a ten-line stanza, the envoy to the Venus; it is combined in six-line stanzas in the envoy to the Clerk's Tale; in a five-line stanza, the genuineness of which has been doubted, as envoy to Purse, see under that heading, Section IV here; also in an imperfectly preserved roundel near the close of the Parlement of Foules. In the (perhaps genuine) Ballad of Pity, or Complaint to his Lady, occurs a brief example of terza rima; see Section V here.

The nine and ten-line stanzas are treated by Schipper, Engl. Metrik I : 430, as original forms; the six-line is a French form, see *ibid.* p. 425. For the roundel-structure and origin see *ibid.* p. 431; for the "ballad" see *ibid.* III : 927, I : 426 ff.

Skeat, in his list of Chaucer's stanzas, VI : lviii ff., includes examples from Merciless Beaute, Against Women Unconstant, Womanly Noblesse, To Rosemounde. The authenticity of these poems is not unquestioned, see Section V here.

The possible variants of the five-beat line are discussed by Schipper, Engl. Metrik I : 440 ff., Grundriss pp. 208-210, ten Brink, Sprache und Versk. § 307 ff., Skeat VI : lxxxii ff. Schipper's list of points requiring consideration is, hovering accent, reversal of accent, lack of upbeat, double upbeat and double unaccented syllable, elision or suppression of syllables, the cesura.

While maintaining Chaucer's debt to Boccaccio and to Dante in the treatment of the five-beat line, I would assert his own probable originality in the five-beat couplet. It is unnecessary to search the works of medieval French poets for isolated examples of such a metre, or even to insist upon the fact that Chaucer had been writing ten-syllabled couplets at the ends of his seven-line stanzas, while Boccaccio used a similar couplet to close his eight-line stanzas, so well known to Chaucer. Given a man of great artistic ability, as was Chaucer, and the passage from the familiar four-beat couplet through the five-beat line to the writing of five-beat couplets is not so difficult as to require explanation.

E. Modes of Varying the Line-Flow

1. The Cesura.

Mayor, in his Chapters on English Metre, ed. 1901 p. 303, says of the "caesura" of classical metres, "It is essential to the harmony of a line that some one or more of its feet should be divided between two different words. This division is called *caesura* or 'cutting.' There are two kinds of caesura, the *masculine, strong,* or *monosyllabic* caesura, where only the first syllable of the foot is in the preceding word; and the *feminine, weak,* or *trochaic* caesura, where the first two syllables of a dactyl are in the preceding word, and only the remaining short syllable in the word which follows." The example given is:

Formosam | resonare | doces | Amaryllida silvas.

Here there are strong cesuras in the second and the fourth foot, and a weak cesura in the third.

In the fourth chapter of his History of French Versification, Oxford 1903, Kastner discusses the French cesura. He defines it as "a pause in the interior of the line, dividing the line into so many parts, which pause indicates the end of a rhythmical period and enables the voice to rest after a given number of syllables." . . .

In a note Kastner remarks that the nature of the classical cesura differs essentially from that of French verse, and that the term is not a very happy one, as applied to French verse.

It appears from the above that the classical conception of a cesura was the interplay of the speech unit and the rhythmical unit, the partial avoidance of words coinciding in form with the foot, of *e. g.*, a dactylic movement made up of words in themselves dactyls. This conception of the cesura is however not that of Old French verse. There it is the pause necessary during the utterance of a ten or twelve-syllabled line; a pause conditioned by the sense, or at least not incompatible with it, and usually dividing the verse very nearly in halves. Thus the classical notion of *a* cesura was in France replaced by the notion of *the* cesura; and instead of being merely the convenient name for a form of variety in verse-pattern (as in Latin), the term becomes in French the indication of a somewhat rigid physical phenomenon.

The heavy medial pause of Old English alliterative verse bears to this latter a strong resemblance; but when we examine the five-beat line of Chaucer, we recognize a difference in his verse-management, as compared with either Old English or Old French, which has caused critics to speak of his "movable cesura." Thus, Schipper, Engl. Metrik I : 450; ten Brink, Sprache und Versk. § 305. The latter ascribes Chaucer's freedom in pause-position to his study of Italian, an opinion also glanced at by Skeat VI : lxxxix. Schipper in his Grundriss p. 208 (note) cites ten Brink's opinion with some doubt.

In view of Chaucer's complete departure from both the classical and the French idea of the cesura, it is hard for many of his readers to see why this terminology should be applied to him. In the examination and dissection of any single line, we may for convenience' sake speak of the position of the pause; but directly the lines are combined into Chaucer's characteristically free and flowing paragraphs,—the first in the Canterbury Tales is of eighteen lines,— it seems a misnomer to speak of the position of the pause, much more of the cesura, which latter implies fixity. Thus Lowell, in his essay on Chaucer, calls the cesural pause "a purely imaginary thing in accentual metres." Yet Ellis, discussing Chaucer's "cesura", EEPron. I : 335, defines it as "the terminating of a word at the end of the second measure or in the middle of the third, or else more rarely at the end of the third or middle of the fourth measure." Inasmuch as Ellis adds that words forming a logical whole must be considered as parts of the same word (*e. g.*, "That slepen *al the night* with open eye"), it is evident that to him the cesura was a sense-pause, occurring in Chaucer in one of four positions in the line. Schipper, Engl. Metrik I : 450, considers Ellis' remarks as insufficient; he finds six principal types of "cesura", with two other less frequent possibilities after the first or after the fourth beat.

This classification is termed "excellent" by Gayley and Scott in their Methods and Materials of Literary Criticism, p. 481, and has been very generally used by editors of fifteenth century texts.

The basis upon which it rests is, however, subjective. In many Chaucerian lines a distinct syntactical pause enables all students to agree upon the position of the "cesura"; and in those cases the manuscripts, our only evidence of any antiquity, usually coincide in the placing of their bar. But in many other cases the disagreement among the MSS in this respect is as marked as their textual disagreement; and we are obliged to feel that here, as in the writing or neglect of the final -e, the scribes are no sure guide. The noble Ellesmere manuscript writes:

> So priketh hem nature in hir corages

and

> The hooly blisful martir for to seke,

without indication of pause; but other MSS mark off the lines after *nature* and *martir*. Other lines are marked by the Ellesmere in a way contrary to the probable practice of a modern reader, *e. g.*, line 32 of the Prologue,

> That I was / of hir felaweshipe anon,

a line which is marked by Schipper, *op. cit.* I : 458, as having its "cesura" after *of,* but as being one of the verses possessing, according to Schipper, an almost imperceptible ("verwischte") cesura. Nevertheless, most modern English readers would probably render the line with a slight recover of the breath after the somewhat emphatic word *I.*

The question of the true nature of pause in verse has never yet been settled; but it seems to many students of Chaucer as if there were a clear distinction between the pause made evident by sentence structure and the fractional delay perhaps needed to regulate the breath in a line having no logical break. There seems also to be a very marked distinction between lines containing different ideas, which require pauses of readjustment as the enumerating mind moves among them,

> Trouthe and honour, fredom and curtesye,

and lines rising in an unbroken crescendo of idea to their close,

> He was a verray parfit gentil knight.

In the case above mentioned, of the line having no real logical break, the point at which the delay is made must be in part dependent upon the place of rhetorical emphasis and in part upon length of preceding phrase. In fact, the whole matter, for Chaucer at least, is less position of pause than length of phrase. There is found the true variety, a variety which is discovered by study not of line, but of paragraph. The consideration of pauses as a special feature of versification, apart from the phrases among which they occur, is as if an artist drew his line, not to indicate form, but for the sake of the line itself.

2. Reversal of Rhythm, or "Substituted Trochee."
Very common in the first foot of the line:

Redy to wenden on my pilgrimage	Prol. 21
Caught in a trappe, if it were deed or bledde	Prol. 145

In the second foot:

Of brend gold was the caas, and eke the harneys	
	Kn. Tale 2038

In the third foot:

To telle yow al the condicioun	Prol. 38

Rare after the third foot; but:

And thanne his neighebour right as himselve	Prol. 535

Except at the opening of the line,—and often there also,—this reversal is marked, and calls the reader's ear to the idea contained in these words. When the substituted foot is a dissyllable, especially one of mere conjunctive value, like *after, under, whoso,* it seems to me better to treat it, not with Schipper as a case of "hovering accent", but as one of those lighter, inconspicuous irregularities which are of no effect rhetorically, although as necessary to ideal rhythm as is regularity. When the substituted foot is however composed of two monosyllables, the effect is usually more emphatic, and brings out strongly the word-idea.

See Ellis, EEPron. I : 333, Schipper, Engl. Metrik I : 459-62, Saintsbury, Hist. Eng. Prosody I : 146.

3. Elision or Slurring; Contraction or Syncope; Hiatus.
Under the name Elision, says ten Brink, Sprache und Versk. § 269, we include the various phenomena consequent upon the fusion into one syllable of a final vowel and a following initial vowel.

This fusion may be complete, one vowel disappearing:

Wel coude he sitte on horse and faire ryde	Prol. 94

Or a diphthongal union may result:

. . . . . . so mery a companye	Prol. 764
By eterne word to dyen in prisoun	Kn. Tale 251

This licence is very common in Italian.

By Contraction or Syncope is here meant the neglect in pronunciation of an unaccented medial vowel occurring after a consonant and before a liquid, a nasal, or -th.

And thenk(e)th heer com(e)th my mortal enemy	Kn. Tale 785
And ev(e)r he rood the hindreste of our route	Prol. 622

This licence does not occur in Italian or in French. See
ten Brink as above, §§ 269-272; Schipper, Engl. Metrik. I : 465-
69; Skeat, in the Aldine Chaucer, Essay on Language and
Versification, § ix, and Oxford Chaucer VI : xciii; Child, *op.
cit.,* summarized in Ellis, EEPron. I : 360 ff.; Saintsbury, Eng.
Prosody I : 172-173; Brydges, Athen. 1904 I : 83.

Hiatus is the opposite of elision, the separate enunciation of a
final vowel and of the immediately following initial vowel. It is
common in Old English and Italian verse.

<blockquote>I have, God wot, a large feeld to | ere   Kn. Tale 28</blockquote>

See Ellis, EEPron. I : 363, Schipper, Engl. Metrik. I : 467.

On the whole subject of syllable-measurement in Chaucer see
Die Silbenmessung in Chaucer's fünftaktigem Verse. E. Hampel.
diss. Halle. 1898, pp. 45.

4. Headless Lines, or lines without the opening unaccented syllable.
In the text of Chaucer at present received as sound, we find lines
like

<blockquote>Twenty bokes clad in blak or red   Prol. 294
In a goune of faldyng to the kne   Prol. 391</blockquote>

where the verse, normally of ten to twelve syllables opening with
an unstressed syllable, is without the initial unaccented syllable, thus
containing in some cases but nine. It is scarcely possible that
Dryden, in his allusion to Chaucer's lines as "sometimes lame for
want of half a foot" etc. (see under A above), was referring to
such lines; and the early editors do not appear to have noticed
any deficiency. Urry prints the lines above cited with the short
opening foot; and Morell, in 1737, was the first to pause over the
peculiar reading; see the extract from his preface cited under A
above. Tyrwhitt combated Morell, and refused to accept the possibility that the heroic line could be of nine syllables; he considered
such verses as due to scribal errors, see his Essay, note 60. In the
text, accordingly, he eliminated them; and those above cited read,
in his edition,

<blockquote>A twenty bokes, clothed in black or red
All in a goune of falding to the knee.</blockquote>

Skeat took up the subject in some paragraphs appended to Tyrwhitt's Essay as printed with the revised Aldine Chaucer of 1866;
but he is mistaken in his claim, Oxford Chaucer VI : lxxxviii note,
of being the first to notice the peculiarity; see remark on Morell
above. Skeat there accepted the licence as Chaucerian; but ten
Brink, in his Sprache und Versk. § 307, and also Lowell in his
essay on Chaucer, declared such lines impossible to Chaucer. The
subject was discussed in detail in: Ueber das Fehlen des Auftakts

32

in Chaucers Heroischem Verse. M. Freudenberger. Leipzig, 1889,
reviewed Koeppel, Anglia Beibl. 1 : 88-90; Koch in Littblatt 1890
p. 452.

Freudenberger in his opening pages enumerates the opinions
of his predecessors, pointing out that Ellis EEPron. I : 333 and
Schipper Engl. Metrik I § 188 concede the licence only when
the first word of the line has full stress and is capable of a
compensatory emphasis. Zupitza, in his ed. of the Prologue, 1871,
accepts such lines even when the first syllable is weak, as in the
second example above; Koch, reluctantly conceding Freudenberger's
proofs, Engl. Stud. 15 : 401, says that outside this one freedom he
considers all departures from the norm as due to scribal error, and
would emend them. Zupitza, Archiv 94 : 443, is of a different
opinion; he thinks that Chaucer may have occasionally omitted a
syllable in the pause, as a form of variant; see the following
paragraph here. Pollard, in his ed. of the Knight's Tale, 1903, p. 81,
terms lines beginning with a foot consisting of a single weak
syllable "a blot on Chaucer's versification." See Ellis and Schipper
as above cited. Saintsbury, Hist. Eng. Prosody I : 170, asserts the
existence of this licence in both the four-beat and the five-beat
verse of Chaucer, though regretting its appearance in the latter.

5. "Lydgate Lines", or lines lacking a medial unaccented syllable.

This line is conveniently termed the "Lydgate line", from its
somewhat frequent use, so far as can be determined from the texts
yet edited, by John Lydgate. Its peculiarity is that an unaccented
syllable is lacking at a verse-pause, so that that pause comes, with
harsh effect, between two syllables carrying stress. For example:

My tale is doon | for my wit is thinne   Merch. Tale 438

Schipper, Engl. Metrik I : 463, Zupitza in Archiv 94 : 443, accept
(Schipper doubtfully) the occasional existence of such lines in the
Chaucerian text; Koch (as above) would refuse them; Skeat VI :
xcii gives two cases, one being that above cited, and says that the
MSS are "sadly unanimous"; Saintsbury, Hist. Eng. Prosody I :
171 note, 175 note, considers the instances in Chaucer so few as to
be negligible, probably mere scribal errors.

Prof. Saintsbury's own remarks, *ibid.* pp. 165-66, that we do not
know what Chaucer really wrote, and that modern texts have been
constructed by inferential hypothesis, are so entirely justifiable that he
cannot with consistency speak of the "Lydgate lines" in Chaucer as
demonstrably few. Here, as previously, it must be said that the details
of Chaucer's line-movement are not matters of certainty. That there
was a consciousness, possibly a dislike, of such lines in the fifteenth
century, almost at the time when Lydgate was presumably writing them,
may be argued from two copies of his St. Edmund, where the many
cases of this movement in MS Harley 2278 have been to great extent
removed in the later copy, Ashmole 46. See Horstmann, Altengl.

Legenden, 1881, pp. 376 ff., and my paper in Univ. of Chicago Decennial
Publ. VII, p. 23.

Browne, reviewing Saintsbury (Mod. Lang. Notes 22 : 122), objects
to his dismissal of the "Lydgate line", and cites:
"To be or not to be, that is the question." Hamlet III :sc. 1. But
the juxtaposition of accents in the Shaksperean verse is rhetorical,
not a necessity, and the verse is of the full ten syllables. Skeat, printing the Chaucerian line above quoted, puts a dash after *doon*, as if to
imply compensatory pause. Nor can such a verse as MLTale 666 be
treated as of this type, since no unaccented syllable is lacking.

6. Trisyllabic Feet.

In the text at present received as sound, we may find a double
(instead of single) unaccented syllable at the beginning of a line:

> With a thredbare cope, as is a poure scoler   Prol. 260

Or at the "cesura":

> His heed was balled | that shoon as any glas   Prol. 198

This form of line, sometimes called respectively "double upbeat",
and "epic cesura", has been discussed by Ellis, EEPron. III : 648-9;
Ellis accepts the trisyllabic measures. Schipper, Engl. Metrik I :
464, Grundriss p. 210, says that such feet are frequent in Chaucer.
Ten Brink, Sprache und Versk. § 307, (2), (3), would in most
cases remove the trisyllabic foot by emending the text. Skeat VI :
lxxxvi-xcii thinks that ten Brink has failed to understand the effect
of the cesura; he gives several cases, pp. xci, xcii, of the redundant
syllable at the cesura, and considers that there is no need to elide
the unaccented vowel preceding the cesura; it should be fully pronounced. Saintsbury, Hist. Eng. Prosody I : 171 ff., defends "actual
trisyllabic" feet, as well as slurring and elision, as a factor making
for variety and charm. The subject was also discussed in detail,
for Chaucer, in: Ueber zweisilbige Senkung und epische Caesur
bei Chaucer. O. Bischoff. diss. Königsberg, 1897. Also in Engl.
Stud. 24 : 353 ff.; 25 : 339-398.

In Part I of his monograph Bischoff endeavors to prove that
there is in Chaucer no dissyllabic thesis except possibly at the
cesura. In Part II he arrives at the conclusion that there is always
elision at the cesura, and that, in consequence, the existence of
"epic cesura" in Chaucer is doubtful.

Our confidence in Bischoff's work is not increased when he combats
the existence of the "epic cesura" in nondramatic poetry later than
Chaucer, and terms incorrect Schipper's scansion of Paradise Lost I : 202,

> Created húgest | that swim the Ocean stréam.

For this Bischoff (Engl. Stud. 25 : 363) would substitute

> Created húgest | thát swim the Ocean stréam.

7. Alexandrines, or Six-beat Lines.

The existence of six-beat lines in Chaucer's five-beat verse was
accepted with reluctance by Ellis, EEPron. III : 649; one of his
examples is:

> But sore wepte sche if oon of hem were deed   Prol. 148

Schipper, Engl. Metrik I : 464-5, denies the existence of Alexandrines in Chaucer; *ibid.* 451 he gives this line as a case of epic cesura, the *sche* being an extra syllable. He considers Ellis mistaken. Ten Brink, Sprache und Versk. § 307, comments on the line above cited that it looks like an Alexandrine, but that emendment will rectify it; apparently he does not recognize such a variant in Chaucer. Skeat prints:

> But sore weep she if oon of hem were deed,

and in his note on the line says that *she if oon* should be treated as one foot, the *she* being very light. In his essay on versification, vol. VI, he makes no mention of Alexandrines.

It should be noted that although Skeat in his text and Zupitza in his ed. of the Prologue (1882) print *weep*, the eight MSS reproduced for the Chaucer Society all read *wepte (wepped)*.

Saintsbury, Hist. Eng. Prosody, I : 174-5 and note, believes in the existence of Alexandrines in Chaucer's verse; the example he gives is:

> Westward right swich another in the opposite   Kn. Tale 1036

Upon which McKerrow, reviewing Saintsbury, Mod. Lang. Review 2 : 69 note, remarks that *Westward* may be a "foolish gloss", which has crept into the text.

8. Variation in Line-Weight.

In English heroic verse the line may upon occasion be possessed of more than five stress-capable syllables, or of less than five. A standard example of the former is Milton's

> Rocks, caves, lakes, fens, bogs, dens, and shades of death.
> > Paradise Lost, II : 621.

A clear example of the latter from Chaucer is the line already cited

> Or breke it at a renning with his heed.

Another form of variety, exceedingly frequent in Milton, is the line light in one portion and heavy in another. Thus, from Chaucer,

> And for to drinken strong wyn, reed as blood   Prol. 635

Here the first three syllables are light, and four heavy monosyllables are grouped together at the end of the line.

9. Accent.

The variable accent of French words naturalized into English has been discussed by Tyrwhitt in his Essay § xvii; by Ellis, EEPron. I : 330-33; by Schipper, Engl. Metrik I : 442-448; by ten Brink, Sprache und Versk. §§ 283 ff.; by Skeat VI : xcii-xciii.

F. Alliteration, Rime, Style, &c.

Alliteration

Chaucer's Alliteration. F. Lindner. Jahrbuch 1875, pp. 311-335.
Discussed by ten Brink, Sprache und Versk. § 334.

The same paper, revised and altered, in English, is in the Ch.
Soc. Essays, part III.

Chaucer's alliteration is discussed by ten Brink, Sprache und
Versk. §§ 335-343.

The Alliteration of Chaucer. C. F. McClumpha. diss. Leipzig,
n. d., pp. 96.

Ueber Alliteration in den Werken Chaucers, mit Ausschluss der
Canterbury Tales. E. Petzold, diss. Marburg, 1869, pp. 98.

Rime

The rimes of Chaucer have been discussed by Ellis, EEPron.
I : 241 ff., ten Brink, Sprache und Versk. §§ 321-333, Skeat VI :
xxxi-lviii. His rimes, like those of Gower and other Early English
poets, are purer and stricter than those of English poets since the
invention of printing. Certain licences he uses:
(a) Identical or Grammatical Rime.

> Albeit that I can nat soune his style,
> Ne can nat climben over so heigh a style.   Sq. Tale 97-98

> The holy blisful martir for to seke,
> That hem hath holpen whan that they were seke.   Prol. 16-17

Ten Brink, *op. cit.* § 330, Skeat VI : xlix-l, speak of these repeated rimes as composed of words different in sense although
alike in form. But see
Chaucer's Identical Rimes. E. P. Morton. Mod. Lang. Notes
18 : 73-4.

This freedom is rare in modern poets; Milton has *ruth: Ruth* in
his Sonnet IV, and Tennyson rimes *eave: eve.*

(b) Cheap Rime, or rime merely of suffix.
Softly : openly, goodnesse : soothfastnesse, namore : evermore. See
ten Brink, op. cit. § 330.

(c) Broken Rime, or the rime of a dissyllable with two words.
See Ellis, EEPron. I : 318-20; ten Brink *op. cit.* §§ 328-330;
Schipper, Engl. Metrik I : 301 ; Skeat VI : xlviii.

(d) Dialect Rime, or the use of a rime-word from other than Chaucer's usual dialect. See Skeat VI : xxiii-xxiv, Lounsbury, Studies I : 387.

(e) Impure Rime, which in Chaucer appears as the riming of close and open vowels or of short and long vowels.

> For of this world the feith is al agoon!
> Alas! what sholden straunge to me doon.   Troilus II : 410-11.

> A long surcote of pers upon he hadde,
> And by his syde he bar a rusty blade.   Prol. 619-20.

See ten Brink, *op. cit.* §§ 325-326; Skeat VI : xxxi ff.; E. W. Bowen on the confusion between close and open ō in Chaucer's rimes, Engl. Stud. 20 : 341-4.

A comment by G. R. Noyes on "A Peculiar Rime in Chaucer", Mod. Lang. Notes 19 : 256, is corrected by J. S. P. Tatlock, *ibid.* 20 : 126.

A much greater variation in the character of the riming vowels is by modern poets regarded as permissible; see Brander Matthews in Longman's Magazine for Sept. 1898, pp. 449-459, A. G. Newcomer and others in the Nation, 1899 I: 63, 83, 109, 145, and 1898 I: 129, 147, II: 241, 310.

(f) Another form of inexact rime is assonance, or the disagreement of the consonantal elements of the rime.

> Syke: endyte: whyte.   Troilus II : 884-887.

See ten Brink, *op. cit.* § 329; Lounsbury, Studies I : 394 ff.; Skeat VI : lvi-lvii, opposing Lounsbury.

The Rime Test

It was argued by Bradshaw and by ten Brink (see Temp. Preface pp. 107-110, and Studien p. 22) that Chaucer did not rime together words etymologically ending in -y and those ending in -ye. Largely on this ground, Bradshaw separated Chaucer's genuine works from the spurious. See Lounsbury, Studies I : 372, 388, Skeat VI : lvii ff. The occurrence of *chivalrye: Gy* in the undoubted tale of Sir Thopas has occasioned some discussion and has given Saintsbury, Hist. of Criticism I : 450, Hist. Eng. Prosody I : 145 note, opportunity to express his agnosticism. See ten Brink, Sprache und Versk. § 327, Lounsbury, Studies I : 388.

For Chaucer's "economy in rime" see Lowes, Publ. Mod. Lang. Assn. 20 : 797 ff. For his elaborate treatment of rime see the Venus and the envoy to the Clerk's Tale, where the changes are rung on a small set of rimes; Lydgate imitates his master in this. For medial rime see the Anelida.

Regarding the avoidance of rimes in -y and -ye by Chaucer, it is curious to note his apparent fondness for introducing rimes of -ē and of -ye in close conjunction; see Wife of Bath's prol. 31-34, 93-96, 513-516, Nun's Priest's Tale 609-612, Summoner's Tale 499-502, Second Nun's Tale 134-137, etc.

Rime-Indexes have been published by the Chaucer Society, to the Canterbury Tales (Ellesmere MS) by Cromie; to Troilus and Cressida by Skeat; to the Minor Poems by Marshall and Porter. See 2d series Nos. XLV (XLVI, XLVII), LXXXIV, LXXVIII, (LXXX).

Style

Das Sprichwort bei Chaucer. W. Haeckel. Leipzig, 1890, pp. 77.
> Reviewed Koeppel, Anglia Beiblatt 2 : 169-173; Hippe, Engl. Stud. 18 : 232; Schröer, Ztschr. f. vergl. Littgesch. 4 : 261. See further Andrae, Anglia Beiblatt 3 : 276-282, 4 : 330.

Das Bild bei Chaucer F. Klaeber. Berlin, 1893, pp. 450. diss. *ibid.* 1892, pp. 36.
> Reviewed Andrae, Anglia Beiblatt 5 : 33-37; Nation 1893 II : 158.

Die Versicherungen bei Chaucer. H. Lange, diss. Halle, 1891, pp. 55.
> Reviewed Kaluza, Engl. Stud. 22 : 77.

Ueber Chaucers Naturschilderungen. E. Ballerstedt. diss. Göttingen, 1891, pp. 92.
> On this point see also the chapter in F. W. Moorman's ed. of Browne's Britannia's Pastorals, in Quellen und Forschungen 81 (1897), and Moorman's The Interpretation of Nature in English Poetry from Beowulf to Shakespeare, in Quellen und Forschungen 95 (1905).
> This latter is reviewed with praise by C. H. Herford, Mod. Lang. Review 2 : 179-181.
> See also the chapter in Alice E. Pratt's diss., The Use of Color in the Verse of the English Romantic Poets, Univ. of Chicago 1898; and C. Weichardt, Die Entwicklung des Naturgefühls in der mittelengl. Dichtung vor Chaucer. diss. Kiel, 1900, pp. 96.

On the question of wordpairs in Chaucer see John Earle, Philology of the English Tongue, Oxford 1892, §§ 77, 78. Earle's theory is opposed by O. F. Emerson, Mod. Lang. Notes 8 : 403-411; to which Earle replied *ibid.* 9 : 121-124, see Emerson *ibid.* 9 : 423-427. Cp. also Lounsbury, Studies II : 153-4, Kittredge in Harvard Studies I : 61-62. Paul Meyer ascribes the same tendency to Caxton, Furnivall to the Bible and Prayerbook; see Athen. 1895 I : 284. Saintsbury, Hist. of Eng. Prosody I : 149, alludes to the "well-known reduplication of synonyms." See:

Abwechselung und Tautologie. Zwei Eigentümlichkeiten des alt- und mittelenglischen Stiles. L. Kellner. Engl. Stud. 20 : 1-24.

Chaucer's tendency to repetition is noted Section III F here. "Epanophora", or the beginning of successive lines with the same word or phrase, is mentioned by Saintsbury, Hist. Eng. Prosody I : 149.

Chaucer's use of padding phrases has not received adequate treatment. See Lange's dissertation on Die Versicherungen . . . etc., mentioned above, and Chaucer's Verse-Tags as a Part of his Narrative Machinery. C. M. Hathaway. Jour. Gc. Phil., 5 : 476-484.

The occurrence of such phrases in rime is of course more frequent than in other positions. We may note the difficulty of a rime for *other,* and Chaucer's consequent use of the awkward locution *my leve brother,* Manc. Tale 117-118, Mill. Tale 661-662, MLheadlink 51-52, HoFame 815-816, 795-796, better used in KnTale 323-4.

A paper on the Rhetoric of Verse in Chaucer, by J. W. Bright, is abstracted at some length in Publ. Mod. Lang. Assn. 16: xl.-xliii. A paper by Woodbridge on Chaucer's Classicism is in Jour. Gc. Phil. 1 : 111.

G. Glossaries and Dictionaries

The first glossary in an edition of Chaucer was that appended to the Speght Chaucer of 1598. This glossary was preceded by the Vocabula Chauceriana of 1594, as described below; and Spenser's Shepherd's Calendar, 1579, was drawn upon by the author of the Vocabula. No dictionary previous to those of Skinner (1671), and Junius (before 1677, though not published until 1743), systematically included Chaucerian words, although Cowel's Interpreter of 1607 and Blount's Glossographia of 1656 made reference to and explained various Chaucerian passages, especially legal phrases.

Spenser's (and E. K.'s) explanations and usages were largely of simple, we may say colloquial, terms, such as *unnethes, sicker, whilom, yode.* His vocabulary, disapproved of by his contemporaries Sidney, Daniel, and Ben Jonson, is discussed by Wagner in his dissertation On Spenser's Use of Archaisms, Halle, 1879, 60 pages. Wagner gives, on pp. 13-20, a list of Spenserian words out of use in Spenser's own time, and on pp. 11-12 a list of words from the dialect of East Lancashire found in Spenser. See also Herford's ed. of the Shepherd's Calendar, Lond. and N. Y. 1897, introd. pp. xlviii ff. Herford remarks that Spenser's archaic terms are not all Chaucerian, which is true also of the Vocabula Chauceriana, see below. Undoubtedly the revival of "Spenserian" vocabulary by the early Romanticists, Prior, Akenside, Shenstone, and Thomson, did much to bring Early English words again into literary usage; and our understanding of such terms as *eft, glee, whilom*, etc., is due to in the transactions of the (London) Philological Society, 1865, vol.

For an annotated list of English dictionaries see H. B. Wheatley in the transactions of the (London) Philological Society, 1865, vol. 17, pp. 219-293; and see the preface to Worcester's dictionary. The New English Dictionary, with its copious examples of word usages, chronologically arranged, is of especial interest to the student of Chaucer. Stratmann's Middle English Dictionary has long been inadequate.

Vocabula Chauceriana quaedam se- | lectiora, et minus | vulgaria ipsae ho- | die Poetarum deliciae, vnà cum | eorum significatis. | In gratiam omnium huius linguae studioso- | rum praecipuè vero Peomatum, discerp- | ta, & in hunc ordinem digesta. | Eodem Authore Stellis, ac herbis vis est, sed maxima verbis.

[Forms the last part of the following work:]
Grammatica | Anglicana, | praecipuè quatenus à La- | tina differt, ad | unicam P. Rami | methodum concinnata. | In quae perspicuè docetur quicquid ad hu- | ius linguae cognitionem requiritur | Authore P. G. | Cantabrigiae | Ex officina Iohannis Legatt. | Extant Londoni ad insigne Solis in Coemiterio D. Pauli 1594.

According to Lowndes, *s. v.* Grammatica Anglicana, only one copy known, in the Grenville Library of the Brit. Mus. The Brit. Mus. Cat. ascribes it to "P. Greenwood?"

Collation: A-E in eights. Title as above, A^1 recto; complimentary stanza by A. C. on verso. A^2-A^4, Lectori Salutem (Epistola). Grammatica Anglicana, etc., A^5-C^6. Dictionariolum vocum Anglicarum, quae passim in libello occurrunt, C^7-E^1. Analysis Grammatica ad nostrae huius artis praecepta unicè conformata, E^2-E^4. Vocabula Chauceriana, E^5-E^8.

The words are arranged in columns, grouped under the letters of the alphabet, accompanied in parallel columns by their meanings, briefly given. The list of the words themselves, with a few of the meanings in parentheses, is as follows: ander, anempst, antique (auncient), to appall; bale (ruth, pinching care, miserie), banne, barne, behest, belt (girdle), to bidde, bilive, blandishment, to blazon, bleake (a storme), to blend, to boote, to bourd, bowne, bowrs (lodgings, rooms, secret places of aboade), breme (bitter, chill or cold), to busse, bust (to goe about, or meddle); to carroll (to sing, daunce), carre (chariot or wagon), to cleape, coint (queint, nicely strange), to con (to can), cragge (necke), to craule; to deare (to trouble, molest, or grieve), deele, to deeme, din (noise), to doffe, to don, drerie (dolsome, unluckie, terrible);

ennaunter, erst; to feime (to rage, to chafe), to flite, freme; gab (a lie), to garre, glee (mirth, melodie), to greete (to weepe, mourne, lament), guerdon; hight; ick (I), ilke; keene (sharpe, fierce), to kenne, kerne, kirke, kole (pottage broth); lamkins (young lambs), lasse (wench, maide, or girl), lay (song, dittie, or tune), to leake (to play, to sport as children doe), leife, to ligge, lither, lore (practise, deede), to lout (to reuerence, to doe obeyance with the legge), lundey (sturdy, stubborn, forward); macht, meede, to mell, meth, mickle, midding (dunghill), to ming (to speake of, to shew in words), mirke, marke (darke, obscure), mone (lamentation, sorrow, waylinge); neve (fist), nooke; to pight (to pitch, set downe, addresse); quell (to abate, or kill); rayes, to reede, recke, reeke, ruth; sam (together), sarke, scathe, to shend, sib, sith (times), to sneb (checke or controll), soote (sweete), source, spell (a charme, verse, or worde used of exorcists in their magicall conclusions, but sometimes used in better part, as Godspell, for Gods spell), stanke (faint, wearie), starke, stowre or stownd (fit, passion, perplexitie); teene (revengfull wrath, inveterate malice), to thoile (to suffer, permit to be willing, to impart to another), to thrill, throb (a sigh, groane); uncouth (unknowne, unkent, strange); to waxen, weede, to weene, welkin, weele, to wend, to weete, whilke, whilom, to wield, wight (any live creature), wimble (nimble, quick, deliver), to wite, woode, to wonne, wracke, to wreake; yore (long agoe, afore time), to yeede (to goe, to wende). Finis.

Of these 120 words, about 40 are used by Spenser in the Shepherd's Calendar, published 15 years before the Grammatica Anglicana, and are given in the later work explanations almost identical with those of Spenser. About 35 of the words do not occur either in Spenser or in the blackletter Works of Chaucer.

The Grammatica Anglicana, with this Vocabula, is to be ed. by M. Rösler and R. Brotanek, Halle, in the series of Eng. grammars under Brotanek's supervision.

Speght. The Chaucer of 1598 contains, after the list of Lydgate's works, beginning on the next recto, sig. Aaaa i, 7 leaves which are filled with "The old and obscure words of Chaucer, explaned." The words are arranged three columns to a page, with brief explanation of each; a little over 2000 are thus treated. There are no references to the text, and the interpretation given is often a guess from the context, cp. *blackburied, clum, herawdes, momblishnesse,* etc. In a few cases the editor honestly left the explanation unattempted, *e. g., hoppesteres, ruell bone.* In some other cases the reader is referred to the Annotations, which follow later in the volume, Bbbb iii, after lists of Chaucer's French words and of most of the authors cited by him. These are headed "Corrections of some faults, and Annotations vpon some places"; they include various parallels from Seneca and from the Greek, comments on astrological allusions, explanations of *begin the board, the orders four, sell shields, go to vigile, magic natural, vernacle, curfew, Gawyn with his olde courtesye, Valerie and Theophrast, warriangles, dan Burnell the Asse, wine Ape, the lords son of Windsor, dulcarnon, heysugge,* etc. These Annotations fill eight pages, and are accompanied by corrections upon the text, which include a passage from the Rime of Sir Thopas omitted from the body of the book.

One of two explanations from the glossary are of interest. The words *lollards, londles* are explained together as "breakers of fasting daies & runnagates"; the word *floyting* is annotated, perhaps by guess, as "whistling"; *rade vore* is interpreted as "tapistry, or loome work." Observe the explanation of *floyting* as whistling.

Before the appearance of Speght's second edition in 1602 Francis Thynne had written his Animadversions; and the glossary of that edition incorporates some of his suggestions thus offered, and shows other differences which may or may not be due to his advice. The words *hoppesteres* and *ruell bone* are now both annotated; the former is explained as "(gubernaculum tenentes) pilotes"; the latter is assigned a derivation from French "riole, diversely coloured." The notes on *autentike, dulcarnon, harrolds,* etc., are adopted or emended from Thynne's suggestions; and some additions are made, cp. the word *iape* and the eight lines of verse there quoted as being written in a lady's Chaucer from which the work had been erased. This is found, we may remark, in the MS Rawl. Poet. 149, see Section III p. 186 here. A long note on *peruise* is also added, but without any connection with the Paradisus or mention of the church porch. Otherwise, the differences in the 1602 glossary are the incorporation of the annotations of 1598, and a more exact alphabetical arrangement. The 1602 glossary fills 22½ pages, in triple columns.

Skinner. Etymologicon Linguae Anglicanae, seu Explicatio vocum Anglicarum Etymologica ex propriis fontibus, etc. Lond. 1671. By Stephen Skinner.

To the General Glossary are added four appendices, one of botanical terms, one "vocum Forensium tum antiquarum & jam obsoletarum . . . . Etymologica expositio"; another "Originationes omnium vocum antiquarum Anglicarum quae usque a Wilhelmo Victore invaluerunt" . . . etc.; the last of proper names. The third appendix includes many Chaucerian words, for about 350 of which reference is made to his works, these "works" comprising poems now rejected as spurious, but printed as his in the Speght editions. Gower, Piers Plowman, and Juliana Berners are also frequently referred to. Errors are many, especially those arising from attempts to explain misprinted words, cp. for example *clenge* for *elynge.*

Thomas: The glossary to the Urry Chaucer of 1721 was by Timothy Thomas; according to Corser's Collectanea IV : 329, its preparation delayed the work more than two years. It is of about 6000 words, with frequent citations from the Speght glossary, a few notes from Kynaston, and some guesswork-interpretations borrowed from Skinner; e. g. *belle Isaude, ferne yere, blackburied, thombe of golde.* Some errors of its own it also has, cp. *heved, scholeie;* but as a whole it is remarkable with what care and success Thomas examined MSS and earlier editions and contended with the distorted text of Urry. Note some of his conjectures as to pronunciation, under *alouth* as to *Rome,* and under *sone;* and observe how clearly he is aware of the kind of errors possible to scribes, see under *afine, agre, cry,* etc. He occasionally uses Lydgate to throw light on a passage.

Junius: Francis Junius, 1589-1677, was born in Germany, brought up in Holland, lived many years in England, and bequeathed his valuable philological library to the Bodleian library at Oxford. His Chaucer interest is evinced not only by his mass of collections for an edition—see Liddell in Athen. 1897 I : 779 —but by the great number of Chaucerian citations in his Etymologicum Linguae Anglicanae, ed. by Lye in 1743. There are 468 references to Chaucer in this work, 79 of which were added by Lye; and most are accompanied by extracts, frequently lengthy, printed in blackletter. Chaucer and Gawain Douglas are the only English authors freely cited; note the remark in Liddell's letter as above, that Junius had also made collections based upon Douglas' version of the Aeneid; Lydgate is mentioned a half-dozen times. The notes are still of value, and the work easily obtained.

Tyrwhitt. The glossary appended to Tyrwhitt's Canterbury Tales of 1775-8 is, with the annotations, the most valuable portion of Tyrwhitt's work. The notes, often extensive and always acute, are about 640 in number; there are about 4300 words in the Glossary, which includes not only words in the Cant. Tales, but in the other poems of Chaucer. Some errors by Skinner and Urry are corrected, e. g., *belle Isaude, heved, nale;* some words insufficiently annotated are more fully treated, e. g., *clum, hoppesteres, parvis;* and oversights are very rare, cp. *minoresse* for *moveresse,* Rom. of the Rose, line 149. This had been corrected by Thynne in his Animadversions on Speght's 1598 Chaucer, and altered by Speght in the 1602 edition; Skeat's note on the passage is insufficient. Todd, in his Illustrations, points out Tyrwhitt's oversight. Tyrwhitt, with admirable frankness, appended to his Glossary a list of 57 "words and phrases not understood."

In the Retrospective Review 14 : 307 (1826) and in the Lowndes-Bohn Bibliographer's Manual, *s. v.* Chaucer, is the statement that Tyrwhitt "conspicuously availed himself" of Morell's work in his notes and glossary. This is repeated in the Bell Chaucer of 1854, I : 59, but is rejected by Lounsbury, Studies I : 297, and see *ibid.* p. 302. A comparison of the annotations upon the Prologue and Knight's Tale, as made by Morell, by Tyrwhitt, and by Skeat, would yield interesting results.

Tyrwhitt's glossary has been often reprinted, sometimes at the close of an edition of the Works, as by Bell in 1782, sometimes condensed and arranged at the foot of the page, as in the "Routledge" editions of the Canterbury Tales.

The 1778 volume V of the Cant. Tales, which contained the Glossary only, may sometimes be picked up separately second-hand for a very small price.

Todd. The last section of Todd's Illustrations is a Glossary covering the extracts from Gower and Chaucer which he prints. It comprises about 560 words; Todd says on pp. xlv-vi of his introduction that his work is founded on Tyrwhitt's, "with occasional but respectful difference of opinion and with some augmentation." The "augmentations" are very slight; for the occasional differences see *e. g.* under *catel, dub.* Todd points out that Thynne had explained *minoresse,*—see ante under Tyrwhitt's glossary—and that Brathwait, in 1665, had explained *gnoffe,* a word not understood by Tyrwhitt. See also Todd's remarks on the words *gat-toothed, goliardeys,* etc.

Bell. Robert Bell appended to his edition of Chaucer, 1854-56, a glossary which, he there states, was prepared entirely new, and not derived from that of Tyrwhitt; his improved text, he says, rendered this necessary. Bell has not added much to Tyrwhitt's annotations; he has a conjecture to offer on *wyntermyte* or *vitremyte,* and his note on *leveselle* is clear as far as it goes; but some explanations, *e. g.* on *goliardeys, radevore, poudremarchant,* are evasive. His list of words numbers about 4600.

Skeat. The glossary appended by Skeat to his Oxford Chaucer, *q. v.,* may be obtained separately, Oxford 1899.

Flügel. A concordance to the works of Chaucer, by Professor Ewald Flügel, is nearing completion for the Chaucer Society.

SECTION VII.

BIBLIOGRAPHICAL

A. Some English Libraries

See:—the article on Libraries in the Encyclopedia Britannica; Edwards' Memoirs of Libraries, London 1859; Madan, Books in Manuscript, London 1893; Rye's Records and Record-Searching, London 1897; Garnett's Essays in Librarianship and Bibliography, London 1899; Fletcher's English Book-Collectors, London 1902; Quaritch's Dictionary of English Book-Collectors, in progress; Macray's Annals of the Bodleian Library, Oxford 1890; Bradshaw's Collected Papers, Cambridge 1889; Sinker's Library of Trinity College, Cambridge 1891.

Catalogues of MSS and printed books, where of value to Chaucerian students, are mentioned below or under the sections on manuscripts, III B and IV A here.

Photographic reproductions may be arranged for in Oxford through the Photographic Department of the Oxford University Press. The latest mode of reproduction, the Rotary Bromide (white on black), is less expensive than the usual print or than the employment of copyists; it costs, for work done in Oxford, a single page or opening 11 by 9 inches, one and fourpence; for same 8½ by 5¾ inches, eightpence. The University Press can also execute work at the British Museum or in Cambridge, for which special arrangement must be made; or photographs can be taken, at the Museum, by artists known to the administration. In all cases permission must be obtained by written application, which must specify the page or pages to be reproduced. For further notes on photography in foreign libraries see Nation 1908 I : 214, 258.

Admission to the various libraries is discussed below.

The Library of the British Museum. This library, belonging to the nation, and housed in the Museum building in Great Russell Street, London, West Central District, is the growth partly of individual gift, partly of purchase made by Parliamentary grant, partly of material accruing under the Copyright Act of 1842. To the first of these sources it owes the oldest and most valuable portion of its collections; the four libraries which constitute the nucleus of the Museum library are those called respectively the Royal, the Cotton, the Harley, and the Sloane, from their former owners or donors the Hanoverian Kings, Sir Robert Bruce Cotton, Robert Harley Earl of Oxford, and Sir Hans Sloane. Although these and other libraries, the Arundel, Egerton, Lansdowne, etc., are now an integral part of

510

the national collection, the books and manuscripts are still known, both for deference' and for convenience' sake, by the names of their original owners; and a volume is marked *Lansdowne* 851, *Harley* 7333, etc., indicating the collection of which it once formed a part. The classification *Adds.* (Additionals) indicates a MS acquired by purchase.

Royal. It was not until the accession of the Georges that the purchasing of books became a matter of personal interest to the Sovereign. When George II, in 1757, transferred his library to the nation, it numbered about 12,000 volumes, 2,000 of which were in manuscript.

The characteristic mark of a MS of this collection is Royal or Reg. (Regum) followed by an Arabic numeral, a letter of the alphabet, and a Roman numeral, indicating case and shelf-marks. Thus, Royal 18 D ii. Catalogue by Casley, London 1734.

Cotton. The Cottonian library far surpasses in value and interest that collected by the English Kings. Sir Robert Bruce Cotton, 1570-1631, who claimed descent from the Bruce of Scotland and cousinship with King James I of England, became involved in political difficulties, and was deprived of his collection by government; the books were however restored to his son, and in 1700 his great-grandson, Sir John Cotton, presented them to the nation. There was at that time no public repository for the collection, and it was stored first in one palace, then in another. In 1731, while it was lying at Ashburnham House, London, along with the King's own volumes, there occurred the famous fire which so seriously injured many of the manuscripts, and destroyed not a few. The unique and priceless copy of the Beowulf, for example, was scorched and mutilated.

The shelfmark of a Cotton MS is noteworthy. The first owner of the MSS kept them in fourteen cases, upon the tops of which were busts of the twelve Caesars and of Faustina and Cleopatra. The volumes were marked accordingly: Cotton Julius B iv, Cotton Cleopatra D vii, Cotton Vitellius A xv, etc.

A catalogue of the MSS, by Planta, was published London 1802 folio.

Harley. Robert Harley Earl of Oxford began purchasing in 1705; ten years later he owned 2,500 MSS, and at his death he possessed 6,000, a large part of them valuable for English history. His son the second earl continued the collection, but after his death without issue the first Earl's daughter sold the collection to the nation for £10,000.

The shelfmark is *Harley* followed by a numeral, Harley 372, Harley 2255, etc.

A catalogue, 4 vols. folio (7639 MSS), by Wanley, Casley, and others, was published London 1808-12.

Sloane. The library of Sir Hans Sloane became the property of the nation in 1753; and an Act of Parliament was then passed providing "one General Repository" for this and the Cotton and Harley collections. Money for the building was raised by a lottery, and Montagu House, now the site of the British Museum, was purchased. No grant of public money was however made for more than fifty years. Then, in 1807, money was appropriated for buying the MSS of Lord Lansdowne; in 1829 the Egerton MSS were bequeathed; the collection of the Earl of Arundel was given by the Royal Society in 1831; in 1846 the Hon. Thomas Grenville bequeathed his magnificent collection of early printed books; and in 1857 the present reading-room was opened to the public.

The British Museum Library contained in 1902 perhaps two million printed books, and about 55,000 MSS.

Access to the national library, with freedom to copy, may be arranged by filling out a form obtainable from the Director of the British Museum. The student must be vouched for by a householder of London, not a boarding-house, lodging-house, or hotel keeper. Explanation of the student's purpose is necessary, as the Museum has not unlimited space at its disposal. The form, when filled out, is deposited in the Museum, and a non-transferable ticket, for three or six months, is issued; this ticket must be shown on demand at the entrance of the Reading-room or of the Manuscript Room. When the student leaves London, this ticket is formally surrendered and put on file; and written application, when further work is desired, is all that is necessary for renewal.

The Bodleian Library at Oxford. The first founder of the University Library at Oxford was Humphrey Duke of Gloucester, the younger brother of King Henry V and the uncle of Henry VI; died 1447. Gloucester, a man of literary enthusiasms, a patron of writers both English and Italian, and a collector, gave to the University, then almost without books, about 600 manuscripts, which were delivered between 1439 and 1446. The catalogue of his gifts may be found in Anstey's Munimenta Academica, Rolls Series, II : 758 ff. But owing partly to the lack of proper housing and care, mainly to the iconoclasm of the Commission of Edward VI, all these MSS but three are now gone. See Macray, pp. 8-13.

For particulars regarding Gloucester, his "Italian character", his share in the Early Renaissance, etc., see the article in the

Dict. Nat. Biog.; Einstein's Italian Renaissance in England, N. Y. 1902; Anglia 27 : 381 and references there cited, *e. g.* Warton-Hazlitt, III : 47-52.

About the middle of the fifteenth century a portion of the present library building was erected by the University, Gloucester being a contributor; but by 1560 not only had all the books of the collection disappeared, but the fittings of the library itself were ruthlessly torn out and sold. Near the end of the century, in 1597-8, Sir Thomas Bodley, an Oxford graduate, a successful statesman, and an enthusiast for learning, refitted the rooms built a hundred years earlier, and began a series of gifts of MSS and books continued until his death in 1613. The restored and enlarged reading-room was named from the first founder Duke Humphrey's Library; but the Library as a whole bears the name of its restorer and second founder. Bodley's example as a donor was followed by many others, and, as in the case of the British Museum Library already described, these volumes receive their catalogue mark from their original owners. The principal MS collections of interest to a student of Chaucer, now incorporated in the Bodleian, are the Ashmole, the Bodley, the Digby, the Fairfax, the Laud, the Rawlinson and the Selden. See Macray as cited for notes, and Madan as cited for catalogues of MSS.

This library is poorer in funds than that of the British Museum; its staff is small, its helpers lads, and there is no such supervision of readers as in the Museum. Few reference books are accessible to the reader's hand, as compared with the 20,000 on the lower shelves of the Museum Reading-room; and the insufficient heat and total absence of any lighting arrangements make the wonderful old-world library in some respects an unpractical one. Since the opening of the Radcliffe Camera, or "annex" reading-room, in a closely adjoining building, to which all but the more valuable books may be carried after Bodleian hours, evening work of some kinds may be pursued by the student. Periodicals and most reference books are kept in the Radcliffe. The Library contained in 1902 about 600,000 books and 31,000 MSS. Librarian, E. W. B. Nicholson, M. A.; sub-librarian, Falconer Madan, M. A.

Admission is given upon the written introduction of a resident Master of Arts. An American student without acquaintance in Oxford should apply, if a man, to the Non-Collegiate Delegacy; if a woman, to the Secretary of the Association for the Education of Women at Oxford.

Volumes in the possession of Oxford colleges may in almost any case be used at the Bodleian. The student should first inquire of the Bodleian authorities if the Library will undertake the charge; written application should then be made to the

33

Librarian of the college in question, explaining the purpose for which use of the volume is desired, and requesting the loan for a specific period. The various colleges differ in their mode of dealing with such a request; in some cases the librarian himself will appear at the Bodleian within twenty-four hours and leave the volume, usually asking to see the student personally. In other cases, the matter must be formally laid before the governing board of the college, and a delay ensues; but the request is almost never refused. When examination of the codex is finished, the student should notify the College librarian. It is advisable that the American student who has but a summer's vacation for work in England should make any requests for loans of MSS before the Colleges close for the summer; for in cases where formal action is necessary, that cannot take place in the absence of members of the College's governing board.

Cambridge: the University Library. Henry Bradshaw, librarian of the University of Cambridge from 1867 until his death in 1886, has summed up in one of his Collected Papers, pp. 181 ff., the state of the Library as he saw it in 1869. He emphasizes the gaps in its history, the losses it has suffered, the miscellaneous nature of its contents, its lack of cataloguing and of classification. Although great gifts have occasionally been made to the Library, it can show no such list of donors as Oxford. For notes upon the peculiar history and organization of the Library see Bradshaw's paper; his own efforts and immense reputation as a bibliographer have done more for the Library than has any single benefactor. The present librarian is Francis J. H. Jenkinson, Esq.

Rye, in his Records and Record Searching, p. 155, has emphasized what he calls the "cramped and illiberal rules" of Cambridge, which require all non-members of the University to be endorsed by two members of the Senate. An American student without acquaintance in Cambridge should address himself, with explanation of the work desired, to Mr. Jenkinson. The mark of a University Library MS is a double letter, followed by a shelf-numeral and by a volume-numeral; thus, Dd iv, 24 or Ii iii, 21.

The college libraries of Cambridge vary as do those of Oxford in their mode of dealing with requests for loans, or for access to their books. The prompt and generous hospitality of Trinity, which has within its own walls every facility for workers, is known to all students; other Cambridge libraries will, in most cases, place their volumes in the University Library for examination, although Corpus Christi and Magdalen, for example, are bound by the strict rules of their benefactors, Archbishop Parker and Samuel Pepys.

B. Some Students of Chaucer

John Shirley, born 1366?, died 1456. Shirley has been discussed
by Otto Gaertner in his dissertation on John Shirley, sein Leben
und Wirken, Halle 1904; this was unfavorably reviewed by me
in Anglia Bcibl. 16 : 360-62; Shirley's work as a compiler of
commonplace-books has recently been treated by me in Anglia
30 : 320-348, under the title Ashmole 59 and Other Shirley
Manuscripts.

We know little more of Shirley than the data given by Stow
in his Survey, see ed. by Thoms. 1842, p. 139-40, that he lived
to the age of ninety, was "a great traveller in divers countries",
dwelt in London in his latter years, and was a devoted admirer
and indefatigable copyist of Chaucer and Lydgate. To the
meagre notice in the Dict. Nat. Biog. something might be added
on the MS commonplace-books which Shirley left behind him,
and which are an important source of information as to the
authenticity and occasion of many poems by Chaucer and by
Lydgate. These commonplace-books, and the Shirley MSS
generally, are not listed accurately in the Dict. Nat. Biog., the
Oxford Chaucer, or any of the articles based upon Skeat; the
true list is, as given by me in Anglia loc. cit., MSS Adds.
16165, Ashmole 59, Sion College, Trinity College Cambridge R
3, 20, Harvard University, and four leaves of Harley 78. The
MSS Adds. 5467 and Harley 7333, though showing Shirley's
influence (especially the Harley), are not in Shirley's hand;
and the same is true of Harley 2251 and Adds. 34360, which are
in part derived from a lost Shirley, see Anglia 28 : 1 ff. Of
the volumes in Shirley's own hand, the Harvard MS contains
nothing by Chaucer, and the Sion College MS, a copy of the
prose translation of De Guileville, contains of Chaucer only an
inserted copy of the ABC. The Ashmole volume is, as I have
tried to show in Anglia 30 above cited, a most untrustworthy
piece of work executed in the last days of Shirley's life; there
remain for students the Adds. and Trinity MSS, volumes independent of one another and containing much of Chaucer's work,
though always under suspicion of tinkering by Shirley.

There is no copy of the Canterbury Tales in Shirley's writing,
but that in Harley 7333 was transcribed from his work, retaining his spelling and notes; it is of interest typically, see Section
III F here. The Boece is copied by Shirley in the Adds. MS;
there is no copy by him or derived from him of the Astrolabe,
the Troilus, the Legend of Good Women, the House of Fame,
the Book of the Duchesse, the Former Age, or the envoys to
Bukton and to Scogan, though the House of Fame must have
existed in one of his MSS, see under that heading, Section IV
here. The Trinity MS contains Fortune, Mars, Venus, Sted-

fastnesse, Gentilesse, Words to Adam (unique), two copies of
Truth, and part of Anelida. The Adds. MS has the whole of
Anelida, beside the Boece as mentioned, and a Balade marked
as Chaucer's but never printed with his works, see Mod. Lang.
Notes 19 : 35-38 and refs. there to Furnivall. Ashmole 59,
as well as Trinity, has copies of Fortune, Gentilesse, and Venus.
Harley 78, followed by the secondary Adds. 34360, has copies
of Pity and the questionable continuation the Ballad of Pity.
The ABC is in the Sion MS. The secondary Harley 7333 has
the Anelida, the Mars, the Parlement of Foules, Purse, Gentilesse, and Stedfastnesse; and the still further removed Harley
2251 has Purse and Fortune; in the former it is accompanied
by its partial sister Adds. 34360 in a continuation bewailing
imprisonment, see Anglia 28 : 3. This continuation is present
as a separate poem, without any ascription to Chaucer, in
Harley 7333.

Beside this mass of copies of Chaucer, Shirley has preserved
to us an unusual body of evidence regarding their authenticity
or occasion. The Words to Adam exists only in his Trinity MS,
where it is marked as by Chaucer; our ascription of the ABC
to Chaucer rests on Shirley's writing of Chaucer's name beside
his Sion College text; for the authenticity of Mars, Venus, Pity,
and Stedfastnesse, we have no direct testimony other than
Shirley's; and for the authenticity of the Anelida we have only
one other marking.

The errors chargeable to him are: the assertion that the
Truth was written on Chaucer's deathbed, which Skeat calls
"probably a mere bad guess", but which is defended by ten
Brink, Hist. Eng. Lit. II : 205; the statement that the Chronicle
(see Section V here) was "made" by Chaucer; this is censured
by ten Brink *ibid.* III : 272 and by Furnivall, but an interpretation which frees Shirley from suspicion is offered by Skeat
I : 53. Furnivall, Trial Forew. p. 120, also blames Shirley for
ascribing the Ballad of Pity to Chaucer; but the authenticity of
that poem is defended by Skeat, see Section V here. The marking of the Venus envoy as Thomas Chaucer's, and the tacking
on of that envoy to the Fortune, both distortions introduced by
the Ashmole MS, are to be viewed as errors due to Shirley's
great age when the Ashmole was written.

The question of the text preserved by Shirley in these copies
is another and very different matter. Two copies by him of the
same poem present no such agreements as do for instance the
independently transcribed MSS Fairfax 16 and Bodley 638.
Koch, in Engl. Stud. 27 : 10-12, has made some comparisons of
Shirley's divergences from himself, while discussing the likelihood of Chaucer's revising his own work; he remarks p. 16
that Shirley seems to write usually from memory. On the

other hand, Furnivall has selected for inclusion in the One-Text Print, as the "best" text of each poem, Shirleyan copies of Anelida, Gentilesse, Stedfastnesse, Venus, and of course the Words to Adam. A minute examination of Shirley's texts, with a view to learning whether his constant variations are due to memory transcription, desire for clearness and emphasis, or the progressive breaking-up of the inflexional system utilized by Chaucer, is a desideratum in the textual study of the Minor Poems. See my suggestions in Anglia 30 : 320-348.

That Shirley wrote his codices with his own hand is stated in the verse table of contents prefixed to Adds. 16165, cp. also the table of contents to another (lost) MS preserved by Stow in Adds. 29729. The former is printed by Gaertner, *op. cit.* p. 63. The Chaucer Society has reproduced a page of Adds. 16165 in its Autotypes, and two pages of the Harvard volume are reproduced by Robinson, Harvard Studies V. Another mark of a Shirleyan codex is the long "gossippy" headings, for specimens of which see Ch. Soc. PT 101, 146, SPT p. 47. His spelling is also an idiosyncrasy, his *elike* for *alike,* his *beon, seon,* for *been, seen,* his *nuwe, nexst,* for *newe, next,* etc. See the Ch. Soc. prints; see Skeat I : 76, Schick, Temple of Glass pp. xxii-xxiv. MSS not in his hand, as especially Harley 7333, thus may show traces of a Shirley origin in their spelling and headings.

From the character of those headings, his tables of contents with their instructions to return the book, and his pedagogical marginal notes, I have inferred that he was a semi-professional lender of books. He also dabbled in verse-making and executed translations himself, see the lines sent to him by Sellyng, transcribed in Harley 7333, and the contents of Adds. 5467 as described by Gaertner *op. cit.;* cp. also his verse-tables of contents and his Chronicle, for which latter see Section V here.

According to John Stow's note, Survey ed. Thoms. 1876, p. 140, some of Shirley's MSS passed to him: "I haue seene them, and partly do possess them." The Shirley MS at Trinity College, Cambridge, was for some time in Stow's custody, and from it he made many copies, preserved to us in his MS Adds. 29729; the MS Harley 2251 is also in part derived from the Trinity MS, see Anglia 28 : 1 ff.; Ashmole 59 was at some time annotated by Stow. The existence of other Shirley codices, now lost, is discussed in Anglia 30 : 320-348.

William Caxton, 1422?-1491?: Born in Kent, apprenticed to a London mercer, settled in Flanders soon after to enlarge his commercial experience, and remained there from about 1441 to about 1476. Here he rose to the important post of Governor of the English trading colony, and was thus brought into contact with the reigning House of Burgundy. At this time the chivalric and literary brilliance of the Burgundian court was at its height; Caxton's interest in romantic fiction, probably already warm, was greatly stimulated by the English born Duchess Margaret of Burgundy, who encouraged his efforts at translation and compilation. The Recuyell of the Historyes of Troye, translated by Caxton from French into English, was presented to the duchess about 1471. Caxton then seems to have resigned his official position, and entered Margaret's service. So many copies of the Recuyell were in demand that, as Caxton tells us in the epilogue to its third book, published about 1474, he was obliged to turn to the new art of printing to supply would-be readers. He mastered the craft, returned to England, set up his press at Westminster in 1477, and devoted the rest of his life to the publication of romances, devotional books, didactic manuals, and poetry; his labors as a printer were more than paralleled by his work as translator and compiler. His business success was great; he was favored of king and court; and his probity and piety are most interestingly revealed in his various prefaces and epilogues, especially the famous proheme to the second edition of the Canterbury Tales. Though the pioneer in England of the great art of democracy, Caxton used it to the preservation of the most aristocratic of literary forms; and thus, as Raleigh says (The English Novel, 1894, p. 18) "secured to English literature continuity of development." His bits of original writing by way of epilogues and introductions have value in themselves as monuments of English prose. He is probably best remembered by his Recuyell, his Golden Legend, his two editions of the Canterbury Tales, and his publication of Malory's Morte d'Arthur; but there remain, whole or in fragments, about 100 works from his press. The value of a Caxton, or of even a few leaves of a Caxton, is now enormous. Quaritch prices the perfect copy of the second edition of the Canterbury Tales which is in his hands at £2500.

For notes on Caxton see:

The Biography and Typography of William Caxton. W. Blades. London, 2 vols., 4to, 1861-63, condensed into 1 vol. octavo 1877, second ed. 1882. Some additions and corrections to Blades may be found in Gordon Duff's William Caxton, pubd. by the Caxton Club of Chicago, 1905; cp. also the Athen. 1894 II : 715 1895 I : 284, 474, 772; 1896 I : 283, 346, 779, II : 129; 1898 I : 661; 1899 I : 371.

On Caxton's two eds. of the Canterbury Tales see Hammond in Mod. Phil. 3 : 159 ff.

Various of Caxton's texts have been reprinted by the Early English Text Society, see their list of publications; some prefaces and epilogues are in Flügel's Neuenglisches Lesebuch;

the Cambridge University Press has issued a facsimile of his print of Anelida; for his conclusion to the House of Fame see under that heading, Section IV here.

The edition of the Canterbury Tales by de Worde in 1498, which differs from the Caxtons, has not yet been examined.

From 1500 to the 18th century there were but three editors of Chaucer,—Thynne, Stow, and Speght; for each of these see under his edition of the works, Section II D here.

Lewis Theobald, died 1744. Churton Collins, in a paper on The Porson of Shaksperean Criticism, included in his Essays and Studies, rehabilitates the reputation of Theobald, pointing out the debt which the present text of Shakspere owes to Theobald's scholarship and insight, and giving an ample list of his emendations. Collins speaks of Theobald's knowledge of Early English and Anglo-Saxon, and of his "frequent and apt quotations from the Canterbury Tales."

An examination of Theobald's edition of Shakspere (1733) reveals no large amount of Chaucerian scholarship. I find the following: wordnotes on *bale* in Coriolanus and on *housel* and *eisel* in Hamlet; emendations supported by the Chaucerian text are *weyward* to *weird* in Macbeth, *y'are* to *yare* in Cymbeline, *grey as grass* to *grey as glass* in the Two Gent. of Verona, *would woman* to *wood woman* in the same play, *stricture* to *strict ure* in Measure for Measure. On Troilus and Cressida Theobald comments that Shakspere took more from Caxton's print of the Troy-legend than from "Lollius or Chaucer"; his only note implying Shakspere's knowledge of the text of Chaucer—and that perhaps also his best note on Chaucer—is the remark on Twelfth Night, Act II, Sc. 4, . . "Patience on a monument Smiling at grief", of which Theobald says that Shakspere perhaps had in mind Chaucer's Parlement of Foules:

> Dame Pacience sitting there I fonde
> With face pale, upon an hill of sonde.

Upon which passage it may be noted that the "hill of sand" is not in the Teseide description which Chaucer is closely translating.

Theobald also compares As You Like It with Gamelyn, and refers the Twelfth Night line, "Cressida was a beggar", to the (pseudo-Chaucerian) Testament of Cressida.

Taken altogether, these constitute no large body of Chaucerian notes; but though the "frequency" of Theobald's references to Chaucer may be doubted, there is no question of their "aptness", nor of the unusualness of his knowledge at that period. He may be compared with Tyrwhitt for his abundance of classical learning, perhaps even in his English reading; and there is a parallel also in the sagacity and sobriety with which each scholar executed his selfappointed task.

Henry Bradshaw, 1831-1886. Head of the University Library, Cambridge, from 1867 until his death. The only piece of Chaucer work which Bradshaw published is included in his Collected Papers (posthumous); and Prothero, in the Dict. Nat. Biog., says of Bradshaw, "The amount of his published work is small, and the reputation which he enjoyed among his contemporaries will be almost unintelligible to those who never knew him, and who are unaware how much of his labour took shape in the productions of others." As a bibliographer, a specialist in ecclesiastical antiquities, and in the work of the early printers, Bradshaw was second to none in his generation. A memoir by Prothero was published Cambridge 1889, and a most intimate and sympathetic paper is in A. C Benson's Essays, 1896, pp. 252-267. See Blades' Caxton pp. 55, 295, Lounsbury, Studies I : 267, Acad. 1886 I : 130, 147.

Bernhard ten Brink, 1841-1892. Born in Amsterdam, but educated in Germany, and professor in a German university from 1865 until his death; from 1873 on, a professor in the University of Strassburg. He published his Chaucer Studien in 1870, his Chaucers Sprache und Verkunst in 1884; both are fundamental for the student. His history of English literature, also of great value for the worker in Early English, was interrupted by his death. A full bibliography of his writings may be found in Engl. Stud. 17 : 186-7, following a brief sketch of his life and work by Kölbing, from which these facts are taken.

James Russell Lowell, born in Cambridge, U. S. A., in 1819, died in 1891. Lowell's study of Chaucer, like his paper on Dante, is of the character of a literary essay, written, however, with ripe fulness of knowledge and penetrant appreciation. This essay was originally published in the *North American Review* for July 1870; it is included in the volume of Lowell's works entitled My Study Windows. No student of Chaucer can afford to overlook this paper; see Furnivall, Trial Forew. p. 28, and the dedication to that work. Lowell's earlier Conversations on the English Poets (1845) also included a paper on Chaucer.

Essays on Chaucer by other writers are of a far different character, and the mass of thirdhand and usually slight papers on various aspects of Chaucer's life and art to be found in the lesser literary journals are not here catalogued; see Poole's Index. Collections of studies or notes are:—the Chaucer Society's Essays on Chaucer (twenty-two papers published in six parts in their second

Series), many of which are now of small value; the Studies in
Chaucer by Lounsbury, noted in the Reference List here; the
volume of papers upon Chaucer pubd. by the Royal Historical
Society in 1900 as the Chaucer Memorial Lectures, under the
editorship of Percy W. Ames. The contents of this last are:—
introd. by the editor.—The Contemporaries of Chaucer, by H. M.
Imbert-Terry.—The Paston Letters, with special reference to the
social life of the XIV and XV centuries, by Samuel Davey.—
Italian Influence on Chaucer, by W. E. A. Axon.—The Portraits
of Geoffrey Chaucer (with illustrations), by M. H. Spielmann.—
The Life and Characteristics of Chaucer, by Percy W. Ames.—
None of these Essays, except that by Spielmann, has any independent value; Spielmann's was also pubd. by the Chaucer Society, 2d
series, No. 31. The volume is revd. Athen. 1900 II : 440.

Works of some extent upon Chaucer are:—Matthew Browne's
Chaucer's England, London 1889, 2 vols. This set of papers,
written by W. B. Rands under the pseudonym above, is still of
value and interest.—F. G. Fleay's Guide to Chaucer and Spenser,
London 1877, is very severely reviewed by Furnivall, Acad. 1877
II : 525.—Chaucer's Liv og Digtning, by Jespersen, Copenhagen
1893, I have not seen.—Root's Poetry of Chaucer is mentioned
in the Reference List here.

Shorter papers are the essay of Mrs. Browning, in her Book
of the Poets, 1842, 1863, the Chaucer-portion of which was reprinted in Ch. Soc. Essays, part II; the papers of Alexander
Smith in his Dreamthorp, London 1863, of Hazlitt in his Essays
on the English Poets, and of Swinburne in the Fortnightly Review
1880 II : 708. The reviews of Skeat by Quiller Couch and by Ker,
reprinted as essays in their Adventures in Criticism and Essays in
Medieval Literature, are entered under their proper place in this
book.

Francis James Child, born in Boston, U. S. A., in 1825, died 1896.
He entered Harvard College in 1842, took a foremost place
among his classmates, and upon graduation entered the service
of his college, in which he remained until his death. During a
leave of absence he studied in Germany, but sought no doctor's
degree; this was later conferred on him by Göttingen. His
post at Harvard for 25 years was the professorship of Rhetoric
and Oratory; in 1876 the special chair of English was founded,
and Child became its first incumbent.

He was the general editor of the series of British Poets
(about 150 vols.), published at Boston from 1853 on, and prepared for this his Spenser, which appeared in 1855. The
edition of Chaucer was to have been from his hand, but he
abandoned the project, thinking the time not ripe. He published, however, in 1863, in the Memoirs of the American
Academy, his laborious paper entitled "Observations on the
Language of Chaucer", a work which marks an epoch in the
study of the poet, and in which "he not only defined the problems and provided many solutions, but gave a perfect model of
method." Skeat has said that "it ought never to be forgotten
that the only full and almost complete solution of the question
of the right scansion of Chaucer's Canterbury Tales is due to

what Mr. Ellis rightly terms 'the wonderful industry, acuteness, and accuracy of Prof. Child.'"

This paper, and another upon the language of Gower, are buried in the Memoirs above mentioned for 1863 and 1873. A few copies were struck off separately, but are very hard to find. Ellis condensed and rearranged them in vol. I of his Early English Pronunciation, 1869, but according to Professor Kittredge this is by no means a good substitute for the originals.

In 1867-8 Child gave the money to begin the labors of the Chaucer Society, and to him accordingly Furnivall dedicates its first publications. The last and the monumental work of Child's life was his English and Scottish Ballads. From the sketch of his life by Kittredge, which is prefixed to that work, these notes have been taken; to it the student is referred for a better understanding of one of the greatest of American scholars and teachers.

The Chaucer Society and Dr. F. J. Furnivall.

The Chaucer Society was founded in 1868 by Dr. Furnivall, "to do honor to Chaucer, and to let the lovers and students of him see how far the best unprinted manuscripts of his works differed from the printed texts". "The Society's publications are issued in two Series, of which the first contains the different texts of Chaucer's works; and the second such originals of and essays on those as can be procured, with other illustrative treatises, and Supplementary Tales." Annual subscription, two guineas; the Hon. Secretary is W. A. Dalziel, 67 Victoria Road, Finsbury Park, London. The Society's publishers are Messrs. Trübner and Company.

Dr. Furnivall is at more than eighty still the laborious editor-in-chief of the Society, and also the president and active editor of the Early English Text Society, the New Shakspere Society, the Ballad Society, etc. Since 1884 he has been the recipient of a pension on the civil list, as State recognition of his great and generously given services to the cause of English letters and scholarship. The Athenaeum of 1899 I : 268 said: "It is not too much to say that if English philologists can hold up their heads in the society of their European fellows it is almost entirely due to his selfforgetting industry and perseverance." In 1900, on the occasion of Furnivall's seventy-fifth birthday, there was issued *An English Miscellany,* composed of fifty papers by friends and fellowlaborers, with poems to him, an account of the meeting held to celebrate the occasion, and a bibliography of his work. The Chaucer papers included in this volume are by Liddell, McCormick, Mather, and Morris, see under the headings of the Parson's Tale, Troilus, the Knight's Tale, and the Doctor's Tale, here. The volume was published Oxford, 1901.

The recognition awarded the Chaucer Society, like that to the Early English Text Society, was somewhat slow on the part of the great English journals. The Athenaeum of 1865 I: 90 had mentioned the founding of the Early English Text Society in terms which called forth a protest from Furnivall *ibid*, p. 128; in the same journal for 1867 II: 435 is a short paragraph heralding the Chaucer Society, and on page 467 is printed the Society's prospectus. The work of the two Societies is regularly though briefly mentioned thereafter in the Athenaeum's columns; and the Chaucer-material, which from 1828 to 1864 had been scanty except for the reviews of the Horne modernizations in 1841 (page 107), of Nicolas' life of Chaucer in 1844 (page 125), and of Saunders in 1847 (page 950), becomes frequent, and is made matter of discussion and controversy. But the first serious public recognition of the Society's work, according to Furnivall, was in the Edinburgh Review of 1870, in the opening article, written by Professor Baynes of St. Andrew's University. Note also the cordial review in Athen. 1871 II ; 392.

Publications of the Chaucer Society

First Series

Issue for 1868. I. The Prologue and Knight's Tale, of the Canterbury Tales, in 6 parallel Texts (from the 6 MSS named below), together with Tables, showing the Groups of the Tales, and their varying order in 38 MSS of the Tales, and in 5 old printed editions, also Specimens from several MSS of the "Moveable Prologues" of the Canterbury Tales,—The Shipman's Prologue, and Franklin's Prologue,—when moved from their right places, and of the Substitutes for them. (The Six-Text, Part I.)

Furnivall marks the Trial Tables "now superseded"; it is not possible to discuss upon their authority the question of Tale-grouping in different MSS, as the Tables give no clue to the state of the Links.

The Specimens of Moveable Prologues are numbered I to IV and paged from 1 to 57. With No. XXV of the First Series (Part IV of the Six-Text) was issued Part V of these Specimens, being Specimens of the various Readings in the Doctor-Pardoner Link, etc., paged from 58 to 69. With No. XXX (Part V of the Six-Text) were issued Parts VI to VIII of these Specimens, paged from 70 to 80, and including: VI. Specimens of the various Readings of the Wife-taking Lines . . . in the Merchant's Tale, and of the Doubtful Lines, 1358-61, omitted by the Ellesmere MS in the same Tale. VII. Two Test Lines in the Clerk's Tale. VIII. Two Test Lines in the Second Nun's Tale.

It will be noticed that the pagination of these Specimens is separate from that of the Six-Text.

II-VII. II. The Prologue and Knight's Tale from the Ellesmere MS, Part I; III. Hengwrt MS, 154, Pt. I; IV. Cambridge

MS Gg iv, 27, Pt. I; V. Corpus MS, Oxford, Pt. I; VI. Petworth MS, Pt. I; VII. Lansdowne MS, 851, Pt. I. (Separate
issues of the texts forming Part I of the Six-Text.)

On misprints in the Ellesmere text see Flügel in Anglia 30 : 401.

Issue for 1869. VIII-XIII. VIII. The Miller's, Reeve's, and
Cook's Tales:
Ellesmere MS, Part II; IX. Hengwrt MS, Pt. II; X. Cambridge MS, Pt. II; XI. Corpus MS Pt. II; XII. Petworth
MS Pt. II; XIII. Lansdowne MS Pt. II, with an Appendix
of "Gamelyn" from six MSS. (Separate issues of the Texts
forming the Six-Text, Part II, No. XIV.)

Gamelyn is supplied in the Ellesmere from Royal 18 C ii, in the
Hengwrt from Harley 1758, in the Cambridge from Sloane 1685;
the other MSS have the Tale.

Issue for 1870. XIV. The Miller's, Reeve's, and Cook's Tales, with
an Appendix of the Spurious Tale of Gamelyn, in 6 parallel
Texts. (Six-Text, Part II.)

See above for texts of Gamelyn.

Issue for 1871. XV. The Man of Law's, Shipman's, and Prioress's
Tales, with Chaucer's own Tale of Sir Thopas, in 6 parallel
Texts from the MSS above named, and 10 coloured drawings
of Tellers of Tales, after the originals in the Ellesmere MS.
(Six-Text, Part III.)

XVI. The Man of Law's Tale, from the Ellesmere MS,
Part III.

XVII. The Man of Law's Tale, from the Cambridge MS,
Part III.

XVIII. The Man of Law's Tale from the Corpus MS,
Part III.

XIX. The Shipman's, Prioress's, and Man of Law's Tales,
from the Petworth MS, Part III.

XX. The Man of Law's Tale, from the Lansdowne MS,
Part III. (Each with woodcuts of fourteen drawings of Tellers
of Tales in the Ellesmere MS.)

Reviewed Athen. 1871 II : 392.

XXI. A Parallel-Text edition of Chaucer's Minor Poems.
Part I : 1. The Dethe of Blaunche the Duchesse, from
Thynne's ed. of 1532, the Fairfax MS 16, and Tanner MS 346;
2. the Compleynt to Pite, 3. the Parlament of Foules, and
4. the Compleynt of Mars, each from six MSS.

The MSS of Pite are:—Tanner 346, Fairfax 16, Bodley 638, Harley 78, Univ. Libr. Cambr. Ff i, 6, Trin. Coll. Cambr. R 3, 19. The MSS of the Parlement are:—Univ. Libr. Cambr. Gg iv, 27, Trin. Coll. Cambr. R 3, 19, Caxton's ed., Harley 7333, St John's Coll. Oxford 57, Univ. Libr. Cambr. Ff i 6. The MSS of the Mars are:—Fairfax 16, Tanner 346, Notary's ed., Harley 7333, Trin. Coll. Cambr. R 3, 20, Selden B, 24.

XXII. Supplementary Parallel-Texts of Chaucer's Minor Poems, Part I, containing 1. The Parlament of Foules, from three MSS. [Reprinted in LIX, First Series.]

The three MSS are:—Tanner 346, Digby 181, Selden B 14. The note above as to reprinting is from the Society's list; I do not find that it took place, although the cover of LIX announces six Texts; only one page of the Tanner-Digby-Selden is in LIX.

XXIII. Odd Texts of Chaucer's Minor Poems, Part I, containing 1. two MS fragments of The Parlament of Foules; 2. the two differing versions of the Prologue to the Legende of Good Women, arranged so as to show their differences; 3. an Appendix of Poems attributed to Chaucer, i. The Balade of Pitee by Chauciers, ii. The Cronycle made by Chaucer, both from MSS written by Shirley, Chaucer's contemporary.

The fragments of the Parlament are from Hh iv, 12 and Laud 416; the two versions of the Prologue are from Gg iv, 27 and Fairfax 16; the Balade is from Harley 78, the "Cronycle" (p. vi ff.) from Ashmole 59. A flyleaf has Newfangleness, from Cott. Cleop. D vii, with denial by Furnivall of its authenticity, dated 1879, and issued with LX, see below.

XXIV. A One-Text Print of Chaucer's Minor Poems, being the best Text from the Parallel-Text Edition, Part I, containing, I. The Dethe of Blaunche the Duchesse, II. The Compleynt to Pite, III. The Parlament of Foules, IV. The Compleynt of Mars, V. The ABC, with its original from De Guileville's Pélérinage de la Vie humaine (edited from the best Paris MSS by M. Paul Meyer).

Blaunche is from the Fairfax MS, Pite from the Fairfax, the Parlement from Gg iv, 27, Mars from the Fairfax, the ABC from Univ. Libr. Cambr. Ff v, 30.

Issue for 1872. XXV. Chaucer's Tale of Melibe, the Monk's, Nun's-Priest's, Doctor's, Pardoner's, Wife of Bath's, Friar's, and Summoner's Tales, in 6 parallel Texts from the MSS above named, with the remaining 13 coloured drawings of Tellers of Tales, after the originals in the Ellesmere MS, and with Specimens of the Variations of 30 MSS in the Doctor-Pardoner Link. (Six-Text, Part IV.)

In the copies as issued the Specimens appear after p. 332; see note on them under Issue for 1868, above.

Koch, ed. of Pard. Tale p. xxi, says that the Six-Text Pardoner's Tale was reprinted 1888.

XXVI. The Wife's, Friar's, and Summoner's Tales, from the Ellesmere MS, with 9 woodcuts of Tale-Tellers. (Part IV.) [That is, part IV of the separate print of the Ellesmere.]

XXVII. The Wife's, Friar's, Summoner's, Monk's, and Nun's-Priest's Tales, from the Hengwrt MS, with 23 woodcuts of the Tellers of the Tales. (Part III.) [That is, part III of the Hengwrt MS.]

Woodcuts of Tale Tellers drawn from the Ellesmere MS.

XXVIII. The Wife's, Friar's, and Summoner's Tales, from the Cambridge MS, with 9 woodcuts of Tale-Tellers. (Part IV.) [That is, part IV of the Cambridge MS.]

XXIX. A Treatise on the Astrolabe, addressed to his son Lowys, in 1391 A. D., by Geoffrey Chaucer, edited by the Rev. Prof. Walter W. Skeat, M. A.

Issue for 1873. XXX. The Six-Text Canterbury Tales, Part V, containing the Clerk's and Merchant's Tales.

Issue for 1874. XXXI. The Six-Text, Part VI, containing the Squire's and Franklin's Tales.

With this were issued Parts VI to VIII of the Specimens, see above under Issue for 1868.

XXXII. The Clerk's, Merchant's, Squire's, Franklin's, Doctor's, Pardoner's, Shipman's, Prioress's Tales, Sir Thopas, Melibeus, Monk's, Nun's-Priest's, Second Nun's Tales; Ellesmere MS, Part V.

XXXIII. The Clerk's, Merchant's, Squire's, Franklin's, Doctor's, Pardoner's, Shipman's, Prioress's Tales, Sir Thopas, Melibeus, Monk's, Nun's-Priest's, Second Nun's Tales; Cambridge MS, Part V.

XXXIV. Squire's, Wife of Bath's, Friar's, Summoner's, Clerk's, Merchant's, Franklin's Tales; Corpus MS, Part IV.

XXXV. Squire's, Merchant's, Wife of Bath's, Friar's, Summoner's, Clerk's, Franklin's, Second Nun's Tales; Petworth MS, Part IV.

XXXVI. Squire's, Wife of Bath's, Friar's, Summoner's, Clerk's, Merchant's, Franklin's Tales; Lansdowne MS, Part IV.

Issue for 1875. XXXVII. The Six-Text, Part VII, the Second Nun's, Canon's-Yeoman's, and Manciple's Tales, with the Blank-Parson Link.

Page 301 was issued with No. XLIX.

XXXVIII. Second Nun's, Canon's-Yeoman's, Manciple's Tales; Ellesmere MS, Part VI.

XXXIX. Manciple's, Man of Law's, Squire's, Merchant's, Franklin's, Second Nun's, Clerk's, Doctor's, Pardoner's, Shipman's, Prioress's Tales, Sir Thopas, Melibeus; Hengwrt MS, Part IV.

XL. Second Nun's, Canon's Yeoman's, Manciple's Tales; Cambridge MS, Part VI.

XLI. Second Nun's, Canon's-Yeoman's, Doctor's, Pardoner's, Shipman's, Prioress's Tales, Sir Thopas, Melibeus, Monk's, Nun's-Priest's, Manciple's Tales; Corpus MS, Part V.

XLII. Second Nun's, Canon's-Yeoman's, Doctor's, Pardoner's Tales, Sir Thopas, Melibeus, Monk's, Nun's-Priest's, Manciple's Tales; Petworth MS, Part V.

XLIII. Second Nun's, Canon's-Yeoman's, Doctor's, Pardoner's, Shipman's, Prioress' Tales, Sir Thopas, Melibeus, Monk's, Nun's-Priest's, Manciple's Tales; Lansdowne MS, Part V.

XLIV. A detaild Comparison of the Troylus and Cryseyde with Boccaccio's Filostrato, with a Translation of all Passages used by Chaucer, and an Abstract of the Parts not used, by W. Michael Rossetti, Esq., and with a print of the Troylus from the Harleian MS 3943. Part I.

XLV. Ryme-Index to the Ellesmere MS of the Canterbury Tales, by Henry Cromie, Esq., M. A. In 8vo for the separate Ellesmere MS.

XLVI. Ryme-Index to the Ellesmere MS, by Henry Cromie, Esq., M. A. In Royal 4to for the Six-Text.

XLVII. Notes and Corrections for the 8vo Ryme-Index, by H. Cromie, Esq., M. A.

Issue for 1876. XLVIII. Autotype Specimens of the Chief Chaucer MSS, Part I, 16 autotypes, with a Note on the MSS, by Dr. F. J. Furnivall.

The MSS are:—Harley 7334 (two pages), Lansdowne 851 (two pages), Corpus, Sloane 1685, Adds. 10340 (two pages), Ii iii, 21, Royal 18 C ii, Hengwrt, Harley 1758, Adds. 16165, Harley 7333, Christ Church, Adds. 5140.

Issue for 1877. XLIX. The Six-Text, Part VIII, containing the Parson's Tale, with a Table of its Contents; and Mr. Cromie's Notes and Corrections for the 4to Ryme-Index.

Page 301 of the Six-Text was issued with this.

L-LV. L. The Parson's Tale, Ellesmere MS, Part VII; LI.
Hengwrt MS, Part V; LII Cambridge MS, Part VII; LIII.
Corpus MS, Part VI; LIV. Petworth MS, Part VI; LV.
Lansdowne MS, Part VI.

The imperfect Parson's Tale of the Hengwrt is filled out from
Christ Church and from Adds. 5140; the Cambridge gaps, here
and elsewhere, are supplied from Harley 1758 and Sloane 1685;
Corpus is completed by Selden and Hatton.
These, with PT part II and the Autotypes, are reviewed by
Koch, Anglia 3 : 179.

Issue for 1878. LVI. Autotype Specimens of the Chief Chaucer
MSS, Part II; 9 from the Cambridge MS Gg iv 27, and 1 from
Lord Leconfield's MS. [the Petworth].

See note on 1877 issues.

LVII. A Parallel-Text edition of Chaucer's Minor Poems,
Part II : 5. The ABC, from 6 MSS; 6. The Mother of God,
from 3 MSS; 7. Anelida and Arcyte, from 5 MSS and Caxton's print; 8. The Former Age, from 2 MSS (with the Latin
original, and Chaucer's prose Englishing) ; 9. To his Scrivener,
from Shirley's MS and Stowe's print; 10. The House of Fame,
from 2 MSS and Caxton's and Thynne's prints.

The texts of the ABC are :—Ff v, 30, St. John's College Cambr.
G 21, Glasgow, Laud 740, Gg iv, 27, Fairfax 16. The MSS of the
Mother of God are :—Phillipps 8151, Selden B, 24, and Advocates'
Library Edinburgh 18. 2. 8. The MSS of Anelida are :—Harley
7333, Fairfax 16, Tanner 346, Harley 372, Digby 181, Caxton.
The texts of Former Age are :—Ii iii, 21, Hh iv, 12. The
Words to Adam Scrivener are from Trin. Coll. Cambr. R 3, 20.
The House of Fame is from Fairfax 16, Caxton, Thynne, Bodley
638. See note on 1877 issues.

Issue for 1879. LVIII. A Parallel-Text edition of Chaucer's Minor
Poems, Part III, completing the Parallel-Text, and containing :
11. The Legend of Good Women from 5 MSS and Thynne's
print. 12. Truth from 6 MSS; 13. The Compleynt of Venus
from 6 MSS; 14. The Envoy to Scogan from 3 MSS; 15.
Marriage, or the Envoy to Bukton, from 1 MS and Notary's
and Thynne's prints; 16. Gentilesse from 6 MSS; 17. Proverbs
from 3 MSS; 18. Stedfastness from 6 MSS; 19. Fortune from
6 MSS; 20. Chaucer to his empty Purse, from 6 MSS.

The texts of the Legend are :—Gg iv, 27, Fairfax 16, Tanner
346, R 3, 19, Selden B 24, and Thynne's print of 1532. The texts
of Truth are :—Adds. 10340, Gg iv, 27, the Ellesmere, Cotton
Cleopatra D vii, R 3, 20. The texts of the Venus are :—R 3, 20,
Ashmole 59, Tanner 346, Fairfax 16, Ff i, 6, Selden B 24. The texts
of Scogan are :—Gg iv, 27, Fairfax 16, Pepys 2006. The texts
of Bukton are :—Fairfax 16, and the prints named above. The

texts of Gentilesse are:—Ashmole 59, R 3, 20, Harley 7333, Cotton Cleop. D vii, Harley 7578, Adds. 22139. The texts of Proverbs are:—Adds. 16165, Fairfax 16, Harley 7578. The texts of Stedfastness are:—Harley 7333, R 3, 20, Cotton Cleop. D vii, Fairfax 16, Adds. 22139, Harley 7578. The texts of Fortune are:— Ii iii, 21, Ashmole 59, R 3, 20, Fairfax 16, Bodley 638, Harley 2251. The texts of Purse are:—Fairfax 16, Harley 7333, Ff i, 6, Pepys 2006, Adds. 22139, Harley 2251.

See Koch in Anglia 4: Anz. 93-117.

Issue for 1880. LIX. Supplementary Parallel-Texts of Chaucer's Minor Poems, Part II: 1a. The Parlament of Foules from 3 MSS; 2. The ABC from 6 MSS; 3. Anelida and Arcite from 6 MSS; 4. The Legend of Good Women, in whole or part from 4 MSS; 5. The Complaint of Mars from 3 MSS; 6. Truth from 6 MSS; 7. The Compleynt of Venus from 3 MSS; 8. Gentilesse from 3 MSS; 9. Lack of Stedfastness from Thynne's print and 2 MSS; 10. Fortune from 2 MSS and Caxton's print.

The texts of the Parlement are:—Fairfax 16, Bodley 638, Longleat 258. The texts of the ABC are:—Harley 2251, Bedford, Speght's print of 1602, Pepys 2006 (two copies), Harley 7578. The texts of the Anelida are:—Adds. 16165, Bodley 638, Longleat 258, R 3, 20, Ff i, 6, Pepys 2006. The texts of the Legend are:—Bodley 638, Adds. 9832, Pepys 2006, Adds. 12524. The texts of the Mars are:—Pepys 2006 (two copies), and Longleat 258. The texts of Truth are:—Harley 7333, Fairfax 16 (two copies), Adds. 22139, Lansdowne 699, and Caxton's print. The texts of the Venus are:— Notary's print and two copies from the Pepys MS 2006. The texts of Gentilesse are:—Caxton's print, Harley 2251, R 14, 51. The texts of Stedfastness are:—Thynne's ed. of 1532, R 14, 51, the Bannatyne MS. The texts of Fortune are:—Lansdowne 699, Pepys 2006, and Caxton's print.

See note ante under No. XXII.

See Koch in Jahresber. 1880, pp. 226-7.

LX. Odd Texts of Chaucer's Minor Poems, Part II, containing, 3. The ABC, from 2 MSS; 4. The House of Fame, from the Pepys MS, etc.; 5. The Legend of Good Women, from 3 MSS; 6. The Dethe of Blaunche the Duchesse from 1 MS; 7. The Complaint to Pity from 2 MSS; 8. The Parlament of Foules from 1 MS; 9. Truth from 3 MSS; 10. Envoy to Scogan from 1 MS; 11. Purse from 1 MS.

The texts of the ABC are:—Sion College, Bodley 638. The text of the House of Fame is from Pepys 2006. The texts of the Legend are:—Adds. 28617, Ff i, 6, Rawl. C 86. The Duchesse is from Bodley 638. Pity is from Harley 7578 and Longleat 258. The Parlement is from Pepys 2006. Truth is from Selden B 24, Kk i, 5, Corpus 203. Scogan is from Caxton's text. Purse is from Caxton's text.

The flyleaf mentioned under XXIII was issued with this part.

See Koch in Jahresber. 1880, p. 227.

LXI. A One-Text Print of Chaucer's Minor Poems, Part II,

34

containing, VI. Mother of God; VII. Anelida; VIII. The Former Age; IX. Adam Scrivener; X. The House of Fame; XI. Legende; XII. Truth; XIII. Venus; XIV. Scogan; XV. Marriage; XVI. Gentilesse; XVII. Proverbs; XVIII. Stedfastness; XIX. Fortune; XX. Purse.

VI is from MS Phillipps 8151; VII is from Harley 7333; VIII is from Ii iii, 21; IX is from R 3, 20; X is from Fairfax 16; XI is from Gg iv, 27; XII is from Adds. 10340; XIII is from R 3, 20; XIV is from Gg iv, 27; XV is from Fairfax 16; XVI is from Ashmole 59; XVII is from Adds. 16165; XVIII is from Harley 7333; XIX is from Ii iii, 21; XX is from Fairfax 16. See Koch in Jahresber. 1880, p. 228; in Anglia 4 : Anz. 111.

LXII. Autotype Specimens of the chief Chaucer MSS, Part III; 2 from Henry V's MS of the Troilus, when he was Prince of Wales (now Mr. Bacon Frank's); 1 from Shirley's MS of the ABC at Sion Coll.

Issue for 1881. LXIII. A Parallel-Text edition of Chaucer's Troilus & Criseyde from the Campsall MS, before 1415 A. D. (written for Henry V when Prince of Wales), Harleian MS 2280, and Cambr. Univ. Libr. Gg iv 27. Part I. Books 1 and 2.

Issue for 1882. LXIV. A Parallel-Text edition of Chaucer's Troilus & Criseyde from the Campsall MS, before 1415 A. D. (written for Henry V when Prince of Wales), Harleian MS 2280, and Cambr. Univ. Libr. Gg iv, 27. Part II. Books 3, 4, 5.

Reviewed by Koch, Anglia 6 : Anz. pp. 80-91; see Littblatt 1885, p. 324.

Issue for 1883. LXV. Part II of Mr. W. M. Rossetti's Comparison of Chaucer's Troylus and Cryseyde with Boccaccio's Filostrato, completing the work.

Issue for 1884 is to be LXVI-LXXI. 6 Appendixes to the 6 MSS of the Six-Text, with Woodcuts and colord Lithographs of 6 Tellers of Tales and of 6 emblematical Figures from the Cambridge Univ. MS Gg iv, 27, etc., and Process Engravings, for the Ellesmere MS Part, of the 23 Ellesmere MS Miniatures. The Hengwrt MS, Part VI, contains the Canon's-Yeoman's Tale from the Lichfield MS.

[Not published]

LXXII. The Six-Text, Part IX, with colord Lithographs of 6 Tellers of Tales and 6 emblematical Figures from the Cambridge Univ. MS Gg iv, 27; Forewords, Title-pages for the three volumes, etc.; and Prof. Hiram Corson's Index to the Subjects and Names of the Canterbury Tales.

[Not published]

Issue for 1885. LXXIII. The Harleian MS 7334 of The Canterbury Tales, with woodcuts of 23 Tellers of Tales from the Ellesmere MS, etc.

LXXIV. Autotype Specimens of the chief Chaucer MSS. Part IV. The Ellesmere.

[One page.]

Issue for 1886. LXXV. Chaucer's Boece from the Cambridge University MS Ii iii, 21.

LXXVI. Chaucer's Boece from the Additional MS 10340 in the British Museum, as edited by the Rev. Dr. R. Morris for the E. E. Text Soc. in 1868.

As Appendix to this, pp. 180-84, are printed the texts of Former Age and Fortune from MS Ii iii, 21.

LXXVII. More Odd Texts of Chaucer's Minor Poems, containing 1. The Compleynte to Pite; 2. The Complaint of the Anelida and Arcite; 3. Truth; 4. Lack of Stedfastness; 5. Fortune; 6. Purse. Appendix : I. The Balade of Pite. II. Roundels (Mercilesse Beaute).

1 is from Phillipps 9053,=Adds. 34360. 2 is from the same MS. 3 is from Phillipps 8299, Hatton 73, Selden B 10. 4 is from Hatton 73. 5 is from Selden B 10. 6 is from Phillipps 9053=Adds. 34360.
The Balade of Pite is from the same Phillipps MS, Mercilesse Beaute from Pepys 2006.
The More Odd Texts was issued in 1891.

Issue for 1887. LXXVIII. A Ryme-Index to Chaucer's Minor Poems, by Miss Isabel Marshall and Miss Lela Porter, in Royal 4to for the Parallel-Text.

Issue for 1888. LXXIX. A One-Text Print of Chaucer's Troilus, from the Campsall MS, before 1415 A. D.

Issue for 1889. LXXX. A Ryme-Index to Chaucer's Minor Poems, by Miss Isabel Marshall and Miss Lela Porter, in 8vo for the One-Text print of the Minor Poems.

Issue for 1890. LXXXI. Parallel-Text Specimens of all accessible unprinted Chaucer MSS: The Pardoner's Prolog and Tale, edited by Prof. Zupitza, Ph. D. Part I, from 7 MSS: Cambridge Dd iv, 24, Christ Church, Additional 5140, Devonshire, Haistwell (or Egerton 2726), Ingilby, Northumberland: the Dd Group.

LXXXII. The Romaunt of the Rose, from Thynne's print, 1532, ed. F. J. Furnivall.

Not yet issued (1907).

Issue for 1891. LXXXIII. A Parallel text of the Romaunt of the Rose (of which the first 1705 lines are most probably Chaucer's), from the unique MS at Glasgow, and its French original, Le Roman de la Rose, edited by Dr. Max Kaluza. Part I.

On Kaluza's work see p. 452 here.

LXXXIV. A Rime-Index to Chaucer's Troilus, by Prof. Skeat, Litt. D.

Issue for 1892. LXXXV. Parallel-Text Specimens of all accessible unprinted Chaucer MSS: The Pardoner's Prolog and Tale, edited by Prof. Zupitza, Ph. D. Part II, from 10 MSS.

The MSS are:—Phillipps 6570, Bodley 686, Harley 7335, Paris f. angl. 39, Selden B 14, Trin. Coll. Cambr. R 3, 3, Rawl. Poet. 223, Glasgow V. 1, 1, Adds. 25718, Hatton Donat. 1.

Issue for 1893. LXXXVI. Parallel-Text Specimens of all accessible unprinted Chaucer MSS: The Pardoner's Prolog and Tale, edited by Prof. Zupitza, Ph. D. Part III, from 6 MSS.

The MSS are:—Sloane 1686, Trin. Coll. Cambr. R 3, 15, New Coll. Oxford 314, Harley 7333, Helmingham, Ii iii, 26.

Issue for 1894. LXXXVII. A Parallel-Text of 3 more MSS of Chaucer's Troilus; the St. John's L 1, Corpus, Cambridge, and Harl. 1239 Brit. Mus., put forth by Dr. F. J. Furnivall. Part I, Books I-III, with a Note by G. C. Macaulay, M. A.

Preface dated 1895, Macaulay's note dated 1896.

Issue for 1895. LXXXVIII. A Parallel-Text of 3 more MSS of Chaucer's Troilus, Part II, Books IV-V.

Issue for 1896 will be:—LXXXIX. Prof. McCormick's Introduction to Chaucer's Troilus, discussing its MSS, its Text, its Metre and Grammar.

[Now announced for 1907; see XCVIII below.]

Parallel Texts of Troilus, Part III.

Issue for 1897. XC. Parallel-Text Specimens of all accessible unprinted MSS: The Pardoner's Prolog and Tale. Part IV, from 17 MSS, edited by the late Prof. Zupitza, Ph. D., and Prof. John Koch, Ph. D.

The MSS are:—Barlow 20, Bodley 414, Cholmondeley-Norton, Delamere, Harley 1758, Laud 600, Laud 739, Lichfield, Lincoln Cathedral A 4, 18, Mm ii, 5, Phillipps 8136, Phillipps 8137, Rawl. Poet. 149, Royal 17 D xv, Royal 18 C ii, Sloane 1685, Trinity Coll. Oxford 49.

On p. xlvii of this issue is:—Preliminary Chart of the MSS of the Canterbury Tales, by Mark H. Liddell, from Prof. Zupitza's Notes and his Edition of the Specimens of the MSS of the Pardoner's Tale published by the Chaucer Society.

Issue for 1898. XCI. Parallel-Text Specimens, Part V: The Pardoner's Prolog and Tale, a Six-Text, from 3 MSS and three blackletters, edited by Prof. John Koch, Ph. D., and Dr. F. J. Furnivall.

> The texts are:—Adds. 35286, Ashburnham Appendix 124, 127, Caxton's first and second prints, Thynne's first print (1532).

> A Supplement. The Pardoner's Prolog and Tale from the Paper MS of the College of Physicians, London, and a Reproduction of Mr. Paul Hardy's pen-and-ink Drawing of the Yard of the Tabard Inn on the Morning of the 17th of April, 1387.

> A note by Furnivall at the close of the introduction is dated March, 1900.

Issue for 1899. XCII. Parallel-Text Specimens, Part VI. The Clerk's Tale, a Six-Text Print from 6 MSS not containing the Pardoner's Tale, put forth by Dr. F. J. Furnivall.

> The six MSS are:—Sion College, Rawl. Poet. 141, Ashburnham Appendix 126, Harley 1239, Naples, Holkham 667.

Issue for 1900. XCIII. Parallel-Text Specimens, Part VII: The Clerk's Tale from the Phillipps MS 8299 and the Longleat MS, put forth by Dr. F. J. Furnivall.

> The Longleat is completed from Hodson 39.

XCIV. Parallel-Text Specimens, Part VIII. The Pardoner's Prolog and Tale from the Hodson MS 39, put forth by Dr. F. J. Furnivall, with an Introduction by Prof. John Koch, Ph. D.

> Marked as second supplement to Part XCI. Continues the pagination of Part V, No. XCI above.
> Koch's introduction is dated Oct. 1901.

Issue for 1901. XCV. The Cambridge MS Dd iv, 24 of the Canterbury Tales, completed by the Egerton MS 2726 (the Haistwell MS), edited by F. J. Furnivall. Part I.

Issue for 1902. XCVI. The Same, Part II.

> Appendix, pp. 679 ff., contains:—Lines and parts of lines from Skeat's edition, left out of the MSS.—The Hymn of Chaucer's Oxford Clerk Nicholas, from Arundel MS 248, in English and in Latin.—Woodcuts of Paintings of the 23 Tellers of the Canterbury Tales, copied from the Ellesmere MS and cut by Mr. W. H. Hooper.—Woodcuts of 6 Tellers of 6 of the Canterbury Tales, the Reeve, Cook, Wife of Bath, Pardoner, Monk, and Manciple, and of 6 allegorical Figures for the Parson's Tale, Envy and Charity, Gluttony and Abstinence, Lechery and Chastity, copied from MS Gg iv, 27 in the Cambridge University Library, and cut, by Mr. W. H. Hooper.

> Furnivall's preface is dated 1903.

XCVII. Parallel-Text Specimens, Part IX. An introduction to the 8 Specimens of Chaucer's Clerk's Tale, by Prof. John Koch, Ph. D.

Issue for 1907 [none in 1903-6] will probably be,

XCVIII. Specimen-Extracts from nine unprinted MSS of Chaucer's Troilus, with an Introduction on the MSS, Metre, and Grammar of the Poem, by Dr. W. H. McCormick.

[See No. LXXXIX above.]

Second Series

Issue for 1868. 1. Early English Pronunciation, with especial reference to Shakspere and Chaucer, by Alexander J. Ellis, Esq., F. R. S. Part I. This work includes an amalgamation of Prof. F. J. Child's two Papers on the use of the final e by Chaucer (in T. Wright's ed. of The Canterb. Tales) and by Gower (in Dr. Pauli's ed. of the Confessio Amantis).

For note on this work, which was published jointly by the Chaucer and the Early English Text Societies, see p. 475 here.

2. Essays on Chaucer, his Words and Works, Part I: 1. Prof. Ebert's Review of Sandras's Étude sur Chaucer, translated by J. W. van Rees Hoets, M. A.; 2. A 13th-century Latin Treatise on the Chilindre (of the Shipman's Tale), edited by Mr. E. Brock.

3. A Temporary Preface to the Society's Six-Text edition of Chaucer's Canterbury Tales, Part I, attempting to show the right Order of the Tales, and the Days and Stages of the Pilgrimage, etc., by F. J. Furnivall, Esq., M. A.

Issue for 1869. 4. Early English Pronunciation, with especial reference to Shakspere and Chaucer, by Alexander J. Ellis, Esq., F. R. S. Part II.

Issue for 1870. 5. Early English Pronunciation, with especial reference to Shakspere and Chaucer, by Alexander J. Ellis, Esq., F. R. S. Part III.

Ellis and the Six-Text are reviewed Athen. 1871 II: 392-3.

Issue for 1871. 6. Trial-Forewords to my Parallel-Text edition of Chaucer's Minor Poems for the Chaucer Society (with a try to set Chaucer's Works in their right order of Time), by Fredk. J. Furnivall. Part I.

Pages 125-128 of this book, being Additions and Corrections, were issued with No. 7. Pages 129-148, Further Additions and Corrections, were issued with No. 10.

Issue for 1872. 7. Originals and Analogues of some of Chaucer's Canterbury Tales, Part I. 1. The original of the Man of Law's Tale of Constance, from the French Chronicle of Nicholas Trivet, Arundel MS 56, ab. 1340 A. D., collated with the later copy, ab. 1400, in the National Library at Stockholm; copied and edited, with a translation, by Mr. Edmund Brock. 2. The

Tale of "Merelaus the Emperor", englisht from the Gesta Romanorum by Thomas Hoccleve, in Harl. MS 7333; and 3. Part of Matthew Paris's Vita Offae Primi, both stories illustrating incidents in the Man of Law's Tale. 4. Two French Fabliaux like the Reeve's Tale. 5. Two Latin Stories like the Friar's Tale.

See note on No. 6 above.

Issue for 1873. 8. Albertano of Brescia's Liber Consilii et Consolationis, A. D. 1246 (the Latin source of the French original of Chaucer's Melibe), edited from the MSS, by Dr. Thor Sundby.

Issue for 1874. 9. Essays on Chaucer, his Words and Works, Part II: 3. John of Hoveden's Practica Chilindri, edited from the MS, with a translation, by Mr. E. Brock. 4. Chaucer's use of the final e, by Joseph Payne, Esq. 5. Mrs. E. Barrett-Browning on Chaucer: being those parts of her review of the Book of the Poets, 1842, which relate to him; here reprinted by leave of Mr. Robert Browning. 6. Professor Bernhard ten Brink's critical edition of Chaucer's Compleynte to Pite.

Issue for 1875. 10. Originals and Analogues of Chaucer's Canterbury Tales, Part II. 6. Alphonsus of Lincoln, a Story like the Prioress's Tale. 7. How Reynard caught Chanticleer, the Source of the Nun's-Priest's Tale. 8. Two Italian Stories, and a Latin one, like the Pardoner's Tale. 9. The Tale of the Priest's Bladder, a story like the Summoner's Tale, being "Li dis de le Vescie a Prestre", par Jakes de Basiw. 10. Petrarch's Latin Tale of Griseldis (with Boccaccio's Story from which it was re-told), the original of the Clerk's Tale. 11. Five Versions of a Pear-tree Story like that in the Merchant's Tale. 12. Four Versions of the Life of Saint Cecilia, the original of the Second Nun's Tale. Edited by F. J. Furnivall.

See note on No. 6 above.

11. Early English Pronunciation, with especial reference to Shakspere and Chaucer, by Alexander J. Ellis, Esq., F. R. S. Part IV.

12. Life-Records of Chaucer, Part I, The Robberies of Chaucer by Richard Brerelay and others at Westminster, and at Hatcham, Surrey, on Tuesday, Sept. 6, 1390, with some Account of the Robbers, from the Enrolments in the Public Record Office, by Walford D. Selby, Esq., of the Public Record Office.

13. Thynne's Animadversions (1599) on Speght's *Chaucers Workes,* re-edited from the unique MS in the Bridgewater Library by Fredk. J. Furnivall, with fresh Lives of William and Francis Thynne, and the only known fragment of The Pilgrim's Tale.

Published 1876, for this society and the EETS jointly. Reprints Kingsley's preface to the 1865 EETS ed. of the Animadversions, and adds much valuable material.

Issue for 1876. 14. Life-Records of Chaucer, Part II. The Household Ordinances of King Edward II, June 1323 (as englisht by Francis Tate in March 1601 A. D.), with extracts from those of King Edward IV, to show the probable duties of Chaucer as Valet or Yeoman of the Chamber, and Esquire, to Edward III, of whose Household Book no MS is known; together with Chaucer's Oath as Controller of the Customs, and an enlargd Autotype of Hoccleve's Portrait of Chaucer, edited by F. J. Furnivall.

This, with Nos. 15, 16, 17, reviewed by Koch, Anglia 2 : 532-45.

15. Originals and Analogues of Chaucer's Canterbury Tales, Part III. 13. The Story of Constance, for the Man of Law's Tale. 14. The Boy killd by a Jew for singing "Gaude Maria," an Analogue of the Prioress's Tale. 15. The Paris Beggar-boy murdered by a Jew for singing "Alma Redemptoris mater"; an Analogue of the Prioress's Tale, with a Poem by Lydgate. Edited by F. J. Furnivall.

See note on No. 14.

16. Essays on Chaucer, his Words and Works, Part III. 7. Chaucer's Prioress, her Nun Chaplain and 3 Priests, illustrated from the Paper Survey of St. Mary's Abbey, Winchester, by F. J. Furnivall. 8. Alliteration in Chaucer, by Dr. Paul Lindner. 9. Chaucer a Wicliffite; a critical Examination of the Parson's Tale, by Herr Hugo Simon. 10. The sources of the Wife of Bath's Prologue: Chaucer not a Borrower from John of Salisbury, by the Rev. W. W. Woollcombe.

See note on No. 14.

17. Supplementary Canterbury Tales: 1. The Tale of Beryn, with a Prologue of the merry Adventure of the Pardoner with a Tapster at Canterbury, re-edited from the Duke of Northumberland's unique MS, by Fredk. J. Furnivall. Part I, the Text, with Wm. Smith's Map of Canterbury in 1588, now first engravd from his unique MS, and Ogilby's Plan of the Road from London to Canterbury in 1675.

See note on No. 14.

Issue for 1878 (none in 1877). 18. Essays on Chaucer, his Words
and Works, Part IV. 11. On *here* and *there* in Chaucer (his
Pronunciation of the two e's), by Dr. R. F. Weymouth. 12. On
(a) An Original Version of the Knight's Tale; (b) the Date
(1381) and Personages of the Parlament of Foules; (c) on
Anelida and Arcite, on Lollius, on Chaucer, and Boccaccio, etc.,
by Dr. John Koch, with a fragment of a later Palamon and
Ersyte from the Dublin MS D 4, 18.

> Weymouth's paper is also printed in the Transactions of the
> Philological Society vol. for 1877-9, Appendix 1. Koch's paper is
> transl. from his article in Engl. Stud. 1. He reviews this issue in
> Anglia 3:187.

Issue for 1884 (none in 1879, 1880, 1881, 1882, 1883).
19. Essays on Chaucer, his Words and Works, Part V:
13. Chaucer's Pardoner: his character illustrated by documents
of his time, by Dr. J. J. Jusserand. 14. Why the Romaunt of the
Rose is not Chaucer's, by Prof. Skeat, M. A. 15. Chaucer's Schip-
man, and his Barge "The Maudelayne", by P. Q. Karkeek, Esq.
16. Chaucer's Parson's Tale compared with Frère Lorens's
Somme de Vices et de Vertus, by Wilhelm Eilers, Ph. D.,
1882, englisht 1884. 17. On Chaucer's Reputed Works, by T. L.
Kington-Oliphant, M. A.

> Reviewed by Koch, Anglia 8 : Anz. pp. 154-7.

Issue for 1886 (none in 1885). 20. Originals and Analogs of the
Canterbury Tales, Part IV. Eastern Analogs I, by W. A.
Clouston.

21. Life-Records of Chaucer, Part III (a) Chaucer as
Page in the Household of the Countess of Ulster, by Edward
A. Bond, LL. D. Chief Librarian. (b) Chaucer as Forester of
North Petherton, Somerset, 1390-1400, by Walford D. Selby,
Esq. With an Appendix by Walter Rye, Esq., on I, Chaucer's
Grandfather; II, Chaucer's connection with Lynn and Norfolk.

> Bond's discovery was first printed Fortn. Rev. 6: 28-35.
> Rye's notes appeared Athen. 1881 I: 165, Acad. 1886 I: 77.

Issue for 1887. 22. Originals and Analogs of the Canterbury Tales,
Part V (completing the volume). Eastern Analogs II, by
W. A. Clouston.

23. John Lane's Continuation of Chaucer's Squire's Tale,
edited by F. J. Furnivall from the 2 MSS in the Bodleian
Library, Oxford, A. D. 1616, 1630. Part I.

24. Supplementary Canterbury Tales: 2. The Tale of Beryn,
Part II. Forewords by F. J. Furnivall, Notes by F. Vipan,
M. A. etc., and Glossary by W. G. Stone; with an Essay on
Analogs of the Tale, by W. A. Clouston.

Issue for 1888. 25. Early English Pronunciation, with especial reference to Shakspere and Chaucer, by Alexander J. Ellis, Esq., F. R. S. Part V and last.

Inadvertently marked, on cover and titlepage, as No. 27 for 1889.

Issue for 1889. 26. John Lane's Continuation of Chaucer's Squire's Tale. Part II, with an Essay on the Magical Elements in the Squire's Tale, and Analogs, by W. A. Clouston.

Issue for 1890. 27. The Chronology of Chaucer's Writings, by John Koch, Ph. D., Berlin.

For note on this work, see p. 71 here.

Issue for 1891. 28. Observations on the Language of Chaucer's Troilus (a study of its MSS, their words and forms), by Prof. George Lyman Kittredge, M. A.

Issued in 1894.

Issue for 1892. 29. Essays on Chaucer, his Words and Works, Part VI. 18. On Chaucer's Queen Anelyda. By Prof. Cowell, LL. D. 19. On the Historical Personages of Chaucer's "Squyeres Tale", and of the spurious "Chaucers Dreme." By Alois Brandl, Ph. D. 20. On Chaucer's Use of the Kentish Dialect. By the Rev. Prof. Skeat, Litt. D. 21. The Romaunt of the Rose: Fragment B. By. the Rev. Prof. Skeat, Litt. D. 22. Chaucer's "Saint Loy." By W. M. Rossetti, Esq.

Rossetti's paper is dated 1894. On Brandl's paper see p. 314 here.

Issue for 1898 (no issues for 1893-97). 30. Some Notes on the Road from London to Canterbury in the Middle Ages. Edited by Henry Littlehales.

Contains two maps, one in part from the Ordnance Maps, one a reproduction of Ogilby's of 1675. Part I=The Route or Routes. Part II= 1. Dr. Furnivall's Table of Allusions; 2. The Appearance of the Country in the Middle Ages; 3. Of Pilgrimages; 4. Of Pilgrims' Signs. Pages 48-50 of Part II contain lists of MS pictures illustrating XIV century life.

Issue for 1900 (no issue for 1899). 31. The Portraits of Geoffrey Chaucer. An Essay written on the Occasion of the Quincentenary of the Poet's Death. By M. H. Spielmann.

"Published simultaneously in the Magazine of Art (July-Aug.-Sep. 1900) and in the volume of Chaucer Lectures issued by the Royal Society of Literature in celebration of the quincentenary of the poet's death. Fifty copies were then reprinted separately, with a few minor but necessary corrections, and from one of these the present Reprint, with further modifications, has been made for the second series of the Chaucer Society's publications." (Dec. 1900.)

Rev. by Koch, Engl. Stud. 30 : 445-50.

32. Life-Records o' Chaucer. IV. Enrolments and Documents
from the Public Record Office, the Town Clerk's Office, Guildhall, London, and other Sources; comprising all known records
relating to Geoffrey Chaucer. By R. E. G. Kirk, Esq.

With 58 pages of "Forewords" by Kirk, summing up all now
known of the poet's life.

Issue for 1901.   33. Richard Brathwait's Comments, in 1665,
upon Chaucer's Tales of the Miller and the Wife of Bath,
edited with an introduction by C. F. E. Spurgeon.

Rev. by Koch, Engl. Stud. 30 :458-60.

Issue for 1902. 34. Supplementary Canterbury Tales. 3. A New
Ploughman's Tale : Thomas Hoccleve's Legend of the Virgin
and her sleeveless Garment, with a spurious Link, edited from
MS clii, Christ Church, Oxford (Chaucer's Canterbury Tales),
by Arthur Beatty, Ph. D., University of Wisconsin, U. S. A.
Paralleled with another copy from Mr. Israel Gollancz's edition
of Hoccleve's Minor Poems Part II, from the Ashburnham
quarto MS 133.

35. The Pardoner's Prolog and Tale, by Geoffrey Chaucer.
A Critical Edition by John Koch.

Pubd. Berlin 1902; adopted as a publication by the Chaucer
Society. For note see Reference List here.

Issue for 1903. 36. Analogues of Chaucer's Canterbury Pilgrimage
(April 1386) and his Putting-up Joust Scaffolds, etc., in West
Smithfield (May 1390). Being the Expenses of the Aragonese
Ambassadors for 58 days in England, 21 July to 16 Sept. 1415,
including their four days' Journey from London to Canterbury
and back, 31 July—3 August, 1415. And the Cost of Erecting
Scaffolds, etc. in West Smithfield for the Joust between Don
Philip Boyl, knight, of Aragon, and John Asteley, Esq., on
Jan. 30, 1442, with Henry VI's Allowance of Materials for the
said Joust. Edited by R. E. G. Kirk and F. J. Furnivall.

Issued in 1906.

37. The Development and Chronology of Chaucer's Works,
by John S. P. Tatlock, Ph. D., Assistant Professor of English
in the University of Michigan.

Issued in 1907.

38. The Evolution of the Canterbury Tales, by Prof. W. W.
Skeat, Litt. D.

Issued in 1907. For note see Reference List here.

Issue for 1904. 39. Studies in Chaucer's House of Fame, by Wilbur Owen Sypherd, Ph. D., Professor of English in Delaware College, U. S. A.

Issued in 1907. Noted in Nation 1908 I : 512.

40. Chaucer's Troilus and Boccaccio's Filostrato and Filocolo, by Karl Jung, Ph. D.

Issue for 1905, to appear in 1908. 41. Five Hundred Years of Chaucer Criticisms and Allusions, 1387-1900 A. D., by Miss Caroline F. E. Spurgeon and Miss Evelyn Fox. Part I.

42. Studies in Chaucer's Troilus, by W. S. McCormick.

REFERENCE LIST

In this List are included the names of writers and works frequently cited in the foregoing pages; for monographs to which but a single reference is made, see Index. For the publication of British learned societies down to 1864 see Lowndes as below, Appendix, vol. VI; and see the British Museum Catalogue, s.v. *Academies.* For the Transactions of such societies see the Official Yearbook of the Scientific and Learned Societies of Great Britain and Ireland, published by Griffin annually since 1884; these meetings are also usually summarized in the Athenaeum or the Academy. For German dissertations and programs see the Bibliographischer Monatsbericht über neu erschienene Schul- und Universitätsschriften, published by Fock, Leipzig, monthly since 1889. For lists of works on English subjects see the Jahresbericht über die Erscheinungen auf dem Gebiete der germanischen Philologie, Berlin 1879 ff.; and the Uebersicht published with Anglia since 1894. For articles in the principal literary magazines see Poole's Index as below.

To the names of journals containing longer and more important Chaucer articles, *e. g.,* Anglia, Englische Studien, Modern Philology, a condensed list of such articles is appended. With journals containing principally brief articles and notes this method has not been followed, *e. g.,* Athenaeum, Notes and Queries.

In many cases journal references are given by volume and page, Arabic numerals being used; in the cases of the Academy, Athenaeum, and New York Nation, journals which divide each year into two volumes, the reference is by the year, followed by the Roman numeral I or II and by the page. In the cases of the Deutsche Litteraturzeitung and the Literaturblatt the reference is by year and page. Notes and Queries is not cited in the usual form of series, volume and page, but by the year, followed by I or II and by the page. Arabic numerals are used for all journals, however different their own procedure, *e. g.,* that of the Archiv; for works complete in several volumes, such as editions of Chaucer, Roman numerals are used.

Acad. Academy, London 1869 ff. Weekly.

Amer. Jour. Phil. American Journal of Philology, Baltimore 1886 ff. Quarterly.

Ames. See under Dibdin, below.

Anglia. Anglia, Zeitschrift für englische Philologie, Halle 1878 ff. Quarterly. Anglia Beiblatt, containing reviews, has appeared since 1890. Before that date, such articles were appended, with separate pagination, to each volume of Anglia, under the title of the Anzeiger. With Anglia has also appeared since 1894 a yearly Uebersicht of literature in the English field; the 1894 issue covered 1891.

542

The more important articles are by Schoepke on Dryden in vol.
2 ; by Wood on Chaucer and James I in vol. 3 ; by Bech on the
Legend in vol. 5 ; by Lange on Chaucer and Douglas in vol. 6 ;
by Uhlemann on Chaucer and Pope in vol. 6 ; by Graef on Chaucer's
present tenses in vol. 12 ; by Koeppel (source-notes) in vols. 13,
14 ; by Lücke on the Constance-story in vol. 14 ; by Holthausen
on Theodulus in vol. 16 ; by Flügel (*q.v.*) in vols. 18, 21, 22, 23, 24,
30 ; by Boll on Ptolemy in vol. 21 ; by Ballmann on Chaucer's
influence upon drama in vol. 25. Long reviews of Chaucerian
monographs and eds., by Koch, are in vols. 2, 3, 4, 6.

Animadversions. Francis Thynne's remarks upon Speght's ed. of
Chaucer of 1598, see p. 125 here.

Anz. Anzeiger, see above under Anglia.

Archiv. Archiv für das Studium der neueren Sprachen und Litera-
turen. 1846 ff. Founded by Ludwig Herrig. Quarterly.

Important papers are by Fiedler on Chaucer's use of Latin, in
vol. 2 ; by Gesenius on the Paris MS in vol. 5 ; by Koeppel on
Chaucer-sources in vols. 84, 86, 87, 90, 101 ; long paper by Koch on
the PoFoules text in vols. 111, 112.

Athen. Athenaeum, London 1828 ff. Weekly.

Auction Prices. Auction Prices of Books. L. S. Livingston, N. Y.
1905, 4 vols.

Bagford. John Bagford, died 1716, was a buyer of books on commission, in the exercise of which vocation he formed two collections,
that termed the Bagford Ballads, and pubd. by the Ballad Society
in 1878, and the mass of titlepages and book fragments now in the
British Museum. He published in 1707 proposals for a history of
printing, which was however never published ; but he is frequently
referred to as an authority in Dibdin's Typographical Antiquities ;
see also Dibdin's Bibliomania, pp. 326-331 (1876), Hearne's Remarks
and Collections, and the letter to him by Hearne printed as
appendix to Hearne's Robert of Gloucester, II : 596-606. In this
letter Hearne speaks of an Account of the Works of Chaucer sent
him by Bagford ; this is apparently unprinted, but accounts of the
various early printers are mentioned in the Harleian Catalogue of
Manuscripts, where Bagford's collections are listed as nos. 5910
and 5892-5988. Bagford was possessed of no real scholarship ; to
him are due the errors regarding editions of Chaucer of 1495,
1520, 1522 ; and his name is held in detestation by booklovers
because of the reckless mutilation to which he subjected valuable
books for the sake of his collection of titlepages.

Bausteine. Zeitschrift für neuenglische Wortforschung. Berlin
1905 ff.

Beibl. See under Anglia, above.

Bernard, Catalogus. Catalogi manuscriptorum Angliae et Hiberniae
in unum collecti.

By Edward Bernard and others, Oxford 1697, folio.

About two-fifths of this work is devoted to manuscripts contained in the Bodleian ; these are numbered continuously up to
8716 ; and the student often finds early MS-references, *e.g.* to
"Bernard 1479", a system of nomenclature now abjured in favor
of specific classification, *e.g.,* Laud 416. For several classes of

MSS in the Bodleian, as Madan points out (Books in Manuscript p. 171), this "Old Catalogue" is still the only list; a
revision of it is to form vols. I and II of Madan's Summary Catalogue, *q.v.* Other libraries catalogued in Bernard are those of
Oxford and Cambridge colleges, the Cambridge University Library,
and many small institutions and private libraries.

Bibl. de l'école des Chartes. Bibliothèque de l'école des Chartes,
Paris 1839 ff.

Blades. Blades' life of Caxton, for which see p. 518 here. Reference
is here made to the octavo edition of 1882 in one volume.

Book Prices. See Prices of Books, by Henry B. Wheatley, Lond.
1898; see under Auction Prices, under Book Prices Current;
see list of famous book sales in Fletcher's English Book Collectors, Lond. 1902, or in Quaritch's English Book Collectors, in
progress; see notes of early prices in Lowndes, of modern in
the Athenaeum and New York Nation.

Book Prices Current. Compiled by J. H. Slater, Lond. 1891 and
annually. "Fairly well done", says Sonnenschein.

Bradshaw. Memoir of Henry Bradshaw, by G. W. Prothero, Lond.
1888.

Collected Papers of Henry Bradshaw, posthumously pubd.
Cambridge 1889.

This latter contains Bradshaw's paper on the Skeleton of the
Canterbury Tales. For note on Bradshaw see p. 520.

Brandl, Grdr. In Paul's Grundriss der germanischen Philologie,
Strassburg 1891, new ed. 1897, vol. II, the article on Mittelenglische Literatur is by A. Brandl; pp. 672-682 are on Chaucer.

This rapid summary contains nothing of value to the student.
Spurious poems included in the Morris Chaucer are discussed
as genuine, *e.g.,* Mother of Nurture, Praise of Women; it
is stated that Chaucer collected sixty old books for his Legend of
Good Women (p. 681), and that the Wife of Bath's prologue was
sent to Scogan with the Envoy to deter him from marriage; the
theory of Chaucer's eight years' love-sickness is accepted, see p. 43
here; the Prioress' Tale is termed a "Verspottung kindischer
Legenden."

Brit. Mus. Cat. British Museum Library Catalogue of Printed
Books. In 215 parts, dated Lond. 1882-3; in process of printing
up to 1890. From 1900 dates the publication of a Supplement,
containing the titles of books added to the Library during 1882-
1899.

Brit. Quart. British Quarterly Review, Lond. 1845 ff.

Brunet. Manuel du Libraire et de l'Amateur de Livres. 6 vols.,
Paris 1810, 5th ed. 1860-65. By J. C. Brunet. Supplement by
P. Deschamps and G. Brunet, Paris 1878-80.

Cambridge Hist. Eng. Lit. History of English Literature. Edited
by A. W. Ward and A. R. Waller; to be completed in eight vols.
Vol. I, Cambridge 1907; vol. II, 1908. In vol. II is found the
study of Chaucer, by Saintsbury, and a bibliography of Chaucer,

the latter unfortunately executed with inaccuracy and slovenliness; see pp. 139, 141, and the prefatory note, here, and Nation 1908 I : 575.

Centrblatt. Literarisches Centralblatt für Deutschland. Leipzig 1850 ff.

Centrblatt f. Bibliothekswesen. Centralblatt für Bibliothekswesen, Leipzig 1884 ff.

Chalmers. Works of the English Poets from Chaucer to Cowper, ed. by A. Chalmers, as noted p. 135 here.

Ch. Mem. Lect. Chaucer Memorial Lectures, as described p. 521 here.

Ch. Soc. Chaucer Society. See pp. 522 ff. here for list of publications and note on Dr. Furnivall, the founder of the Society. The works of the Society most frequently cited are:—

> *Essays. Life-Records. Originals and Analogues. Odd Texts* (OT) and *More Odd Texts* (MOT) of Chaucer's Minor Poems. *Parallel Texts* (PT) and *Supplementary Parallel Texts* (SPT) of Chaucer's Minor Poems.
> *Six-Text,* the Six-Text print of the Canterbury Tales. *Specimens* (Parallel-Text Specimens of all Unprinted MSS). *Specimens of Moveable Prologues.*
> The principal works by Dr. Furnivall for the Society here cited are his Temporary Preface and his Trial Forewords.

Contemp. Rev. Contemporary Review, Lond. 1866 ff.

Copinger. See under Hain, below.

Corp. Script. Lat. Corpus Scriptorum Ecclesiasticorum Latinorum. Vienna, in progress.

Corser. Collectanea Anglo-Poetica. ed. Corser, Chetham Society 1860-83, 11 vols.

Courthope, Hist. Eng. Poetry. History of English Poetry, W. J. Courthope, Lond. 1895 ff.

> Chapter VII of vol. I treats of Chaucer. Courthope's work, though containing some suggestive comments, is careless to an extraordinary degree. On pp. 251-52, especially, he accumulates errors by asserting that the authenticity of the Romaunt is doubtful because it is not in "Shirley's MS" nor the Thynne print of 1532, all the contents of which latter are "unquestionably genuine." As Shirley left several MSS, which do not together constitute a complete canon of Chaucer; as the Romaunt *is* in the 1532 Thynne; and as that print of Chaucer is more than half of spurious material, it is evident that Courthope has paid no real attention to the pages of Skeat, from whom he says that he derives his facts.

CT=Canterbury Tales.

Decenn. Publ. Decennial Publications of the University of Chicago. Chicago 1902-3.

Dial. Chicago 1880 ff. Fortnightly.

Dibdin. Typographical Antiquities: or the History of Printing in England, Scotland and Ireland, etc.—Begun by the late Joseph Ames,—considerably augmented by William Herbert,—and now greatly enlarged, with copious notes, by the Reverend Thomas Frognall Dibdin. Lond. 1810-19, 4 vols.

Ames' work was pubd. in 1749, Herbert's in 1785. The book, although antiquated and needing much revision and addition, is not yet superseded. Blades' study of Caxton has replaced one portion, and the Handlists of the Bibliographical Society, *q.v.*, constitute the sketch of a work which will ultimately cover the rest of Dibdin's field.

Dict. Nat. Biog. Dictionary of National Biography. Lond. 1885 ff., in 63 vols., with 3 vols. of Supplement. Edited by Leslie Stephen to vol. 22; vols. 22-27 by Stephen and Sidney Lee; subsequently by Sidney Lee. Now appearing (1908) in revised and cheaper edition.

A standard work of reference, with some weaknesses and errors. The life of Chaucer, by Hales, is inadequate; the note on John Stow contains misstatements regarding MSS, see Anglia 28 : 25; and the assertion, in the life of Henry Scogan, that he was author of Chaucer's Truth, is castigated by Flügel in Anglia 21 : 258.

DLZ. Deutsche Litteraturzeitung, Berlin 1880 ff.

Du Cange. Glossarium mediae et infimae Latinitatis. 1678. ed. Henschel, 10 vols. 1882-88.

Ebert. Allgemeine Geschichte der Literatur des Mittelalters im Abendlande bis zum beginne des 11ten Jahrhunderts. A. Ebert. Leipzig, 3 vols., 1880-89.

Edinb. Rev. Edinburgh Review. 1802 ff.

EEPron., see Ellis below.

EETS. Early English Text Society. Founded 1864; prints annually one or more volumes.

Ellis, EEPron. Early English Pronunciation, by A. J. Ellis; see p. 475 here.

Encycl. Brit. Encyclopedia Britannica, the article upon Chaucer in which, by Minto, is criticised p. 40 here.

Eng. Misc. An English Miscellany, presented to Dr. Furnivall in honor of his 75th birthday. Pubd. Oxford 1901.

This book contains 50 articles by friends and fellow-workers, with a bibliography of Furnivall's own work. The Chaucer-articles are by Liddell (Parson's Tale), McCormick (Troilus), Mather (Knight's Tale), and Morris (The Physician in Chaucer).

Engl. Stud. Englische Studien, 1877 ff. Quarterly, pubd. Leipzig since 1900.

The more important articles are by Kölbing in vols. 1, 2, 11, 21; by Koch in vols. 1, 27, and reviews of Chaucerian literature in vols. 15, 30, 36, 37; by Rambeau in vol. 3; by Fick in vol. 9, Lindner in vol. 11, both on the Romaunt; by Brandl on the Squire's Tale in vol. 12, overthrown by Kittredge in vol. 13; by Kittredge on Froissart and Chaucer in vol. 26; by Kellner on Boethius text-variants in vol. 14; by ten Brink in vol. 17; by Koeppel in vols. 17 and 20; by Kaluza in vols. 13 and 20 on the Romaunt; by Schade on Pope's versions of Chaucer in vols. 25, 26; by Bischoff on metre in vol. 26; by Lange on the Romaunt in vols. 29, 31.

Flügel. Chaucerian articles by Professor Ewald Flügel are to be found in Anglia vol. 18 (on the Wife of Bath and Ptolemy), vol. 21 on minor Chaucer-points, vol. 22 (list of MSS of the Minor Poems), vol. 23 (textual notes on the Minor Poems and notes on the Prologue), vol. 24 (Gower and Chaucer). Notes on the Prologue by Flügel are also contained in Jour. Ge. Phil. vol. 1; and in Dial vol. 18 is a review of the Oxford Chaucer.

Neuengl. Lesebuch. Neuenglisches Lesebuch, ed. Flügel, Halle 1895, vol. I.

Furnivall. For note on Dr. F. J. Furnivall, editor-in-chief of the Chaucer Society, etc., see p. 522 here. The original works by Furnivall most frequently referred to here are:—*Temp. Pref.,* Temporary Preface, see p. 166, and *Trial Forew.,* Trial Forewords, see p. 352 here.

Garnett and Gosse, Eng. Lit. English Literature, an Illustrated Record. By Richard Garnett and Edmund Gosse. In 4 vols., Lond. and N. Y. 1903 ff.

   Chaucer is treated in vol. 1, chap. V. A rapid recapitulation of the established facts and conventional comment; mainly based on Skeat.

Gent. Mag. Gentleman's Magazine. London 1731 ff.

Germania. Germania. Stuttgart 1856 ff. Quarterly.

Giorn. stor. della lett. ital. Giornale storico della lettatura italiana. Turin and Rome 1883 ff.

Godwin, Life. See p. 38 here for full title of Godwin's Life of Chaucer, also for critical note. References here are to the edition of 1803, in 2 vols. quarto.

Gordon Duff. Early Printed Books. E. Gordon Duff, Lond. 1893. Accompanied by: Early English Printing. A Series of Facsimiles, Lond. 1896. (40 photographic facsimiles in portfolio.) For Gordon Duff's book on Caxton see p. 518 here; for his part in the Handlists see below under that heading.

Grdr. Grundriss der germanischen Philologie, ed. H. Paul. Strassburg 1891 ff., second ed. 1897 ff. Articles by Paul and others. The article on Middle English Literature is by A. Brandl, those on English prosody by Luick and by Schipper.

Gröber, Grdr. Grundriss der romanischen Philologie, ed. by G. Gröber. Strassburg 1888 ff. Articles by Gröber and others. The papers on Latin literature and on French literature are both by Gröber.

Hain. Repertorium Bibliographicum, in quo libri omnes ab arte typographica inventa usque ad annum MD typis expressi ordine alphabetico vel simpliciter enumerantur vel adcuratius recensentur. Opera Ludovici Hain. 2 vols. Stuttgart and Paris 1826-38. Corrections and Additions, by W. Copinger, Lond. 1895-1902. Appendices ad Hainii-Copingeri repertorium bibliographicum (etc.). D. Reichling, Munich 1905 ff.

Hales. Folia Litteraria, N. Y. 1893, reprints the brief Chaucer-notes earlier published in Academy and Athenaeum, 1874-1893.

Halliwell, Minor Poems. Minor Poems of Dan John Lydgate, ed. J. O. Halliwell, Lond. 1840.

Hammond. In the Decennial Publications of the University of Chicago, vol. VII, is a paper by E. P. Hammond on the text of the Parlement of Foules, see p. 387 here. In Modern Philology vol. 3 is a paper on the Order of the Canterbury Tales and Caxton's two editions; in Anglia, vols. 28 and 30, are papers on MSS chiefly Lydgatian in content, but including two or three of Chaucer's minor poems. In Mod. Lang. Notes, vols. 19 and 20, are papers on the Chaucerian MSS Pepys 2006 and Longleat 258, also notes on St. Loy and on Lollius. In vol. 23 is a note on the editing of the Minor Poems.

Handlists. Handlists of English Printers, 1501-1556. London, printed for the Bibliographical Society. Part I, 1895. Part II, 1896. Part I, by E. Gordon Duff, contains lists of the work of de Worde, Notary, the two Faques, Skot. Part II, by Gordon Duff, Plomer, and Procter, contains lists of the work of Pynson, Copland, J. Rastell, Treveris, Bankes, Andrewe, W. Rastell, Godfray, Byddell.

"Tentative preliminary" lists, including all works of which the existence is asserted on good authority. With mention of the English public libraries where copies can be found, and of private libraries where mention is permitted. Lists only; titles and dates given, but no further particulars.

Hazlitt, Handbook. Handbook to the Popular, Poetical, and Dramatic Literature of Great Britain, from the Invention of Printing to the Restoration. W. C. Hazlitt, Lond. 1867.

The Handbook was continued by Collections and Notes, of which four series have been published, with two supplements and a general index.

Harvard Studies. Studies and Notes in Philology and Literature. Published under the direction of the Modern Language Departments of Harvard University. 1892 ff.

Vol. I contains Kittredge's paper on the Romaunt; vol. II, Manly's study of the language of the Legend of Good Women; Kittredge's Observations on the language of the Troilus comprises the third volume; vol. V, the memorial to Child, includes Manly on the Mars and Garrett on the House of Fame.

Hearne, Remarks and Collections. Published by the Oxford Historical Society, 1885-1902, 6 vols. Hearne is also author of a Letter to Bagford, printed at the end of vol. II of Hearne's ed. of Robert of Gloucester, Oxford 1724, pp. 596-606. See under Bagford, above.

Hertzberg. Chaucer's Canterbury-Geschichten, aus dem englischen von Wilhelm Hertzberg. See p. 236 here

Hist. MSS. Comm. The Royal Commission on Historical Manuscripts owned by Institutions and Private Families was appointed in 1869. Its first Report appeared in 1874, and there have since been issued 16 more, with a large number of volumes of prints from manuscripts, their prefaces giving descriptions of the codices examined by the Commissioners. A number of Chaucer MSS receive brief mention in these Reports,—the Campsall MS of the Troilus, two Longleat MSS, the Ashburnham codices now owned as on p. 193 ff. here. As the main purpose of the Commission is historical, general literature receives but slight attention. See Appendix B to Gross' Sources and Literature of English History, N. Y. 1900.

Hortis. Studj sulle Opere Latine del Boccaccio. Trieste 1879.

Jahrbuch. Jahrbuch für romanische und englische Sprache und Literatur. Berlin 1859 ff.

James. Catalogue of Western Manuscripts in the Library of Trinity College, Cambridge. M. R. James. Cambridge, Eng., 1900-04, 4 vols. See p. 192 here.

Jour. Compar. Lit. Journal of Comparative Literature, N. Y. 1903. Four numbers only?

Jour. Gc. Phil. Journal of Germanic Philology, Urbana, Ill., U. S. A. With vol. 5 the title is changed to Journal of English and Germanic Philology.

> In vol. 1 are papers by Woodbridge and by Flügel; in 2 is Broatch's paper on Troilus; vol. 5 contains Hathaway on Chaucer's Verse-Tags; in vol. 6 Jones discusses the Squire's Tale, Holt edits Stedfastnesse, and Gelbach has a note on the Monk's Tale.

Jour. of Philol. Journal of Philology, Lond. 1868 ff.

Jusserand, Lit. Hist. Histoire littéraire du peuple anglaise, J. J. Jusserand. Paris 1894 ff., transl. into English N. Y. 1895 (vol. I) as the Literary History of the English People. Severely handled by Churton Collins in his Ephemera Critica, pp. 193 ff. Careless in detail, *e. g.,* his reference to Caxton's two editions of Chaucer's *Works.*

Kissner. Chaucer in seinen Beziehungen zur italienischen Literatur. Marburg 1867. See p. 74 here.

Kittredge, Observations. Observations on the Language of Chaucer's Troilus. Harvard Studies III and Chaucer Society; see p. 400 here. Professor Kittredge's other Chaucerian papers are: on friends of Chaucer, in Publ. Mod. Lang. Assn. 16 and in Mod. Phil. 1; on Chaucer and Maximianus, in Amer. Jour. Phil. 9; on Chaucer and Froissart, in Engl. Stud. 26; a note on Chaucer's Pardoner in the Atlantic Monthly for 1893; a paper against Brandl's historical explanation of the Squire's Tale, in Engl. Stud. 13; and long reviews of Lounsbury and of the Oxford Chaucer, Nation 1892 I, 1894 II and 1895 I.

Koch. Ausgew. Klein. Dicht. Ausgewählte kleinere Dichtungen Chaucers, . . etc. See p. 352 here.

Crit. Ed. A Critical Edition of some of Chaucer's Minor Poems; for note see p. 352 here.

Chronology. Chronology of Chaucer's Writings. See p. 71, p. 167, here.

Ed. Pard. Tale. The Pardoner's Prolog and Tale, a Critical Edition; see pp. 112, 169 here. The elaborate text-construction of this monograph is rendered useless by the editor's assumption that in any MS what is true of one Tale is true of the codex. Koch has many reviews of Chaucerian literature in the journals: Engl. Stud. 15, 27, 30, 36, 37; Anglia 2, 3, 4 Anz., 5 Anz., 7 Anz., 8 Anz.; Littblatt 3, 6, 11, 24. In Archiv 111 and 112 is a long textual paper on the Parl. of Foules, see p. 387 here; and see *ibid.* for Koch's critical ed. of the same poem. In Ch. Soc. Essays is a transl. of his notes in Engl. Stud. 1.

Koeppel, E. Source-notes in Anglia 13 and 14; similar papers in Archiv 84, 86, 87, 90, 101; reviews in Engl. Stud. 17, 20, 30, and Littblatt 14, 15.

Littblatt. Litteraturblatt für germanische und romanische Philologie, 1880 ff. Since 1890 pubd. at Leipzig. Papers from this journal noted here are mainly reviews.

Litt. Verein Stuttgart. Bibliothek des litterarischen Vereins in Stuttgart. Publishes annually one or two early German works; over 240 volumes have thus appeared.

Lounsbury, Studies. Studies in Chaucer, T. R. Lounsbury, N. Y. 1892, 3 vols. Vol. I, the Life of Chaucer, the Chaucer Legend, the Text of Chaucer, the Writings of Chaucer; vol. II, the Romance of the Rose, the Learning of Chaucer, the Relations of Chaucer to the English Language and to the Religion of his Time; vol. III, Chaucer in Literary History, Chaucer as a Literary Artist. For reviews see Acad. 1892 I : 173 (Pollard); Amer. Jour. Phil. 19 : 439-445 (Garnett); Athen. 1892 I . 462; Atlantic Monthly 69 : 554; Dial 12 : 351 (Emerson); Mod. Lang. Notes 7 : 164 (McClumpha); Nation 1892 I : 214, 231 (Kittredge); Public Opinion 12 : 415; Sat. Review 73 : 185.

Lounsbury's work has very great merits, and a few minor faults. His theory regarding the Romaunt is accepted by no other scholar; some of his remarks on pronunciation, etc., are combated by Skeat, VI : 1 ff.; the treatment of the eight monographs contained in the book as distinct pieces of work occasions some repetition, which is furthered by a diffuse style; and the absence of bibliographical references is regrettable. But the mass of information brought together and presented in a form interesting and stimulating to both student and general reader renders the work of permanent value. The second chapter, on the Chaucer-Legend, and the last two of the work, might be singled out as especially important.

Lowndes. The Bibliographer's Manual of English Literature, containing an Account of Rare, Curious, and Useful Books published in or relating to Great Britain and Ireland, from the Invention of Printing; with Bibliographical and Critical Notices, Collations of the rarer Articles, and the Prices at which they have been sold. By William Thomas Lowndes.

> Originally pubd. in 1834, revised by H G. Bohn in 1857-64; re-edition of this in 6 vols., Lond. 1890. Vol. VI is an appendix containing lists of the publications of learned societies and of special presses.
> As will be seen from the dates, this work extends no further than 1864. It is full of errors and insufficiencies, but no other compilation has yet taken its place.

Macaulay. Works of John Gower, Oxford 1899, 4 vols. Reviewed Archiv 105 : 390, 110 : 197 (Toulmin Smith); Engl. Stud. 32 : 251 (Spies); Amer. Jour. Phil. 24 (Hamilton); Quart. Rev. 1903, pp. 437-458 (Ker), repubd. in Ker's Essays on Medieval Literature.

> In the Acad. 1895 I : 315, see *ibid.* II : 71, 91, Macaulay announced his discovery of the supposedly lost poem by Gower, the Speculum Meditantis.

Macray, Annals. Annals of the Bodleian Library. W. D. Macray. Oxford 1890.

Madan. Books in Manuscript. A Short Introduction to their Study and Use, with a chapter on Records. Falconer Madan. Lond. 1893.

> *Summ. Cat.* A Summary Catalogue of Western Manuscripts in the Bodleian Library at Oxford which have not hitherto been catalogued in the quarto series. Falconer Madan. Oxford, 5 vols.; vols. III-V already pubd., vols. I and II to be a revision of Bernard, *q. v.* above.

Memoir, see under Bradshaw above.

Mod. Lang. Notes. Modern Language Notes, Baltimore 1886 ff. Fortnightly.

Mod. Lang. Review. Modern Language Review. Cambridge, Engd., 1906 ff., quarterly. Successor to Mod. Lang. Quart., *q. v.*

Mod. Lang. Quart. Appeared as Modern Language Quarterly July 1897, Nov. 1897, London. With March 1898 assumed the title Modern Quarterly of Language and Literature, Vol. I, having also on its title page Modern Language Quarterly Vol. II. This volume has a fifth number, August 1899, which is included in the index of that volume, but with separate bracketed pagination. From July 1900 (Vol. III, No. 1) the journal is again entitled Modern Language Quarterly; it ceased in 1904, and was succeeded in 1906 by the Modern Language Review, as above.

Mod. Phil. Modern Philology, Chicago 1903 ff., quarterly.

Vol. I contains Kittredge's paper on Chaucer's friends, Tatlock on the dates of Troilus and of the Legend, Emerson's notes on the Prologue. Vol. 2 includes Canby's paper on the Pardoner's Tale. In vol. 3 are Lowes on lines of the Book of the Duchesse, Hammond on the order of the Cant. Tales, Schoch on the Romaunt, Tatlock on Chaucer and Dante, Brown on the "little clergeon", and Hamilton on "ventaille." Vol. 4 contains Dargan on the Cock and Fox stories, Young on Boccaccio and Chaucer, Hendrickson on Chaucer and Petrarch, Hamilton on Trotula.

Mon. Germ. Monumenta Germanica Historica. Berlin 1826 ff.

Moore. For Moore's paper on textual criticism of Dante see pp. 111-13, 248 here.

Morley, Eng. Writers. English Writers, by Henry Morley. Lond. 1887 ff., 11 vols. Vol. V contains the discussion of Chaucer, see p. 41 here.

Morris. Richard Morris, 1833-1894, was editor of various volumes for the EETS, of the 1866 Aldine Chaucer (see p. 140 here), and of portions of the Cant. Tales for school use. With Skeat he also began the Specimens of Early English (Oxford 1874), which like the school eds. of the Cant. Tales later underwent revision by Skeat.

MOT. More Odd Texts, see Index.

Nation. New York 1865 ff. Weekly.

Nichols, Lit. Anecd. Literary Anecdotes of the Eighteenth Century, J. Nichols. 9 vols., Lond. 1812-16.

Nord. Tidskr. Nordisk Tidskrift for Filologi. Copenhagen 1874 ff.

N. and Q. Notes and Queries. Lond. 1849 ff. Weekly.

Notices et Extraits. Notices et extraits des manuscrits de la bibliothèque du roi. Paris 1787 ff.

Appears at irregular intervals, with titles varying in accordance with French politics,—bibliothèque nationale, bibliothèque imperiale, etc.

OT. Odd Texts, see Index.

Palæography. For notes on this subject see E. Maunde Thompson's Manual of Greek and Latin Palæography, chaps. 18 and 19 of which deal with the English medieval hand; the same writer has papers on the history of English handwriting in vol. V of the Transactions of the Bibliographical Society, and on medieval hands in Bibliographica, vol. III. See Wright's Courthand Restored, ed. by Martin, Lond. 1879; see Wattenbach, Das Schriftwesen im Mittelalter, 3d ed. 1896; see Sir T. Duffus Hardy's introd. to vol. III of the Descriptive Catalogue of Materials relating to the History of Great Britain and Ireland, 1871; see Madan's Books in Manuscript as above. For reproductions of MS pages see Skeat's Twelve Facsimiles; see the Chaucer Society Autotypes; and single pages in the Oxford Chaucer, in Garnett and Gosse.

Patrologia. Patrologiæ Cursus Completus seu Biblioteca Universalis ... omnium SS. Patrum Doctorum Scriptorumque Eccleciasticorum. ed. J. P. Migne. 222 vols. of the Latin Fathers, to the 13th century. 166 vols. of the Greek Fathers, to the 15th century.

Texts defaced by frequent misprints, but the most complete and the cheapest collection yet available.

Philologus. Göttingen 1846 ff.

Polit., Rel., and Love Poems. Political, Religious, and Love Poems, ed. F. J. Furnivall, EETS 1866. A revised ed. was pubd. in 1903.

Pollard, Primer. Chaucer. By A. W. Pollard. In the series of Literature Primers. Lond. 1893, re-ed. 1903.

Pollard is also ed. of the Cant. Tales in various forms, and joint ed. of the Globe Chaucer; see Index. Reviews by him (of Skeat) are in Acad. 1889 I : 179, of Lowes in Acad. 1906 I : 61, 227.

Poole's Index. Index to Periodical Literature, ed. W. F. Poole. Vol. I, 1802-1881; II, 1882-87; III, 1887-92; IV, 1892-96; V, 1897-1901. Continued by the American Library Association (W. I. Fletcher *et al.*, editors) as the Annual Literary Index, later the Annual Library Index. Pubd. New York. Collected in volumes at intervals as above.

PT. Parallel Texts, see Index.

Publ. Mod. Lang. Assn. Publications of the Modern Language Association of America, 1884 ff. An annual volume, to which are appended the Proceedings of the Association, paged in Roman numerals; many papers thus summarized are printed elsewhere, *e. g.* Anglia, Jour. Gc. Phil., Mod. Phil.

Vol. 5 contains Kent on Chaucer's negatives; vol. 11, Manly on the Squire's Tale, Price on Troilus; vol. 16, Schofield on the Franklin's Tale, Mead on the Wife of Bath's Tale, Kittredge on Lewis Johan; vol. 18 contains Petersen on Chaucer and Trivet; in vols. 19 and 20 are Lowes' papers on the Legend of Good Women; vol. 21 contains Brown on the Prioress' Tale and Tatlock on date of the Prologue; vol. 22 includes A. S. Cook on Cressida and Cipriani on the Romaunt.

Quaritch. His General Catalogue of Books, 1887-92, is of value. See his Catalogues of Rare and Valuable Books on sale, issued monthly. See his Dictionary of English Book Collectors, 13 parts thus far published, in progress. See the Dict. Nat. Biog., supplement, for life of the elder Quaritch, the prince of English booksellers.

Quart. Rev. Quarterly Review, London 1808 ff.

Quellen und Forschungen . zur Sprache und Culturgeschichte der germanischen Völker. Strassburg 1874 ff.

Reliq. Antiq. Reliquiæ Antiquæ, ed. J. O. Halliwell-Phillipps and Thomas Wright. 2 vols., Lond. 1841-43.

Retrosp. Review. Retrospective Review, Lond, 1820-54.

Ritson, Bibl. Poet. Bibliographia Poetica: a Catalogue of English Poets . . . . Lond. 1802. Cited p. 38 here.

> Ritson was a student of great energy, and of unusual accuracy, but of a bitter and savage disposition; see remark on his treatment of Warton, below.

Romania. Paris, 1872 ff. Quarterly.

Rolls Series. A work so marked belongs to the series of Chronicles and Memorials of Great Britain and Ireland during the Middle Ages, published under the direction of the Master of the Rolls, and comprising the medieval chroniclers, historical poets, etc. See Appendix C to Gross' Sources and Literature of English History, N. Y. 1900.

Root, Poetry of Chaucer. The Poetry of Chaucer, by Robert K. Root. Boston and N. Y. 1906.

> A painstaking and cautious piece of work, safe for the student's use, but lacking suggestiveness. See p. 72 here.

Sandras, Étude. Étude sur G. Chaucer considéré comme Imitateur des Trouvères. E. G. Sandras, Paris 1859. For note see p. 73 here.

Sandys, Hist. Class. Scholarship. History of Classical Scholarship. J. E. Sandys, Cambridge 1903.

Saunders. For his modernization of the Canterbury Tales see p. 230 here.

Schick, Temple of Glass. Lydgate's Temple of Glass, ed. J. Schick for EETS, 1891.

Schipper, Engl. Metrik. Englische Metrik, von J. Schipper. See p. 478, 490, here.

Schofield, Hist. Eng. Lit. English Literature from the Norman Conquest to Chaucer. W. H. Schofield. Lond. and N. Y. 1906.

> The first of two volumes dealing with the literary history of England from the Conquest to Elizabeth.

Shakspere Jahrbuch. Jahrbuch der deutschen Shakspere-Gesellschaft. Berlin, etc., 1865 ff.

Sitz. ber. der Akad. d. Wiss. Sitzungsberichte der kaiserlichen Akademie der Wissenschaften (philosophisch-historische Classe), Vienna 1848 ff.

Six-Text, of the Canterbury Tales, see Index.

Skeat, I, II, III, IV, V, VI, VII. For these volumes of the Oxford Chaucer see note on that work, p. 144-46 here.

> *Canon.* See p. 55 here.
>
> *ed. Minor Poems,* see p. 351 here.
>
> *Twelve Facsimiles* of Old English Manuscripts. Oxford 1892.
>
> *Evolution of the Canterbury Tales.* Chaucer Society, 1907.
>
> Here, as in the text of his Oxford Chaucer, Professor Skeat has constructed an extensive theory upon limited and

insecure evidence. For Skeat's numerous articles upon the Romaunt and upon the authenticity of works ascribed to Chaucer, see under the separate headings in Section V here.

Soc. d. anc. textes franc. Société des anciens textes français. Paris 1875 ff. Publishes annually two or more volumes of Early French texts.

Sonnenschein. Two extensive volumes of bibliographical references have been compiled and pubd. by W. Swan Sonnenschein, Lond. 1894 and 1895; these are entitled The Best Books, and The Reader's Guide, the latter being supplement to the former. Both are fully indexed, and form an excellent guide to the general student in all fields of work.

Specimens, Specimens of Moveable Prologues, see Index.

Spelman, Glossarium. Glossarium Archaiologicum, etc. Lond., 3d ed. 1687.

SPT, Supplementary Parallel Texts, see Index.

STS. Scottish Text Society, founded 1884. Publishes annually one or more Scottish texts.

Studj di filol. rom. Studj di filologia romanza. Rome 1885 ff.

Tanner. Compiler of the Biblioteca Britannico-Hibernica, see p. 38 here.

Tatlock, Devel. and Chronol. of Chaucer's Works. Development and Chronology of Chaucer's Works. J. S. P. Tatlock. Chaucer Society, 1907.

An interestingly executed monograph, showing much thought, in which however the discussion outweighs the facts. Reviewed Nation 1908 I : 220.

See also Professor Tatlock's articles in Mod. Phil. 1 (p. 381 here) and 3 (p. 82 here); in the Publ. Mod. Lang. Assn. 21 (p. 163 here); and his review of French as noted p. 382 here.

Temp. Pref. Furnivall's Temporary Preface, see p. 166 here.

Ten Brink, Hist. Eng. Lit. This work appeared in German as Geschichte der englischen Literatur, vol. I, Berlin 1877, vol. II part 1 Berlin 1889. The latter extended to the accession of Elizabeth; part 2 of vol. II, to the death of Surrey, was passing through the press when the author's sudden death occurred in 1892. The finishing touches were put to this portion of the work by Professor Alois Brandl, though the Appendix, to which ten Brink had frequently referred as his History progressed, exists but in fragmentary notes. The English translation of vol. I and of vol. II part 1 was read by the author and received his emendations; these, pubd. 1883 (again 1889) and 1893, are therefore more authoritative than the original German. Part 2 of vol. II has also been transl. into English; in this volume reference is made to the work as of three volumes, in accordance with the English format.

See Acad. 1889 I : 249-50 (Herford); Anglia Beibl. 10 : 289-

92 (Binz) ; Centralblatt 1900, p. 206; Mod. Lang. Notes 6 : 290-96 (McClumpha).

Chaucer is treated in vol. II. The only drawback to the use of this work by students is its lack of bibliographical references, which ten Brink felt himself compelled to omit. No subsequent writer upon the subject has brought to his work ten Brink's combination of firsthand knowledge as to technical detail, fine literary appreciation, and suggestive genius.

Sprache und Versk. Chaucers Sprache und Verskunst, see p. 478 here

Studien. Chaucer. Studien zur Geschichte seiner Entwicklung und zur Chronologie seiner Schriften. Münster 1870.

In this epoch-making work was first fully discussed the development of Chaucer's genius under the pressure of external influences; and the division of Chaucer's works into "periods" accordingly was first made here. Some of ten Brink's results are questioned by modern scholars; but of this, as of his other works, it is still true that students must reckon with his theories and suggestions.

See note on ten Brink, p. 520 here; and see Index.

Trans. Amer. Philol. Assn. Transactions of the American Philological Association, Boston 1869 ff.

Trial Forew. Furnivall's Trial Forewords, see p. 352 here.

Tyrwhitt, Account of the Works of Chaucer: *Essay: Introductory Discourse.* For the first of these papers by Tyrwhitt, accompanying his edition of the Canterbury Tales, see p. 210 here, under *Canon.* For his Essay on the Language and Versification of Chaucer, see p. 471-2 here, also p. 482. His Introductory Discourse is noted p. 210 here, under *Sources.*

Ward, Catalogue. Catalogue of Romances in the Manuscript Department of the British Museum. H. L. D. Ward. 2 vols., Lond. 1883, 1893. The death of Ward (1906) leaves the work incomplete.

Warton-Hazlitt. Thomas Warton's History of English Poetry was published as follows: vol. I in 1774, with dissertations on the origin of Romantic Fiction in Europe and on the introduction of learning into England; vol. II in 1778; vol. III, with a dissertation on the Gesta Romanorum, in 1781. A second edition of vol. I appeared in 1775, also "Emendations and Additions" to vol. II, in which use is made of Tyrwhitt's ed. of the Canterbury Tales. At Warton's death, in 1790, he left a small portion of a projected vol. IV, which would have continued the History to Pope; this was however carried no further, and the History does not go beyond the reign of Elizabeth.

In 1824 the work was issued under the editorship of Richard Price, with notes by Ritson, Douce, and other antiquaries; this was reissued, with further changes, in 1840. In 1871 appeared the

edition at present current, in 4 vols., edited by W. C. Hazlitt with the co-operation of a number of scholars, including Furnivall and Henry Sweet. The prefaces and dissertations are placed in vol. I; vol. II covers the time from the Anglo-Saxon period to Chaucer; vol. III, Chaucer to Surrey; vol. IV, Writers of the XVI century. According to a statement made by Furnivall in Trial Forew. p. 99, he is the adviser alluded to in Hazlitt's preface p. ix, at whose suggestion "the wrong, obsolete, and insufficient parts" of Warton were cut out, and "made right by insertions in . . . brackets." Also "large additions" were made, and "all the notes incorporated with the texts."

Of this edition Sidney Lee says in the Dict. Nat. Biog., art. *Warton*, that Warton's text was "ruthlessly abbreviated or extended in an illadvised attempt to bring the information up to the latest level of philological research." Of the work in its original form Lee says that it "is impregnated by an intellectual vigor which reconciles the educated reader to almost all its irregularities and defects." In these opinions every Early English student will coincide. For all scholarly purposes, the first edition of Warton is much the most desirable, though reference is made to Warton-Hazlitt because of its greater accessibility. It is not possible to discover from the edition of 1871 what Warton's original statements were, *e.g.*, Warton said, "There is a further proof that the *Floure and the Lefe* preceded the *Confessio Amantis"*; which in 1871 becomes "There is [an indication] that the [writer of the] *Flower and the Leaf* [studied] the *Confessio Amantis."*

Another edition of the first Warton has not the "Emendations and Additions" at the end of vol. II, but has at the close of vol. III a separately paged "Observations on the Three First Volumes of the History of English Poetry, in a Familiar Letter to the Author." This letter, of 1782, is by Joseph Ritson, and is expressed in Ritson's usual violent and abusive style. He terms Warton's work "an injudicious farrago, a gallimaufry of things which do and do not belong to the subject,—a continued tissue of falsehood from beginning to end." He advises Warton to consult Tyrwhitt in revising his work; and it may be noted that the Emendations and Additions, when they appeared, contained, as above remarked, frequent allusions to Tyrwhitt. Ritson was severely censured for the disregard of decency in this attack upon Warton.

On Warton see Courthope, Hist. Eng. Poetry I, preface.

Wright. Anecdota Litteraria. Lond. 1844. A collection of English, French, and Latin poems of the 13th century.

Anglo-Latin Satirical Poets of the Twelfth Century. 2 vols. Rolls Series, Lond. 1872.

Political Poems and Songs from Edward III to Henry VIII. 2 vols., Rolls Series, Lond. 1859-61.

Specimens of Lyric Poetry of the Reign of Edward I. Lond. 1842.

Thomas Wright, English antiquary, 1819-1877, was author or editor of over 120 works dealing with medieval England and its literature; his studies have been printed by the Percy Society, the Camden Society, the Rolls Series, and the Roxburghe Club, etc. He was well known and of high reputation in his own time, but later opinion of him is thus summed up by Lee in Dict. Nat. Biog.:—"Nearly all his philological books are defaced by errors of transcription and extraordinary misinterpretations of Latin and

Early English and Early French words and phrases. But as a pioneer in the study of Anglo-Saxon and medieval literature and on British archaeology he deserves grateful remembrance." Wright and Halliwell together edited the Reliq. Antiq., *q.v.*

Wülker, Altengl. Lesebuch. Altenglisches Lesebuch, ed. R. P. Wülker. Halle 1874, 2 vols.

    Gesch. d. engl. Lit. Geschichte der englischen Literatur. Leipzig 1896. Of no independent value.

Ztschr. f. roman. Phil. Zeitschrift für romanische Philologie. Halle 1877 ff.

Ztschr. f. vergl. Littgesch. Zeitschrift für vergleichende Litteraturgeschichte. New Series, Berlin 1887 ff.

INDEX